BOOK SELECTION AND CENSORSHIP IN THE SIXTIES

BOOK SELECTION AND CENSORSHIP IN THE SIXTIES

edited by Eric Moon

R. R. BOWKER COMPANY, NEW YORK & LONDON 1969

Published by the R. R. Bowker Co. (A XEROX COMPANY)
1180 Avenue of the Americas, New York, N.Y. 10036
© 1969 Xerox Corporation.

Library of Congress Card Number: 78–79423
Standard Book Number: 8352–0205–4

Printed and Bound in the United States of America.

Foreword

This book is primarily an anthology of articles written for *Library Journal* during the decade of the 1960's—at least, up through the first few months of 1969. That so much material on the subjects of book selection and censorship should have appeared in such a comparatively short span of time is testimony to the problems that surrounded this central discipline in librarianship in this period. That so much of it appeared in one magazine is perhaps only indicative of a hobbyhorse interest of the editor's.

Three pieces are published here for the first time: the review by Ervin Gaines of the changing climate and its influence on censorship trends since the late fifties; the account by Kenneth Kister of a unique library school course in intellectual freedom; and the editor's introduction on the theory and practice of book selection.

The dates at the head of individual chapters are the dates of the issues of *Library Journal* in which each of these articles first appeared. In several symposia-type articles reprinted here, a number of librarians and others are identified by position and institution. These are given as they appeared in the original *Library Journal* articles, and many of these authors have now moved on to other assignments. A list of contributors at the end of this volume properly identifies the current positions and institutions of these contributors. In today's highly mobile world, it is perhaps advisable to note that "current" in this context means as of June 1969.

ERIC MOON

Contents

PART I: BOOK SELECTION

MAGAZINES & NEWS PUBLICATIONS

AUDIO-VISUAL MATERIALS

CHILDREN'S BOOKS

SELECTION TOOLS AND REVIEWING

PART II: BOOK CENSORSHIP

VIEWS ON CENSORSHIP—OUTSIDE THE PROFESSION

LIBRARY ASSOCIATIONS DEBATE CENSORSHIP

CASE HISTORIES

THE POLITICS OF CENSORSHIP

THE LIBRARY SCHOOL'S RESPONSIBILITY

PART 1: BOOK SELECTION

Theory
Surveys
Magazines & News Publications
Audio-visual Materials
Children's Books
Selection Tools and Reviewing

INTRODUCTION

The Blue and the Grey:
Theory and Practice
in Book Selection

by ERIC MOON

When is a librarian's decision not to include a book in his library collection an act of book selection, and when is it censorship? Is there, in fact, any discernible difference in the two terms: book selection and censorship? This topic was discussed so lucidly and ably, long ago, by Lester Asheim in what has become a classic essay in the literature of librarianship, "Not Censorship, but Selection," that raising it again may appear to be an exercise in redundancy.

It needs to be discussed anew, however, because it remains a core question, a continuing problem, a point of vulnerability for the library, particularly the public library, because its objectives remain the least well defined among the institutions of the library world. In today's turbulent society one of the interesting confrontations is that between the individual and the institution— or the system. The decisions and motives of public institutions and the people who run them are coming, and will continue to come, under closer and more critical scrutiny, and individuals and groups can be expected to question, with increasing frequency, whether society's institutions are operated for their benefit or whether some of these institutions have simply become self-perpetuating entities, operated in accordance with some obscure, abstract set of principles which have little relevance for the individual the institution is supposed to serve.

Although most of the noisier pressures on public libraries are set off by group opposition to controversial publications which the library *has* selected and added to its collection, the defense of the positive book selection decision is not really the crux of the problem. This is not to suggest that defending such decisions is always easy or comfortable, but logically one *can* defend the inclusion of almost anything in a library collection under the broad umbrella of intellectual freedom, the Library Bill of Rights and other such pronouncements of the profession. The more difficult exercise, for the librarian, is the defense of the negative book selection decision; that is, book rejection, or the refusal to buy a book or periodical that an individual reader wants or needs. This is the point at which the reader may find it difficult to distinguish between library book selection and library censorship, since for him the end result is the same. When the library decides not to buy or supply the book he wants, the library, he may well conclude, has taken a decision against *his* interests.

In whose interest, then, is such a decision made? Failing the satisfaction of getting the book he wants, this reader, at the very least, wants a logical explanation of why this institutional decision should prevail over his need. And this is the point of vulnerability—because most of the policies and philosophies on which book selection practice rests are very shaky props. They appear to be—and the more so if you compare the policy pronouncements with the evidence of the library shelves—a series of prismatic evasions, of ad hoc excuses for whatever decision suits the book selector's whim of the moment.

One has only to examine some of the popular phrases from the lexicon of book selection policies to begin to sympathize with the reader's difficulties in distinguishing between book selection and censorship. There are other words and phrases which rarely get committed to print in such documents as book selection policies but which occur with some frequency when librarians discuss book selection among themselves. Every time I have asked a number of librarians why they failed to add a particular book to their collections, I have been surprised by the number who replied, simply, "Because it is trash." Several chapters in this book, particularly those reporting on surveys of book selection practice, will document the frequency with which this value judgment is rendered, and the incredible range of its apparent applicability. It may be worth noting that "trash" and other equivalent terms are also rather large in the vocabulary of the pressure groups and censors who operate outside the library walls.

The librarian, of course, unless he lacks all public relations (and common) sense, does not tell the reader that the book he wants is trash. He wraps up the message in institutional verbiage, the language of the book selection policy. He may tell the reader that the book in question does not meet all the requirements of the library's book selection "standards." With this argument, particularly if he is faced with an acute or knowledgeable reader, the librarian is already walking in quicksand.

A learned Justice once said that trying to come to grips with a definition of obscenity was like trying to catch a greased pig. Applying consistent standards in book selection, as some librarians profess to be able to do, is considerably more difficult, perhaps like trying to lasso an eel. It ought to be obvious that book selection is not a measurable technique like circulation control or cost accounting. There is no slide rule which will cope with the complexities of calculation involved. This is why the written book selection policy is really of very little help when one gets down to the hard, specific case. What one then has to solve is a difficult equation which involves not just the individual book but also the library collection (and the judgments *it* reflects) and the individual reader who wants the particular book (and perhaps no other). At best, the policy will serve as a rough, rule-of-thumb guide, but at worst, it is used too often as a defense mechanism because there is no library which could defend all of its inclusions, or its exclusions either, on the basis of its written policy.

Again, other chapters of this book will document the quality and consistency of librarians' pronouncements on the "literary" or other standards they apply in the book selection process. These need not be repeated here, but by way of illustration it is worth noting that the librarian who declares that John Updike does not meet the literary standards of her library's collection, when the latter includes the works of the late author of *Peyton Place,* is doing one of three things: either she is saying that the library has *no* standards, or she is revealing that the general level of the collection is determined by standards which would not be considered remotely literary, or she is lying about the real reason for excluding Updike. Does the Updike reader see book selection principles at work here, or the hand of the censor?

Such clear value contrasts are not apparent in all cases, but a good many others illustrate the vulnerability of library pronouncements on book selection policy. In 1968, for example, the book selection policies of the St. Paul Public Library received a rather warm press after the revelation that the library had rejected Myra Breckenridge because "The book is well-written, but it has no literary merit." The same library defended its inclusion of *Valley of the Dolls,* even though the book had "no redeeming features," because the library felt it had an obligation "to show facets of our era such as the misuse of pills." Commenting on the St. Paul fracas with whimsical punch, the *Staff Bulletin* of the Youngstown and Mahoning County Library, after noting that the St. Paul Public Library had no written book selection policy, suggested: "If they get one, it will probably be well-written but without literary merit."

Another recent example may illustrate a different point about standards in book selection. When Norman Mailer's *Why Are We in Vietnam?* was published I reviewed it for *Library Journal* and panned it as a bad book (Eliot Fremont-Smith, in the *New York Times,* incidentally, said it was brilliant). Some time later, a librarian friend accosted me jubilantly at a convention. He had been glad to see my review, he said, because it supported his library's decision not to buy the Mailer book. My friend was somewhat perplexed when I told him I thought the library was wrong, that the Mailer book should have been added to the collection.

"But you said yourself the Mailer book was a bad one. Are you advocating that the library buy bad books?" he asked. It was a naive question which might have been answered with another question: "Are you so sure your library *doesn't* buy bad books?" Instead, I tried to explain that, had I been making the book selection decision in his library, I would have bought the book because: 1) Mailer is unquestionably a major figure in contemporary American literature; 2) Everything he writes is of immense public interest, and among the suburban public of this particular library there are surely many people who would want to read *any* book he produces; and 3) The implied topic of the book, and its rather obscure central theme, are closely related to important social and political concerns of the day—especially so in the Washington, D.C. area where this library (and a good many others which did not buy the Mailer novel) was located. My friend could not buy book selection philosophies as elastic or elusive as these.

Standards as applied to book selection, nevertheless, must be elastic, and the message may be gradually becoming clearer to more librarians. This may, indeed, be the healthiest and most obvious impact that today's social upheavals are having upon the public library. As libraries, at long last, have begun to reach out for a public whom they and their book selection policies have ignored for years, they begin to discover that those policies which satisfied at least a large part of the known or predictable needs of a white middle class public which libraries, along with other social institutions, had made their own, are wildly irrelevant when applied to service to the new residents of the cities: the black, the foreign-speaking, the miscellaneous poor. Thus, Daniel Fader, advocating the use of books which could never have "passed" under old book selection policies, becomes a new prophet. And Marie Davis, president of ALA's Adult Services Division, warns that "book selection policies, based on 'balanced collections' and 'literary merit,' do not recognize the full thrust of [today's] modes of expression and all that they imply."

Not only the old, fixed ideas about content standards are being called into question; some of the rigid attitudes about form are also under fire. Resistance to the paperback wanes. Out in Venice, California, new-breed librarian Don Roberts declares that fifty percent of the library collection should be "electric." If you can get nine-track stereo on airplanes, he asks, why not in libraries? And Lowell Martin reminds the Enoch Pratt Free Library—and others who read his report, *Baltimore Reaches Out*—that "It is easy but not accurate to draw a sharp line with book readers on one side and the great unwashed on the other. This amounts to designating one kind of printed page as the real thing and excluding others." Martin, too, is arguing that libraries must get away from their obsession with the book.

The growing recognition that "the community" and the traditional library public are by no means the same thing has put a strain on book selection policies which may once have seemed secure in their generalities, and have exposed the hollowness of those various phrases that relate the library's book selection practice to "the needs of the community." Our individual reader, still in confrontation with the librarian who has rejected the book he wants, may well call up one of these phrases in his own cause. OK, he says, *I'm* part of the community. What about my needs?

What, indeed, do the policy statements mean when they talk about the needs of the community? In a very small town, perhaps, it may be possible for the librarian to sense the general tenor and tone of the community, and to have some knowledge of group interests. But even in such a community the possibility that the librarian will understand the inner beliefs and concerns of even a majority of individuals must be viewed skeptically. I would not even place any large bets on the certainty of my predictions on the reading tastes and desires of my own family; even less would I have the temerity to prejudge those of my neighbors. And in the large city, to talk in these terms about the community is ludicrous. When we begin to talk about the community in the mass, when we forget for one moment that the mass is made up of individuals, library book selection has already begun to operate on very suspect principles.

Among all the arguments raised when one questions book selection practice, the most unconvincing are those concerned with that amorphous body, "the public." Most alarming is the widespread, often unconscious, superciliousness of librarians who talk about the lack of "maturity" or "sophistication" of their reading public. In an age when mass communications reach into every corner of society, it is hard to understand the easy dismissal of the possibility (probability?) that the whole range of taste and all shades of opinion exist within *every* community. The quantity distribution varies, certainly, with each community, but few librarians would be prepared or able to defend the proposition that the library should serve only majority tastes and opinions.

Yet, forced to admit that our troublesome reader's needs *are* part of the community's needs, the librarian can fall into this box through reliance on another concept deeply embedded in the excuse vocabulary of book selection: the "demand" factor. As a defense for a policy decision, "demand" is a veritable Maginot Line. One might be forgiven for assuming, for example, that many controversial books would rank high among the books in demand. Yet it is amazing how often librarians have indicated "no demand" for such books, even when they were selling by the tens of thousands in bookstores. But even eliminating the element of controversiality, might not our reader, given the "demand" excuse, point to the shelves and ask the librarian how many times there has been active demand for, say, the poems of Wallace Stevens, or for Bacon's *Advancement of Learning*? How much demand is demand? And how is it measured? Does the library just listen to the vocal readers, or those who come in weekly with their batch of request cards after reading the *New York Times Book Review*? How much do libraries know of the unexpressed demands, of the disappointments of readers who never find what they want on the shelves?

Before we proceed to other matters one more concept from the book selection policies deserves mention: the muddled theory of "balance" in library collections. This is a sacred cow, propagated in all the most noble pronouncements of the profession (like the Library Bill of Rights), but every librarian knows that the theory is indefensible against the evidence of the library shelves. Rare is the library that gives as much weight to publications favorable to either communism or fascism as to democracy. And radical right pressures on libraries have gained some strength from the general truth of their argument that library collections tend to favor liberal over conservative points of view. And how often does one witness a balance between material on heterosexuality and homosexuality? Or between Christianity and atheism?

There is, nevertheless, one way in which many libraries have managed to create and preserve an impression of balance. The seesaw analogy explains it best. Even if they are not evenly matched in weight, if you put two people as near as possible to the middle of a seesaw, the ends of the seesaw will not go up or down too much. The further out your people move, the harder it is to maintain a balance. Libraries—and who can say how consciously?—have preserved an appearance of balance in just this way, by staying generally as close as possible to the safe, respectable middle; by never placing too much emphasis on the outer edges, the fringe groups, the dissident or dissenting opinions, the impolite or abrasive voices. Here is one substantial reason why, in this time of social revolution, the relevance of libraries is called into question.

While librarians have talked of applying, or trying to apply, some vaguely consistent standards to book selection, what has been more evident has been the widespread adherence to a rather pernicious double standard. Thus, the polite or "harmless" or insipid book does not really have to be very good to reach the library shelves of most public libraries, is not subjected to the same rigorous interrogation as that book or magazine which treads ground that the conformists fear to approach. The book or magazine which is, or even may be, controversial has, on the other hand, to be a near masterpiece, supported by almost unanimous critical opinion, before libraries will offer it the sanctity of the shelves—and certainly the *open* shelves.

If libraries *must* apply a flagrant double standard, one wonders whether the present one shouldn't be reversed in its emphases. Better, it seems to me, that the shelves be full of books which provoke thought and reaction in the mind and heart, and even perhaps a movement of the reader's juices, than that they be full of textual pap.

If this essay, thus far, appears to be thoroughly negative, defeatist, hopeless, it is not meant to be. It is intended to undermine the certainties of those who think book selection can be done by rote or formula, of those who believe themselves "safe" in their decisions if only they have a written policy, of those who ascribe fallibility or prejudice only to others. Daniel Melcher once told me that he'd asked a librarian what she did about burying her book selection mistakes. The librarian answered: "I don't make any." That librarian has not even learned the first mandatory lessons for the book selection practitioner: that we are all of us nearly as often wrong as right; that the only person who can be absolutely certain that a book is good is the reader for whom that book *is* good; that book selection, in short, is a fallible, human, prejudice-ridden technique.

Book selection, however, is not a *uniformly* difficult process. Some selection decisions, it would appear, are easy to the point of being automatic, others appear to be much more difficult. But it is interesting to examine whether the strengths and weaknesses of library collections coincide with the areas of comparative ease and difficulty in the selection process.

Most librarians, for example, would probably be prepared to accept that retrospective book selection is easier than current book selection. Time and society have rendered their withering judgments on the older books, have eliminated the transient, the ephemeral, and have given a stamp of approval and permanence (sometimes an erratic permanence) to the survivors. There is no such perspective to help us in deciding upon the merits of current books. Society's hurried mass judgments, such as the best seller lists; the unpredict-

able irascibility or benignity of critics and reviewers (they are human, too!);
the imprecision of some of the criteria written into book selection policies, such
as the reputation of the publisher—all of these factors, and others, may mis-
lead the book selector in any one of several directions. If this proposition is
basically correct, the conclusion one might draw from it is that the library
shelves might be expected, in general, more adequately to represent the time-
tested books than the more doubtful contemporary pretenders.

But it isn't so. I proved it to myself a number of times when I was a book
selector, with carefully checked tests. I have had it sadly, and repeatedly,
proven to me as a library user. And I checked it out again, in a small way, a
few years ago, and reported the findings in an article called "A View from the
Front," reprinted in this volume. When one can find a Thomas Wolfe novel in
only one quarter of the libraries one checks, or a collected Milton in less than
half of them, and at the same time one does find the shelves crowded with the
dross from the last several years' best seller lists, it does not appear that the
greater ease of retrospective book selection leads to better shelf representation.
I must stress that I am talking about books *on the shelves*, where readers want
them, not entries for books in the catalog (though, frequently, they are missing
also). I never knew an empty-handed reader who left the library deliriously
happy with having found a catalog entry.

To take a second "degree of difficulty" proposition, most librarians would
probably agree that it is generally easier to select "factual" books than to select
what is sometimes called "creative literature." The factual books, those which
assist the library in fulfilling its informational mission, can be measured against
something, perhaps their predecessors. Does the new book add anything new?
Does it provide later information? Does it have a special viewpoint? Is it
addressed to a special audience? Is it accurate? Does the library need anything
else in this subject area? These are *relatively* easy, practical decisions to make,
even if one has to call occasionally upon subject specialists for assistance.

Where book selection gets much tougher (and this applies equally to
reviewing) is when one is dealing with current creative writing—poetry,
drama, fiction, perhaps some philosophy, history. Here every man's judgment
is *not* as good as the next's, and no one's is certain. How, for example, do you
assess the worth of a new play? Can you measure the new dramatist, with any
accuracy, against Shakespeare or Shaw, or even Arthur Miller? What would
you prove, if you could? Subject content is no help either. You cannot decide
on the basis of whether or not the library needs another play about infidelity or
doctors, miscegenation or religion. The play, the poem, the novel is only
measurable against itself, and perhaps against what we know of ourselves and
the world around us, today and through all the yesterdays.

So, if our proposition is correct this time, we should expect that the factual
or informational representation in public libraries would be our strength,
would be more supportable than the fiction or creative literature sections. But
is it so? Let me illustrate by adapting and updating some remarks made by
Dan Lacy in 1961:

"I wonder how many people have come to our libraries in the last month
to borrow a book on the Vietnam problem [Lacy was talking about Berlin

then]. What if a considerable number of the population *did* want to find out something about the Vietnam problem? In a community of 20,000 people, let's not be extravagant and say 50% or 30% or 20%, but suppose one percent of the 20,000 came into the library and said, 'I want a book about the Vietnam problem.' Your service, of course, would have collapsed after the first dozen arrived."

And so to a third proposition: that it is very much more difficult to select books for the small library than for the very large. There do not appear to be too many holes in this one. It is, of course, harder to select a very small number of representative titles from today's overwhelming publishing output than it is to buy most of them. Every housewife knows that the smaller the budget, the more difficult the shopping becomes; she has to be more certain about what the essentials are. But this is too simple a view of the responsibilities of selection, and this proposition falls in practice because it has the same glaring hole that the other two have. The "easier" selection problem *does* lead to better collections in the large libraries, in the sense that those collections have more range; but it is by no means always easier to find on the shelves of a large library the book one wants, when one wants it, than it is in the smaller library—whether the book be fairly current or a classic.

The reason why all three of these apparently reasonable propositions begin to look dubious when measured against the evidence of the shelves is that most libraries have tended to sacrifice depth in favor of range. Most library collections would be considerably more *useful* if some of the obsessive concern about "quality" in book selection were matched with an equal concern about *quantity*. A library needs not just specific titles and adequate coverage of subject areas but varying quantities of specific titles related to the varying intensities of reader interest and need.

In general, the larger libraries have dealt no more satisfactorily with the quantity problem than have their smaller brethren. Also, the academic libraries have done no better with it than the public libraries. Some of the larger academic libraries, indeed, have been so concerned with the status of statistics and with the widest possible range of titles that their book selection practices tend to lead to a very curious result: the more esoteric the reader's need, the better able is the large research library to satisfy it; and conversely, the more predictable the need, the more dismal is the library's performance. The degree to which the academic libraries have ignored the quantity problem has, in fact, accentuated the problems and difficulties of the public library—difficulties which in recent years have been encapsulated, inaccurately, in the phrase, "the student problem."

There is some evidence that some of the newer academic institutions may have learned the vulnerability of the "range at the expense of depth" philosophy. A considerable swing in the other direction is apparent in the approach, for example, of the new Federal City College in Washington, D.C. The following is quoted from the college's information leaflet on its media center, which began operating in the fall of 1968:

"In its first year the basic book collection will include 18,000 titles. The Center also will have a section containing *200,000 duplicate volumes,* seventy-five percent of which will be paperbacks. These will be available to students on loan for as long as they are enrolled at FCC.

"Books in the basic collection cannot be taken from the Center by either faculty or students. Circulating hardbound books will be subject to recall when the demand is great, but paperback books may be kept by any student for months or even years. A student may borrow up to 50 books on this basis."

This example is startling because it is so exceptional. Undoubtedly, many librarians will consider this duplication ratio as excessive. We would not be surprised if it proved, in time, to be still less than adequate.

Any storekeeper who devoted as little careful attention to the quantity factor as most libraries, even if his judgments about the quality of his products were impeccable, would very probably go bankrupt. The shopper who goes to a supermarket, for example, for something as basic as a bar of soap and several times doesn't find it because the management consistently miscalculates customer needs, would very quickly stop using that supermarket. If reader dissatisfaction in libraries had the same immediate economic consequences as customer dissatisfaction has upon the store, libraries also would quickly be in deep trouble.

The principal reason why shelf collections are so frequently inadequate in meeting reader needs is that the book selection process stops too early, operates too much in limbo. A tedious and often unnecessary amount of time can be spent on the decision to include or exclude a particular title, but beyond that not much happens. The statistics that are so laboriously compiled by libraries reveal little that is helpful about the usage of specific books. Many modern circulation systems have removed even the last remnant of elementary evidence about usage from the book: the old date label. And rare is the library where trained personnel are assigned fulltime to the care and study of the book collection *and its usage*. When libraries assign the same priority to the content of the collection as they do at present to the mechanics of the collection, for example in technical processes, library collections may take on a relevance many do not exhibit today.

CHAPTER

1 *Book Rejection:*
Is It Censorship?

(JUNE 15, 1962)

"I personally feel on much stronger ground defending the *inclusion* of a book than I do defending the exclusion of a book from a public library collection." Wouldn't Lj consider doing something "on the obverse of the coin—how and when to reject a book"?

This was the opinion expressed by Lelia B. Saunders, assistant director of the Arlington (Virginia) County Libraries, on her approach to book selection and censorship.

By way of illustration, Miss Saunders pointed out that, while *Tropic of Cancer* was banned in many other libraries in the greater Washington, D.C. area, her library had copies, and very few objections had been lodged by Arlington citizens.

In contrast, the library had been besieged with complaints, directly and in the press, because it refused to buy Carleton Putnam's incendiary book, *Race and Reason.* This decision was later reversed, but Miss Saunders explained that the original rejection decision was based on "a staff review, a LIBRARY JOURNAL review, a *National Review* review and a statement in the fall from the American Anthropological Society which rejected in committee, 192 to 0, Mr. Putnam's thesis of Negro inferiority to white, biologically and in innate mental ability. We felt that the book engendered racial hatred and that Mr. Putnam advanced scientific theories without providing any proof except the author's own statements."

Basically, the problem Miss Saunders wanted discussed was, to use her own words "How far is a public library obligated to go in providing controversial material, which would otherwise be rejected? . . . One side of the question says the public library *should* add questionable material, particularly in the controversial fields, so that its readers can make up their own minds. On the other hand, books of scientific unreliability or those fostering intolerance or racial or religious hatred are not to be added."

Miss Saunders' question is one that is being asked all over the country. How far do we go in the quest for impartiality? We have recently heard a library school teacher, who is also a member of a local library board, express concern because copies of the Putnam book and other publications representing views of right wing extremists have found their way into that local library usually by gift.

Liberal minded librarians have repeatedly affirmed that a library must stock books representing all points of view on a controversial question. Putnam's view is an ugly one, and certainly cannot be defended scientifically. But it is a view held by a considerable number of people, and their views perhaps *cannot* be presented rationally or scientifically. Should the Putnam book therefore be represented in a public library collection? Should the Birch Society publications? Can one know how the opposition thinks and operates (the argument used for stocking pro-Communist books) without having their views represented in the collection?

Or is there a tendency for liberals only to be liberal on behalf of the things they believe in? Are they not as bad as the censors they attack if they repeatedly reject books they don't agree with, or which they believe to be "unsound," even though these books may represent a considerable segment of public opinion?

How, in short, does a librarian reject a book, particularly a controversial book, without incurring charges of censorship?

Miss Saunders' comments and some of these questions were sent to a number of librarians who have been much concerned with problems of book selection and censorship. The point was not to discuss the Putnam book specifically, but the problem which it seems to illustrate so well.

Below the views of some of those who responded are presented. Several, in covering letters, admitted that the problem raised was an exceptionally difficult one, and one or two said they were not satisfied that they had come to grips with it.

Jerome Cushman, Librarian, New Orleans Public Library, Louisiana: If this were the most perfect of worlds, your question "How does a librarian reject a book—particularly a controversial book—without incurring charges of censorship?" would have a ready-made, simple answer.

A book is rejected because it does not come up to the standards required by the library as adjudicated by staff and librarian.

In the last analysis one can say, "I'm the librarian and as far as book selection goes, the buck stops here."

Life in the jungle of book selection is not easy. The problem of public policy, pressures that are exerted by those who feel that the book should be in the library, the librarian as an unconscious censor, and whether or not the librarian is necessarily the best judge of a work, all enter the tangled forest together.

Let's dispose of the last point first.

For better or worse, whether he is capable or not, the librarian must assume the final responsibility of rejecting a book for the library. Collective leadership does not work here. At best, a Board of Trustees can take the heat off the librarian, but this is not book selection. Selection belongs where responsibility can be assessed. It is equally untenable for a librarian to hide behind a Book Selection Committee, or for that matter, a book selection policy. A book selection policy is a guidepost, preferably set out in general terms to be acted upon by reasonable and trained librarians. Proper library growth can be stultified when a book selection policy becomes a weapon to be used as an excuse for rejection. There is real danger that a dogmatic approach to book selection can result in the error of failure to consider the book as a whole. The problem of liberal versus conservative is now so tangled that both terms, within the framework of book selection, are becoming meaningless. The viewpoint of the reviewing authority rather than the validity of the book often becomes a controlling factor.

The most persistent irritant these days is the crusading spirit exemplified by groups who are vocal in their devotion to democratic principles. They would not think of asking that a book be removed from library shelves, but they exert fiendish pressure in seeing that multiple copies are placed in the library, without cost to the book budget. Book selection becomes blurred in the face of this type of pressure. Librarians do not wish to be considered censors and they many times inevitably allow the books to be placed in the library, often against their professional judgment. Book selection policies can meet this situation only halfway. Personal courage and conviction must come the other half of the distance.

Public policy has many ramifications. In all of this concern for book selection and book rejection (since both are identical) one could well keep in mind the basic task of the library as a community resource, as well as a deep respect for its mission.

It seems equally important to think of the responsibilities of librarianship, remembering that while book selection at best is subjective, the maintenance of the integrity of an institution which reflects the freedom of the mind must do so objectively and in the highest service of the multi-sided individuals who make up the public.

I know that in some degree the librarian will act in accordance with his skill, his convictions, and the loud, large voice of his conscience.

Edwin Castagna, Director, Enoch Pratt Free Library, Baltimore, Maryland: One way to a sure footing on the slippery ground where you reject a controversial book is to have a book selection statement on exclusion as well as inclusion. The Enoch Pratt Free Library has such a statement. The following staff reviews apply some of its principles. "For instances" are probably better than generalizations.

In excluding Emmett McLoughlin's *Crime and Immorality in the Catholic*

Church, several reviews were used. One of them gives cogent reasons for exclusion: "He generalizes from insufficient data, makes false deductions, disregards evidence, uses emotional and abusive epithets—in short, furnishes textbook illustrations of all the common types of fallacious reasoning. I went to the trouble to verify some of his references and statistics. The statistics, though accurate, were old, dating from 1880–1885–87, and 1910 (p. 56, 57, 64) but were offered to prove statements in contemporary conditions."

Rosalie M. Gordon's *Nine Men Against America* was excluded upon the basis of this review: "This book is an outstanding example of determining one's conclusions and arguing emotionally therefrom. It is full of historical mis-apprehension, specious reasoning, outright smear and the emotionally charged vocabulary which seems characteristic of much of this type of right wing opinion. It is possible to build a respectable case of sorts against the Supreme Court but fair-minded persons will give little credence to views which show so little fundamental faith in American Institutions. John Frank's *Marble Palace,* recently published, offers a refreshing contrast."

If we apply recognized criteria, we will get through pretty well. Every-body falls down now and then. And when you make a misstep you can expect to be called to account. Nobody forced us into librarianship. The public has an interest in what we select and reject. We made ourselves targets when we became public servants. If we get hit occasionally, we shouldn't cry over it. Controversy is one indication we are alive. A doctor diagnoses and prescribes even though he doesn't know everything about human tissues and diseases. And he can take his lumps and still get a fair night's sleep. Agility in walking the slippery path will be improved if we have to dodge brickbats while we are trying to stay on our feet.

(*Because it is, in our view, one of the best statements of its kind, we quote below a passage from "Book Selection Policies," Enoch Pratt Free Library, 2d. edition, 1961, p. 12—Ed.*)

Public opinion tends to change with time and circumstances. It is at times hasty and emotional (witness, for example, the ban on German in schools during World War I). Since librarians do not claim to be exempt from these transitory currents of feeling, they believe that public opinion, even when shared by themselves, is scarcely a safe guide for book selection and exclusion in a library with a duty toward the future as well as the present.

In view of the above considerations, the Library observes the following general rules:

On questions on which there are two or more widely supported opinions or theories, and about which definite facts have not been established or which by their very nature are not susceptible of factual proof, the Library will pro-vide material on both or all sides as far as availability permits. An attempt is made to provide books that give evidence of a sincere desire to get at the facts, and seem to be written in a reasonable fashion, and as a result of careful study. The Library may, on the other hand, decide to exclude sensational, violent, or inflammatory books, and those that contain demonstrably false statements and undocumented accusations. For exceptions, see the paragraph below.

The Library may exclude from its collection a majority of the books presenting views that are regarded by a consensus of responsible opinion—civic, scientific, religious, and educational—as unsound, and have been so regarded over a period of years. For the use of students and scholars, however, the Library collection may include a few representative and prominent books which, when published, favored practices which have since come to be regarded as either anti-social or positively illegal, e.g., it possesses a number of anti-bellum works in favor of slavery, which are of great value to students of the period. Since such books and pamphlets are difficult to obtain except currently, the Library recognizes its obligation to future scholarship to include a very few prominent examples of current materials of an anti-social nature. These are usually kept for reference use only. For their historical value, the Library also purchases works of world or national figures whose views, though they may be widely rejected, have affected events. Such books usually circulate, although in rare cases they may be kept for reference use.

Stuart C. Sherman, Librarian, Providence Public Library, Rhode Island: To record in 500 words a defense for book rejection may be compared to the feat of recording the Lord's Prayer on the head of a pin.

It is easy to reject books, but it is often difficult to justify the reasons, and even more difficult to satisfy certain readers of the reasons for rejection.

In the Address given at the dedication of the Providence Public Library building in 1900, Arnold Green, a trustee of the library and father of former Senator Theodore Francis Green (a trustee for 59 years), stated: "As trustees of the public library we have no opinions . . . In the disputes of history, the bickerings and eulogies of biography we take no part. . . . Our business is to furnish, so far as we are able, the means for acquiring information and then to say: Come, study, think and decide."

The chief responsibility of librarians is to gather and make available the best books in all fields representing all points of view for all types of readers. Since book selection is indirectly a winnowing process, it defers or drops from consideration many books which fail to meet accepted standards. But to many persons the absence of a book in a library collection is considered censorship. Such persons accuse the library of denying others the right to know.

Library standards for rejecting a book must, therefore, be as carefully considered as the standards for selection. We may be challenged for rejecting a book, and we should be prepared to defend our reasons.

Book rejection, just as book selection, presupposes acceptance of the principles of the *Library Bill of Rights* and *The Freedom to Read*. What, then, are the justifiable grounds for rejection?

1. LEGAL. Books which represent treason, libel or pornography.

2. FINANCIAL. The ability of every library to purchase books is largely governed by the extent of its book budget. The limitation of funds places a limit on what we can buy, which forces librarians to reject many which cannot qualify for selection.

3. STANDARDS OF SELECTION. The absence of certain standards in a book may be considered grounds for rejection. Among these standards are the authority of the author, the reputation of the publisher, literary style or clarity of expression, format, etc.

4. LIBRARY POLICY. Just as in book selection, rejection will vary with the nature and size of the library. In general, books may be rejected if the nature of the community is such that the book would be too technical or erudite (e.g. *The Parasitology of the Salamander*); if there is no industry or ethnic group that would demand its presence; if the book collection has an adequate, up-to-date coverage of the subject; or if the subject is the responsibility of another library in the community. Books should be rejected only when they fail to meet thoughtfully approved library policy.

Librarians often give such reasons for rejecting books as "controversial," or "it might offend certain people." These are indefensible reasons. The fact that a work is controversial is, in the context of the *Library Bill of Rights*, the best reason for its inclusion in a public library collection.

Having a book on our shelves implies no automatic approval of its contents, nor should the absence of a book imply our condemnation of it.

In book rejection, as in book selection, objectivity on the part of the librarian is essential. A book must never be rejected because our opinion persuades us that it is inappropriate. Librarians must possess subject knowledge, a familiarity with publishing and the ability to evaluate, but this is no area for personal opinion.

Ray Smith, Director, Mason City Public Library, Iowa: As the Fiske study showed (*Book Selection and Censorship* by Marjorie Fiske, Berkeley, University of California Press, 1959), most censorship in libraries has probably been quietly accomplished by librarians themselves, through rejection of potentially controversial books.

Such rejection for social or political opinion, or for manner of literary expression, solidly defies the Freedom to Read statement of ALA, which ought to be adopted as a minimal book selection policy by every library board and be on the agenda of every state association to this end. This policy, interpreted and defended by the community librarian, must be the backbone without which a crucial freedom may not stand erect.

For example, in March, 1961, several Iowa libraries rejected three Russian Embassy gift pamphlets containing information about the 1961 Soviet Communist Party Congress, much of it already printed in newspapers and magazines. This was an unwise rejection, drawing unfavorable publicity to libraries. It was an attempt to foreclose the risk of controversy. But the risk and the miracle of freedom are inseparable—for libraries no less than the press.

Proposition One of the Freedom to Read statement asserts that: "It is in the public interest for publishers and librarians to make available the widest diversity of views and expressions, including those which are unorthodox or unpopular with the majority."

Rejection of medical or scientific material for inaccuracy is a different thing. Here, *cooperative inquiry* by librarian and qualified professional people —an approach rather than a formula—may determine acquisition or rejection. For example, we rejected a book on cancer because of medical advice that it contains harmful misinformation.

Central to the issue of book rejection is the proposition that when a librarian surrenders his right of selection under pressure he becomes only a more or less gracious purveyor—not an intellectually desirable role, and one with a growing shadow across the community. He may be called upon, for example, to decide how extensively, in terms of balance and limited budget, he can represent extremist publications. In most libraries the shelves themselves speak to the reader—and they should not reflect, by their numbers or their omissions, pressures of fear or prejudice.

It is not always understood by readers that selection among the 15,000 titles published in one year means rejection of others, within book budget limits. Yet wherever there seems to be a living option in opinion or theory, access somewhere in the library system or by interlibrary loan from research collections has special importance for titles outside the range of the smaller or medium sized library.

What is apparently needed by most libraries is a fuller interpretation to the community of book selection policy. And, needed also, since rejection is negative, is strength through positive selection in sensitive areas.

Zada Taylor, Librarian, West Valley Regional Branch, Los Angeles Public Library, California: A librarian cannot reject a book, particularly a controversial book, without incurring charges of censorship. It may be an insignificant charge with only local implications, but in this day and age a librarian must be prepared to face this charge daily. This is a "sign of our times" and is not the librarian's problem alone. Each in his own way, educator, scientist, doctor, lawyer, is faced with the same basic problem. Mass communication and turbulent times accentuate and foster sensitivity to these problems and leave no convenient holes in which to bury our heads.

Blank statements tend to be idealistic and gloss over the hard face of reality, but I feel every librarian must be prepared with sound, unemotional and impersonal arguments to justify exclusion and/or combat the charge of censorship.

My personal feelings are strongly in favor of including controversial material, even questionable material, unless it is presented emotionally and blatantly without merit and for no other reason than to incite. It seems to me that public libraries are obligated to make available as much material, on all sides of all questions, as is possible within the standards set by the community. My reasons for this are not just those of making both sides immediately available but also have to do with the future and having available in years to come such material that may be of great value to students and historians. Currently we have the Birch Society—15 or 20 years ago we had the Townsend Plan and Technocracy—and a little before that there was *Uncle Tom's Cabin!*

John F. Anderson, Director, Knoxville Public Library, Tennessee: In the minds of many people, book selection becomes censorship when someone disagrees with the decision to exclude a title. The public librarian will often be subject either to charges of censorship or promiscuous buying. He cannot hide behind the excuse of insufficient funds, since most libraries have enough money to purchase titles demanded by the community. If there is a lack of funds, more often than not there is a willing donor who will force the selection decision on a controversial book.

A fundamental question relating to inclusion and exclusion of material on controversial topics is raised upon reading the Library Bill of Rights. How far should a public library go in "resisting all abridgement of the free access to ideas and full freedom of expression." Librarians are taught the fundamentals of evaluating material for library purchase; then in practice they are confronted with the demand that material be included that does not meet the standards of sound factual authority. At what point do and should our standards for quality break down before the "free access to ideas" provision? Are we to use the principle of sound factual authority only with noncontroversial materials?

My concern as a public librarian is for proper use of materials in the controversial area. Many of our users of nonfiction materials are high school young people working on "research papers." When materials are made fully accessible, there is a real possibility that the "controversial scale" is not balanced in actual reader selection. Few adult or young readers follow a program of reading both sides of an issue. If the library has accepted material lacking sound factual authority in its effort to present all sides, then it may find itself offering unreliable proposals to a number of readers without any counterbalance.

I believe that the public library should be a strong center for impartial information and education in the community. I would hope that the public library would have the reputation for good accurate material. I do not think the library need *equally* balance its collection in controversial areas, particularly if the material available attacks responsible laws or medical or scientific facts.

Defending the purchase of material upon the grounds of freedom of expression and freedom to read may be easier than defending a rejection; but if we are to exercise no judgment, then we might better become public book store retailers, using clerks to order and stock only what is asked for. We should represent both (or all) sides of an issue (when is an issue no longer controversial—upon unanimous opinion?), but only by careful selection of the most reputable material. If we do less, we lose our obligation to select, and then become a center for propaganda from all sides.

Donald V. Black, Physics Librarian, University of California, Los Angeles, and Editor, "Newsletter on Intellectual Freedom": Book selection has always been a precarious business and frequently, whether we admit it to ourselves or not, the real criterion used to reject a book is some slight personal prejudice. It is precisely for this reason that book selection is frequently done by committee. But committees, too, can be subject to prejudice.

The stock phrase, "in keeping with the usual practices of book selection," is usually quoted to justify the presence of some book in a library, but it is equally valid to justify the rejection of a book. The difficulty comes in explaining just what the "usual practices" of book selection are. The criteria used will vary according to the type of library, and in accordance with the stated goals of the larger institution, of which the library may be a part. An academic library, for example, may have a goal of completeness in one or more subjects. Most public libraries do not have such a goal.

But despite the differences, there would seem to be at least one common factor: *usefulness* to the clientele of the specific library. Rejection of a book can be based on this factor. In a scientific library, if a book does not meet a certain level of technical proficiency, if it does not contribute to the advancement of knowledge in the subject discipline of which it treats, it may not be useful to the particular clientele of that library. Thus, it would be rejected for that reason, even though it might be quite satisfactory for a high school science class. A book such as *Race and Reason* might well be rejected on the basis that it would serve no purpose, that is, be of little use. But such a view of a book ceases to be valid as soon as a controversy arises concerning it. Thus, in any controversial matter, all materials of any bearing whatsoever on the controversy then become useful, so that each individual may be free to form his own opinion.

In book selection there is danger in relying on reviews which appear in journals having nation-wide circulation, and on the opinion of "experts" in distant cities, because distant reviewers or experts cannot determine the usefulness of a particular item in a particular place. It must also be recognized that usefulness changes with time. If a book is rejected because of a lack of usefulness, one must always be watchful that a need does not develop in the future for the material contained in that previously useless book.

An academic library can afford to wait for many years for use to develop. Most public libraries cannot. If the potential use is not immediate, then the items should not be purchased.

In Arlington a use for *Race and Reason* developed just as soon as there was a controversy concerning the book. It was at that point that the reviewers' opinions concerning the book became of no importance, and the book should have been added to the collection. (*It was—Ed.*)

Materials published by the John Birch Society, or approved by them, could be examined in the same light. If, in a given community, there is no interest in politics, if no one cares about the John Birch Society, or its counterparts on the far left, then there would be no need to have materials concerning the John Birch Society or left wing organizations, because there would be no use for them. Barring lack of funds for any purchase whatsoever, then, potential usefulness becomes the only valid criterion for book selection or rejection.

Robert B. Downs, Dean of Library Administration, University of Illinois Libraries, Urbana: Nearly 40 years' inculcation in the policies and practices of university library book selection doubtless disqualifies me from attempting to answer the question of how and when to reject a book—certainly in the form stated by Miss Saunders.

In several respects, the university librarian and the public or school librarian live in different worlds. The true university is traditionally a community of scholars, and its librarian is unlikely to be concerned with the reading of children and adolescents, people of limited educational background, and the general public. As is implicit in its name, the university library is universal in scope, and literally nothing is foreign to the potential concerns of its clientele. All eras, ancient and modern, all languages, no matter how esoteric, and every subject however exotic—from A to Z, or from ooo to 999—are encompassed in its wide-ranging resources.

Is there, then, no limit or restriction to be placed on the growth of a university library collection? Naturally, there are practical limitations caused by shortages of funds, lack of space, varying emphases in curricula and research programs, and the enormous volume of contemporary publishing.

No more than his colleagues in other branches of librarianship, too, can the university librarian disregard or ignore the increasing costs of technical processing, forcing him to reject, or at least to apply rigid standards of selection to, materials of ephemeral interest and value simply because of the expense of cataloging, classifying, binding, and shelving.

In the realm of controversial literature, however, the university librarian is seldom subjected to the kinds of pressures so frequently felt by the public and school librarian. On the contrary, university faculty members and students thrive on controversy. They find in an atmosphere of intellectual ferment the ideal environment for teaching and scholarship. Dedicated to the search for truth, it is a *sine qua non* that they have access to all shades of opinion on ethics, morals, philosophy, religion, politics and government, economics, art, education, literature, and innumerable other facets of the complex universe in which we live. For them, the library must represent in every debatable area the entire spectrum, from extreme left to extreme right. The world is the university's oyster, and the library carries the sword with which to open it. Thus, books, if rejected, are excluded for the fundamental reason that they have been judged to contribute nothing significant to the endless quest for the advancement of learning.

CHAPTER

2 *The Actual Enemy*

(JULY, 1962)

by WILLIAM L. EMERSON

Thomas Mann once said that order and simplification are the first steps toward the mastery of a subject—the actual enemy is the unknown. The problems connected with the evaluation and selection of books do seem at least disorderly if not downright chaotic when one realizes that since 1921 there have been—even allowing for duplication—over 400 articles appearing in *Library Literature* under the headings, "Book Selection," and "Public Libraries —Book Selection." Let me hastily confess that I didn't read these articles. Counting them alone convinced me that reading them was no way to attempt to bring order and simplification into the problems connected with the evaluation and selection of books in the sciences.

If we do not plunge into this morass of material, how then might we begin to bring some semblance of order and simplification into the problem? I should like to begin by recommending for the book selector in any field, Carter and Bonk's *Building Library Collections* published by the Scarecrow Press in 1959. The opening chapter on "Principles of Book Selection" is of interest, not only because it lists most of the various principles that have come into professional discussion about book selection but also because it shows what conceivably might develop if a selector tried to follow any of these principles. If one follows demand or "give 'em what they want" theory one will obviously end up with a quite different collection than if one follows the value or "give 'em what they *should* want" theory. The core of the problem is one of finding as precisely as possible the fulcrum between these two extremes. Once found, there remains the continuing problem of keeping the collection somehow balanced between these two points. To paraphrase a famous statement, "Eternal vigilance is the price of a well-balanced book collection."

There is, however, a prerequisite to eternal vigilance. This prerequisite is a knowledge of what we are being vigilant for or vigilant against. Book selectors must, as Carter and Bonk state:

> . . . make judgments and choices from a clearly realized point of view and not from some nebulous, imprecise feelings which they have never translated into real understanding.
>
> The best way of assuring that such clear realizations will be achieved is to have a written statement of book selection policy. This statement should include an outline of the general purposes that the library is attempting to serve as well as a statement of the specific aims which arise out of the particular community's needs.[1]

There is only one disagreement I have with this statement. I do not think that having a written book selection policy statement is the "best" way, I think it is the *only* way. Unless some program for the basis of selection has been worked out, there will be no yardstick by which one can evaluate. Unless a book selector can operate from the basis of a statement, each of his selections might almost as well be based on coin flipping.

In the sciences as in any field, the drawing up of a comprehensive book selection policy statement is the first step in introducing some order and simplification into book selection. May I quote the three short paragraphs from the Long Beach Public Library book selection policy statement that pertain to science. After discussing the requirement of having all sides to social and political questions in accordance with the ALA's *Library Bill of Rights*, the book selection policy statement goes on to say:

> However, in the scientific and technical fields controversial and doubtful material should be avoided. Science generally is a field in which a distinction should be made between sciences and pseudo-science. The librarian, to avoid misusing funds and misleading patrons of the library, should attempt to draw this distinction, both in acquisition of materials and in classifying. When help to distinguish is needed, the librarian should rely on reliable professional journals, scientific reviews and specialists in the community.
>
> It is the library's policy to buy very selectively in medicine, surgery, psychiatry, and related fields. Books on diagnosis and treatment are not purchased for the general public for obvious reasons.
>
> Special care is necessary in the purchase of health and medical books in which subject matter or treatment is not recognized by reputable scientific authority. Careful examination of such books may rule out those which are unsound scientifically or potentially harmful. In doubtful cases, it is necessary to wait for authoritative reviews in reliable professional journals as a basis for selection.[2]

It will not always be easy to follow such a policy. The flying saucer controversy is a case in point. The adherents, dare I say fanatics, maintain that science has not yet caught up with this phenomenon. Thus confronted, can the science librarian do anything but reply, "This may be true but our book selection policy statement for the sciences gives us an objective formula for selection. At such time as flying saucer phenomena become scientifically acceptable, we will be most happy to treat them as such." The adherents will be unsatisfied, but the librarian will have a firm ground for defense.

In some respects the selection of books in the fields of science and technology, aside from the embattled fields of some of the social sciences, can be relatively painless, although it may be time consuming. Anthony Standen to the contrary, science is not a sacred cow. Science, by its very nature, as Louis N. Ridenour states, ". . . enjoys the property of having an agreed body of discipline and an agreed storehouse of objective information, which is shared by scientists the world around."[3]

Ridenour stated this in an article which should be required reading for every librarian selecting books in the sciences. It appeared as the chapter, "Science and Pseudo-Science," in the book, *Freedom of Book Selection*, published by ALA in 1954.

Science, then, represents a demonstrable and respectable body of knowledge. Accepting this basis, should not almost the entire weight of the book collection in the sciences consist of books which would have the approval of the scientific community? If *this* principle is accepted, then the question of how to evaluate books in the sciences could be reduced to the answering of a simple question, "Is the book scientifically acceptable?" Answering such a question requires reliance on such journals as *Scientific American, Science, Nature, Physics Today,* and the publications of the various scientific professional associations. It requires placing less reliance on *Publishers' Weekly, Kirkus, Booklist,* and the more commonly used book selection tools. Of these more familiar tools, I believe *Library Journal* to be the most reliable: although outside of this generalized belief I have but one bit of factual evidence to support such a statement. It is to be recognized, of course, that placing more dependence on scientific journals will sacrifice immediacy to reliability.

The public librarian can also rely on the publications of such agencies as the American Heart Association, the Arthritis and Rheumatism Foundation, the American Cancer Society, and other such nonprofit, public service agencies which try to disseminate the latest scientifically acceptable information. That the information they give may later be modified or even radically changed is not the point. At any given moment in time they are trying to disseminate the current information that reliably represents the state of knowledge.

Answering the question of scientific acceptability also requires placing less reliance on the *Standard Catalog for Public Libraries* than on such—if I may use the term in this context—a biblical-like aid as the *AAAS Science Book List* published by the American Association for the Advancement of Science in 1959. Although primarily aimed for the reading of young people, most of the books on the list are not beyond the comprehension of unscientifically oriented adults. As the introduction states,

> . . . not only have all of the books included in this list been suggested by
> professionals and specialists in their fields, but they have been read and evalu-

ated by senior high school students and college undergraduates majoring and already well grounded in the various fields of science and mathematics.[4]

By relying on such tools, the book selector can have a good deal of assurance that the books chosen reflect a high degree of scientific reliability.

There remains another major aspect of the problem. From these remarks so far it has been obvious that the underlying assumption has been that the value theory of book selection should probably be basic in choosing titles in the sciences. While it seems apparent to me that primary consideration should be given to the value theory, some attention must be paid to the demand theory. A public library collection, like any other collection, should bear some resemblance to the needs of its users.

A first step in the gathering of objective information on this point might be to find out what books, what fields of science, the readers are using. Lord Kelvin was fond of repeating that, "Until you can measure something you can know nothing about it." Two years ago in an effort to gather some information on book use in the Science-Industry Department of the Main Long Beach Public Library every book from the department that appeared on the microfilm circulation record for a two week period was transcribed to a Keysort punched card which was then coded to bring out certain data. I shall not bore you with a detailed analysis of the findings. Suffice to say that in this department, which contains the 300's, the 500's and the 600's in the Dewey Classification, the 300's accounted for about 32 percent of the department circulation, the 500's for about 19 percent, and the 600's for about 49 percent. It was interesting to us to note that the 610's and 620's alone accounted for almost 27 percent of the department circulation.

After completing this study we felt less in sympathy with Lord Kelvin's statement than we did with the reply once made to it: "Yes, but you can measure something and still not know very much about it." If we did know very little, we had at least learned which areas were in greatest use and where numerically at least the collection needed greatest strengthening.

In this analysis of circulation, books in the 610's accounted for over 10 percent of the department's circulation. Books on health and nutrition made up no small part of this figure. Sometime after our study was completed, a very useful list appeared in the LIBRARY JOURNAL for February 15, 1960 entitled, "Nutrition for Lay Readers," written by Helen S. Mitchell, Dean of the School of Home Economics at the University of Massachusetts. This annotated list contained 27 acceptable titles and 14 unacceptable titles. Acceptable and unacceptable, that is, as books for the lay public judged by the scientifically trained people working in the fields of nutrition and public health. The Science-Industry Department collection contained a healthy number in each category —or should I say an unhealthy number? While we have not yet withdrawn any titles not recommended, we did purchase all the recommended titles which we did not have and duplicated those recommended titles which were already represented. We are not replacing any of the nonrecommended titles as they are worn out or are lost. We hope that in the not too distant future Gaylord

Hauser, Adelle Davis, and D. C. Jarvis will follow the fading act usually attributed to old soldiers.

This general area brings us to an important consideration. Many public library patrons actually turn to books in the areas of science for nonscientific reasons. They do not seek objective analysis of factual data. They seek solace, comfort, or something that will bolster their own preconceived ideas of life or of some aspect of life. Martin Gardner's *Fads and Fallacies in the Name of Science* is an enlightening discussion of many of the unusual ideas that have been offered to and accepted by people under the guise of science.

In 1955 in New York there appeared a delightful off-Broadway musical called "The Shoe String Revue." One of its many high points was a production of the Medea legend as it might ostensibly be retold by Walt Disney. In the closing moments of this number, Jason, who has just seen his fiancée and future father-in-law burned to a crisp, is not downcast. As he says to Medea, "A bright, sunny, golden future can still be ours if only we wish hard enough. Education, planning, hard work, all these things have their place but for results give me a good, solid wish every time." Perhaps this wishful Jason bears some similarity of character to some of those who have accepted as scientifically valid some of the rosy nostrums that have been offered in the name of science.

No librarian needs to be told that some patrons want and seem to need this strong belief in pseudo-science. As Jean Rostand has said in his book, *Error and Deception in Science:*

> Pseudo-sciences are important factors in our social life. If we were to take stock of the followers of radiesthesia, of astrology, of metaphysics, etc., we should discover that they far outnumber the more earth-bound scientists. Nor do these mystifiers need to expend a great deal of their energy on propaganda;— their armies require little encouragement.[5]

The numbers of these armies who patronize the public library are, after all, also supporters of the public library and some attempt should be made to meet their needs. If some of the titles of books which satisfy their needs are in the medicine and health classification, shouldn't some effort be made to see that these books are not potentially medically harmful? Our own local Public Health Department has always been most willing to help us if the reviewing media leave room for doubt. Also, our patrons have seemed to appreciate booklists which the Science-Industry Department issues occasionally which call attention to recommended titles of books about health and disease and which also give the reason for not purchasing certain titles in these fields.

If other titles in the science classification actually represent the nonscientific wishful thinking that some patrons find helpful, does not the library have an obligation to the scientific community, to science itself, to see that some degree of differentiation separates science from pseudo-science? Might not and should not some arbitrary subclassification be assigned to the 500's and 600's for pseudo-science? Or, as an alternative, might not these titles join others in that peculiar fictive cosmos of the 100's which has been somewhat quaintly called "Occult Sciences"? Surely this is one of the most flagrant contradictions in terms that our profession has perpetrated!

If I have digressed somewhat from the basic problem of evaluation and selection, it is because the problem does not necessarily end there. If it is necessary to acquire and classify some of these so-called nonfiction titles, surely we should not honor them by calling them science. As Ridenour has stated in the article already quoted:

> In sum, then, science generally, is a field in which a distinction—an objective distinction—can be drawn between responsible and irresponsible work, between the trained worker and the quack, and between science and pseudo-science. The librarian, to avoid misusing funds for acquisitions and misleading clients of the library, should attempt to draw this distinction, both in acquisition and in classifying, and where advice is needed to permit this to be done, the librarian's scientific colleagues, I am sure, will be ready with that advice.[6]

In conclusion, if we recognize the validity of science as an organized body of knowledge; if we prepare our book selection policy statement for the sciences to reflect this recognition; if we seek scientifically reputable guides; if, with the dross we find must be present, we take care to see that it can be recognized as dross; if, in short, we follow some of the aims and methods of science itself, we will have introduced some objective procedure, some fundamental order into the process needed for the solution of the problems of evaluation, selection, and classification of books in the sciences. As Thomas Mann once said, "Order and simplification are the first steps toward the mastery of a subject—the actual enemy is the unknown."

REFERENCES:

1. Mary Duncan Carter and Wallace J. Bonk. *Building Library Collections*. Scarecrow Press, New York. 1959. p. 25
2. Long Beach Public Library. *Policy and Procedure Manual*. Long Beach, California. 1958. (mimeo) p. 18
3. Louis N. Ridenour. "Science and Pseudo-Science" in *Freedom of Book Selection*. American Library Association, Chicago. 1954. p. 42
4. *The AAAS Science Book List*. American Association for the Advancement of Science and the National Science Foundation, Washington, D.C. 1959. p. 4
5. Jean Rostand. *Error and Deception in Science*. Basic Books, New York. 1960. p. 30
6. Louis N. Ridenour. ibid. p. 21

CHAPTER

3 *"I May, I Might, I Must"*

(FEBRUARY 1, 1963)

by DOROTHY M. BRODERICK

In a poem entitled "I May, I Might, I Must," Marianne Moore writes, "If you will tell me why the fen/appears impassable, I then/will tell you why I think that I/can get across it if I try." Rarely has a title been so important to a poem—for it takes us from the point of having permission to act, then moves on to consideration of action, ending with determination to do the job.

I am going to set down some of the strongest reasons I know that "appear" to make consistent, impartial, scientific book selection impossible. And in examining these obstacles, I hope to demonstrate that the job can be done if only we will try.

SHAKY CONCEPTS

I started to label this section "false premises" but have settled for the phrase "shaky concepts." The word false implies value judgments which I am not yet ready to make. I am willing to go only so far as to say that the following concepts, each of which represents a generally accepted principle, seem to me to be still vulnerable.

Shaky concept number one: We tend to believe that the process of book selection is an orderly one; that it can be handled by learning a few basic principles in library school and by writing a book selection policy. I am all in favor of written book selection policies; I am a little disturbed by the great faith being placed in them. They are fast taking on the dangerous aspect of an intellectual Maginot line.

Shaky concept number two: We tend to believe that the "Freedom to Read" document is a concrete statement rather than a series of slogans. We also appear to believe that freedom to read as a process (as opposed to *The* statement) is an unlimited freedom.

Shaky concept number three: This is really a part of two, but is so vital that I have made it independent. This concept is that the public library has a responsibility to provide materials on all sides of all questions.

Shaky concept number four: That the public library, as a unit of government, has a responsibility, first and foremost to the community which has given it its legal entity.

GROUND RULES

In discussing these shaky concepts, I am not considering the research library, but the library designed for popular use. It may be that we should have a fifth shaky concept, namely that many librarians appear to believe that the same principles of book selection are applicable in a public library as in a university library. I do not believe this to be possible and would like to stress that nothing in this article is to be interpreted as applying to a research library.

RESPONSIBLE TO WHOM?

Every person I know in the library field, be he friend, casual acquaintance or opponent, is in agreement that the public library has responsibilities. But, when we ask "responsible to whom and for what?" not even a kaleidoscope produces as many variegated patterns.

While it is the local community that gives us our existence, our responsibility is primarily, as Margaret Monroe has said so well, to those "few fundamental values upon which human society is based, and which have been determined by a consensus of responsible opinion distilled from all fields of knowledge over the total period of man's culture."[1]

Therefore, when we talk about all sides of all questions, we are engaged in academic discussion, stimulating perhaps, but impractical in practice. Even if a library had space and money to provide all sides of all questions, it would not want to do so. The real question is how many sides of which questions?

Some questions have been removed from the arena of public debate. We do not believe, for example, that murder is the solution to personal conflicts between people. An author who set forth the premise that we had a perfect right to murder our mother-in-law or co-worker simply because she had made our lives intolerable should find no space on the public library shelf.

FLUORIDATION AND VACCINATION

On the other hand, the question of fluoridation of water is still very much in the arena of debate and the pro and con should be represented. I would not buy a book that claimed fluoridation was a Communist conspiracy. I *would* buy one that discussed the question in terms of the individual's right to decide for himself whether he wants to take preventive medication. To further clarify this point, let us note that, as far as we know, decaying teeth are not contagious and that we cannot equate them with vaccination laws established by the community. When an individual's personal behavior endangers the community health, the individual must yield. That is the essence of democratic life.

We are now in the middle of the freedom to read question—freedom to read what? One of the things that confuses this issue is the continued use of the word censorship. I would strike it forever from library literature. We may be good or bad selectors; we cannot be censors. For censorship is a legal process. It is the bringing to bear on a book, the legal arm of the community to effectively deprive all citizens from buying, and consequently from reading, a book. All the public library says when it does not purchase a book is that in our considered judgment the purchase of a particular title is not a legitimate use of public funds. Interested parties can still buy the book if they wish.

I think I am willing to go on record as believing in the adult's right to *buy* any book. It is an oddity of the so-called right-wing groups who pride themselves on the role of the individual as opposed to governmental action, that they are the people most dedicated to "protecting" the very individuals they claim to champion.

Let us look at the limitations on the freedom to read within the context of Margaret Monroe's statement that "the library takes no responsibility for telling people what to think but does take responsibility for proposing what they shall think about.[2] Whether Miss Monroe would agree with my examples is unknown to me. That I am presuming to expand on the best statement ever made in library literature is the height of audacity.

Freedom is bounded by the lines of legality, morality, ethics and community standards. In terms of the legal boundary, let us look at the subject of the United States Supreme Court. In recent years, the Court has made itself highly unpopular with a segment of the population because of its rulings on civil rights. It has been settled long ago that the Supreme Court represents "The law of the land." The public library's responsibility is to uphold that law just as much as any other unit of government should. Therefore, we can and should buy books which question the wisdom of the decisions as well as those in agreement with the Court. We should not buy books which advocate refusal to live within the framework of the decisions while working to alter them. In essence, we are saying, you may agree or disagree all you like but you must do it within the accepted framework of civilized behavior. This is our only defense against anarchy.

My personal philosophy of life is such that morality and ethics are synonyms. However, because of the strong religious foundations of our country, they are not generally thought of as synonymous. Therefore, I distinguish morality as those precepts generally accepted as God given, e.g. Thou shalt love thy neighbor. Ethics are man derived principles of behavior.

With this distinction, I would say that hate arousing books are immoral and logically rejected by the public library. That they may also be demonstrated as inaccurate is a further help in taking this stand. When a book plays on the fears of the reader, encourages his bigotry, it has no place in the library. Such books as Carleton Putnam's *Race and Reason* and Blanshard's *American Freedom and Catholic Power* fall into this category. You are undoubtedly surprised at the inclusion of Blanshard here, but I do not see how we can be consistent in this area unless we recognize that the illusion of scholarship is more dangerous than the purely emotional approach. All men are entitled to their opinions, no man is entitled to distort the facts to justify his opinion.

The fundamental ethic of American life is that all men are created equal, and while we are still a million light years away from seeing it practiced, we have as a nation, haphazardly and erratically worked toward it. This ethic is the basis for the first ten amendments to the Constitution and while we may argue over how much freedom of speech, for example, we may not argue about it as a right of man.

One of the real problem questions for many librarians is what happens when an ethic which is part of the nation's standards comes in conflict with local community standards. It is not a question that can be answered by a clever phrase in a book selection policy. It cannot even be answered the same way twice, for it would be ridiculous of us to pretend that we do not all make numerous compromises. What every librarian and board of trustees must determine together is what few principles are beyond compromise.

Our problem would be much easier if the attackers were consistent. Why, for example, the great concern with *Tropic of Cancer,* a book many people may buy or borrow but few will read; and the relative unconcern with *The Carpetbaggers,* as trashy a novel as I have encountered in years, but imminently readable from most people's standards? Why do the hard core segregationists shout, "You cannot legislate social behavior," and then surround themselves with local laws that legislate against social intercourse?

Inconsistency is not the exclusive property of other people; each of us has his share and every library in the country suffers from it. It does not come to southern segregationists and by-pass northern liberals; it does not infect the John Birchers and avoid the Communists. Thus we find libraries with *Das Kapital* behind locked doors, if they own it at all, and *Mein Kampf* circulating freely.

There are two major fallacies in our thinking about book selection practices. One is that we, as librarians, have no right to make value judgments; that our sole responsibility is to give people what they want. If this is the case, then there is no justification for requiring training and education for our jobs. The second, and far greater fallacy, is that a community is a completely homogeneous group.

The question cannot be phrased in an either-or sentence: do we give people what they want; or do we give them what we think is good for them? The question is, which demands do we satisfy? And, do we make our decisions solely on the basis of the number of demands or on the quality of the demands?

Within every community, there are segments with opinions contrary to the majority. Sometimes these opinions are destructive, sometimes, constructive. The library's responsibility, in my opinion (and here I have formulated a new law, "There are two sides to every question on which I have not made up my mind"), is to support constructive thinking. This is not difficult to identify with a little knowledge of history; history demonstrates that ideas cannot be eradicated by witch hunts and inquisitions; history shows that clinging to the status quo leads to annihilation or a mere fading away; history proves that fear eventually defeats itself.

The public library cannot be simply an institution dedicated to the status quo. It must also lead men to consider new ideas; it must have the foresight to recognize the future while it is still the present.

We must constantly bear in mind that all ideas that have moved mankind forward have been originally greeted with fear and sometimes with violence. From Copernicus to Galileo, to Darwin, to Einstein, men have trembled at the thought that the world was not what it appeared to be. Yet mankind has not only survived, it has prospered when the fear settled down and objectivity took over.

None of the questions I have raised nor the answers I have offered are simple. I have not said it would be easy to do the job; I have said only that it must be done. I think it requires nothing but intelligence, unswerving logic and a strong sense of purpose.

To accomplish the task, the library profession needs the best brains and the most courageous men it can find to man the barricades. I reject absolutely the Lj letter writer who defined our profession "as one kind of honest employment for modest remuneration and with modest job satisfactions." There is no other public institution in America with the same degree of freedom and the large number of valid reasons for exercising that freedom as the public library. It is time we saw our profession for what it can be—the most exciting, challenging and exacting job in the country. We need to have faith without allowing it to become dogmatism; we need to have self-confidence without it degenerating into egotism; we need the ability to question without becoming confirmed skeptics. Most of all we need Marianne Moore's conviction that the job can be done if only we will try.

REFERENCES

[1] Monroe, Margaret. *The Library's Collection in a Time of Crisis.* "*Wilson Library Bulletin,*" January 1962.
[2] *Ibid.*

4 Meeting Demands: A Library Imperative

(FEBRUARY 1, 1963)

by MARGARET E. MONROE

The sturdy defense, presented with a cocksure swing of the head, "I believe in giving people what they ask for," is often the response to an exhortation that the "demand theory" of book selection, or the "demand theory" of reader assistance, lacks something in its approach to the public library's collection and services.

Why has furnishing the reader with what he asks for been put on the defensive? What is there that makes a reader's request a paltry thing? The defenders of the demand theory stoutly assert the privilege of the reader to go his own merry way to damnation without a librarian rushing to his rescue with a reading ladder just before the flames close in.

> Dost thou think, because thou art virtuous,
> there shall be no more cakes and ale?

Can it be said that readers have abused the privilege of the public library? Taxpayers (nonreaders all!) question whether each must buy his neighbors' cakes and ale. Has the librarian—administrator of the community information center and director of a significant educational institution—settled for the role of proprietor of a house of respite reading? Thus the battle is engaged.

Let me speak a word for demand as a basis for library service—not as a theory but as an actuality. Bluntly, if there is no demand, there is no service. The library's collection exists even when idle on the shelves; the staff remains available even if there are no takers; but services exist only in the librarian's act of assisting a reader who *wants* the service. So demand is the most precious thing a librarian can ask: it is the reader's testimony of faith that the library may have something he really wants; it denotes the flexing of a mental muscle, a function to be fed and cultivated.

What are the problems the librarian faces in meeting readers' demands? Some demands upon the librarian may be outside the objectives of the library to provide; some demands may not be stated in terms of the real wants of the reader; some demands may not go far enough to provide the assistance the reader could well use. Demand is only the first element in the complex equation of service. Librarians clarify requests daily and suggest additional materials or services once they understand the reader's purposes. There can be no simple commandment in librarianship: Thou shalt meet demand. Perhaps the closest the librarian can come to a formulation is: Thou shalt listen to and attempt to understand the reader's demand.

RELEASING THE READER
FROM BONDAGE TO HIS DEMAND

As Harry Miller Lydenberg pointed out (*Bulletin of the New York Public Library*, March, 1936, p. 187), the general reader would often be in the embarrassing position of "starving in the midst of plenty" if it were not for the help the librarian provides in selecting from the wealth of possibilities the materials which he needs. The reader, aware that librarians answer questions, fashions his dilemma into a "question" so that it may be "answered" and the dilemma solved. "Do you have a book about personality?" he asks. Hopefully the librarian has such a book as he may need, although it may not be a book "about personality." The skillful librarian, at home among books and sensitive to the reader's difficulty in posing the problem which needs solution, releases the reader from the bondage of his inexact demand.

Charles Elliott, a British librarian of distinction, has commented that the reader should be given "not what he wants, not what we think he ought to want, but . . . the best that he is able to assimilate." (Charles Elliott, *Library Publicity and Service*. London: Grafton, 1951, p. 27.) This is no counsel to the creation of a frustrated readership. This is, instead, a rejection of reader service limited to the request from a reader whose conception of the library's potential is incapable of envisioning the satisfaction of his need at its best level. Elliott is counseling the librarian to open up the library's resources relevant to this particular reader's needs, interests, and abilities. Let the reader choose from knowledge of the wealth of possibilities, not out of ignorance or poverty of imagination.

RELEASING THE LIBRARIAN
FROM SUBSERVIENCE TO DEMAND

In these days of heavy library use and tremendous outpouring of publications, librarians must establish priorities among demands for books and services. No librarian can afford to be at the mercy of a particular demand. The most effective path to establishing priorities among demands for service is through clarification of library objectives and a full knowledge of the relevant needs of library users. A "demand theory" can never relieve a library of the obligation to clear objectives, and no statement of objectives phrased solely in terms of "meeting demands" is plausible since obviously there are demands which could conceivably be made of any library which never would be filled. The statement of *which* demands will be honored constitutes a statement of library objectives.

With a statement of library objectives in hand, the study of the library's community then becomes relevant to the identification of those needs which the library will attempt to meet. Then, when demand comes knocking loudly on the door, as librarians we are ready to answer: "Yes, I'll be pleased to talk with your group about books on insurance," or "No, I am sorry, we are not able to release staff to work on that project for you, but we'll be glad to give you a start with the bibliography"; or "Yes, our program specialist will be glad to help your committee with planning and I know that we have books and films on your topic." The librarian with full knowledge of his community and its needs is released from subservience to demand but cultivates and guides demand to fulfill the library's objectives.

The ability of the librarian to anticipate demand—in books or services—is a major factor in achieving excellence of library function. When important and legitimate demands arrive, the materials are there and the staff prepared to provide the information and the help required. Quick, effective response to demand has much more to commend it than merely the stout iteration that "our responsibility is to meet demands." Let us not scurry like mice at the sound of a demand but lead like lions in the filling of important needs which the reader's demand identifies.

EDUCATING DEMAND

The problems posed by the "demand theory" of collections and services are not confined to the need for clarification and amplification of the reader's request nor to the librarian's perception of priorities among demands. The quality of service performed by a library is directly related to the quality of demand from its community. The library, therefore, if it is to improve its service must be in a position to educate its readers' demands.

If, as the foregoing discussion has consistently implied, librarians are to determine *which* demands they will meet in terms of library objectives and community needs, then they must be in a position not only to *reject* demands which are unsuited to the library's purposes or are less significant in the light of community needs, but they must also be in a position to *encourage* the demand for services which will enable the library to fulfill its objectives and to meet community needs. If, for example, a library's service is not to remain on the primitive level of supplying casual reading or providing quick information, then its readers must be ready to demand more significant materials and more complex services. If the readers are not making these more important demands, then they must be encouraged to do so.

To the supporters of the "demand theory" the education of the reader's demand may seem the very height of manipulation and brain-washing. Let me suggest that it has become acutely necessary in our time to distinguish between manipulation and education lest our proper fear of manipulation deprive us of education, that essential function upon which the continuity of civilization depends. The librarian's education of demand should *release*, not control, the curiosities and interests of its readers; it will *increase* the diversity of materials to be read, viewed, and heard, not limit the range; it will *improve* the skill with which the library user makes independent judgments, not substitute the librarian's judgment for his own.

How can the public librarian function to improve the quality of demand so that these proper educational results are achieved? Let me suggest four approaches.

First, we interpret to our users and potential users the range of materials and services which are available to them, and make this clear in terms of relevant interests, talking to parents as parents, church members as church members, businessmen as businessmen. We seek them out to tell them about the materials and services they can "demand" from the library.

Second, we can provide our users with the opportunity to become more competent library users. As skills in using the library catalog and bibliographies, as skills in reading and in critical judgment of ideas to be found in books and films—as these skills are improved they will be more frequently exercised, and demand will mount.

Third, as public librarians we work with others in our community to create the climate for those things which produce demands for significant library service: the climate for intellectual curiosity, for scientific investigation of problems, for informed decision-making, for delight in reading. As the community climate for such values improves, demand for significant use of the library increases. The public library cannot control the community climate, but it, together with its colleague agencies, can cast the weight of its influence toward these social values.

Finally, in the daily service to readers we can exploit each request for service to its fullest usefulness for the reader who asks for help. Yes, "exploit," not the reader but rather the occasion for the reader's benefit. Such exploitation of the occasion avoids overburdening the reader with unwanted materials or assistance, but opens up the materials and services which will meet the *reader's* purpose and which are within *his* interest and ability to use with satisfaction.

One of the pleasantest remarks to the ears of a public librarian is the comment from the city mayor, the clubwoman, the businessman, the student, the lawyer, the city editor, the teenager: "Oh, I never realized we could get this here, and you've been so helpful!" This is the mark of a first step in *educating demand* and in improved library service.

In sum, the public library is a community service that functions only through meeting demands, and at the same time it is a social institution with particular responsibilities which it can fulfill only as it encourages its public to make increasingly significant demands upon it. It encourages an improved quality of demand through raising public expectation of library service and through stimulating public aspiration for knowledge and ideas. The public demand is the seed of intellectual life which the library nourishes and cultivates for the best uses of the individual and for the purposes of society.

5 *The Fallacy of "Balance" in Public Library Book Selection*

(FEBRUARY 1, 1966)

by RONALD A. LANDOR

A representative of the group that caused a furor in Long Beach, California, by seeking to impose its novel, alien and disruptive views of book selection upon the public library there, defined Liberal books as "those which advocate or advance the cause of 'one-world' socialist government." She defined Conservative books largely as those in opposition to this cause, and demanded equal expenditures for Conservative and Liberal books.

Clearly, this view bears no closer relation to bibliographic reality than do the bizarre persuasions, of which it is a characteristic expression, to political reality.

In Max Frisch's play, *The Firebugs*, there is a poor deluded householder who helps the arsonists burn his house down as they burned down other houses in his community. That householder is all the people of good will who are peculiarly vulnerable to those who would cripple or destroy them.

What could be more naive than letting the extremists foist upon us the conditions under which we consider the problem that their acts present to us? They provide the terms and we accept them. But accepting their terms of discourse is the first step toward accepting their definitions of these terms. Accept their definitions and you go a considerable way toward accepting their version of political reality. There may still be room for disagreement within their universe of discourse—but upon their terms. And it cannot be too strongly emphasized that these terms do not describe a real but an imaginary world.

This Liberal-Conservative bit is the extremists' game, and it is a shell game. But what is under the shells is a good deal more significant than the phony labels put upon them.

To define the terms of a problem is to influence or control its solution. We must emphatically reject the notion that we have to achieve some kind of mythical balance of Conservative and Liberal books in our public library collections.

Book selection implies discrimination according to a criterion of excellence. Is a particular book of a kind that belongs in a public, as distinct from a special or private, collection? Is it a good book of its kind? The answer to these questions is posited upon criteria of qualitative, not quantitative, values. Surely, nothing else that a librarian does has a sounder claim to be considered the distinctive contribution of his vocation than book selection. What would you think of a librarian who is not competent or is not inclined to apply the appropriate criteria to this function?

Let us be realistic and act upon the recognition that there are enemies of the public library as well as friends. If librarians would not be the dupes of their enemies, they should not adopt their principles. The most seemingly virtuous principles can be used for destructive ends. Principles are useless when divorced from reality, and mischievous when they lead us where we do not and should not want to go.

Could any self-respecting librarian agree to a balance of book-reviewing media in which there are LIBRARY JOURNAL, *Bookweek, Saturday Review, The New York Review of Books, The Atlantic,* and the *New York Times Book Review* on one side of the scale; and, on the other—presumably exactly balancing it—*The American Legion Magazine, The Dan Smoot Report, The Manion Forum, Counter-attack, The Wanderer,* and the Santa Ana *Register?* This is a sample of what is wanted by those who cry loudest for "balance."

The conviction that every book on politics bears, or should bear, either a Liberal or a Conservative label is, as we know, characteristic of a simple mentality. We do not wish to fall into the trap of looking at the world as if every part of it must be seen as either Red—or Red, White, and Blue. "Stick it on the left and color it Red" is simple enough but it is not illuminating.

It is a delusion to suppose that a line can be drawn, capable of separating the expression of political views into two neat halves of the same weight, labeled Liberal and Conservative respectively, which in some way it is the curious business of librarians to keep in balance in their collections. To be not only fair but also competent, librarians must be absolutely partial—partial to the book or other library material that is first-rate, no matter upon which side of some hypothetical line the views expressed in it may fall.

A sane community is one that seeks to identify its real problems and to discuss them rationally. The public library is more likely to be helpful in this quest if its materials are selected according to criteria of excellence and not by a balancing act. We are commissioned by our communities to select books on the basis of their intrinsic value, and not upon their imagined power to balance other books. It is the inherent worth of a book, determined according to our best informed judgment, that makes it appropriate public library material. What place does an irresponsible, badly-written, highly tendentious, sensationalistic book have in a public library, except possibly as an item in a display of literary trash? If we are deliberately to spend public money on trash, let us at least partly redeem its value in fulfilling the educational function for which the library is established by designating it as such.

Political writings of this caliber have no more place on the shelves of the public library than does hard-core pornography. No public library in the country can afford to buy whatever is published on every subject, and few can afford or even have the desire to buy "everything," even on only *one* subject of general interest. There are, of course, large research libraries that do attempt to buy in this way in a particular, limited field. But public libraries are not customarily able to indulge in this luxury. All public libraries are obliged to spend money discriminately on every subject.

Discrimination is the fundamental principle of book selection. But how does it apply in a particular instance; for example, in a Presidential election. One assumes that every public library in the country would want writings by and about the major candidates, but not necessarily their complete works or the works of some of their more zany followers. If a librarian does not understand that there is political pornography as well as sexual, political science fiction as well as the conventional brand, he is unqualified to select books discriminately in this field.

It is fairly well established that, as librarians, we are not required to pass judgment upon the truth or the soundness of the views expressed in the books we select for our collections; our concern is with the quality of their expression. (Of course, validity is never wholly distinct from style, but as far as book selection is concerned we should be able to make the distinction without cavil.) A considerable diversity and conflict of views will invariably be represented in any public library whose materials have been selected upon this principle.

The problem of books on communism is no different from that of books on any other subject of vital and disputed concern. The ostrich is not the public library's mascot. But there may be—indeed, there is—a perennial problem of attempted censorship of library materials, raised now in relation to one subject of popular interest and then to another.

At present, sex has become the center of interest for self-appointed censors of the library. To be really with it, library meetings should not be discussing Conservative-Liberal library materials but heterosexual and homosexual ones —how to achieve a proportional representation of the Straight and the Gay in a really well-balanced collection.

There are all sorts of ways that library materials might be balanced upon the basis of opposing interests, values, and opinions. Furthermore, the idea of balance has numerous relations.

There is, for example, the dictum that the collection should represent All Points of View. Since every book expresses a view distinct from that of every other, the addition of any book to the collection disturbs the "balance," however slightly.

Special pleading for O.K. values is also closely related to the notion of balance. That a book is "for" or "against" Patriotism, Morality, or Religion—or, for that matter, Freedom, Democracy, or Civil Rights—hardly seems sufficient reason for either its automatic selection or rejection. "For America First" and "We shall overcome" may be seen as admirable sentiments or not, depending upon one's point of view, but they are not principles of book selection.

Neither, to be sure, is Public Demand. When a librarian says of a good book, "It will be a shelf-sitter," this may not only be a bad guess and a weak excuse for rejecting it; it is often also a presumptuous downgrading of the public's intelligence, which must be assumed to be at least as considerable as our own.

By the same token, to yield to a vociferous and extended public campaign that seeks to gain greater representation for, or to exclude a particular viewpoint from, the collection can hardly be thought the exercise of book selection either.

As we know from the Fiske report, there is a silent veto that operates here too. A weasel approach to book selection taken by librarians who either lack the courage of their convictions or else lack convictions is most conveniently covered by the shibboleth of Public Demand.

All varieties of the balance of power approach to book selection open the way for bitter factional disputes in the community. Hearings by City Councils, who are appealed to over the head of the librarian, are naturally encouraged. The library itself becomes a battleground. Every request by a patron for library purchase of a particular book or periodical becomes a political act— with the decision on the request being made, not on the grounds of whether or not the book would add recognizable literary or educational value to the collection, but on the basis of whether or not it would "balance" it.

In order to balance a collection properly, it would be necessary to label the items in it—to label not only those expressing Conservative or Liberal viewpoints but those expressing every other kind of view. All significant items in opposition to anything else would have to be labeled, either in part or in whole, if we were to maintain the balance.

The American Library Association has said: "Labeling is an attempt to prejudice the reader, and as such, it is a censor's tool. Labeling violates the Library Bill of Rights."

Labeling makes it easy for the patron to pass judgment upon a book before he has read it. Whatever other objectives this procedure might serve, it would surely not be an educational one.

Labeling is not to be confused with classifying, any more than censoring should be confused with selecting. The author or publisher supplies the title of a book, the librarian supplies the subject heading and classification number. But we had better let the reader provide his own labels.

The republic of letters and the democratic society that supports it are the best guarantees we have that all relevant and important points of view will be heard from. If we look out for the quality of the library materials that we select for our collections, we can safely allow the balance to look out for itself.

6 *"Problem" Fiction*

(FEBRUARY 1, 1962)

by ERIC MOON

Marjorie Fiske, in her now famous report on book selection in California school and public libraries, found: "When it comes to actual practice, nearly two-thirds of all librarians who have a say in book selection reported instances where the controversiality of a book or author resulted in a decision not to buy" (*Book Selection and Censorship*, by Marjorie Fiske, University of California Press, 1959). She revealed also that nearly one-fifth habitually avoid buying any material which is known to be controversial or, more horrifyingly, "which they believe *might become* controversial."

Another section of this report—incidentally, one of the most fascinating books yet written on book selection—declares that two-thirds of the public librarians who contributed to the study "used the words quality and demand as they discussed library objectives, and by far the greatest weight was to be found on the side of demand. Among the 69 public librarians who described their philosophies in these terms, 38 believe that the library's chief function is to meet public requests; five are primarily value-oriented, and the rest hold mixed or contradictory views."

We puzzled long over what seemed to us the antithetical quality of these two statements in juxtaposition. Surely the most controversial books are also frequently the books most in demand. The best-seller lists would appear to offer some confirmation of this. Yet these California librarians professed to be influenced, positively on the one hand by public demand, negatively on the other by controversiality. Is it only California librarians who hold such illogical beliefs? We decided to try to find out.

We compiled a list of 20 fiction titles published during the past two or three years—books which, for one reason or another, might be considered controversial, and which, for the most part, might have been in heavy demand. Such books, we felt, might pose problems in book selection, particularly for libraries without clear-cut policies or convictions.

This list was sent to a number of libraries, large and small (but with an emphasis on the medium-sized and larger libraries, where we thought the excuse of a shoestring budget might be used less often), in every state of the union. We asked each library to indicate how many copies had been bought of each title on the list (for the library system); whether these copies were freely available on the open shelves or whether their circulation was restricted in some way; and if they did not buy certain titles, to indicate reasons for rejection.

It was probably one of the simplest questionnaires ever. We invited comments, but the only other question we asked was: "How, and by whom, are books selected for your library?" Yet we had doubts whether we would get enough of the questionnaires returned to make this small survey of any use. If librarians avoid controversial books, wouldn't they be likely to avoid answering something as controversial as this list?

We need not have worried. Nearly three-quarters (actually 113, or 74.8 per cent) of the 151 questionnaires we sent out were returned. We'd like to thank all these librarians for their spontaneous cooperation, and for the frank and helpful replies they sent in. Only two or three librarians indicated that they didn't want their libraries named specifically. A substantial number expressed interest in the results, and one—whose book selection seemed beyond reproach—confessed to awaiting them "anxiously." A Texas librarian said: "This is one questionnaire that we enjoyed," and a New York librarian asked us, not too seriously, "Why is Lj circulating lists of dirty books?"

Many expressed serious concern over the problem of the selection of controversial fiction. "This is one of the growing problems of public libraries," said John Eastlick (Denver Public Library). He expressed his belief that there is "a rising objection—on behalf of the general public—to sensationalized fiction." The librarian of a small library in Vermont said "we would like to know the best way of handling it." Perhaps the best evidence that this is a live problem with at least two edges, is the comment by Margaret Fulmer, librarian of the Whittier (California) Public Library:

"There is complaint about current fiction. There is the reader whose protest was expressed by his call for 'good clean Christian novels.' There is the reader who felt her right to read was abridged because we didn't yet have a copy of *Lolita*, although it was at the time in the rental collection. Yesterday afternoon the staff at the circulation desk had a strongly expressed objection to John Updike's *Rabbit, Run*."

An interesting question was raised by an Arizona librarian: why didn't the questionnaire "also ask for reasons why we purchased the books we did?" We didn't think of it: we wish we had.

Only one return professed open skepticism about the results. The librarian of a large county library in Maryland asked: "What good purpose do you hope to show from this kind of survey?" That library has since been ordered to remove from its shelves the three copies of *Tropic of Cancer* which it had at the time of the questionnaire. One of our objectives was the hope of producing evidence of practice in other libraries which might give support to a library faced with just this kind of situation.

The 20 titles on which we queried libraries are shown below. On the questionnaire they were listed in alphabetical author order: here they are listed according to the number of libraries which bought each title.

	LIBRARIES WHICH PURCHASED		NO. OF COPIES
AUTHOR AND TITLE	NO.	%	PURCHASED
O'Hara, John. *From the Terrace*	105	92.9	1720
Lawrence, D. H. *Lady Chatterley's Lover*	93	82.3	876
Nabokov, Vladimir. *Lolita*	87	77.9	1357
Updike, John. *Rabbit, Run*	76	67.2	583
Durrell, Lawrence. *Black Book*	68	60.2	369
Moravia, Alberto. *Wayward Wife*	68	60.2	311
Mailer, Norman. *Deer Park*	61	53.9	341
Miller, Henry. *Tropic of Cancer*	58	51.3	530
Vittorini, Elio. *The Dark and the Light*	54	47.8	219
Lytton, David. *The Goddam White Man*	49	43.4	271
Bourjaily, Vance. *Confessions of a Spent Youth*	38	33.6	275
Caldwell, Erskine. *Jenny by Nature*	35	30.9	184
Wallace, Irving. *The Chapman Report*	35	30.9	423
Kerouac, Jack. *Doctor Sax*	31	27.4	194
Mayfield, Julian. *The Grand Parade*	31	27.4	247
Peyrefitte, Roger. *Knights of Malta*	31	27.4	102
Peacock, Jere. *Valhalla*	28	24.8	67
Metalious, Grace. *Return to Peyton Place*	27	23.9	144
Robbins, Harold. *The Carpetbaggers*	26	23.0	405
Harvey, Frank. *The Lion Pit*	20	17.7	89

A librarian in Wisconsin expressed curiosity about "why these particular 20 titles were chosen." No explanation would seem to be required for the Nabokov, Lawrence and Miller titles. They, and a number of others such as *The Carpetbaggers* and *The Chapman Report* were clearly books which had created controversies. Many of the others dealt frankly—and the reviews said so—with the sensitive subject of sex, or used language which might offend tender minds. Some titles included were not particularly controversial, but the authors *were* on the basis of previous work, e.g. Caldwell, O'Hara, Moravia. Question: 'Do an author's subsequent works suffer banishment if a previous title (*God's Little Acre, Woman of Rome*) has created pressures on the book selector?

The Peyrefitte book was included as one which might conceivably have offended religious susceptibilities in some areas. Two others dealt with the "color problem"; the Mayfield book tackling it on the home front, the Lytton book (whose very title, we thought, might be sufficient to assure its exclusion from some libraries) dealt with color clashes at a distance—in South Africa. Question: Is the truth harder to take when it's nearer home? Kerouac was included for no better reason than to find out how "far out" libraries were prepared to go in order to be representative of current "schools" of writing. Most of our reasons and our questions were confirmed as relevant by the returns.

One other explanation before we get down to results. We deliberately mixed books of literary quality with others that were meretricious potboilers, exploiting sensation with the best-seller list as a goal. The objective here was to discover what, if any, was the relationship between literary standards, public demand, and controversial content as determining factors in public library book selection.

The results, in our view, if disappointing in some specific instances, are encouraging as a whole, and provide a more substantial defense against charges of public library "censorship" than we dared expect after the evidence of the Fiske Report. Eight of the 20 titles were bought by more than half of the responding libraries, and what is more significant is that all the eight writers whose works are at the top of the list are authors of some stature—a clear indication that literary standards in many libraries outweigh the problem of pressures and controversy. Certainly, we did not expect to find *Tropic of Cancer* in more than half the libraries, nor *Lolita* in 87 per cent of them.

That demand takes a back seat in cases where literary quality is lacking or in doubt is also clearly evidenced by the low standings on the above list of such titles as *The Carpetbaggers, Valhalla* and *Return to Peyton Place,* all of which ran well up on the best-seller lists.

If there are disappointments they are that writers of the calibre of Vittorini and Bourjaily were not bought by more libraries, and that such poor books as the Caldwell title and *The Chapman Report* were bought by so many. Appropriate in this connection is the comment recorded by the Los Angeles Public Library:

"We do not feel that our collection is the better for having chosen *The Carpetbaggers* rather than *The Chapman Report* (or that another library is the better for having purchased both or neither). We do feel that we are the better for having both Moravia and Vittorini."

Between the established writers like Durrell and Lawrence, and the best-seller sensationalists, there seems to be a no-man's-land in which librarians do not often buy, and in which they are motivated by a combination of caution, the absence of heavy demand pressures, and a distinct lack of knowledge. The number of occasions on which the phrase "not known" or "never heard of it" was applied to an author or title is disturbing evidence that some librarians do not know either their books or their selection sources as well as professional bookmen should. This is particularly evident in the case of foreign writers such as Vittorini or Peyrefitte.

The figures quoted above for total "number of copies purchased" are not particularly significant except for purposes of comparison between individual titles. Some libraries indicated only whether they had a book in stock or not, without showing quantities; some large libraries gave figures for main library copies only or said they were unable to provide "system" figures. The totals are therefore certainly well below "actual" figures.

The totals are also influenced considerably in certain cases by the holdings of one or two very large libraries. For example 395 of the 530 copies of *Tropic of Cancer* are held by three large library systems, leaving only 135 copies among the other 55 libraries which have the book in stock. One library system has 420 copies of *Lolita,* another has 375 of the O'Hara book. An exceptional case is *The Carpetbaggers,* with three libraries holding 347 of the 405 copies, leaving only 58 to be shared by the other 23 libraries. In the case of a number of titles on the list it is evident that the majority of libraries have no more than a "token" single copy.

Only copies listed as in "permanent" stock and fully cataloged were counted in the totals. Some of the returns indicated use of extra noncataloged paperback copies to soak up heavy initial demand—this was particularly common in the case of *Lady Chatterley's Lover.* Others used rental or lending library copies from McNaughton, American Lending Library or similar sources for the same purpose. One library (Brooklyn) gave totals for both permanent and pay collection copies. These, in a few cases, were astounding: Brooklyn holds 151 "permanent" copies of *Lady Chatterley,* and has another 476 copies in pay collections; for *Lolita* the figures are 149 and 803 respectively; *Tropic of Cancer,* 95 and 275; *The Chapman Report,* 82 permanent and 521 pay collection copies.

Holdings of the 20 titles by individual libraries covered the complete range from zero to 20. Twelve libraries (10.6 per cent of total returns) had from 16 to 20 titles each; 32 libraries (28.3 per cent) had from 11 to 15 titles; 38 libraries (33.6 per cent) bought 6 to 10 titles; and 31 libraries (27.5 per cent) had 5 or less.

Analyzed by geographical areas,* the returns showed that readers in the North-east can expect the widest range of controversial novels to be available on the shelves of their public libraries. Here the coverage of the books listed ranged from a low of 3 titles in two libraries to a high of 20 in one, with an average of 10.5 titles per library.

There was a remarkable similarity (numerically) between the libraries in the western and southern states. In the South, the range was from a low of one title to a high of 19 (one library in each case), with an average of 9.1 titles per library. The Western States yielded an identical average, and a title range from one to 18 (again, one library in each case).

The area where selection is most rigid (restrictive?) is the Midwest, which averaged only 7.5 titles per library. At one end of the range were two libraries

* *The geographical breakdown was as follows:* WEST (*30 libraries*): *Alaska, Arizona, California, Colorado, Hawaii, Idaho, Montana, Nevada, New Mexico, Oklahoma, Oregon, Texas, Utah, Washington, Wyoming.*
MIDWEST (*34 libraries*): *Illinois, Indiana, Iowa, Kansas, Michigan, Minnesota, Missouri, Nebraska, N. Dakota, Ohio, S. Dakota, Wisconsin.*
SOUTH (*21 libraries*): *Alabama, Arkansas, Delaware, Florida, Georgia, Kentucky, Louisiana, Maryland, Mississippi, N. Carolina, S. Carolina, Tennessee, Virginia, W. Virginia.*
NORTH-EAST (*28 libraries*): *Connecticut, Maine, Massachusetts, New Hampshire, New Jersey, New York, Pennsylvania, Rhode Island, Vermont.*

with 16 titles each; at the other were *nine* libraries with two or less titles, one of these being the only library submitting a return which indicated not one of the 20 titles in stock.

An example of the difference between these four geographical areas (and we will examine the reactions to individual titles more fully later) is that while *Lady Chatterley's Lover* is available in better than 85 per cent of the libraries elsewhere (West, 86.7 per cent; South, 85.7; North-east, 89.3), in the Midwest it can be found in only 70.6 per cent of the libraries responding. It is difficult to make value judgments on the basis of these figures, however, for other variations reflect, if anything, to the credit of the Midwestern group of libraries. They had, for example, far fewer copies of *Return to Peyton Place* than libraries in other areas, and there are some who will find this evidence of wise conservation of book funds.

A further analysis by size of library proved at least one thing—that the widest choice is not always to be found in the largest libraries. The only two libraries which offered the whole range of 20 titles were both smallish libraries serving less than 50,000 population—Bethpage, New York, and Fair Lawn, New Jersey. Two other small libraries that were well up, each with 16 of the 20 titles, were Salina, Kansas, and Mason City, Iowa.

The other eight libraries in which more than 15 of the titles may be found *are* all among the giants, each serving over 250,000 population: Birmingham, Brooklyn, Charlotte and Mecklenburg, Los Angeles, Philadelphia, Queens, Rochester and San Francisco. At the other end of the scale, there were five libraries in this largest population group which had only half a dozen or less of the listed titles.

Generally, the poorest showing was made by the smallest libraries, below 25,000 population, and those in the second largest population group, 100,000–250,000. It is interesting—indeed intriguing—that this latter group provided the lowest average of all, 6.8 titles per library, and that 50 per cent of the 22 libraries in the group had no more than six titles.

Now the question that has to be raised, sooner or later, in connection with these figures and comments, is: "How many of the 20 titles listed *should* the public library patron expect to find in his local library?" Since the librarians who responded to our questionnaire laid their cards so openly on the table, it is incumbent upon the compiler of the list to offer an opinion without hedging.

A public library, in our view, has an obligation to offer a reasonable representation of current as well as classic literature. In order to meet this obligation, we would feel that we *had* to stock at least 11 of these 20 titles, whatever the size of the library. They would be the books by Bourjaily, Durrell, Kerouac, Lawrence, Mailer, Miller, Moravia, Nabokov, O'Hara, Updike and Vittorini. With the slightest evidence of demand or interest on the part of the public, we'd want to add to those the books by Lytton, Mayfield and Peyrefitte—and in the larger libraries we would expect to find them automatically. The remaining six titles are difficult to defend by any principles of book selection which involve standards, literary or otherwise.

We recognize that these are opinions only, not edicts. However, they are opinions based on a reading of the 20 books and some experience in book selection for public libraries, large and small—and the reading is firmer ground than is evident in some of the questionnaire returns. But there are no sure bets in book selection, no rules without exceptions. Our feelings on this subject are nicely stated by J. F. W. Bryon in the January 1961 issue of *The Librarian and Book World:*

"One is taken aback by the effrontery of some colleagues' virtual claim to omniscience in their book selection. It is an imprecise process, at best frustrating and unsatisfactory and at worst embarrassing, since the materials dealt with are the fallible, ephemeral product of the human mind, and the public for whom they are sifted and culled, doubtless with conscientious heart-searching, is fallible in its judgment, capricious in its tastes and, above all, fluctuating in composition and needs. I have never known a conscientious book selector who did not admit dismay on seeing, in other libraries than his own, books which he had not bought, or even known about, but which he realized would be useful to his own readers. In any event, even if one's selection is impeccable, what of the minorities?"

There were a few—very few—among the librarians who responded to this survey who admitted to doubts and the possibility of inconsistency. Among such statements was the one from the Knoxville (Tennessee) Public Library: "We do realize that literary criticism involves debatable issues and we are conscious that our selection reveals inconsistencies in judgment."

One librarian who agrees with us that a library's bookstock should include a representative collection of contemporary literature is Ford Rockwell (Wichita Public Library). He said, of current literature: "We don't buy all of it. We don't necessarily like, or have to like, what we do purchase. But we do select sufficient to reflect what is being written in our day. This is not the first age of 'problem fiction' nor will it be the last . . . Rather than practice censorship and playing 'goodie-goodie' we might better practice selection, recognizing that literature was always a wide open market."

The extremes on either side of this philosophy are well represented by comments from two New York public libraries. Henry R. Meisels, director of the Bethpage Public Library, which had all of the 20 listed books, expresses what is probably more a public relations than a book *selection* policy: "It is our policy to make every effort to furnish any title demanded by our public." The Syracuse Public Library, on the other hand, marked 17 of the 20 titles as "not purchased—because regarded as 'problem fiction'." It is to be hoped that this library's *Gold Star List of American Fiction*, which has been selling to other libraries for 46 years, demonstrates more convincing selection principles.

Of all the comments on the questionnaires the one we most liked—perhaps because it is closely akin to the basic principle of justice that it is better to allow ten criminals to go free rather than convict one innocent man—was offered by James Marvin, librarian of the Cedar Rapids, Iowa, Public Library: "We attempt to add a variety of fiction, providing a wide field of choice to our patrons. Although we may not always do so, we would rather run the risk of having a novel of inferior quality than deny to our public the privilege of sampling for themselves a controversial book of quality."

One thing that emerges clearly from this survey is that many libraries do not apply a consistent standard in the selection of fiction. If a novel contains material that is likely to be controversial, it is often expected to have considerably more virtues—reputation, literary merit—to offset this disability than is required of more "harmless" fiction. Forrest Mills, librarian of the Racine Public Library, put his finger on this point of the double, or multiple, standard:

"The questionnaire recalled to mind a paradox in our selection policy. I often find myself justifying exclusion of a *Peyton Place* or *Lion Pit* on the basis of inferior craftsmanship, style or what not. Yet, during the course of a year we will, without serious question (but with some misgiving), add a dozen or so fiction titles ranging in quality from the Avalon type to Elizabeth Seifert and a cut or two above. My justification of this contradiction seems to revolve about the intention of the author—the audience he is trying to reach, and what he is trying to say.

"In effect, I suppose, our practice is this: a book with a harmless theme designed principally to entertain and characterized by a style ranging from trite to mediocre to fair is judged less vigorously than a book addressed to a serious, challenging or controversial theme. It is in recognition of this double standard, I suppose, that we severely limit the quantity acquired of the harmless items."

It is "library policy to exclude weak, incompetent, intentionally sensational writing." This was the reason given by the Free Library of Philadelphia for excluding four of the titles on our list of 20. The reason is fair enough, but it is, like most of the book selection policy statements we have seen, open wide to interpretation. Much depends on the degree to which the expressed intent and the performance demonstrate a consistent relationship. In Philadelphia's case, the practice and the policy were, in our view, reasonably consistent. The Free Library rejected *Return to Peyton Place, Valhalla, The Carpetbaggers* and *The Chapman Report*.

Having analyzed some of the facts and figures emerging from the survey, we should now like to examine some of the reasoning, the policies and practices which produce those facts and figures.

Public librarians must, at some time or another, be called upon to explain or defend their book selection policies. They may be faced with the irate patron who can't borrow from the library the book he wants to read, or the one who wants to know why the library *did* buy another book he doesn't want to read. "You bought that junk. Why not the book *I* want?" Or they may be faced with nothing worse than a curious library periodical editor with an academic interest in such matters. How do librarians defend their decisions? What reasons do they give for decisions *not* to buy certain books? Here are some that were offered in connection with our list of recent controversial fiction.

There are, first, the libraries which offer only as reasons for rejection, limited budgets or lack of demand. An example is the New Jersey library which had five of the titles listed and said: "All other books not purchased because we had no demand for them." Or the library in Washington which said: "Since our budget is very small we are inclined to by-pass dubious titles, particularly if we have no requests on file for them." This library by-passed 15 titles.

These reasons we find less than convincing. A limited budget demands careful book selection in all categories, but it should not materially affect principles related to standards and it certainly is no reason for excluding a book on the basis of the controversiality of its subject matter. So far as demand is concerned, we find it difficult to believe that many of the books we listed were not asked for. But even if this were so, doesn't the average library buy many books not specifically requested by readers? And are there not some books, and the works of some authors, which should be stocked by libraries without the impetus of demand? How often does the average public library receive actual requests for Milton's *Comus* or Bacon's *Advancement of Learning*? Admittedly these are dead and respected authors—but so is Lawrence.

Then there are the libraries whose returns showed an attempt to base selection decisions on such factors as literary quality or the author's integrity. Some of these were admirable, and the selections made were consonant with the principles expressed. Others were not very convincing. A South Dakota librarian said: "If a book seems to be controversial, we have followed the rather conservative policy of waiting to see if its literary merit makes it essential for our collection." This raises a number of questions. The only books (of those listed) in stock at this library are David Lytton's *The Goddam White Man* and Moravia's *Wayward Wife*. Do these have *more* literary merit than all the other books listed? How long does it take for a book to acquire literary merit? And how does the South Dakota library discover that a book has subsequently acquired this literary quality?

Much more common than judgments on literary merit or quality were judgments on content, assessments of moral values or taste, and a protective attitude towards a public described with alarming frequency and condescension as "unsophisticated."

"Questionable taste" was the phrase used by an Idaho librarian, while the return from an Arizona county library annotated 11 of the 20 titles with the curt comment "trash in subject." Among the books this Arizona library *did* buy were *Return to Peyton Place*, *Valhalla* and *The Chapman Report*.

Typical of many comments about the "unsophisticated" public was one from a library in Kansas: "We have a rather unsophisticated reading public and those books dealing with such subjects as detailed illicit love affairs are not in demand." The only titles in stock were *Lady Chatterley* (one of the classic "illicit love affairs" of all time) and the O'Hara book. We have always considered love affairs something of an O'Hara specialty. And we wondered about that "illicit": are there books dealing with *licit* love affairs?

One Wisconsin librarian felt that the patron needed to be protected both from his own ignorance and from the evils of advertising and best-seller lists. Among her comments were: "Often, almost always, patron does not know content of book he is requesting and is embarrassed by it . . . Best-seller lists and prolific advertising create a false demand for these titles. I wish that more book reviewing media would have the courage of the *Chicago Tribune* which is not listing these so-called 'problem' titles with their best-seller listing. More power to them."

A variation on "sophistication," or the lack of it, was "maturity." A North Dakota library bemoaned the fact that it had "no way of restricting such books to the mature readers who are ready for them." What sort of test does a library apply to determine whether a reader is mature or if he is *ready* for a particular book? Some did, of course, mention specifically the common problem of the younger reader.

A Vermont librarian confessed to some heart-searching on this score: "We dislike purchasing books for limited circulation but feel taxpayers have a right to the books they request. But parents sometimes object to the availability of these books to young people." An Iowa librarian lost no sleep over this, but simply passed the responsibility back where it belongs, with the parents. "Parents with YP reading complaints," he said, "are referred to our newly attractive YP section."

There were libraries that didn't buy some of the listed titles because of the possibility of theft, like the New York library which said: "We find 'problem fiction' made available for free circulation all too often disappear from the shelves."

Among some of the larger libraries there appears to be almost a trend towards discrimination against fiction generally. The Carnegie Library of Pittsburgh, for example, limits "fiction to 5 per cent of city funds, and all endowment income is spent for nonfiction." The librarian at Springfield, Massachusetts, declared: "For several years the City Library has decreased the number of fiction titles purchased. The poor quality of fiction, the high cost of books, and a book budget which has not increased substantially have contributed to this decision." *Is* fiction generally of poorer quality than nonfiction? Is the artificial division between fiction and nonfiction a reasonable basis for allocation of the book budget?

The bogey word "censorship," let it be said, was seldom raised, although a Louisiana librarian admitted, with disarming honesty, "We do not censor books, except those advocating integration or communism." The librarian at Mobile, Alabama, declared roundly: "Mobile has NO censorship problems as regards moral values in fiction."

Finally, there were those librarians who presented, as their reason for not buying certain titles, the unassailable plea of ignorance. "Author unknown," said a Montana librarian of eight of the 20 books listed. "Never heard of it," said an Oklahoma librarian of nine books on the list. The latter continued: "I'm not ashamed to admit that I have not heard of nine titles on the list, and I claim that I read and check book selection information as much as the next librarian. . . . One reason that we do not make a great attempt to supply current fiction is because it is 'Current' and therefore 'Dead' within 90 days of publication. Also, almost without exception, within 60 days of publication, they are available in paperbacks."

Leaving aside the dubious logic that suggests a publisher would issue a large paperback edition of a book that only has another 30 days to live, and the fact that very few books *are* available in paperback within two months of hardback publication, this librarian did voice a fairly common illusion. A West Virginia librarian, for example, whose library had only one of the 20 titles said: "Available in paperbacks if the patron really wants to read any of the ones listed."

We checked the latest edition of *Paperbound Books in Print,* and found that 11 of the 20 titles we listed are now available in paperback form. At least one of those, *Tropic of Cancer,* has been issued in paperback since our survey was completed. We do not wish to condone the practice of not buying a hardback copy if a paperback edition is available; merely to correct the widespread impression that nearly all popular fiction titles *are* available in paperbacks.

Most of the comments recorded above were general observations applied to or incited by our list as a whole. We analyzed also (where they were specific enough to analyze) the reasons given for exclusion of individual titles on the Lj questionnaire.

BOURJAILY, Vance. *Confessions of a Spent Youth.*

Fifteen libraries did not buy this because of poor or unfavorable reviews; one mentioned Lj's recommendation "for large fiction collections" and another that there were more minus than plus signs in *Book Review Digest.* How do libraries which depend solely or heavily upon reviews strike a balance between favorable and unfavorable reviews? Almost all the reviews had something good to say about this book, and those in the *New York Herald Tribune Book Review* and *Saturday Review* were very enthusiastic. The latter said: "A singularly honest and intelligent book about our difficult times."

Seven didn't buy the Bourjaily book because they had no requests for it; another five had not heard of the author, the title or both; five found it lacking in literary quality ("literary merit insufficient to compensate for sexual frankness"); four found the subject matter unsuitable for their communities; and two were resting on a "wait and see" policy.

CALDWELL, Erskine. *Jenny by Nature.*

The libraries that omitted this book did so largely on the basis of unfavorable or unenthusiastic reviews or because it lacked literary merit. There were 16 in each of these categories, and it seems that many agree with one librarian's comment: "Latter-day Caldwell seems to have nothing to recommend it." Ten mentioned a lack of demand for this book, and one said his library had "no demand for Caldwell as a whole." Eight found the subject or theme of even this harmless and trivial little item undesirable.

DURRELL, Lawrence. *Black Book.*

The main reason given for exclusion of *Black Book* was lack of demand or reader interest. Only two librarians dared to criticize Durrell's literary quality, and only four voiced specific objections to the content ("crude offensive language and emphasis on sexual activities"). The reviews, which in general were very commendatory, were cited by another four libraries as a reason for not buying the book.

HARVEY, Frank. *The Lion Pit.*

This was condemned on every score: reviews (which *were* bad), lack of demand and literary merit both, its content (particularly emphasis on sex again), and a variety of inconclusive reasons like "unsuitable," "unimportant," etc.

KEROUAC, Jack. *Doctor Sax.*

Bad reviews were the most common reason cited in this case, with many quoting the Kirkus comment, "incoherent fugue." The book did receive, incidentally, two very favorable reviews in Lj and *Time*, the latter describing it as "Kerouac's best book." Among those who claimed a lack of demand, three said that previous books by Kerouac had proved unpopular. There were still two (un-hip) librarians who said "author unknown."

LAWRENCE, D. H. *Lady Chatterley's Lover.*

Very few gave *any* reason for exclusion of this book. Boston mentioned a "long standing State court injunction" and one library didn't buy it because it "couldn't be placed on the open shelves." Paperbacks were more often mentioned in connection with this title than any other. Three used the availability of a paperback edition as an excuse not to buy it; a substantial number mentioned buying extra paperback copies to help stem the heavy demand.

Two libraries were using delaying tactics and said that they would buy in the future for the "serious student of Lawrence" or "the discriminating reader." The latter added, "sensationalism created a demand which would have required many copies to meet. Will put in a copy . . . now that the sensation-seeker is asking for *The Carpetbaggers*." Is he really the same reader?

LYTTON, David. *The Goddam White Man.*

This book received reviews as favorable as an author could hope for, from the *Times Literary Supplement*—"brilliantly written . . . carries immense conviction"—to inclusion in the always conservative ALA *Booklist*. Seven librarians must have read only the Peter Abrahams review in *Saturday Review* (the only negative one among the majors), for they mentioned reviews as the reason for not buying.

Half a dozen objected to the content. Three librarians, two in Tennessee and one in West Virginia, agreed that the book's "racial theme would make it unpopular here." A Colorado library commented: "When racial problems were so much in the news we decided not to add a book which was full of sex and violence and added nothing to the understanding of the South African situation."

There were the usual sprinkling of libraries which hadn't heard of the book or which hadn't bought because of lack of requests. Four libraries complained about a surfeit of novels on Africa, and three didn't buy this one because of its title, which one Mississippi library felt was "a bit much." A Louisiana librarian commented: "No special reason for exclusion (of any) except David Lytton's book, the title of which is offensive."

MAILER, Norman. *Deer Park*.

The major reason given for exclusion of the Mailer book was its lack of literary quality (10 libraries). Only five objected specifically to the content, and only five called upon reviews to support rejection. An interesting judgment was made by the Enoch Pratt Free Library, which found *Deer Park* inferior to *What Makes Sammy Run* in conveying an understanding of Hollywood.

MAYFIELD, Julian. *The Grand Parade*.

Only one library (the same one in Colorado which objected to the Lytton book) stated specifically that this wasn't bought *because* it emphasized the racial theme, but seven altogether did count it out on content. It should be noted that, although Southern libraries bought less copies than any other area of the Lytton book, more of them bought the Mayfield book than did libraries in the Midwest. Mostly, demand was the factor cited for nonpurchase in this case.

METALIOUS, Grace. *Return to Peyton Place*.

If few literary judgments were made in some other instances, librarians felt on surer ground in backing their critical abilities on this title. More than 25 per cent rejected Metalious on the basis of literary quality. Many referred to *Peyton Place*. Some said they bought the sequel because they had the original; others gave this as the reason why they didn't buy the sequel; and some said they wouldn't buy either. The nicest comment came from a librarian who said *Peyton Place* didn't seem worth returning to.

MILLER, Henry. *Tropic of Cancer*.

Among the usual reasons for rejection, only content (6 libraries) and lack of demand (3 libraries) were offered. One library in Texas said: "Had no requests until banned. Then had seven. Did not think this showed enough demand." Nobody mentioned reviews.

Three libraries, all in Massachusetts, did not buy because of an obscenity case pending in the State. One Vermont library had ordered the book, but the Massachusetts jobber could not supply it. A Colorado library was awaiting the outcome of litigation, and two other libraries were still debating whether to buy or not.

The position has probably changed drastically on this title since our survey. The Los Angeles Public Library, the Free Library of Philadelphia and the Montgomery (Maryland) County Library are only three libraries which reported *Tropic of Cancer* as being in stock or on order, and which have subsequently withdrawn all copies or cancelled orders. So widespread is the campaign against this book by the police and other self-appointed censors, that there are doubtless other cases.

MORAVIA, Alberto. *Wayward Wife*.

Reasons for rejection were again sparse. Eight libraries indicated a lack of demand, and one of these said short stories were generally unpopular. One library confirmed our suspicion that the works of some authors suffer banishment as a whole. We do not "purchase *any* of this author's writings," was the comment. Only one library dismissed Moravia on grounds of literary merit. The library which called this book "poorly written" had *The Lion Pit, Jenny by Nature* and *The Chapman Report.*

NABOKOV, Vladimir. *Lolita.*

Very few reasons were given for nonpurchase of *Lolita.* Six objected to the content, and three offered reviews as their authority. All of these quoted the trite Kirkus comment: "literary pornography." One unusual reason was "price": "At $5, too expensive to duplicate in volume"—so this library didn't buy it at all.

O'HARA, John. *From the Terrace.*

O'Hara yielded nothing, except a comment from Boston Public Library, which turned it down on grounds of "literary quality." Another library held strong views on the other side: "O'Hara's novels certainly represent literate writing that is among the best of the mid-century."

PEACOCK, Jere. *Valhalla.*

This was turned down overwhelmingly on the strength of reviews, 20 libraries in all giving this reason, and six of them quoting the LIBRARY JOURNAL review in particular. Although eight libraries rejected it because it lacked literary merit, the Brooklyn Public Library bought it for the main library only, "due to indications of ability to write."

PEYREFITTE, Roger. *Knights of Malta.*

The usual variety of reasons applied in this case, but in addition at least half a dozen libraries said the book had "limited appeal," another three described it as "difficult reading," and 11 libraries had just "missed it" or "lost it in the shuffle." The St. Louis and San Antonio public libraries described it as "anti-clerical," and Denver felt "this could be offensive to our Catholic readers, since the author is sneering, mocking and flippant."

ROBBINS, Harold. *The Carpetbaggers.*

Nineteen libraries turned down this title because it lacked literary quality, 12 because of its content, and 14 because of unfavorable reviews. Four of the latter mentioned the Lj review, which, said one, "states the case splendidly."

UPDIKE, John. *Rabbit, Run.*

This book, a strong candidate for the National Book Award last year, "did not sound particularly significant" to a Connecticut librarian. The reviews, which were generally magnificent, were the reason four libraries did *not* buy. A Massachusetts librarian said: "This was a tough one to exclude. Unlike Wallace it has literary merit—but not enough."

VITTORINI, Elio. *The Dark and the Light.*

This title appeared not to be very well known. Ten libraries had no demand for it, and four others, even so long after publication, had it "still under consideration." The one comment which deserves recording is that of a Delaware library: "Not enough interest in *lesser* Italian writers."

WALLACE, Irving. *The Chapman Report.*

The reviews persuaded 15 libraries not to buy this book, and an equal number judged its literary quality below par. Eleven dismissed it because of its content. Some libraries which had bought it were in the process of changing their minds. "A slip up," said the Mobile Public Library. "It is so poorly written that it should never have been added, and it will soon be withdrawn." Another library which bought it said that "in reviewing the evidence we feel that our logic was on tenuous grounds."

It will be seen from the comments above that the main factors which influence libraries in their decisions, so far as controversial fiction is concerned, are reviews, the literary quality, subject content, and local demand. In answer to our question, "How and by whom are books selected for your library," however, we discovered that published reviews are the pre-eminent factor.

Forty-one of the 113 libraries submitting returns indicated that they relied solely or primarily upon published reviews. Another 22 made their decisions on the basis of a combination of published and staff reviews. Eleven relied primarily on staff reviewing. Only four, despite the findings of the Fiske Report, cited demand as the *primary* factor, though many others admitted it to be influential. An unusual breakdown was submitted by a New York library, which selected "75 per cent by careful reading of reviews, 25 per cent by demand and publishers' blurbs."

Although we did not ask which review media libraries used as book selection sources, many cited them. Those which were mentioned were:

	NO. OF LIBRARIES
LIBRARY JOURNAL	21
KIRKUS SERVICE	13
BOOKLIST	12
SATURDAY REVIEW	12
NEW YORK TIMES BOOK REVIEW	10
PUBLISHERS' WEEKLY	4
BOOK REVIEW DIGEST	3
N.Y. HERALD TRIBUNE BOOK REVIEW	3
ATLANTIC	1
WISCONSIN LIBRARY BULLETIN	1

Most often, of course, these were cited as being used in various combinations. One or two librarians indicated those periodicals on which they placed greatest reliance, for example:

"Heavy reliance on Kirkus" (Santa Barbara Public Library, California).

"Largest reliance on Kirkus and Lj; secondary reliance on *Saturday Review* and *New York Times*" (Racine Public Library, Wisconsin).

"Rely heavily on Lj and *Booklist,* less heavily on Kirkus" (Wethersfield Public Library, Connecticut).

"Published reviews, notably LIBRARY JOURNAL, influence decision in doubtful cases" (Free Library of Philadelphia).

RESTRICTIVE PRACTICES

"There are two stages at which a librarian's practices in regard to controversial materials become manifest," says the Fiske Report, "in the act of book selection itself, and in circulation procedures." What happens to some of these controversial books *after* they get into the library (if they do) is, of course, a matter of some interest. We asked libraries not only to indicate whether they bought the titles we listed, but also to say whether the books were on the open shelves. Selection is only the first stage in book *provision*, and the availability of those books purchased is a factor of at least equal importance.

Statistics by themselves are more than ever open to interpretation in this area. It would be possible to feel encouraged by the fact that 54 (nearly half) of the responding libraries indicated that all the books they purchased from our fiction list were available on the open shelves. But a substantial number of these libraries were the same ones who purchased very few of the titles, thus cutting off the problem of availability at the source.

Every title on the list was somewhere on the "restricted" shelves, with D. H. Lawrence (or his creation, *Lady Chatterley*) the chief victim. This book was restricted in 41 libraries (44 per cent of those replying). Lawrence's nearest contender for the "hidden" treatment was Nabokov, whose *Lolita* has not, even three years after publication, reached the open shelves in 27 libraries which bought it.

Forty-one per cent (24 libraries) of those who bought *Tropic of Cancer* keep it under cover, and John O'Hara's *From the Terrace*, bought more heavily than any other title listed, is nevertheless restricted in 17 libraries.

The only other titles to receive restricted treatment in a dozen or more libraries are: Mailer's *Deer Park* (16); Durrell's *Black Book* (13); and Updike's *Rabbit, Run* (12). Vance Bourjaily finds himself in the company of Grace Metalious, Harold Robbins and Irving Wallace as a "restricted" author in 7 libraries. Least often hidden from public view are Vittorini and Peyrefitte, only one library in each case feeling that these were too dangerous for the open shelves.

One of the more positive statements of principle came from the Jackson (Miss.) Public Library: "If we buy a controversial title at all, we make it fully available, a policy with which none of our readers have so far taken serious issue." The Birmingham (Alabama) Public Library *sounded* more cautious: "Our policy is to restrict as few books as possible, but because of wide use of the library by young people we attempt to be careful in selection." In fact— and this illustrates how such statements can be misinterpreted if not considered in relation to practice—the Birmingham library was among those which purchased nearly all the controversial titles we listed. Seventeen were in stock, and only Lawrence was on the restricted shelves. The Jackson library had 12 of the 20 titles.

Many were the variations in practice, but only two chief reasons were cited frequently for keeping books off the open shelves; theft, and the younger reader. A comment that combined these reasons came from a Vermont librarian: "I do not believe in closed shelves, but experience with *Lady Chatterley's Lover* has forced me to put that book on closed shelf. We had a run on the book from the local high school and one copy was stolen from the shelves. Some way had to be found to keep it out of the hands of sensation seekers who would read it for that purpose only."

There were various interpretations of "restricted circulation," but only a couple of libraries reached the point of complete absurdity: they bought, in one case Lawrence, in another Miller, and then didn't catalog these titles or reveal that they were available.

The common interpretation of "restricted" is summed up in the Minneapolis Public Library's note: "Shelved in stacks—but freely available on request." In short, we have it but you have to have the nerve to ask for it. Only readers of Durrell, Nabokov or Lawrence among our terrible twenty need follow this routine at Minneapolis.

Almost as common was "restriction" according to some arbitrary age level. Louisville (Kentucky) Public Library, for example, said: "Most of these books are placed in the stacks area. They are fully cataloged and given without question to anyone having an adult borrower's card, which is issued to ninth graders and up."

The Missoula (Montana) Public Library supported our belief that there is a pretty direct relationship between controversiality and demand. Six of the eight titles this library bought had been "placed on restricted circulation after complaints were received." The librarian added: "We do not purchase if we think the book may have to have restricted circulation, unless the demand warrants purchase."

Two large libraries, Milwaukee and Wayne County, have *grades* of restriction. Restricted, said Milwaukee, means "for adult circulation only"; "reference" means for adults only and restricted to use in the library. Eight of the listed titles were in the first category, and three (Caldwell, Miller and Wallace) were confined to quarters. At Wayne County, only Durrell and Bourjaily attain the isolated eminence of the reference shelves. Six other titles were indicated as restricted in the Wayne County Library in the sense that they were "not available to the high school age without parental permission."

The Los Angeles Public Library also uses parental permission as a safety valve. Some titles—12 from the Lj list—are available on open shelves but "are marked on the book pocket with a line, indicating that they may not be circulated to holders of Children's or intermediate cards (under age of 18, or below senior level in High School) without permission from parents or special school assignments." Some fiction at Los Angeles is "kept permanently in the stacks because of experience with excessive theft or unlicensed long-term 'borrowing.' Many such books are translations of foreign novels, used as 'ponies' in classes." The only titles from the Lj list in this latter category at Los Angeles seem to be ponies of a rather different color—Kerouac, Lawrence, Miller, Nabokov.

Only one library among those submitting returns to our questionnaire mentioned a practice which seems contrary to ALA's statement on "Labeling Library Materials." A Washington county library indicated that five of the six titles in stock from the Lj list "are available on open shelves but are starred as a guide to those who wish to avoid this type of book." Although the ALA statement seems primarily concerned with labeling in connection with books advocating political ideologies, the purpose remains the same here. One section of the ALA statement reads: "Labeling is an attempt to prejudice the reader, and as such, it is a censor's tool." However, like most censor's weapons, labeling is of the boomerang family. The Washington county library commented further, of the books that are starred, "some deliberately seek them, others avoid them."

In summary, the evidence we collected suggests that about half our public libraries follow practices and principles which allow little scope for charges of censorship, and which remain firm and constant even in the face of controversial materials and public pressures. The other 50 percent cover the spectrum from weather-vane vacillation to rigidly restrictive or protective practices.

We began this article with some questions about the Fiske Report. We can find no more appropriate conclusion than to agree absolutely with one other of Marjorie Fiske's comments: "It is doubtful whether many librarians would agree that consistency is always a virtue in book selection, but it is also doubtful whether many are quite aware of the extent of their inconsistencies in buying controversial books."

CHAPTER

7 *"Problem Nonfiction"*

(OCTOBER 1, 1962)

by DOROTHY M. BRODERICK

This report was undertaken at the suggestion of several librarians who felt that nonfiction offered a fruitful field for study. Many of the librarians participating in the survey said, "Thank you for initiating this much needed survey." Only one said, "I am returning your questionnaire on 'Problem Nonfiction' in a virgin condition. While we do have an occasional complaint on a book found to be 'objectionable' by a reader, the so-called problem book is no problem here." We are grateful that the majority of librarians are not as parochial in their viewpoint and completed the questionnaire even when they personally did not feel the problem's impact.

The pitfalls inherent in this survey were many and we note them here to preclude readers making assumptions that are not warranted from the data. In the first place, the purpose differed from the Lj fiction survey. There, we were striving to determine how librarians balanced demand against controversy. Here, we were seeking to discover the "balance" of library collections. As small a sample as this (24 titles) will not produce anything near conclusive results, though the results ought to provide food for thought and discussion (*see* Table).

The first problem to be overcome was whether to survey in depth one or two areas or cover lightly five. We selected five, namely, nutrition, race, sex, politics (U.N. and Cuba), politics (Communism and the FBI). The selection of the titles in each category was made by Eric Moon and Dorothy Broderick and requires a word of explanation.

In nutrition, the Jarvis and Taller book were obvious choices, both having wide publicity and popularity. The Leverton and Pollach titles were selected as solid titles covering the same areas, which have the approval of medical groups. Both titles were on a list published in Lj (*see* "Nutrition Books for Lay Readers," by Helen S. Mitchell, Lj, Feb. 15, '60), which was reproduced widely by state health agencies and other interested groups. However, there is no particular reason why a library should have bought these two when it might already own several equally good titles. This must be kept constantly in mind.

The race issue is with us and all five titles were, to us, obvious choices. Baldwin is more than a Negro writer, being one of the most articulate of American authors, and his book was on ALA's Notable Books List for 1961. Hays speaks for the moderates; King for the new-Negro. Putnam is the segregationist's answer; Lillian Smith's volume a classic in the field. Because the Smith comes in two editions, we counted copies owned of the 1949 edition as well as the 1961.

Sex is an obvious choice for a problem area and the Kinsey, Mead and Van de Velde titles were automatic selections. Stone's book is the one most often recommended by doctors and is as reputable a title on birth control as can be found. West's book is one of the few medically and psychiatrically approved titles on homosexuality for the lay reader. It is neither a defense nor an attack, but an objective handling of a difficult subject.

We divided politics into separate areas, the first covered a violently anti–United Nations title in the Copp and Peck; Cousins providing the equally passionate pro viewpoint. On Cuba, Weyl is violently anti; Mills violently pro; Matthews generally conceded to be middle-of-the-road.

Communism was also an obvious area for study and Hoover's book was used because we were sure his reputation was such that all libraries would buy it. (They did.) Ketchum's is not outstanding, but the format and approach make it more likely to appeal to the average reader. Marx, being Marx, should go without saying. Schwarz, despite the deceptive title, is the extreme right-wing view. The Whitehead book was tossed in as a control item more than as a "problem" book. It is readable, the reviews were good, and as a best seller it had little chance of being marked "Don't know."

Some of these titles are much better than others. Some have had more publicity and better reviews than others. And here is a good time to note that Moon and Broderick are not in agreement on how a librarian *ought* to react to these books. This basic disagreement between the compilers we feel, served as a protection against personal bias.

There was considerable confusion about the use of the word "problem" in connection with some of the titles. A book does not have to provoke a flaming controversy for it to be a problem to book selectors. All books written out of extreme conviction are problems in that they are open to charges of nonobjectivity, emotionalism and/or sensationalism. Several of the titles on this list are just that type of book, and a librarian buying or rejecting could do so for apparently sound principle without being open to the charge of prejudice.

We asked for the number of copies purchased but since what we really wished to know was whether the title was available to the public, we counted gift books as purchased. We assume that gifts are not added unless they meet the library's general standards of selection and are rightfully counted.

CONCLUSIONS

On the whole, the libraries in the sample came off very well, though the averages are in many cases misleading. The average represents the total forest, but there were some very sick individual trees present. The Table shows how many libraries bought how many copies of which books, using 226 libraries as the workable sample.

As is immediately obvious from the chart, social problems were the best covered by libraries. In the top ten, only Jarvis and Kinsey do not fall into this area in one way or another. Of the four titles owned by less than 50 per cent of the libraries, three are definitely troublesome. The reasons for selection or rejection of these 14 titles will be set forth later under each book. At the moment, let us look at the overall categories for patterns or lack of.

NUTRITION

As was to be expected, the two "problem" books were owned by most of the libraries. While fewer libraries bought Taller than Jarvis, they bought more copies. The question of medical competence disturbed some librarians and they frankly stated that they were in a dilemma when it came to popular do-it-yourself health books.

Six libraries originally bought the Taller but withdrew it from circulation when the government instituted action. Two expressed great concern, one calling the book "dangerous," but indicated the reserve list was too heavy for them to withdraw it. One librarian, speaking, we felt, for the majority, said, "Readers take these diet books with a grain of salt. . . . We have books on meat diets, vegetarian diets, hay diets, pro and con eye exercises, pro and con fluoridation, etc."

RACE

The averages here are very good with Baldwin and King in the top ten, and Smith eleventh. Putnam ran a poor twenty-third and Hays, moderate that he is, came very close to the middle. It would appear that libraries are more liberal than conservative when it comes to buying books concerned with racial issues. However, unlike most of the other categories, the same libraries are responsible for the nonbuying totals. Libraries tended to either buy everything or nothing, and there are about 40 libraries in the sample where a borrower would be hard put to read about the major internal issue of our society. Those not buying race books made such comments as, "We have a potential situation in regard to race relations here so we are very careful about what we buy." This is in contrast to the librarians who bought most of the titles because, "These are significant books on a vital issue." Nonbuying libraries also claimed that periodical literature covered the subject as far as their needs were concerned.

SEX

This was the only category that some librarian did not preface the page with, "No interest in this subject in our area." While Kinsey was the only title to make the top ten, Mead and Van de Velde ranked high, and the comments were numerous. About *Ideal Marriage,* "Most popular of all our marriage titles over many years. Marriage counselors not always in agreement on this one. Borrowers are however." Aside from the usual comment, "Standard title," the recommendation by doctors of Velde's book was stressed. The most unique reason for buying it was, "Recently purchased because of high recommendation in Robertson Davies' book, *A Voice from the Attic.*" One librarian, in rejecting the same book said, "Had definite proof it was not good for people with unhealthy minds." She volunteered further, "Would borrow for any adult who requested it. Nobody has." Who would dare?

Mead's book was not bought by 43 libraries and aside from the usual, "No demand," the reason given was, "Have similar material." That there is nothing similar to Mead's approach seems beyond discussion and one wonders whether these librarians are aware of the actual content or just the title.

Three-quarters of the libraries buying sex books keep them in "Protective custody." Those not buying, do not do so because, "This type material disappears from shelves." This was a major complaint by libraries keeping their sex books locked up. Strange (or is it?), libraries keeping them on open shelves reported little or no theft or mutilation.

Another complaint about sex books was that they "Wear out." The annoyance that some books were used enough to need constant replacing was so obvious that one did not know whether to laugh or cry. Books are rejected because of "No demand," and are also rejected because the libraries "Cannot afford to replace."

POLITICS

Six of the ten titles are in the top ten of books bought and reasons why will be noted under each title. Of the other four, Matthews did best, though hardly well. Reasons for rejection of the Matthews, Mills, Wcyl and Copp and Peck titles generally rested on the lack of objectivity. One librarian said, "Doubt these are of lasting value." Others noted, "Magazines take care of coverage." There were, of course, the usual "Lack of Demand," "No interest in subject," and "Did not see." It should be reassuring to the critics that extremes are rejected with equality, neither the right nor the left coming off ahead.

GEOGRAPHIC DISTRIBUTION

Unlike the fiction survey, there was no geographic pattern obvious from the nonbuying habits. Twenty-two libraries bought ten or less of the titles, low score being five. They range from New Hampshire, and Vermont, up and down the eastern seaboard, across the country to Maui County Library in

Hawaii. The single most given reason for not buying more books was the size of the library. Side by side with this went a limited budget.

Eleven libraries bought all 24 titles, and 18 libraries bought 23. Again there was little geographic consistency, though the northeast held the edge thanks to the concentration of large metropolitan libraries.

LEAST BOUGHT TITLES

WEST, Donald. *Other Man.*

Seventy-three per cent of the libraries (164) did not buy this book. It was generally rejected with the single word, "Homosexuality" or the phrase, "Subject matter." A few librarians simply "Missed it," others cited other material they owned. However, the majority said frankly, "Never considered getting it." The comment most worthy of being pondered for its implications was, "We haven't adequate 'controlled' reading. Problem would have been to reach the patron who would benefit by reading it."

PUTNAM, Carleton. *Race and Reason.*

This was not bought by 135 libraries. Despite the publicity given to it as a problem book in libraries, many librarians marked it "Don't know this." A few have it but do not catalog it, treating it as "Pamphlet material." The libraries buying it felt that it represented a viewpoint which the library must have in its collection. Those rejecting it did so on its lack of accuracy and highly emotional tone unsuited to a supposedly scientific subject. One librarian buying it, (the only race book the library owned) said, "It opened my eyes to the real argument of the segregationists. I knew that most arguments finally got around to intermarriage as the final one, but I had never realized how dependent it was on the selection of a geneticist until I read this argument."

STONE, Abraham. *Planned Parenthood.*

Reasons for rejecting this ranged from those libraries in Connecticut and Massachusetts that noted there is a state law against dissemination of birth control information, to the ever present, "No demand." A few libraries noted they owned *Babies by Choice or Chance* or had other material, but on the whole it would appear that the subject matter is too dangerous for general library purchase.

POLLACH, H. *How to Reduce Surely and Safely.*

The low score for this one stems primarily from "missed," or "bought another." Both of which could easily happen, though it raises the question of whether a book must be sensational or offbeat for it to come to the attention of book selectors.

MOST BOUGHT TITLES

HOOVER, J. Edgar. *Masters of Deceit.*

All 226 libraries bought, most of them noting, "There was never a question about buying this." There is little doubt that Hoover's reputation is such that librarians would buy him even if he put his name to a telephone directory. One librarian with tongue in cheek (we know because of his other marvelous comments) said, "It is possible that any library journal sending out question-naires asking reason for selecting this book is subversive." Libraries averaged over ten copies of this book and some of them were gifts. As one Iowa librarian said, "The donation was from some wild-eyed local group of Communist hunters."

WHITEHEAD, Don. *FBI Story*.

"What's controversial about this?" was the most often asked question. All but two libraries bought it, one noting it had "similar material" and the other not saying. Two librarians asked why we didn't use Max Lowenthal's *Federal Bureau of Investigation* which is strongly anti-FBI if we wanted a controver-sial title. We leave it to participating libraries to see how their balance is on this score.

MARX, Karl. *Das Kapital*.

We asked for this in "any English edition" and most replies said, "Cannot imagine a library not owning this." Tell it to the 14 who feel they can do without it. One library that did not own it said, plaintively we felt, "Wish we did." The others couldn't care less, or at least didn't seem to.

SCHWARZ, Fred. *You Can Trust the Communists*.

This ranks high because of the publisher's distribution of gift copies and very few of the libraries owning it actually spent money for it. A good many of the comments were decidedly apologetic for accepting the gifts and it would appear that left to themselves, librarians probably would not give much shelf space to the extreme right-wing. Of those rejecting it, one said, "Style and content didn't lend confidence in the author."

JARVIS, D. C. *Folk Medicine*.

Jarvis owes his popularity to demand and the *Booklist* review. One library rejected it with the comment, "We avoid panaceas." A beautiful line—except that the same library owns 66 copies of *Calories Don't Count*. The majority of the libraries not buying it cited medical reviews as the major reason.

KINSEY, Alfred. *Sexual Behavior in the Human Female*.

"Standard," demand, patron requests, were the phrases that appeared most often here. Those not buying it found it "too technical" for their communities or cited "no demand." A certain number, as noted earlier, did not buy it because it disappears from the shelves.

BALDWIN, James. *Nobody Knows My Name*.

Eighteen of the 28 libraries not buying this were northern libraries, who gave as their reasons, "No Negro population," or "Little interest in the race question here." Baldwin was the author most often bought because of "patron requests," and it became clear that the American public can have as good books in its libraries as it demands. Three librarians went out of their way to note that they were not buying *Another Country*.

KING, Martin Luther. *Stride Toward Freedom.*

King's stature as spokesman for the new-Negro was most often cited as the reason for purchase. One Mississippi librarian stated frankly, "The only book which I did not buy because of prejudice against the author was Martin King's *Stride Toward Freedom.*" Such honesty was appreciated by the surveyor.

COUSINS, Norman. *In Place of Folly.*

The author's reputation and good reviews were the major reasons for selection of this. "No demand," the reason for its rejection. Librarians were careful to point out that they had anti–U.N. material even though they had not bought *Betrayal at the U.N.*, the opposite book on our list.

KETCHUM, Richard. *What Is Communism?*

This was the surprise book among the top ten and its success is attributable to its attractive format which makes it a title added to young adult collections as well as adult. While most buying librarians felt it was of "average" quality, they felt its approach made it worth adding. "Bought another," was the primary reason for rejection.

MISCELLANEOUS OBSERVATIONS

We asked librarians to send along a copy of their book selection policy when they had one. We received 55 policies and a number of libraries promised to send theirs along as soon as it was finished. We did no correlating between what they said their policy was and the actual practice of selection, leaving that to a future study.

What became very clear was that librarians think of a book selection policy, not as a tool whose presence makes for smooth operations, but merely as a weapon against attack. Most of those not having a policy said, "My fingers are crossed, but we don't need one. There is no interference of any kind with our policies." Others showed the usual misconception of what constitutes a policy, outlining for us *sources* of selection, not principles.

It is this confusion that prevents more consistency in the selection process, and while selection is admittedly the most difficult and demanding task, it would be more orderly if more librarians demonstrated an understanding of the process. Our favorite comment was from the librarian who said what was needed was not a book selection policy but a personnel policy which assured the hiring of professionals capable of sublimating their personal prejudices.

The mobility of librarians was never made clearer than by the number of questionnaires that said, "I was not here when these were selected/rejected." But only a few of these demonstrated concern with going back and filling in the gaps. Selection, it would seem, is an immediate process, a point of no return for many librarians, and a book once missed is missed forever.

In summary, there were libraries that agreed with Margaret Mead when she wrote, "For in order to think creatively, men need the stimulus of contrast." They balanced their collections without second thoughts about "demand," preferring to represent points of view which they felt would provide the

AUTHOR & TITLE	LIBRARIES WHICH PURCHASED		NO. OF COPIES PURCHASED
	NO.	%	
Hoover, *Masters of Deceit*	226	100.0	2625
Whitehead, *FBI Story*	224	99.0	2098
Marx, *Das Kapital*	212	93.8	1754
Schwarz, *You Can Trust the Communists*	211	93.3	1394
Jarvis, *Folk Medicine*	205	90.7	1191
Kinsey, *Sexual Behavior in the Human Female*	201	88.9	1227
Baldwin, *Nobody Knows My Name*	198	87.6	1082
King, *Stride Toward Freedom*	198	87.6	1044
Cousins, *In Place of Folly*	195	86.3	838
Ketchum, *What Is Communism?*	190	84.0	1165
Smith, *Killers of the Dream*	184	81.4	846
Mead, *Male and Female*	183	80.9	862
Taller, *Calories Don't Count*	182	80.5	1224
Van de Velde, *Ideal Marriage*	181	80.0	1510
Matthews, *Cuban Story*	163	72.1	619
Hays, *Southern Moderate Speaks*	152	67.3	457
Leverton, *Food Becomes You*	149	65.8	544
Mills, *Listen, Yankee*	128	56.6	513
Weyl, *Red Star over Cuba*	128	56.6	419
Copp & Peck, *Betrayal at the U.N.*	113	50.0	284
Pollach, *How to Reduce Surely and Safely*	107	47.3	484
Stone, *Planned Parenthood*	102	45.0	382
Putnam, *Race and Reason*	91	40.0	214
West, *Other Man*	62	27.0	148

contrast for thoughtful decisions. It is unfortunate that only Americans living in good sized cities are extended this opportunity.

To the libraries that buy only what is requested, we offer a quote from Stuart Chase: "Especially important are the areas of public ignorance. . . . An urgent responsibility for leaders in a democracy is to locate areas of ignorance and arouse interest in and action on important issues."

To lead or to follow is the only choice we have.

CHAPTER

8 *On the Shelf*

(JANUARY 15, 1964)

by ERIC MOON

Many years ago, first in a relatively small branch library, then in a large central library, we conducted some experiments in what we then called "saturation buying." We compiled lists of all the works of a number of classic or contemporary authors which we knew to be in demand, then checked the *shelves* (not the catalog) to see how many were there. More often than not the outstanding titles were not present.

We then bought a predetermined number of copies of each missing title and placed them on the shelves on a recorded day. Several weeks later we checked the shelves again, and once more multiple copies were purchased of each missing title. This process was continued until the point was reached where a specific title began to "show" pretty consistently on the shelf. At that point we took a count of the number of copies in stock.

The documentation on this little project has long since disappeared, but we remember clearly that with more than 40 copies of some Hemingway titles in stock (in a branch library serving some 25,000 people) it was difficult to find *on the shelf* a copy, for example, of *For Whom the Bell Tolls*.

The thinking behind these ancient experiments went something like this:

1) There are a number of absolutely basic, standard works which the reader might justifiably expect to be *readily* available in any library worth the name.

2) There are a number of readers who do not automatically "ask the librarian" when they do not find on the shelf the book they want. How many leave the library regularly disappointed because *the* book is not there?

3) Most librarians would agree that the emphasis in their collections, and the priority in their book expenditures, should be in favor of the books that last rather than the passing froth of today or yesterday. While it may be justifiable to send to the Rental Collection, or keep on a long reserve list, the reader who wants *The Three Sirens* or some such, the reader who wants a copy of *Hamlet* ought to have better-than-even chance of finding one when he wants it.

4) Probably the weakest tooth in that old saw, "the right book for the right reader at the right time," is the last one. The man who wants his *Hamlet* now is not enchanted by the response that "it's in the catalog" when he does not find it on the shelf.

So, long ago, we set out to discover what it takes in quantity to give the reader who wants quality a reasonable chance of getting it when he wants it.

Our memory of these experiments was stirred by the list in Lj, compiled by Caroline Hieber, of books which the college-bound student should have or should be reading. How often, we wondered, would the eager student in search of one or other of these mostly standard titles be disappointed when he visited his local public library?

Are librarians still prone to be satisfied with copies recorded in the catalog or shelf-list, or do they check their shelves regularly enough to know that some items are never there? Do copies slumber in reserve stacks while empty spaces adorn the open shelves? Are we so busy buying the "new" titles that we too rarely go back and check our shelf representation of the "old" ones?

Well, we like answers, even to our own questions. We selected 20 titles from the fiction and nonfiction works listed by Miss Hieber and checked the shelves of eight New York and New Jersey public libraries, varying in size from the gigantic city library to the medium-sized suburban library.

We chose titles which we thought most librarians would agree were basic stock items, and our choice was justified by the fact that nearly all the titles were "in stock" in nearly all the libraries we visited. We also chose titles which were all available in paperback. This, we thought, gave the libraries an extra advantage, since some of the eager readers would have bought their own copies, thus lessening pressure on the library, and also, the library that needed to duplicate fairly heavily in order to satisfy demand for these titles *could* do so, without wrecking the book fund, by buying extra paperback editions.

What did we find? Were the books generally "on the shelf"? Space does not permit elaboration here, but the results were quite interesting in their variety. While seven out of eight could produce *Sister Carrie*, only four had *Vanity Fair* on the shelf, and none could supply *Lord of the Flies*—and three didn't have a Milton in sight! For more, as the serial writers say, see next installment.

9 *The View from the Front*

(FEBRUARY 1, 1964)

by ERIC MOON

My preceding article introduced, and left hanging inconclusively, the story of a small experiment. A continuation was promised, and this is it.

The investigation recorded here was, it must be emphasized, no very intense or scientific research project designed to produce devastating conclusions. It was no more than an exercise in inquiry, a lightning foray prompted by curiosity and an old hobbyhorse interest. If it is worth reporting, it may be because the factors involved—the bookstock, and the reader who tries to use it—are central in library service. And just as the doctor sometimes finds it difficult to see a situation through his patient's eyes, so the practicing librarian does not always see his shelves from the reader's side of the aisle.

When I first received the list of books which tempted me to take an old hobbyhorse out for another ride (*see* "Paperbacks for College-Bound Students," Lj, Jan. 15, pp. 185–7), I wondered whether there was really any point in publishing it. It seemed such a basic and general list: surely, there would be few libraries, college or public, or even in the better high schools, where all or most of these works would not be available. But then I remembered some experiments from my practicing-librarian days which had shattered such easy assumptions, and remembered, too, the frequent frustrations of more recent years as a public library user who often wants a specific book at a particular time—and rarely finds it. It depends, you see, what you mean by "available." The point of the list was not that these are books which most libraries should possess, but that they are books of some permanence for which the list indicates a likely steady demand. Were sufficient *copies* being supplied to satisfy this demand?

The limits of the inquiry were quite narrow. The tables list the 20 fiction and 20 nonfiction titles selected from the "college-bound" list. The fiction titles were checked against the shelves of eight libraries in New York and New Jersey, the nonfiction titles in six.

In the case of fiction the catalogs of these libraries were bypassed altogether, on the assumption, hopefully with justification, that there would be none among these libraries which did not have all 20 titles "in stock." Classification peculiarities were frequent enough to make it mandatory to travel to the shelves via the catalog in the case of nonfiction, if one were to be absolutely sure that all possible places had been checked. This enforced extra step at least served the purpose of supporting the validity of the assumption that these were titles which were being stocked pretty generally. Only four of the 20 nonfiction titles were not in stock in all six libraries visited.

				LIBRARY					
FICTION	A	B	C	D	E	F	G	H	TOTAL
AUSTEN, Jane. *Pride and Prejudice*	√	√	√	√	o	o	√	√	6
CAMUS, Albert. *The Stranger*	o	√	√	o	o	o	o	o	2
CONRAD, Joseph. *Lord Jim*	o	o	o	√	o	o	√	√	3
DICKENS, Charles. *Great Expectations*	o	√	√	√	o	√	√	o	5
DOSTOYEVSKY, Fyodor. *Brothers Karamazov*	√	√	√	√	o	√	√	√	7
DREISER, Theodore. *Sister Carrie*	√	√	√	√	√	o	√	√	7
ELLISON, Ralph. *Invisible Man*	√	o	o	o	√	o	√	√	4
FLAUBERT, Gustave. *Madame Bovary*	√	√	√	o	√	o	√	√	6
GOLDING, William. *Lord of the Flies*	o	o	o	o	o	o	o	o	0
HAWTHORNE, Nathaniel. *House of the Seven Gables*	o	√	√	√	o	√	√	√	6
HEMINGWAY, Ernest. *The Sun Also Rises*	√	√	√	√	√	√	√	o	7
LAWRENCE, D. H. *Sons and Lovers*	o	o	√	o	√	o	√	√	4
LEWIS, Sinclair. *Main Street*	√	√	√	√	o	√	√	√	7
MAUGHAM, W. Somerset. *Of Human Bondage*	o	√	o	√	o	√	√	√	5
SILONE, Ignazio. *Bread and Wine*	√	o	√	o	√	o	√	√	5
STEINBECK, John. *The Grapes of Wrath*	√	o	√	o	√	o	√	o	4
THACKERAY, W. M. *Vanity Fair*	√	o	o	√	o	o	√	√	4
WILDER, Thornton. *Bridge of San Luis Rey*	√	√	√	√	o	o	√	√	6
WOLFE, Thomas. *Look Homeward, Angel*	o	o	o	√	√	o	o	o	2
WRIGHT, Richard. *Native Son*	o	√	o	o	o	√	o	o	2
TOTAL	11	12	13	12	8	7	16	13	

But the concern—and let this be stressed again—was not with copies recorded in the catalog, nor with the possibilities of interbranch or interlibrary loan, nor yet with the nuggets to be mined in basement reserve stacks. I was looking at the shelves as the general reader sees them, trying to ascertain what chance he has in some sample public libraries of getting what for him may be "the right book *at the right time.*" Having, I considered, weighted things in favor of the libraries with the selection of titles, I recorded only what I found, or did not find, on the open shelves.

In the tables, A and B represent the main libraries of very large metropolitan systems; C is a branch of another large city system; and D through H are the main libraries of medium-sized systems in New Jersey serving, in ascending order, from about 23,000 to 77,000 population, according to the 23rd edition of the *American Library Directory.*

	LIBRARY						
NONFICTION	A	D	E	F	G	H	TOTAL
MACLEISH, Archibald. *J. B.*	√	√	√	o	√	√	5
MILLER, Arthur. *Death of a Salesman*	o	√	o	o	o	√	2
MILTON, John. *Paradise Lost*	√	o	o	o	√	√	3
ROSTAND, Edmond. *Cyrano de Bergerac*	o	√	√	o	o	√	3
SHAW, G. Bernard. *Saint Joan*	√	√	√	o	√	√	5
STRUNK, William. *Elements of Style*	o	√	o	√	o	o	2
BRINTON, Crane. *Ideas and Men*	o	√	√	o	√	√	4
PLATO. *Dialogues*	√	o	√	o	√	√	4
RUSSELL, Bertrand. *History of Western Philosophy*	o	√	o	o	o	√	2
CONANT, James. *Modern Science and Modern Man*	√	√	o	X	√	√	4
GAMOW, George. *One, Two, Three, Infinity*	√	√	√	√	√	√	6
WHITEHEAD, Alfred N. *Science and the Modern World*	o	o	X	X	X	√	1
FRANKLIN, Benjamin. *Autobiography*	√	√	√	o	√	√	5
HERSEY, John. *Hiroshima*	o	o	√	o	√	√	3
SANDBURG, Carl. *Abraham Lincoln*	√	o	√	√	√	√	5
DE TOCQUEVILLE, Alexis. *Democracy in America*	o	X	√	√	√	√	4
GALBRAITH, J. K. *The Affluent Society*	o	√	√	√	√	√	5
WHITE, T. H. *The Making of the President*	√	o	√	o	o	√	3
BARZUN, Jacques. *The Teacher in America*	√	√	o	√	√	o	4
VAN DOREN, Mark. *Liberal Education*	o	X	√	o	X	o	1
TOTAL	10	12	13	6	13	17	

√ = One or more copies on shelf.
o = No copies on shelf.
X = Title not recorded in catalog.

It is at once apparent that the size of the library, at least within this sample, doesn't affect the reader's chances much, one way or the other. The "best" shelf results were obtained in the two largest of the medium-sized New Jersey libraries, the "worst" were found in the third largest of this group. And the branch library did about as well, in the case of fiction, as did the two very large main libraries in the New York City area. Also, the New York City results were very close to the average result in the suburban libraries of New Jersey.

While the working assumption was that the good library would have a majority of these books on the shelf, it could be argued (and probably will be by some) that the libraries performing the liveliest service might very well be those with fewest of these titles "in," since in such libraries the copies might be assumed to be actively working and in circulation.

Some of the evidence, indeed, seemed to point in this direction. On the one hand, the library which had the highest percentage of these titles represented on the shelves was the dingiest I visited. The building was a rented factory or store, unprepossessing within and without; the shelves were stygian and crowded, the bookstock ragged, aging, and unappealing in its over-all physical condition. On the other hand, the library where fewest of the titles could be found was by far the most attractive and modern of the group of libraries visited. It looked lovely and alive, used the most modern methods, had plenty of staff around, but only 13 of the 40 titles I was looking for were on the shelves.

Not all the evidence, however, pointed toward such a simple and face-saving conclusion. The library with the second highest number of shelf-present titles is one of the busiest in New Jersey and, for its size, one of the busiest in the country. The stock is of very high quality and brightly attractive in appearance. Though the premises are old and somewhat overcrowded, they are still well-lit, well-arranged, and exude vitality of service.

So what does one conclude? It seemed evident, despite librarians' concern for quality—supported to some extent by the fact that nearly all titles were in stock in the majority of the libraries—many have not solved, perhaps have not even tackled, the more difficult equation involving both quality and quantity. When, in all the vast area served collectively by these libraries, the reader has a very slim chance of finding on public library shelves a particular book by Camus or Wolfe, or Whitehead, or Van Doren, the problem of duplication of standard works clearly requires more attention.

This will be pounced upon, perhaps, as an over-simplification, but it is not said without some awareness of the many factors involved. First and foremost, there is every librarian's perpetual nightmare—space. "Our shelves are jammed already. Where are we going to put all these extra copies on the open shelves, even supposing we had the budget to provide them?"

I am not suggesting that the need is for more books on the shelves: in some places there were too many already. What is required is that the *balance* of what is there needs to be examined more thoroughly and with greater frequency in many libraries. In *every* library I visited there were glistening examples of stagnant little pools formed by 1963's popular flood. (Hiram Haydn's *Hands of Esau* must have averaged about four or five dormant, giant shelf copies per library). One library had a shelf-full of Milton in the basement (the dust revealed that this had been the poet's resting place for many a long day), but where some of the greatest poems in the English language should have been—on the shelf—there was only a void.

Another aspect of the question of balance was illustrated in several of the libraries. Even within the output of some of the authors I was checking, it was not unusual to find multiple copies of the least heralded, least wanted, or least successful books, while his major landmarks were commonly absent. In one library, there was a shelf and a half full of tatty copies of *Pendennis* and *The Newcomes*, but ne'er a *Vanity Fair*. While *Winter of Our Discontent* formed a solid phalanx on some shelves, it was like looking for gold to find a copy of *The Grapes of Wrath* or *Of Mice and Men*. Do some libraries, when they decide to order replacement copies of the standard items, still buy on the "three of each" system, without ascertaining from the shelves that six copies of one of an author's works might be desirable, while one copy of some of his dull thuds would be more than adequate?

It is possible to conclude from another observation that some of the obeisance we pay "the books that last" is not much more than lip service. Often the most dismal editions of any I found on the shelves were those of the works of Conrad, Hawthorne, Dickens, Thackeray, Milton. If librarians believe in the best, they surely might do more to promote it than this. Appearance, to be sure, is not everything, and the determined reader of the good things will seek them out and accept them whatever their garb. But the younger readers of today have been reared in a jazzily packaged world, and what their eyes pass over their hearts will seldom reach. The classics deserve at least an equal chance of being seen among their brightly plastic-jacketed "new" neighbors on the shelves.

This story started, not without design, in a paperback announcement issue of Lj. I am fond of fine editions of books, particularly great books, and would contribute no ounce of support to the replacement of the hardcover volume by the paperback invader. But I know, also, as a librarian, that the duplication problem is one of gigantic proportions. Unless book budgets are destined to fly through the present low roof (something which does not appear to be in immediate prospect), paperbacks may offer perhaps the only practical remedy for the shelf shortages that do the library's quality-image lasting and repeated harm.

All the books I chose to check against library shelves are available in paperback editions, and this fact bears upon the problem and the findings from a number of different directions:

1) The publication of a title in a paper edition makes it available, in most cases, at a reasonably low price to a much larger reading audience. One might assume, though I am aware of no evidence pro or con, that this would reduce the demand upon libraries, particularly by students, for copies of these books.

2) Whether or not the potential demand has been reduced by paperback publication, it is clear that many of these books are *not* available in sufficient quantity in most public libraries. For example, despite the thousands of copies sold in paperback, *Lord of the Flies* was nowhere to be found in any of the

libraries I visited: it is undeniably a book of sufficient quality and popularity to merit more copies than libraries are presently buying.

3) If the budget is the principal barrier, or excuse, two remedies tower above all others for those libraries which are prepared to back quality with quantity. One is to buy less of the flotsam which is washed up each week or month by promotion-activated demand; the other is to support the basic, hardcover editions of the good books with a small army of paperback editions.

4) Some studies have indicated that many of today's readers, given a choice of a paperback and a hardcover edition, will choose the paperback, for reasons of portability, informality, or sheer packaging appeal. Certainly the sprightly, and often artistic paperback is to be preferred to some of those gothic monstrosities of tired old editions which litter the shelves of some libraries.

Having dispensed mostly criticism, I must conclude by saying, nevertheless, that the results of this investigation were much more encouraging than my expectations. A number of the chosen titles (and, of course, others of similar quality) *were* available in many cases. However, most of the libraries visited would rank fairly high nationally, in their budgets, support, and bookstock, for their respective sizes. What a wider sample would have produced is anyone's guess.

Perhaps it *would* pay some libraries to check Miss Hieber's list in Lj. But check the shelves—not the catalog. I never knew a reader who wanted a book "right now" who left the library wildly enthused by finding a catalog entry for it.

CHAPTER

10 *"Problem"* *Books Revisited*

(MAY 15, 1964)

by RAYMOND B. AGLER

In 1962 LIBRARY JOURNAL reported the results of two surveys of public library practice and policy in the selection of controversial books, "'Problem' Fiction," and "'Problem' Nonfiction." These two surveys, which were directed primarily at medium-sized and large libraries throughout the country, eventually led to the present in-depth study of the selection of "problem" books—both fiction and nonfiction—by libraries in a well-defined geographical area. Four suburban Philadelphia counties—Bucks, Chester, Delaware, and Montgomery—were selected for study. Since most of the libraries in this area are small public libraries, it was thought that such a sampling might provide an interesting comparison with the earlier Lj studies.

Questionnaires covering the "problem" titles (20 fiction and 24 nonfiction) were sent to the 77 libraries in the Delaware Valley area. Librarians were asked to state their reasons for selection or rejection of the titles, and to indicate whether the books were freely available on the open shelves, or restricted in any way. Fifty-six libraries (over 72 percent of the sample) responded, with a fair representation from each of the four counties. Since the sample included a wide range of library situations in terms of size of book budgets (from $200 to $10,000), population served (primarily small however, with only seven libraries serving over 25,000), it was felt that the survey provides a fairly accurate image of book selection practices in the area.

GROUNDWORK

The first task to be undertaken was a thorough examination of the books and of the critical opinion that appeared in the reviewing media. Five reviewing sources were consulted: *ALA Booklist*, Kirkus, LIBRARY JOURNAL, *New York Times Book Review,* and *Saturday Review.* These five were selected since they were the sources most frequently cited by the *Book Review Digest* and by the librarians who cooperated in the Lj fiction survey. Other sources checked were the *Fiction Catalog* and the *Standard Catalog for Public Libraries.*

The 20 fiction titles were fairly easily judged on the basis of reviews. Three categories of quality became evident: nine titles were almost unanimously received with favor; four were considered to be of medium quality; and the remaining seven were received with almost universal disfavor. In the analysis of data, these three groupings were considered separately.

Titles in the nonfiction areas proved to be more difficult to categorize according to quality level. Reviews were generally more difficult to delineate as concretely favorable or unfavorable, although there were several titles about which there could be little doubt in terms of high or low quality. The most obvious difference noted between titles selected for the two lists was that the nonfiction titles included many more high quality items than the fiction list. Because of these "built-in" difficulties, no division of high quality versus low quality was made in the analysis of "problem" nonfiction, although a general indication of the quality of each title is indicated.

HIGH QUALITY FICTION

In one respect, the selection scorecard on high quality fiction titles provides a welcome note of optimism. Nabokov, Updike, Lawrence, and Durrell—four of fiction's most controversial, and widely praised problem children—took the top four places. The one conspicuously low in the scale is Miller. Moravia, Lytton, Vittorini, and Peyrefitte may not be essential choices for the small library's collection, but the record shows that these latter four titles got their position at the bottom of the chart through injudicious reasoning or ignorance of the books' existence.

Literary excellence, favorable reviews, and public interest were the main reasons cited for purchase of *Lolita, Rabbit, Run, Lady Chatterley's Lover,* and *The Black Book.* Specific reasons included curiosity about and requests for *Lolita,* the fact that Pennsylvanian Updike is something of a "local" author, the importance of Lawrence in modern literature, and *The Black Book* as an illustration of the genesis of the "Alexandria" quartet. Restricted circulation was noted in the case of two titles: three of the 34 libraries housing *Lolita* muffle her style in the rare air of the closed shelf, while five of the 21 libraries owning the unexpurgated *Lady Chatterley* keep her enclosed.

Comments concerning rejection of these titles provided alarming examples of uninformed or dictatorial opinion, or worse—clearly defined cases of self-censorship. Lawrence and Durrell received the brunt of angry remarks, with Nabokov running a close third.

Five librarians closed the door on *Lady Chatterley* for the simple reason that she has a "record," and has received this treatment in the past. These librarians noted previous bans, or the novel's "bad reputation," as ample evidence to warrant rejection. Three others pronounced the novel's content "unsuitable," and there were two reported instances of board orders to withdraw the book. One librarian said emphatically, "We have no shelf space for this sort of trash." Four librarians suggested that readers who were anxious enough to obtain *Lady Chatterley* could easily get a copy from any drugstore paperback collection. Two libraries noted cost as a factor; only one claimed lack of demand.

Nearly half of the libraries which did not buy *The Black Book* gave no reason for its rejection, but comments from those who did respond included "in poor taste" and "unsuitable." Four librarians pointed out that the work was rejected in the interest of economy since it parallels the later tetralogy which was considered by critics to be more significant.

All but two of the 22 librarians who held negative views on Nabokov gave their reasons for rejecting *Lolita*. Twelve of the dissenters condemned the

"PROBLEM" FICTION

AUTHOR AND TITLE	LIBRARIES WHICH PURCHASED		DON'T KNOW OR NO COMMENT
	NUMBER	PERCENT	PERCENT
HIGH QUALITY:			
Nabokov, Vladimir. *Lolita*	34	60.7	3.6
Updike, John. *Rabbit, Run*	25	44.6	42.9
Lawrence, D. H. *Lady Chatterley's Lover*	21	37.5	35.7
Durrell, Lawrence. *The Black Book*	17	30.4	48.2
Moravia, Alberto. *Wayward Wife*	7	12.5	58.9
Lytton, David. *The Goddam White Man*	6	10.7	58.9
Miller, Henry. *Tropic of Cancer*	5	8.9	32.1
Vittorini, Elio. *The Dark and the Light*	4	7.1	89.3
Peyrefitte, Roger. *Knights of Malta*	3	5.4	80.4
MEDIUM QUALITY:			
O'Hara, John. *From the Terrace*	40	71.4	17.9
Bourjaily, Vance. *Confessions of a Spent Youth*	10	17.9	57.1
Mayfield, Julian. *The Grand Parade*	4	7.1	78.6
Kerouac, Jack. *Dr. Sax*	3	5.4	71.4
LOW QUALITY:			
Robbins, Harold. *The Carpetbaggers*	22	37.6	37.6
Wallace, Irving. *The Chapman Report*	20	35.7	37.6
Mailer, Norman. *Deer Park*	18	32.1	44.6
Caldwell, Erskine. *Jenny by Nature*	15	26.7	33.9
Metalious, Grace. *Return to Peyton Place*	14	25.0	7.5
Peacock, Jere. *Valhalla*	10	17.1	48.2
Harvey, Frank. *The Lion Pit*	5	8.8	69.6

theme as "lewd," "sordid," or "unsuitable." Another dismissed the book as "not worth considering." One library got no requests, and therefore, no *Lolita*.

Twenty of the 31 who did not purchase Updike declined to comment. Five had no knowledge of the title, while three cited lack of funds and three others objected to the content. One librarian who *did* buy had waited a year until her budget was strong enough to allow for purchase of this "special" item.

In fifth and sixth positions on the list were the *Wayward Wife* and *The Goddam White Man*. Reasons for selection included favorable reviews for both; the prominence of Moravia as an author; and the literary excellence of Lytton, as well as current interest in African affairs. On the negative side, 11 libraries had not heard of the *Wayward Wife*, while 14 indicated no reader interest. One librarian preferred that members of her community get themselves a paperback copy elsewhere. Lytton was missed by 20 libraries; eight cited lack of demand; two, bad reviews (no sources given); and three noted "offensive" *title*.

Eleven libraries bought *Tropic of Cancer* on the basis of the author's prominence, status of the novel as a dominant influence on other contemporary writers, favorable opinion of literary critics, and strong reader interest. Of these eleven, only five stood firm in their decision. Two Montgomery County librarians decided to wait out the county's ban on the book with *Tropic* waiting with them on their office shelves. Of the four others who removed the novel from circulation, two jumped onto the shirttails of the Philadelphia censors, stating that they were "cooperating" with other local bans. The remaining two withdrew the book in anticipation that there *might* be a local fight.

Seven librarians who did not buy *Tropic* took to the high ground on the fairly defensible platform that the book is too expensive ($7.50). Three of these also mentioned that reviews published at the time of *Tropic*'s appearance here were partly unfavorable. Eleven thought the book offensive (and in one case "dangerous"), but only two of these librarians mentioned having read the book. Some specific comments: "No place in our community's library for trash"; "Too many four-letter words"; "In poor taste for us"; and "Too heady for public consumption."

Vittorini and Peyrefitte, authors of considerable standing in Europe, were virtually ignored by the Delaware Valley libraries, with an overwhelming number declaring that they had never heard of the titles. Two librarians felt that they had committed an oversight in the case of *The Dark and the Light*, and were considering purchase on the basis of reviews. One rejected Peyrefitte because the reviews were not solely full of praise, and another stated flatly, "Not for public libraries."

MEDIUM QUALITY FICTION

The record of selection practice in the case of the four medium quality novels provides clear evidence of the over-riding influence of "demand." Had sound principles of literary merit been observed, the percentages of libraries purchasing these titles should have remained fairly constant (and small). In practice, however, O'Hara was bought by more libraries than any of the other titles. *From the Terrace* is surely not the worst novel on the list, but not by a considerable length could it be considered the most critically well received of the 20 titles.

Of the 30 libraries that bought O'Hara on the basis of demand—some simply stating "best seller" as their reason—11 indicated that the author's popularity had prompted them to order the title immediately, without consulting reviews as a precaution. Three felt that the book stood high in literary merit and one librarian decided to buy and allow the public to "make up its own mind." Three libraries without the novel objected to O'Hara on moral grounds; three quarrelled with the price; only two claimed unfamiliarity.

Nineteen librarians could not recall having seen or heard of *Confessions of a Spent Youth*, number two on the list. Favorable reviews and reader requests were responsible for seven purchases. Three libraries joined in derisive comment: one labelled Bourjaily "unsuitable for our readers"; two others were satisfied to stop at calling the book "trash."

The Grand Parade did not elicit a grand following among the counties' librarians. Twenty-seven declined to comment on its absence; 17 others stated that they had not heard of it; and four found fault with the author's frankness concerning sex. The four loners who bought the book did not state their reasons for selection.

The author's reputation as the best of the "far-out young writers" was the main consideration in the selection of the Kerouac title by three libraries. Three others found *Dr. Sax* "depressing" or "ridiculous"; three found Kerouac a poor choice on the basis of professional reviews which recommended the book only for larger collections; and another three mentioned that earlier works of the author were available in their collections.

LOW QUALITY FICTION

Again, the fact most conclusively evident from the returns is that too many libraries consider demand before quality. Demand is a valid consideration in book selection if demand is construed to be synonymous with consciously studied community needs and interests. And in order to best reflect such needs and interests, selection should be made only within the framework of quality standards. Unfortunately, like Mae West's diamonds, goodness (quality) had nothing to do with the getting of the seven titles in this category.

Persistent demand accounted for the purchase of Robbins' popular mistake by 18 out of a total of 22 libraries. Seven, however, envisioned eventual withdrawal. More libraries bought multiple copies of *The Carpetbaggers* than any other of the 44 titles on the list, with 18 libraries purchasing two copies, and 12 buying three or more. One library with no funds to spend on Durrell was able to scrape up enough money for three copies of Robbins. Two historically-minded librarians leaped at the opportunity to add another item to their resources on the ever-raging Civil War. (Let us hope that they had to look no further than the dust jacket to discover their mistake.) Nineteen of those who rejected Robbins supplied colorful reasons. Six put down "sexy" or "too sexy" (did all six mean the same thing?); others wrote "junk, junk, junk," "trashy," "I wouldn't waste the taxpayer's money," and "a vile book." Three who indicated that Robbins did not measure up to expected literary standards, described the book with more rational adjectives, such as "weak plot," "intentionally sensational," and "mediocre." Five libraries confine *The Carpetbaggers* to the cupboard.

Wallace's much-condemned treatment of suburbia sexualis was bought by 20 libraries, with half of those leaving us mystified as to why. Five committed themselves to demand, one added a gift copy, and another cited "glowing" reviews (none were found). Three expressed regret at having made a mistake—cause for a slight bit of optimism. Those who didn't buy were also tight-lipped concerning why, but five indicated objections to the book's lurid aspects, and there was one case of the library board's putting up the bar.

Only half of the libraries owning *Deer Park* offered reasons for its inclusion—five cited author's prominence; one, favorable reviews (which ones?); and three, requests. Unfamiliarity, budget problems, and failure to accumulate the requisite number of requests were among the reasons for abstention. One library removed the book at the request of the board of trustees, and six others based their objections on the bold handling of sex. One over-judicious librarian has been pondering purchase for the last eight years; her return stated simply, "still considering." Three librarians who had Mailer's earlier novel, *The Naked and the Dead*, felt that this was the better choice to offer their readers.

Jenny was purchased mainly on the premise of Caldwell's popularity, as evidenced by requests. In one case, the librarian read the book after her concession to demand and felt that she had made a mistake. Another who bought the title for the rental collection noted that Caldwell made a smashing good fund raiser. Only one library keeps Caldwell on the closed shelf. Almost half of the 41 libraries which do not offer this novel a place in their collections gave no reasons. Two libraries pointed out that they had earlier and better works by the author (*God's Little Acre* or *Tobacco Road*). Five resorted to name calling: "too sexy," "bad taste," and "too controversial." Only four noted unfavorable reviews.

Fourteen libraries joined in the dreary trek back to *Peyton Place*, all for rather shaky reasons. Eight bowed to requests; one purchased with an eye to increasing the manna from the rental collection. Another well-meaning, but somewhat misguided librarian confided that, "This bit of trash was bought to satisfy reader demand. It will shortly be withdrawn and readers told that it has been lost." Of the 37 libraries which took a stand against the title, four based their opinion on a first-hand reading, ten cited unfavorable reviews, and only one aired the budget problem. For once, no one was unfamiliar with the book. The more vociferous replies labeled Metalious "distasteful," "offensive," "trash," or more emphatically, "cheap trash." One librarian refused to buy this sequel since she had been forced to withdraw *Peyton Place* because "too many teen-agers were requesting it."

Peacock's *Valhalla* seemed to be an embarrassment to the ten libraries which purchased it. Only one stuck to the defensible reasoning that several reviewers thought Peacock a promising young writer, and that this, his first novel, was not a complete failure. Four promised withdrawal at the first sign of a frayed edge (more "lost" books?), one writing, "I was unaware of its lewdness when ordered." Twenty-seven librarians were unfamiliar with the title or gave no reason for rejection. Others cited unfavorable reviews, lack of demand and funds.

Only two of the five librarians who selected Harvey's *The Lion Pit* stated their reasons: one added a gift copy without consulting reviews; the other noted requests. Twenty had not heard of the title; six listed "no requests";

"PROBLEM" NONFICTION

AUTHOR AND TITLE	LIBRARIES WHICH PURCHASED NUMBER	PERCENT	DON'T KNOW OR NO COMMENT PERCENT
NUTRITION:			
Jarvis, D. C. *Folk Medicine*	39	69.6	19.6
Taller, Herman. *Calories Don't Count*	19	33.9	21.4
Leverton, Ruth. *Food Becomes You*	3	5.4	89.3
Pollack, Herbert. *How To Reduce Safely and Surely*	2	3.6	94.6
RACE:			
Baldwin, James. *Nobody Knows My Name*	26	46.4	14.3
King, Martin Luther. *Stride Toward Freedom*	16	28.6	57.1
Smith, Lillian. *Killers of the Dream*	11	19.6	28.6
Putnam, Carleton. *Race and Reason*	9	16.1	60.7
Hays, Brooks. *A Southern Moderate Speaks*	7	12.5	75.0
SEX:			
Mead, Margaret. *Male and Female*	18	32.1	58.9
Kinsey, Alfred. *Sexual Behavior in the Human Female*	17	30.4	3.6
Van de Velde, Theodoor H. *Ideal Marriage*	14	25.0	75.0
Stone, Abraham. *Planned Parenthood*	10	17.9	35.7
West, Donald J. *The Other Man*	2	3.6	92.9
POLITICS:			
Hoover, J. Edgar. *Masters of Deceit*	53	94.6	1.8
Whitehead, Donald F. *The FBI Story*	52	92.9	1.8
Schwarz, Fred. *You Can Trust the Communists*	41	73.2	19.6
Marx, Karl. *Das Kapital*	35	62.5	17.9
Cousins, Norman. *In Place of Folly*	21	37.5	21.4
Matthews, Herbert L. *The Cuban Story*	14	25.0	55.4
Ketchum, Richard. *What is Communism?*	9	16.1	44.6
Mills, C. Wright. *Listen, Yankee*	9	16.1	7.1
Weyl, Nathaniel. *Red Star over Cuba*	7	12.5	62.5
Copp, DeWitt and Peck, Marshall. *Betrayal at the UN*	2	3.6	25.0

three cited unfavorable reviews; and three labelled Harvey "unsuitable." One case of board interference resulted in the removal of the book.

NUTRITION

While a minority of 17 libraries abstained from embarking on the flood of public curiosity concerning *Folk Medicine* (which was widely condemned by the medical profession as being potentially harmful), 23 out of the 39 who indulged themselves bought on the basis of demand. Five librarians regretted the purchase. Reviews were not mentioned as a basis for either selection or rejection. One librarian who bought the book was happy to report that she had as yet had "no cases of casualties from eating honey and vinegar."

Second among the nutrition titles was *Calories Don't Count*. Quality and the good interests of the public apparently didn't count much either for the 19 libraries that purchased Taller. "Requests" was given as the chief reason for selection. Three libraries received gift copies and three others that paid for their copies with money, which does count, bought in quantity. Some of the 37 libraries that stood on the opposing side were apparently unsure of why, although one claimed that Taller was "too specialized" for her reading public. Of the 18 libraries rejecting the book for sound, intelligently expressed reasons, ten mentioned personally reading or examining the book and finding it inaccurate or misleading. Eight others consulted authoritative reviews. One said, "It is my policy to wait for qualified opinion before selecting in areas where popular medical advice is offered."

As for the other two diet books, Leverton was largely overlooked, while Pollack almost won the race for obscurity. Thirty-five libraries missed *Food Becomes You,* and 43 were not acquainted with *How To Reduce Safely and Surely.* Those who purchased the two books mentioned need and "solid, reputable advice." The only library commenting on the rejection of Pollack said, "We try to avoid fad books." This same library bought *Folk Medicine* and *Race and Reason.*

RACE

Baldwin was selected mainly on his reputation, with several libraries noting community need, timeliness, or favorable reviews as added incentives. One librarian selected the title to satisfy the demand created by the book's inclusion on a school reading list. Eight libraries expressed unfamiliarity with the title, the same number lacked sufficient funds, and four rejected the book on the basis of no demand.

Nearly half of the libraries purchasing King's account of progress toward desegregation in the South based their decision on excellent reviews. Five purchased on the authority of the author's reputation. Those who neglected to buy offered little in the way of comment. Thirty-two either had not heard of it or said nothing. One rejected on the premise that the library already offered enough material on race problems.

Killers of the Dream was bought on the strength of the author's reputation and the book's status as a classic on the subject of race problems. Of the 45 who did not buy, 22 were concerned mainly with the lack of demand. One library mentioned that other books filled their need in this area, and six others excused themselves on the basis of budget limitations.

Putnam's distressingly fanatical and fallacious theory on race was received in six libraries as a gift, the only reason offered for inclusion in all six cases; three others did not comment. Two libraries restrict the title to the reference collection (for which there is some justification). Most of the 47 libraries which did not purchase were apparently unaware of the book's existence. Only three rejected on the basis of reviews (which were hard to find), and one stated, "We have other material in the collection which expresses this viewpoint more logically."

Four libraries chose Hays to represent the southern moderate's viewpoint on race problems, while three mentioned timeliness and favorable reviews. The majority of librarians (42) who did not buy were unfamiliar with the title; 20 stated lack of demand.

SEX

Anthropologist Mead's fine study of growing up in the simple versus the complex culture, was purchased by nine libraries on the basis of the author's reputation, and by three others because of the work's inclusion in the *Standard Catalog*. Twenty-four libraries missed the title, while three lacked enough money and two felt the need for material was amply provided in other sources.

Selection criteria for Kinsey's study were the author's reputation, the work's position as a classic of its kind, and need. Five libraries keep their copies on closed shelves and one library restricts its copy to reference use in the library. Most frequently noted reason for rejection was "too specialized," or "limited use here." Three stated that the book could be borrowed through interlibrary loan should the need arise. Eleven cited the problem of expense ($8) and four felt that their communities had no need for the work.

Van de Velde's excellent marriage manual was stocked because of its status as a standard, highly recommended work, demand (3), usefulness (2), recommendation of a local churchman (1), and in one instance, the recommendation of another library.

Stone's well-balanced, temperate survey of birth control methods was bought by nine libraries on the basis of reliability and need; one bought as the result of a local physician's recommendation. Twenty did not buy because of lack of demand, six because of lack of funds. Seventeen had not heard of the title.

The Other Man was the most widely unknown title on the list, with 50 out of 56 libraries noting unfamiliarity. This skillful handling of the difficult subject of homosexuality was well received in the specialized reviewing media, but gained little notice or publicity in the mass media. Two libraries bought on the basis of usefulness, and two others rejected it on the grounds of already having suitable materials on the subject.

POLITICS

Hoover's *Masters of Deceit* and Whitehead's *The FBI Story* were nearly universally bought. The enormous popularity of the Hoover book and the popular appeal of the author were noted by 31 libraries, while favorable reviews accounted for purchase by another 17. Reviews were also responsible for the acquisition of Whitehead by 28 libraries, and the book's usefulness with students was the determining factor for eight others. The few who did not buy either book cited lack of enough money.

The third place spot was held by Schwarz, whose somewhat inflammatory description of Communist techniques and activity was available in 41 libraries, with 19 of these having received gift copies from the publisher. Down in seventh position was Ketchum's concise and dispassionate explanation of Communism, which was bought by a smattering of nine libraries. Four praised its usefulness to students and two listed high quality as their guide. The majority of those who did not purchase Schwarz or Ketchum either missed the books or failed to comment.

Das Kapital's status as a classic of modern political and economic ideology was cited by most of the libraries owning this title. One librarian pointed out that it was a Great Books selection. Of the libraries not offering Marx, nine pleaded lack of funds and two felt no need for it.

In the fifth and tenth spots on the list were the Cousins and Copp books on the UN. Author's reputation was the most widely reported reason for selection of Cousins' partisan, but even-tempered approach to the subject, while lack of demand, other books in the area, and budget problems were cited by the rejectors. The Copp title, which could logically have been rejected on the grounds of superficiality and lack of documentation, was bought by only two librarians, one failing to comment and the other on the premise of presenting all points of view on controversial topics.

The three titles on Cuba scored as follows: 14 libraries bought journalist Matthews' nonpartisan account of events in Cuba, with six adding the book on the basis of reviews, three because it "adequately presented all points of view," and one because it presented a "sound, realistic" account. Three of the nine libraries that bought Mills' heatedly pro-Cuban tirade mentioned their goal of presenting all points of view on controversial issues. More libraries than usual offered thoughtful reasons for rejecting this book, with 17 citing biased presentation and two pointing out distortion of facts. Unfavorable reviews accounted for ten rejections. Weyl's violently anti-Cuba title was purchased by a small minority of seven, of which two selected it to balance Mills. Eleven libraries felt that other material filled the need, and 12 did not know the book.

BOOK BUDGETS

To test the assumption that the size of a library's book budget might influence the quality of the "problem" books selected, libraries were ranked according to their book funds. Book budgets ranged from a high of $10,000 to a low of $200. Nine libraries at the top of the scale reported book funds between $10,000 and $5000, while the nine libraries at the bottom spent between $600 and $200.

The returns of these 18 libraries were analyzed according to high versus low quality titles selected in both fiction and nonfiction. Only those nonfiction books on which reviews were unanimously unfavorable were counted as low quality selections. No consistent relationship between size of budget and quality of titles selected was discernible. In fact, selection of low quality titles was represented in widely scattered fashion in both groups, except for two well-reasoned replies from the small-budget group and two equally sound returns from the large-budget libraries. The only conclusive fact determined by this analysis was the obvious one that libraries with more money were able to purchase more titles. Out of the total of 44 books, an average of 20.8 was bought by the top nine libraries, while the bottom nine purchased an average of three each.

SELECTION RESPONSIBILITY

It was also thought that in the selection of "problem" books practice might differ measurably between libraries where the librarian alone is responsible for book selection and those in which a board committee selects the books, with or without the aid of the librarian. In nearly half (44 percent) of the libraries surveyed, book selection is the duty of the librarian without the aid of library trustees. The remaining libraries select books by librarian-board committee. Here, too, there was no strong emergent pattern of good or haphazard book selection by either group. There was a fair amount of inconsistency or mistaken judgment in both groups, as well as scattered examples of sound, critical practice.

POLICY STATEMENTS

Another variable tested was the effect of a written book selection policy statement on the quality of titles selected. Libraries which had a written policy were asked to include a copy with their return. Six libraries complied.

The most sophisticated selection statement included the *Library Bill of Rights* (officially adopted by the library board), as well as the library's own policies in dealing with materials in the areas of religion, science and pseudo-science, and other controversial areas. This statement outlined the library's position regarding standards of quality expected of books to be added to its collection, both those purchased and those received as gifts. In this library, books were selected by the librarian. Twelve of the 44 "problem" titles were available, including four fiction and seven nonfiction high quality titles. There was only one lapse of judgment. The comment on the purchase of *Calories Don't Count* was: "The great number of requests got me in a weak moment."

Another fairly elaborate book selection statement included an excellent analysis of the library's objective of presenting materials representing all points of view on controversial issues, and its policy of nondiscrimination against writers because of race, nationality, and religious or political convictions. The library applied the same standards of quality to books added as gifts as to those purchased. It also sought to relate the selection of books to consciously studied community needs; demand alone was not considered a primary factor. Both the *Library Bill of Rights* and the *Freedom to Read Statement* had been formally adopted by the library board. Responsibility for selection rested with the librarian who was "advised" by a library board book committee. This library purchased eight titles: two quality titles from the fiction list and five from the nonfiction. Questionably, the library bought *Folk Medicine* on the basis of "requests," contradicting its stated policy of considering need above demand.

A third well-worded policy statement dealt primarily with standards of quality expected of materials to be added to the collection. The library purchased books of timely or permanent value, conforming to standards of accuracy, authority, and a clear and readable presentation. It sought to eliminate the cheap and trivial, the deliberately distorted or sensational. Here again, both the *Library Bill of Rights* and the *Freedom to Read Statement* had been officially adopted by the trustees. Gifts were added only on the same terms as books purchased. One interesting and unique exception was made to the library's stated goals: if a number of active borrowers requested a given substandard title, it might be purchased from money set aside each year, the amount not to exceed one percent of the library's annual book budget. About $30 a year was provided for such a fund.

A look at this library's record of selection shows 19 titles which are worth mentioning specifically. Quality fiction titles which were added in line with the library's policy included the Bourjaily, Lytton, Nabokov, O'Hara, and Updike books. Low quality fiction titles, out of line with the stated objectives, were those by Caldwell, Mailer, Robbins, and Wallace. In the nonfiction category, King, Cousins, Matthews, Weyl, Hoover, Marx, Schwarz, and Whitehead fell justifiably within the policy framework, while Jarvis and Taller were out of bounds.

This library's selection record also pointed up some rather curious omissions. It purchased none of the five standard works on sex, three of which are listed in the *Standard Catalog for Public Libraries*. Only one of the titles on race relations was purchased, with the three other quality titles being omitted. In the nutrition category, only the two questionable titles were bought. Concerning the reasons for selection or rejection of these titles, the librarian wrote: "The majority of these books were selected before my present appointment. Therefore, I cannot give specific reasons for selection or rejection. Our enclosed book selection policy statement, however, should—and I think *does*—answer this question."

A fourth library sent along a copy of its short, simply-worded, but nonetheless workable statement. It was primarily concerned with setting forth standards of quality, defining the aim and purpose of the collection, and outlining techniques of selection to be employed. Full responsibility rested with the librarian. Apparently, the policy statement was kept well in mind, for the library's record of purchase included 15 high quality titles, six in fiction and nine in nonfiction, with no glaringly low quality titles.

Two other libraries aimed their effort toward defining the library's role in the community and in prescribing goals to be achieved in building their collections. The two libraries were considerably far removed from one another in size of book budgets. One, with a book fund well within the upper-bracket range, purchased five quality fiction titles and 13 quality nonfiction. The other library, operating on a considerably smaller book budget, purchased eight quality titles, five fiction and three nonfiction.

It is worth noting that five of these librarians were more articulate and rational in their comments concerning selection or rejection than the large majority of respondents. In three cases, no low quality purchases were made, while in two others, only one questionable title was bought. The margin of error in the case of the one remaining library rose to nearly one-third of its total purchases. In the light of this evidence, one may conclude that the adoption of a written book selection policy statement, while offering no guarantee of perfect selection practice, does contribute measurably to consistent application of quality standards.

AVAILABILITY OF SELECTION TOOLS

The high incidence of blank spaces and "don't knows" which occurred so frequently in the questionnaires might lead one to suspect that a good many librarians in these small libraries were unable to keep abreast of current publishing because of a possible lack of access to reviewing media and book selection aids. Unfortunately, the questionnaire did not query librarians on the availability of book selection aids. This information, however, was available from three other surveys of libraries in Chester, Delaware, and Montgomery counties. The data, which had been gathered but not used in these other studies, provided the titles of book selection tools available in 42 libraries, or 75 percent of the 56 libraries included in the present survey. Only the five book selection aids most frequently cited by *Book Review Digest* were counted. The number of libraries subscribing to Kirkus was expectedly low. *ALA Booklist*, LIBRARY JOURNAL, and the *New York Times Book Review* were available in a respectably high proportion of the libraries for which data was reported. The tally was:

REVIEW MEDIA	NUMBER OF LIBRARIES	PERCENT OF LIBRARIES (N = 42)
New York Times Book Review	37	88
ALA Booklist	31	74
LIBRARY JOURNAL	25	60
Saturday Review	22	52
Kirkus	8	19

To further test the relationship between unfamiliarity with titles and availability of reviews, an analysis was made of six titles—recommended by the majority of reviewers, but not widely purchased—and the selection aids in which they were reviewed. The results are as follows:

AUTHOR AND TITLE	REVIEWED	LISTED	PERCENT OF DON'T KNOWS OR NO COMMENT
Lytton. *The Goddam White Man*	ALA, Kirkus, Lj, NY Times, SR		58.9
Moravia. *Wayward Wife*	Lj, NY Times, SR	Fiction Catalog	58.9
Vittorini. *The Dark and the Light*	ALA, Kirkus, Lj, NY Times, SR	Fiction Catalog	89.2
King. *Stride Toward Freedom*	ALA, Kirkus, Lj, NY Times, SR	Standard Catalog for Public Libraries (starred)	57.1
Leverton. *Food Becomes You*	ALA, Lj	Standard Catalog for Public Libraries	89.2
Mead. *Male and Female*	ALA, Kirkus, Lj, NY Times, SR	Standard Catalog for Public Libraries (double starred)	58.9

An examination of the overall availability of reviews in popular media in relation to the percentage of the sample indicating unfamiliarity with individual titles or declining to comment on their rejection showed that several titles, both high and low quality, were excusably "obscure" among the libraries sampled. This was especially true in the case of the Harvey, Pollack, Leverton, and West titles. However, several low quality titles, equally ignored in popular reviewing media, were considerably more widely held, notably Schwarz' *You Can Trust the Communists* and Taller's *Calories Don't Count*. In some cases publishers' advertisements or the general reputation of the author undoubtedly reduced the unfamiliarity factor.

COMPARISON OF SAMPLES

It was anticipated that this study might reveal relative patterns of conservative versus liberal policies in the selection of controversial books among the larger libraries included in the earlier Lj studies and the smaller libraries represented in the present survey. There is strong evidence to support the conclusion that the smaller libraries tend to be more conservative in the selection of "problem" books. The most striking case in point is furnished by the record of proportionate purchases between the two samples in fiction. The record of eight fiction titles, four high quality and four low quality, fell into this startling pattern (below):

	PERCENT OF LIBRARIES WHICH PURCHASED	
AUTHOR AND TITLE	LIBRARY JOURNAL SAMPLE	DELAWARE VALLEY SAMPLE
Lawrence. *Lady Chatterley's Lover*	82.3	39.2
Durrell. *The Black Book*	60.2	33.5
Moravia. *Wayward Wife*	60.2	14.2
Miller. *Tropic of Cancer*	51.3	8.8
Caldwell. *Jenny by Nature*	30.9	26.7
Wallace. *The Chapman Report*	30.9	35.7
Metalious. *Return to Peyton Place*	23.9	25.0
Robbins. *The Carpetbaggers*	23.0	39.2

The comparison reveals really striking imbalances on the high quality level, while on the low quality titles, the percentages are more nearly in line. The proportion of purchase by the small libraries actually exceeds that of the larger libraries on each low quality title except for Caldwell. This is taken to mean that the small library selector is less concerned with quality and more willing to follow the dictates of demand.

The most obvious difference in the record of nonfiction purchases appears in the total number of titles bought. More than half of the libraries in the Lj sample purchased 20 of the 24 nonfiction titles, but only five titles were bought by more than half of the Delaware Valley libraries. This may be due to the difference in book budgets at the disposal of the two groups; or it may mean that the smaller libraries do not buy "problem" nonfiction; or that they buy more heavily in fiction than in nonfiction.

A further analysis of nonfiction purchases could not be carried out because neither the Lj nor the Delaware Valley questionnaire asked libraries to list equivalent titles where these were appropriate.

CONCLUSIONS

The study offers several important generalizations concerning the selection of "problem" books in the small and medium-sized libraries sampled. First, the reasons given for selection or rejection of fiction were considerably more emotion-centered and subjective than those applied to nonfiction. It must be granted that controversial novels can cause considerable difficulty to the selector of library materials. However, the disturbing aspect of selection practices represented in this study pertain to the *kind* and *quality* of reasons given for selection or rejection. Are "too heady for public consumption," or simply "a dangerous book" defensible or intelligent reasons for rejecting a book? And what of the basis for such remarks? Only a slight number of librarians claimed to have read these books. Where do such comments appear in reputably published reviews?

The embarrassing comments offered as criteria for not selecting such works as those by Miller, Lawrence, and Durrell furnish evidence that no small segment of these librarians yielded to the pressures of anticipated trouble. Others relied on word-of-mouth criticism in forming their decisions not to buy.

What can be said by way of explanation? The majority of Delaware Valley libraries do not receive adequate financial support, which creates a host of problems affecting the selection of library materials. One of these problems is the lack of trained personnel able to devote the time required to do a reasonably good job in selection. In addition, the dependence on private as well as public sources for support, and the uncertainty of receiving adequate operating funds from year to year leave the small town and suburban community library much more vulnerable to real or anticipated pressures than the library in the large city. Public demand, therefore, becomes of overriding influence in book selection.

What should be done to improve book selection practice in these libraries? First of all the library should define its position and responsibilities in the selection of books for its collection. ALA's *Library Bill of Rights* and the *Freedom to Read Statement* are excellent guide posts. Those libraries presently without a book selection policy statement should give immediate thought to adopting one. Library literature abounds with ideas for building such a statement around consciously considered general aims and specific community needs. The Enoch Pratt Free Library has long had the reputation of having originated one of the most widely and highly regarded book selection statements. Though it is designed to guide the building and maintenance of a large, sophisticated collection for a major city, the statement nonetheless provides libraries of any size with a great many ideas and an excellent list of criteria in the fair judgment of books. After discussion and adoption of a book selection statement by the library board, it would be well for the library to seek allies in the community by publicizing the statement through the news media and through interested civic organizations.

Finally, the development of cooperative library systems can contribute to the improvement of book selection practices in small libraries. The Pennsylvania library development plan with its District Center libraries gives local librarians an opportunity to meet together for the discussion of new books, to examine approval copies of books being considered for purchase, and to gain access to the widest possible variety of book selection aids and reviewing media.

11 *In, Out,*

or Neglected?

Part I

(JANUARY 1, 1966)

by ERIC MOON

The pages of periodicals, newspapers, and book review media will shortly be blooming with lists of the chosen, the best, the notable books of 1965. The survey on which this article is based attempted to take a somewhat different look at the 1965 publishing scene and to produce a rather different kind of list.

The survey started with the theory that book selection is most difficult when the budget is very small and the area of choice vast. This, it seemed to us, is precisely the dilemma of the small public library faced with today's publishing flood. And this was the motivation behind three questions we sent to about 60 librarians who have voiced opinions on book selection or who have had considerable book selection experience. Each of them was asked to name:

1) One adult book (fiction, nonfiction, or reference) published in 1965 which should be on the shelves of virtually every public library, whatever its budget or size.

2) One adult book published in 1965 which should *not* be on the shelves of any public library (other than for local or special collection reasons).

3) One book published in 1965 which has considerable merit but which, for some reason (such as insufficient notice in the review media, insufficient promotion by the publisher, its format—for example, paperback only, its controversial nature, etc.), is likely to be neglected or purchased less widely by public libraries than it deserves to be.

Before we present the lists that emerged from these questions, a few cautionary words are in order. Clearly, what we were asking for were opinions—and that is what we got from nearly 50 respondents. Some gave us their own, others took a consensus of their staff. We very deliberately did not ask for "best" or "worst" books of 1965; our concern was with books that might have wide or narrow applicability for public library shelves, and with books that might deserve more attention than some deserving books receive. Some respondents were not entirely clear about this distinction, but it is worth repeating that we were not looking for comparative judgments so much as for clues or discoveries that might help other libraries, particularly the smaller ones.

Some respondents, particularly a few who clearly enjoy books and the stimulation of any book selection exercise, cheated a little on their answers. Some went beyond the boundaries of 1965, others could not restrict themselves to one title in the various categories. None of this seemed important to us, so we listed their titles and comments anyway; it was interest and challenge we were after, not science, immaculate statistics, or a Q.E.D.

THE "IN" BOOKS

Two books dominated the answers to the first question—which adult book of 1965 should be on the shelves of virtually every public library of any size? They were Theodore Sorensen's *Kennedy*, which garnered nine votes, and Samuel Eliot Morison's *Oxford History of the American People*, which received eight. Both books, at $10 and $12.50 respectively, are well above the average nonfiction price.

There was only one near contender to these two giants, Theodore H. White's *The Making of the President, 1964*, which received five votes—the only other book for which more than two respondents voted in answer to the first question in our survey. Thus, our top three were all books the primary interest of which is historical.

Actually, there was one other book up there at the top with the big three: the *World Almanac*, for which six respondents voted. Our questionnaire had included reference books, but what we were hoping to uncover was a *new* reference book of wide appeal, not an old reference shelf "Bible" like the *Almanac*.

Only seven other books received as many as two votes in this category, although the first three were also named once each in answer to our third question. The seven which received two votes each were: Claude Brown's *Manchild in the Promised Land;* Kenneth B. Clark's *Dark Ghetto; Congress and the Nation, 1945–1964;* Bel Kaufman's *Up the Down Staircase;* Nikos Kazantzakis's *Report to Greco;* Flannery O'Connor's *Everything That Rises Must Converge;* and Arthur Schlesinger's *A Thousand Days.*

Twenty other books received one vote apiece from our respondents. The complete list follows:

SORENSEN, Theodore C. *Kennedy.* Harper, $10 (9)
MORISON, Samuel Eliot. *Oxford History of the American People.* Oxford, $12.50 (8)

WORLD ALMANAC and Book of Facts for 1965. N.Y. World Telegram & Sun, $2.50 (6)
WHITE, Theodore H. *The Making of the President, 1964.* Atheneum, $6.95 (5)

BROWN, Claude. *Manchild in the Promised Land,* Macmillan, $5.95 (2)
CLARK, Kenneth B. *Dark Ghetto.* Harper, $5.95 (2)
CONGRESS AND THE NATION, 1945–1964. Congressional Quarterly, $27.50 (2)
KAUFMAN, Bel. *Up the Down Staircase.* Prentice-Hall, $4.95 (2)
KAZANTZAKIS, Nikos. *Report to Greco.* Simon and Schuster, $7.50 (2)
O'CONNOR, Flannery. *Everything That Rises Must Converge.* Farrar, $5.50 (2)
SCHLESINGER, Arthur M., Jr. *A Thousand Days.* Houghton, $9 (2)

ALBEE, Edward. *Tiny Alice.* Atheneum, $4.50
BEHRMAN, S. N. *The Suspended Drawing Room.* Stein & Day, $5.95
BELLOW, Saul. *Herzog.* Viking, $5.75
BENET, William Rose. *Reader's Encyclopedia.* 7th ed. Crowell, $8.95
BOOKS IN PRINT, 1965. Bowker, $18
BOWLE, John. *Henry VIII.* Little, Brown, $6.50
BROWER, David, ed. *Not Man Apart.* Sierra Club, $25
CRONIN, Vincent. *Louis XIV.* Houghton, $6.95
DOUGLAS, William O. *A Wilderness Bill of Rights.* Little, Brown, $5.95
FOWLER, H. W. *A Dictionary of Modern English Usage;* ed. by Sir Ernest Gowers. Oxford, $6
GOODMAN, Paul. *People or Personnel.* Random, $4.95
HUMPHREY, William. *The Ordways.* Knopf, $5.95
LAPP, Ralph E. *The New Priesthood: the Scientific Elite and the Uses of Power.* Harper & Row, $4.95
LORD, Priscilla S. and FOLEY, Daniel J. *Folk Arts and Crafts of New England.* Chilton, $17.50
LORD, Walter. *The Past That Would Not Die.* Harper, $5.95
LOWELL, Robert. *For the Union Dead.* Farrar, $3.95
MANNING, Harvey, ed. *The Wild Cascades.* Sierra Club, $20
STATISTICAL ABSTRACT OF THE UNITED STATES. US Bureau of the Census, $3.75
WARREN, Robert Penn. *Who Speaks for the Negro?* Random, $5.95
YOUNG, Wayland. *Eros Denied.* Grove, $7.50

This list of "essential" books for public libraries is perhaps a curious one when viewed in its entirety, but it has a number of points of specific interest. First, among the old staples cited in the reference area—*World Almanac, Books in Print,* the *Statistical Abstract*—there is one new reference title which several people considered to be of broad interest. Everett Moore (UCLA) describes *Congress and the Nation* as "a remarkable compendium of the what, when, where, how, and why of our national life during the postwar years." Eleanor Smith (Brooklyn P.L.), who named the same book in our third category ("likely to be neglected"), said: "We are strongly recommending that our branches purchase [it] for their reference collections. . . . Since it is published by Congressional Quarterly, it is quite probable that many libraries may not know about it, and its price might deter its purchase by some." Mrs.

Smith adds that it is "one of the most valuable reference tools published in the last decade."

The historical emphasis in the list is obvious, and it is perhaps healthy that a couple of titles—*Henry VIII* and *Louis XIV*—take us beyond American history. Also obvious is the awareness among our contributors of the importance of the civil rights issue and the need for libraries to make widely available the best material on this subject. It was this reasoning that dictated our own choice of Claude Brown over Sorensen and White. Nowhere better than in this book can one find the real meaning of the urban crisis, the crippling dimensions of the drug problem, or the picture of what the Negro is trying to escape, so vividly spelled out. While the language may occasionally cause a tremor in some faint hearts, this book seems to us essential reading for teen-agers as well as adults who want to understand what is happening in their own society and what is at the base of much of its present turmoil.

Some of the selections, however, appear to us to be hobbyhorse choices and, while undoubtedly valuable books, hard to defend as selections for the small library—which must first have the "essentials." The two Sierra Club books, for example, might more appropriately appear in our third category (where one, in fact, was chosen), as books which may not be purchased as widely as they deserve to be, rather than in this group of books for every public library. The same reasoning would seem to apply to *Folk Arts and Crafts of New England.*

One further point bears stressing again, at the risk of repetition. There are a number of quite expensive books in this list, and if our respondents' choices are in any way typical of general practice, we take this to be a healthy trend in book selection. In our experience, the expensive book is too often passed by in favor of two or three cheaper and, usually, less adequate books—the "bargain" psychology. William Chait (Dayton P.L.) put his finger on this point in defending his choice of the Morison book. "Too often," he said, "small libraries buy the inadequate history because of price."

THE "OUT" BOOKS

Our second question—which 1965 books should not be on public library shelves?—yielded fewest answers in terms of concrete titles, but elicited many comments and a variety of nervous wrigglings. Perhaps the charges of internal censorship which have often been made against libraries and librarians have made this kind of selection pronouncement unpopular or unpalatable.

Even some respondents who did name a title in this category confessed to not liking the exercise much. As Martha Boaz (USC Library School) said: "It conflicts with my whole philosophy of book selection." J. Periam Danton (Berkeley Library School) voiced the most specific, and probably most valid, objection to the question: " 'Any public library' must include the great collections in New York, Chicago, Detroit, Los Angeles, Philadelphia, and Baltimore, with their tremendously varied clientele. I don't believe there is any adult book published in 1965 which might not legitimately find a place on the shelves of one of these libraries."

There were some who put the basically pious reason succinctly, as did Bradford Harrison III (President, Conservative Library Association) who said: "I do not believe in censorship, but in free access to books." Ervin Gaines (Minneapolis P.L.) reached about the same conclusion, it seemed to us, but in a more interesting manner: "In theory, no book should be excluded. The fact is that books are excluded because budgets are limited and public taste is underdeveloped. But to say that anything in print should not come to rest in a library is to say something preposterous. I might be able to name a book that I would buy *last*, but that is not what you asked me."

One of the most interesting negative responses came from Homer Fletcher (Vallejo P.L., California), who said he wouldn't name a book in this category in this or any other year. "Even though a library is limited on book funds, this should not limit the outlook of the librarian in searching out ideas which are provocative, views which are stimulating, statements which are unorthodox. In fact, the smaller the book fund the more diligent should be this search for the uncommon, the heretical, the nonconforming . . . We are not really worth our salt if we do not purchase one really provocative book, even if it displaces five or 105 bland diet ones."

At the other end of the opinion scale were Joseph Klimberger (Nassau Library System) and Allan Angoff (Teaneck P.L., New Jersey). The former found the question hard to answer because "there is so much trash published that the selection of a single book as the ultimate of trash is beyond my poor abilities." Angoff said he found the other questions difficult, but for this one "I could have given you 100 or even 500 bad books without any difficulty."

What we were looking for here—we thought this might be apparent—were titles that might serve as examples of *types* that might fairly be excluded by libraries which never have enough copies of the essential books anyway (which means *all* libraries). John Hopkins (Free Library of Philadelphia), although he did not name a title in this category, understood the point. He said: "What I would like to do is cite a work of nonfiction that honest men could agree was dishonest. Theory represented as fact. Or something fallacious in its reasoning on an important subject. Something like the Carleton Putnam book of a few years ago. I can't think of anything comparable."

Well, what did get chosen? Two celebrities shared top (or bottom?) honors: Jean Harlow for *Today Is Tonight*, and Oscar Levant for *The Memoirs of an Amnesiac*, each of which gathered three votes.

Three other books received two votes apiece: Lenny Bruce's *How To Talk Dirty and Influence People*, Dan Greenburg's *How to Be a Jewish Mother*, and Terry Southern and Mason Hoffenberg's *Candy*. Another 18 books were each mentioned once. Here is the complete list:

HARLOW, Jean. *Today Is Tonight*. Grove, $5 (3)
LEVANT, Oscar. *The Memoirs of an Amnesiac*. Putnam, $5.95 (3)

BRUCE, Lenny. *How To Talk Dirty and Influence People*. Trident, $5 (2)
GREENBURG, Dan. *How to Be a Jewish Mother*. Trident, $2.95 (2)
SOUTHERN, Terry, and HOFFENBERG, Mason. *Candy*. Putnam, $5 (2)

CARSON, Johnny. *Happiness Is a Dry Martini*. Doubleday, $1.95
CROON, J. H. *Encyclopedia of the Classical World*. Prentice-Hall, $5.50
DAVIS, Adelle. *Let's Get Well*. Harcourt, $4.50
HALL, Desmond. *I Give You Oscar Wilde: a Biographical Novel*. NAL; World,
$5.95
HIMES, Chester. *Pinktoes*. Putnam, $5
HOWELLS, J. Harvey. *A House of Glass*. Appleton, $5.95
KRAFFT-EBING, Richard von. *Psychopathia Sexualis*. Stein & Day, $10
LENNON, John. *A Spaniard in the Works*. Simon & Schuster, $2.50
MAILER, Norman. *An American Dream*. Dial, $4.95
NYOITI, Sakurazawa. *You Are All Sanpaku*. University Bks., $4.95
O'BRIEN, Edna. *August Is a Wicked Month*. Simon & Schuster, $3.95
OLMSTED, Lorena. *To Love a Stranger*. Avalon, $2.95
POLLINI, Francis. *Glover*. Putnam, $5.95
SHAW, Irwin. *Voices of a Summer Day*. Dial, $4.95
WINSOR, Kathleen. *Wanderers Eastward, Wanderers West*. Random, $7.95
WOLFE, Tom. *The Kandy-Kolored Tangerine-Flake Streamline Baby*. Farrar,
$5.50
WOUK, Herman. *Don't Stop the Carnival*. Doubleday, $4.95
YOUNG, Marguerite. *Miss MacIntosh, My Darling*. Scribner, $10.95

This list is particularly ripe for comment. Our first reaction was mild incredulity that works by writers of such wide appeal as Norman Mailer, Irwin Shaw, and Herman Wouk should be named by librarians for exclusion from the majority of public libraries. Whatever the librarian's personal opinions, these choices seem unrealistic at best. Pandering to public demand is one thing; completely ignoring public taste quite another.

Almost as surprising is the inclusion here of the highly-touted *Miss Mac-Intosh, My Darling*, of which Frank Sessa (Miami P.L.) said: "We bought it, but we think it is probably the greatest waste of paper we have encountered in a long time. It is almost unreadable; there is little or no plot, and the whole thing seems pointless."

There were some obvious "types" among the chosen, such as the production-line romance. Dorothy Curley (Northbrook P.L., Illinois) pointed out that she chose *To Love a Stranger* "simply as illustrative of the kind of ill-written romance every library can do without." She added that "The smaller the library, the less trivia it can afford, and *To Love a Stranger* stands as the arch-image of the trivial." This was echoed by Walter Dziura (Hingham P.L., Massachusetts, and editor of Faxon's *Bulletin of Bibliography*), who nominated "any title bearing the Arcadia or Avalon imprint" for exclusion from public libraries.

Another "type" which is frequently subjected to more rigorous inspection than some other subject areas is the "health" book. Two examples were uncovered by our survey. One was the Adelle Davis book, of which Mabel Fischer (Fort Worth P.L.) said: "Purports to be a documented study of therapeutic effects of proper nutrition—especially in stress situations—but is actually full of author's conclusive statements which are only half or less of the truth . . . The Foreword contains a physician's warning against the reader's self-diagnosis. But public librarians should remember people's propensity for self-diagnosis and treatment."

The other health sample was of a more exotic variety, *You Are All Sanpaku,* a book which recommends the system of "macrobiotics" as the way to well-being and good health. This one was named by Katherine O'Brien (NYPL).

The nonbooks flourished in this list: Dan Greenburg, Johnny Carson, John Lennon, for example. Gerald Somers (Kellogg P.L., Green Bay, Wisconsin) seemed to find Tom Wolfe in this category also: he commented "The Beatles are in demand, too." Harlow and Levant, the title-winners in this category, were each cited as examples of "so what" ephemera.

Candy, Pinktoes, and perhaps a few others were chosen for fairly obvious reasons; whether those reasons are defensible or not is the subject of continuing debate. Harriet Goode (Detroit P.L.) described *Pinktoes* as a "sensational exploitation of race relations." And Ford Rockwell (Wichita P.L.) called *Candy* "a bit of deliberate over-indulgence which actually charms a very few readers." That might be hard to prove, even statistically!

Lenny Bruce's book is charged with the same kind of prurience that the police of some cities found in his nightclub act. Martha Boaz (USC) pointed out that the book "has been banned in Britain as obscene, immoral, indecent." So, of course, at various times, have been *Ulysses, Lolita, Lady Chatterley,* et al. William Chait (Dayton P.L.) commented, apropos *How To Talk Dirty . . . ,* "Our prurient society loves this junk, but should libraries buy only to avoid criticism of censorship or to prove that they are free institutions?"

A few items were just dismissed as incompetent, shoddy, or generally worthless. Lillian Bradshaw (Dallas P.L.) found *I Give You Oscar Wilde* "particularly dreadful; research bad and overly sentimental." John Pine (Smithtown P.L., New York) cited *A House of Glass* as "one of several banal novels" he had reviewed during the year for Lj. Richard Gardner (outgoing editor of *Choice*) named the *Encyclopedia of the Classical World* on the basis of its "inaccuracy and misinformation."

Finally, one other "type": the poor rewrites of literary classics—mentioned by no one else—was nominated for library oblivion by Joseph Klimberger (Nassau Library System). He described the Prentice-Hall series, "Graded Readers for Students of English as a Second Language," as representative of "a type of the worst offences against good taste and lowest literary standards . . . These books are rewrites of literary masterpieces in poor English, poor taste, and are not for consumption as a first, second, or third language."

"NEGLECTED" BOOKS?

Our third question, designed to uncover some books of merit which may not otherwise have received sufficient attention, prompted by far the most interesting answers—perhaps because the question was the most interesting of the three.

Only four books were nominated more than once, and none more than twice. The four which collected two votes apiece were: William Eastlake's novel, *Castle Keep;* the Henry Miller trilogy, *The Rosy Crucifixion;* Jan Myrdal's *Report from a Chinese Village;* and poet M. B. Tolson's *Harlem Gallery.* Another 44 titles, mentioned once each, illustrate the diversity of response to this question. The complete list follows:

EASTLAKE, William. *Castle Keep.* Simon & Schuster, $5.95 (2)

MILLER, Henry. *The Rosy Crucifixion* trilogy (*Nexus, Sexus,* and *Plexus*). Grove, 95¢, $1.25, $1.25 (2)

MYRDAL, Jan. *Report from a Chinese Village.* Pantheon, $6.95 (2)

TOLSON, M. B. *Harlem Gallery.* Book 1: *The Creator.* Twayne, $4 (2)

ALPEROVITZ, Gar. *Atomic Diplomacy.* Simon & Schuster, $7.50

AMMONS, A. R. *Corson's Inlet.* Cornell, $3.95

BELFRAGE, Sally. *Freedom Summer.* Viking, $5

BOLL, Heinrich. *The Clown.* McGraw-Hill, $5

BORGSTROM, Georg. *The Hungry Planet.* Macmillan, $7.95

BROWER, David, ed. *Not Man Apart.* Sierra Club, $25

BROWN, Claude. *Manchild in the Promised Land.* Macmillan, $5.95

BURGESS, Anthony. *The Long Day Wanes.* Norton, $6.95

CARTHY, J. D. and EBLING, F. J. *The Natural History of Aggression.* Academic Pr., $5

CLARK, Kenneth B. *Dark Ghetto.* Harper, $4.95

CONGRESS AND THE NATION, 1945–1964. Congressional Quarterly, $27.50

DABBS, James McBride. *Who Speaks for the South?* Funk & Wagnall, $5.95

DAVIS, Kenneth S. *Experience of War: the United States in World War II.* Doubleday, $7.95

DRAPER, Hal. *Berkeley: the New Student Revolt.* Grove, 95¢

EBERHART, Richard. *Selected Poems, 1930–1965.* New Directions, $1.75

EDITORIAL RESEARCH REPORTS. Congressional Quarterly, $84

ENDORE, Guy. *Satan's Saint.* Crown, $4.95

FIRST, Ruth. *117 Days.* Stein & Day, $4.95

FORD, Jesse Hill. *The Liberation of Lord Byron Jones.* Little, Brown, $5.95

FUSSELL, Edwin. *Frontier: American Literature and the American West.* Princeton, $8.50

GASNER, Beverley. *Nina Upstairs.* Knopf, $3.95

GINGER, Ray. *Age of Excess.* Macmillan, $5.95

GIRODIAS, Maurice, ed. *The Olympia Reader.* Grove, $12.50

GIRONELLA, José M. *Phantoms and Fugitives.* Sheed, $3.95

GRISHAM, R. A., Jr., ed. *Encyclopedia of U.S. Government Benefits.* Wm. H. Wise, $7.95

HENDERSON, N. *Prince Eugene of Savoy.* Praeger, $6.95

KOHL, Herbert. *Age of Complexity.* NAL, 75¢

LEDUC, Violette. *La Batarde.* Farrar, $6.95

MALCOLM X. *The Autobiography of Malcolm X.* Grove, $7.50

MELMAN, Seymour. *Our Depleted Society.* Holt, $5.95

MOINOT, Pierre. *An Ancient Enemy.* Doubleday, $4.50

MONTEIRO, Luis de Sttau. *A Man of Means.* Knopf, $3.95

NIEBUHR, Reinhold, and others. *Mississippi Black Paper.* Random, $4.95

OGBURN, Charlton, Jr. *The Gold of the River Sea.* Morrow, $6.95

PERKINS, Ralph. *The Prospective Teacher's Knowledge of Library Fundamentals.* Scarecrow, $4.50

PFEFFER, Leo. *This Honorable Court.* Beacon, $10.95

PRIESTLEY, J. B. *Man and Time*. Doubleday, $12.95
REDFORD, Polly. *Raccoons and Eagles*. Dutton, $4.95
SHAW, Robert. *The Flag*. Harcourt, $4.95
SNIDER, Delbert A. *Economic Myth and Reality*. Prentice-Hall, $4.95
TANIZAKI, Junichiro. *Diary of a Mad Old Man*. Knopf, $3.95
TOLKIEN, J. R. R. *Tree and Leaf*. Houghton, $4
UNTERMEYER, Jean Starr. *Private Collection*. Knopf, $5.95
VICTORIA, Queen. *Dearest Child: the Letters of Queen Victoria to the Princess Royal, 1858–1861*. Holt, $5.95

In this third question we cited a number of possible reasons why certain kinds of books sometimes tend to get overlooked or purchased less widely than they deserve to be. Our list of suggestions did not set out to be comprehensive, but many of the books listed were obviously chosen for reasons given in the question.

Katherine O'Brien (NYPL) said: "Paperback format is no longer a real detriment, I think, to generous purchase." Several respondents clearly disagreed with this view, among them Richard Gardner (*Choice*) who picked *Age of Complexity* as an important book which might be overlooked by many libraries because it appeared only in paperback.

One respondent, Alan Thomas (Ferguson Library, Stamford, Connecticut) appeared to think that paperback format might be used as an excuse to cover up other reasons for nonpurchase. He said: "I cannot resist scoring Grove Press for another publishing decision . . . Libraries are wary of Henry Miller as a matter of course. I believe that the appearance of the trilogy, *Nexus, Sexus,* and *Plexus* in paperback editions only will deter some libraries from purchasing the set. It gives them an 'out.' I believe another Grove Press publication, *Berkeley: the New Student Revolt*, which was well reviewed and which does a good job of presenting one side of a controversial occurrence, would have been purchased more widely had it been brought out in hard covers."

It was clear also that some of our respondents felt there are some subject areas which still make library book selectors nervous. Paramount among these, of course, is sex, which probably explains the presence on this list of the books by Tanizaki, Miller, Girodias, and Endore, among others. Martha Boaz (USC) noted that Tanizaki has been mentioned as a Nobel Prize candidate, but added that "libraries may be reluctant to stock his books because of his treatment of sex."

Guy Endore's *Satan's Saint* may have been neglected by some libraries because of its subject matter (it is about the Marquis de Sade), but Everett Moore (UCLA) claimed also that it "has not been given much of a chance by the review media. The story of how a good many publishers shunned the book is well known. It seems strangely in keeping that the reviews should find it unworthy of their notice. I'm one who believes that it is the unpopular, distasteful, shocking content of the book that has frightened the reviews and made them unwilling to acknowledge that the book exists."

One respondent blamed the publisher and others for sensationalism in connection with another book. Alan Thomas (Ferguson Library) said that *La*

Batarde "has been published in the United States with a fanfare of publicity which has given it an aura of sensationalism it does not deserve. . . . The Janet Flanner notice, the book's cause celebre status in France, its title, the theme of lesbianism (which has been emphasized), all point to a salacious feminine Frank Harris kind of autobiography. I fear this build-up may result in rejection by some timid book selectors . . . I hope that I am wrong in thinking that the purchase of so ably written and unsensational a book will be curtailed by this cry of wolf."

On this list, books on the race question are again prominent, perhaps indicating that this, too, is a subject still avoided in some degree by some libraries. Poetry is, without doubt, an area which is grossly neglected in many public libraries, and Negro poet Tolson's two votes may have resulted from an awareness of both the factors just mentioned. Ray Smith (Mason City P.L., Iowa) says: "Now 65, Tolson has been praised by writers as diverse as Tate and Shapiro, but till this year has been almost ignored—Shapiro says because he has written *as* a Negro poet."

Another book which gathered two votes was Myrdal's *Report from a Chinese Village*. Ervin Gaines (Minneapolis P.L.) commented: "It has been reviewed in the more specialized journals, and rather favorably, but because it is narrow in scope and because it deals with China, the book might well be omitted from library collections. Why do I think this is unfortunate? Because our knowledge of China is limited. What books we have about China are distorted either by the preconception of the authors or by the obstacles imposed by the government itself. Often a careful study on a small theme can provide the insights and the facts that will support larger generalizations. . . . In the political and social areas of knowledge Myrdal's book gets high scores, but it is almost certainly not going to show up in many small libraries across the land. And that is too bad."

The book which takes a controversial position on political issues is still likely to be excluded from some libraries for just that reason, according to some of our respondents. For example, Gerald Somers (Kellogg P.L., Green Bay, Wisconsin) says that Alperovitz's *Atomic Diplomacy* has a disturbing thesis: "that considerations of power politics outweighed humane considerations in the decision to use the atomic bomb on Japan. In view of today's confrontations of power blocs and the unpopularity of dissent in America's foreign policy methods, I think this book merits more attention than it has received to date. I can conceive of libraries not purchasing it because of its controversial stand, not because it is poorly researched or written."

Editorial Research Reports was named by Robert Hirst (Mills College of Education, New York) as a reference work "of the highest value, but virtually unknown." We feel, in view of the difficulty we had in tracing much information about it, that Mr. Hirst may very well be correct. "The number of libraries subscribing to it," said Hirst, "is shockingly small. The promotion is routine. The value received for the money is outstanding."

Finally, because fiction gets more hard knocks than praise these days, let us end with glowing words from two librarians for *Castle Keep*. Dorothy Curley (Northbrook P.L.) nominated it, she said, "because Eastlake always gets overlooked. His first two novels, both splendid, are no longer available even in paperback. He speaks too quietly, perhaps. He specializes in neither sensation nor charm. He is precise, low-keyed, in control. *Castle Keep* is a departure. It shows a good deal of influence by Heller, but it is Hellerism much cooled and tempered. I'd judge it a major book that will be spoken of with respect 50 years from now—if we can just keep a few copies in circulation in the meantime."

Just as enthusiastic about Eastlake was Riva Bresler (Los Angeles P.L.) who saw him also as "a young contemporary writer of great ability who is sometimes passed over because his work is not characteristic of trends in modern fiction."

Our survey does not quite end here. As the results recorded in this article now stand, they are clearly a compendium of theory and opinion from some knowledgeable book selectors. We have gone one stage further. We compiled a composite list of the titles which were cited in answer to our three questions and sent this to some 200 public libraries across the country. Without indicating the criteria by which the titles were chosen, we simply asked these libraries to indicate which books they had purchased or had on order.

We shall report on Phase II, as the project boys would put it, and then we shall see how the theories and guesses about "in" books, "out" books, or "neglected" books match up against the actual selection and buying practices of a number of public libraries, large, medium, and small.

12 In, Out, or Neglected? Part II

(FEBRUARY 1, 1966)

by ERIC MOON

Bellow, Kaufman, White: these three authors, it seems clear, wrote the *library* best-sellers of 1965. This is one of the more tangible results of an Lj book selection survey, the first part of which appeared in the January 1, 1966 issue.

The three lists resulting from the survey which appeared in the January 1 article, were then amalgamated into one list which was sent to 200 libraries of varying size in all parts of the country. These libraries were asked to indicate which of the 95 listed titles they had purchased or had on order. This article records the results of that second stage of the survey, as compiled from returns from 124 libraries in 47 states.

THE "IN" BOOKS

What follows is the list of books chosen by our selection panel in answer to the first question in stage one of the survey, i.e., the books which they thought should be in virtually every public library. The list has now been rearranged in order of the number of libraries in which each title was actually represented in stage two of the survey.

BELLOW. *Herzog.*	124
KAUFMAN. *Up the Down Staircase.*	124
WHITE. *The Making of the President, 1964.*	124
MORISON. *Oxford History of the American People.*	122
WORLD ALMANAC . . . 1965.	122

The most obvious comment here is that, if our panel did indeed select some of the most essential books of 1965 for public library shelves, so did a large number of the responding libraries. The degree of harmony, in our view, is remarkable.

Of the 29 titles chosen in this category by our selection panel, three were in all 124 libraries. Ten of the titles (just over one-third) were in 90 percent or more of the libraries, and 16 were represented in 75 percent or more of the responding libraries.

Only five titles were held by less than 50 percent of the libraries in our sample—and of these five titles we questioned three in the January 1 article: Lord & Foley because of its heavy regional interest, and the two expensive Sierra Club books (Manning and Brower) as hardly essential for *every* public library, desirable as they undoubtedly are for many.

The most seriously neglected title in this list is Wayland Young's *Eros Denied* which, in our earlier survey, was described by Bill Katz as a book which "should be required reading for every teenager contemplating sex"! Like many other titles that appear on the other lists below, this one was probably ducked by many libraries because of its unabashed treatment of sexual subjects and language.

THE "OUT" BOOKS

Did the libraries responding to the second part of our survey again agree with our selection panel about the books the latter named for exclusion from public libraries? Indeed, they did not! The harmony between our theorists and practi-

tioners was restricted to a very few titles in this category, as the following list
(again arranged in order of the number of libraries holding each title) clearly
indicates:

WOUK. *Don't Stop the Carnival.*	119
SHAW. *Voices of a Summer Day.*	111
YOUNG. *Miss MacIntosh, My Darling.*	101
LEVANT. *Memoirs of an Amnesiac.*	96
WINSOR. *Wanderers Eastward, Wanderers West.*	91
MAILER. *An American Dream.*	87
WOLFE. *The Kandy-Kolored Tangerine-Flake Streamline Baby.*	75
GREENBERG. *How to Be a Jewish Mother.*	59
DAVIS. *Let's Get Well.*	47
KRAFFT-EBING. *Psychopathia Sexualis.*	38
O'BRIEN. *August Is a Wicked Month.*	37
LENNON. *A Spaniard in the Works.*	30
CROON. *Encyclopedia of the Classical World.*	29
SOUTHERN. *Candy.*	28
HALL. *I Give You Oscar Wilde.*	21
CARSON. *Happiness Is a Dry Martini.*	18
HOWELLS. *A House of Glass.*	16
OLMSTED. *To Love a Stranger.*	16
POLLINI. *Glover.*	13
BRUCE. *How to Talk Dirty and Influence People.*	11
HARLOW. *Today Is Tonight.*	8
HIMES. *Pinktoes.*	8

The difference is apparent at the outset here. While our panel managed to
pick three books which are in every responding library, they were unable to
pick one title which is in none of these libraries. They did, however, choose
three titles which are in less than ten percent of the libraries, and half the listed
books (11) are in less than 25 percent of the libraries.

There are some interesting contrasts between the selection panel's list and
the returns from the libraries. Jean Harlow and Oscar Levant, for example,
shared the "lead" among the titles picked by our selectors for public library
"exclusion." The Harlow choice was clearly supported by the selection of most
responding libraries, but long-suffering Oscar was right up there with the
winners.

Our biggest surprise was to find Krafft-Ebing in better than 30 percent of
the responding libraries; and even *Candy* did better than we expected. The
list, nevertheless, raises some interesting questions about value judgments and
standards of selection. Is Kathleen Winsor of higher quality than Terry
Southern? Or Lorena Olmsted better than Chester Himes? Or John Lennon
than Francis Pollini? Or do we again see the old double standard at work here:
the one that requires less rigid quality standards of the trivial and "harmless"
book than of the book which treads perhaps more dangerous ground?

It was no surprise to find Wouk, Irwin Shaw, and Marguerite Young, in
stock in most libraries. Our selectors, we believe, were setting unreasonable
standards when they nominated these titles for exclusion.

"NEGLECTED" BOOKS?

And so to the third list. Were our selectors correct in their guesses at the 1965 books of merit which might, for various reasons, be neglected by a majority of public libraries? They were, as humans usually are, right some of the time and wrong some of the time, as the following list shows.

DAVIS. *Experience of War.*	104
FORD. *The Liberation of Lord Byron Jones.*	104
BROWN. *Manchild in the Promised Land.*	94
MYRDAL. *Report from a Chinese Village.*	93
BOLL. *The Clown.*	89
EASTLAKE. *Castle Keep.*	89
OGBURN. *The Gold of the River Sea.*	88
VICTORIA, Queen. *Dearest Child.*	86
CLARK. *Dark Ghetto.*	84
GASNER. *Nina Upstairs.*	83
PRIESTLEY. *Man and Time.*	77
MOINOT. *An Ancient Enemy.*	74
REDFORD. *Raccoons and Eagles.*	74
TOLKIEN. *Tree and Leaf.*	74
BELFRAGE. *Freedom Summer.*	70
DABBS. *Who Speaks for the South?*	70
CONGRESS AND THE NATION.	69
GINGER. *Age of Excess.*	65
GRISHAM. *Encyclopedia of US Benefits.*	64
MELMAN. *Our Depleted Society.*	64
SHAW. *The Flag.*	64
UNTERMEYER. *Private Collection.*	64
BURGESS. *The Long Day Wanes.*	60
FUSSELL. *Frontier: American Literature and the American West.*	60
MALCOLM X. *The Autobiography*	59
PFEFFER. *This Honorable Court.*	56
NIEBUHR. *Mississippi Black Paper.*	55
BORGSTROM. *The Hungry Planet.*	51
SNIDER. *Economic Myth and Reality.*	50
TANIZAKI. *Diary of a Mad Old Man.*	47
EDITORIAL RESEARCH REPORTS.	46
HENDERSON. *Prince Eugene of Savoy.*	44
ALPEROVITZ. *Atomic Diplomacy.*	44
MONTEIRO. *A Man of Means.*	44
HIRST. *117 Days.*	43
GIRONELLA. *Phantoms and Fugitives.*	36
DRAPER. *Berkeley: the New Student Revolt.*	35
LEDUC. *La Batarde.*	30
EBERHART. *Selected Poems.*	28
PERKINS. *The Prospective Teacher's Knowledge of Library Fundamentals.*	26
TOLSON. *Harlem Gallery.*	25
BROWER. *Not Man Apart.*	21

AMMONS. *Corson's Inlet.* 19
ENDORE. *Satan's Saint.* 19
CARTHY & EBLING. *The National History of Aggression.* 8
MILLER. *The Rosy Crucifixion.* .... 7·3°
GIRODIAS. *The Olympia Reader.* 7
KOHL. *Age of Complexity.* 5

° *One library purchased only* Plexus, *one-third of the Miller trilogy.*

Our selectors did, in fact, pick a majority of books which turned out to be neglected by a majority of the libraries responding. If those titles are as meritorious as our selectors thought, this list may bear further checking by many libraries. Twenty-six of the 48 titles chosen by our selection panel are in less than half the libraries; 11 titles are in less than 25 percent of the libraries; and four titles are in less than 10 percent of the libraries.

Among our original selectors, first prize must go to Richard Gardner of *Choice,* who picked Kohl's *Age of Complexity* as a worthy book which he thought might be neglected by public libraries because it was published in paperback only. When only five out of 124 libraries buy a book, it may fairly be said to be neglected. The lesson for publishers seems obvious: if they want public libraries to buy a book, they must put out a hard cover edition. Hal Draper's *Berkeley* also finished fairly low on the list, perhaps for the same reason.

Another book published only in paperback appeared near the bottom of the list: Henry Miller's trilogy, *The Rosy Crucifixion.* We picked this as a likely neglected title, but we would share the opinion of Alan Thomas, who also chose it, that the paperback format is probably more excuse than reason for the avoidance of this title. Down there solidly on the bottom with Miller is his erstwhile Parisian publisher, Maurice Girodias, whose superb anthology of erotica clearly scared the hell out of most public library book selectors.

The only title which is very low down on this list for which there is no obvious explanation is Carthy & Ebling's *The Natural History of Aggression.* This collection of papers from a London biology institute should certainly be in more of the larger libraries. One can only assume that it was one of those books which received insufficient notice in the media and was thus "missed" by the vast majority of libraries.

One other generalization is permissible on the strength of these returns: if sex is the surest path to exclusion from the majority of public libraries, meter is almost as effective in insuring the absence of a book from the shelves. Witness the poor showing of poets Eberhart (28 libraries), Tolson (25), and Ammons (19). Only Robert Lowell, of the poets on any of these lists, reached a majority (86) of the responding libraries. In Eberhart's case, the excuse might be offered by some libraries that they have other collections or selections, but no such reason validly explains the low standing of the books by either Tolson or Ammons.

We did some more playing with this survey, mainly for the benefit of those who like to have as much of the statistical story as possible.

First, the 124 libraries who checked their holdings for us were located in 47 states. No replies were received from Alaska, Louisiana, South Carolina, or the District of Columbia. The responding libraries fell into the following population categories, based on the figure given for "population served" in the 24th edition of the *American Library Directory*:

		NO. OF LIBRARIES
A.	Less than 10,000	7
B.	10,001–25,000	18
C.	25,001–50,000	22
D.	50,001–100,000	15
E.	100,001–250,000	26
F.	250,001–500,000	18
G.	500,000 and over	18

The list of titles was, in fact, sent to a larger proportion of small and medium-sized libraries than the above table indicates, but the returns followed the general pattern. The larger libraries always provide a greater percentage of replies, thus tending to unbalance the statistics somewhat in favor of the more substantial libraries.

We also analyzed the number of titles (from the three lists) held by libraries in the above population categories. The results are shown in the table below.

Since these figures reveal something about quantity but not much about quality of selection, we also made three further analyses. In the first, we checked the half-dozen titles which were selected by the smallest minority of libraries: the books by Kohl (5 libraries), Girodias (7), Miller (7.3), Carthy (8), Harlow (8), and Himes (8). Our purpose was to find out whether these titles, which were generally passed by, were concentrated in a few libraries. In general, they were.

The Bangor (Maine) Public Library held five of the six titles; the Public Library of Cincinnati and Hamilton County (Ohio) had four. Three of the six titles were in each of: Cherry Hill (N.J.) Public Library, Milwaukee Public Library, Norfolk (Va.) Public Library, San Francisco Public Library, and the Wayne County (Mich.) Public Library. Three other libraries held two titles each: the Buffalo and Erie County (N.Y.) Public Library, the Public Library

NO. OF TITLES	NO. OF LIBS. BY POPULATION							NO. OF LIBS
(95)	A	B	C	D	E	F	G	(124)
0–9		1						1
10–19	3	4	1		1			9
20–29	4	6	4	1			1	16
30–39		5	8	5	2	1		21
40–49		1	3	4	2	2		12
50–59		1	2	3	6	3	1	16
60–69			2	2	13	6	7	30
70–79			1		2	5	3	11
80–89			1			1	5	7
90 +							1	1

of Fort Wayne and Allen County (Ind.), and the Newark (N.J.) Public Library. Twelve other libraries held one each of the six titles in question.

We thought it might be interesting to know also which titles were least likely to be found in even the libraries holding the largest number of listed books; and at the other end of the scale, which titles might be most commonly found in those libraries with the smallest holdings.

The first check was made against the holdings of the 19 libraries which had 70 or more titles in stock or on order. The titles most often missing from this group were as follows:

TITLE	NO. OF LIBS. IN WHICH BOOK IS NOT IN STOCK
HOWELLS. *A House of Glass.*	15
KOHL. *Age of Complexity.*	15
HARLOW. *Today Is Tonight.*	14
OLMSTED. *To Love a Stranger.*	14
CARTHY. *Natural History of Aggression.*	13
GIRODIAS. *The Olympia Reader.*	13
HIMES. *Pinktoes.*	13
MILLER. *The Rosy Crucifixion.*	13
BRUCE. *How to Talk Dirty* . . .	12
CARSON. *Happiness Is a Dry Martini.*	12
AMMONS. *Corson's Inlet.*	11
ENDORE. *Satan's Saint.*	11
HALL. *I Give You Oscar Wilde.*	11
POLLINI. *Glover.*	10

This list could be extended further, but the above are the titles which are missing from more than half those libraries which had the most extensive holdings among the libraries which submitted returns. There were actually 39 titles which were held by *all* this group of 19 libraries, and 56 titles which were missing in one or more of them.

The most extensive holdings among this group were those of the Public Library of Cincinnati and Hamilton County, which had 91 of the 95 titles we listed. A very surprising second was the Bangor (Maine) Public Library, which had 86 titles. As can be seen from the population breakdown (p. 636), all but two of the libraries with more than 70 titles came within the three largest population groups. The two exceptions were Bangor (serving a population of 38,912), and Cherry Hill, N.J. (serving a population of 44,000). The latter held 77 titles out of the 95 listed.

At the other end of the scale, we checked the holdings of the ten libraries which each held less than 20 of the 95 listed titles, to see which titles one might have most hope of finding even in such limited collections. Heading the list, of course, were the books by Bellow, Kaufman, and White, which were in all libraries submitting returns. Other titles most commonly held by this group were:

TITLE	NO. OF LIBS.
BENET. *Reader's Encyclopedia.*	8
HUMPHREY. *The Ordways.*	8
MORISON. *Oxford History of the American People.* ...	8
WOUK. *Don't Stop the Carnival.*	8
FOWLER. *Dictionary of Modern English Usage.*	6
BOOKS IN PRINT 1965.	5
SORENSEN. *Kennedy.*	5
WORLD ALMANAC.	5
SHAW. *Voices of a Summer Day.*	4
STATISTICAL ABSTRACT OF THE U.S.	4
WINSOR. *Wanderers Eastward . . .*	4
DAVIS. *Experience of War.*	3
FORD. *Liberation of Lord Byron Jones.*	3
MAILER. *An American Dream.*	3
O'CONNOR. *Everything That Rises*	3
SCHLESINGER. *A Thousand Days.*	3

Seven other titles were held by two libraries each, and 15 titles appeared once each among these ten libraries. Altogether, the ten libraries with the smallest holdings had, collectively, 41 of the 95 listed titles. All libraries in this group were in the two lowest population categories, with two exceptions: the Middle Georgia Regional Library, serving a population, according to the *ALD*, of 214,156—which had 17 titles; and the Pulaski County Free Library, Virginia, which serves a population of 27,258, and had 18 of the 95 titles.

Not the South, however, but New England claims the two libraries which had the lowest number of titles among all the responding libraries: the Sayles Free Public Library, Lincoln, Rhode Island (8); and the Newmarket (N.H.) Public Library (10).

13 *Satisfaction Point*

(MAY 15, 1968)

by ERIC MOON

How many public library branches throughout the country possess 40 or more copies of *Who's Afraid of Virginia Woolf?* Or 50 copies of *Manchild in the Promised Land?* Perhaps the more significant question is: How many librarians believe that this number of copies—of these and a great many other books—may be necessary?

George Moreland's article in the May 15, 1968 issue of Lj on the recent Montgomery County Libraries' paperback experiment reveals once again the enormous chasm that yawns between library book selection practices and actual reader needs. Taking a national average, the Montgomery County Libraries are fairly affluent, and certainly, they are better stocked than many public libraries we have seen. Yet, the branch librarians involved in this project must have learned a great deal about the inadequacies of their libraries' holdings.

To take the two examples with which this editorial begins, the three branches for which statistics are given in Mr. Moreland's article held, at the beginning of the experiment, five, two, and two copies, respectively, of the Albee book. At the end of the project they had 45, 32, and 42. In the case of Claude Brown's book (a book of enormous relevance in today's troubled society), the holdings rose from four, two, and two copies to 51, 56, and 17. And the library with 56 copies still had not reached "satisfaction point"—this being defined as "the number of copies needed to guarantee that *at least one copy* would be in each branch at all times." Another among the many staggering discrepancies between practice and need is illustrated by Arthur Miller's

The Crucible: the Davis Library, which had *no* copies at the beginning of the project, wound up with 30, and had still not reached satisfaction point.

The Montgomery County experiment was prompted, in part, by an earlier user survey which had revealed that the greatest cause of dissatisfaction among library patrons was that they could never find the books they wanted *on the shelves.* They might in most cases have been able to determine that the books were in stock but, as we have said before, we never knew a reader who wanted a book and left the library enchanted with having found a catalog entry for it.

We are not suggesting that every library should try to reach "satisfaction point" for every ephemeral bestseller published, but there are a great many books of lasting worth and quality that the library user ought reasonably to expect to find available on the shelves at most times.

Libraries spend altogether too much time on the initial selection and acquisition of a book and altogether too little on bookstock control thereafter. Much more active and continuous shelf scrutiny is necessary to determine whether a book, once bought, is ever really *available.* The storekeeper, who sells a product for profit, knows that it isn't enough just to put it on the shelf initially; he must make sure that it is continually available while there are customers for it. The profit for the librarian in being as diligent about his shelf stock is greater reader satisfaction—and the consequent possibility of broader patron support.

A determined attack also needs to be made on the too-common library goal of acquiring the largest possible number of *titles.* This disease is most prevalent in the larger research libraries—where there is *some* justification for it—but it pervades even the smallest institutions. The result of this policy is satisfaction of the more esoteric demands and an escalating level of failure on the titles needed by the largest number of patrons.

Thirdly—and this may be the most acceptable of these observations—most library book budgets need to be not just increased but tripled or quadrupled before there can be much hope of reaching any very general satisfaction point. Even with increase of this magnitude, the goal could still not be achieved without more realistic economic practices. It would be possible to avoid the escalation of staff costs which we insist must accompany much larger book budgets—IF more of these book funds were spent for heavy duplication (rather than more and more titles)—IF more of the heavy demand were soaked up through the purchase of paperback copies—and IF librarians didn't insist on undermining the economic gains that paperbacks make possible by then adding the heavy costs of elaborate cataloging, processing, and record keeping.

Book selection will never reach satisfaction point until we give as much emphasis to the word "quantity" as we do to that more pious word "quality."

14 Statistical Wailing Wall: A Nationwide Survey

(JUNE 1, 1968)

by BILL KATZ

The average public librarian will not be cuddling-up with a book of modern American poetry tonight. Neither will the reader who looks to the library for poetry.

This is hardly a surprise, but it pretty well sums up the findings of a recent survey. Curious to discover both attitudes and book buying policies, I asked some 200 librarians to check their poetry holdings against a selective list. I noted 16 individual titles, three anthologies, and three poetry magazines (*see* Table A). Emphasis was primarily, although not exclusively, on poetry of the 1960's. The choice of this or that title will be explained a bit later, but on the whole it was a matter of personal taste.

I received 149 replies. The majority were from libraries in urban centers of over 100,000. None came back from communities of less than 10,000. Geographically, every state except Delaware was represented. While extrapolation may be dangerous, it seems to me that the results are at least indicative of how poetry is approached in most public libraries.

And now to the statistical wailing wall. Only 52 of the 149 libraries claimed more than one-half of the individual titles; another 67 had between one-quarter and one-half; and four libraries exceeded credibility by admitting to not a single volume (*see* Table B). San Francisco and Cleveland took honors, with 14 out of the 16 titles. Close behind, with 13 entries apiece, were Detroit, St. Louis, Kansas City, and Charlotte.

Individual poets aside, almost all libraries had at least one anthology, and approximately 55 percent checked off all three titles listed on my questionnaire.

Of the three magazines listed, *Poetry* was favored in 120 libraries, but the two little magazines were noted only by San Francisco and Los Angeles.

Three poets—Lenore Kandel, Robert Kelly, and Paul Blackburn—should receive some type of prize for total nonrecognition. Cleveland had one copy of Kelly's poems; San Francisco purchased several copies of Kandel's *The Love Book;* and, for some unexplained reason, the Enid Public Library in Oklahoma boasted the only copy of Blackburn's poems.

Two years ago Eric Moon asked librarians about book selection policies ("In, Out, or Neglected?" *LJ*, January 1, 1966, p. 57–64; February 1, 1966, p.

TABLE A

		NO. OF COPIES PURCHASED
BERRYMAN, John.	*77 Dream Songs* (Farrar, 1964)	222
BLACKBURN, Paul.	*The Reardon Poems* (Madison, Wis.: Perishable, 1967)	1
DICKEY, James.	*Buckdancer's Choice* (Wesleyan, 1965)	216
DUNCAN, Robert.	*Roots and Branches* (Scribner, 1964)	95
FIELD, Edward.	*Stand Up Friend With Me* (Grove, 1963)	84
GINSBERG, Allen.	*Kaddish and Other Poems* (City Lights, 1961)	70
KANDEL, Lenore.	*The Love Book* (San Francisco: Stolen Paper Review, 1966)	?
KELLY, Robert.	*Round Dances* (New York: Trobar, 1964)	2
KINNELL, Galway.	*Flower Herding on Mount Monadnock* (Houghton Mifflin, 1964)	121
LEVERTOV, Denise.	*Jacob's Ladder* (New Directions, 1961)	69
LOWELL, Robert.	*For the Union Dead* (Farrar, 1964)	380
METCALFE, James.	*Poem Portraits* (Doubleday, any edition)	142
NASH, Ogden.	*Marriage Lines* (Little, 1964)	423
OLSON, Charles.	*The Maximus Poems* (Jargon/ Corinth-Citadel, 1960)	35
PLATH, Sylvia.	*Ariel* (Harper, 1966)	272
ROETHE, Theodore.	*The Far Field* (Doubleday, 1964)	360

Note: A 17th title by Anne Sexton was included in the original questionnaire, but was deleted here when it was discovered that an error had been made in the title.

ANTHOLOGIES:

ROSENTHAL, M. L.	*The New Modern Poetry* (Macmillan, 1967)	454
ALLEN, Donald.	*The New American Poetry* (Grove, 1960)	366
UNTERMEYER, Louis.	*Modern American Poetry* (Harcourt, 1962 edition)	506
MAGAZINES:	*Poetry; Kayak; El Corno Emplumado*	

633–37) and discovered that, next to sex, "meter is almost as effective in insuring the absence of a book. . . . Only Robert Lowell reached a majority of the responding libraries." Matters haven't changed much; Lowell was the favored poet in our poll. His close competitor is Ogden Nash (*see* Table C).

Of considerably more interest to us than the statistics were the comments by librarians. We asked reasons for having or not having a title and for reactions to the whole matter of modern poetry in the public library.

There was almost complete unanimity on one point: reviews are the main guide for the purchasing of poetry. Outside of the professional journals, the *New York Times* and *Saturday Review* were mentioned almost as frequently as *Kirkus. Library Journal, Choice,* and *Booklist,* in that order, are the professional magazines most consulted. Oddly enough, *Poetry* magazine, while found in almost all libraries, was one of the last sources consulted. Little magazines are a total loss.

Anthologies figured high because a number of librarians feel that they supplement or make up for the lack of individual titles. One might not argue with the supplementary aspects, particularly since anthologies also serve reference work via *Granger,* but to consider them as a substitute for a particular poet's work is much like giving a Hemingway fan a book of short stories with one of the writer's included, and letting it go at that.

Other factors mentioned in selection were listings in standard bibliographies and "best" lists; the reputation of a particular publisher; and, only five times, personal preference of the librarian. Much was made of lack of demand, but not one librarian noted a specific title on my list which was purchased *because of* demand.

Larger libraries tended to purchase multiple copies, up to 25 or 30 of Lowell or Nash. Still, no poet will enjoy the monetary returns of a best seller from library sales.

After I compiled the data, I sent the results to the living, listed poets. Some were good enough to reply. Allen Ginsberg, who finished 11th in a field of 16 had this to say: "That *any* library at all, A.D. 1967, has copies of my City Lights book is due to the miraculously eccentric professional competence of some of the librarians . . . it's hopeful that there are a lot of rebel librarians."

A professional surveyor or statistician could point to my figures and report with some confidence that there are about as many rebel librarians as purchased Ginsberg's *Kaddish.* That's 40 out of 149, or roughly 20 percent. Not an impressive number, but one Dewey among a thousand catalogers, or one leader among as many sheep, can sometimes bring about miraculous changes.

Admittedly, this is a biased conclusion, yet I have an abiding mistrust of surveys, even my own, and little faith in averages. Fortunately, there isn't such an animal as an average librarian.

I wish to establish my biases immediately, primarily because what follows will *not* shape up into that familiar dart game called Aggression—the one where Nixon or LBJ is on target. In my type of poll the face you find on the board is that of the average librarian. A few seem to enjoy the positioning, even ask for it. Take, for example, the confident masochist who requested dart board billing when he replied: "Poetry is dead." My favorite is the lady who fired back the questionnaire with a simple question of her own: "Who are these people?"

"These people," with one exception, are to be found in any representative discussion of what is happening in poetry today. However, only the first nine (excluding Metcalfe, including Duncan) received enough attention to be listed in *Book Review Digest*. Cutting it even thinner, only five of the top nine are in the *Standard Catalog for Public Libraries*, and of these, three are Pulitzer Prize winners, a fourth is a recent National Book award winner, and the fifth is Nash.

Public library fame came a bit late for Sylvia Plath, yet her *Ariel* is found in 121 libraries. I am not suggesting death is a sure path to the library shelf, but it helps. Roethke's first books of poems were remaindered, and only when he began winning prizes did he garner enough reviews to earn a place in *Book Review Digest*. Plath has yet to be elevated to immortality in the *Standard Catalog*, and Roethke was not listed until the 1959–63 volume, published the year after he died.

Reputation, age, and the stamp of approval by the reviewers and the lists is all it takes to make the grade, at least in libraries where poetry is purchased. Even poets with substantial reputations fight the lists all the way. Take the case of Ginsberg, Levertov, and Olson. The titles I listed are not in *Book Review Digest*, certainly not in the *Standard Catalog*. Still, in some 40 libraries, Ginsberg and Levertov are cataloged without benefit of mass reviews. Olson may make it yet. What it seems to come down to is that the more involved the library, the better its collection; the less there is dependence on faceless committees, the more there is on the librarian's own taste, judgment, and reading. Edward Field had some comments on this: "Surely Allen Ginsberg's *Kaddish* has sold many more copies in bookstores all over the world than any of Lowell's books have, but librarians think on conventional lines and buy the respectable authors."

Lack of reviews, if not standard lists, was the most common complaint or excuse offered by respondents for not having this or that title. I think the point well taken. This is illustrated by the fate of Kandel, Kelly, and Blackburn. Aside from a review in *Poetry* magazine of Kelly's *Round Dances*, nothing is to be found in media mentioned by librarians from Kandel or Blackburn. What is more, none is listed in *Books in Print*, and all were published by little presses in limited editions. I listed them for two reasons. To use the vernacular of the marketplace, like the better known Ginsberg, Levertov, and Olson, I think they are comers. All are young, all promise to make a name for themselves. Equally important, they represent a common misunderstanding or downright bias on the part of public librarians.

An otherwise intelligent respondent explained the lack of the three: "As you can ascertain by a quick look at unchecked items these are all publications of vanity presses, except one . . . Vanity press items are usually not even ordered on approval." There is considerable difference between a small publisher or a little press and a vanity house. Normally the latter swamps libraries with free copies, is a big business, and churns out badly printed volumes.

Blackburn's poetry was published in a beautifully designed limited edition by craftsmen; Kelly, who admits to having issued no more than 150 copies of his work, did it under the imprint of the Trobar press, which also issued Blackburn's earlier poems and work by Louis Zukofsky and Jerome Rothenberg; the Kandel verse came from an equally small but distinguished press.

The importance of small publishers and poetry cannot be overemphasized. Economics dictates that they play a major role in the development of modern poetry. As any publisher will tell you, even a well-known poet is lucky to sell 1000 copies of his work. Consequently, more for prestige than for profit, the commercial publishers bring out some 500–600 volumes a year. With the exception of university presses and a few publishers such as Grove and New Directions, a young poet finds it more difficult to find a publisher for his work than to get it into the average public library. He rarely can afford a vanity press, so he turns to the duplicating machine and the hand press. A check of *Trace* or Len Fulton's *Small Press Review* will indicate the volume of such publishing—probably 1000 to 1500 individual titles a year.

TABLE B

DISTRIBUTION OF TITLES BY SIZE OF LIBRARY

No. of Titles	Population Served						
POETS (16)	Less than 25,000 (7)	25–50,000 (25)	50–100,000 (19)	100–250,000 (47)	250–500,000 (21)	Over 500,000 (30)	Total Libraries (149)
0 titles	1	2	1				4
1 title	1	1	2				4
2 titles	3	2	1				6
3 "		3		2			5
4 "		3	2	5			10
5 "		3	7	4	2		16
6 "			1	9		1	11
7 "		5	1	5	2	3	16
8 "		2		8	4	1	15
9 "	1	1	2	9	3	4	20
10 "		1	1	4	4	9	19
11 "	1	1	1	2	2	1	8
12 "		1			2	5	8
13 "					1	5	6
14 "						1	1
15 "							0
16 "							0
ANTHOLOGIES (3)							
0 titles	2	1	2	1			6
1 title		1	3	5	3	2	14
2 titles	2	8	8	19	3	6	46
3 "	2	12	7	20	18	24	83

Poetry magazine, which librarians apparently shelve but rarely read, talks about many of these small press publications. *El Corno Emplumado* and *Kayak* are two representative and, I think, superior little mags that carry on in the *Poetry* tradition. The poetry of Kandel, Kelly, and Blackburn (and the hundreds they represent) is not only extensively published in literary magazines but is well reviewed by those same magazines.

My plunge into statistics was prompted by the article, "On the Shelf Poetry in the Public Library," which appeared as the lead item in the March 9, 1967 issue of the *Times Literary Supplement*. This poll of 35 British libraries produced much the same dismal results as my own survey. Apparently, the English librarian is no more fond of the moderns than is his American counterpart. The *TLS* article noted:

> A librarian who is genuinely interested in doing a good job is unlikely not to hear about the best of [small press poetry]. . . . One would not complain about pandering to popular requests if the librarian were at the same time making some systematic effort to lay the foundations of a decent poetry catalogue, to ensure that—whatever its unpopularity—a representative collection of modern poetry is at least available on their shelves.

I said, earlier in this article, that the lack of reviews in the common review media found in libraries was an acceptable excuse for the absence from the library shelves of some of the poets on my list. Still, is the librarian entirely blameless? I think not, and nothing illustrates my position better than the fate of two of the poets, Kandel and James Metcalfe.

Frankly, I wasn't even sure who James Metcalfe was, although a check of my survey results will show that librarians know him better than one half of the other poets listed. Looking about for the traditional red herring, I had thought about including such winners as Edgar Guest and Ella Wheeler Wilcox, whom, the Fort Wayne Public Library in Indiana tells me, the public prefers. They seemed too obvious, so an Albany colleague suggested Metcalfe as a poet to include. A check of *Books in Print* showed that he had written several works and that all were published by a reputable firm. Most of his poetry first gained fame in newspaper columns.

When 61 librarians reported some 80 copies of his *Poem Portraits*—or more than double the number of copies of Edward Field's *Stand Up Friend With Me*—I thought it time to check out Mr. Metcalfe. He is not found in any list, and a 20-year search of individual magazine indexes and *Book Review Digest* showed nothing. In desperation, I looked to *Biography Index* and did find three entries: one in a work not available in our library, and two obituary notices. Apparently he died in 1960 (if he lives, forgive me) and, aside from being a diligent poet and newspaperman, is best known by the FBI as the man who helped to end the career of John Dillinger who was shot in front of that movie house.

My question, which may be naive, is: how did Metcalfe's poetry get into so many libraries when he received even less notice than Kandel? If reviews are the major swing-point for exclusion or inclusion, just what reviews were those 61 librarians reading? My ignorance was shared, incidentally, by the poets I contacted and by the editor of *Kayak*, who is considerably more knowledgeable about poetry than I. He asked: "Who is James Metcalfe and what are his *Poem Portraits?*"

No one had any problem with Kandel—at least, no one except my librarian respondents. This side of Ginsberg's *Howl*, few poetry titles have received as much publicity as Kandel's *Love Book*. According to *Saturday Review*, September 30, 1967, more than 20,000 copies have been sold. The runaway best seller owes most of its success to the San Francisco police, who confiscated the 122 lines of poetry in December 1966. The cops thought it dirty but, by January, a judge had ordered them to return the copies of the book to the dealers. Since then, publisher Jeff Berner has agreed "to donate one per cent royalties to the San Francisco Policemen's Benevolent Association in gratitude for helping the book's sales."

An assessment of Mrs. Kandel's contribution to modern poetry is beyond my purpose, though I do think she is pretty good. But, if popularity is any criterion, and it seems to be with librarians, why has she been so neglected? Lack of reviews? Possibly, but anyone with even the most remote contact with modern poetry should have recognized her immediately. Can it be that Mr. Metcalfe, with a different style and content, is so much superior? One is left with the feeling that some librarians evaluate poets somewhat in the same manner as the San Francisco police do.

A certain amount of antagonism showed itself in the survey. As one librarian put it: "I'm unprepared for the new poetry; I don't understand it. How many others have had the same experience?" To answer her query, close to 15 of the 60 or so who bothered to jot notes on the questionnaire. For example: "It is quite clear that many poets are only slightly concerned with presenting their ideas in an intelligible manner. For better or for worse American poetry has changed . . ." and: "It has been said that the poetry of today is not understandable, and freedom of thought without responsibility is evident in modern poetry." Many of those who complained, however, made a good showing on the list. And while I hardly agree with their views, I think they do much to explain the real reason for younger poets not being purchased by many librarians. Librarians are as representative of the middle class as the patron, and the poets are often attacking their blessed virtues and attitudes.

Identification with the patron was considerably more evident than identification with the poet. Here, one suspects, is the real reason for the strong showing of Metcalfe and the "safe" poets in the library. Yet, once again, the rebels raised a howl; among them, the most consistent note of optimism was that modern poetry is finding new, imaginative audiences. Such, at least, was the report from such libraries as King County in Seattle; Brooklyn and Queens Borough; Madison; Scarsdale; Nashua, New Hampshire; and perhaps a dozen more, ranging from the Washoe County Library in Reno to the Minneapolis Public Library. The most satisfying note was struck by one librarian who did not wish to be identified: "Modern poetry is well received in this area. So well received, in fact, that copies frequently disappear after one circulation."

Heartening statistics were offered by Daniel Teisberg of the Minneapolis Public Library:

On May 18, 1967, we found that 50 percent (nine out of 18) of the poetry books . . . were in circulation. This compares with 74 percent (60 out of 81) of the fiction; 60 percent (54 out of 89) of the nonfiction; 95 percent (19 out of 20) of the mysteries; and 83 percent (five out of six) of the science fiction. While this suggests that poetry will not replace mysteries and science fiction in popularity, it indicates a greater interest in poetry than we had previously believed.

Students, both in high schools and colleges, were credited for most of the poetry circulation—at least in the modern poetry section. Assignments account for a given amount of the interest, but even where demand was admittedly small, it was helped along by an imaginative librarian. Poetry readings and programs, newspapers and television stations, book marks and lists—all were responsible for sparking poetry circulation. In the September 1965 issue of *Owl*

TABLE C

NUMBER AND SIZE OF LIBRARIES CHECKING INDIVIDUAL TITLES

POETS	Less than 25,000 (7)	25–50,000 (25)	50–100,000 (19)	100–250,000 (47)	250–500,000 (21)	Over 500,000 (30)	Total Libraries (149)
1. Lowell	3	24	15	44	21	30	137
2. Nash	5	18	14	44	20	30	131
3. Roethke	4	17	16	42	19	29	127
4. Plath	2	16	13	41	19	30	121
5. Berryman	3	14	10	38	19	30	114
6. Dickey	1	13	11	31	15	29	100
7. Kinnell	2	10	6	30	15	26	89
8. Metcalfe	1	6	2	19	13	20	61
9. Field	1	4	3	15	11	23	57
10. Duncan	1	5	3	13	11	23	56

Note: All the above, except Metcalfe, are listed in Book Review Digest

POETS	Less than 25,000 (7)	25–50,000 (25)	50–100,000 (19)	100–250,000 (47)	250–500,000 (21)	Over 500,000 (30)	Total Libraries (149)
11. Ginsberg	2	4	4	6	6	18	40
12. Levertov	1	3	4	7	8	17	40
13. Olson	1	1	1	2	5	14	24
14. Kelly						1	1
15. Kandel						1	1
16. Blackburn		1					1

ANTHOLOGIES

	Less than 25,000 (7)	25–50,000 (25)	50–100,000 (19)	100–250,000 (47)	250–500,000 (21)	Over 500,000 (30)	Total Libraries (149)
1. Untermeyer	5	17	15	40	29	27	133
2. Rosenthal	3	16	12	43	16	25	115
3. Allen	3	16	9	37	18	27	110

MAGAZINES

	Less than 25,000 (7)	25–50,000 (25)	50–100,000 (19)	100–250,000 (47)	250–500,000 (21)	Over 500,000 (30)	Total Libraries (149)
1. *Poetry*	3	10	15	42	19	29	118
2. *El Corno Emplumado*						2	2
3. *Kayak*						1	1

Among the Colophons, Eleanor Smith, then of the Brooklyn Public Library, suggested methods of involving the public with the muse. And anyone who wants to know how to set up a meaningful poetry session, with modern poets as guests, is advised to contact Mrs. Kenneth Hirschl of the Carnegie Library of Pittsburg—or, for that matter, almost any of the large urban libraries.

All of this, of course, assumes a knowledge and a faith in poetry. A majority of the respondents to this survey seem not so sure that it is worth the effort. Aside from reviews, the common complaint was simply that there is no demand for poetry. Identification of the public library's mission with demand or, as the *TLS* puts it, "pandering," was all too evident in our survey. I firmly believe that those who build a collection only on the basis of demand are dead wrong, and a trifle muddled in their approach to what libraries are all about. Some of the answers laid it right on the line, but I suspect that the many who did not reply, particularly from the smaller libraries, are confident that the image they see in the mirror is the image of the public they serve.

Lest anyone believe that the urban centers have an edge on poetry, let me quote from a letter from Richard Burns of the Falls Church Public Library in Virginia (population, 12,000). He set a bit of a record by having the best collection of poetry of any small library in the survey. He says:

> The alternative to the placation theory is a notion that I have long argued: that is, in book selection the first consideration be given to the total collection, the second to the possible readers of the book. I feel there is a core collection of books which should be available in every library. Additionally, there must be a wide representative group of new material in which experimentation and development is freshly emerging. These basic materials must be purchased without regard to how many people may or may not read them. If they *never* circulate, they must be there.

Burns, who knows his collection and his public, reports that poetry does circulate. Granted, it is not always this simple. Witness the librarian with a fair to good showing in this survey who noted that it was an easy job to check my list, "as all of the books were gathering dust on the shelf." K. Richard Greene of the Free Public Library of Woodbridge in New Jersey, a highly sympathetic rebel, is representative of a number of librarians who support the poetry collection, but with misgivings. "Let us both lower our prejudices," he said, "and confess that modern poetry is not a hot item in most public libraries. It is not easy for a library to buy a book of poems that will never leave the shelf while the public is demanding other books."

No, but it may be the librarian's responsibility. Poets, at least, who are also a bit of the public, seem to think so, if Robert Kelly's views mean anything. Commenting on his poor showing in the survey, Kelly posed a rhetorical query about himself and all the younger members of the fraternity:

> What is to be done? . . . Nothing will change until librarians adopt a coherent policy about acquiring poetry books, turn aside from their charybdic circulation figures, and get down to their responsibility of building and presenting to the public a collection of what *is* happening and has happened. There used to be a branch of the NYPL up in Spanish Harlem that carried shiny new multiple

sets of Dickens, unopened year after year. It was not wrong for them to be there. Somebody *knew* that writing in English had been touched by Dickens, a conscience molded or warped by him, and that someday, someone would pick it up.

Well, what *is* to be done to improve poetry collections? Kelly goes on to suggest that library schools might help by teaching that "contemporary arts are *immediately* important in the public library, out of all proportion to their specific circulation statistics." He points out, as do many respondents, that current review media are inadequate. There's a qualitative as well as a quantitative side to this problem, as the Denver Public Library noted: "Although we collect comments from all major book review sources, we feel that these are of little help. Too many poetry books receive unqualified praise, so that reviews are not really too useful." James Bryan of the Newark Public Library asks: "How is the librarian to select from so many reviews that say, in effect, the same darn thing over and over again?"

The feeling is shared by Kelly, who dismisses many reviews as "tara-diddle," and by Edward Field, who says:

> I'm not sure that it is only the lack of reviews that discourages librarians from ordering poetry books, but perhaps the dullness of the reviews that could only appeal to other poets. Poetry is very hard to review, and I admit I have never attempted it myself.

Having reviewed poetry myself, I'm not sure, either, what's to be done to liven things up a bit. One reason for the lack of critical tone in such reviews is the natural desire of the reviewer to give the poet more than an even break. But I'd like to suggest that more librarians read the reviews in *Poetry, Partisan Review,* the *New York Review of Books* and, of course, the little mags. Here, fellow poets tend to wield the axe, and with considerably less charity than is found in most of the library publications.

The final solution, however, rests pretty much with the librarian, and particularly Mr. Ginsberg's "eccentric professional." This is the man or woman who not only buys poetry but reads it. I'm optimistic enough to believe that there are more of these rebels in public libraries than my dismal statistics indicate. Which brings me to the letter from Ogden Nash, a fitting conclusion. Mr. Nash says:

> I am filled with great delight, and even greater astonishment, at the results of your survey. I spend so much time wondering what the hell I am doing and why I am doing it that a bit of news like this does wonders for my wilting ego. I dread the day, however, when you finally persuade the librarians to take a second look at their collections.

The late Randall Jarrell explained why Ogden Nash is at the top of any library collection: "He doesn't write down to his public . . . I mean, he doesn't have to write down." I wonder when public librarians will deserve the same kind of tribute.

15 *The Two-Million Dollar Question: A Survey of Libraries on Long Island*

(JUNE 1, 1968)

by INGE JUDD and JOHN C. PINE

In a speech at the 1966 New York Library Association Conference in Syracuse, Dan Lacy, then managing director of the American Book Publishers Council, lamented the fact that poetry is the poor stepchild of American publishing and virtually has to be subsidized in one form or another in order to exist at all. The publishing firms lose money on poetry, but continue to bring it out, not only for reasons of prestige, but because they recognize that poetry is important. If librarians would only recognize the importance of poetry, Mr. Lacy seemed to be saying in his tactful way, poetry would no longer be the poor stepchild of publishing. The burgeoning library market has in fact revitalized publishing, but poetry has not shared in the general prosperity.

Inspired by Dan Lacy's remarks, the writers of this article decided that it might be useful to make a poetry survey of public libraries on Long Island. The actual survey was conducted by Mrs. Judd as the basis for a Master's Report in partial fulfillment of the requirements for a MLS degree at the Graduate School of Library Science at C. W. Post College, a branch of Long Island University. We knew from the beginning that poetry is not being bought in great quantities (there are statistics enough on that), but what we hoped to find out was what this meant in terms of individual libraries of varying sizes and budgets. What did it mean in Roslyn and Riverhead and Rego Park?

A questionnaire was sent to the libraries surveyed in order to gain some idea of the attitudes, background, and buying habits of the librarians respon-

sible for book selection in the field of poetry. When the replies to the questionnaire were compared with the results of the survey, there was found to be a
wide discrepancy between what the librarians profess to believe and what they
actually practice. We cannot account for this discrepancy, but we know it
exists, and it is more ominous and disturbing than the simple fact, which
everybody knows, that librarians do not buy poetry. It reveals a professional
laxity which can only bode ill for our profession at a time when the demands
made on it are greater than ever before.

A list of 40 of the most important and highly praised volumes of contemporary poetry, published between the years 1960 and 1966 inclusive, were
checked against the holdings of 151 public libraries in Queens and Nassau and
Suffolk Counties. All 40 titles received favorable reviews in *Library Journal*
and other book review periodicals most frequently consulted by librarians.
Almost without exception, the professional library journals recommended the
books for purchase by all libraries.

THE 40 TITLES SURVEYED

The 40 poetry titles chosen for the survey were as follows:

Ammons, A. R. *Corson's Inlet*.
Berry, Wendell. *The Broken Ground*.
Bock, Frederick. *The Fountains of Regardlessness*.
Booth, Philip. *Weathers and Edges*.
Coxe, Louis. *The Last Hero and Other Poems*.
Davison, Peter. *The Breaking of the Day and Other Poems*.
Dugan, Alan. *Poems*.
Dugan, Alan. *Poems 2*.
Evans, Abbie Huston. *Fact of Crystal*.
Field, Edward. *Stand Up, Friend, With Me*.
Francis, Robert. *Orb Weaver*.
Freeman, Arthur. *Estrangements*.
Haines, John. *Winter News*.
Ignatow, David. *Say Pardon*.
Jarrell, Randall. *The Woman at the Washington Zoo*.
Kinnell, Galway. *Flower Herding on Mount Monadnock*.
L'Heureux, John. *Quick as Dandelions*.
Logan, John. *Ghosts of the Heart*.
Matthews, Jack. *An Almanac of Twilight*.
Miller, Vassar. *My Bones Being Wiser*.
Moses, W. R. *Identities*.
O'Gorman, Ned. *The Buzzard and the Peacock*.
Oliver, Mary. *No Voyage and Other Poems*.
Plath, Sylvia. *The Colossus and Other Poems*.
Rich, Adrienne. *Necessities of Life*.
Scott, Winfield Townley. *Change of Weather*.
Sexton, Anne. *Live or Die*.
Simpson, Louis. *At the End of the Open Road*.
Squires, Radcliffe. *Fingers of Hermes*.

Stafford, William. *Traveling Through the Dark.*
Stanford, Ann. *The Weathercock.*
Starbuck, George. *Bone Thoughts.*
Stoutenburg, Adrien. *Heroes, Advise Us.*
Swenson, May. *To Mix with Time.*
Van Duyn, Mona. *A Time of Bees.*
Vance, Thomas. *Skeleton of Light.*
Vazakas, Byron. *The Equal Tribunals.*
Vliet, R. G. *Events and Celebrations.*
Whitbread, Thomas. *Four Infinitives.*
Wilbur, Richard. *Advice to a Prophet.*

To determine how many of the selected poetry titles were purchased, the union catalogs of the Nassau Library System and Suffolk Cooperative Library System and the public catalog of the Queens Borough Public Library were consulted. When all the returns were in, it was found that the 151 libraries surveyed purchased a total of 549 copies of the selected poetry titles. This is an average of 3.6 volumes per library. The 151 libraries, with a combined book budget of over two million dollars, spent approximately $1,698 (less discount) for these 549 volumes, or about $13.32 per library. When Dan Lacy was addressing a rapt audience of concerned librarians in the Syracuse War Memorial, this was what he was referring to. This is why poetry must be subsidized in the most affluent society in the history of the world. Librarians in North Babylon and Syosset and Laurelton do not buy the best contemporary poetry being published.

As might be expected, the Language and Literature Division of the Queens Borough Public Library, with a budget of $22,000, purchased 33 of the 40 titles, more than any other library. It did not purchase, for one reason or another, seven of the most highly regarded volumes of poetry published since 1960.

Fifty-three of the 151 libraries, however, neglected to buy a single title out of the list of 40. Twenty-nine of these libraries had less than $5000 a year to spend for books, periodicals, and binding. But budgetary limitations were not always the reason for poor representation of poetry. One Suffolk library, with a budget of $56,000 for books alone, did not purchase a single title; another Suffolk library with a book budget of $29,000 matched this record, as also did two others, one in Nassau and one in Suffolk, with budgets of $16,500 (books, periodicals, binding) and $23,150 (books only) respectively.

In sharp contrast, one Suffolk library, with only $609 to spend for books, periodicals, and binding, had 11 of the 40 titles in its collection. At first, we thought this small library was a unique example of what could happen when the librarian was interested in more than lip service to poetry. We subsequently learned however, that the reason why the library had so many of the titles was that it had received all of them, in a short period of time, under the Greenaway Plan. Apparently the library was not happy with the arrangement because it later withdrew from the Plan. Now, like most of the other libraries in Long Island, it can happily ignore poetry.

The questionnaire, mailed to all but one of the 151 libraries, was made as simple as possible in order to encourage a large response. The following questions were asked:

1) Do you consider current poetry as important to your literature collection as traditional poetry and well-established modern poetry?

2) In deciding what books to buy, do you read critical reviews of current poetry as regularly as reviews of books in other fields?

3) Do you read these reviews: a) in library journals? b) in other magazines as well?

4) Do you allocate a certain percentage of your total book budget for each subject?

5) Do you include poetry in your book purchases regularly?

6) Does the subject division among the libraries in the Suffolk (or Nassau) system limit your purchase of poetry?

7) Do you believe that favorably reviewed current poetry must be preserved and fostered, and that this is a public library responsibility?

7a) If yes, do you think that this responsibility exists regardless of an active readers' interest in poetry?

8) Are you in the habit of reading poetry for your own enjoyment?

9) Does your academic background include courses in literature, such as: a) undergraduate major? b) graduate courses?

A LIVELY RESPONSE

The response was lively and immediate, indicating that librarians, whether they buy poetry or not, are interested in discussing it. One hundred and ten replies were received, 90 of them submitted in the first three weeks.

Over half the librarians unequivocally stated their belief that the public library not only has an obligation to preserve and foster the best poetry being published, but that it should assume this obligation and responsibility even in the absence of an active community interest in poetry. In theory, at least, they would seem to agree with Robert D. Leigh, in *The Public Library in the United States*, that a primary aim of most librarians is "to seek to give people an opportunity to improve their capacity for appreciation and production in cultural fields."

That there is a hidden—or perhaps not so hidden—interest in poetry among the general public was indicated by a CBS network television program, presented on August 16, 1962, entitled "Americans: a Portrait in Verses." The program presented "a kaleidoscopic picture of the American people, from the earthy types of Spoon River to the measured coffee-spoon lives of Prufrock and his drawing-room friends talking of Michelangelo, from Sandburg's sidewalk philosophers to Cummings' 'sweet old aunt etcetera.'" During the program, selections from the works of Frost, Benet, Emerson, Whitman, Emily Dickinson, Ogden Nash, Marianne Moore, and Allen Ginsberg were read by a cast of distinguished actors. The reaction to the program was unexpectedly enthusiastic, and 54,000 listeners asked CBS for a bibliography of the poetry presented!

To return to the questionnaire, 65 of the 110 librarians answered both parts of Question 7 in the affirmative, without any reservations. Fifteen who agreed with Question 7 but had reservations about 7a, offered such comments as: "to a degree"; "Yes, for large libraries; no, for small branches which have resources of a library system available to them"; "within certain limits of practicality and budget and use considerations"; "Must regard readers' interests, but do purchase better known modern poets"; "Yes, however severe shelf and budget limitations curtail ability of small branch to do much"; "I believe this, but our book budget is so small, I can't afford to practice it as I'd like." In contrast with these guarded replies, one librarian stated bluntly: "You can't force people to read what they don't want."

Four librarians got into a semantic quarrel over fostering and preserving poetry. "Preserved perhaps—not fostered," said one. "Fostered yes, but not necessarily preserved," argued two others, while the fourth wrote, "Foster would be more the college responsibility, preserving could be the libraries' responsibility."

One librarian agrees to Question 7 "as far as budget permits," and to 7a if the collection is to be "well-rounded." "Though current poetry should be bought more widely than it is," he adds, "perhaps one reason that it is not centers around too little publicity given to the poets and their works." "Now, now, does the public library have such a responsibility?" asks another librarian in reply to Question 7. "Perhaps the college/university library has it, largely because professors will demand poetry . . . the trouble with most public library and college /university acquisition is that the contemporary is regarded as most important; items with an historical future are postponed."

Nine librarians answered "yes" to Question 7 and "no" to 7a; a few answered with a question mark; and only six of the 110 librarians gave a categorical "no" to both parts of Question 7.

In reply to Question 1, 60 librarians stated that they considered current poetry to be as important in their literature collections as traditional poetry and well-established modern poetry. In addition, the following comments were expressed: "Poetry, however, except the *very* fine poems and poets, just sits in this small branch"; "Most calls for poetry are almost certainly school assignments here"; "important for a small readership as well as to introduce new poets to readers who might be interested but not aware of their works"; "If of good quality." In view of the fact that a clear majority of the respondents believe current poetry to be as important as traditional poetry, the results of the survey make one wonder just how well traditional poetry and well-established modern poetry is represented in the libraries surveyed. Or, as one observer noted, with friends such as this who needs enemies?

Forty-nine of the 110 librarians (30 of whom had answered in the affirmative to both parts of Question 7) did not consider current poetry to be as important as traditional poetry and well-established modern poetry. The following reasons were given: "primarily, there is no reader demand for it"; "based on demand—requests are for traditional mainly"; "in most branches current poetry tends not to circulate, but an effort is made to select a sampling, e.g., Lowell, Updike, etc."; "to be frank, a large part of our poetry readership are college and high school students with assignments. We need more of well-established than of other poetry. We will buy modern with good reviews, but in small quantities." Four librarians took the quite reasonable position that current poetry, although important, is not as important as traditional poetry.

Seventy-two of the 110 librarians stated, in answer to Question 2, that they read critical reviews of current poetry as regularly as reviews of current books in other fields. "Please note," commented a librarian who answered this question in the negative, "for some time we received all the poetry (new and new editions) from the Suffolk Cooperative Library System in their Greenaway Plan. We have withdrawn from the plan because our poetry collection became out of proportion in our small library." We sympathize with this librarian, but would like to state for the record that this is the only case we have been able to note of a poetry collection becoming out of proportion to the rest of the collection! "No, because poetry reviews are harder to come by," commented another librarian. "Let us be realistic," cautioned still another, ". . . poetry does not get the attention of the press that is given to biography and fiction. When *Life* did the big piece on Berryman, and the *New York Times Magazine* wrote up Betjeman, I read the articles. But I don't go looking for them."

All but one of the librarians indicated that they read the poetry reviews in the library periodicals. Other magazines mentioned (and number of times mentioned) as book review sources for current poetry are the *New York Times Book Review* (32), *Saturday Review* (29), *Choice* (8), *Kirkus* (8), *New York Review of Books* (8), *Poetry* (7), *Atlantic Monthly* (4), *Book Buyers' Guide* (4), *Publishers' Weekly* (4), *Time* (4), *Harper's* (3), *Times Literary Supplement* (3), *New Yorker* (2), *American News* (1), *Book Week* (1), *English Journal* (1), *Hudson Review* (1), *Kenyon Review* (1), and *Yale Review* (1). A list of sources that ranges from the *American News* to the *Yale Review* cannot be said to lack diversity! One Suffolk librarian said emphatically, "We simply do not read reviews of poetry."

In answer to Question 4, only 21 librarians said that they allocate a certain amount of their book budget for each subject.

REVIEWS LESS RELIABLE?

Sixty-five of the 110 librarians replied in the affirmative to Question 5. Thirty-three librarians admit that they do not purchase poetry on a regular basis. A librarian in Queens notes that "several weeks can go by without any poetry appearing on a book selection list." "When poetry appears with good reviews," he adds, "I generally buy, with no prejudice as to whether it is contemporary or traditional." Another Queens librarian finds "the necessarily subjectivity of an individual's response" to be a major stumbling block to the purchase of poetry. "Reviews in this area are often less reliable than in any other field," he adds. "I will be much more eager to purchase a collection which I have examined personally and responded to, than I will a collection for which I have merely seen some favorable reviews. And then, my enthusiastic response does not ensure that of an appreciable number of my borrowers. Thus, most librarians, especially those who read even less poetry than I, prefer to wait for a tradition of approbation to be established before purchasing with confidence."

A reply such as this makes vividly clear the barriers, grammatical and other-wise, that contemporary poets must hurdle before being allowed into the sacrosanct halls of some public libraries.

In reply to Question 6, which was addressed to librarians in Nassau and Suffolk Counties, where nearly all public libraries are members of cooperative systems, all but two replied that the subject division among the libraries did not limit their purchase of poetry. The same librarian who absolutely refuses to read reviews of poetry again added a special note to her answer to Question 6. "We scarcely are affected by the Suffolk System," she wrote. "We do not purchase books via the System, hence we are free to arrange our own subject divisions." The two librarians who answered in the affirmative to Question 6 gave the following explanations: "In a sense, of course, since our book budget is only $6500. Naturally demand will play an important part in selection. The fact that we can inter-loan those books requested only occasionally does limit our purchase of current poetry"; "Modern American poetry is neither the area (for which) we get Central Book Aid (N.Y. State) money nor the area we get under Suffolk's Greenaway Plan. However, we still buy." It will be seen from the results of this survey and from the comments of several librarians that the Greenaway Plan is not working very effectively in either Nassau or Suffolk County, at least in regard to poetry.

THE LIBRARIANS

The educational background of the librarians was wide and varied. Forty-nine of the 110 librarians had completed some graduate work in literature. Only 24 did not have any special training in the field. Sixty of the librarians stated that they read poetry for their own personal enjoyment. There appears to be little relationship between the personal enjoyment of poetry and a special academic background in literature.

A large part of the difficulty revealed by this survey seems to be implicit in the comment of the Queens librarian who distrusts the reviews of contempo-rary poetry as well as his own taste, although obviously favoring the latter. But is it the librarian's functcon to decide for his patrons just which poets should be included in his collection, without regard to responsible critical opinion? Despite the clear majority of the librarians who stated their belief that the public library has an obligation and responsibility to preserve and foster the best contemporary poetry being published regardless of reader interest, it is clear that reader interest or demand is very much on their minds. The judg-ment of posterity does not appear to concern them greatly.

One librarian did not reveal the slightest discrepancy between what he professes to believe and what he practices. He returned his unanswered questionnaire with the following comment: "Our borrowers are not at all interested in poetry. Only read on assignment. People do not like modern poetry at all."

As if in reply, another librarian commented, simply and eloquently (even poetically), "I am glad someone took up the issue. I believe in the beauty of language . . . and the importance of poetry."

TEN MOST WIDELY PURCHASED TITLES

TITLE	NO. OF LIBRARIES
Poems, Alan Dugan	62
The Woman at the Washington Zoo, Randall Jarrell	40
To Mix With Time, May Swenson	30
Live or Die, Anne Sexton	29
Flower Herding on Mount Monadnock, Galway Kinnell	28
Corson's Inlet, A. R. Ammons	26
At the End of the Open Road, Louis Simpson	25
Traveling Through the Dark, William Stafford	25
Advice to a Prophet, Richard Wilbur	25
Poems 2, Alan Dugan	19

TEN LEAST WIDELY PURCHASED TITLES

TITLE	NO. OF LIBRARIES
The Fountains of Regardlessness, Frederick Bock	2
The Breaking of the Day, Peter Davison	2
Ghosts of the Heart, John Logan	2
Skeleton of Light, Thomas Vance	3
The Equal Tribunals, Byron Vazakas	3
An Almanac of Twilight, Jack Matthews	4
The Colossus, Sylvia Plath	4
Say Pardon, David Ignatow	5
Bone Thoughts, George Starbuck	5
Four Infinitives, Thomas Whitbread	5

16 *Demand for Dissent?*

(OCTOBER 15, 1964)

by JOHN N. BERRY III

Goldwater's famous sentences had become a cliché before we turned off our TV set. The Cow Palace was nearly empty. We were suddenly aware of our ignorance af the extremism that caused all the shouting. We remembered those unrelated events starting in Dallas last November. Murders in Mississippi, riots in Harlem and Rochester, bitter clamor about the John Birch Society, ". . . a republic, not a democracy," Cuban exiles picketing in New York, "impeach Earl Warren." We heard Malcolm X say, "A man with a rifle or club can only be stopped by a man with a rifle or club." Someone else whispered about "the fascist takeover of the GOP," "Zionist reds," and the "international communist conspiracy."

When we were young, in a comfortable suburb in New Jersey, we learned about the "melting pot" and we sang kindergarten songs with lyrics that went: "Walk up to the kind policeman." We wouldn't have believed in Harlem, or lynching, or police brutality. We had never seen a slum, or a communist. The only "race problem" was far away in the south, the only fascist was far away in Germany, and no one had ever picketed, or protested, or rioted in our neighborhood.

One institution in that happy island of middle class security had given us strength in other moments of fear, and information to dispel our ignorance. The public library, rich store of information on everything (so we had been told), would help us now to find out what an "extremist" is, just as it had provided Dr. Spock to tell us that our children were normal, and their illnesses common.

The library had let us down occasionally, but not in serious matters. We bought a paper copy of *Tropic* at the drug store, and we found our own *Fannie Farmer* in the drawer under the dish towels. We were really more relieved than let down to know that our kids wouldn't find *God's Little Acre* or *Peyton Place* there to sneak into their own reading.

So we went down to the public library to find out about the "extreme," but all we found was the same old middle.

Because our library was as much a prisoner of the suburb as we were, we decided to find out if other public libraries would supply the information we wanted.

The problem quickly boiled down to a brief exploration of the literature of the fringes of political and social thought. Our emphasis changed from "extremism" to more general dissent, and we decided to conduct a survey.

The purpose of this survey was to test the operation in public library practice of these widely accepted principles:

"The collection must contain the various opinions which apply to important, complicated, and controversial questions, including unpopular and unorthodox positions. . . .

"Non book materials should be an integral part of the collection and, within limits of availability and usefulness, should be provided to the same degree of range and inclusiveness as books."—*Public Library Service*, the ALA standards of 1956.

"There should be the fullest practicable provision of material presenting all points of view concerning the problems and issues of our times, international, national, and local; and books and other reading matter of sound factual authority should not be proscribed or removed from library shelves because of partisan or doctrinal disapproval."—*Library Bill of Rights*.

With this purpose in mind we began to select from the heap of "far-out" periodicals that we had collected from everywhere on the spectrum of opinion. The titles selected meet at least one of the following criteria:

1. They serve as the sounding board for an organization that espouses a cause or position that is controversial, widely publicized, and of high current interest, either as the group's official organ or unofficial spokesman. Those chosen in this category were the National Association for the Advancement of Colored People's *The Crisis; Corelator*, from the Congress of Racial Equality; *The Militant*, representing the Socialist Workers Party; the black Muslims' *Muhammed Speaks; The Worker*, for the Communist Party of the USA; *Church & State*, from Protestants and Other Americans for the Separation of Church and State; the AFL-CIO publication entitled *The American Federationist;* Jimmy Hoffa's *The International Teamster;* and unofficially representing the John Birch Society, *American Opinion*.

2. They present a unique opinion or unusual coverage of current issues, from the right or left. Here find *Human Events*, the "insider's newsletter" of the right; the racist *The Augusta Courier; American Mercury*, for being generally anti—Jews, Negroes, and Leftists; *I. F. Stone's Weekly*, a highly individualized liberal-left newssheet; another independent dissenter, M. S. Arnoni's *The Minority of One; Freedomways*, a high quality quarterly of the

Negro freedom movement; *The Progressive*, with its slightly left of center, general political criticism; the *National Guardian*, a progressive left-over from the days of Henry Wallace's quixotic crusade; and *The Cross and the Flag*, Gerald L. K. Smith's long published Jew-baiting, white supremacist organ of the Christian Nationalist Crusade.

3. We needed a point of reference, and a familiar title or two, so we added, from the *Reader's Guide, The Nation, National Review*, and *Ebony*.

This roster of dissent was mailed to 120 public libraries, 100 of which returned completed questionnaires. Most included some comment, many long explanations, and one "took the fifth amendment." A summary of the results follows:

TITLE	PAID SUBSCRIPTION	GIFT
Nation	94	0
National Review	80	5
Ebony	84	0
Human Events	16	45
American Mercury	53	1
American Fed'ist	30	20
Crisis	41	4
Church & State	2	39
Nat'l Guardian	33	5
Progressive	29	9
Int'l Teamster	6	30
Freedomways	12	2
I. F. Stone's Wkly	4	8
Worker	9	3
American Opinion	7	3
Minority of One	6	2
Muhammed Speaks	2	1
Corelator	1	1
Cross and the Flag	0	2
Militant	1	1
Augusta Courier	0	0

When someone asks for a particular publication the librarian's first reaction is to justify not having it in the collection. These justifications made up the majority of the comments that came back with our questionnaire. One librarian said: "Why aren't the periodicals that give unbiased news sufficient?" Another was more articulate: ". . . smaller libraries must devote space to the better known and indexed periodicals." Someone else had another reason: "Negro population here is less than one percent; no significant labor union membership here. . . . Catholic population here is in vast majority." A large city library said: "We are willing to purchase any of these titles if demand for them would develop." From these comments, and others like them, we found our first clue to library practice in the selection of periodicals. Briefly stated, selection practice is based upon demand and the availability of indexing. The three most widely held titles in this survey were *The Nation, National Review,* and *Ebony,* all well known, and all indexed in the *Reader's Guide. Ebony* has the largest circulation of those on our list, some 750,000 readers in the US.

An earlier editorial in Lj discussed the concept of "tested usefulness." When one is dealing with the vast literature of dissent, this concept, selecting material to meet current demand, is even more fatal to good library service. Many of these publications are relatively unknown, even though they are unique in opinion or in their representation of an important organization. That minority of the general public that uses public libraries is unfamiliar with them, and has been conditioned not to expect this kind of material in the public library anyway. Demand for *I. F. Stone's Weekly,* to use an example, will not just "develop." The same 1956 standards from which the principles to be tested in this survey were derived also commit the public library to the function of education. It is, therefore, incumbent upon librarians, not only to provide dissenting views, but to educate the public to the existence of these views wherever they are available. In this regard it was disappointing to note that less than half of the libraries surveyed placed any publication other than *Ebony, American Mercury,* the *National Review,* or *The Nation* on public display. It is unlikely that their publics will ever come into contact with the more dissident publications on our list through any other agency. Thus, there can never be demand until the public is aware of the existence of this body of literature.

A second criterion for periodical selection practice was indicated by the great number of libraries that told us they selected their periodicals from those available in published indexes, especially the *Reader's Guide.* As one criterion for the selection of material this is valid, and helpful. To use it to reject periodicals is not valid; indeed, it is dangerous. The periodical index, especially the *Reader's Guide,* represents another manifestation of "tested usefulness." Yet a majority of the libraries in cities of less than 150,000 reject some material on this basis. Two cases will illustrate at least two dangers inherent in selecting only from periodicals for which published indexing is available.

It is no secret that in its early days the *National Review* had troubles, and employed a great many tactics to build its circulation. A few years ago nearly every library in the US received a letter on Cornell University stationery, signed by several leading historians and political scientists, urging the librarians to vote *National Review* into the *Reader's Guide.* The campaign was successful, as it should have been, and the magazine is now included. The implications of this tactic are obvious. While *National Review* is certainly a legitimate addition to the index, one wonders if others could employ the same tactic with equal success.

The other case could apply to several titles on our list, those that represent important organizations but are not indexed in *Reader's Guide.* The most dramatic example is *The American Federationist.* If the ALA, NEA, US Chamber of Commerce, AMA, PTA, and National Audubon Society are worthy of representation (through their periodicals) in *Reader's Guide,* why not the AFL-CIO? The point, which must be obvious by now, is that selecting from an index is the same thing as selecting on the basis of demand. The public library exists as much for the members of the AFL-CIO, John Birch Society, Communist Party, and Muslims as it does for the bird watchers. If the publications of these organizations are deemed not to be of "permanent reference value," a debatable point, their current opinions are still as important to balanced library collections as any, *Reader's Guide* or not. It is as important, probably more important, that the general public (let alone the members of these organizations) have access to these opinions.

When we are told daily that communism is the central issue of our times, it is appalling that only 12 libraries out of 100 receive *The Worker,* and these in cities of over 500,000 population, where seven of them place the magazine on closed shelves.

If the race problem is your candidate for major issue (as a recent opinion poll indicated), then it is more appalling that only three libraries receive *Muhammed Speaks* (and one of these subscribes for the local police); yet the position of the "black" Muslims is common conversation everywhere, and most people know about Cassius Clay and Malcolm X. To carry this point a step further, less than half of the libraries surveyed receive the following official or unofficial organs of major US organizations: *The Crisis, Corelator, Muhammed Speaks, The Worker, The American Federationist, The International Teamster,* and *American Opinion.*

In smaller libraries (those in cities of less than 500,000 people) the majority receive only *Ebony, The Nation, National Review, Human Events,* and *American Mercury.* After these the most popular titles in small libraries are *The American Federationist* and *Church & State.* These seven most popular titles, especially the four which are not indexed, raise very serious questions about library selection practices.

Human Events, the right-wing tabloid, is received by 60 percent of the libraries surveyed. Founded in 1944, its editors tell us: "In reporting the news, *Human Events* is objective; it aims for accurate presentation of the facts. But it is *not* impartial. It looks at events through eyes that are biased in favor of limited constitutional government, local self-government, private enterprise and individual freedom." Under a front page reprint of a Chicago *Tribune* editorial entitled "Arm-Twisting Poverty Bill Through Congress" there is the following commentary for those who have read the reprint: "If the person reading it shrugs his shoulders and says—as do all Socialists (who now call themselves liberals): 'That's the way to get things done!' then that person is either blind to the future consequences of this type of power or is impatient for the arrival of dictatorship—upon the innocent assumption that the dictator will hold the same beliefs as he does. If on the other hand the Chicago *Tribune* editorial raises the reader's blood to the boiling point, then he is a genuine fighter for freedom."

Out of 61 libraries that receive *Human Events,* 45 have gift subscriptions. Usually the magazine finds a local donor, and usually it is accepted by the library (several of our respondents reported this tactic). *Church & State,* often as anti-Catholic as it is zealous for the separation of church and state, is similarly generous. Of 41 libraries that receive it, 39 get it as a gift. Of the 36 subscriptions to *The International Teamster,* 30 are gifts. We agree that these publications should be in libraries, but for the right reasons. The sobering implication of these findings is that there are tactics that can be employed to influence library collections quite independent of selection principles and policies. The gift campaigns of *Human Events* and *Church & State,* and the *Reader's Guide* election campaign of *National Review* are probably only the beginning. The current election campaign suggests that ideological pressure will increase in the coming months, and years.

For those who haven't read *American Mercury* lately, H. L. Mencken is gone. So is his spirit, to be replaced by views which are anathema to Jews, Negroes, and all but arch-conservatives. The magazine has been dropped from the *Reader's Guide,* but it lingers on in 54 libraries, we suspect by default. If the popularity of *American Mercury* is the result of consciously applied selection principles then we wonder why every other title on our list was not in every library that still gets the *Mercury.* It is certainly an inconsistency that more libraries receive, and pay for, *American Mercury* than they do all but the top four periodicals on our list. The implication of this, and of our earlier findings, is that practice and principles are widely divergent in the selection of periodicals.

One librarian, after refusing to answer our questionnaire, said: " . . . who can say how much or how far, or what too much emphasis on the issues this grouping of publications mostly represents will do to starve other functions of the library?" Another, Harold Roth, director of the East Orange (N.J.) Public Library, wrote: " . . . I question that the existence of partisan publications of a current nature on the shelf is the answer to the question. . . . I find . . . that there are some arbitrary restrictions placed upon us by the indexing publications and by the long range need for bibliographic access and use of the material. . . . How far do we go? Whose interests do we select for . . . ours or the public? How much of the spectrum do we need to expose . . . ?"

To answer Mr. Roth's last question first, it seems obvious that libraries should have the official publications of the largest labor unions, the largest and most active Negro rights organizations, the most controversial black supremacy group, something representing opposition to the Negro movement, and the most important communist publication in the US. They deal with the central issues of the current election campaign, and of our times.

The other questions relate to cost. The whole list, if a library had to pay for all of them, would only cost about $110. Subtract only the obviously available gifts and it amounts to just under $60. This is less than Cobbett's *Chamber Music* and Smith's *Classified Shakespeare Bibliography,* two items recommended by the Reference Services Division of ALA for small and medium-sized libraries. The need for the information in these two seems small indeed compared to the range of information and opinion available in the periodicals we listed.

The implication that books, or secondary sources, would do a better job than current polemic periodicals was made in several comments. We submit that secondary sources have at least two great disadvantages: they are always out-of-date, and they report and interpret what might be better understood in the original. Two titles suggested as substitutes will illustrate both points. Eric Lincoln's *Black Muslims in America* was viciously attacked by the Muslims as biased and it does not, of course, include the implications of the defection of Malcolm X. The Communist Party would never espouse Hoover's *Masters of Deceit*. Any historian worthy of the name will readily admit that primary sources are the only valid historical evidence. It is only logical, then, to go to the primary source for information. Daniel Melcher, in an editorial discussing a speech by Senator Fulbright, sums it up this way: "Will your library contain what was actually said by the Senator, as distinct from what others said he said?". It is equally important that the library contain the information or opinion expressed fast, within a day or week after it was articulated. Only the periodical can provide this speed.

There is a brighter side to the results. We were surprised by many individual libraries. St. Louis and Dallas were the stars, with more titles than any others. Lillian Bradshaw at Dallas listed several periodicals we didn't know about, and surely the Dallas Public Library has outstanding representation of dissenting opinions. Others, among the many with strong collections, are Los Angeles, San Francisco, Honolulu, Boston, Detroit, Brooklyn, Buffalo and Erie County, Syracuse, Rochester, Akron, Cleveland, Cincinnati and Hamilton County, and Seattle, Milwaukee, Philadelphia, and Pittsburgh.

An analysis by regions showed no significant differences between any one part of the US and another. This too is healthy.

We have already noted that smaller libraries tend to have fewer titles. This was certainly expected, but the surprise here was that coverage fell off dramatically immediately as the size of the city served descended lower than 500,000 persons, a much higher point on the population scale than we had expected.

Replies were received from every state except Arizona, District of Columbia, Kentucky, Maine, and Wyoming. The total response was gratifying, just over 80 percent.

The variety of comment was interesting. Here are a few examples:

"We shall be taking a Birch Society publication, in this instance at the request of liberals in the community who desire firsthand information."

"As an ear to 'down There' we subscribe to P.D. East's *Petal Paper* (formerly published at Hattiesburg, Miss., but because of threats against Mr. East, address now: Southeast Publishing Co., 1603 Reuben St., Montgomery, Ala.) monthly."

"One selection criterion for this library: That periodicals to be put into the collection must be clearly identified as to sponsorship, or issuing agency . . . the reader should be able to determine 'Who says so?' "

A common reaction: "I'm surprised we don't take this one (*I. F. Stone's Weekly, Corelator, The Crisis*) and have entered a subscription."

"I think this questionnaire is unnecessary. In my opinion this is 'busy' work with very little good to be realized."

Several libraries offered substitute titles representing other opinions, and certainly, one inconclusive aspect of this survey is the fact that many of these opinions could be represented by a number of titles. Those mentioned most frequently were: *Studies on the Left, Firing Line, Civil Liberties* (ACLU), *AFL-CIO News, Dan Smoot Report, World Marxist Review,* and *New America.*

Our approach to publishers of the periodicals elicited the following responses:

Gerald L. K. Smith of *The Cross and the Flag* wrote: "*The Cross and the Flag,* although a highly controversial journal, is recognized by our opposition as being the most consistent expression of the viewpoint espoused to be found in America. We are ready to offer this publication free to any and all libraries . . ."

From R. N. Ober of *American Opinion:* "Actually, relatively few libraries subscribe to the magazine, apparently because we are not listed in the *Reader's Guide.*"

"*Human Events* is in relatively few libraries in relation to the total number of such institutions. At this time, it is our estimate that it is found in 1000 to 1200 libraries," said K. W. Ingwalson, Publisher.

M. S. Arnoni, who is *The Minority of One,* was most enthusiastic: "Indeed we should like to be helpful to your survey, which we welcome and believe to be of great importance." He then sent us a detailed circulation breakdown indicating, among other things, that *The Minority of One* is often given to libraries, but that the gift subscription is seldom renewed.

Looking at the end result, there is one thing of which we are certain: public libraries are willing to cooperate with any analysis of their activities, and most answer with enthusiasm, and considerably more information than is requested. Many tried to anticipate the conclusions, and many did, by offering justifications for the titles they did not receive. It should be pointed out that this list was not necessarily a recommendation. It is the writer's opinion, however, that most of the titles listed, especially those representing significant organizations, can be justified for library collections.

Finally, does library practice measure up to those lofty principles upon which this survey was based? The answer is inconclusive for several reasons. We were unable to tap every source of dissent, and libraries may subscribe to other titles that offer the opinions of those we listed. Our sample, while geographically representative, is small, and may or may not support generalizations from the data collected. At any rate we offer a tentative answer.

In many libraries the attempt to provide material presenting all points of view is an emphatic success. More often, however, it is eroded by the reliance on selection criteria of doubtful validity—demand and available indexing—or it is left to chance. It is easy to accept the crutch of the index, even though the purpose of that index is not to influence selection. It is easy, as well, to continue a subscription once entered. More important, periodical selection can be influenced by tactical devices, the gift in particular, unrelated to library selection policies or principles.

This survey, although tentative, like so many studies of the selection problem that have preceded it, tends to reinforce our nagging suspicions. We are left with the feeling that public libraries in the United States continue, very cautiously, to cling to the middle of the road.

17 The Foreign Press in U.S. Libraries

(FEBRUARY 1, 1966)

by CAROL WALL

It is a truism that each nation's well-being depends upon the well-being of other nations. Whatever your politics, you could probably be convinced that the day of US isolationism is dead, for better or worse.

You might agree, as well, that foreign policy is sometimes made in response to public opinion. This is not to say that every majority view is reflected in some State Department position, but only that the popular consensus is one factor in the promulgation of the official US policy toward the rest of the world.

The same is true, in part anyway, of other nations. It is also true in most countries that the public opinion to which leaders respond is often molded, and sometimes twisted out of its former shape, by the interpretations and propaganda in the official response, or in the policy officially adopted.

In short, public opinion helps mold official policy, and official policy, at the same time, tends to shape public opinion. Thus, in order to understand the international position of a given nation you must try to know the point of view of that nation's citizens, and to understand it.

Popular beliefs are seldom the product of scholarly research or careful study. It is easy to prove the divergence between the academic conclusion and the popular belief. By the same logic, it is obvious that popular opinion is reflected in the popular press, not in the nation's scholarly journals. You get a more accurate idea of what Americans think from such sources as *Time, Newsweek, Look,* or the *Daily News,* than you do from the *American Political Science Review* or *Foreign Affairs Quarterly.* Thus if you want to predict or understand the changes in US foreign policy, your best source, short of polling the public itself, is the popular press in the US. Americans who want to know how the world reacts to our foreign policy, or what people and governments in other nations believe, should, it follows, read the popular periodical publications from other countries.

"The Library Bill of Rights" states that "There should be the fullest practicable provision of material presenting all points of view concerning the problems and issues of our times, international, national, and local. . . ." This survey was conducted under the premise that periodicals from other countries, popular periodicals, are important to the successful achievement of that aim. A foreigner could find current American opinion reflected in the daily press and "slick" magazines of the US. Can an American, through his public library, gain access to similar sources for determining the point of view of people in another country?

The technique of this survey was based on John Berry's "Demand for Dissent?" which studied public library practices in the selection of periodicals expressing minority political opinions in the US.

A questionnaire was sent to every third library in the US with a total budget of $25,000 or more, as listed in the *American Library Directory*. The $25,000 minimum budget was an attempt to limit the size of the sample and to question libraries which could best afford a larger periodical collection. The many pleas of poverty in the returns suggest that this minimum wasn't high enough.

The questionnaire listed 94 foreign news periodicals selected from *Atlas*, a periodical which attempts to inform US readers about foreign opinion by printing excerpts of material from the foreign press.

The list, with the number of library subscribers to each title, follows:

AL AHRAM (Egypt)	0
AL AKHBAR (Egypt)	0
AL GOUMHOURIA (Egypt)	0
ANHEMBI (Brazil)	0
ARTS (France)	3
ASIA MAGAZINE (Hong Kong)	3
CARREFOUR (France)	0
CHRIST UND WELT (West Germany)	1
CORRIERE DELLA SERRA (Italy)	1
DAGENS NYHETER (Sweden)	1
DAILY EXPRESS (England)	0
DAILY MAIL (England)	1
DAILY MIRROR (Australia)	0
DAILY TELEGRAPH (England)	0
DEUTSCHE ZEITUNG (West Germany)	2
DIARIO DE NOTICIAS (Brazil)	0
DRUM (Ghana)	0
EASTERN WORLD (England)	0
ECONOMIST (England)	33
ELEFTHERIA (Greece)	0

EPOCA (Italy)	0
O ESTADO DE SAO PAULO (Brazil)	0
L'EXPRESS (France)	2
L'EXPRESSO (Italy)	0
FAR EASTERN ECONOMIC REVIEW	
(Hong Kong)	7
LE FIGARO (France)	2
LE FIGARO LITTERAIRE (France)	3
FORUM (Republic of South Africa)	0
FORUM SERVICE (England)	1
FRANCE OBSERVATEUR (France)	1
FRANKFURTER ALLGEMEINE ZEITUNG	
(West Germany)	3
HINDU WEEKLY REVIEW (India)	1
INTERNATIONAL AFFAIRS (USSR)	1
IZVESTIA (Russia)	0
JERUSALEM POST (Israel)	1
JEUNE AFRIQUE (Tunis)	0
JORNAL DO BRASIL (Brazil)	0
KURIER (Austria)	0
LINK (India)	0
LITERATURNAYA GAZETA (USSR)	0
LUDMAS MATY (Hungary)	0
MAINICHI SHIMBUN (Japan)	0
MANCHESTER GUARDIAN (England)	52
LE MONDE (France)	2
LE MONDE DIPLOMATIQUE (France)	0
IL MONDO (Italy)	1
LA NACION (Argentina)	1
NEPSZABADSAG (Hungary)	0
NEUE ZURCHER ZEITUNG (Switzerland)	1
NEUES DEUTSCHLAND (East Germany)	0
NEW COMMONWEALTH (England)	1
NEW STATESMAN (England)	23
LES NOUVELLES LITTERAIRES (France)	0
NOVY MIR (USSR)	0
OBSERVER (England)	5
L'OSSERVATORE POLITICO LETTERARIO (Italy)	0
PALANTE (Cuba)	0
PARIS-MATCH (France)	23
PEKING REVIEW (China)	0
PHILIPPINES FREE PRESS (Philippines)	1
PICTURES OF GREECE (Greece)	0
POLISH PERSPECTIVES (Poland)	0
POLITYKA (Czechoslovakia)	0
PRAVDA (USSR)	0
PREUVES (France)	1
QUADRANT (Australia)	0
THE QUEEN (England)	2
QUEST (India)	1
RENMIN RIBAO (China)......................	0

THE REPORTER (Kenya)	1
REVIEW OF INTERNATIONAL AFFAIRS (Yugoslavia)	1
SPECTATOR (England)	13
DER SPIEGEL (West Germany)	3
LA STAMPA (Italy)	0
STATESMAN; WEEK-END REVIEW (Pakistan)	1
STATIST (England)	2
STERN (West Germany)	0
SUDDEUTSCHE ZEITUNG (West Germany)	0
SUNDAY TELEGRAPH (England)	2
SUNDAY TIMES (England)	2
SURVEY (England)	0
SWISS REVIEW OF WORLD AFFAIRS (Switzerland) ..	2
TABLET (England)	3
TIMES (England)	16
VDI NACHRICHTEN (West Germany)	1
WEEKLY NEWS (New Zealand)	1
DIE WELT (West Germany)	0
DIE WELTWOCHE (Switzerland)	0
WEST AFRICA (England)	0
WEST AFRICAN PILOT (Nigeria)	1
DIE ZEIT (West Germany)	2
ZERI POPULLIT (Albania)	0

The list was sent to 335 libraries, of which 250 (74 percent) replied. Questionnaires were returned from every state except Alaska and Hawaii. A simple tabulation of the results reveals several interesting, if not appalling, facts.

Novy Mir, Pravda, and *Izvestia,* three of the most representative popular publications from the Soviet Union, were not received by any of the responding libraries. A single subscription to *Corriere Della Serra* and another to *Il Mondo* were the total holdings from Italy. Of the eight titles listed from all of Africa, only single copies of *The Jerusalem Post* (Israel), *The Reporter* (Kenya), and the *West African Pilot* (Nigeria) were reported. Not one of the 250 libraries received Ghana's, English-language, *Drum,* which is widely circulated throughout the world. *Die Welt,* the most widely circulated paper in West Germany, is not received by any library in the sample.

From the communist bloc in Eastern Europe, represented by eight titles on the list, libraries receive a single copy of *International Affairs* (USSR) and one of the *Review of International Affairs* (Yugoslavia). Poland, Hungary, Czechoslovakia, East Germany, and Albania each publish popular magazines, none of which are received by libraries in the sample.

India, with three titles on the list, is represented in the 250 libraries by one subscription to each of two, although all three are published in English. For Asia as a whole there were ten titles on the list. Of the 14 subscriptions to Asian titles, ten are divided between two publications from Hong Kong, *Far Eastern Economic Review* and *Asia Magazine.* One library receives the *Philippines Free Press.* China's two entries, both of which publish English editions, are not received.

The combined holdings of the 250 libraries amount to 233 copies of 45 titles. Nearly 60 percent (148) of the libraries reported that they did not receive a single title on the list. Of the 233 copies received, just under 60 percent (137) are accounted for by subscriptions to five British publications: *The Spectator, The Economist, The Times, The Manchester Guardian,* and *The New Statesman.*

The questionnaire asked libraries to list other foreign titles received, though not named in the sample from *Atlas.* They reported 55 subscriptions to the *Illustrated London News,* Britain's high society pictorial. Another popular title not listed in the survey sample was the slick French pictorial *Réalités,* which is received by 23 libraries. Such foreign embassy publications as *Venezuela Up to Date, Coming Events in Britain, Korean Report,* and *Saudi Arabia Today* were among the top 30 titles received. These government publications are usually free to libraries. *Soviet Life,* the US/USSR exchange publication, is received by nine libraries.

The average library in the sample devotes 2.7 percent of its total periodical holdings to foreign titles. Libraries with budgets ranging from $25,000 to $39,999 carry 1.6 percent foreign titles in their periodicals collection; those with $40,000 to $74,999 average 1.5 percent, while the larger libraries ($75,000 and up) carry 3.8 percent foreign serials.

The first, and most obvious, conclusion that can be drawn from these results is that most US public libraries do not provide foreign periodicals from countries with official positions or strong public sentiment that is opposed to US foreign policy. The USSR, Eastern Europe, Asia, Africa, China, and even nonaligned India are virtually without representation in US libraries. The opinions of friendly critics as well as those of unfriendly adversaries in the world are just not available. The public library is obviously not the place to go to for the opinions of the foreign press. It is not the place to locate current information and opinion "concerning the problems and issues of our times."

The causes most frequently cited by librarians for the lack of foreign periodicals were 1) the language barrier, 2) lack of funds, and 3) the lack of demand. "We do not have a great foreign population in our community," reported one librarian. Another said, "I sincerely wish I could say 'yes' to something—but this is the center of the US—maybe someday, but not now." More revealing was, "I guess the Hatfields and the McCoys, the Ledbetters and the other descendents of the Wild West, couldn't care less."

One "small" librarian complained, "It would seem that small libraries—or even larger rural libraries such as we—would get none of these. Will this study be really useful outside university, college, and large public libraries?"

Beginning with the first excuse, the language barrier, the findings of the survey suggest, at least, that this is but a small factor in the decision to select or reject many of the titles listed. In the first place, a full 40 percent are available in English, many from areas that were virtually not represented. A few examples will suffice. China's *Peking Review,* the four titles from India, and Russia's *International Affairs* are published in English. *Polish Perspectives, The Reporter* (Kenya), *Drum* (Ghana), the *Philippines Free Press,* and

Forum (Republic of South Africa) have also broken the English barrier. None of these examples, nor the areas and countries they represent, are adequately covered in the library collections.

The budget excuse, according to these findings, seems equally invalid. Libraries with less money to spend subscribed to more of the periodicals than was expected. Those with the smallest budgets in the sample ($25,000 to $39,999) devoted 1.6 percent of their total periodical collections to foreign titles, and the 88 libraries in this category subscribed to 24 of the titles listed. The 80 medium budget libraries ($40,000 to $74,999) despite their greater funds, received only 11 of the titles listed and devote just 1.5 percent of their serials collections to foreign titles. The 82 larger libraries ($75,000 and up) did better. They receive 32 of the listed titles and devote 3.8 percent of their total periodical holdings to those from abroad. In short, the weakest holdings were in the relatively better endowed libraries in the $40,000 to $74,999 budget range. The very rich are stronger, but the very poor seem to give the lie to the view that a lack of material is directly related to a lower budget.

One cannot statistically prove the demand for opinions from abroad. To use the lack of popular demand as the criteria for selection, however, has repeatedly been questioned in the professional journals. The best argument seems to be based on the premise that if the public is ignorant of certain material it cannot demand it. Since libraries do not provide a wide range of current foreign opinion and information and since, in most communities, foreign periodiacls are not easy to obtain, obviously the public will not know what to ask for. Any American schoolboy can discourse upon the "domino theory" in Southeast Asia, but how many can recite the program of the Viet Cong for Vietnam? If, as librarians keep telling themselves, the public library is an educational institution and an information center, then it is within its responsibility to provide material from foreign nations, and to publicize its availability. To beg off because no one asks is to abrogate its basic *raison d'être* as a public service.

Finally, it seems obvious from this survey that there is really no pattern nor any well defined criteria in most public libraries for the selection of periodicals representing foreign views. The preponderance of pro-western, European titles seems to be related to the fact that they are already fairly well-known in the US, and easy to obtain.

The popularity of embassy publications and "give-aways" suggests that it is easy to get material, some of it questionable, into library collections if you have the money to donate copies. The gift periodicals also suggest the absence of selection criteria, except demand, cost, and language.

In summary, public library selection of foreign periodicals is not balanced, does not provide access to the full range of opinion nor information on various important areas in the world. Libraries can, of course, partly meet the need by subscribing to US sources such as *Atlas*. Still, this will not fulfill their obligation to provide current information and opinion, directly from the source, in the shortest possible time.

Selection in this area, as in so many others, is haphazard, and timid. Even the largest libraries lack representation from those important parts of the world that are likely to disagree with the US. Rather than attribute this gap in library collections to any stated causes, this evidence suggests that librarians are not yet ready to accept the importance of foreign opinion and the foreign press to an informed US populace.

CHAPTER

18 Where It's At

by SANFORD BERMAN

(DECEMBER 15, 1968)

The Black Militant reads. But not *Jet, Ebony,* and Booker T. Washington. He turns to W. E. B. DuBois, Frantz Fanon, Malcolm X, LeRoi Jones, Stokely Carmichael, Eldridge Cleaver, *Freedomways, Soulbook, The Journal of Black Poetry,* and *Black Dialogue.*

The "peacenik" and "New Leftist" read. But not Norman Podhoretz, Max Ascoli, the *Nation,* and *New Republic.* They want Herbert Marcuse, Staughton Lynd, Conor Cruise O'Brien, Tom Hayden, Paul Goodman, Tariq Ali, Daniel Cohn-Bendit, *Ramparts, New Left Notes,* the *Guardian* (New York), *WIN,* and *Liberation.*

The Spanish-speaking, proud, and angry "Chicano" reads. But not *Selecciones del Reader's Digest.* He demands Reies Tijerina, Che Guevara, Corky Gonzalez, Cesar Chavez, and the lately-erupted papers and magazines of the *barrio.*

The folk-rocking, "turned-on," bead-wearing, long-haired generation reads. But not Norman Vincent Peale and the *New York Times.* It prefers Allen Ginsberg, Ed Sanders, Gary Snyder, the "underground press," A. S. Neill, Prince Kropotkin, Charles Bukowski, Jerry Rubin, and experimental, taboo-busting, life-affirming mags like the *San Francisco Earthquake, Realist, City Lights Journal, Boss,* and *Caterpillar.*

Does the black militant, political rebel, Chicano, or Establishment-shy youth find what he wants in the neighborhood or college library? No, baby. And it doesn't require a year-long, carefully-conducted, foundation-funded study to prove it. Everybody *knows* it.

The point is this: No amount of talk at library conferences and round tables about "relevancy" and "social responsibility" is itself going to enliven, enrich, un-barnacle, and, yes, *controversialize* library collections. Only librarians *themselves* can actually make their wares relevant to the *whole* community they serve: not just the respectable, well-shaven, white middle class (who, in any event, ought to know what's going on elsewhere from more trustworthy sources than *Time/Life*), but also the dissidents, the increasingly self-aware minorities, the forces in motion.

If this appears to suggest that most libraries are insufferably "square," that the profession is murdering its own noble "Bill of Rights" by ignoring it, and that literally millions of deprived, oppressed, and disaffected, yet wonderfully creative, sensitive, and energetic people simply don't find much nourishment or stimulation in the library—well, that's right.

So what do we do about it? Here are a few scattershot proposals:

Buy the *Directory of Little Magazines* (Dustbooks, 5218 Scottwood Road, Paradise, Calif. 95969; $2) and Robert H. Muller's *From Radical Left to Extreme Right* (Campus Publishers, 711 North University Ave., Ann Arbor, Mich, 48108; $4.75). Request samples. Then begin stocking both "little mags" and at least two or three items from each of Muller's six categories.

Pages 53–54 in the *Directory* list the newspapers that compose the Underground Press Syndicate. Each enjoys a unique personality, due to editor and locale, but all exchange material freely and for the most part are serviced by LNS (Liberation News Service). So, except for large research libraries that choose to document-in-depth the whole "underground movement," there's no need to subscribe to more than the *nearest* UPS paper. If the budget permits, also take the *Los Angeles Free Press, San Francisco Express-Times,* or *Berkeley Barb*. These are easily the best of the genre. (Incidentally, UPS coverage of events like the Columbia University rebellion, 1968 "French Revolution," and Chicago street-demonstrations during the Democratic Convention has been fuller, livelier, and more genuine than in the orthodox media.)

Visit the offbeat bookshops in town to discover new publications and trends (in Los Angeles, as examples: The Free Press Kazoos and Papa Bach). Another two ways to keep up-to-date on nonmainstream publishing: *The Small Press Review,* a quarterly Dustbooks publication, priced at $3.50 yearly, furnishes data on "small-press books and magazines worldwide," recording new, changed, and discontinued titles, political and literary alike; while the quadri-monthly *Trace* (Villiers Publications, Ltd., P.O. Box 1068, Hollywood, Calif. 90028; $4 annually) contains a usefully annotated "evolving directory" of "little" publishers and magazines.

Consciously try to represent significant, though perhaps unconventional, groups and ideas. (N.B. This doesn't mean *approving* them.) Purchase or beg the pertinent mags, books, and pamphlets. For instance, a library in New York or California that doesn't have *something* issued by the Black Panthers or Peace and Freedom Party just isn't with it. Any college without some "student power" organ like *The Activist, Young Socialist,* or *CAW!* is playing at make-believe. Collections that fail to reflect the turmoil and new directions inside organized labor (e.g., through H. W. Benson's crusading *Union Democracy in*

Action and AFT's *Changing Education*) deny their patrons important insights and information. A library that doesn't stock *The Modern Utopian* in effect blots out for its readers the exciting developments in community-building and human ecology that practically no other publication reports. And the library ostensibly serving teenagers that offers nothing on conscientious objection and the draft probably doesn't deserve to be patronized by young people at all. (The *News Notes* published by the Central Committee for Conscientious Objectors costs only the price of a postcard request.)

ED. NOTE: *When this manuscript arrived we queried Mr. Berman about the omission of voices from the right. He replied: "As you probably gather, I'm sympathetic toward the four groups I treated. Beyond that, however, they share a number of characteristics that completely distinguish them from rightwing movements: all favor immediate and thoroughgoing change; all oppose the political status quo and social orthodoxy; to at least some extent, they all interact with one another; all have produced distinct life-styles or 'countercultures,' ramifying into literature, art, philosophy, and even dress; all operate with extremely limited resources; all demand demilitarization, both at home and abroad; and all have been maligned, patronized, or merely ignored by the mass media. Plainly, while right-wing elements may also be discontented and highly active, the comparison ends there. Their spokesmen appear daily over the airwaves, their organizations enjoy heavy support from benefactors like Schick and Eversharp, etc. I simply regard them as neither as dynamic, numerous, nor neglected as the black militants, Chicanos, etc."*

Mr. Berman added: "They are distinctly worth attention, though," and suggested that LJ invite the Conservative Library Association to prepare a similar paper.

Rather than restrict the invitation to this apparently moribund organization (we have heard nothing of it in more than a year), we took this opportunity to invite anyone who has as much enthusiasm for, and knowledge of, the publications of the right as Mr. Berman had in the areas he has covered, to prepare a similar article covering the other end of the political spectrum.

TOWARD RELEVANCY: A CHECKLIST OF PERIODICALS

Activist. 27½ West College St., Oberlin, Ohio 44074. Quarterly. $3. (A student publication whose advisors include Tom Hayden, David McReynolds, and Raya Dunayevskaya)

Albany Liberator. 172 N. Pearl St., Albany, N.Y. 12207. ("Newspaper of ghetto communities in Albany, Schenectady, and Troy, connected to Black Power group, and a challenge to local Hearst journalism")

Ally. P.O. Box 9276, Berkeley, Calif. 94709. Monthly. $4. ("A newspaper for servicemen," concentrating on dissidence and anti-war activity within the Armed Forces)

Berkeley Barb. P.O. Box 5017, Berkeley, Calif. 94705. Weekly. $5. (editor: Max Scherr)

Black Dialogue. 642 Laguna St., San Francisco, Calif. Quarterly. $1.75 (A "black magazine for black people," containing essays, poetry, plays, art, articles, and reviews)

Black Panther. Ministry of Information, Black Panther Party, Box 2967, Custom House, San Francisco, Calif. 94126. Weekly. $7.50 (A no-holds-barred forum for ghetto militants)

Black Politics. P.O. Box 1233, Berkeley, Calif. 94700. Monthly. $6. ("A journal of liberation")

Black Theatre. New Lafayette Theatre, 200 W. 135 St. (Room 103), New York, N.Y. 10027. Bi-monthly. $1.50. ("A periodical of the black theatre and arts movement," born in mid-1968 and edited by dramatist Ed Bullins.)

Black Vanguard. 526½ Mayberry Drive, Danville, Ill. 61832. Semimonthly. $5. (The accent is local, but contents and tone typify black militancy throughout the North and West)

Bond. Room 633, 156 Fifth Ave., New York, N.Y. 10010. $6. (East-coast counterpart to the Berkeley *Ally*)

Boss. Box 231, Village Station, New York, N.Y. 10014. Semi-annual. $2. (An avant-garde potpourri, confected by Reginald Gay)

Broadside. Statewide ed. Peace and Freedom Party of Los Angeles County, 619 S. Bonnie Brae, Los Angeles, Calif. 90057. Biweekly. $3.

Caterpillar. 36 Greene St., New York, N.Y. 10013. Quarterly. $5. (A vibrant, attractive package of art and literature, finely edited by Clayton Eshleman)

CAW! Box 332, Cooper Station, New York, N.Y. 10003. Bimonthly. $5. for 12 issues. (An amalgam of poetry, graphics, essays, songs, and rebellion, published by the New York Regional Office of SDS)

Changing Education. American Federation of Teachers, AFL–CIO, 1012 14th St., N.W., Washington, D.C. 20005. Quarterly. $4. (Subscribers also receive the AFT newspaper, *American Teacher*)

Chicano Student Movement. P.O. Box 31322, Los Angeles, Calif. 90031. (A member of the Chicano Press Association, which is "bound to service and dedication to the Mexican American people")

City Lights Journal. 261 Columbus Ave., San Francisco, Calif. 94111. Annual. $2.50. (A book-size, always stimulating volume, edited by poet-publisher Lawrence Ferlinghetti)

Civil Liberties. American Civil Liberties Union, 156 Fifth Ave., New York, N.Y. 10010. Monthly. 5 cents per issue. (National organ of the ACLU, important for news and symposia on free speech, police malpractice, and minority rights)

Con safos. P.O. Box 31004, Los Angeles, Calif. 90031. Quarterly. $2. (A new vehicle for Mexican-American art, literature, and opinion)

Freedomways. 799 Broadway, New York, N.Y. 10003. Quarterly. $3.50. ("A review of the freedom movement")

Great Speckled Bird. Atlanta Cooperative News Project, Inc., 187 14th St., N.E., Atlanta, Ga. 30309. Weekly. $6. (The Deep South's lone "underground" voice, not yet listed in the *Dustbooks Directory*)

El Grito. Quinto Sol Publications, 2214 Durant, Suite 2, Berkeley, Calif. 94704. Quarterly. $4. ("A journal of contemporary Mexican-American thought," the emphasis "about equally divided between fiction, poetry, and social commentary")

Guardian. 197 East 4th St., New York, N.Y. 10009. Weekly. $7. (A 20-page tabloid "dedicated to the principle that the capitalist system which governs the United States and exploits the world must be dismantled and replaced by a socialist model . . .")

Independent Socialist. P.O. Box 910, Berkeley, Calif. 94701. Monthly. $1.

(News and analysis from the perspective of the Independent Socialist Clubs of America, a prime force in the creation of Peace-and-Freedom parties)

Intercontinental Press. P.O. Box 635, Madison Square Station, New York, N.Y. 10010. 26 issues per year. $7.50. (Specializing in "political analysis and interpretation of events of particular interest to the labor, socialist, colonial independence and black liberation movements"; each 24-page number represents a global kaleidoscope of radical activity—and the often savage repression it evokes.)

Journal of Black Poetry. 1308 Masonic Avenue (No. 4), San Francisco, Calif. 94117. Quarterly. $3.80. (Le-Roi Jones, Larry Neal, and Clarence Major are contributing editors)

The Kudzu. Box 22502, Jackson, Miss. 39205. $2.50 for 18 issues. ("Put out by the Miss. Student News Project, it hopes to appeal mainly to Miss. whites who want change here toward freedom and peace")

El Lado. 1306 N. Western Avenue, Chicago, Ill. 60622. Bimonthly. $5. (A Midwestern equivalent of *La Raza* and *El Papel*)

Liberation. 5 Beekman St., New York, N.Y. 10038. Monthly. $7. (Founded by the late A. J. Muste and currently edited by Dave Dellinger)

Los Angeles Free Press. 7813 Beverly Blvd., Los Angeles, Calif. 90036. Weekly. $5. (Art Kunkin edits; Ron Cobb and Ed Badajos draw devastating cartoons; Nat Freedland, Lawrence Lipton, and KPFK-broadcaster Frank Greenwood contribute distinctive columns)

The Magdalene Syndrome Gazette. 946 Orient St., Chico, Calif. 94117. Irreg. Free. (Mainly "brash, youthful, alive, and singing" verse in a "100%, undeodorized, no-blush American" idiom.)

El Malcriado. P.O. Box 130, Delano, Calif. 62315. Biweekly. $3.50. (Organ of the United Farm Workers Organizing Committee, AFL–CIO, now conducting a nation-wide boycott of California grapes. Available in both Spanish- and English-language editions)

Mississippi Newsletter. Freedom Information Service, Box 120, Tougaloo, Miss. 39174. Biweekly. $3. (A mimeographed six-to-eight-page paper. According to I. F. Stone, "one of the best grassroots publications to come across our desk")

Modern Utopian. 2441 Le Conte, Berkeley, Calif. 94709. Bimonthly. $4.

Movement. 330 Grove St., San Francisco, Calif. 94102. Monthly. $2. (A newspaper, national in scope, geared to young activists, black and white alike)

New Left Notes. Room 206, 1608 West Madison St., Chicago, Ill. 60612. Weekly. $10. (The much-quoted tabloid issued by Students for a Democratic Society)

News from Nowhere. 424½ First St., DeKalb, Ill. 60115. Monthly. $1.80. (Published by the Dekalb Peace and Freedom Party and intended as a catalyst for community action and dialogue, the maiden issue featured moving first-hand reports by Chicago war-protesters and notes on a new "black history" course at NIU)

News Notes. Central Committee for Conscientious Objectors, 2016 Walnut St., Philadelphia, Pa. 19103. Bimonthly. Free. (The Committee also publishes a $1 *Handbook for Conscientious Objectors,* now in its 9th ed.)

Open Skull. Open Skull Press, 1379 Masonic Ave., San Francisco, Calif. 94117. Irregular. $1 per issue. (Lively, free-wheeling correspondence between offbeat philosopher/bard/rebels like Dan Georgakas, Eric Oatman, Bukowski, and editor Doug Blazek)

Our Generation. 3837 St.-Laurent Blvd., Montreal 18, Canada. $5. ("Largest circulation quarterly of dissent in Canada and of the New Left in North America")

El Papel. P.O. Box 7167, Albuquerque, N.M. 87104. (The most authoritative source for news of the Alianza Federal de Mercedes, captained by fiery Reies Tijerina, and the revolt—or re-awakening—it has spawned among Chicanos throughout the Southwest)

Paper Tiger. 39 E. Springfield St., Boston, Mass. 02118. ("Monthly publication of the adult new left")

Radical America. c/o Paul Buhle, 1237 Spaight, Madison, Wis. 53703. Bimonthly. $3. ("Well reflects the spirit, strategy, and tactics of the angry young militants . . . hell-bent on turning society inside-out.")

Radical's Digest. 516 Fifth Ave., New York, N.Y. 10036. Monthly. $5. (Editor Joe Dubovy scours nearly 200 "movement periodicals" for "significant" material to reprint, condense, or synthesize. Among the sources are gutsy, "troublemaking," tell-it-like-it-is publications such as *Now,* bulletin of the National Welfare Rights Organization, *Basta,* a "Lower East Side newspaper," *Campus Underground* [401½ Main St., Cedar Falls, Iowa], "serving the campus community in the mid-West, and throughout the country," the Progressive Labor Party's *Challenge,* and *DRUM Newsletter,* issued by the Dodge Revolutionary Union Movement, an organization of Black workers at the Hamtramck assembly plant of the Chrysler Corp.")

Ramparts. 495 Beach St., San Francisco, Calif. 94133. Monthly. $8.50. (The nation's foremost muckraker, numbering Robert Scheer, Donald Duncan, Jean Lacouture, Carl Oglesby, Jack Newfield, and Noam Chomsky among its writer-editors)

La Raza. P.O. Box 31004, Los Angeles, Calif. 90031. Biweekly. $2.50. ("There is a new determination and a new spirit in the Mexican American Community, a mood of change for improvement, and *La Raza* intends to be here whenever it happens")

Realist. 595 Broadway, New York, N.Y. 10012. Monthly. $3. (Founder-editor Paul Krassner does most of the writing, but other contributors range from Terry Southern and Norman Mailer to Dr. Albert Ellis and Ed Fisher)

Salted Feathers. c/o Dick Bakken, 3206 N.E. 12th Ave., Portland, Ore. 97212. Irregular. $5. (First-rate poetry, interviews, drawings, and photos. Upcoming number will be "a large 200-page special double issue . . . entitled *Ginsberg/Portland,*" containing previously unpublished poems and all the lectures Ginsberg delivered during a controversial one-week visit to Portland last spring)

San Francisco Earthquake. City Lights Books, 261 Columbus Ave., San Francisco, Calif. 94133. Quarterly. $4. (A cornucopia of ultra-modern poetry, fiction, and graphics)

San Francisco Express-Times. 15 Lafayette St., San Francisco, Calif. 94103.

Weekly. $6. (Editor Marvin Garson, once a Free Speech activist, emphasizes social and political themes)

Soulbook. P.O. Box 1097, Berkeley, Calif. 94701. Quarterly. $3. (An instrument of the "Black Renaissance")

Southern Patriot. Southern Conference Educational Fund, 3210 W. Broadway, Louisville, Ky. 40211. Monthly. $3. (A leading voice of dissent from the South)

Union Democracy in Action. 31 Union Square, New York, N.Y. 10003. Monthly. $3. (A four-page wholly independent newsletter)

Village Voice. Sheridan Square, New York, N.Y. 10014. Weekly. $5. (Precursor of today's "underground press" and still notable for topical comment as well as fine art, movie, and theater criticism. Nat Hentoff, David McReynolds, and Jules Feiffer appear regularly)

Vocations for Social Change. Monthly. Donations. 2010 B Street, Hayward, Calif. 94541. Free. (A unique employment directory that "seeks to encourage Americans to choose life-styles and jobs which represent an effort to stimulate basic changes in the institutional framework in order to foster greater democracy, individual freedom, social and economic justice, and world peace." Categories include Community Organizing, Co-ops, Schools and Colleges, Press, Peace and the Draft, and Arts)

WIN Magazine. War Resisters League, 5 Beekman St., New York, N.Y. 10038. Semi-monthly. $5. ("Radical-pacifist," edited by Jim Peck, one of the earliest Freedom Riders)

Young Socialist. P.O. Box 471, Cooper Station, New York, N.Y. 10003. Bi-monthly. $1.25 (Organ of the Young Socialist Alliance, youth wing of the Trotskyist Socialist Workers Party. Excellent for treatment of the current tumult in France)

19 *Where It's Also At*

(MAY 1, 1969)

by HENRY P. DURKIN

Sanford Berman's article on how to "enrich" library periodical collections was unashamedly biased in favor of the left. I am grateful for the opportunity to correct a one-sided presentation by recommending publications of the responsible right in America.

Unlike Mr. Berman, however, I see nothing to be gained in publicizing a paper or magazine which specializes in four-letter words, preaches racial or religious hatred, or expounds totalitarian propaganda. I do not choose to write about such periodicals because to do so would only give them a respect and recognition they do not deserve. It is far better that the lunatic fringe of bigots be ignored.

Clearly, though, there should be no censorship of such materials—by a librarian or anyone else. The First Amendment protects freedom of speech for all, even bigots. The foundation of our democratic heritage demands that a wide variety of belief and unbelief be represented in our society. Only by having access to all shades of opinion will it be possible to engage in the meaningful dialogue we all desire, and achieve what Ernst Angst calls "the viable society."

As a conservative, I can never argue for censorship, only for good judgment. And good judgment demands a fair representation of viewpoints.

Before presenting my list of conservative publications, I must correct Mr. Berman's statement that the right wing does not have dynamic nor numerous spokesmen and periodicals. Well over a thousand papers and magazines can be called "right wing," but whether they can also be called conservative is another matter. Equally, there must be a distinction made about left-wing called liberal.

Fundamentally, conservatives believe in the principles of democracy and freedom, just as liberals do. The disagreement is only about the means of achieving the full implementation of these desirable goals.

Having read at one time or another most of the periodicals Mr. Berman recommends, it is quite refreshing to turn to a conservative newspaper or magazine and find good grammar, literate commentary on political and social issues, and honest opinions about what can be done to make our society a better place for all people.

In order to maintain the fair balance of politically-oriented journals in libraries, consider several or all of the following:

America's Future. 642 Main St., New Rochelle, N.Y. 10802. Weekly. $5, but free to libraries and educational institutions. (A review of news, books, and public affairs, supporting the belief in the freedom of the individual.)

Battle Line. 328 Pennsylvania Ave., S.E., Washington, D.C. 20003. Monthly. $10. (Official publication of the American Conservative Union, devoted to interpreting the events in the nation's capital.)

Christian Economics. 3030 West 6th St., Los Angeles, Calif. 90005. Bi-weekly. $3. (Editorial policy upholds the free market economy and proposes application of Christian principles to all economic activities.)

Combat. Box 182, Murray Hill Station, New York, N.Y. 10016. Bi-weekly. $24. (Newsletter analyzing totalitarian groups. Contains valuable information about the revolutionary struggle of today.)

The Freeman. Irvington-on-Hudson, N.Y. 10533. Monthly. $5. (Champions individual freedom through limited government.)

Human Events. 422 First St., S.E., Washington, D.C. 20003. Weekly. $12.50. (Contains three regular features: "This Week in Washington," "Capital Briefs," and "Spotlight on Congress." Also carries feature articles and a wide array of conservative columnists. Publishes bound and indexed annual volumes.)

Insight on the News. Box 581, Coral Gables, Fla. 33134. Bi-weekly. $5. (Just what the name suggests: a look behind the issues and the men who shape them.)

Jewish Press. 2427 Surf Ave., Brooklyn, N.Y. Weekly. $7.50. (America's largest circulation Anglo-Jewish weekly. Has excellent coverage of socio-political issues and penetrating commentary by Associate Editor Meir Kahane.)

Latin American Report. 301 Langford Building, 121 S.E. First St., Miami, Fla. 33131. Monthly. $10. (Authoritative news digest on the political climate south of the border, as it affects the United States. Published by the highly respected Citizens Committee for a Free Cuba.)

The Manion Forum. St. Joseph Bank Building, South Bend, Ind. Weekly. $5. (Transcripts of broadcasts by Clarence Manion, former dean of Notre Dame University Law School. Each issue is devoted to a single topic or guest interview.)

Modern Age. 154 East Superior St., Chicago, Ill. 60611. Quarterly. $4. (An erudite journal favoring the intellectual conservative viewpoint. Focuses on the evils of depersonalization in what it calls a "welfare-oriented" society.)

National Review. 150 East 35 St., New York, N.Y. 10016. Bi-weekly. $10. (Perhaps the leading journal of conservative thought in America today. Edited by William F. Buckley Jr., ably assisted by James Burnham, M. Stanton Evans, Ralph deToledano, John Chamberlain, William F. Rickenbacker, Henry Hazlitt, and other distinguished commentators.)

National Review Bulletin. 150 East 35 St., New York, N.Y. 10016. Bi-weekly, alternates with *National Review* magazine. $7. (A tightly-written eight-page newsletter of fact and opinion.)

The New Guard. 1221 Massachusetts Ave., N.W., Washington, D.C. 20005. Monthly. $4. (Organ of Young Americans for Freedom, the nation's largest conservative youth organization. Detailed coverage of YAF activities, feature articles on foreign and domestic issues, humor and how-to-do-it columns, and an excellent "Report on the Left.")

New Individualist Review. Ida Noyes Hall, University of Chicago, Chicago, Ill. 60637. Quarterly. $3. (Bills itself as "a journal of classical liberal thought," i.e. libertarianism.)

Rally. Box 1028, Larchmont, N.Y. 10538. (A bright, handsomely produced monthly journal, written and edited by young conservatives. Although it was only published for a year and a half, it acquired a solid reputation for wit and audacity, balanced by thoughtful and well-informed articles. A limited number of all 18 issues are available from the publisher: $17, loose; $22, bound and indexed.)

Religion and Society. Box 56, Bayport, Minn. Bi-monthly. $5. (Deals with the application of Christianity to moral and social problems.)

Tactics. Box 3541, Arlington, Va. 22203. Monthly. $10. (Designed for the informed person who seeks to use his influence to help maintain and expand America's freedoms.)

The Top of the News. Sheraton Park Hotel, Washington, D.C. 20008. Weekly. $15. (Reprint of radio commentary by Fulton Lewis III. Often ahead of the daily press in reporting trends in national politics.)

Triumph. 927 Fifteenth St., N.W., Washington, D.C. 20005. Monthly. $7.50 (Independent Catholic publication, providing well-thought-out commentary by editor L. Brent Rozell and feature articles on controversial Church-State developments.)

The Wanderer. 128 East 10 St., St. Paul, Minn. Weekly. $7. (Contains news briefs, syndicated columnists, special features. Coverage ranges from the teen scene to Medicare, and then some.)

Washington Report. 123 North Wacker Dr., Chicago, Ill. 60606. Weekly. $12. (Reports on policies affecting national security, as seen by the staff of the American Security Council.)

Westwood Village Square. Box 24904, West Los Angeles, Calif. 90024. Quarterly. $3. (Politics à la hippie, if you will. But without four-letter words or rhapsodies to Che, Ho, Mao and the rest. Pop, op, and mod artwork galore, groovy articles and free posters in each issue. Pow!)

CHAPTER

20 *Controversy on Film*

(FEBRUARY 1, 1963)

by GEORGE HOLLOWAY

The composite film review of *Operation Abolition* which appeared in the *ALA Bulletin* (May 1961, pp. 424–5) was compiled from the
comments of five members of the Booklist Film Review Subcommittee of the
ALA Audio-Visual Committee. It was an unfavorable review, rejecting the
film for public libraries.

I first became aware of this controversial film six months earlier, in
November 1960, at the same time that I was introduced to Dr. Fred Schwartz
and his Christian Anti-Communist Crusade. His school held in Philadelphia
that month drew attention to this film, and a list of anti-communism films was
given to me with a special note that *Operation Abolition* be seriously considered for our collection.

Quite a few Free Library of Philadelphia staff members, including the
director, Mr. Greenaway, and some of his Advisory Council, previewed it in
the Film Department, and its implications were recognized.

The pros and cons began to appear in the press, so in self-defense and to
allow time to investigate its validity (no credits appear on the film), I put the
film up for the Booklist Film Review Committee's consideration. The final
review did not appear in the *Booklist* but in the *ALA Bulletin* because the
Booklist accepts only reviews of recommended items.

Since that time, the film department file on anti-communism films at the
Free Library of Philadelphia has grown to two inches thick. We had one title
from the Christian Anti-Communist Crusade's list (*Nightmare in Red*) before

the *Operation Abolition* furor, and subsequently bought another (*Revolt in Hungary*).

In the *ALA Bulletin* review we stated: " . . . perhaps these few excellent scenes will appear later in a more objective and impartial documentary report of student rioting and Communist activity in the United States." Now a film has appeared that purports to be just that.

It is called *Autopsy on Operation Abolition*. It was produced by Impact Films, which is the film division of the Catechetical Guild of St. Paul, Minnesota. The Guild publishes teaching materials for Catholic schools and has distributed what is called "responsible anti-communism" literature. The narrator of this film is Father Louis Twomey, S.J., of Loyola University. In his introduction he says that the film might better be called an inquest on *Operation Abolition*. The film consists of interviews with 12 persons concerned with the San Francisco riots in May 1960, most of whom were present sometime during the hearings and some of whom were seen in the original film.

Clips from the original *Operation Abolition* film were interspersed with these later interviews, analyzing the events that took place back in May 1960. For example, in one such clip from the House Committee on Un-American Activities film, State Assemblyman O'Connell is shown addressing the students in Union Square, San Francisco. This is followed by an interview with Mr. O'Connell in his office, where he reflects on what occurred that Black Friday. This goes on for an hour.

The opinion of those who previewed *Autopsy* at the Free Library was that, without the original *Operation Abolition*, it had little meaning. The American Civil Liberties Union representative who attended our preview thought it impartial and hoped we would buy it. The representative and other supporters of the Christian Anti-Communism Crusade felt it decidedly favored the opponents of *Operation Abolition*, or the liberal viewpoint.

I felt the narrator gave the impression of being unbiased, but the spokesmen selected for the liberal viewpoint came across better than those for the conservative side. At least both sides were recognized in this film. Still, it did very little to help me decide who was in the right. As Father Twomey put it: "It is uncertain who the real victims are—who are the good guys and who are the bad guys." Communists are quick to support and join in the civil liberties and civil rights pronouncements of reputable groups, thus lending coloration which is confusing to liberals and conservatives alike.

Now we come to a third film, *Operation Correction*, produced by the ACLU of Northern California to refute the implication made by the original film (*Operation Abolition*) that all opposition to the House Committee on Un-American Activities is communist inspired, and to point out errors in the arrangement of filmed sequences. The former point is by far the most important. This is the proposition that is the most difficult to prove or disprove.

Several of us previewed *Operation Correction* at a meeting sponsored by the Philadelphia Chapter of ACLU. The majority of the ACLU members, after its screening, thought the film did not present their side to the best advantage and resorted to much the same type of propaganda pitch as was present in the original film. Also, the need to have the original seen was recognized. Even to those who had seen the original film, *Operation Correction* was still confusing.

A list of special criteria to consider in film selection follows this article. It was extracted from the first and second editions of the *Book Selection Policies* of the Enoch Pratt Free Library and from the ALA *Booklist* criteria and suggestions for film reviews.

Using these criteria, I feel we can justify rejection of the first film certainly, and also the last (i.e. *Operation Abolition* and *Operation Correction*). Possibly we can also reject the second—*Autopsy on Operation Abolition*—since it relies so much on the original. Of particular relevance in the criteria are the phrases: "films which are little more than propaganda for special interest groups are not acquired," and "film content must be valid, true to fact . . . should contain no half truths nor generalizations." Remember that these are criteria for *public library* film collections—not special or university libraries.

I noticed that the Yeshiva University *Film Library Newsletter*, December 1961, listed *Operation Abolition* with the following note: "This film is being made available to schools and universities for study and analysis purposes only. All requests should be made in writing on official stationery, indicating the purpose for showing it and the audience to whom it is to be shown. A bibliography of suggested readings or a background for utilization of the film is available."

Fortunately we do not have to go through the extensive investigation outlined in this article for every title and subject we add to our film collection at the Free Library of Philadelphia. But it is a beneficial exercise to do it once or twice, if only to test our selection policy.

I want to emphasize one more point from the list of special criteria below. This is the emotional impact and persuasive power of the film medium. A Roper survey found that we are most inclined to believe what we see on television. Next most believable medium is the newspaper, then radio, and last, magazines. More people believe what they see and hear than what they read. The public library, in making available the products of the film medium for group use, has a definite responsibility to provide only filmed material concerning which the truth is evident beyond any shadow of a doubt.

SPECIAL CRITERIA TO CONSIDER
IN FILM SELECTION

Films, unlike most other library materials, are selected for group use rather than for individuals, not only because of their cost, which usually limits purchase to one print of each title, but because it is felt that films in adult education serve their purpose best when accompanied by group discussion. All films purchased for the Library's collection are 16mm. sound. Emphasis is placed on subjects of community and national significance, particularly in the fields of intercultural relations, international understanding and significant social problems which lend themselves to group discussion. Outstanding documentaries, subjects of general adult interest, both cultural and practical, examples of experimental techniques of film making, and productions which stimulate the creative imagination of children are also included. No attempt is made to build up an archival collection, but films which represent the history and development of the motion picture and which lead to an understanding and appreciation of this medium as an art form may be purchased.

Films produced primarily for classroom use are not included since, like other teaching materials, they are the responsibility of the schools. Highly technical material is rejected as being more suitable for a university or specialized collection. Teacher training materials are purchased only if they are suitable for wider community use. Industrial training films for a specific technique are not purchased, but general supervisory training films as well as vocational guidance films on an adult level are considered. How-to-do-it materials on hobbies and sports of wide interest are occasionally purchased.

The Library's policy of accepting sponsored films on loan or deposit is similar to its policy regarding gift materials. Sponsored films which are little more than advertisements of commercial products or propaganda for special interest groups are not acquired.

The ALA *Booklist* criteria and suggestions for film reviews remind us that the same general principles as used in the selection of other materials are used in the evaluation of films. But some special considerations are needed due to the powerful impact of visual and audio presentation. The emotional impact and persuasive powers of this medium have been found to be much greater than those of printed materials, and a film reaches large numbers of people whom the library staff never sees and with whom, therefore, direct contact is not possible. For these reasons and because films are so expensive and cannot be skimmed, the Films Department staff, together with experts both from other departments of the Library and from other agencies in the community, preview each film that is being considered for acquisition.

The following criteria are used as guides: the importance of the content of the film to the Library's objectives and the effectiveness of its presentation; the superiority of the film medium in the particular case under consideration over other media of communication; the type of group for which it is adapted; and easy, inexpensive availability of the film from other sources. More explicitly, the film content must be valid, true to fact, true to life, true to text (if based on writing). It should contain no half truths nor generalizations. Subject matter should be of lasting value or timely importance. It should be presented in a manner suited to its content, with no condescension, no loaded words, avoiding cheapness, preachiness and coy humor. The film is an art form and should be judged for its style, imagination, originality and other aesthetic qualities in much the same manner as books. A film should have these technical qualities: imaginative photography, sense of movement and change; good clear understandable sound; imaginative narration.

21 *The Practical Record Selector: A "Plaine and Easie" Introduction*

(MAY 1, 1963)

by GORDON STEVENSON

POLYMATHES: *Stay, brother Philomathes, what haste? Whither go you so fast?*

PHILOMATHES: *To seek out an old friend of mine.*

POLYMATHES: *But before you go I pray you repeat some of the discourses which you had yesternight at Master Sophobulus his banquet, for commonly he is not without both wise and learned guests.*

PHILOMATHES: *It is true indeed, and yesternight there were a number of excellent scholars, both gentlemen and others, but all the propose (i.e. subject) which then was discoursed upon was music.*

POLYMATHES: *I trust you were contented to suffer others to speak of that matter.*

PHILOMATHES: *I would that had been the worst, for I was compelled to discover mine own ignorance and confess that I knew nothing at all in it . . . Upon shame of mine ignorance I go now to seek out mine old friend to make myself his scholar.*

And so it was that in London, in 1597, Philomathes, bent on the acquisition of knowledge, set out to find a "master" and make of himself a scholar. This dialogue is from *A Plaine and Easie Introduction to Practicall Musicke*, by a certain Thomas Morley ("Batcheler of musick, & one of the gent. of hir Majesties Royall Chappell")—a book that is neither plain, nor easy, but which is eminently practical.

Like many people today, Philomathes knows nothing about music, and he is the first to admit it. The thing that reminds us that this took place in 1597 and not 1963, is that today Philomathes would not seek out a master, but would go to his public library in search of enlightenment. Once at the library, our friend would in all probability find a collection of phonograph records. How well this collection would serve his needs, would depend, of course, on what his needs are, and which of these needs the library has decided to serve as a matter of policy.

We now have Philomathes in the library. He finds his way to the record collection and, curious fellow that he is, he quickly strikes up a conversation with the librarian:

PHILOMATHES: *In selecting records, where do you begin?*

LIBRARIAN: *With knowledge, of course. And with my own great love of great music. We never buy anything but the very greatest of music, and this played only by the greatest musicians.*

PHILOMATHES: *Oh? But specifically, where do you begin?*

LIBRARIAN: *Well, in the beginning was and still is "Schwann."*

PHILOMATHES: *Swan? What is this swan of which you speak?*

LIBRARIAN: *No, no, no. It's "Schwann," not swan. It's a list of the 30,000 LP records that are currently available. I hesitate to think what life would be like without swan. I mean "Schwann." Now you have me doing it.*

PHILOMATHES: *But what about all those books about music I see on your shelves. I see there are books by men like Reese, Bukofzer, Lang, and many great scholars in music. Do these help in record selection?*

LIBRARIAN: *No, those books are about music, not about records. Besides, I avoid them like the plague. Music is to be listened to, not read about, and I have an ear for music. I also took piano lessons when I was in the fifth grade.*

PHILOMATHES: *Yes, but how do you decide what records to buy?*

LIBRARIAN: *I buy recordings of "good" music. Why don't you go away?*

PHILOMATHES: *But how do you know what is "good"? And for whom is it good?*

LIBRARIAN: *Everybody knows what good music is. It is great music, and I'm beginning to get bored with you.*

PHILOMATHES: *But how do you . . . Oh well, it's obvious I'm getting nowhere; so just give me a recording of Leadbelly's "Last Session" and I'll be on my way.*

LIBRARIAN: *Leadbelly! Are you a nut or something? Where do you think you are? This is a library, my friend, not the Ethnomusicological Archives.*

PHILOMATHES: *But isn't your motto "The right book for the right person at the right time," or something like that? And what's the difference if it's a book or a record?*

LIBRARIAN: *You can have whatever book you want, right or wrong; but you, my friend, are in the Record Department, and I decide what is good and what is not good for you when it comes to music. You might think that this fellow Leadbelly is important, but I know better. Now, how about this recording of the Budapest String Quartet playing the Beethoven Opus 135?*

So Philomathes leaves the Record Department a little frustrated, since he did not get what he wanted, and no one gave him a good reason why.

Giving people what they want may not be your idea of record selection, but I am convinced that a public library record collection is for all of its patrons, not just some of them; and that all or most of them should get something of what they want (obviously, all of them will not get everything they want). And along with what they want, you can give them quite a bit of what they should want, what you would like them to want, and what would make our musical culture better if they did want.

To this end, the following suggestions are designed to be plain, easy and practical. They deal only with recordings of music, for nonmusic records are another matter. Music specialists will be annoyed at some of these ideas; but I hope they will offer some comfort to the nonspecialist.

We talk about record collections as if they had little connection with other library services. Record services should originate and grow as part of a program of music services. There are many serious and challenging aspects of our musical culture in which the library can play an important role, and in some of these, records are of little value. Get a picture of the total musical life of your community, set up goals, *then* see where records fit into your plans.

The practical selector realizes that music, like the library itself, means many things to many people; and it behooves him to give his public credit for knowing what they like and what they don't like—for they are in somewhat of a better position to know what music means to them than he is. All of his patrons may not like the kind of music he would prefer them to like, but if in the music of their choice, people find esthetic satisfaction, relaxation, peace or amusement, then this music (regardless of where it originates or what we call it) is not without a certain nobility of purpose.

This is not to say that the librarian will not try to educate his patrons; but he should begin by finding out what music means to them and why. Lifetime listening habits are not easily changed; yet library record borrowers are generally a foolhardy lot, and will give almost anything at least one hearing.

Coordinating records with books, and people. When you provide books about music for your patrons see that they have records to go with the books. Machlis' *The Enjoyment of Music,* Grout's *A History of Western Music,* J. T. Howard's *Modern Music,* B. H. Haggin's *Music for the Man Who Enjoys Hamlet,* and the like, not to mention books on biography, folk music and jazz, gain real meaning when used with recordings of the music discussed. For every book about music, there are a dozen phonograph records that will enhance the significance of the book for the reader—try to get the three of them together: the patron, the book and the record.

The "Comparison Game." In the major reviewing media this game has reached the point of absurdity. Practically all judgments are subjective, seldom are historical or musicological criteria used. This game is too expensive for the library. Concentrate on building a collection of *music,* not a collection of performances or interpretations. Don't even try to keep up with the latest darling of the opera stage or lion of the keyboard. The most important and basic function of your classic record collection will be served equally well by the Toscanini, the Reiner, the Walter, or any of the other umpteen versions of Beethoven's "Eroica" symphony.

The Standard Repertory. The S.R. is something you have to live with, so you should find out what it is and how it got that way (see Mueller's *The American Symphony Orchestra*). The S.R. was formed under circumstances that were quite different from those that prevail in our society today, yet it remains as firmly entrenched as ever. The miracle of the LP record should have made the concept obsolete, but it didn't. For many, the S.R. is the only excuse for having a record collection, for others it is a strangling, suffocating force that prevents the collection from functioning as a vital educational media and a forum for important and timely issues. You must work both with S.R. and against it. If you include nothing but S.R. titles, you won't have room for anything else—and it is this "anything else" that gives the collection vitality and one of the basic justifications for existence. If your collection is big enough (around 2,000 titles) you can see that S.R. items are well represented and still have room to do a lot of imaginative things. Smaller collections are advised to include a continually changing selection of S.R. titles, not attempting to be comprehensive. The S.R. includes practically nothing written before 1750, and very little written after 1900, and only comparatively little in between. This is a rather severe limitation to place on the collection.

Background reading for the selector. Keep an eye out for books that discuss music in the context of our society. Books like Jacques Barzun's *Music in American Life,* Cecil Smith's *Worlds of Music,* Paul S. Carpenter's *Music, an Art and a Business,* Virgil Thomson's *The State of Music,* and Lang's *One Hundred Years of Music in America;* and articles like Mueller's "The Social Nature of Musical Taste" (*Journal of Research in Music Education,* Vol. IV, No. 2), and Charles Rosen's "The Proper Study of Music" (*Perspectives of New Music,* Fall, 1962)—in other words, material that deals with music, not as an art form, but as a product of our society.

Other background reading. If you read nothing but record-reviewing magazines you will get a very distorted idea of what is going on in music in this country. Minimum monthly browsing in the "serious" field are *Musical America* and the *Music Journal* (the "Current Chronicle" of the *Musical Quarterly* is excellent but very technical). If you have the interest and inclination, there are a lot more music magazines on every conceivable musical subject, from *Accordion World* to Unesco's *World of Music,* many of which should help sharpen your awareness of important issues and developments in the field of music that may influence your record selection policies.

Contemporary "serious" music. A total collection of around 1,000 titles should include at least 50 recordings by contemporary U.S. composers. Don't try to keep a "standard" group of contemporaries in the catalog, there is simply too much good material available to choose from. When a record is discarded, replace it with a new title by the same composer, or a title by a composer new to your collection. Many record reviewers seem utterly incapable of adequately evaluating contemporary music—so don't place too much faith in what the reviewers say about it. Two outstanding exceptions are Alfred Frankenstein

(*High Fidelity*) and William Flanagan (*Hi Fi/Stereo Review*). Arthur Cohn's *The Collector's 20th-Century Music* (Lippincott, 1961) is a most useful guide.

The local scene. Coordinate some of your purchases with local concerts, if there are any; and tie them in with your collection through displays and record lists.

When you find a good cause, support it. When recording companies do attempt to bring out titles that are of a significant cultural value, but offer little chance of commercial success, go out of your way to find out if you can use the material (e.g. Decca's recordings of the New York Pro Musica ensemble, the Yale Poet series, the Record Hunter's M.G.M. reprint series, to mention only three of dozens of notable adventures in culture).

Watch those small labels. The small record producer plays an indispensable role in bringing out music that would otherwise be lost to the record-listening public. Idealistic, bold, and imaginative, the catalogs of these small producers deserve your careful attention.

The "well-rounded" collection. Some convincing arguments have been marshaled to show why the well-rounded book collection is not practical. Records are different. Music is a virtually unknown world to the layman. Only a well-rounded collection will give him room to move around in and permit him to discover the many forms that music has taken and the various roles it plays in the lives of men.

Double check. Check your holdings from a number of different angles. Consider it historically: are major styles and periods represented? Are all important forms represented? Are various instrumental and vocal media represented? For information on these matters, turn to the books on your shelves, books like Alec Harman's *Man and His Music*, Peter Garvie's *Music and Western Man*, Peter Hansen's *Twentieth Century Music*, and specialized books like Alec Robertson's *Chamber Music*. Don't specialize in performers: build up a variety of conductors, orchestras, singers and instrumentalists.

There is more, but this will do for a start. Oh yes, if somebody named Philomathes stops in and requests something you don't have, you might consider his request very seriously as a possible purchase.

22 *Programed Materials*

(MAY 15, 1963)

by THEODORE C. HINES

The teaching machine approach to learning has made a great stir in education since 1959. Just now the dust is beginning to clear. It is suddenly possible to see that the library implications are perhaps different from those originally supposed, and much more immediately important. But background first, conclusions afterward.

The basic concept behind the teaching machine is that of programed instruction. The machine presents a carefully constructed series of learning steps—the program—to the user who is required to react to each step as it is presented. The user then has his learning "reinforced" when the program immediately tells him whether or not his reaction is correct.

Unlike a textbook, a program of this kind requires constant active participation from the user. Unlike a textbook, too, it gives him constant checks on his own progress. If he sticks to the rules and if the program is properly written, the user must understand each section before he goes on successfully to the next.

The teaching machine itself is simply a mechanical device designed to present such a program to the user. About a year ago, there were 24 different machines in full-scale production, 21 more in limited production and 35 others in various stages of development. With very few exceptions, a program produced for one machine cannot be used on another.

There are good reasons for the variety of designs among teaching machines, although it seems hard to justify quite so many different designs. For large scale school use, the problems caused by this multiplicity of mechanical devices are not really serious ones. In library situations, however, the problems resemble those which would arise if every make of phonograph record were different in shape, size and speed from most of the others—and playing each required a completely different phonograph.

THE LIBRARY AS A SOURCE
OF PROGRAMED MATERIALS

For this reason, the six or so articles which have appeared thus far in library journals about this new phenomenon have approached the library implications of teaching machines quite cautiously. They have explained what the new approach is all about; they have suggested that librarians inform themselves and the public; and they have concluded that we should think about the use of programs and machines. Some have mentioned, in passing, the programed book. Mainly, the function of these articles has been simply to provide background information. Even the reviews of books about teaching machines seem directed chiefly at school librarians and are meant to draw their attention to what classroom teachers are up to, with scarcely any implication that some aspects of programed instruction just might overflow into the library.

Librarians ought to be more concerned than this. The goals of libraries frequently have been summed up as the provision of information, education and recreation. In recent years, librarians have been forced into greater realization of the importance of the informational and educational goals. If education is one of the major functions of libraries, then surely the truly distinctive educational role which libraries can perform is that of helping the reader in individual self-education, whether he needs it for school, work or personal interest. In school and public libraries alike, librarians have supplemented formal classroom education in this way for years.

The programed instruction approach to learning is intended for individual self-instruction. The user can go through the program at his own speed and at times of his own choice. Using a program is a solitary occupation like reading a book, not a group occupation like classroom lectures. The user is neither held back nor harried ahead to keep pace with the rest of the class.

Yet the effect of following a program through is more like that achieved by classroom instruction than it is like trying to learn the same material by oneself from a standard text, especially since most standard texts are intended for use in classroom situations.

In public, school and college libraries alike, then, if the programed instruction technique really works, providing programed materials certainly seems an essential step. This is a method of self-instruction peculiarly adapted to the kind of educational job libraries can do best.

But buying a teaching machine means expanding library services to include a new medium, just as the decisions to accept phonograph records, films and filmstrips did. The evaluation and acceptance of a new medium which requires new devices and new techniques is bound to take time. This is especially true since teaching machine design is not standardized, and since any given machine can accept only a limited number of the available programs.

From the librarian's point of view, it would be most pleasing if there were a device compatible with all or most of the existing programs. It would be valuable, too, if this device were readily portable and hence easily circulated for home use; if it were relatively cheap and required no electrical connections; if it posed no really major problems in the library situation, and required no extensive instruction before use.

As it happens, such a device exists. It is the invention, probably, of a German named Gutenberg, and is called the printed book.

IS THE MACHINE REALLY NECESSARY?

Some of the articles on teaching machines in library journals have mentioned the programed book. There are programs available in book or sheet form which require no machine at all. With some of them, the user must move a slide or mask down the printed page. Others do not even require a device of this simple kind. One major list of 122 programs, including almost all of those supposedly available in September 1962, indicated that 94.3 percent of all programs listed could be purchased in printed form for use without a machine. In fact, this was the only form in which 31.1 percent of these programs were to be available, as compared to 6.6 percent in machine format only.

Does the printed form of program presentation work as well as the machine form? The answer depends largely on the material to be presented, the program and the user. The machine (or some of the machines) can, for example, handle types of programs or information which cannot be printed. They can prevent cheating. They may be so designed as to give the teacher or programer evidence of places in the program where the student has trouble. They may provide an objective record of the length of time a student takes to complete a program, or of which parts of certain types of programs are most useful. For certain uses, the machines may be cheaper than some printed programs. Most of these advantages are of value in the school situation rather than in the library.

In comparison tests of the same program as presented by machine and in book form, eight separate studies show no significant difference between the two forms in mastery of the material by the user.

Buying a teaching machine pushes the library into a new medium. But the printed program has the old familiar form of ink on paper, and what the library must deal with is a new concept, not a new device. If the printed book is an effective way of presenting programed material, and if most programs are now available in printed form, then the need for libraries to do something constructive about programs is immediate.

WHAT PROGRAMED MATERIALS ARE NOW AVAILABLE?

It is hard to say exactly how many of these programed books are actually available because the bibliography of the field is in a particularly messy kind of infancy. One thing is sure: many programed books are available and many more are in progress or being planned.

Three of the major encyclopedia publishers are producing simple machines and/or programed texts for both the home and school markets. TMI-Grolier, first in the field, offers two machine models and a large number of programs in both book and machine form. Encyclopaedia Britannica Press has a large number of programs in what it calls TEMAC form, a special booklike folder with a sliding mask, and apparently has plans to program most of the high school curriculum. Field Enterprises is producing a gamelike device with programs and quizzes on discs (the CycloTeacher) in connection with the World Book.

There are now at least 50 commercial publishers or producers of programs for sale. Thirty-seven of them produce programs in book or sheet form. While many of the producers are new to publishing—and more behave as if they were—there are certainly enough of the great and well-established names. In addition to Encyclopaedia Britannica, Grolier and World Book, these include Addison-Wesley; Appleton; Collier-Macmillan; Doubleday; Harcourt, Brace and World; Holt, Rinehart and Winston; McGraw-Hill; Prentice-Hall; and Wiley. Harcourt, Brace and World alone, for example, is said by one source to have 50 programed texts in progress.

A bibliography issued early in 1962, which included published programs and those projected for publication, listed some 630 items. This figure is probably more indicative of interest than real performance, but it speaks well for the interest. At least one manufacturer (U.S. Industries) is offering a "TutorCenter" to libraries. This is a machine-and-book package, costing in the four-figure range.

It should be clear by now that the nation's educators are becoming more and more deeply involved with programed instruction. The number of schools adopting or experimenting with the method is enormous, still growing, and includes practically every progressive system in the country. Such national awareness will have, is having, an influence on libraries too.

SIX SUGGESTED STEPS FOR LIBRARIES

At this point it seems possible and necessary to draw up a tentative list, in rough priority order, of the steps libraries should take toward understanding and use of programed materials.

1. The size, scope and nature of the programed instruction movement show that it is a major social and educational phenomenon. Librarians need to inform themselves about it, and to provide informative materials for their users.

The beginning of a beginning in this area might well include the following books. A. A. Lumsdaine and Robert Glaser's sourcebook *Teaching Machines and Programmed Learning,* published by the Department of Audio-Visual Instruction of the National Education Association really sums up developments previous to 1960. David Cram's *Explaining Teaching Machines and Programming* (San Francisco, Fearon Publishers, 1961) is a most ingenious paperback. It explains programed instruction by programing it, and illustrates various techniques by using them. Benjamin Fine's *Teaching Machines* (Sterling, 1962) is another good general book, rather more popular in style than William Deterline's excellent *Introduction to Programmed Instruction* (Prentice-Hall, 1962).

These books only scratch the surface, of course. McGraw and Wiley, for example, among many others, have good new titles in preparation, or issued as this is written.

2. The widespread availability of machines and printed materials specifically intended for home use means that libraries should be prepared to assist their users to evaluate them, just as they now provide guidance in the selection of encyclopedias and other materials. Librarians should work for adequate reviewing of programs, which does not now exist. Pending adequate reviewing (and even after), they should apply the same evaluative criteria now applied to book materials. A very good article on the subject, "Evaluating Teaching Machines and Programs" by James G. Holland, may be found in *Teachers College Record* 63:56–70 (October, 1961).

It is also suggested that libraries purchase samples at least of Encyclopaedia Britannica TEMAC materials, TMI-Grolier texts and the World Book's CycloTeacher for examination by users. Larger libraries might also consider purchase of the reasonably priced TMI MinMax I machine for exhibit purposes.

3. Libraries ought to provide, for themselves and their users, the basic lists of programs. The two most indispensable are James D. Finn and Donald G. Perrin's *Teaching Machines and Programed Learning; a Survey of the Industry, 1962* and The Center for Programed Instruction's *Programs '62; A Guide to Programed Instructional Materials Available to Educators by September 1962*. Both are available from the Government Printing Office, both 1962 imprints. Finn and Perrin (OE-34019) costs only 55 cents, and includes good background information and much on machines, plus directories of programs, manufacturers and publishers. The directory of programs, however, is so lacking in elementary bibliographic data as to be shocking by any normal standards; still, it provides cues as to what may exist. *Programs '62* is more thorough in this respect, but is full of ghosts and omits programs "which have little or no relevance to the school curriculum." It also omits copyright dates. A new version (*Programs '63*, of course) was published the following year.

The great majority of published programs do not appear in CBI, PW, or BIP. Nor do they have LC numbers. This bibliographic deficiency is probably a major factor in library neglect of programed instruction. Established general publishers are nearly as guilty of the failure to list their materials as machine men.

4. Libraries should provide printed programs (requiring no machine) whenever they meet the needs of the library clientele and if program format makes this feasible. The desire of the general public for good self-instructional materials should not be sold short.

Some programs look like normal books, but others are more erratic from the library viewpoint. Many are paperbound. Many have sliders or come in folders. Others include extra pamphlet material, or are pamphlets themselves. Some are designed to be written in, and it will require experimentation to see if borrowers can refrain from writing in library copies. Some are spiral bound or in loose sheets. Then, too, programed books seem more expensive than more normal books of the same length, because developmental costs for good programs are so high.

But these are all problems that require only the adaptation of existing methods. Besides, it is simple enough to ease into the situation by buying Doubleday TutorTexts to start with—a start many libraries seem to have made without quite realizing that these are programed books. Doubleday *has* had its books listed in conventional sources.

5. Many teachers and industries are doing their own programing. Libraries should consider providing material on *how to program,* either for use by programers, or simply because manuals on programing constitute good explanations of the programing method of instruction even for readers who do not intend to try the technique.

6. Libraries also should consider seriously the use of programed instruction as a method for teaching people *to use libraries.* There has been at least one machine experiment of this kind. At least three commercial programs are being written.

Librarians might consider programing experimentally such materials themselves, possibly in collaboration with experienced programers. Freshman library instruction has been tried in this way at Southern Illinois University.

All of the above suggestions are tentative. None involves machines. None involves unusual expenditures, except perhaps the last. Paradoxically, however, the quantity of material available in reasonably conventional form may lead libraries to serious consideration of machine use earlier than might otherwise have been expected. Libraries using programed books are able to experiment with the concept of programed instruction in the library situation without first committing themselves to mechanical devices.

Finally, libraries should not simply experiment with programed instruction; they should then evaluate the results of their experiments and, when necessary, adapt library procedures to user needs and convenience, in this field as in all others.

CHAPTER

23 *A Plea for Sanity*

(SEPTEMBER 1, 1964)

by DANIEL MELCHER

Educational Media Index. A project of the Educational Media Council. N.Y.: McGraw-Hill, 1964. 14 vols. 64-17810. $62.45, the set; $79.95, with supplements (first supplements to be issued in 1965); prices for individual volumes from publisher.

Fun's fun and a joke's a joke, but when people are asked to marvel over a "great breakthrough in electronic data processing" which turns out to be nothing more than a botched job of shingled varityping, it's time to speak up for sanity.

According to the press releases, the new *Educational Media Index* is "an entirely new approach to index compilation," and "the enormity of the project obviated the traditional bibliographic and graphic arts techniques." The press release goes on to say that the producers "devised a sequential card system which combines graphic arts techniques with an ingenious use of conventional data processing equipment." This looks very impressive, especially when boxed in 14 separate volumes. However, let's take a look behind the gobbledygook. For those unused to the data processing argot, here is a brief glossary of translations of the terms used in the prospectus for *EMI:*

"A mnemonic code of three, four or five characters was assigned to each primary source." *Translation:* Producers' and distributors' names are abbreviated.

"Sources were provided with an effort-saving structured response form." *Translation:* Questionnaires were sent to producers and distributors.

"The editorial work is paralleled by a machine processing effort that translates the worksheets into decks of punched cards." *Translation:* The entries are typed on cards which are then punched for ease of sorting.

"Automated techniques have been devised for extracting from the data base, etc." *Translation:* We sort and photograph the cards.

"The system permits custom searching of the data base—for example, the custom print-out could be made of 1) filmstrips, 2) arranged for teaching French, 3) to adults, 4) released since 1958, and 5) arranged alphabetically, 6) by source translation." *Interpretation:* If it is too much trouble for you simply to open the language volume to the "French Language—Study and Teaching" section (which has only eight filmstrips graded for adults anyway), we will be glad (for a stiff price) to go to our card file and pull out the same entries for you and make a special copy of them. If you want to be sure that all the filmstrips which could be used with adults for the teaching of French are actually found, including those that may have been misclassified in our 14 volumes, we can if you like search our entire files, 500,000 cards. Such a search will, to be sure, be prohibitively expensive—still it is theoretically possible.

One could simply pass with averted gaze over the childish pretense that the composing typewriter coupled with a shingling mechanism and an IBM card sorter constitute "advanced data processing techniques" if it were not for the fact that it was precisely this mumbo-jumbo that misled the earnest and well-intentioned sponsors of the *Educational Media Index* into wasting half a million dollars of the taxpayers' money. The committee was persuaded that the world of the future would never be won with the old-fashioned techniques of Wilson and Bowker and the Library of Congress, and decided instead on "the electronic data processing approach," which was the more interesting inasmuch as it carried with it a grant from the US Office of Education which would permit the committee to employ a full-time executive secretary and open a New York office.

The *Educational Media Index* provides, it is claimed, about 30,000 listings of nonbook instructional materials arranged by subject with title indexes. Most of the listings are for films and filmstrips. Also included are assorted records, phonotapes, charts, maps, models and mock-ups, flat pictures, slides, and programmed instructional materials. Entries give source, year, running time, grade range, price, and brief annotation. Symbols distinguish the various media one from another. The type is an unjustified, sans-serif, varitype face in a two-column arrangement.

The listings are presented under 17 broad subject groupings in 13 separate volumes, each grouping (sometimes two in a volume) with its own internal subject sequence and title index. There is also a 14th volume containing a master title index. The subject headings are said to have been "based on" Sears, although there is very little evidence to support this.

To present the *EMI* as a 14-volume work is rather misleading, since most of the volumes are very slim, one having only 64 pages, and another only 83. Furthermore, the entire set offers hardly more information about films and filmstrips than did the last big (1953) cumulation of the Wilson *Educational Film Guide* (11,000 films) and the 1954 Wilson *Filmstrip Guide* (5,883 strips).

In general, if you have a file of the Wilson *Guides* up until their discontinuation in 1962, cherish them. They contain far more information about films and filmstrips than is to be found in *EMI*, better annotations, a more usable arrangement, and vastly better cross references. For the period since 1962, you will probably depend for information about films less on the *EMI* than upon the EFLA (Educational Film Library Association) ratings, the catalogs of the various film libraries, and the Library of Congress *Catalog of Motion Pictures and Film Strips,* though the *EMI* may have its uses when it comes to spotting phonotapes, models, charts, etc. Another source of information on free instructional materials is the series of publications of the Educators Progress Service. (Why is it that so few libraries subscribe to the LC *Catalog of Motion Pictures and Film Strips?* By last report there were only 84 subscribers beyond the 1300 institutions which have a blanket subscription to all the LC book catalogs. It's only $8 a year.)

It is unfortunate that the *Educational Media Index* is weakest just where its multi-volume breakdown demands most strength, namely in cross-indexing. One of the deciding factors in the decision to go "electronic" was the feeling that audiovisual aids could not adequately be organized by conventional indexing methods. It was stated in committee that whereas few books are entered under more than two or three headings in the average catalog, it might be necessary to enter a multi-faceted film under as many as 20 different headings. It is interesting to note that the automation which was supposed to provide greater depth in subject indexing actually led to a result in which few items are entered more than once!

The sponsors speak of the "unusual difficulties of accommodating 10,000 subject headings and 20,000 subject cross-references." The volume arrangement has compounded these difficulties 17 times, for both editors and users.

The first problem of a prospective user is to decide which volume is likely to contain the information he is seeking. Suppose, for instance, he is interested in cooperative agriculture. If he starts with Volume 9, INDUSTRIAL AND AGRICULTURAL EDUCATION, he will find eight films listed under "Agriculture, Cooperative" and "Agriculture, Cooperative-Virginia." He will also be referred to two other films listed under another subject in Volume 9. But he will not be referred to the listings in Volumes 2, 4, 12, and 13 on this subject. He won't know, without checking each volume, that additional items appear under "Agriculture, Cooperative" in the GEOGRAPHY AND HISTORY volume, in the BUSINESS EDUCATION AND TRAINING volume, in the ECONOMICS AND POLITICAL SCIENCE volume, or in the INTERMEDIATE GRADES 4–6 volume.

If our user is a sixth grade teacher, and looks in the INTERMEDIATE GRADES volume for films on agriculture, he will miss films graded for junior high school which appear in the volumes mentioned—films which might be suitable for his students even though they are one year below junior high school. He will also miss at least ten films graded for kindergarten through sixth grade which appear in the PRE-SCHOOL AND PRIMARY GRADES volume, but which do not appear in the INTERMEDIATE GRADES volume, even though they belong there as well.

Not only are there no cross-references between volumes, but the cross-references within the volumes are unbelievably careless in many places. In

Volume 1, of a sample 56 *see also* references checked, 42 referred to subjects which did not exist! In the same volume, 142 cross-references indicating that a particular title would be found under another subject heading were checked. In 46 cases either the subject didn't exist or the title cross-referenced could not be found under the subject. Sixteen of the titles involved referred to "Reading (Elementary)," which doesn't exist in Volume 1.

Blind references are not limited to the text. They are also to be found in the indexes. Weston Woods Studios is listed in the Directory of Sources, and since many of their titles are recommended by EFLA, these titles were checked in the index to Volume 1. Entries for *Stone Soup, The Story About Ping, Curious George Rides a Bike,* and *Caps for Sale* were all found in the index, with the indication that they were to be found under "Children's Stories." However, not one of these is in fact listed under that heading. *The Five Chinese Brothers* is supposed to be in "Illustrated Books, Children's," a subject section which doesn't exist, and in "Reading," where it isn't listed either.

Besides having cross-references with nothing at the other end, *EMI* lacks cross-references where they are needed. There are no cross-references between "Art" and "Painting" in Volume 2, and no indication under either heading that there are also listings under the individual artists' names. There are no cross-references between "Grain" and "Corn," between "Grain" and "Wheat," between "Flowers" and "Wildflowers," or "Flowers" and "Plants," and there are many more examples.

Another peculiarity is found in the indexing of literary classics. In Volume 1 there are headings for "Stevenson, Robert Louis: Treasure Island" and "Treasure Island: Stevenson, Robert Louis." Under the first are two records, each called *La Isla del Tesoro.* Under the second is a film of *Treasure Island.* There are no cross-references at all between these listings.

Since our estimate of the number of entries in the Master Title Index is only 27,000, as compared to the 30,000 now claimed by the *EMI* sponsors, and the 50,000 claimed earlier, and also because the total falls so far short of the total for the Wilson *Guides,* we did a spot check of the 1964–65 catalog of Coronet Films, a distributor listed in the *EMI*'s Directory of Sources. The first four pages of the Coronet catalog contain 53 film listings. Out of this number, 21 could not be found at all in *EMI*. Eight films were listed in the index, but not in the text of any of the volumes. Two films listed in the Master Title Index as being in Volume 7 were not found there, but turned up instead in Volume 1. Thus, in all, only 32 of the 53 films were found at all, and of these, two were found in a volume other than that indicated by the Master Title Index.

EMI might be forgiven for not listing four of the 21 missing films which Coronet indicates were in production as of March 1, 1964, if the April-June 1964 LC *Catalog* didn't contain three of the four. Every one of the missing films which was issued before 1962 (14 in all) will be found in the Wilson *Educational Film Guide* and its supplements. The remaining six films, issued from 1962–64, will be found in the LC *Catalog.*

According to the press releases, 2400 film sources were identified during the editorial process. Only about 1000, however, appear in the guide to sources. Fifty-two of the first 125 sources listed in the 1962 supplement to the Wilson *Educational Film Guide* do not appear in the *EMI*. Conspicuous absentees include Air France, American Friends Service Committee, H. J. Heinz Co., Coca-Cola, Dartmouth College, and Cornell University, among many others.

A check of the programmed materials listings revealed that here also the *EMI* falls far short of adequate coverage. There are over 250 programmed learning materials listed in the 1964 edition of *Textbooks in Print,* which incidentally was published before *EMI* went to press. A total of 163 programmed learning materials were counted in the indexes of the 13 *EMI* volumes (only 126 could be found in the Master Title Index).

Though the *EMI* volumes are very attractively bound, the man who designed the bindings was apparently not asked to help with the text. There are no running heads at all. Thus, if a user opens the double volume on SCIENCE AND ENGINEERING, he has no running heads to tell him whether he has opened to the Science or the Engineering index or main section. The arrangement of the title indexes is also poor, for want of adequate indention to distinguish the alphabetical title entries and the unalphabetized subject references.

The great effort expended in assigning original mnemonics to the names of the sources might better have been devoted to a study of the way others abbreviate distributors' names. Wilson, for instance, abbreviates American Red Cross as "AmRedCross," while *EMI* designates it "ARC." The Wilson abbreviation is readily recognizable, while the *EMI* system necessitates constant reference to the Directory of Sources for translation.

How is it possible for so much earnest effort to come to so little? No one could fault the proposal to do a first-class guide to audiovisual materials. No one could fault the idea of making government money available, if needed to make this possible. No one could fault the way in which the committee started by bringing together and consulting with those with experience in the field. It is hard to criticize McGraw-Hill for agreeing to sell the Educational Media Council the services it said it wanted, though it was clear that no business-minded publisher, McGraw-Hill or anyone else, would have done this kind of job in this kind of way at his own expense. The fault can only be ascribed to the current credulity about "data processing." (It has gotten so that if you don't give your new project "data processing" overtones, you don't get your grant.)

There are many in the library profession who *know* that the LC *Subject Headings* list wasn't built in a day. The trouble starts when they are asked to check their brains outside the committee room while some brash young machinery salesman who doesn't know the difference between a "see also" and a "refer from" says soothingly, "Now don't worry, just leave everything to our technical men." It makes no difference whether the "data base" of his technology is a simple deck of typed cards or a "sophisticated" computer. He won't be able to get any worthwhile "data processing" out of it without the active help of those who know how "sophisticated" even a good card catalog must be.

24 Music in Medium-Sized Libraries

(MARCH 15, 1965)

by GORDON STEVENSON

"In considering whatever materials and services your library provides for its community in the area of music, how would you describe your current services? Are they adequate, inadequate, or don't you know?"

I suspect that if librarians had been asked this question before they opened their morning mail that day last November when they received our questionnaire, many more of them would have replied rather optimistically. However, by the time they read through the questions, they must have realized that "music services," as implied in the questionnaire, constituted a rather broad coverage of music materials. Some of the questionnaires that escaped the wastepaper basket had these replies: 76 librarians believe their services are inadequate, 61 give themselves a rating of adequate, and 24 do not know how they rate.

One library in New Jersey, serving a metropolitan community of over 50,000 population, has 350 books about music, no records, no printed music, and is providing adequate services. Another library, a West Virginia county library serving a population of over 60,000 has 500 books about music, 5000 records, 1500 pieces of music, and provides inadequate service. These self-evaluatons were made by professional librarians—the first a head librarian, the second a part-time music librarian—who should be qualified to evaluate the adequacy of their work. Obviously, the important question is not whether their services are or are not adequate, but "what constitutes adequate public library music services?"

The answer to this question depends on answers to such questions as these: What public? What music? What type of library? What kind of service? Service to whom? Who decides? How do they decide?

Decisions on the library's role in our musical culture involves us in many thorny problems, some musical, some social, many involving techniques of librarianship, and they all must be solved within the framework of the library's function, aims, and responsibilities. How much thought has gone into these matters, I do not know; but in practice, every public library has found its own working solutions. In some cases this was evident in returned questionnaires with five words written across the top: "We have no music materials." At the other extreme we find, even in many medium-sized communities, working examples of Alfons Ott's suggestion that "the finest and most important function of the popular [i.e. public] library is to provide an enduring and vital rallying-point for the musical public in the broadest sense of the term" (*Music in Education,* Unesco, 1955). Between the two extremes there are several large areas of agreement. These, along with information on current practice, will someday form the basis for the establishment of standards. With this in mind, I report here on a survey of certain aspects of music in a group of public libraries serving communities of between 50,000 and 100,000 population.

This particular group of libraries was chosen because I felt that their problems are typical of those that face the profession as a whole. Few of them are large enough to have music departments or art and music departments; generally they must do with whatever musical knowledge they can muster from present staffs, and the status of music in these libraries is, more often than not, in the hands of a chief administrator who is busy running a library.

The following information was gathered from 174 replies received from a mailing to 310 libraries throughout the United States.

The three basic types of library materials relating to music are the printed word, the printed musical note, and the sound recording. Each has its own unique set of symbols and each is used by the borrower—often by three different borrowers—in a different way and for different reasons. The librarian who collects all three types of material must consult three different sets of selection tools, find three sources for acquisitions, and once he has the material in hand, his problems have just begun, for he is faced with three different physical formats, each of which presents its own problems of processing, cataloging, storing, and handling.

Comparatively few of our 174 libraries collect all three types of material, possibly only a fourth of them—it is hard to say exactly because we have to decide what constitutes a "collection of printed music" (ten titles? 100? 1000?). Happily, I can report that all libraries have at least a few books about music. All but 27 libraries provided a count of their book holdings in the 780's. They are smaller than expected:

BOOKS IN THE 780's	NO. OF LIBRARIES
100 or less	14
101–300	50
301–500	28
501–1000	38
More than 1000	17

The *Standard Catalog* (1959) and its *Supplements* 1–4 list a total of around 360 titles in the 780's. Sixty-seven (around 45 percent) of the above libraries have fewer than 350 titles in this area. During the past 12 months, 126 libraries reported adding a total of 4,832 books about music, an average of about 39 titles each. The ALA *Booklist* and Lj each list or review close to 60 titles annually.

Phonograph records present an entirely different picture. Thirty-three of our libraries do not have record collections and another 13 did not give us a count of their holdings. Those who did provide statistics have amassed a grand total of 191,910 records:

RECORDS	NO. OF LIBRARIES
500 or less	44
501–1000	26
1001–5000	51
More than 5000	7

Annual expenditures and acquisitions reflect the growing importance of recorded sound. Last year 115 of our libraries added a total of 26,151 records. Ninety-six libraries reported their expenditures during the past 12 months, or the amounts currently budgeted for records. The total is impressive: slightly over $86,000 was spent on records by these libraries.

In the general picture, printed music hardly rates at all. Seventy-four libraries have no such collections. Those that have collections and provided statistics fall into the following groups:

PRINTED MUSIC	NO. OF LIBRARIES
100 or less	34
101–200	8
201–300	1
301–500	11
501–750	5
751–1000	6
More than 1000	12

The total resources of these 77 libraries is 65,853 pieces of printed music; but the greater part of it is in the 18 libraries that account for over 54,000 of the reported titles. Most of the collections were static last year, or so it seems from the fact that 57 libraries reported adding 1,847 titles, and only five libraries accounted for more than 50 percent of these titles.

There is little to go on as regards standards of quantity in this area. One would think that a general collection of various types of music could begin with 500 titles. On the other hand, E. T. Bryant (*Music Librarianship*, 1959) and the Canadian Music Library Association's *Standards for Music Collections in Medium-sized Libraries* (1959) agree that a minimum basic collection can consist of around 275 titles. According to these standards, 35 of our libraries have at least basic collections. I am not going to try to answer the question of whether more libraries should have such collections, but think you will be interested in the reasons given for the lack of them.

Few librarians were willing to state unequivocally that this is not a legitimate public library service. Only six came right out and said so. Twenty-three librarians felt that their communities either had no need for printed music, or if they did, they had neglected to request it from the library in any quantity that would justify the library spending money on it. Six other librarians indicated that this sort of material is available elsewhere in the community or through some cooperative arrangement with another library. Only one librarian stated that her library faced other, more pressing responsibilities. Nevertheless, this thought was implicit in many of the reasons checked. In descending order of frequency, here are the reasons why the bulk of our libraries are not collecting printed music: insufficient funds, insufficient staff, lack of a staff member qualified to organize a collection, lack of space or storage facilities, lack of selection tools and other information. Since most of these problems come up and are solved when dealing with the LP record, we are inclined to think that, though these are all perfectly acceptable excuses, the basic reasons are more complex.

The lack of channels of information is certainly a serious problem, and with this in mind I took the opportunity to test several pet theories. I wrote: "Few of the library selection tools includes printed music. Please check any of the following which, if started, you think would be helpful in selecting printed music for a medium-sized public library collection." Thirty-two librarians apparently did not look with much enthusiasm on any of my brain children. The others provoked this response: 57 librarians thought that at least one would be useful, 47 voted for two, and 38 were interested in all three. Here are the suggestions with the total number of votes each received: a) The inclusion of selected music titles in the *Booklist,* 82; b) A few reviews of printed music in each issue of Lj, 97; c) The compilation and publication of a *Standard Catalog of Music,* 86.

Generally speaking, our libraries either collect music in a wide variety of performing media (e.g., piano music, chamber music, organ music, miniature scores, popular songs, folk music, etc.), or they collect only song books. I expected to find many libraries with collections of miniature scores selected in conjunction with record collections, but turned to light only two outside of the libraries with wide-ranging general collections of music. Here and there among the smaller collections there were some unusual types of selected performing media represented, and this seems to indicate that either there was no systematic plan or the materials had been acquired as gifts. In a half dozen collections it was clear that selections were purposely made in one or two specific media.

In gathering information on the organization of the materials I was chiefly interested in identifying libraries that have music departments or art and music departments. I was surprised to find nine music departments, two "music rooms," one "music area," eight art and music departments, one art-music-films department, and one library with printed music, records, and films in one department. These are libraries with large holdings of all three types of material, though two of them do not collect printed music—the idea of a "music department" without printed music is an idea that implies something quite different from what we are used to thinking of as a music department; yet this seems to be the direction in which we are heading. The idea of the "music room," which was quite popular about 20 years ago, seems to be on the wane. With only three exceptions, the foregoing departments all have at least one full-time music librarian or art-music librarian. In the others, one staff member devotes from 25 to 75 percent of his time to music services.

The greater part of the libraries reported that no one on the staff is assigned exclusive responsibility for music services. It is impossible to spell out the percentage of time spent on music in these libraries, but 29 libraries gave the approximate amount of time one person spends on music. For the most part, they ranged from 15 to 50 percent. In one-third of the reporting libraries, the head librarian takes the responsibility for the selection of materials, sometimes with the help of other staff members. Otherwise, the selection of materials can fall to about anyone on the staff: the adult services librarian, assistant librarian, reference librarian, cataloger, head of circulation.

Public service programs of any extraordinary interest are few. Three-quarters of the libraries had nothing to report. Seven libraries have live concerts, 13 have record concerts, six have radio programs, and three have lectures on music. Other activities mentioned were cooperation with local symphony orchestras, several music appreciation courses, and cooperation with local college music appreciation classes. Individually considered, some of these programs are quite exciting and imaginative, but there certainly is no overall trend.

Few librarians have made surveys, formal or informal, of music in their communities, but this is not to say they may not know quite a bit about this aspect of community life. I raised the question because music-making, outside of public concerts, is a private activity—it is possible that many communities are much more musical than we think.

Fifty five percent of the reporting libraries receive some form of help from other libraries, principally the loan of materials. About the same number of libraries share their materials. It remains to be seen to what extent the resources of interlibrary loan can be used to the best advantage in providing access to *all* types of music materials. There is a reluctance to "get involved" with the interlibrary loan of LP records. The record clubs send thousands of records through the mails every month, so fear of damage in transit should not be a problem (what other reasons do we have for not loaning them?). The interlibrary loan of printed music is going to have to be investigated further. Is the Interlibrary Loan Code being correctly interpreted by the nonspecialist? (You would be surprised at the number of librarians who call *all* printed music "sheet music," whether it's a vocal score, a miniature score, or a popular song.) Have music librarians read it lately to see if it does reflect their recommended policies?

I did not attempt to survey the services performed by state libraries in supporting local library music services. Nor did I attempt to examine the place of music materials in regional or cooperative systems.

Before drawing any conclusions, the reader will understand that I realize that a library's contribution to the musical life of its community cannot be measured by the quantity of material it houses. The quality of material and the use to which it is put are measures of its value, and this survey was not intended to investigate such services as readers' advisor, listeners' advisor, or reference.

The survey has raised the question of what materials are necessary for adequate music services in medium-sized public libraries. The majority of responding librarians are agreed that the best way they can serve the musical interests of their communities is by providing collections of records. These collections are much larger than was to be expected. Wheeler and Goldhor, in their *Practical Administration of Public Libraries* write that "public library record collections average about 500 discs," but the libraries in our survey have an average of 1500 discs; and of the 128 that provided these statistics, only 44 have fewer than 500 discs.

This great interest in records does not seem to have produced any spectacular increase in books about music. For the most part, those who go to the library in search of the printed note will be disappointed. But insofar as I was able to measure the opinions of the librarians—and I am optimistic—there is an interest in extending library service to this smaller, less vocal segment of the community.

CHAPTER

25 *Resistance and Reluctance in Record Selection*

(FEBRUARY 1, 1968)

by BARBARA HAGIST

If book collections had been developed with the principles of selection used by today's record librarians, libraries would contain only incunabula and classic literature. Libraries are not keeping abreast of public tastes or technological advancements in the selection of newer media.

Nonbook materials must be treated with the same seriousness and consideration books receive. Much time and effort is spent keeping current with the literary scene. Record selection policies, however, generally reflect the past rather than present needs of the community.

In updating its record selection policy, the Fine Arts Department of the Tulsa City-County Library System sent out a nationwide record-selection survey to all public libraries serving cities of over 100,000 population (130 libraries). This was matched by a survey of patrons in the Tulsa Central Library. The results show a difference in thinking between librarians and the community. The widest gulf is in the area of stereophonic records and types of musical and spoken recordings in the collections.

Since their appearance in 1957, stereophonic records have been resisted by record libraries. One response by public librarians demonstrated this resistance: 74 of the 105 librarians replied that 0–4 percent of the collection consisted of stereophonic records; only one library's collection consisted of over 70 percent.

More revealing is the percentage of current record orders being placed for stereo. Seventy-three out of 101 libraries reported only 0–4 percent of the total record order for stereophonic recordings; only five libraries reported over 70 percent. This pinpoints current actions and opinions of libraries regarding stereophonic recordings.

The public library's reluctance to adopt stereophonic sound reproduction is not shared by the public. Questionnaires given to adult patrons of the Tulsa Central Library asked their needs regarding monaural and stereophonic sound reproduction. The sample studied consisted of two groups of 200 patrons each—those using the record collection and those using the library for other purposes. Table One reports the results of the survey.

TABLE ONE

PHONOGRAPH EQUIPMENT ACCESSIBLE
TO LIBRARY PATRONS

EQUIPMENT	GROUP A	GROUP B
	RECORD COLLECTION	
	USERS	NONUSERS
Stereophonic	61.5%	50.5%
Monaural	37.0	26.5
No Working Equip.	1.5	23.0

Fifty-four percent not using library recordings stated they would use the record collection if there were more stereophonic recordings. Fifty-nine percent of the record users said they would make greater use of the collection if more stereophonic recordings were included.

The record librarian's defense of the monaural recording is difficult to understand. A stereophonic record, when played with a phonograph needle intended for monaural use only, will be ruined. But (with the exception of portable, inexpensive phonograph equipment) all phonograph equipment sold commercially is stereophonic. Much of the inexpensive equipment, though not having speakers for stereophonic sound reproduction, is sold with a stereophonic stylus. Monaural set owners can play stereo records safely by substituting a stereophonic pickup cartridge. Very shortly all phonograph equipment will be stereophonic or equipped to play stereo records. Already the market for classical records is 90 percent stereo.

The price differential which justified the choice of a monaural over a stereo recording of the same work has disappeared. Most record companies sell mono and stereo recordings at the same price. The next step is to stop the manufacture of monaural records altogether, which London and Deutsche Grammophon have already done.

The question of stereophonic and monaural recordings has been decided in favor of stereophonic. For libraries to continue to purchase monaural recordings is close to absurdity. The present issue about which libraries should be concerned is stereophonic tape.

In 1947, tape manufacturers generally felt tape would supplant the phonograph record. The long-playing monaural recording appeared on the scene and changed the prediction. Today, the future again remains uncertain. Using the stereophonic principle, tape is flourishing as never before. Significant

improvements are being made in the tape and in its method of sound reproduction.

The future may hold a place for both the disc and tape, or one may gain
public acceptance over the other. Meanwhile, the library should be alert to
developments in these areas, and consider prerecorded tape as an addition to
library collections.

Record librarians again remain out of touch with the general public with
regard to composition and content of the record collection. Principles of record
selection should be based upon basic principles used in the general selection
policy of the library. Few library collections consist of over 50 percent classical
literature, yet 49 of the 92 responding public libraries have collections consist-
ing of 70 percent or more classical records. Eighty-one have collections
composed of 50 percent or more classical recordings.

Forty-two and one-half percent of the record collection users prefer classical music, as compared with 28 percent who prefer popular. Opposite results
were revealed by patrons not using the record collection, with 29 percent
indicating a preference for classical music, and 44.5 percent for popular. These
figures seem to reflect the predominance of classical recordings in the Tulsa
Central Library.

TABLE TWO

INDIVIDUAL LISTENING TASTES
OF PUBLIC LIBRARY PATRONS

CATEGORIES	PREFERENCES OF PATRONS	
	USING/ NOT USING	
RECORDINGS	THE RECORD COLLECTION	
Classical	42.5%	29.0%
Folk	8.0	9.5
Spoken	4.0	.5
Religious	1.5	3.0
Country	5.0	4.5
Jazz	11.0	9.0
Popular	28.0	44.5

Forty-one percent of the nonusers said they would use the collection if
more records other than classical were added. Forty-nine percent of the group
using library records stated they would make greater use of the collection if
additional records other than classical were available.

Record librarians are developing classical collections to achieve the educational and cultural goals of the library. Selection of spoken and musical recordings caters to the needs and demands of the users and refutes library objectives.

Librarians are creating a crisis when they restrict the educational and
cultural goals of the collection to classical recordings alone. To bring the best
of jazz, spoken and instructional records, ethnic folk, popular, Broadway
musicals, and soundtracks into the collection is in keeping with the library's

tradition of service to everyone. By keeping the standards of selection high in these categories, the educational and recreational needs of the individual can be satisfied, and library objectives and standards met as well.

If the library is to be a center for all types of cultural experience, record librarians should aim for comprehensive collections. Classical recordings from the standard repertoire generally form the basis for record selection, but this area represents a very minute quantity of world culture. The standard repertoire dates from about 1750–1900, representing almost purely European composition.

Jazz, which is often ignored by record librarians, is one of the finest representations of American culture and our only original musical innovation. Popular music, including Broadway musicals and movie soundtracks, certainly reflects the present era. Folk music represents many cultures and historical periods.

Spoken records are increasing in quantity and quality. Recordings of plays, poetry, and readings greatly enhance the book stock of a library. In addition to recording literature, spoken records are important in recording speeches and events. Records of instruction in foreign languages, typing and shorthand dictation are much in demand and serve a valid educational function.

Some aspects of popular music seem to hold the least justification for library expenditure. This is not to exclude the entire popular scene. As in current fiction, there is great variance in the quality of composition. Much ephemeral material is produced which does not meet the library's standards of selection on grounds of composition and lasting value.

Quality of performance as well as composition must be considered. Even if performed by the New York Philharmonic, "Coming To Take Me Away" by Napoleon XIV would not be acceptable for a library collection on the basis of weak composition. Much popular music, such as "Yesterday" composed by John Lennon and Paul McCartney of the Beatles, when performed by legitimate groups varying in style from Lawrence Welk to Ramsey Lewis, meets both standards of composition and performance. The same selection, when performed without taste or valid arrangement, can be rendered unfit for library collections.

These principles hold for all types of musical and spoken recordings. An amateurish performance of Beethoven's *Fifth Symphony* or Shakespeare's *MacBeth* exclude them from a library collection, even though the compositions have merit and value.

Popular music, when judged fairly and intelligently by library standards of selection, can and should be included in library record collections. Judgment on the part of the record librarian must not be confused with taste, which can mean prejudice and censorship in record selection. To select recordings on the basis of personal taste is to violate all principles of librarianship.

If it is to continue to prosper, the public library must adapt more easily to change. The public is deciding whether to embrace the stereophonic tape or remain with the stereophonic recording. Musicians are wondering if mechanical innovation will make the composer of the future a computer and the musician an electrical engineer. It is predicted that in the foreseeable future we may record on tape activated by heat or by laser beams, turning on 15/16 revolutions, and offered in a spool the size of a silver dollar, with several hours playing time. The phonograph may have no needle, the sound being picked up by a light beam. Manufacturers are marketing devices which make practical the use of video tapes in the home. Yet librarians are debating whether to accept the Beatles or stereophonic recordings.

Knowledge today no longer needs a traditional binding. It appears on discs, tapes, and film. This is an era of innovation in the field of information distribution. Yet few libraries are fully committed to collections in these media. Libraries that have made commitments to nonbook materials assume that to open the door to creative people is to accept their ideas, whatever the shape or form.

26 The Twelve-Year-Old "Adult" Reader

(MAY 15, 1965)

by DOROTHY M. BRODERICK

There is really no such animal as the 12-year-old adult reader, but since people insist on talking about him, let us accept the phrase and merely note that there is the 12-year-old on his way to becoming an adult reader. That is, if he finds the books that push him forward.

The trouble with adults in our society, librarians included, is that not being adult readers themselves, they have little concept of the ultimate goal, and even less understanding of the means by which one reaches it. This defect gets in their way when it comes to trying to guide young people along the road to maturity.

You know that psychologist's game in which he says black and you say white; he says hot and you say dog—and he makes a little note because the proper answer was cold? I'd like to play it with the phrase "adult reader." When the results were tallied, the survey would probably show that most responses boiled down to "sex" and "dirty words." We worry so much about sex and dirty words that we pay almost no attention to the meaning of a book, and it is its meaning, its maturity level, that determines whether a book is adult reading or merely reading that adults do. And there is a difference.

Since this discussion must be narrowed within workable limits, I have chosen to limit it to books written specifically for young people. I am further limiting myself to fiction titles.

To begin with, let's define the word adult. If we had to determine the single outstanding characteristic of an adult, it would be his self-acceptance. This trait cannot come early in life, for to know our limitations we must have tried and failed; to know our abilities, we must have tried and succeeded. Only experience provides the knowledge on which such acceptance can be based. Acceptance includes, in turn, two very important characteristics: first a sense of humor, defined as the ability to laugh at oneself; then the ability to resent injustice when it does not affect us personally. No credit is due to anyone for feeling indignation when he is affected; the line that separates the mature person is his empathy, his involvement with the human race. Empathy is really just the other face of self-acceptance: it means that we recognize no man is infallible, that we accept another man's weaknesses as we do our own.

Unfortunately, these are not what our society considers signs of maturity. The mature person, by current definition, asks, "What's in it for me?" Sexual freedom, money, prestige, and good looks are the symbols of adulthood. Almost everyone recognizes how spurious these measurable symbols really are, for in the end it is only the intangible qualities of love and a sense of security that count. If you doubt this, think for a brief moment about that particularly pathetic product of American life, Marilyn Monroe, a woman who, by our standards, "had everything," while in reality she had nothing because self-acceptance was beyond her.

A TIME OF UNCERTAINTY

Now let us look at the child and see what characteristics of childhood are important to our discussion. First, childhood is *not* the happiest time of anyone's life, nor should it be, for that would mean that somewhere along the way the individual had ceased to grow. It is a time of dependency, a condition that precludes happiness. It is a time of uncertainty and confusion, when concrete facts are learned easily and abstract concepts create crises for the child. The child does not know who he is or even what he wants to become. The characteristic that makes childhood bearable is the knowledge that "this too shall pass away"—in brief, that there is a future toward which the child is willing to move. In many ways, we have taken this dream from him by allowing him privileges which were formerly reserved for adults.

Is it unrealistic to believe that the right books can help the child to move from his state of uncertainty into the adult state of self-acceptance? If it is, we have no business being librarians, for without such faith, we have no reason for existing. I do not claim that books and libraries alone can stem the tide of materialism in our society; but I do maintain that we have no right to ride it. We have a fundamental responsibility to exercise judgment in seeing that children are offered the possibility of growing into mature, happy adults. We cannot guarantee the results. But we can, and must, create an atmosphere which offers the child the chance.

SOME IRRELEVANT STATISTCS

Certain misconceptions currently plague us whenever this type of discussion arises. We should clear up the confusion about the difference between facts and truth. They are not synonymous. Facts can be taught; truth can be learned only through experience and an ability to generalize. We tend to believe that a child who can master the fundamentals of nuclear physics can also read *Madame Bovary*. That the two subjects have nothing in common seems to have escaped both the teachers and the librarians of the world. Facts never require the learner to make a value judgment—they are either correct or incorrect. Truth always requires value judgments.

Librarians are particularly adept at confusing facts and truth, and our major emphasis is on facts, presented as if they had a predetermined value. Take two statements based on an increase in circulation figures: 1) more people are reading books today; 2) people are reading more books today. Either or both of these statements may be facts, verifiable by research. Neither has anything to do with value judgment unless we know the quality of the books being read and the impact they have on the readers. Sadly, the only impact we dramatize is the measurable one. When a Cleveland councilman announced that he made $50,000 a year on the stock market by reading books, the Cleveland Public Library was overrun with people. A-ha! Books can make us rich; dash to the library. Books can help us cook better, build a better mouse trap—run, don't walk, to the library.)

Someday I would like to see an article on libraries in the local paper that stressed the intangibles that books provide the reader, because no one will ever convince me that 80 million circulations of the *First Book of the American Revolution* outweigh one circulation of *Johnny Tremain*. The best statement on this was made by James Baldwin, and though you may have already read it in LIBRARY JOURNAL, let me repeat part of it here:

> You think your pain and heartbreak are unprecedented in the history of the world, but then you read. It was books that taught me that the things that tormented me the most were the very things that connected me with all the people who were alive, or who had ever been alive.

There it is: from books, a growing sense of identity, accompanied by the sense of involvement with the human race.

ARITHMETIC OF DESPAIR

If we are going to help children grow through reading, the first step we must take is to sharpen our own reading abilities. We must take time to analyze books instead of devouring them; and we must take even more time to relate the books to the world of reality, not some sentimental remembrance of things past.

Here is reality:

Item one, a news story: Are you aware that the greatest increase in venereal disease in the United States is in children between the ages of 11 and 15? Can we, in good conscience, spend time and energy arguing over whether the presence of a "hell" or "damn" in a book will corrupt young people when they are facing far more serious problems? The question is no longer Should I kiss him goodnight? but, how far do I go?

Item two: Do you know that there has been an increase of 300 percent in child suicides in the past three years; and that doctors estimate that 50 attempts are made for every successful suicide? What drives children to this act? What makes the future so dim they are unwilling to move toward it?

Item three, a letter to Ann Landers, may help answer that question:

> Dear Ann: Please help me. I am 12 years old and very unhappy. My mother lets me do whatever I want and it is a terrible thing to know that nobody is ever going to say "No" to you. If I told my mother I was going to kill myself she would say, "If that's what you want to do Honey, go ahead."
>
> My best friend Beverly has a mother who says, "You can't do it and I don't want to hear any more." Then it's all settled.
>
> Sometimes I ask my mother for permission to do things I don't want to do at all. If she would say "No" it would help me out a lot. I am not a very good writer but I hope you understand what I am trying to say.

I hope you do too. . . .

The mother of that girl is not much different from those of us who refuse to make adult judgments about some very flabby books because we think we are giving them what they want. What young people want is guidance, and the librarian who is willing to forget the word "popular" has a chance of offering it to them. Any book can be popular, regardless of its quality, if the librarian is personally enthusiastic, and has the courage to challenge the young people he is working with.

I never felt I was violating some God-given commandment when I openly expressed to the junior high students I worked with, disapproval of their taste. When they asked why we didn't own Nancy Drew, for example, I gave them the only answer I could: because they're lousy books. When they asked why we didn't own more "Nurse Stories" I told them: we own the good ones; the bad ones aren't worth the money.

Was I giving them a trauma? Insulting them? Perhaps. But there is a saying that we must die a little in order to grow again. I was and am willing to take people where I find them; but I am not and never will, God willing, be reconciled to leaving them at the point at which I encounter them. The highest compliment I have ever received from a graduate student was when she said, "You are the first person who ever made me reach." That is my job as a teacher; it is the way I saw my job as a librarian working with children.

DATES AND CONVERTIBLES

Too many librarians feel that the frothy world of dates and convertibles, of football heroes, and beautiful girls don't really do any harm. After all, it's just fun. But is it just fun? Don't these books perpetuate an image that leads young people to behave as in the following news story:

> As Margaret Mary Little walked home from her third day at Torrance High School, a carload of teenagers pulled up alongside her. One yelled:
> "We don't want misfits in our school."
> Then, three boys and two girls jumped out. The others watched, she said, as one boy ripped her skirt and her blouse, and, with a rusty razor blade, slashed her cheek and forearm.

"Worse will happen if you come back to school," the boy shouted as the car drove away. Police are looking for them.

Margaret walked three blocks home. The slashes—four on her cheek, five on her arm—were minor. She told investigating officers later that she didn't know whether she would return tomorrow to the school, where she is new.

Margaret, 15, is a cerebral palsy victim. She has been handicapped since birth.°

Weren't these young people doing what they considered proper—eliminating an unpleasant item that marred the romantic world they like to think is the real one?

There are things to be gotten from the teenage romance, but they aren't the things I want young people to be getting. One wonders if the authors and editors recognize the shallowness and basic immorality of the values they are presenting. As *The Lively Art of Picture Books* film makes so clear, we cannot get out of a book what has not been put into it. And that is the difference between the hack writer and the person who writes because he has something inside him that has to be communicated.

Where we go astray in book evaluation is when we allow the author's good intentions to override his lack of writing skill. If there is anything worse than a bad book with a banal plot, it is a bad book on an important subject. Too many authors are providing superficial answers to complex problems. Take, for example, Regina Woody's *Wisdom to Know,* a book which purports to treat of mental health. It has the amazing quality of not having one single mentally healthy person in it. Our heroine, who is 17, has never had a date because—get this—she would rather have no date than face the possibility that the boy will not ask her a second time. And she's the healthiest person in the book.

Unfortunately, our standard response to book selection these days seems to be "We need a book on the subject." The only valid response is "We need a *good* book on the subject." Do we need a biography of Werner von Braun so badly that we can allow the author to pass over with a wave of the hand the fact that von Braun was responsible for Hitler's rocketry program that all but wiped out England? *Do we ever need a fact more than we need truth?*

In *And Now Miguel,* Krumgold has Miguel say, "To become something different from what you are, it takes more than being strong." Krumgold is talking about faith, an admittedly old-fashioned concept these days. The quote has particular application to our future. Do we want to become something different from what we are? Would we like to reach the point where lists drawn up of "popular" books in a given library (or, by our national list compilers) were also lists of quality? Would we like to sharpen our own responses to books and reach the point where we were mature enough ourselves to read *It's Like This, Cat* and *Catcher in the Rye* without having them shake our stability? *Would we, in short, like to become professional librarians instead of dispensers of books?*

° *A subsequent story reported that Margaret Mary Little inflicted the slashes upon herself. Several people were quick to bring this to my attention. My reply: the facts of the story have been altered; its truth has not been, in fact, it has been strengthened. How much more desperate to scar oneself, how much more alone and open to the silent forces of hostility that girl must have been than the first story indicated.*

Perhaps our trouble is that we equate the popularity of the books with our own popularity. It is a malady of our society that too many adults want to be popular rather than respected. The two are not necessarily opposed, but if we must choose between being respected and loved, we have no alternative but to choose the former. To do otherwise is to destroy our role in the child's world.

ROADS TO MATURITY

Let us now look at some books in relationship to the needs of young readers. I make no claim that reading these books will miraculously solve their personal problems; they do, however, have enough content to challenge anyone who wants to think "the long, long thoughts of childhood."

One of the most pressing problems for the 12-year-old is his awakening realization that his parents are not infallible. He has known this for some time: it began the first time he was blamed and punished for something he did not do. But, as an abstract concept, it presents large problems. For one thing, it undermines his sense of security at the very time when he is most in need of security. He hides all this behind a hypercritical attitude, an attitude that literally forces him to move into the outer world. This step toward independence, the breaking of the home bonds, is essential if he is to move toward maturity.

Onion John, The Rock and the Willow, and *It's Like This, Cat,* to mention just three excellent books, offer the child reader the opportunity to see the doubts other young people have about their parents. We must not be like the librarian at ALA who told Miss Nordstom that *Cat* was not a good book because Dave did not respect his parents. We must be among those who understand that life is science: for every action, a reaction. If we wish to teach good, we must show evil; if we wish to demonstrate honesty, we must show the dangers of cheating.

A fact is a fact, but for every value there is an opposite. The following conversation in *Avalanche!* speaks for itself: Our hero asks, "Why do all these things happen? Why can't people live happy and ordinary lives?"

"Happy and ordinary aren't the same," said Hans Peter slowly. "I believe you're only happy if you *know* you're happy. And you only know that after you've been miserable."

It occurs to me each time I read this exceptional book that one reason our society has so many problems with middle-class youths is that they have been pampered so thoroughly they have no basis upon which to judge their own good fortune. They have nothing to compare it with. We have very few books which do a really good job of depicting non-middle-class realities. But in reading *To Beat a Tiger,* we would have to be totally insensitive not to recognize the standards of behavior inflicted upon people by war and poverty.

Our young people may not be able to understand what adults are talking about when they tell them, "What's the matter with you? We give you everything you want. What more can you ask for?"

They can ask for the only thing they really have a right to expect from adults—leadership, not buddy-buddy companionship. An 18-year-old girl in Darien, Connecticut put it this way:

"When we were 15 and 16 almost all the girls who were my friends had one thing in common—they hated their mothers. It's hard to explain to people who look at your house and your clothes and everything you have and wonder what in the world you could complain about. It's hard to tell anyone what's wrong when they say you and your mother are just like sisters. But if you were 12 or 13 and a girl, you'd know because you'd see your mother wearing a 7 or a 9, a junior size, and putting on eyelashes and acting as though she is your sister. They were always pushing you into parties with boys and dating, and acting as though you'd be an old maid. And then when you'd want to do something that an adult would do they'd say you were just a baby."

Are we prepared to assume responsibility for telling these young people that they are unique, that no one else has ever suffered from their problems? Or, do we recognize that books can do for them what they did for James Baldwin—provide them with an understanding that other people not only have suffered, but survived to become creative geniuses. Not all children hate their parents, even briefly, but all children do have moments of great doubts, which are accompanied by almost overwhelming guilt. Books which depict conflict between parents and children are far less objectionable than books which are totally devoid of relationships between children and adults. It simply is not normal for a growing child to be unaware of, or uninfluenced by, the adults in his world. No matter how good or how bad the parents, they play a tremendous role in the child's life, and the book which notes casually that our hero or heroine has parents, then drops them from sight, is a pretty bad book.

THE ADOLESCENT SUBCULTURE

It is true that sometimes that role is positive, sometimes it is negative, but all too often in our current society that role is one of neutrality. The complexities of our society have forced the adult to make numerous compromises; he lives with a very uncertain set of ethics. For example, he may have long since renounced organized religion, but he sends his children to church every Sunday; a situation that must arouse confusion within the children. The uncertainty arouses in the adult a sense of guilt, guilt which keeps him from actively trying to transmit his values to his children. This forces the children to evolve their own; the void must be filled, and so a subculture evolves, that of the gang.

We had a dramatic example of this last year in Cleveland when a four-year-old boy was killed in a hit-skip accident. The four boys who were in the car that killed the boy went to a dance that night and vowed silence. Eventually the police tracked them down and the newspaper reported the following exchange (I almost said conversation, but that would be a misnomer) between one of the mothers and her son:

"If only you had told what happened—that would be courage."

"But, ma, you just don't tell—it's the unwritten law," the boy protested.

"What law?—The law of the jungle?" the mother exclaimed.

The boys involved in this incident were not thugs but they were victims of preadolescent thinking, they still clung to the black-and-white world of childhood when they were old enough to be driving lethal weapons. But if parents and society do not communicate to them the complexities involved in reaching rational decisions, how can they do other than live by such simple codes as: you don't tell? At least it has the advantage of being consistent, and never underestimate the need all of us have to live in a consistent world.

It would be senseless to try and talk to such boys about moral values. The way these words are used today makes them sound like products you can buy in the large economy size at the supermarket. And these young people know better. They know, not only that their parents are fallible, but that the adult world is a hypocritical one. Now, to a certain extent we are all hypocrites, because we are human and cannot always possess the strength to practice what we preach, and the child would have to be deaf, dumb, and blind not to know that discrepancies exist.

However, there is a broader sense in which we are hypocrites. There is a very particular time when all the talk about morality becomes just that—talk. And that is when it comes in conflict with the great American ideal: success. Last spring we *Peanuts* fans suffered while Lucy made Linus the subject of her science fair project. She took Linus' blanket away and stood with a stop watch, timing the various stages he went through before passing out from the tension caused by removal of his security symbol. The last panel in this series shows Charlie Brown saying, "You know, Lucy, you really puzzle me . . . What sort of person are you who would enter her own brother in a science fair?" To which Lucy replies, "I won, didn't I?" Charlie stands there, his usual dejected self, saying, "That's always been a problem with me . . . I've never known how to argue with success."

Charlie Brown is not alone in not knowing how to argue with success. Few of us do; and fewer even want to. We are fortunate to have an author team that not only wants to argue, but does so in a most realistic, vivid way. Annabel and Edgar Johnson have consistently demonstrated an ability to give the young reader perspective about the adult world of hypocrisy where what seems like success on the surface is really fool's gold underneath. Any librarian who has read these books should have no trouble making them the most popular books in any collection. Of course, the operative phrase is, "the librarian who reads . . ."

Beyond these problems of presenting adult hypocrisy, or problems with parents, lurks a larger one: namely, the differentiation between hypocrisy and adult prerogatives. It is hypocrisy to tell a child he must not cheat in school and then boast of how we cheat the income tax men or the boss. It is not hypocrisy to tell a young person that he must not drink or indulge in sexual relationships and then do either or both ourselves. Drinking and sex are matters of judgment—judgments young people are unqualified to make, and *they know it,* even if we don't.

Would not a discussion group built around the mature teenage books provide a natural lead-in for the leader to raise some of these questions?

Would we not be helping young people to define for themselves the nature of limitations and prerogatives?

But even if we have neither the time nor the ability to arrange formal discussion groups, we can, at the very least, be offering our readers those books which will stimulate them to talk among themselves. The measure of a good book is two-fold; first, we want our friend to read it; secondly, we want to talk with him about it. I cannot conceive of discussions over Cokes built around DuJardin's books. What is there to say?

And so, the good books, the ones I would push and plug and praise, are those in which children are shown as having genuine relationships with their parents and the adults of the world. Such books must depict these relationships realistically, showing the ambivalence, that mixture of love and hate, antagonism and attraction, that permeates all but the most superficial contacts between people.

Such books exist, not in the quantity of the manufactured teenage romances, but Mary Stolz, Annabel and Edgar Johnson, Joseph Krumgold, Jean George, and Emily Neville are slowly providing us with a nucleus of books with which we can start the 12-year-old on the road to maturity. We might even contemplate making the trip ourselves.

27 *Carping Critics, Instant Experts*

(SEPTEMBER 15, 1965)

by DOROTHY M. BRODERICK

In Jazz Country, the hero, Tom Curtis, says "I heard somebody playing trumpet, and it was as if that trumpet player were ten feet tall and had just found out he was going to live forever. I mean, he played as if he were feeling so good that he had to let some joy out or he'd explode. And he made *me* feel glad just to be listening." Some of our writers must be feeling ten feet tall these days, for 1965 has been a banner year for thought-provoking books, and those who would bury juvenile publishing had better take another look at the corpse. Like Old Dry Frye, it's mighty mobile.

Prospective grave-diggers of juvenile writing are a diverse crew. Some find too many "adult overtones" in children's books; some find too *few* adult overtones; others decry the overemphasis on realism (defined as anything less than total happiness). Still others complain that realism is impossible because librarians get upset about portraits of minority groups.

The very diversity of criticism should prove something: that each reader brings as much of himself to a book as the author did. Hentoff makes this point strongly in describing the jazz artist who must tell a story—expose himself—to an audience. In a given audience some do "listen underneath" to the story being told; others feign attention but are thinking of the rent bill or buying a new car; still others pay no attention at all because to hear and understand will upset their illusions, and to hear but not understand will shatter their egos. The latter, like Hentoff's jazz critic find it easier to dismiss the performer than admit their shortcomings, and this seems to be the case with our "instant critics." They never blame the writer or the editor, but only the librarians, who by default hold the purse-strings and thus determine the poor quality of juvenile books.

WITH FRIENDS LIKE THESE . . .

It is difficult for one who has spent most of his adult life becoming reasonably informed about children's books to take the "instant experts" in stride, for enough of our supposed allies, our fellow librarians, do fall into the cliché category of "With friends like these, who needs enemies?" Take for example our long fight over *Harriet the Spy*. The opposition has decided Harriet is immoral; that is that, and they wish the rest of us would shut up. Back in 1907 Alice Jordan wrote, "With the definition of moral tone often lies the root of our diverse opinions regarding the merit of this book or that." We are still having trouble defining "moral tone."

Our so-called "book selection standards" provide little help here, being nebulous enough to permit us to apply them to whatever opinion we want to hold. If we don't hear the author's story as he intended it, we can provide our own, or none, and find all kinds of faults with the work at hand. One wonders if the librarians who dislike Harriet so much will also object to Gilly Ground in *Dorp Dead*, another unconventional, even experimental, children's book. If they do, more self-appointed experts will arise to damn us.

Yet, admitting that some librarians are guilty of everything charged (and of some crimes the critics didn't notice); and also that much is wrong with juvenile publishing, let's examine some criticisms to see which approach reality.

We can begin with Gore Vidal's charge (*N.Y. Review of Books*, Dec. 3, 1964) that children's librarians have no interest in fantasy these days. He describes us as hulking women with an obsessive passion for diesel trucks. Now, let us grant that among us we have a full range of neurotics. But lovers of diesel trucks? We may be fond of Mary Ann, Mike Mulligan's steamshovel, and Little Toot is a lovable tugboat; but we also manage to appreciate *The Borrowers, The Children of Green Knowe,* and C. S. Lewis' Narnia books. Vidal's charge is prompted by his discovery that American children don't read E. Nesbit these days. Maybe not; but we can be sure that those who do have gotten their copies from the public library, not as gifts from Auntie. And equating E. Nesbit with pure fantasy shows Mr. Vidal's limitations, not ours.

Then there is Mrs. Heilbrun's "Life in Safe Doses" in the May 9, 1965 New York *Times* Book Review Section, which can serve as a prototype for these articles. Having read a handful of them, Mrs. Heilbrun decided that the trouble with teenage books is that they don't provide a vision of the adult world.

What makes the charge so fascinating is her list of the adult authors she'd have them read: D. H. Lawrence, Salinger, Bellow, Mailer, Hemingway. Has any century before ours produced a better collection of adolescents writing in the guise of adults? Is Hemingway's vision of women as rabbits hopping in and out of sleeping bags more mature than the average teenager's view of sex? Are Lawrence's obsession with his mother, Bellow's strange concept of virility, and

Mailer's rantings "visions of the adult world?" Even an affirmative answer would not necessarily imply that these authors can help the teenager in his own search for identity, or lead him to maturity.

But the Vidals and the Heilbruns, after all, are amateurs. Let's examine some charges made by a working juvenile editor.

WORRIED EDITORS

In an article on presenting the Negro in children's books (*Top of the News,* April 1965) Jean Colby charged librarians with keeping editors and authors from creating honest masterpieces because we, their best market, won't buy them. We want them "toned down." The charge is documented by Mrs. Colby's personal experiences as an editor, and no one can doubt she is telling the truth as she sees it. The question is, is she seeing enough? The piece made me think of the peddlar in *Caps for Sale,* standing under the tree shaking his fist, and saying, "You monkeys, you. Give me back my caps." Only this time it's "You librarians, you. Give me back my job." For certain assumptions underlie each line of this article, which really treats the roles of the editor and the librarian.

Its main assumption is that all editors operate under the same system of mindreading and fear of salesmen. This is an interesting system, but I question how widely it is practiced. I have met many juvenile editors, worked intimately with some, called a few "friend," yet not once has any of them asked my permission to publish a book. Perhaps there are librarians who can claim to be constantly consulted; if so they would do well to come forward and say so.

Good editors produce books that meet their own standards of integrity and taste without undue concern about anyone else's. They read manuscripts the way a librarian reads a new book, hoping a new jewel will appear on the scene. When the manuscript presents believable characters, an appropriate atmosphere, and plausible plot, there is an involvement that precludes outside worries. It is hard to imagine that in the midst of an exciting discovery an editor suddenly looks up and says "Oh, but the librarians will never let me make money on this."

There *are* some editors who won't publish a book until some librarian has approved it, but they are in a minority, and if they prefer to abdicate their prime responsibility—accepting or rejecting a manuscript, it's their business.

MISS MAU MAU AND OTHERS

Let's pass on to "You librarians (what a nice, all-encompassing sound!) know the answer." Which librarians? The ones who will buy *Jazz Country,* or those who'll reject it? Mary, the wife of the trumpet player, is a wonderfully true portrait of the Negro who hates white people. Her husband calls her "Miss Mau Mau" and the reader often wants to tell her off. Her reconstruction is a fascinating study in reverse prejudice.

Or are we discussing the librarians who will buy Natalie Savage Carlson's

The Empty Schoolhouse? With so much talk about the outside agitators who stir up the Negroes in their fight for equality, Mrs. Carlson has chosen to depict the other invaders, the professional bigots who can't stand to see a school peacefully integrated. At one point the narrator, who is a cleaning girl at a motel (and likes the job) is washing the sidewalk when Mr. Buzzard and Mr. Alligator, her nicknames for the agitators, come out the door. One of them kicks her bucket and says "Get out of my way, nigger." How simple it would have been to simply eliminate the word "nigger" from the sentence. Yet we all know the word rings of a truth we may not like but can't ignore. Any child who has watched the television coverage of the race riots is fully aware of the bigot's vocabulary.

If this book had been written to offend no one, and with an eye to what the salesmen might think, it would have been narrated by a highly intellectual girl with visions of being the first woman president. The bigots would have had a pristine vocabulary. And it would have been a pretty mediocre book. As it stands it may not sell many copies in Mississippi or Alabama or Louisiana, where it is set, but at least no one will have to apologize for buying it.

We might term 1965 the year of the social novel, for it is not only the racial theme that is covered by the authors who feel ten feet tall. In Emily Neville's new book *Berries Goodman,* both the overprotective Jewish mother and the "some of my best friends are, but let's not live next door to them" gentiles are bound to squirm. Anyone who has lived in suburbia will identify each character in *Berries*. How many of us will therefore reason that it's not up to *It's Like This Cat?* We often charge that an author is going downhill only when he hits us where we live. When he writes about other people's foibles, he's great.

With a very different setting but an equally hard-hitting theme, Thelma Nurenberg's *My Cousin, the Arab* takes as its heroine a German Jew, a talented teenager living in an Israeli kibbutz. Despite having lost her father to a German gas chamber, she persists in thinking of herself as German and resents being in Israel. Here the portraits of class and caste consciousness among Jewish exiles are beautifully drawn. Furthermore, during the fighting some of the finest people in the book are killed—a rather startling development by some standards.

It seems then that the answer to Mrs. Colby's question is almost ludicrously simple. How do you present minorities in children's books? As people.

GILLY'S ADVICE

Finally, in our look at the carping critics, let's remember they seldom read broadly enough to get the full picture of juvenile publishing. Critics of adult writing read the best books and cover an area with intense study; juvenile critics rarely bother. They suffer from the malady of thinking that anyone who can read automatically qualifies as a juvenile reviewer; having a child or two makes them infallible.

If our self-appointed critics can read *Dorp Dead* without realizing that juvenile writing is very much alive, they aren't terribly good at reading. This book alone would make 1965 memorable: if some of our authors are feeling ten feet tall, Julia Cunningham stands 100 feet high. We can say of her book what was said many years ago: "Works like this are as a mirror: if an ass looks in you cannot expect an angel to look out." The critics might remember their complaints tell us more about them and their inadequacies, than they do about children's book publishing. I don't expect they'll take my advice; but like Gilly's to Kobalt, I wish they would *Dorp Dead*.

28 *A Study in Conflicting Values*

(MAY 15, 1966)

by DOROTHY M. BRODERICK

No book is complete without a reader; no book is great if it does not stimulate the reader's mind, luring him into new worlds of thought, and if it does not touch his heart, forcing him to grow in understanding himself and other people. The books I have chosen to discuss here have this quality, and another very special virtue that distinguishes them from many great books.

The books I have chosen should also be distinguished from those which fall into the special category we have evolved at Western Reserve—the N-U-N books, *not* to be confused with non-books. N-U-N books are Nice, Useful, Needed. They do a job for us; we could not easily exist without them.

But neither can we live without the provocative book: the book that becomes a part of the reader's life. I have chosen the word "provocative" because I don't consider it essential that we approve or disapprove of the books in question. The vital point is that these books by simply existing add dimensions to our thinking and responses—and, yes, add flavor to our arguments; for argue we do. I also prefer "provocative" because the alternative is "controversial," and for better or worse, in our day and age, "controversial" has a nasty meaning. It alerts us to the fact that this book is dangerous, will stir up discussion and possibly bring complaints, in short cause us a bit of trouble if we add it to our collection.

Before talking about the books themselves, it is necessary to establish some definitions in my personal dictionary. For this purpose, imagine three married couples, each of whom has set aside a certain amount of mad-money to be spent every month.

The first couple has decided to use the money to build a record collection. They argue, quietly, over the choice: he wants to buy Mozart's Clarinet Concerto in A Major; she wants Mahler's 4th Symphony. This argument is a question of *taste,* and the chances are that whoever wins this month, the other person will be willing to live with the decision. In fact, next month's money will probably go for the rejected record.

Couple Number Two has also decided to build a record collection. He wants to buy Mozart; she wants to buy Mantovani. This argument will be settled less easily because this couple's problem is one of *education.* One does not instinctively prefer Mozart to the daily offerings of radio and television.

Couple Number Three has a more serious problem. He wants to buy Mozart (consistent men, aren't they?), and she wants to buy Johnnie Walker Black Label. Each is demonstrating excellent *taste,* but no matter how they solve the immediate problem they are in for a long hard fight, for they are arguing over conflicting *values.*

Whenever we make a decision, that decision is based on one or more of the three terms described. And when we argue our decisions or judgments, the ground rules for arguing differ in each of the three cases. One cannot argue a question of values as if it were a matter of taste. To do so only muddies the water and resolves nothing.

While I wish to discuss a conflict in values largely as it is found in the book world, I must stress first that our battle is in no way unique; the conflict permeates our society. If you watched the CBS-TV documentary *Sixteen in Webster Groves,* a presentation of the attitudes, values, and mores of the 16-year-olds in Webster Groves, Missouri, you probably confirmed once again what many of us have known for too long: that education is not connected with intellectual curiosity; that the genuine student is a misfit. Education in Webster Groves has little to do with developing taste, and the values it inculcates in the youth are questionable, if not deplorable. It is a means to an end: you don't have to like what you learn, you don't have to understand what is taught—just pass the tests, get the grades, and be accepted at a good college. If you have to cheat to achieve these goals, well, that's life. Besides, almost everyone does it.

The few students who had been exposed to the outer world—they called it "downtown," meaning St. Louis—were surprised at what they saw. They encountered poverty for the first time; they saw mentally retarded people and suddenly it dawned on them as one girl put it: "It makes you wonder, have people been honest with you all your life?" The girl thought she might like to be a social worker. These students were misfits in Webster Groves.

Most parents felt that at 16 the children were not out of the diaper stage; they said that 16-year-olds had no business being concerned about civil rights, politics, the outer world. All that was expected of them was that they go to school, pass their driver's test (failing that seemed to be life's nadir), get into college, and "have fun."

It was the most depressing television show I have watched in a long time. The horrors of war in Vietnam paled before the regimentation of Webster Groves, Missouri, U.S.A. At least in Vietnam we are fighting for one of America's soundest values; in Webster Groves, all that is inherent in the American principles of freedom, self-expression, and individuality is being eroded by adult pressures.

If you missed *Sixteen in Webster Groves,* you can capture its essence, in fact some of the very dialogue, in what was 1965's most significant book as far as I am personally concerned, *Two Blocks Apart,*[1] in which Charlotte Mayerson has captured the horrible sterility that plagues the affluent American. Her two characters, Peter Quinn and Juan Gonzales, live in New York City—two blocks apart, but in entirely different worlds. Peter is an upper-middle-class Irish Catholic, Juan a lower-class Puerto Rican Negro, raised a Catholic, but no longer finding within the church anything to add meaning to his life.

Juan, with all his problems, his lack of a decent education, his aloneness in the world, emerges a vital character. He feels, he cares, he dreams; his drive is to be more than what he is or what his parents were. He is a person I would like to know, whose company I would find stimulating. He would be welcome in my home; for no matter what our initial problems were, we could eventually communicate.

Peter Quinn is one of the complacent people of the world. Juan wants something nebulous; Peter knows exactly what he wants. His father and older brother went to Notre Dame, so Notre Dame is essential. And after that: "The one thing I'd like is to be finished with college and have all that worry behind me—all the difficulty of whether I'm going to get in, how my marks are going to be and all that over with. I'd like to be settled down in a good job with enough money to buy all the necessities and some luxuries. . . . And the kind of girl I'd want to marry would be well-mannered, respectable, and good-looking, with a good personality. The important thing is to have a refined girl who knows how to speak, act."

Juan's answer to what he would like is enough to make us all weep: "Me, I'm Puerto Rican, colored, and I'm not going to turn my back on that, but if you ask me, if I could, 'Which would you rather be?' Well, I mean, you've got to face it. I mean anybody would. If you ask me, which I'd rather be, well, man, I'd rather be white."

Juan Gonzales lives in a world of high emotion. Everything to him is important: the streets he can't cross, the swimming pool he can't use, the family he doesn't have. He seeks and finds solace in books.

Nothing shakes Peter Quinn. Nothing? Well . . . the assassination of John F. Kennedy shook him. He felt deprived of something special in his world. Peter says: "He was dead and everybody was stunned. I was terrified. I was really afraid. I said that the world was going to come to an end and I kept thinking about it and thinking about it and I was really more afraid than I have ever been in my life or than I ever will be."

It is one of the few times in the book I didn't want to slug Peter in his orthodontically straightened teeth. Yet even then I felt, as will many readers, that if Kennedy had not been an Irish Catholic, Peter Quinn would have cared less about his assassination. For Peter, John F. Kennedy did not exist as a person, a man with a wife and children, the president of the United States— but as a symbol of the success Peter wants for himself. Peter's concern, his fear, seemed to be for his own world more than the greater tragedy of Kennedy's death.

By contrast, Juan, the "culturally deprived" of our time, has the more highly developed moral sensibility: "You know I felt bad when Kennedy was assassinated because that's wrong, to kill anybody."

In short, Peter, with a private school education, a protecting, loving family, lives in a shell; he is as much, if not more, a captive of his environment as Juan is a captive of his. The major difference is that Juan wants a better world and Peter is completely satisfied with his. He would change nothing—and that, in a 17-year-old, is tragedy worthy of the Greek playwrights.

ESCALATION IN THE CHILDREN'S WAR

With this fairly lengthy digression, I would like to turn to the problem of our conflicting values in evaluating provocative books. We *must* understand what we are arguing about, for we cannot much longer pretend we are arguing about taste when we are really arguing about values. The pretense is neither deliberate nor conscious. If it were we would be having discussion instead of war.

For librarians working with teenagers, the war may be said to have begun in 1951 with *Catcher in the Rye*.[2] For librarians working with children, open warfare did not break out until *Harriet the Spy*[3] arrived on the scene, though skirmishes had occurred for some time. With the more recent publication of *The Long Secret*[4] and *Dorp Dead*,[5] the children's field can be said to be building its own little cache of provocative books. The lines are being drawn and escalation is occurring.

What are the characteristics of these books which cause otherwise gentle ladies to remove their white gloves and come out swinging? They must be something more than what we call great books. Certainly *Johnny Tremain*,[6] *Call It Courage*,[7] and *Charlotte's Web*[8] are great; yet they are not provocative in the sense we mean today. In fact, while all my classes read them, we don't much discuss them—for what is there to say? The student who did not recognize them as great would have so little taste as to make further effort meaningless.

So let us agree that a great book does not automatically provoke the reader. It can be analyzed according to the fundamentals of esthetic criticism and found worthy. But it need not question the world of accepted values—and it is by calling into question established values that a book becomes provocative. We can also agree that a book can be provocative without being great; *Durango Street*[9] and *Ring the Judas Bell*[10] come immediately to mind.

THEME AS IMPLICIT VALUE

The books I am emphasizing here are, I know, provocative; I think they are also great. Others obviously disagree with the latter judgment. On what grounds? Largely a matter of values: people who dislike Harriet and Gilly

Ground do not like to believe that children behave, react emotionally, or think the way these characters behave, react, and think. The books become even more objectionable when the adults in them behave toward children in ways we don't like to believe possible from adults.

It is perfectly human to dislike books whose characters threaten our established world, just as it is equally human to like books whose characters meet with our approval. The danger in this situation is that we lose all perspective and are incapable of making literary judgments because we are too busy making moral ones. Since there is no such thing as an objective judgment, does this mean we cannot ever hope to have anything but perpetual war?

I can't answer that question. All I can do is discuss some books which are very much in the news and see if the problem really is one of conflicting values—or whether the literary style has misled some readers into making moral judgments which are not in the books themselves.

For a beginning, let's take *Dorp Dead* and look at it in relationship to this year's Newbery winner, *I, Juan de Pareja*.[11] There is no objectivity in the following analysis. I love *Dorp Dead* and find *I, Juan* deadly dull and thoroughly objectionable from a number of viewpoints.

But let us look at the books in terms of values, leaving literary taste out of the discussion for the time being. *Dorp Dead* is essentially a story of one individual's fight for freedom. Gilly Ground is as thoroughly an individualist as Harriet is in her own way. Yet for a time he succumbs to Kobalt's values. He finds solace in being well fed, well clothed, and in having a room of his own. He knows what is expected of him; he has a routine that never varies and thus provides security. When the Hunter asks "Are you bewitched, boy?" Gilly responds angrily: "Who are you anyway, going around like a nut with an unloaded gun and no name, acting like the ruler of the earth, interfering with people like me?"

It fascinates me that when Elizabeth Speare in *The Bronze Bow*[12] spells out in one syllable words that "Love is the answer," we admire the book, but when Julia Cunningham uses the same theme, we are not only confused but actually object. Freedom and love go together—one is contingent upon the other. Can we really claim to be arguing over values when Gilly learns that it is better to be uncertain, insecure, but free? Simply because the book has an allegorical structure?

To read some of the reviews of *Dorp Dead* one is forced to believe that many children's librarians have never read an allegory, at least not one which was not previously identified as such. Gilly discovers who the Hunter is—but librarians reading the book object because Gilly doesn't tell them. They ask, "Who is the Hunter and what does he symbolize?" One expects these librarians would read Camus' *The Plague*[13] as a story about rats; and they probably think *The Hound of Heaven* is about dogs.

Other reviewers evade their objections on the ground of "values" or style and quibble about details instead, questioning, for example, the validity of *Dorp Dead* because an orphanage should have been more responsible in investigating Kobalt before placing Gilly with him. Yet what would an investigation have turned up but the fact that Kobalt was an ideal, if somewhat eccentric, citizen? He works hard, makes money, keeps a neat, orderly house. He even has a dog—in good condition at the time the proposed investigation would have taken place. He seems to embody all the values we cherish!

In fact, Miss Cunningham makes a deliberate point through the character of Kobalt, whose name, I choose to believe, is no mere accident. Spelled with a "c" instead of a "k," the word is *cobalt*, a radio-active element which when used in moderation can cure cancer. Used in extreme doses, it destroys. Isn't Miss Cunningham suggesting to us that certain perfectly valid forms of behavior, when carried to extremes, become aberations?

There is another point to be made about *Dorp Dead*, an essential one, I think. Gilly's concern for the dog is all-important, and Miss Cunningham, here, gives us the same message that *Call It Courage* provided: it is when those we love suffer that we become capable of acting, when we would not, could not, act in behalf of ourselves. If Gilly had not loved the dog, he might never have been alerted to his own danger until the time for action was past.

As a teacher, I have to love *Dorp Dead*. It makes my life more exciting and satisfying. Last summer, in Kentucky, I watched a class of 18 adults discuss this book for two hours and during the course of that discussion each one of them grew before my eyes. At the end of the session my invited guest, Mary K. Eakin, stopped being an observer long enough to ask the group, "What do you think Gilly would have thought of Harriet, and Harriet would have thought of Gilly?" The answer, from one student, is memorable: "I don't know what they would have thought of each other—but they would have met, because Harriet would have been coming down that fireplace while Gilly was going up it."

As for the children: A few weeks ago one of my students, Mrs. Eble, a school librarian in the Fairview Park Schools, came into class with stars in her eyes. Seven of her bright sixth graders had had a discussion about *Dorp Dead*, and the insights these children had, the ideas the book stimulated, left both the librarian and the teacher gasping. Was it an accident? Mrs. Eble repeated the situation with another group of sixth graders with the same result. Later the teacher told her he had been trying for so long to get the children to talk, but had never dreamed that given the right book they could achieve such insight and articulateness.

This is not a unique experience: librarians who have bought and are using *Dorp Dead* are discovering that they have been guilty of underestimating children. We preach our faith in children, but too many of us don't really have much respect for their intelligence or common sense.

Now let us compare Gilly's individualism, his fight for freedom, with our Newbery Medal book. The nastiest possible question about *I, Juan de Pareja* is, "Do we really, at this time and place in our history, need a story about a happy slave?" Mrs. Trevino doesn't miss one stereotype: the sly, sneaky, grasping Gypsy; the good master; the happy slave.

Yet, she depicts Juan de Pareja as intelligent, sensitive, observing—and then asks us to believe that such an individual would never see the basic inhumanity of one man being another's property. Let's be as fair as possible. Maybe Juan never was exposed to the horrors of slavery; or never saw a mistreated slave, families separated, men deprived of their virility, women forced to surrender to the amorous advances of their masters. His only conflict is his desire to paint: and what a lovely way out the author offers him. Go to confession, discover that it is not a sin, only illegal, so paint secure in knowing you will reach heaven.

Overlooking all this and even more—like the passing over lightly of the scene where condemned convicts are nailed to the cross to enable the artists to capture the "essence" of the Crucifixion—the book is still a fraud. Or, to be fair to the author, our reactions are fraudulent and sentimental.

At one point in the book Velazquez is quoted as saying, "Art should be Truth; and Truth unadorned, unsentimentalized, is Beauty." If Velazquez did not actually say those words, he certainly lived them. Velazquez painted what he saw—moles on the face, shrewdness in the eyes, the tightness of a man's smile; and, unlike many artists, he refused to make moral judgments about what he saw. An unpopular vocation; but Velazquez had the maturity and talent to make his realistic portraits works of art and hence acceptable to knowledgeable critics.

Yet as I read Velazquez's words, I muttered, "Oh, God, here we go again" in simple despair, not at the statement, but at our consistent willingness to condone—indeed, adore—historical treatments of themes which when presented as modern are condemned. For there is something of a parallel between the realistic portraits of Velazquez and Harriet's candid recordings of the events around her. Harriet records just what she sees and hears. In the beginning, she lacks the maturity to even know she might contemplate making moral judgments. What is important is that Harriet grows before our eyes. She learns that unvarnished truth *can* be painful, not only to her, but to others. Like Velazquez, she will never be able to stop seeing the unadorned truth, but we do know that she will learn; that one can tell the truth only if one acquires the necessary artistic skills.

So to me it is Harriet and Gilly who show the veracity and the values we prize, not Juan, who finds slavery an acceptable way of life. How much longer, after all, can we go on trying to have things both ways? Can we object to Gilly's struggle to find love and freedom and give our most cherished medal to a book which denies the value of freedom? Can we admire Velazquez's realistic portraits while wishing Harriet had never arrived on the scene? Can we respect Velazquez's right to paint realistically and object to Louise Fitzhugh's right to write realistically?

Oh, but Harriet isn't real, the critics will insist. There are no children like her—and if there are, we don't want to know about them. Particularly, we don't want other children to know about her in case they decide to emulate her behavior.

If those are the rules of the game, then rush back and weed your shelves of all subversive reading. Do you want boys reading *Tom Sawyer* and scaring their families into thinking they are dead? Do you want them to learn from Tom how to get a job done by conning your friends into doing it for you?

Next comes *Huckleberry Finn,* whose father is an alcoholic. (All Harriet's father does is have a pre-dinner martini.) Huck's comments on religion are hardly complimentary; he runs away from home, plays hookey, shows no respect for his elders. Small wonder that juvenile delinquency is continually on the rise when we harbor such books!

The list is never ending. Put in its strongest terms, there is no book in your library that someone cannot object to for one reason or another. And all the nice, precise "criteria" we set forth are of no real help because the criteria are subject to interpretation—in other words, to value judgments.

A classic example of the uselessness of precise criteria can be found in *Book Selection in Education*[14] by Hannah Logasa.

The criteria are Miss Logasa's; the comments in parentheses are mine.

"For children, do not place on the shelves books

1. Written in poor English (there go *Strawberry Girl, The Lone Hunt,* in fact all regional stories).

2. Untrue to life, unless they are frankly imaginative (untrue to whose life—yours or mine?).

3. Giving incorrect information, especially in geography, history, science and inventions (why not just stop at giving incorrect information?).

4. In a long series (out you go Laura Ingalls Wilder, *Henry Huggins,* and *Little Eddie*—or does one know how long long is?).

5. Emphasizing murder, cruelty, scenes of violence, and low ideals (that seems safe enough, unless, of course, you are one of those who considers bullfighting cruel, violent, and representing low ideals?).

6. Having themes [sic] as follows: child as a problem (*Caddie Woodlawn* and *Good Master?*); child as a matchmaker; child runaways; boy runaways; getting rich (What? Not treat of our national goal?); childish love affairs (more appropriate, perhaps, for adult book selectors, since most affairs in adult books strike me as terribly childish); weeping, sentimental girl (okay for boys to weep?); the morbid (wish I knew what that meant); the melodramatic (Dickens will do for a beginning); overemphasis on riches (what's with this money bit, anyway?); children who are flip and 'smarty' (banish *Pippi Longstocking* for a start); emphasis on class feeling; *generally, whatever you would not wish your child to be or do."* (Italics mine.)

That last comment is the crux of the matter as far as interpretation is concerned. Does it automatically follow that I want for my children what you want for yours? Does it even follow that we want for Jimmy what we want for Johnny once we know each one's special abilities and limitations?

In an *Introduction to Children's Work* I said: "There can be no hard-and-fast rules as to what is appropriate content because there are many differing views on what is needed to help a child grow into the kind of person we want him to be. There is general agreement about the qualities we want him to have but not about how he can best develop them.

"We want the child to grow into an adult who is happy in his work, who is capable of genuine affection and relationships with other people. We want him to use whatever talents he is blessed with to the best of his ability."[15]

What an optimistic statement that was! Had I been hard-headed rather than inspirational I would have said, "We want our children to be exactly like us, only more so."

The Iowa Supreme Court recently proved the latter statement with a vengeance when it denied Harold Painter custody of his own son. Mr. Painter is a photographer for the Job Corps, he drives a foreign car, and his new wife plays the guitar. He does not go to church; she is a Roman Catholic. The maternal grandparents were awarded custody on the grounds that their home would provide the boy "with a stable, dependable, conventional, middle-class, Middle West background and . . . a solid foundation and secure atmosphere." Though the court admitted the boy would have "more freedom of contact and thought with an opportunity to develop his individual talents" if he lived with his father, it nevertheless took upon itself the right to select the values the boy would grow up with. The case is not settled and one can only pray that higher courts have broader minds.

Is the goal of democracy, then, to produce the *Brave New World* of Huxley, the *1984* of Orwell, to enforce conformity by court decree and in libraries by carefully selecting only those books which treat of the conventional? We have reached the crucial point in our history—not only in the library and school world but in our entire society—where we must ponder the implications of our current policies.

Shall we continue to buy books only for Peter Quinn and the youth of Webster Groves, who will read them to get into college and to reinforce their own sense of superiority; or shall we buy books for Juan Gonzales, who will read them, as James Baldwin read books, to identify himself as a member of the human race, with the knowledge that he is not alone in being different, in suffering?

I refuse to believe that we really want an entire world of Peter Quinns. That would mean the end to art, music, literature, which the Quinns cannot create. I think we also realize that no society could withstand an entire world of creative people. We need a balance, and if history is a reasonable guide, the Peters will always outnumber the artists. But it is balance we must have, for survival.

What I want from the librarians of the world is the guts to provide a book collection that allows children and young people to make their own decisions. I believe that children are capable of far more mature thinking than we give them credit for; that they, even more than we adults, understand the issues of existence and survival. But even more, they own the future; they have possibilities of growth that are no longer ours, and that we cannot calculate; above all, they have a disinterest we cannot claim. A Mississippi Freedom Worker explained recently the gulf that separates youth from us middle-aged, middle-class Neanderthals. He said:

"What we question is whole assumptions, while I think you get excited about specific injustices. I think that's the way it is because you have a lot going for you inside the system, so you're hung up on what you know is best for you; or else you're able to be 'philosophical,' which I think is a middle-class luxury if there ever was one. I don't mean to single you out; it's the way things are. People like you have to think twice about what you say or do, and what so-and-so will think about your opinions, and all that. As you keep saying, it's rough on the white Southerner, and rough on middle-class people, too. Well, in a way, it's *not* rough on us. We may get shot, but we don't sit up half the night worrying and sweating about whether to sign a petition *we* believe in, or whether to come out in favor of something we believe, for fear the papers will call it 'radical.' That's freedom we have—and maybe we shouldn't give it up, even for a lot of money in the poverty program."[16]

That young man outlined for us the real conflict in values in our society. Some of us have comfort, and security, as long as we do not express deviant opinions, run against the crowd. Others of us have freedom, including the greatest freedom granted man, the willingness to die for our beliefs.

Before those choices, it seems more than a little ridiculous that we, who live in comfort and conformity, should be directing so much energy toward keeping young people from the books which make freedom, even at the risk of death, worth achieving. Johnny Tremain discovered that men must fight for the right to stand up: the story repeats itself in Freedom Rides, Sit-Ins, and in Vietnam. For whatever our differences on these subjects, we know that freedom, not comfort, is the issue.

Is it so much to ask that we fight for authors to have the right to offer young people provocative books which may help them to break through the barriers we, the adults, have created to keep them from questioning our comfortable way of life? Considering the number of adults who are going to psychiatrists, taking tranquilizers, having ulcers, and dying young of tension-induced heart attacks, we can hardly claim that our way of life is the ultimate in satisfaction. Can we?

REFERENCES

1. *Two Blocks Apart,* ed. C. L. Mayerson, Holt, 1965.
2. *Catcher in the Rye,* J. D. Salinger, Little, 1951; Modern Library; pa. Bantam.
3. *Harriet the Spy,* Louise Fitzhugh, Harper, 1964.
4. *The Long Secret,* L. Fitzhugh, Harper, 1965.
5. *Dorp Dead,* J. Cunningham, Pantheon, 1965.
6. *Johnny Tremain,* Esther Forbes, Houghton, 1943.
7. *Call It Courage,* Armstrong Sperry, Macmillan, 1940.
8. *Charlotte's Web,* E. B. White, Harper, 1952.
9. *Durango Street,* F. Bonham, Dutton, 1965.
10. *Ring the Judas Bell,* J. Forman, Farrar, Straus, 1965.
11. *I, Juan de Pareja,* Elizabeth Borton de Trevino, Farrar, Straus, 1965.
12. *The Bronze Bow,* Elizabeth G. Speare, Houghton, 1961.
13. *The Plague,* Albert Camus, Knopf, 1946; pa. Vintage.
14. *Book Selection in Education,* Hannah Logasa, Faxon, 1965.
15. *Introduction to Children's Work,* Dorothy Broderick, Wilson, 1965.
16. "The Search for Community," Robert Coles, *New Republic,* Feb. 26, 1966, p. 4.

CHAPTER

29 *The Diamond and the Parrot*

(NOVEMBER 15, 1966)

by ANNE PELLOWSKI

Even if hostile to your beliefs, any book that has been written in honesty, out of love of people, out of good will, is admirable.—Maxim Gorky

Nothing is more repugnant to a child than to be told that his present is merely a preparation for the future, that he is today somehow less than living. He is very much alive to everything that goes on around him, but only in his own peculiar way. The writer has to set himself on that way and then see life—steady and whole. A child is never satisfied with a partial vision or a diluted or disinfected version of life. Whatever we give him must be complete and fullblooded.—B. B. Agarwal

Very few have realized that children's literature is written with the aim of educating them, and education is a worthy undertaking, which decides human destiny. . . . Therefore, children's literature should be judged . . . not only for its ideas and content, but also for its artistry and style.—Hsün Lu[1]

Do these passages have a familiar look, as though encountered once before, perhaps in Hazard, perhaps Lillian Smith? This sensation of *déja vu* occurs frequently when one studies the history and theory of children's literature in other countries. One might conclude from these highly idealistic sentiments that the Soviet, Indian, and Communist Chinese theorists who are quoted above have much in common with each other, as well as with the critics who have served the United States in her development of a children's literature. Let me hasten to add that what all have in common is fairly well balanced by what they disagree on, in theory and in practice.

The quote from Maxim Gorky expresses at best only a small part of his feelings about the purpose of children's literature. In a later essay, he wrote:

> Of special importance is the task of providing children with books that will tell them of the origin of private property and how that property is the main obstacle to man's development today . . .
>
> We must get our leading writers and artists to produce books and albums about the peoples of the world, while the peoples of the USSR can best be described by specialists on local lore . . . These will be able to describe the life and customs of the various nationalities in the process of change and development, thereby inculcating sentiments of internationalism in children. . . .
>
> Children must learn not only to count and measure, but also to imagine and foresee. . . .
>
> The bold and successful experience of several authors who have written books on the future of our construction . . . shows that children can be addressed in simple and attractive language, without the least didacticism and on the most serious themes. Simple and clear style is achieved not by lowering the level of literary standards but through consummate craftsmanship.[2]

Such statements, clearly moral in purpose, give a better indication of what this leading Soviet writer recommended. They are of greatest importance, for Gorky's essays on the subject are perhaps the single most influential force in children's literature of the Communist countries. Even in Communist China, which boasts its own revered theorist in the person of Hsün Lu, it is customary for critics to refer to Gorky's works and to the resulting superiority of children's books in the USSR. This has become less pronounced since the 1960s, but admiration is still evident in the countless Chinese children's books which are modeled on those of the Soviet Union.

In this country, it is Chukovsky whom we have in translation,[3] and who stirs a reponsive echo, through his admirable independence of doctrine, and free aestheticism. But Gorky had little use for Chukovsky and his criticisms, and if the sheer number of current books and articles appearing in Communist countries is any indication, it is Gorky who has had the more intensive and far-reaching influence.

THE ROLE OF IDEOLOGY

What of the children's books which are produced to meet the needs of countries with such an ideology? What happens when, as Hsün Lu recommends, children's books have as one of their main purposes the fostering of the revolutionary spirit?[4] It will probably surprise many to discover that the results are generally good. What is expressed in their theory as devotion to the revolutionary cause most often emerges, in stories about everyday children, as a kind of high moral code, based on what is right and wrong, not on ethical or religious grounds, but in terms of what is for the good of the state and its collective members. To the US librarian, their tone is vaguely reminiscent of the didactic stories so popular in this country in the 19th Century.

But just as Gogol saw no contradiction between doctrine and aesthetic quality, these books don't, for all their morality, suffer in literary merit. Nonfiction books are expertly illustrated and clearly written. Picture books for the very young are most often rhymed, and deal with everyday characters, situations, and objects—the family, the home and its furnishings, food, games, toys, animals, etc. Sometimes these common articles have magical properties or are placed in fantastic dreams. The books are usually produced on mediocre paper, with flimsy covers, but the illustrations and general format are quite good, and each decade shows a marked improvement, especially in the quality of paper.

These general characteristics could be applied to a majority of the children's books produced in any of the Communist countries, but there is one characteristic which can be said to apply to all—the stupendous size of the editions. This is no secret; it has been observed and described by any number of persons. Suffice it to say that its significance has yet to be comprehended. In this country, we speak in hopeful tones of ten books per child in each school library. *There are probably more than this number of books per child in the homes of a good majority of the peoples of the Communist countries.* This is a supposition, but it is based on personal observation and on a very general interpretation of statistics issued by the countries themselves.[5]

Not all of these books inculcate "sentiments of internationalism," as Gorky would have them do. Political expedience often cancels out the effort to show brotherliness. While a great number of the books Chinese children read are "humble-looking books published with the best of taste and unusually inspired in pictures and texts,"[6] other kinds have been described, notably by Virginia Haviland. Miss Haviland, discussing a group of Chinese children's books acquired by the Library of Congress, comments that they reveal "a prevailing element as sharp as that in the earlier doctrinal children's books from Hitler's Germany. Published either in Peiping or Shanghai, these include a few examples of juvenile periodicals. . . . The most sensational book . . . is a story entitled *A Negro Boy Named Paul.* In it, a small American child, lame from polio, receives further injury from a white policeman who will not permit him to approach a school for white children."[7]

One may question, however, whether such bias is unique to Communist literature. In previous eras, it was felt that the child should be sheltered from the harsher political and social realities of life. A child of revolution, a child of this age of advanced audiovisual communication, is no longer afforded the luxury of innocence and ignorance in such matters. He is expected to take a stand not only *for* patriotism but *against* the particular ideology considered most inimical by his country's leaders and politicians. He is supposed to know why aggression is all right for his country but denounced when it appears on "the other side," and all the while he is urged to learn more about the children of other lands, and about peaceful coexistence. And this from books which are out-of-date, stereotyped, one-sided, or incomplete.

The situation is as true of the US as it is of the USSR or China, or almost any country, for that matter. Have we the right to label as shocking or "sensational" the Chinese story mentioned above when in the US the only children's fiction dealing with contemporary life in the Communist countries has to do with an escape from it? It is quite evident that a racial incident in the US occurs about as frequently as an escape across the Berlin wall or over a guarded border. Some might argue that books like *Aunt America* by Marie Bloch are exceptions, but the tone is very much the same as that of the escape books, and early in the book there is a passage in which some of the men in the village (near Kiev) discuss past times, which were perhaps not better than the present:

> "But at least anyone who had the wish and the money could leave. Nowadays, my friends, our frontier is a prison wall. . . ."
> "If they should open it, overnight we would leave."
> "For that matter, even the dogs would follow us?"[8]

Somehow this seems more like wishful thinking on the part of the American author, and it does not ring true in any but the narrowest context.

It is true that we have many traditional folktales, some "classics," and an increasing number of nonfiction books and historical stories, all centered in one or another of the Communist countries. But for the most part, these are concerned with the history and past of the two great powers, the Soviet Union and China, and by no means does the number of titles equal the number of books about our old allies, Russia and China, nor does it anywhere approach the percentage of titles we have on such countries as France, Italy, Germany, or Japan. To corroborate this point one has only to compare the appropriate sections of current basic lists with those of 30 years ago.

Perhaps it is to be expected that ideologies so in conflict can never be seen objectively or be experienced without suspicion, especially when this rapprochement must take place through the medium of books. But official government policy, at least in this country, has encouraged more and more the exchange of ideas, the attempt at some kind of communication. The fact remains that for US children, modern books offer either downright discouragement or they lead to ever greater misunderstanding because they represent the past—not the present, the few—not the many, with a few exceptions, such as Vandivert's *Young Russia*, Appel's *Why the Russians Are the Way They Are, Children of Russia*, and others. But these titles are not typical of the mass of US output.

The depiction of Yugoslavia may be the one exception in this dearth of American juvenile fiction on contemporary life abroad, because of the translations of Ivan Kusan's *Koko and the Ghosts* and *The Mystery of Green Hill* and Nada Curcija-Prodanovic's *Ballerina*. But three books make a very weak exception.

Translation is not the only solution; it is not always the best, either. But it is one which is bypassed most quickly. "Those languages are so terribly difficult!" is the thought which comes first, rather than "What a fine story this is!" It is a little disconcerting to note that in Poland, for example, a child can share not only the same classics as the English-speaking child: *Little Women, The Secret Garden, Anne of Green Gables*, The Leatherstocking series, *Wind in the Willows*, to name only a few; he can also read more recent writers such as Munro Leaf, Pamela Travers, Geoffrey Trease, E. C. Spykman, Arthur Clarke and Eleanor Farjeon. What have we from or about Poland in the English language? Precious little! The excellence of *The Trumpeter of Krakow* and a few good folktale collections do not go far. A slightly revised *Land and People of Poland* and a sketchy *Getting to Know* series book add a little, but the dry fact is never quite as effective as the evocative story. No wonder, then, that the Polish guide at the UN is greeted with blank looks and peculiar answers when she asks children if they know where Poland is located. While her French colleague from Paris gets delightful answers such as "That's where Madeline lives!" and her Swiss counterpart invariably is asked about Heidi, she must cope with "Is Poland in Africa?"[9]

Although Communist countries are obviously most neglected in representation here, other countries don't fare much better in our children's books. We are afflicted by too many US travelers who become quick experts rather than careful observers. Their mistakes are not often those of commission—facts are checked too carefully by most editors. It is the omissions which create the wrong impressions or never allow a total picture to develop.

On many lists one finds these story books recommended on contemporary India: *My Village in India, The Road to Agra, The White Bungalow, "What Then, Raman?," India's Children, Chendru, Rain in the Winds, Gift of the Forest, A Cap for Mul Chand.* They are all acceptable, some more than others. Yet the total picture is overwhelmingly one of *village* life, whereas there is about 30 percent of the population living in the large cities and towns, with children who lead quite different lives. Must we learn about them entirely from nonfiction?

"Why do almost all US books on Mexico picture little burros and barefoot Indian children in sombreros?" questions a Mexican librarian sadly.[10] If you don't believe her, take a careful look at these titles, culled from three standard lists: *The Story of Pancho, Angelo, the Naughty One, The Painted Pig, The Least One, Ramon Makes a Trade, Tacho, Boy of Mexico, A Hero by Mistake, Hat for a Hero, The Poppy Seeds, The Two Uncles of Pablo, Chucho.* Many have excellent illustrations to match basically good stories, but only one or two are completely free of the stereotype.

Why do so many books about other countries have as their central character an American or British child? Is it entirely because this is a more natural situation for the writer to describe, or is it because he cannot or will not attempt to write from a truly native point of view? In a selective list of books about Africa,[11] covering the years 1960–1965, the compilers were able to recommend only nine fictional books, and five of these had American, British, or European children as the protagonists. This to cover a vast continent with more than two dozen countries. In a more recent list of children's fiction on Japan, there were some 55 titles for that country alone![12] (True, less than a third were classified as very good and the remainder were termed only satisfactory, in whole or in part.)

The nonfiction series now on the market have a terrible similarity in tone, format, and even representation, often when dealing with the most diverse nations. Librarians and teachers are guilty of recommending and purchasing them in quantity, simply because there is nothing else available. No one seems to question the fact that a single author can hardly write with the same objectivity about all the countries of the world. Yet there are any number of series which trust to this device (quite apart from the photographic books about individual children, which come out better because of their very limitation). A patronizing tone is immediately deplored in a book of fiction, but slips by unnoticed in many a nonfiction book. Instead of opening with "You could be in the Virgin Islands tomorrow morning if you were to fly from the East Coast of the United States tonight," it would be more correct to begin with the reverse: "You could be in the United States tomorrow morning, if . . ." Is the book really about the Islands, or is it about how and what we in the US think about the Islands?

We seem to be constantly exhorting our children to look for the "likenesses" or "sameness" of children of other lands, while at the same time capitalizing on their easy distraction with the unusual. Make no mistake about it, we *are* different from each other. To point out the infinite variations on this common experience we call life, and to teach children to admire and wonder at them rather than regard them as exotic curiosities, should be our goal. Comparison and self-realization will come on their own, if the child is ready for them.

A TIME OF APPREHENSION

How true and appropriate was Elizabeth Nesbitt's statement that children of today are given few opportunities to *apprehend*, rather than comprehend. It brought to mind the story "Winter Night" by Kay Boyle, which has one of those rare and compelling opening sentences: "There is a time of apprehension that begins with the beginning of darkness, and to which only the speech of love can lend security." For each of those children about to experience a "time of apprehension" about other ways and other peoples, it is up to us to provide enough of the written language of love.

We have some fine books to start with. For, political trends notwithstanding, many delightfully individual human characteristics have remained the same and there is a great deal of validity in such books as *Treasure Trove of the Sun, Big Tiger and Christian, The Good Master, Daughter of the Mountains, Dobry*. But we delude ourselves if we think this is enough to keep our children in the world, not out of it, as Eleanor Farjeon puts it in "The Seventh Princess." The most careful selection, the most critical reviewing, the most perceptive analysis should be given our books about other countries. Wider use should be made of foreign books in their native editions. Many of these collections sit on closed shelves or cupboards because they are considered irreplaceable. Others are on the open shelves but never get used because they are not introduced; yet I can testify from experience in the New York Public Library that they make a most effective substitute or supplement. (When you've run out of material on Russia for the fourth grade, try giving a Russian book to the child to take to his teacher, with the explanation that you don't have a book on what Russian children eat, but you have one showing them doing it and in their own language.)

We tend to dismiss lightly the efforts of other countries to develop a sound children's literature, forgetting that our own went through long periods of didacticism and that even our present-day total production has faults which could bear correction. The same is true of library service to children. Our public and school libraries are not always models to be emulated. Both the philosophy and the practical application have little or no relevance in too many instances. Far better would it be to send abroad experts, advisers, teachers and volunteers equipped with a broader knowledge of the oral and written children's literature which does exist, and with a wider exposure to the patterns of children's book service (not only in libraries) which have proven helpful in many countries, not just in the US. This information is limited in amount, and extremely difficult to locate, but well worth investigating.

We must have wider study of the literature of other countries, so that we are better judges of books about them. Library school students can use such study with greater profit than they might use a survey of some miniscule point in the Newbery or Caldecott books. This can turn up such enchanting comparisons as the difference between Mother Goose songs and this traditional Malayalam lullaby:

Are you a darling baby moon or a fine beautiful lotus flower?
Are you the honey that fills flowers or the light of the full moon?
Are you a new piece of diamond or the whisper of little parrots?
Are you the dancing peacock or the quail that sings a beautiful note?[13]

With such discoveries to be made, there should be few complaints about the effort involved.

The author wishes to thank Jean McGraw, Kathleen Roedder, S. Carolyn Thomas, Carolyn Heidemann, and Mary Villemonte, students in the children's literature classes of the University of Maryland School of Library and Information Services and the University of Wisconsin Library School, for assistance in corroboration of a number of points in this article.

REFERENCES

1. Complete references for these quotations are: Maxim Gorky, *On Literature.* Moscow: Foreign Languages Publishing House, n.d., p. 22; B. B. Agarwal in Prabha Sahasrabudhe, *Writing for Children Today: Why, What, and How?* New Delhi: Bal Bhavan and National Children's Museum, 1963, p. 3; and Hsün Lu, quoted in Po-ch 'ui Ch'ên, *Tso chia yü êrh t'ung wên hsüeh.* Tien-Tsin, People's Publisher, 1957, pp. 2–11.
2. Maxim Gorky, *op. cit.,* pp. 224–227. The two essays cited here seem to be the only ones translated into English. However, there are many editions in Russian, German, Polish, Czech, Chinese, etc., some of these in the Library of Congress.
3. Kornei Chukovsky, *From Two to Five,* ed. and trans. by Miriam Morton. University of California, 1963.
4. Shu-jên Chou, *Lu Hsün lun êrh t'ung chiao yü ho êrh t'ung wên hsüeh.* Shanghai: Youth Press, 1961, Chapter II.

5. For example, *Pechat SSSR*, published yearly in Moscow by the Ministerstvo Kultury, Vsesoiuznaia Knizhnaia Palata, gives statistics for all of the Soviet republics. They must, of course, be interpreted carefully.
6. Claire Huchet Bishop, "What Chinese Children Read," *Commonweal*, Vol. 82, No. 10, May 28, 1965, p. 325.
7. Virginia Haviland, "Serving Those Who Serve Children; a National Reference Library of Children's Books," *Quarterly Journal of the Library of Congress*, Vol. 22, No. 4, Oct. 1965, pp. 311–316.
8. Marie Bloch, *Aunt America*, Atheneum, 1963, p. 14.
9. Reported in a personal conversation.
10. Aurora Labastida, "Children's Books on Mexico," *Top of the News*, Vol. 18, No. 1, Oct. 1961, pp. 40–43.
11. Helen T. Armstrong and Ruth Ann Robinson, "Books on Africa for Children," *Top of the News*, Vol. 21, No. 4, June 1965, pp. 334–337.
12. Miriam Burris, "Japan in Children's Fiction," *Elementary English*, Vol. 43, No. 1, Jan. 1966, pp. 29–38.
13. Quoted by S. Carolyn Thomas in a paper "Children's Literature in Kerala, India," submitted in Course LS 622, University of Wisconsin Library School, summer 1966.

CHILDREN'S BOOKS CITED IN ARTICLE

Note: Citation is not necessarily a recommendation. Please consult article for author's comments.

APPEL, Benjamin. *Why the Russians Are the Way They Are*. Little, 1966
ARORA, Shirley L. *"What Then, Raman?"* Follett, 1960
BATCHELOR, Julie Forsyth. *A Cap for Mul Chand*. Harcourt, 1950
BEHN, Harry. *Two Uncles of Pablo*. Harcourt, 1959
BRENNER, Anita. *Hero by Mistake*. W. R. Scott, 1953
BULLA, Clyde R. *The Poppy Seeds*. Crowell, 1955
Children of Russia (series). Sterling Publishing Company
CURCIJA-PRODANOVIC, Nada. *Ballerina*. Criterion, 1964
DARBOIS, Dominique. *Tacho, Boy of Mexico*. Follett, 1961
GARRETT, Helen. *Angelo, The Naughty One*. Viking, 1944
GIBBS, Alonzo. *The Least Likely One*. Lothrop, 1964
GIDAL, Sonia and Tim. *My Village in India*. Pantheon, 1956
HADER, Berta and Elmer. *The Story of Pancho and The Bull with the Crooked Tail*. Macmillan, 1942
KELLY, Eric P. *Land and People of Poland*. rev. ed., Lippincott, 1964
———. *Trumpeter of Krakow*. Macmillan, 1928
KUSAN, Ivan. *Koko and the Ghost*. Harcourt, 1966
———. *Mystery of Green Hill*. Harcourt, 1962
LOUDEN, Claire and George. *Rain in the Winds*. Hale, 1953
MORROW, Elizabeth H. *The Painted Pig*. Knopf, 1942
MUHLENWEG, Fritz. *Big Tiger and Christian*. Pantheon, 1952
PRISHVIN, M. M. *Treasure Trove of the Sun*. Macmillan, o.p.; Viking, indefinitely out of stock
RANKIN, Louise. *Daughter of the Mountains*. Viking, 1948
RITCHIE, Barbara. *Ramon Makes a Trade*. Parnassus, 1959
SEREDY, Kate. *The Good Master*. Viking, 1935
SHANNON, Monica. *Dobry*. Viking, 1934

SHORTER, Bani. *India's Children*. Viking, 1960

SINGH, R. L., and LOWNSBERY, E. *Gift of the Forest*. McKay, 1958

SOMMERFELT, Aimée. *Road to Agra*. Criterion, 1961

————. *White Bungalow*. Criterion, 1964

SUCKSDORFF, Astrid Bergman. *Chendru: The Boy and the Tiger*. Harcourt, 1960

VANDIVERT, Rita. *Young Russia*. Dodd, 1960

WALLACE, John A. *Getting to Know Poland*. Coward, 1960

30 The

Grand Illusion

(MARCH 15, 1968)

by ELI M. OBOLER

In 1951 a popular song had a line expressing the common plaint, "They tried to tell us we're too young." Who were "they"? "They," of course, were the ones the new generation seems to find especially annoying, the ones who are over 30, or 35, or 40. "They" are trying to tell kids that they are far too young to do what they're doing. Naturally, this leads to resentment on the part of teenagers, and in exasperation and natural reaction, they do even more of whatever it is that "they" try to tell them they are too young to do.

This problem of "the generation gap" ties in with reading and communication. Even Restif de la Bretonne, best known today as a pornographer, in his later years waxed most eloquent on the cause and effect relationship of "bad" books and youthful delinquencies. The Durants tell us in their most recent volume, *Rousseau and Revolution,* that de la Bretonne "berated Rousseau for having unleashed the passions of the young. . . ." He charged, "It is *Emile* that has brought us this arrogant generation, stubborn and insolent and willful, which speaks loudly, and silences the elderly."[1] Today's teenage generation may not be inspired by *Emile*, but it certainly could be described by some of the same adjectives applied by de la Bretonne.

Common among the restrictions on our teenagers are those which, in the case of movies, tell them that particular movies are for those 18 and over only; or, in the case of books, tell them that they cannot buy particular paperbacks at the corner drugstore, or they cannot find in their public libraries the books that they would like to read, or even that, within those public libraries, if they can locate them, they may not *read* them unless they, again, are over the magic age of 18.

This matter of age as related to interest in sexual matters is often ignored in considering how best to give appropriate library services to those between 13 and 18. For many years we have known, on the basis of scientific proof, from Dr. Alfred Kinsey's famous studies and others, that adolescence, particularly for the male, is coincident with the high peak of sexual activity and interest.[2] So we have the interesting paradox that the very period in human life when the human animal is most interested and concerned with sexual activity is the period when he or she is expressly barred from reading material directly concerned with his or her greatest interests. As might be expected, this often leads to difficulties.

To clarify further, the Kinsey report, discussing the adolescent boy, says that "the peak of *capacity* occurs in the fast-growing years prior to adolescence; the peak of actual performance is the middle or later teens."[3] In other words, the typical male high school student is much more preoccupied with sex than even the college student, whom conventional wisdom accepts as the leader in this respect. Kinsey comments on "an intensification of the struggle between the boy's biologic capacity and the sanctions imposed by the older male. . . ."[4] It is about these sanctions and the *realities* of adolescent life that I am writing.

Often, the mistaken impression exists that some kind of mysterious or magic change in brainpower and self-control occurs between the last day of the 17th year of an individual and the first day of his 18th year. This is not so. People mature at different rates, and, indeed, some never mature at all in the psychological or even the physical sense.

INTELLECTUAL FREEDOM FOR TEENS

Our present library rules on access to books of a presumably sexual nature for adolescents are not only outdated; the rules themselves are almost obscene in the commonly accepted sense of being "offensive to . . . decency." What could be more indecent than what Browning, in his mid-Victorian way, referred to in *The Statue and the Bust* when he said:

> The sin I impute to each frustrate ghost
> Is in the unlit lamp and the ungirt loin.

Surely our modern psychology has verified this Victorian rebel's literary attempt to single out the sin of the loin which is girt, when the human physiology calls for the opposite.

Don't misunderstand me. I am advocating neither promiscuity nor the widespread reading of obscene and/or pornographic literature by teenage boys and girls; rather, I am asking that we face up to what our own experience, knowledge, and the scientific facts of life indicate to us.

The 1967 meeting of hundreds of librarians and others interested in the topic of "Intellectual Freedom and the Teenager," sponsored by the ALA Intellectual Freedom Committee, came to several rather interesting conclusions. Among these were that if any group of library users needs protection and a "bill of rights," it is certainly the teenager in America today. A prominent lawyer, Stanley Fleishman, discussing the legal aspects of censorship, asked librarians to check into why they were restricting access to certain books. He wondered if librarians are "truly interested in complete freedom for the young, or are they interested in controlling, directing, and shaping young people in the present cultural molds."[5]

The Supreme Court of the United States, on May 15, 1967, ruled that "neither the Fourteenth Amendment nor the Bill of Rights is for adults alone." Detailed evidence indicates that despite the fact that in many states and local communities adolescents have been denied their just rights, they are still entitled to them. This is certainly another step toward indicating that these days are different from the past, and that if the majority of the Supreme Court of the United States can agree that juveniles are entitled to the safeguards of the Bill of Rights and other parts of the Constitution, surely there should be no differentiation made between laws on censorship for adults and for adolescents.

THE CASE FOR CENSORSHIP

A prominent sociologist, Ernest van den Haag, writing in *Esquire Magazine* for May 1967, under the title *The Case for Pornography Is the Case for Censorship and Vice Versa,* has claimed that censorship on the whole is needed because "if pornography were allowed to proliferate unchecked it might influence both public and private attitudes and sensibilities, and, therefore, ultimate reactions." He says that "certainly books can follow the atmosphere so as to engender a support of abominable and criminal acts."[6] You will note that he gives no evidence to support this, but simply states that it is so. There have been many opinions to the contrary, held by equally prominent sociologists, psychologists, and other authorities, based on research and investigation.

Even if it were true that the reading of so-called "bad" books causes or contributes to socially undesirable behavior, "most believers in censorship apparently reject as too long-range or visionary the corollary that the answer to a bad book is a good one. Rather, their philosophy seems to be that the best answer to a so-called "bad" book is no book.

Let's face it. At this point, we really don't *know* for sure what the actual cause-and-effect relationship is between reading and behavior. As Bergen Evans has stated, "In the realm of sexual customs—the field in which censors are most industrious—the effect of books is very slight. Raping is a much older activity than reading, and men are rarely incited to it by the printed page."

Fortunately, something is being done about this facet of the censorship problem. At the ALA preconference I referred to, one of the major recommendations was that a truly scientific study in depth be made to ascertain the causal relationship, if any, between reading and deviant social behavior. When funds become available, it seems fairly certain that this study will be made. Furthermore, the United States Congress has passed a bill to set up a study commission on the subject. And, most important, this fall the U.S. Supreme Court issued a judgment on a New York case involving the limits of what can be published and made available for teenagers.

But whatever the results of the studies and the verdicts, they cannot really affect the most important part of dealing with teenagers as far as libraries are concerned. Librarians are prone to follow the criteria their professional groups set up, and this is probably more true of those lax in standards than of any other type.

LOOPHOLES IN SELECTION GUIDES

The leaflet entitled *Selecting Materials for School Libraries: Guidelines and Selection Sources to Insure Quality Collections,* prepared by the American Association of School Librarians in 1965, states:

> The individual school library collection should include all facets of the curriculum with materials which reflect different points of view on controversial subjects and which provide opportunities for pupils and teachers to range far and wide in their search for information and inspiration. . . . All materials selected for the school library, in whatever format, should meet high standards of excellence. Materials which deal with current topics should be up-to-date; those which reflect a biased point of view should make the prejudice recognizable.

Let us speculate on the possible effects of following these "guidelines." To begin with, there seems to be a pretty strong indication that school libraries must reflect whatever is in the curriculum: if there were to be no curricular matter connected with sex, surely the library would be obligated, under these guidelines, to bar materials on sex, since they would be unrelated to the particular courses taught.

Another reflection based on these guidelines might be that the injunction about the "up-to-dateness" of materials would imply a rather rigid weeding program. If one were to consider Vietnam, for example, as a "current" topic, then books and other reading materials dated before 1967 could possibly be considered out of date, and therefore not needed in the library, which certainly would hurt any historical study on this important subject.

Librarians have, to a great extent, begged the question of what to do about controversial and censorable materials. To say that "all materials . . . should meet high standards of excellence" is equivalent to saying that "God is good." What would be a *low* standard of excellence? What would be a standard of *less* than excellence? What, indeed, would be a standard? There is no indication in these guidelines to help any school librarian, or school board member, or principal, or even the people most directly concerned—the students.

Let us consult another official publication: *Standards for School Library Programs,* issued by the American Library Association in 1960. This is the latest available set of standards for this branch of the profession and it says that: "A wealth of excellent materials is available for children and young people, but there is no justification for the collections to contain materials that are mediocre in presentation of content." It also says, "Maintaining qualitative standards of selection of materials is essential. All materials are, therefore, carefully evaluated before purchase, and only materials of good quality are obtained."

This sounds very nice. But just what are these "qualitative standards"? Nothing is stated specifically; there is simply a reference to "the established criteria for the evaluation and selection of materials."

Let us try the School Library Bill of Rights. It says that:

It is the responsibility of the school library to . . . provide materials that will enrich and support the curriculum . . . ; to provide materials which stimulate growth in factual knowledge, literary appreciation, esthetic values, and ethical standards . . . ; to provide a background of information which will enable pupils to make intelligent judgments in their daily life; provide materials on opposing sides of controversial issues so that young citizens may develop under guidance the practice of critical reading and thinking; provide materials representative of the many religious, ethnic, and cultural groups and their contributions to our American heritage; . . . to place principle above personal opinion and reason above prejudice in selection of materials of the highest quality in order to assure a comprehensive collection appropriate for the uses of the library.

Once again, some questions are being begged or evaded here. What materials "provide growth in . . . ethical standards"? Would *Little Lord Fauntleroy* be of more value than *Studs Lonigan* to a teenager living in a slum area in one of America's large cities today? How far does one go in attempting to provide "materials on opposing sides of controversial issues"? Practically everything and anything is controversial, and budgets are, after all, limited. Would ten books on religion and one book on atheism be a fair balance? Or should no books on atheism be included in a school library? How far should the school library go in including materials "representative of the many religious, ethnic, and cultural groups" which make up America? If one lives in a town which is 40 percent or 60 percent of one particular religious faith, should 40 percent or 60 percent of the books on religion in that school or public library deal with that particular faith, and should all books which are inimical to that faith be excluded?

A SOLUTION FOR THE LIBRARIAN

After these somewhat negative reflections, here is what I recommend as a simple and constructive proposal: that the librarians, responsible for selecting books, and the trustees, responsible for preparing or approving book selection policies for libraries, should not, at any time, place books in a public or school library specifically for a particular age group. Either a book should be in a library or it should not. If a teenager—a boy or girl under 18, since that is the generally accepted legal age of maturity—has a library card and requests a book which is in the library and which follows the various criteria cited above, he or she should be given that book, regardless of his or her age and no matter what the possible censorable quality of the book may be. If it is good enough to be in the library, it is good enough to be read by anyone who can read it.

The last people in the world to be censors are librarians. Once the decision has been made to add a particular book or magazine to the library, there should be no further censorship or selection that will keep it from anyone wanting it.

Finally, it is clear that trying to solve as complex a problem as the appropriate amount of intellectual freedom to which a teenager is entitled these days is somewhat like giving a pat answer to the question, "How can the U.S. get out of Vietnam with honor and with safety?" The *kind* of answer one gives to such questions as these, rather than the actual details of the answer, is what is important.

Here is a brief credo to which I hope all librarians can subscribe. The librarian should be on the side of the positive, the progressive, the one who seeks new answers rather than the one who goes along entirely with more of the same. What was earlier referred to as "the conventional wisdom" tells us that the older we are, the smarter we are. It also tells us that we must stop the young from finding out too soon what the world is really like. Librarians should disagree with both of these all-too-widely held judgments. The true librarian should be for freedom, for searching, for trying to find new and better answers to important questions, rather than relying on answers that have been given in the past. Getting down to the very basics in librarianship, librarians and library trustees are not, and *must not* try to improve or regulate the morals of today's teenager. The family, church and to some extent, the school (outside of the library) are far better and far more appropriate institutions to see to it that American youth today becomes a mature, responsible, worthwhile, older generation. The library's function in this is to do whatever it can to make the wealth of fine books, so-called good literature, available, even if there are a few four-letter words or pictures of nudes included in the package.

REFERENCES

1. Durant, Will and Ariel. *Rousseau and Revolution* (The Story of Civilization: Part X). Simon and Schuster, 1967, p. 919.
2. Kinsey, Albert C. and others. *Sexual Behavior in the Human Male.* Saunders, 1948, p. 219.
3. *Ibid.*
4. *Ibid.*, p. 222.
5. "Intellectual Freedom and the Teenager," *ALA Bulletin,* July, August 1967, p. 833.
6. The Case for Pornography Is the Case for Censorship and Vice Versa," *Esquire,* May, 1967, p. 134–135.
7. Jennison, Peter. "Freedom to Read," *Public Affairs Pamphlet No. 344,* May, 1963, p. 17.

CHAPTER

31 *Librarians*

and Literature

(AUGUST, 1960)

by DOROTHY M. BRODERICK

In the January 15, 1960 issue of LIBRARY JOURNAL, the editorial, "The Uninvited," lists three examples of the exclusion of librarians from important national committees and says, "If librarians cannot claim, earn, deserve, or receive recognition as experts in their own field—books—they have no right to expect greater status."

Reading this in the privacy of my own living room, I shouted aloud, "Three cheers!" It is a statement that needs repeating over and over again until no one calling himself a librarian will not have heard the call and answered it. We are fond of saying, "Books are our business," and that is how we treat them—as merchandise. The whole profession, as indeed our society, is permeated with the cult of usefulness. The "usefulness" of a book determines whether we accept it or reject it with almost no attention paid to the innate value of the book itself. It is only what the book is good "for" that interests us.

No reputation as literature experts can be gained while operating on this basis. The good literary critic is concerned with the book. He operates on the assumption that a good book will have some potential audience, the size of which does not interest him. Librarians operate on the opposite premise; a large audience for a bad book is more important to us than the quality of the book.

The question is, "Can it be otherwise?" I think it not only can but ought to be, and will develop the reasons for this further on. At the moment, let us look at library book reviews and see if the fundamental assumptions behind the clichés used in them are valid.

Probably we all have a pet phrase that irritates us more than the others. In my case the phrase is, "For the small library." The assumption is made that all small libraries have a lower class reading public while a large library by mere power of numbers will have a few people so odd as to want literary value in the books they read.

This may be true. It also may be true that a small library may be situated in a college town where its public consists primarily of college faculty members, their wives, children, and students at the college. A larger library may be located in a predominately manufacturing town with little or no interest among the people in literary and cultural affairs. Therefore, it is not the size of the library but the make-up of its clientele that determines the nature of the collection. A better wording might be, "For the small-minded library."

Of course the librarian ought to know his public, but if we worked on this assumption we would review books according to their merit and leave the selection to the librarian without degrading his ability to choose wisely by such a questionable cliché.

The whole philosophy of what one buys for a small library needs to be continually re-evaluated. I think of the small library and the large library in terms of monogamy and polygamy. The man who can marry only one woman has a far greater problem in selection than the man who can have a harem. The former must choose one that will last, not be a passing fancy. The latter can have a different wife for his every need and desire and thus can be far less selective with any one of them.

We all know that there is nothing quite so dead as last year's best seller. Yet it is this ephemeral material that is often recommended to the small library while the book of quality, the one that will be re-read for several generations, if not indefinitely, is considered too erudite for purchase. Does this really make sense? Isn't the fundamental principle of wise book selection to build a lasting collection? If not, in what way does the public library differ from a superior rental collection, other than in being free?

FAULKNER + HEMINGWAY = ⅓ ALDRICH

This bug-a-boo of what is suitable for the small library is also found perpetuated in the *Fiction Catalog*. The librarians who vote for the selection of books do not demonstrate any concern with literature. In the 1950 edition of the *Catalog* there are nine titles of Bess Streeter Aldrich with single or double stars. In the same volume, one Faulkner and two Hemingway titles are starred. When our two most important living authors combined are considered one-third as valuable as Bess Streeter Aldrich, we are hardly on our way to earning recognition as literary critics.

Reviews are passing things; but that mediocre value judgments should be perpetuated in standard tools is a disgrace. I have no quarrel with libraries buying a *limited* number of mysteries, westerns, science-fiction or light love novels. I do, however, proclaim loudly that these items have no right to inclusion in a selected buying guide. (Aside to H. W. Wilson: You are not being held responsible for the taste of the profession. I know you only tally the votes and I think you handle the mechanics of publishing the *Catalog* very nicely.)

A look at the contents of the *Fiction Catalog* will tell you much about how expert librarians are in the field of literature, and provide a working guide toward discovery of basic attitudes of the voting librarians. I assume the *Catalog* meets with general approval from the profession; this assumption is made negatively, i.e. there is no printed record of criticism and I've never been in a library that did not own it.

The preface to the supplements sets forth the standards by which books are to be voted for. The voting shall be done, it says, ". . . with emphasis on the usefulness (or otherwise) of each book in their own libraries or systems, in fact, they are instructed not to vote on books not actually known and used."

There are two important points here: books are to be in their own libraries and known to the voters. This means that we may make the following assumptions: books in the *Catalog* are bought by a majority of those voting and are read by the librarians.

Bendix, in her paper, *Some Problems in Book Selection Policies and Practices in Medium-Sized Public Libraries* observed that there was little relationship between the reviews a book received and whether the libraries in her sample bought it. The two books she cited were Nevil Shute's *Beyond the Black Stump* and Rodney Garland's *Heart in Exile*. The former received unanimously bad reviews, the latter's reviews were excellent; the former was bought, the latter not bought. This problem is complicated by the subject matter of the Garland book, homosexuality, but it raises several questions, the most important of which is whether the Garland book was "censored" or whether the long arm of coincidence was operating and the librarians in the five libraries simply felt their publics wouldn't be interested.

The next statement will surprise no one. The Shute book made the *Fiction Catalog*, the Garland book did not. This is not the only example of a book with extremely bad reviews making the *Catalog*. On those slow rainy nights when time hangs heavy take an issue of *Book Review Digest* and the *Fiction Catalog* and play the game yourself. The crime—and it is a crime—is that we buy bad books in the first place and then vote for their inclusion on a list because they are available.

The inclusion of mediocre books might not be bad if we were dealing with a comprehensive list but when a tool is selective the inclusion of one title means the exclusion of others. Among the more interesting titles not found in the *Fiction Catalog* are: Algren's *Man with the Golden Arm;* Beauvoir's *All Men Are Mortal;* Boulle's *Face of a Hero;* Camus' *The Stranger;* Faulkner's *Absalom, Absalom* and *Light in August;* Isherwood's *Berlin Stories;* Joyce's *The Dubliners;* Moravia's *Two Adolescents* and *Women of Rome;* O'Hara's *Appointment in Samarra;* and all of Sartre's works.

Could anyone be at all concerned with modern world literature and not find the excluded titles useful? Are we then safe in assuming that the excluded titles are not in the majority of the libraries and are unread by the librarians? And the question I really would like answered: Why is the second-rate always judged more useful than the first-rate?

We do know that librarians read mysteries. We know this because ten percent of the total entries in the 1950 edition are mysteries. Does anyone actually believe that these approximately 340 mysteries are worth the space they take up? It has been my experience that the most useful mystery is the newest one and once read it can be forgotten. Obviously we would retain a few of the "classics" in the field and this would mean the entries in the *Catalog* would be truly selective.

We need not limit our samples of the reading tastes of librarians to the *Fiction Catalog*. Take a look at Bryan's *The Public Librarian* and compare the percentages of librarians who read *Time* and *Life* as opposed to those who read *Atlantic Monthly* and *Harper's*. Go back to the early issues of *Booklist* and see if you can find that it reviewed Hemingway's *The Sun Also Rises*, Faulkner's *Absalom, Absalom,* or O'Hara's *Appointment in Samarra*. I couldn't. Or look at "The Fifty Notable Books of the Year" lists. A whole thesis could be written on that list and its weaknesses and prejudices.

In the November, 1913 issue of LJ an article by Anne Carroll Moore contains these words, " . . . it is not difficult for an institution to grow if it can keep in advance of what the public has learned to expect." Our public has come to think of us as purveyors of the popular and we give the public no more than it has come to expect. About the only unexpected item these days is the arrival of the photo-charging machine; rarely is the unexpected found to be a book.

We will not become recognized as experts by always running madly to catch up—we should be leaders, not followers. We should be more and more intelligently concerned with new authors and should develop assurance in our own ability to recognize new talent when we encounter it.

The easiest way to become an expert is to read, easy, that is, if the books are made available. As one concerned with modern fiction I borrowed Granville Hicks' book, *The Living Novel,* from a medium sized library. I enjoyed the essays by the 12 new novelists and on my next trip to the library looked for books by the authors involved. I found three titles by the 12 authors. How does a library justify buying books of criticism without also purchasing the books that will make the criticism meaningful?

All of this adds up to two points: the average library discriminates against the discriminating reader and worships the false idol of reading for reading's sake. Reading is not a virtue! It does not rank with the moral values of honesty, charity, or justice with mercy. Reading is a tool and is only as valuable as the use we make of it. Used wisely it makes the world we live in more meaningful; used badly it is time wasted that might better have been spent watching TV, mowing the lawn or baking a cake. It is like the cartoons about the husband's straight-edged razor. When he uses it to shave it serves its purpose; when his wife uses it to cut linoleum its value is destroyed. Like the wife, we are confirmed pragmatists. If the tool at hand does the job that needs doing then it is the right tool. Neither she nor we stop to think of the long term implications of our acts.

Some of these implications have already begun to catch up with us. One reads of more and more libraries having budget battles. Like the schools, we have abdicated our responsibilities and have let the public come to believe it knows as much as we do about our jobs. Perhaps the most fallacious idea of 20th century America is that public support automatically removes from the institution the right or the responsibility to make judgments. It is this ability to make judgments and defend them wisely that determines the public's respect for the institution. Do the publicly supported art museums clutter their walls with Grandma Moses because Pollack and De Koonig are unpopular? Does a public hospital dispense narcotics to addicts on the assumption that the addict is a taxpayer and one must always give the public what it demands?

It is ironical that the two institutions supposedly dedicated to education, the schools and libraries, are the two that have adopted the motto, "Something for everyone." We have let our respective publics think they are educated; we have encouraged them to think that knowledge can be acquired without effort; that learning is fun. Of course it is. But it is also hard work, requiring huge quantities of mental effort on the part of the learner. We do neither them nor ourselves justice by pretending that the sugar coated pills we dispense will magically bestow knowledge.

If we want status, if we want to be recognized as book experts, if we want to convince our public that it needs library school graduates running its libraries and that such librarians are worth high salaries, then we have got to begin to work toward earning that respect. It is not going to be granted on our say-so; we will have to prove it, and the longer we procrastinate, the harder it will be to win the fight.

We have got to begin to read more widely, more wisely, and more critically. We have got to stop thinking of our public as the ten sweet old ladies who come in every Monday for their seven light love and mystery novels, and begin considering the one borrower who wants books that will help him understand the problems of Africa, or the labor movement in America, or just what it is that makes Faulkner a Nobel Prize winner.

I do not wish to be a portender of doom but I would like to remind us that no institution in man's history has managed to survive unless it continually demonstrates that it can do *one* thing better than any other unit is able to do it. We are living through a revolution in the tremendous growth of availability of printed materials. The paperback, to be found absolutely everywhere, has dramatically changed the reading habits of millions of Americans. It has also relieved librarians of the necessity of satisfying mass demands. We are at a stage in our history when we are able to say, with a minimum of inconvenience to anyone, that libraries are places of learning. And yet, most of us are acting as though nothing were changing about us; as though we were still back in the days of the depression when nobody could buy books and everyone wanted to "escape" his problems for an hour or two. If we're not careful, *we* may escape—into oblivion.

32 *Minor Masterpieces and Ghastly Mistakes*

(FEBRUARY 1, 1962)

by JOHN C. PINE

In many respects fiction is the "poor orphan" of the public library. As often as not it is relegated to a corner along with sports and party games. The New York State Library in Albany will send *The Specialist* by "Chic" Sale all over the state, but not Saul Bellow's *Dangling Man* or John Hawkes' *The Cannibal*. Quite obviously their bias is showing. Can anyone seriously doubt that it is an example of what Wellek and Warren describe in their *Theory of Literature* as the "lingering American popular view, disseminated by pedagogues, that the reading of nonfiction [is] instructive and meritorious, that of fiction, harmful or at best self-indulgent . . ."?

Consider also ALA's annual list of notable books. These lists positively brim over with Truth and Optimism writ large. But note how few fiction titles are represented. In 1959 Allen Drury's best-seller made the list, but surely the relevant point about *Advise and Consent* is that it is woefully deficient in just those qualities of style and imagination that distinguish a good novel from a bad one. What made it an obvious choice, one suspects, was the celebrated picture—surely a press agent's dream—of the Messrs. Kennedy and Nixon solemnly looking it over in the shadow of the US Capitol Building. This was simply too much for the average librarian to resist. It was as if God were to have granted an interview to Charlton Heston just prior to the film première of *The Ten Commandments*. James Michener's *Hawaii*, another pseudo-novel, was likewise an obvious choice.

Actually, of the 49 notable books of 1959 chosen by the Notable Books Council of ALA, a mere six were fiction. And this in a year that saw the publication of such truly notable novels as William Faulkner's *The Mansion*, A. E. Ellis' *The Rack*, James Purdy's *Malcolm*, Lillian Smith's *One Hour*, Robert Penn Warren's *The Cave*, Alan Sillitoe's *Saturday Night and Sunday Morning* and Jack Kerouac's *Doctor Sax*.

In 1960 there was a slight improvement: of 46 notable books, eight were novels. Notably absent from the list were Vance Bourjaily's *Confessions of a Spent Youth*, John Updike's *Rabbit, Run*, John Barth's *The Sot-Weed Factor*, William Styron's *Set This House on Fire*, Wright Morris' *Ceremony in Lone Tree*, Claude Mauriac's *The Dinner Party* and Abram Tertz's *The Trial Begins*. The sad truth is that, year after year, the notable novels that are *not* selected tower accusingly over those that are.

"Imagination," Albert Einstein once remarked, "is more important than knowledge." Several years ago when I began to review fiction for LIBRARY JOURNAL, not the least of my qualifications, I believe, was my firm conviction that fiction is important. Literature in the 20th century *means* fiction, just as in other times it has meant poetry or the drama. Perhaps it is not too much of an exaggeration to say that when the library profession gets over its sanctimonious belief in the efficacy of knowledge (the constant fuss that is made over statistics, the glamorizing of informational services) and begins to discover, or rediscover, the power and delight of belles-lettres, it will have finally begun to mature. And just as an aside, it would be interesting to know how many librarians still subscribe to the "lingering popular American view" that the reading of fiction is "harmful or at best self-indulgent."

I have said that one of the best qualifications a fiction reviewer can have is a firm belief that fiction is important. I think it helps to have a little integrity, too. After all, to be genuinely displeased about a bad novel is merely the obverse of being genuinely pleased about a good one. We cannot escape the fact that praise and blame are as inevitable as day and night, no matter how many bland reviews appear to speak otherwise in the pages of LIBRARY JOURNAL, the *New York Times Book Review* and the *Saturday Review*.

In book reviewing absolute candor is imperative. There is nothing particularly high-minded in this. I personally favor speaking frankly for the most practical of reasons. As William Blake put it, "Always be ready to speak your mind, and a base man will avoid you."

After two years of what many well-meaning people consider the thankless task of assessing current fiction, what surprises me more than anything else is not that there are so many *bad* novels being published (and there are quite a few), but that there are as many *good* ones as there are. Since we librarians are so fond of statistics, allow me to indulge in a few statistics of my own. Of the 39 fiction reviews I have written for LIBRARY JOURNAL, 14 were definitely favorable. This is a fairly respectable batting average of .358. And since I do not grade on the curve, as we used to say in college, this batting average is all the more impressive—or at least it is to me. Surely the publishing industry is not doing too badly when a conscientious reviewer who attempts to apply critical standards can recommend over a third of all books reviewed during a two-year period, including such distinguished works as Stig Dagerman's *The Games of Night*, Richard Yates' *Revolutionary Road*, Christopher Davis' *First*

Family, Ruth Rehmann's *Saturday to Monday,* Abram Tertz's *The Trial Begins* and John Hawkes' *The Lime Twig.* Incredibly enough, eight of these 14 titles were first novels!

As for the other side of the ledger, 17 of the 39 reviews were definitely unfavorable. Moreover, the novels that are bad are *very* bad and should never have been published in the first place. Now this is where we must earn our professional standing. The tendency nowadays is to lump everything together indiscriminately (nonbooks as well as books) on the cynical assumption that few people know the difference. Although it is perfectly all right to bandy phrases like "a major novel" and "a minor masterpiece," it isn't considered seemly to criticize too harshly. In the general homogenizing process in which the *Book Review Digest* plus signs almost always triumph over the minus signs—and this is especially misleading to those who are forced to rely on reviews—it becomes virtually impossible to distinguish an Al Hine from a Vance Bourjaily, a Victoria Sackville-West from a Henry Green.

Only eight of the 39 novels reviewed seemed to me neither especially good nor especially bad; that is to say, mediocre. This may seem surprising until one stops to think about it. A mediocre novel is probably more difficult to achieve than either a good novel or a bad one. If a writer is capable of writing a good novel he will usually proceed to do just that. If he isn't capable of writing a good novel he will often deliberately and cynically proceed to write a bad one. "I laughed all the way to the bank," Liberace is supposed to have said. "None of Harold Robbins' novels have sold less than 40,000 copies," Simon & Schuster exclaims proudly in its preview of *The Carpetbaggers,* "some have even done better." Now *The Carpetbaggers* is unadulterated trash—I suspect that no one knows this better than Robbins himself—but apparently he isn't capable of writing a good novel and is too intelligent to settle for a mediocre one.

Harold Robbins is an extreme case and, as pessimistic as I am about reviewers, I really do not believe that *The Carpetbaggers* will be compared to *The Sun Also Rises* or *The Sound and the Fury.* And yet the book reviewing industry continues to grind out its homogenized product in greater quantities than ever before. R. V. Cassill's pretentious *Clem Anderson* is described as "a major novel." Victoria Sackville-West's *No Signposts in the Sea,* dismissed by John Coleman in *The Spectator* as "a short piece of creaking flummery" (Mr. Coleman apparently being the exception that proves the rule), is "a minor masterpiece." Merle Miller's saga of a tape recording, *A Gay and Melancholy Sound,* is highly praised. And an incredibly banal performance by Al Hine entitled *Lord Love a Duck* is dignified by a completely serious review in the newspaper with all the news that's fit to print. To read these reviews is actually to become more cynical than the authors of the books themselves.

And where does this leave novelists of the highest talent and integrity, novelists like Vance Bourjaily, Saul Bellow, John Barth, John Hawkes, Wright Morris? Inevitably the over-inflated reputations of the Al Hines and Merle Millers, in the classic tradition of Gresham's law, lower the reputations of the Hawkes and Bourjailys. No wonder librarians are confused. No wonder they find it more expedient to dismiss all fiction as "entertainment" and turn to Leonard Bernstein to illuminate the joy of music. No wonder they fall back on extraneous factors when deciding whether or not to buy a particular title. Sex, for example. Most libraries will probably rule out *The Carpetbaggers* as unsuitable for library purchase. The depressing part is that many of these same libraries have already ruled out *Confessions of a Spent Youth,* Bourjaily's best book to date, for exactly the same reason. And this despite the fact that Harold Robbins is a complete nonentity as far as the writing of novels is concerned, whereas Bourjaily is one of our most important novelists. Extraneous factors— frank depiction of sex, four-letter words—are so much easier to apply than critical standards.

Ironically, if a single library patron starts clamoring for *The Carpetbaggers* the chances are excellent that the library, now completely upset, will purchase the book. Even extraneous factors, it seems, can be quickly discarded if someone decides to call the tune. In an excess of caution, some reviews in Lj have said "buy if you must" rather than "buy and be damned." "Peace in our time," Neville Chamberlain said in 1938. "Buy if you must," the library profession said in 1962.

The difficulty stems mostly from the lack of confidence that is a corollary of the lack of critical standards. If a library forthrightly rejects *The Carpetbaggers* on the grounds that it is obviously trash and completely without literary merit, it will not have to feel so guilt-ridden about not filling the occasional patron's request. And similarly it will buy *Confessions of a Spent Youth* whether anyone asks for it or not, with the assurance of those who know what is likely to be important 50 or 100 years from now as well as the day after tomorrow.

If we librarians refuse to make ourselves responsible for deciding what books to buy, how can we pretend that our function is not simply a clerical one? By looking up a number in the telephone directory? By carefully compiling a lot of useless statistics and dutifully comparing them with last year's? By making things so confusing to the ordinary patron that he isn't able to find his way out of the building except by asking the librarian?

I cannot leave this subject without adding that it is downright cowardly and hypocritical, as well as a sign of intellectual bankruptcy, to buy *The Carpetbaggers* simply because there happens to be a superficial demand for it, but turn down *Confessions of a Spent Youth* because it is "strong meat" for which there is no *apparent* demand. Future generations will not bless us for this kind of "professional" illogic. It is a ridiculous state of affairs indeed when a public library with a budget of over a million dollars owns 20 copies of *Peyton Place* but not a single copy of Saul Bellow's *Dangling Man,* nor any of the highly regarded novels of Daniel Fuchs. How many public libraries had the foresight to buy Henry Roth's superb *Call It Sleep* when it first appeared back in 1934? Now, over a quarter of a century later, it is again available, thanks to the enthusiasm of critics like Leslie Fiedler and Alfred Kazin. But even now how many public libraries actually have it on their shelves?

I would like to conclude on a hopeful note. After reviewing fiction for several years in LIBRARY JOURNAL, I have come to the conclusion, not only that there are more good novels being published than might have been expected, but that it is possible for a reviewer to be critical and to say exactly what he thinks about the bad novels also, alas, being published. I have made some pretty strong criticisms in my reviewing career, not because I am necessarily full of malice and hate (though I may have my share), but because I think real *criticism* is essential if we are not to be completely submerged in a mountain of junk. In the homogeneous atmosphere in which we now live, nothing could be more significant and important than that a conscientious fiction reviewer should have been able to call a book "a ghastly mistake." This remark alone is worth a dozen "major novels" or "minor masterpieces." And make no mistake about it, the book *was* ghastly.

PART 2: BOOK CENSORSHIP

INTRODUCTION

Intellectual Freedom
from Roth to the Presidential
Commission on Obscenity and
Pornography

by ERVIN J. GAINES

       The years following the decision of the United States Supreme Court in the *Roth* case (1957) were marked by a quickening of public interest in the role of government and the law in setting limits to the content of printed and pictorial material. While there were many moves to repress books, periodicals, and films, both by legal and extra-legal means, including black-listing and boycott, the efforts were often surprisingly counter-productive, bringing into the field intellectually oriented groups who had learned during the McCarthy reign of terror the sterility of silence.

       There is still dispute as to the intrinsic merit of the *Roth* doctrine, but its catalytic effect may have been the most important thing about it, for in its wake came a sudden release of social forces which threatened older values, aroused fears and created new pressures on the cultural attitudes and modes of conduct of the American people. The degree to which literature became engaged in the subsequent revolutionary movements was owing chiefly to the candor of authors who shed conventional restraints and inhibitions long accepted in America. The *Roth* case was not the cause of the literary ferment, but rather in its own way it was a response to the shifting values of a society apparently preoccupied by the pursuit of wealth at home and the cold war abroad. The relatively calm period of the 1950's masked deep self-doubts that were to burst forth in the 60's. Hence *Roth* was more of a surprise than the facts warranted.

       Sexual questions were at the heart of *Roth,* and in the context of what had been happening in the United States, there was ample justification for the

Supreme Court to lay down new guidelines as to what was permissible in public print, especially since there seemed to be a growing disparity between what the law allowed and what society was actually doing. The rules of literary candor were not conforming to social behavior, and this gap between professed beliefs and conduct was leading to an erosion of enforcement. By 1957, American society had progressed so far as to create a demand for a new doctrine on the limits of candor, and that doctrine emerged in *Roth*.

Just how far had society outrun its rules for literature? Perhaps the readiest answer lay in attitudes toward birth control. Early in the century, when Margaret Sanger was the daring and lonely advocate of family planning, the legality of birth control hinged largely on the twin questions of morality and personal freedom, but by the mid 50's birth control was being looked at as a potentially useful social defense against world overpopulation and mass starvation. While the literary pressures were building up before the *Roth* decision, public opinion about birth control was also moving from the overly sensational and scandalized reactions of the 1920's to the sober and technical evaluations of the 1950's. This change in the climate of opinion is important for a comprehension of the issues surrounding *Roth* and the subsequent events both inside and outside our courts.

Christian opposition to birth control, and indeed to any tampering with traditional sexual codes (masturbation, abortion, homosexuality, adultery, fornication, etc.) in the name of higher law, began to seem irrelevant in the face of threat to human survival; at the same time there set in a strong tide of opinion favorable toward civil rights, privacy, and the sanctity of individual decisions with respect to self as distinct from society. Roman Catholic thinking, which had seemed to be so adamantine, began to show itself malleable after all, under heavy pressure from laymen and the lower ranks of the clergy. Scientific and technical break-throughs in birth control, most dramatically in the discovery of the "pill," tended to humanize and personalize the issues of individual rights and to remove them from abstract levels of discussion. The "pill" and the widespread publicity given to it in the mass media increased the confidence of men and women to make their own decisions about their sexual lives, whatever state or church might decree. It should have been no surprise that Pope Paul's encyclical in July, 1968, reaffirming the church's traditional opposition to interference with birth, was met with protest and dismay by clergy and laymen alike.

Coincidental with changes in attitudes and possibilities in birth control were notable shifts in opinion about relations between the sexes, family stability, and even abortion. Stiff legal obstacles to divorce, like those of New York, came under increasing criticism, and in 1967, three states, with surprising suddenness, liberalized abortion laws which had stood unassailed since the 19th century.

Efforts to remove ignorance about sex, which had perhaps been triggered originally by Kinsey's *Sexual Behavior of the Human Male* in the 1940's, continued relentlessly. Technical and scientific studies replaced the philosophical speculations that had been fashionable in the early writings of Havelock Ellis and Sigmund Freud. Data were methodically accumulated, and occasionally some of the findings reached the popular market. Sex gradually achieved the status of respectability as a subject for parlor conversation, but it was sex peculiarly devoid of eroticism.

Educators were not slow to take advantage of the newer freedom suggested by cultural developments. Sex education courses were constructed for public school curricula. A dry and clinical candor about sex tended to make it seem less exciting to children than to their parents, prompting one bored 12-year-old girl to remonstrate, "Everybody is interested in my sex life but me."

The second major social development affecting censorship after 1957 was the revolution in the relationships between young people and adult institutions. The beatniks, and later the hippies, became national curiosities or scandals, depending upon one's point of view, but they were understood by wise heads to be symptomatic of what was described frequently as alienation. While much pontifical nonsense was written about these highly visible rebels, they were something new on the scene, and they invited comment often for the quite superficial reason that they seemed to have an aversion to cleanliness. Politics and morals for the middle class critics of the hippies were less significant than hygiene, for the hippies represented disorder, and disorder threatened the middle class. Nevertheless the withdrawal behavior of the hippies and their sympathizers raised cries of alarm even among those elders who were well-disposed toward them. The chief benefit the rebels seemed to derive from the public discussions was a reluctant willingness by society to re-negotiate the status of children. Although the adult community responded, the frustrations the young felt at the slowness of change stimulated them to militant and aggressive action. The hippie movement faded out to be replaced by student riots and demonstrations as more meaningful expressions of discontent. Even the Beatles passed in a very few years from being the butt of tedious jokes to the higher realms of serious art, worthy of criticism in learned journals. On the campuses there was the solemn moment when, in the early 1960's, Columbia University permitted women to visit men's dormitory rooms on condition that the doors were propped open by a book, and one student complied with a match book. But all of that was before the harsh strife on the same campus in 1968. Discussion on campuses shifted radically and rapidly from peripheral issues like dormitory rules and parietal hours toward serious negotiation aimed to give students a strong voice in their own education. So widespread did disaffection become that political careers at high levels were influenced by student attitudes, and many candidates for elective office wooed votes on the strength of their promises to do something constructive about the youthful revolts. A particularly spectacular reformer, Max Rafferty, in a very few years capitalized on the unrest among the young to catapult himself from an obscure school superintendent's job to serious contention for a seat in the United States Senate. His defeat in 1968 could very well be the high water mark of traditional conservatism toward youth.

Sexual taboos for young people virtually disappeared, and medical departments in liberal colleges freely prescribed birth control pills to coeds. Even segregated education in colleges began to disappear as school after school decided that two sexes in the classroom were better than twice as good as one.

Sex was not the major concern of students, although it often seemed the major issue to adults, whose shock at cohabitation by teenagers wore off slowly. The popular press sensationalized the superficial or anti-social aspects of the student revolt, including the drug issue, but the seriousness and the depth of the student movement became apparent first in the civil rights invasion of the South and later in resistance to the creaky, 30-year-old draft law which was defied with increasing frequency as the Viet Nam War ground on year after year. Underground newspapers began to appear in the more conservative schools, and the independent spirit of youth spread from college down to the high schools. Public school officials, despite their quaint repugnance at long hair on boys and short skirts on girls, found it necessary to capitulate to youths who, when blocked at the school house door, were not loath to strike and to picket against school establishments. The revolt rolled on and spread in spite of anything the adult community could do. Political involvement on the national scene was clearly in the offing as the next logical step for the young, and they constituted an important force in the candidacy of Senator Eugene McCarthy in seeking the presidential nomination in 1968. It now is likely that the voting age will be lowered to 18 everywhere.

The sophistication of the student was, however, in marked contrast to the disorganized but also threatening behavior of the "dropout." For the Negro "dropout," at least, there was the possibility of identification with the racial struggle, and the militancy of the black undereducated youth had its parallels with the white student rebellion. The young person most likely to harm himself or society was largely ignored—the white boy who couldn't make it in school but who had no cause to rally to. He was the truly alienated one. Because most young people still remained relatively docile, it seemed possible to suggest that it was not the massiveness of the revolt by young people but their determination which made the movement significant. But even that illusion vanished in the Chicago clash in August, 1968.

Inevitably books and pictures reflected what was going on among young people, sexually and otherwise. Because naive people mistook the reporting for the cause, the hallucinatory quality of the debate over sex in literature was perhaps the most remarkable thing about it. In 1883, Anthony Comstock, in *Traps for the Young* had stated the case against obscene literature, and nothing of any importance was added thereafter. Neither the vocabulary of the crusade nor the tactics changed in more than 80 years. What altered in the meantime was the thing itself. The literature Comstock deplored and struggled against in his lifetime had long since passed into the camp of respectability to be replaced by newer and far more daring material. It could not be successfully asserted that Sister Carrie was the same kind of girl as Candy. In literature, where there is a threshold of social tolerance determined by a consensus among the many individuals who shape opinions about taste, that threshold visibly lowered in the ten years after *Roth*. In 1957 there had been no *Lady Chatterley's Lover,* no *Tropic of Cancer;* in 1967 not only were those celebrated books in free circulation, there were films like *491, Seventeen, I, a Woman,* and *The Female.* D. H. Lawrence and Henry Miller passed completely out of the arena of discussion to be replaced by Gore Vidal and Philip

Roth. So rapid was the shift in taste that serious doubts were expressed about the wisdom of utterly unbridled sex in literature, leading the Federal government to authorize, albeit somewhat reluctantly, a study of the effect of obscenity on the young people who had access to it.

The importance of the *Roth* decision lay additionally in the fact that for the first time in its history the Supreme Court reached out to take hold of the spiny question of sex in literature. Prior cases had been decided in lower courts, and the presumption had always been abroad in America that the State's authority to control obscenity was unquestioned, and if obscenity could be found in a book it fell outside the law. Except for Justices Black and Douglas, the Supreme Court did not openly attack the prerogatives of state and local governments to legislate. The Court was primarily attempting to create a definition which was more workable and realistic than the old Hicklin rule which had prevailed since the mid 19th century. The Hicklin rule, enunciated by the Lord Chief Justice, Alexander Cockburn, said that "the test of obscenity is this, whether the tendency of the matter charged as obscenity is to deprave and corrupt those . . . into whose hands a publication of this sort may fall." The willingness of our highest court to consider in a fresh light a doctrine that had stood so long was probably a recognition that society had changed more than the man in the street realized. To replace it, the Court forged a new doctrine, which lies at the heart of the *Roth* decision: "whether to the average person, applying contemporary community standards, the dominant theme of the material taken as a whole appeals to prurient interest." Actually, *Roth* merely compressed and codified what Judge John M. Woolsey had said in his eloquent decision in 1933 which led to the admission of Ulysses to the United States. The most important contribution of *Roth*, building upon the Woolsey decision, was the requirement that the total work had to be considered, not a single offending passage, as in the Hicklin rule.

The difficulty with the *Roth* decision, however, lay in its unspoken assumption that there are gradations of taste. The Court said, without intending to, that what the respectable segment of the community accepts will pass muster, but what the underside of the community prefers may get into difficulty with the law. In short, middle class values prevail in the *Roth* doctrine. The Court's blind spot about its bias was to give it trouble in the next decade, as case after case was brought before it. Whether it thought so or not, the Court had declared itself to be the final interpreter of such elusive meanings as may be attached to "average person," "community standards," and "dominant theme." It seems clear in retrospect that the Court was not conscious at the time of *Roth* of the paradox it was creating. The baffling and subtle distinctions between art and smut eluded most people, but since the Court had implied that it knew how to make those distinctions it soon found itself becoming a board of censors, a role for which it is not well suited. Immediately following *Roth* there began a long procession of cases through lower courts and on to Washington. In succession *Tropic of Cancer*, the film *The Lovers*, and *Fanny Hill* were ruled upon, to say nothing of a list of works so lengthy and so insignificant as to fail to engage public attention at all. The Court sought in *Jacobellis* and *Ginzburg* to disentangle itself from its own web of reasoning and to clarify the *Roth* doctrine but only succeeded in further clouding the definitions it had established. *Jacobellis* (which involved *The Lovers*) declared that "community standards" were national rather than local, which cleared up one point, but in its anxiety to show that it was socially responsible and accountable to middle class prejudices, the Court could not resist suggesting that perhaps laws protecting children should be sought. And this concession to conservative views immediately opened up new areas of disagreement. In *Ginzburg*, the Court did not object to the material—a magazine called *Eros*—but did object to the manner of its sale, and thereby popularized that rare word "titillation." At the end of 1967, what had seemed relatively simple in *Roth* had once again become complex, because the Court could not in its sobriety give legal sanction to everything it found unpleasant or embarrassing. While it went a long way toward liberalization, it seemed terribly reluctant to face the consequences of complete freedom, and kept hanging back from the teachings of Justices Black and Douglas, whose stark simplicity was too daring.

If *Roth* substituted one muddle for another, the consequences were not all bad. Because the Court showed a broader tolerance for sexual writings than had been customary in the United States, and because it did let *Fanny Hill* be published, prosecutors became more cautious, and the number of convictions of publishers and booksellers was discouragingly small in the opinion of militant censorship groups, as case after case failed in the courts or never reached trial at all. Many public prosecutors refused to institute proceedings against any material whatsoever, and the pressures, even on outright pornographers, visibly lessened.

On the negative side, the efforts to legislate at the state level increased, as frantic and sometimes ridiculous attempts were made to close the breach opened by *Roth*. New York enacted a law designed to remove young people from the market place of sex literature, and when that statute was upheld in 1968 by the Supreme Court, it immediately became a model for other states to follow. Some jurisdictions enacted laws so harsh in their penalties and so flagrantly unconstitutional in their definitions, that it is certain that they will be tested in future cases and found lacking. In 1966, an attempt, led by California's Superintendent of Public Instruction, Max Rafferty, was made to amend the California constitution to outlaw obscene literature. This contest at the polls in an open referendum attracted national attention because it provided a testing ground of public opinion rarely available in the United States. In the debate preceding the election the constitutional arguments for a free press were pitted directly against those in favor of morality and public safety. The defeat of the amendment by a 3 to 2 vote in a state noted for its militantly conservative elements was a distinct encouragement to the proponents of liberal views, and gave substance to the opinion that the electorate, by and large, is more tolerant than its elected and appointed officials. But the California experience was not by itself a final determinant, and the unconvinced proponents of censorship, dismayed but not persuaded, can be counted on to keep public controversy and court litigation boiling during the years ahead, as laws come to be tested by the courts and as new legislative proposals are fought over in the state capitals around the nation. A typical straw in the wind blew through St. Paul, Minnesota, in 1967, where a vigorous and ambitious city attorney set out on a crusade to drive a local bookseller out of business or, failing that, to force him to submit to the taste standards of the attorney. In a series of raids stretching over several months, the bookseller was charged with multiple violations of the state obscenity statute. After a mixed bag of decisions from the courts, including one mistrial, the crusade was muted, largely because there was no rallying of public opinion to the side of the prosecutor. Instead, the free advertising afforded to the bookseller more than repaid him for the inconvenience and expense of defending himself. While the struggle between the bookseller and the city attorney continued into 1968, without a clear-cut victory for either side, the probabilities seemed to favor the bookseller if he had the staying power to fight off what increasingly looked like official persecution, precisely because the public is less interested in the matter than the prosecutor seems willing to admit.

Such local flurries aside, the fate of sex literature was being placed in the hands of the Federal government, partly as a result of Supreme Court decisions and partly as a result of the stepped up interstate commerce in obscene materials. The Post Office continued to be the Federal agency most deeply involved, and Congress sought to strengthen its power to constrict the circulation of unpleasant materials by allowing citizens to demand that their names be stricken from mailing lists promoting obscene materials. Senator Karl Mundt of South Dakota, after a decade of effort, succeeded in 1967 in persuading Congress to enact into law a bill establishing a Commission to study obscenity. Even so, Senator Mundt's pet bill underwent considerable softening before Congress would agree to adopt it. Persistent objections from publishers, the American Civil Liberties Union, and the American Library Association forced Mundt and other sponsors to tone down the language until, in the final draft, the enabling legislation prescribed what amounts to a call for a scholarly study of the putative effects of obscenity on young people instead of the outright condemnation that had been originally sought. One professional victory for librarians in the long tussle over the bill was in the appointment by President Johnson of Frederick Wagman, Librarian of the University of Michigan and former ALA president, to serve on the Commission. Although the Commission's membership covers the entire spectrum of public attitudes toward obscenity, the recognition given to librarians was a sign of the growing importance of the profession. The chairmanship of the Commission went to Dean William Lockhart of the University of Minnesota, whose known liberality on the issue gave promise of something more constructive than a *parti pris* report seeking stronger criminal laws. The expiration date of the Commission was set at January 31, 1970, which was much too short a time for it to perform effectively.

Church induced censorship also weakened noticeably in the period under examination. The influence of the Vatican Council was paramount in encouraging a more permissive climate, and the discontinuance in 1966 of the *Index of Forbidden Books* indicated the willingness of the Roman Catholic Church to alter some of its historical postures. It would have been too much to expect clerical conservatism to disappear entirely, and many of the censorship battles within the United States were either led or abetted by conservative clerics of all faiths. Operation Yorkville, a particularly militant group in New York, enjoyed strong religious backing from Catholic, Protestant and Jewish clergymen, and the Citizens for Decent Literature, a Cincinnati based anti-obscenity organization, was led by a Catholic layman whose church support was well known. Although clerical opposition was still much in evidence, the solid phalanx of institutional resistance was visible, and many clergymen of all faiths actively supported freedom of expression. Religious energies were gradually turning to other social issues, and organized church opposition could be regarded as a slowly declining force in the area of censorship.

Sex censorship was one thing, political censorship quite another. The American press, which has since the earliest days of the republic consistently defended its right to gather and print news of governmental activities, showed a distinctly selective bias in defending First Amendment rights. Where obscenity questions were the issue in American communities, the prevailing tendency was for editorial comment in newspapers to lean toward a conservative and restrictive view, although individual reporters and columnists and, occasionally, a publisher, sometimes took a forthright stand for freedom to read. But it did not escape notice that there still exists in the public press greater vigilance in defending political prerogatives, while being relatively cool to the proposition that all ideas and opinions ought to move freely through our society, particularly on sexual questions.

Outright, and sometimes ruthless, political censorship which had precipitated a major crisis in American life in the early 1950's, (during the summer days of Senator Joseph McCarthy), in the more recent decade, took on new and interesting guises, some of which may give trouble in the future. Because the national political scene saw no successor to the Wisconsin Senator, right-wing agitation slowly retreated to the private sphere. The John Birch Society enjoyed a brief notoriety in the early 1960's in a flurry of efforts by Society members to interfere with free expression, but its influence peaked out early, and by 1967 was beginning to fade from the American scene.

Instead, and possibly as a manifestation of the increasing subtlety and complexity of American culture, what did appear on the scene was the obverse of censorship: positively manipulated information. Following the Cuban missile crisis in the early 1960's, the American press bitterly assailed the government for alleged attempts to control or manage the news. Three Presidents, Eisenhower, Kennedy, and Johnson, at one time or another in their terms found themselves telling untruths or partial truths on issues of international significance.

While a short period of mutual trust between people and government followed the assassination of President Kennedy, by 1966 the earlier doubts about the candor of the Federal bureaucracy began to reappear. Late in that year it was revealed in a Congressional Committee that the United States Information Service had been subsidizing the authorship of books in furtherance of American foreign policy objectives. A few months later, *Ramparts* magazine set off firecrackers with its revelation that the National Student Association had been heavily subsidized by the CIA through devious financial maneuvers. Matters were not helped by accusations from Governor Romney of Michigan that Federal officials had engaged in deceptive practices in informing him about the progress of the war in Viet Nam.

While the national reaction to those events was one of dismay, the fact that the CIA had long been manipulating public opinion via subsidy was generally condoned, except by the militant young, as being in the long-range interests of the nation in its conflict with Communism. Keen observers and people knowledgeable in government were well aware that CIA practices were scarcely touched by the *Ramparts* revelation, and most Americans remained indifferent to the large infusions of Federal money into organizations trying to influence public opinion either at home or abroad. Nevertheless, there was a growing, if somewhat inarticulate, uneasiness that all was not as it seemed.

The phrase "credibility gap" had a brief currency with respect to the Viet Nam War, as well as lesser issues, and Americans at the end of 1967 were less inclined than they had been in a long time to accept at face value the pronouncements of government officials. Certainly the restlessness of young people was traceable in part to their lack of trust of "people over 30." A watchful cynicism became the dominant American mood, and it was a potentially ugly spirit, particularly in the light of the Negro's frustrations.

Public skepticism was turned on private business as well as on government following the exposure of attempts by General Motors to intimidate Ralph Nader into silence about automobile safety, and the open opposition to the Dow Chemical Company in its role as chief supplier of napalm to the armed forces. On the other hand the Supreme Court's firm determination to strike down loyalty oaths for public employees was a counter sign of the distance America had traveled from the days of the Communist witch hunts. Right-wing activities, however noisy, were not prevailing. Meantime, there was a resurgance on the left reminiscent of the 1930's, and the tie-in both with student rebels through the Students for a Democratic Society (SDS) and black power advocates leavened the American political scene. A growing defiance of authority and a readiness to risk much in expressing opinions became evident in the frequent ritualistic destructions of draft cards, which brought young men into direct clash with their government. The American Civil Liberties Union rallied to the defense of the card-burners and invented a new phrase "symbolic speech," which might strike any linguist as a bit of tautology. The test of how far one might go in expressing opinions without incurring penalties is still in process, but free speech seems on balance to have progressed a good deal farther than most Americans are accustomed to.

The issue of draft resistance was dramatized by Dr. Benjamin Spock, and others, who openly invited government prosecution for their advising young men to resist the draft. The Justice Department responded to the challenge by indicting Spock for conspiracy and, as the year 1967 ended, the battle lines on the issue were being drawn. Spock's conviction in the summer of 1968 was being challenged in the Supreme Court. It is not certain at this writing that all liberal opinion is willing to accept the thesis that the counselling of resistance to orderly governmental process is permissible, but the fact that the proposition is debatable at all is a departure from tradition. Thoreau on civil disobedience is now frequently invoked in support of the activities of Spock and of black power advocates, and a new fervor has entered the debate over whether a higher morality should govern men's expression of opinion during a crisis of conscience. These are deeper matters than normally concern librarians, but they are important as background for the definition of the permissible limits of free speech and a free press.

The major domestic development in the 1960's was the rise of Negro influence. Beginning with the Civil Rights movement in the South, originally under the leadership of Martin Luther King, and abetted by the active intervention of idealistic white students from the North, the arousal of the Negroes had, by 1965, begun to create critical incidents in the rest of the nation. The explosive quality of Negro resistance invited retaliation, and the more eloquent Negro political leaders, authors and entertainers were attacked in a variety of ways, often indirectly. Stokeley Carmichael, Rap Brown, James Baldwin and LeRoi Jones ran afoul of authorities. But whatever ostensible reasons were advanced to justify harassment, their fearless and often brilliant statement of the Negro dilemma was at the root of their conflict with law enforcement authorities. Baldwin's *Another Country* encountered trouble in New Orleans and Chicago, and while obscenity was the pretext, the racial issue lay just under the surface. Similar observations could be made about LeRoi Jones, who was singled out for special attention by Newark police in 1967 during riots in that city, and it was hard to determine just what was the proper mixture of police motives, although it is clear that Negro writings which could somehow be related to obscenity, invited strong counter action from the white community. The Negro's freedom of expression was interdicted with far greater frequency, and for lesser reasons than the white man's.

The Negro drive for equality affected libraries early in the decade, when it was brought home forcibly to Americans that in the South, the Negro often had only limited access, or none, to public libraries. Dramatic sit-ins highlighted the issue and led the American Library Association to sponsor a study of access to libraries which, when published, had unfavorable repercussions in some Northern libraries as well, since the study suggested in strong terms that discrimination in library service, while differently arranged in the North, had some of the same results. Whether the study was erroneous, as some librarians charged, it had the bracing effect of making librarians more conscious than ever of their responsibilities. The American Library Association read some Southern state chapters out of the organization for a time, but by 1967, they had all been readmitted. Although political and social influences were at work to limit equal access to libraries during the stormy 1960's, it was quite clear that librarians themselves were generally committed to the highest ideals of freedom and were working hard against ancient prejudices.

As the social revolution grew in strength, the American Library Association responded with increased activity aimed at shedding its conservatism. The establishment of the *Newsletter on Intellectual Freedom* under the able leadership of Donald Strout and later of LeRoy Merritt, was a significant contribution to the extension of freedom because it recorded patiently and with growing thoroughness the attacks on freedom of expression throughout the nation, and, indeed, abroad as well.

It was impossible to tell from the *Newsletter* whether attacks on libraries increased in number as the years passed or whether the coverage improved. In either case, the reporting was valuable. And if any librarian doubted the energy of those forces which seek to interfere with freedom to read, the 21 lines in the 1963–65 index to the *Newsletter* referring to attacks on *Catcher in the Rye* were persuasive. In those three years Salinger's bright little novel came under fire in California, Oregon, Pennsylvania, Georgia, Colorado, Indiana, Wisconsin, Virginia, Ohio and Connecticut, but still survived.

The *ALA Bulletin* for 6 years featured a regular column on intellectual freedom, which after a short interruption was resumed at the end of 1967. The formal establishment of the Intellectual Freedom Office at ALA headquarters in December, 1967, was the culmination of years of effort by a few librarians to alert the entire profession to the importance of the issue. Articles and books by and about librarians kept intellectual freedom firmly in focus as a major problem for the profession.

But professional self-satisfaction was shattered when proof was produced that censorship was not entirely an external force against which librarians labored in concert. Marjorie Fiske's *Book Selection and Censorship* in the late 1950's brought together the evidence, long suspected but not articulated, that librarians were often guilty of practices they protested in others. Fiske demonstrated that self-censorship by librarians made many books unavailable to readers, and she proved that timidity and fear of controversy motivated librarians more often than honest conviction. Her report, together with the fact that its sales were low, strengthened the determination of more liberal librarians to push the issue harder than ever. The content of library school courses began to include larger doses of discussion about librarians' responsibilities, and the open-mindedness of the younger professionals was often in marked contrast to the excessive caution of their elders. In libraries, as elsewhere, the generation gap was showing.

Militant librarians attempted to push the question of intellectual freedom to the foreground of professional conferences. In 1964, in Washington, D.C., a meeting sponsored by the Intellectual Freedom Committee convened a distinguished panel of men from other professions who urged librarians to act with greater confidence in enlarging the holdings of controversial materials in their institutions. Encouraged by this kind of backing, the Committee drafted a revision of the Library Bill of Rights which clarified ALA's position on censorship and stated emphatically its across-the-board condemnation of any interference in the traffic of ideas. The revised Bill was approved by the American Library Association Council at San Francisco in 1967.

In other ways too did professional associations take their responsibilities seriously. The Massachusetts Library Association joined the Civil Liberties Union in that state in filing an *amicus curiae* brief in *The Tropic of Cancer* case, and later the American Library Association took similar action when Miller's book was an issue before the Supreme Court. These are the only two known instances of library initiative in court cases, although librarians more

than once testified as expert witnesses in defense of books at trials. The boldness and forthright eloquence of some professionals more than offset the dim
and vacillating image of the librarian projected by the Fiske study.

Outside the United States the same kinds of concerns were being ex-
pressed, and it could be assumed that a world-wide change was taking place.
If filthy post-cards were no longer confined to the Paris market, much could be
credited to activities elsewhere. England's sceptered isle allowed the sale of
Lawrence's *Lady Chatterley's Lover* after a sensational court case, but the
British willingness to accept a classic work by a native son did not automatically exempt foreign works from censorship, as was discovered when
Selby's *Last Exit to Brooklyn* was temporarily banned in 1967. And although
Australia and New Zealand kept a fairly sharp eye out for obscenity, these
outer areas of the English speaking world were a minority. Among the Com-
monwealth nations only South Africa and Ireland continued harsh policies, the
one acting out of racism, the other still under the heavy hand of the Catholic
Church. The Soviet Union, after a deep freeze of forty years, began to exhibit
signs of spring. Ehrenberg's *The Thaw* in 1954 foreshadowed one of the most
celebrated events of the mid-century, the publication abroad in the year of
Roth of Pasternak's *Doctor Zhivago*. This successful defiance of Soviet censorship by one of its great authors did much to lower international tensions, and
even though the government struck back by later sending some of its rebels to
jail, the loosening of the bonds of censorship in the Communist world were
unmistakable, particularly in Eastern Europe. Poland and Czechoslovakia were
becoming much more tolerant of criticism and dissent, so much so that the
latter country was re-occupied by the Soviets in 1968.

On obscenity, the most liberal attitudes in the world were exhibited in
Scandinavia. In 1967 the Danish Parliament removed the last strictures from
the printed word, retaining only a slight control over pictures, and Sweden
appeared to be ready to follow suit. The freedom of the Scandinavian countries was the indicator of what might be expected in the Western world during
the latter part of the 20th century.

Special mention should be made of the motion picture. It stood apart from
the printed word for at least three reasons: it was relatively new compared
with printing; its vividness and immediacy evoked faster responses; and its
characteristic as a group medium put it into a different social relationship. If
reading was essentially a private communication between author and the
ultimate consumer, the making and the viewing of films was not accepted by
society in the same way. Films were public in a very special sense. It was not
unexpected, therefore, that freedom in motion pictures lagged. Only with the
Jacobellis case of 1964 was the United States, at last, willing to grant to film
makers anything like the freedom permitted to authors. Restrictions on films
were falling, slowly but with regularity. In early 1969 a bitterly controversial
Swedish film *I Am Curious (Yellow)* was shown uncut in the United States.
Prior censorship exercised by film review boards was finally outlawed by the
Supreme Court, and in the mid-1960's film producers were rapidly achieving
equal status with authors and publishers. The peculiar ability of films to

transcend language and cultural barriers also tended to accelerate the general sense of release from government and institutional control across the world.

Television and live theater endured the same kinds of restrictions as the motion picture, and for similar reasons. In almost its last overt act as the nation's most restrictive city, Boston attempted to delete certain passages from Albee's play, *Who's Afraid of Virginia Woolf?* when it played in that city, but the attempt was so ridiculed that the effort led to the abolition of the censor's role by the city. By the end of the decade, dramas in some cities were featuring nude scenes and suggestive, often deviant, sexual acts, without undue harassment from public authorities. Students at the University of Wisconsin even managed a nude scene in *Peter Pan.*

Television underwent the kind of critical trial that the motion picture had encountered in the 1930's, with frequent attacks centered on the portrayal of violence in children's programs. As a newer medium, and one that is inserted into the home environment, its place in American society has not yet been fully assessed, although, if past experience is any guide, it seems likely that TV will eventually enjoy the same prerogatives as the motion picture.

While adults were wafted aloft on a euphoric cloud of permissiveness, the young were not always so fortunate. Educators took note of a rising tide of attacks in schools, particularly on English teachers and librarians, where the issue was more often than not obscenity, with politics playing a minor role. The National Education Association thought the problem serious enough to call attention to it in 1966, and the National Council of Teachers of English was prompted a year later to call a meeting of professional, educational and civil liberties groups to assess the national situation, and to consider the formation of an inter-disciplinary committee to combat extra-legal pressures on the free flow of ideas. It appeared that the American Library Association would take the lead in creating such a body.

Being in the public sphere and dealing with the young, schools proved particularly vulnerable to public agitation, and activities with schools were frequently subjected to microscopic scrutiny and negative criticism. The rising pressures on schools grew partly out of conservative opposition to the restiveness of young people and partly out of the failure by censors to make their case in court. School administrators were easier to intimidate than judges, and understandably the administrators being in the direct line of fire were readier to yield to pressure than were the classroom teachers and librarians.

Reacting to the events in the larger society, school and public librarians busily reassessed their own traditional attitudes toward young people, whose reading had long been considered subject to the rule of the librarian. The advent of Sputnik, which occurred in 1957 along with the *Roth* decision, caused curriculum demands in high schools to be stepped up; the enriched school programs drove students into libraries and librarians out of their minds. Under the pretext of keeping order, some librarians tried to restrict library use by young people, and this in turn moved the American Library Association to devote a large part of its 1963 convention to a new look at library responsibilities to young people. Concurrently, the national movement toward greater sexual permissiveness led many librarians to the conclusion that discrimination in the handling of materials *vis-à-vis* minors was regressive. A noticeable tendency developed to remove restrictions on what young people might read or borrow.

In retrospect, the lively decade 1957–1967 generated attitudes which enlarged the boundaries of intellectual freedom, and promoted a growth of that freedom which is continuing even further in the present day. The variety and the boldness of controversial material increased; its availability to young people visibly extended. If prophecy has any merit, one might venture to predict that the United States may achieve in the next 10 years what it has struggled so long to establish: the complete freedom of the interchange of ideas, with restrictions by government removed once and for all. And if the prophecy proves accurate, librarians will have played a large part in making it an actuality.

33 *Apologist for Censorship*

(JUNE 1, 1961)

by ROBERT B. DOWNS

James Jackson Kilpatrick's *The Smut Peddlers* (N.Y.: Double-day, 1960) illustrates the perils of over-objectivity. The author, former editor of the Richmond (Va.) *News Leader,* appears to have begun his researches into obscenity and pornography with a reasonably unbiased viewpoint—indeed with a considerable leaning toward freedom and an unfettered press. He emerges embracing and condoning the NODL, the Citizens for Decent Literature, Americans for Moral Decency, and similar extra-legal private pressure groups, and advocating stringent repressive legislation. But throughout, Mr. Kilpatrick attempts to maintain an air of impartiality, carefully weighing the pros and cons with utter fairness. One cannot have it both ways.

How did Mr. Kilpatrick get himself into this sad predicament? Chiefly, it seems, through his investigations of the "obscenity racket," as he calls it—the vast underground traffic, often directed toward children and young people, in dreary "art" photographs, nudist magazines, stag films, and like mail-order trash. Even those liberals who insist that freedom is indivisible are hard put to it to defend such hard-core pornography, certainly in the case of children, reluctant as we may be to make any concessions to the censors. What the censors and professional do-gooders almost invariably overlook, however, is the presence of adequate statutes—federal, state, and municipal—for dealing with this despicable commercialization of sex in the raw. Not satisfied to work through legal channels, the self-appointed censors proceed to take the law into their own hands.

And, unfortunately, once started on their crusades for reform, they are constantly seeking new worlds to conquer. From the nude photographs, cheap sexy magazines, and stag movies, they proceed to books (especially paperbacks), serious moving pictures, the stage, radio and television, determined to give others the courage of their convictions. The consequences are dire. The broadcasting industry is mercilessly plagued by a variety of pressures; magazines and newspapers are oversensitive to public reactions; and Hollywood, as John G. Fuller put it, "is nervous, shaky, and intent on satisfying the fourteen-year-old mind." The only people who have consistently shown a willingness to fight back are the book publishers, librarians, and legitimate theater producers. Mr. Kilpatrick does a neat job of undermining their defenses.

We are witnessing today the frightening spectacle of innumerable veterans organizations, religious bodies, White Citizens Councils, super-patriotic societies, Congressional committees, and other misguided pressure groups working around the clock to place restrictions and limitations on what we may read, or see, or hear. Not realizing or not caring that they are seeking to destroy the basic concept upon which America was founded, the voices calling for conformity, for unanimity of opinion, for eliminating all ideas with which they happen to disagree grow more strident, intolerant and uncompromising. Their opponents are discredited by such epithets as Communists, subversives, fellow travelers, sex perverts, nigger lovers, egg heads, or, as Mr. Kilpatrick contemptuously refers to them, the "literati." It is these busybodies, soul savers, and do-gooders who are urged on by him to bigger and better censorship activities, along with more authority for the Postmaster General to dictate the nation's taste, and more laws to clutter up the statue books. The great moral crusade is fittingly represented by that noted champion of civil rights, Senator Eastland of Mississippi (apparently considered on the side of the angels by Mr. Kilpatrick), who recently introduced into the Congress a bill allowing each state to decide "on the basis of its own public policy, questions of decency and morality" and barring any abridgement of the right of states to enact legislation in this field—thereby nullifying all the safeguards of the Bill of Rights and effectively hamstringing the U.S. Congress and Supreme Court.

The would-be censors almost invariably rest their case on the protection of children. Along with Mr. Kilpatrick, they quote approvingly J. Edgar Hoover, who asserts that "the increase in the number of sex crimes is due precisely to sex literature madly presented in certain magazines. Filthy literature is the great moral wrecker. It is creating criminals faster than jails can be built." The testimony of medical, psychiatric, and sociological authorities outside the police field does not support Mr. Hoover's contention. Two research criminologists, Eleanor and Sheldon Glueck, intensively examined 1000 delinquent boys from the Boston area. The most significant factors contributing to delinquency, they found, were culture conflict, unwholesome family environment, educational deficiencies, socially undesirable use of leisure time (e.g., gambling, drinking, drug addiction, and sex misbehavior), and psychological defects. There was no evidence that erotic or other types of reading matter was a contributing factor in delinquency. In the same vein, George S. Smyth, a prominent children's court judge in New York, listed 878 factors which troubled children; reading was not even on the list, but difficulty in reading was. It is the consensus that delinquent children read much less than the law-abiding.

But granting that it is highly undesirable to expose immature minds to hard-core obscenity and pornography, normal adult readers hardly require such tender coddling. The definitive word on the subject was expressed in 1957 by the U.S. Supreme Court decision in the case of *Butler* v. *Michigan.*

In the same year, an eminent English judge, Justice Stable, was pointing out to a jury that "A mass of literature, great literature, from many angles is wholly unsuitable for reading by adolescents, but that does not mean that the publisher is guilty of a criminal offense for making those works available to the general public."

The two foregoing legal decisions are clear cut, unambiguous, and un-equivocal. As much cannot be said, unfortunately, for the mass of court actions in this controversial field. The most valuable feature of Mr. Kilpatrick's book is his extended historical review of legal precedents, English and American, in obscenity trials, though it makes depressing reading. One is left with an over-all impression of a labyrinth of judicial confusion, quibbling, hair-splitting, widely contradictory views, struggles with definitions, and general futility. The prevailing murkiness is dispelled only occasionally by the enlightened, civilized views of such figures as Augustus and Learned Hand, John M. Woolsey, William O. Douglas, Curtis Bok, and Jerome Frank.

Even the U.S. Supreme Court is not immune to the conflicting, confusing, contradictory opinions that have marked the judicial history of censorship. After curbing police excesses in the *Butler* v. *Michigan* case, and appearing to emancipate motion pictures in the *Burstyn* v. *Wilson* case (involving *The Miracle*), the Court went on later to lose itself in a quagmire, in the *Roth* v. *U.S.* case, attempting to define obscenity and in effect establishing a federal system of censorship, and most recently put motion pictures back in a strait-jacket by ruling that they are not entitled to the protection of the First Amendment, and holding them subject to the vagaries of a maze of local and state censorship boards. Censorship by prior restraint, condemned for books and the press, thus is blessed for another area of mass communication, the cinema.

All is far from lost, however, as long as we have such eloquent spokesmen for the liberal point of view as Justice Douglas, who consistently maintains that "If a board of censors can tell the American people what it is in their best interests to see or to read or to hear, then thought is regimented, authority substituted for liberty, and the great purpose of the First Amendment to keep uncontrolled the freedom of expression is defeated." His colleague, Justice Harlan, concurred. "The federal government," he stated, "has no business, whether under the postal or commerce power, to bar the sale of books because they might lead to any kind of 'thoughts'."

Encouragement and hope may be found also in looking at these matters in historical perspective. Ideas cannot be killed by suppression. There is scarcely any record of a book totally disappearing because of the activities of the censor. Only when the ideas expressed in books lose their interest and signifi-cance do the books vanish.

One might even be able to make a strong case for the thesis that if books have not been attacked by the censor, they are of doubtful literary merit. Consider, for example, some of the authors who have been most frequently under fire in our own era: William Faulkner, James T. Farrell, Somerset Maugham, John O'Hara, C. S. Forester, Ernest Hemingway, John Steinbeck, James Michener, John Dos Passos, Eugene O'Neill, Erskine Caldwell, Aldous Huxley, D. H. Lawrence, George Orwell, George Bernard Shaw, and the whole school of Irish writers. Certainly, 20th century literature would be a poverty stricken and sterile thing without their magic touch.

34 *Censorship Debate*

(AUGUST, 1961)

POLEMICIST AT WORK
by JAMES JACKSON KILPATRICK

For whatever it may be worth, now that your hatchet-man Downs has done his dirty work on my book, I should like to register my strong and emphatic protest against the total misrepresentation embodied in his article. I am no longer astonished at the irrational and hysterical outcries of the professional liberal on the hustings, but I am amazed that so respected a magazine as LIBRARY JOURNAL should have participated in publication of an article that resorts to every contemptible trick of the polemicist at work—guilt by association, exaggeration, misstatement of fact, and the use, ad nauseam, of ad hominem statements.

Mr. Downs says that I emerged from research on my book, *The Smut Peddlers,* "embracing and condoning" various censorship groups "and advocating stringent repressive legislation." He lies. Nowhere in my book do I embrace these various groups; I report on their existence and activities, I present their views in summary, and in the only editorial section of the book I specifically criticize the NODL for some of its sillier listings.

As for advocating "stringent repressive legislation," that idea exists nowhere but in the fevered imagination of Mr. Downs. Far from advocating stringent repressive legislation, I endorsed the very model bill approved by the American Book Publishers Council, and I played an instrumental part in 1960 in persuading the Virginia General Assembly to adopt such a model bill in place of a highly repressive bill that had been introduced. I have repeatedly and publicly opposed prior restraint censorship of motion pictures.

In his remarkable fourth paragraph, Mr. Downs deliberately and maliciously undertakes to link me with "veterans organizations, religious bodies, White Citizens Councils, super-patriotic societies, Congressional committees and other misguided pressure groups working around the clock to place restrictions and limitations on what we may read, or see, or hear." Implicitly, he suggests that I have attempted to discredit opponents of these groups "by such epithets as Communists, subversives, fellow travelers, sex perverts, nigger lovers, egg heads, or, as Mr. Kilpatrick contemptuously refers to them, 'the literati'."

That sentence reveals far more about the curious mind of Mr. Downs than it does about my book. The noun he finds so contemptible was not mine but Mr. Justice Douglas', whose "enlightened and civilized views" he later praises.

Mr. Downs then goes on to make the flat and unqualified statement that in my book I "urge these busy bodies, soul savers, and do-gooders on to bigger and better censorship activities, along with more authority for the Postmaster General to dictate the nation's taste, and more laws to clutter up the statute books." This is an absolute falsehood. I do no such thing. On the contrary, the only counsel I urge upon the Postmaster General is to impose not more censorship, but less.

One more example of Mr. Downs' scurrilous technique and I am done: "The great moral crusade is fittingly represented by that noted champion of civil rights, Senator Eastland of Mississippi (apparently considered on the side of the angels by Mr. Kilpatrick), who recently introduced [a certain] bill . . ." Where did your literary assassin get *that* parenthetical phrase? So far as I can recall, neither Senator Eastland nor the Senator's foolish resolution is even mentioned in my book. I thought his proposal too ludicrous and wrong to be dignified by comment. Yet Mr. Downs charges in the pages of LIBRARY JOURNAL that "apparently" I support the Senator. How did this nonsense become "apparent" to him? Is it your custom to permit your contributors to fling these reckless and wholly unfounded charges against an author in no position to defend himself?

To judge from his article, Mr. Downs has trouble comprehending the English language, but I am willing to give him another chance. I am therefore sending a copy of this letter to him at the University of Illinois. Whatever difficulties he may have encountered in understanding my opinions on censorship, he should have no trouble in comprehending my opinion of his article.

BETWEEN TWO STOOLS
by ROBERT B. DOWNS

Mr. Kilpatrick's screams of protest arise, no doubt, from the fact that he has been caught off base and tagged out.

Judging from his astonishing and intemperate reply, Mr. Kilpatrick does not realize exactly what he has wrought in *The Smut Peddlers*. His intentions, according to his present testimony, were of the purest, but the results he has achieved are a horse of another color.

The principle is now widely accepted in legal circles that a book charged with obscenity should not be condemned on the basis of isolated passages, but rather by the criterion of whether, taken as a whole, it has a libidinous effect. Adhering to the same well-established rule, the total impression created by the Kilpatrick work is favorable to censorship. The author even admits (p. 289) that he probably belongs on the side of "the Philistines," i.e., the censors. Furthermore, he comes to the amazing conclusion (p. 291) that "the Philistines as a group are more lenient, tolerant, sensible, and ready to listen than the literati (the anti-censors) as a group."

Even the words in Mr. Kilpatrick's title *The Smut Peddlers*, semanticists would classify as "loaded," designed to create prejudice and to start the reader off with a bias, as are such phrases as "merchants of filth," recurring throughout the book.

It should be pointed out, for purposes of clarification, that my Lj article "Apologist for Censorship" did not appear in the book review section, nor was it meant to be confined to a discussion of *The Smut Peddlers*. Instead, the book was simply a point of departure for a discussion of the whole climate of censorship in the United States at the present time, without imputing to Mr. Kilpatrick all blame or responsibility for the existing state of affairs. My objections are based on the aid and comfort which the forces of reaction will inevitably derive from his work.

To cite chapter and verse for statements in my article to which Mr. Kilpatrick took most violent exception:

1. *Attitude toward censorship groups.* For the convenience of anyone who would like to form a local NODL committee, the address of the national office is given (p. 246), the procedures followed by such committees are described, and a long statement is quoted from Monsignor Fitzgerald (p. 247) justifying NODL's extra-legal activities. "Also seeking to fill that void [presumably referring to the breakdown of law enforcement and other agencies] are the local chapters of Citizens for Decent Literature, Inc." (p. 247). With every indication of approval, the programs of similar organizations, "working nationally in the field of decent literature," are also presented (p. 249–51). They are given a pat on the back by Mr. Kilpatrick with the statement that "individual and community efforts of the sort recommended by the various decent-literature groups can be effective" (p. 251).

2. *Advocacy of stringent legislation.* Noting the efforts of the Post Office Department to close the mails to "obscene" literature, Mr. Kilpatrick feels that "the statute governing second-class mail offers a feeble weapon in the war upon obscenity" (p. 68), and appears to support the Granahan bill in Congress to grant authority to the Postmaster General to impound mail for 45 instead of 20 days (p. 255–56). Citizens are urged to report to postal officials the receipt through the mails of material which they consider obscene (p. 255). Advocating state and local legislation in preference to federal, Mr. Kilpatrick states that he "would view with equanimity the prosecution of *Big Table* (University of Chicago student magazine banned by the Post Office Department) under a state law or local ordinance" (p. 291). In addition to criminal statutes, he also implicitly places his stamp of approval on state commissions on obscene literature, such as those in Oklahoma, Massachusetts, and Georgia (p. 267–68).

3. *Views on intellectuals.* Mr. Kilpatrick's low opinion of "the literati," a term applied to censorship opponents, was noted above. Elsewhere, he refers to "their caterwauling about the long dark night of suppression and the horrible excesses of the puritans and the Comstocks," and suggests that they "stop that blubbering" (p. 288). He asserts his belief that "the literati are guilty of exaggeration in their bland and hoity-toity certainty that obscene materials really cause no social damage," and his researches have persuaded him that "most of the experts on the literati side are academicians, lady psychologists, book publishers, and lawyers of the ACLU" (p. 289).

4. *On Senator Eastland.* I regret having wronged Mr. Kilpatrick in implying that perhaps he and Senator Eastland were pals, and I am happy to have him dissociate himself *now* from the Senator's incredible proposed constitutional amendment. But, by way of extenuation, it should be noted that no word of criticism appears in *The Smut Peddlers,* and the text of the Senator's bill is quoted along with a discussion of other legislation proposed by Representative Granahan and Senator Kefauver.

Despite the extreme, emotional tone of Mr. Kilpatrick's letter, I confess to some feeling of sympathy for him. He is simply confused, suffering from a split personality on the question of censorship. As a newspaper editor, he naturally wants reading to be free and unrestrained; unfortunately, exposure to former Postmaster General Summerfield's chamber of horrors (now happily abolished) has shaken his faith. Conscientiously attempting to weigh all the pros and cons of censorship, he falls between two stools and fails to present a convincing case for either side.

CHAPTER

35 *A Problem Author Looks at Problem Librarians*

(JUNE 15, 1962)

by IRVING WALLACE

Recently, I was invited to attend an innocuous cocktail party in Los Angeles, California, given for a newly published author of juveniles. A placid punch bowl, mildly spiked, held the center of the room, and around it were grouped many gentle people who were in the juvenile book field. I stood apart, enjoying a smuggled Scotch on the rocks, when suddenly I was accosted by the hostess, who had three pleasant-looking ladies in tow.

The hostess introduced me to the three ladies, identifying them as prominent librarians in the Los Angeles Public Library system. We exchanged banalities, and they beamed upon me, no doubt believing me to be an author of juveniles and no doubt disarmed by my round, benevolent face and warm smile and shy, inoffensive manner.

Suddenly, my hostess said to the librarians, "Of course, ladies, you know who Mr. Wallace is—he wrote *The Chapman Report*."

Well—

I had not seen such physical transformation in the human countenance since last I had dipped into the travail of Dr. Jekyll and Mr. Hyde. The three public librarians actually blanched and recoiled. It was as if I were something that had escaped from a cage. It was as if the nice man they met was not Ted Geisel, known to them as Dr. Seuss, but V. Nabokov, whose only juvenile was a precocious child named Lolita. It was as if the benevolence and sweetness they had read in my expression could now be seen for what it really was—the leer of a sex mad ogre, and worse, far worse, the bloated, unnatural look of the crass commercialist, panderer to low tastes and thief of easy dollars, who had sold out, and knows it in the darkness of lonely nights.

I simply could not let my librarians go, not on this note, for it was suddenly less funny now, and it was important, and I wanted to talk to them. And so I did. Gradually, in the next ten or 15 minutes, their shock and revulsion turned to wonderment ("They laughed when he sat down . . ."), and soon we were able to make normal conversation about books and people and the world in which we lived.

When they had gone, and I had gone, I thought about the meeting. It had surprised them that I was library bred, and book raised, and conscientious about my work, and dedicated (as best one can be) to truth and honesty. It had surprised them that I had tried to write well, and wanted to write well, and would never cease trying to do this. It had surprised them that I did not manufacture best-sellers deliberately ("ah, let me see, let's bake it with two rapes, four adulteries, one perversion, three four-letter words") but wrote what I observed, felt, and believed within my limitations. Yes, I was glad I had talked to them. They may not buy my next books—because they are victims of their milieu, a hushed world where controversy is too often to be avoided—but perhaps they will think twice before declining.

All of which brings me to those of you who are reading this article. As I said, I simply could not let those three public librarians go—without some communication with them—and now I simply cannot let you go, either, without clearing the air. Yes, I have read the sensational article that you may have read, " 'Problem' Fiction," in the February 1, 1962 issue of LIBRARY JOURNAL, and I have found my name among the 20 "problem" authors of the last two or three years. I have also read the widely circulated reprint of part of that article in the April 7 number of *Saturday Review*. And I can say, must say, that while I understand the pressures under which you work, I am appalled at the way so large a number of you think.

Too many of us who write are, to too many of you, merely numbers on your catalog cards and impossibly posed paper faces on book jackets. Perhaps that is as it should be. Perhaps it is our books, our books alone, that should speak for us. Yet, it is evident in the LIBRARY JOURNAL survey on " 'Problem' Fiction," that frequently, too often, we are known and judged not by our work, but by gossip, hearsay, inaccurate reporting, and often by biased reviewing. Because you are overworked and busy, you are susceptible to propaganda, and I feel we who write should counter it. As to those of you who do find the time to read, and can make first-hand judgments, I believe many of you are the victims of your profession, and something should be said of that, too.

Librarians have been valuable to me, and good to me, and still are, and I feel I owe them something as a group—and I have decided what I owe them is some free advice. I am not trying to be offensive, only a little funny, but truly I believe communication between us has now become a necessity. You are deeply concerned with problem fiction produced by problem authors. I am as deeply concerned with problem librarians.

This is no touchy defense of myself or of *The Chapman Report* or some novels produced by Henry Miller, Norman Mailer, Harold Robbins. I strongly feel that the act of writing for publication is one that invites public judgment. If the judgment is sometimes adverse, the author has no right to oppose it. The author asked for judgment, nay, begged for it, and whatever comes next, he should be still. When he should *not* be still, when he should speak up loudly and clearly, is when judgment, be it from the public, the various grades of librarian, the critics, is not based on literary merit but on irrelevant considerations. What I resent is the slyness of some librarians, and the reviewers to whom they pay lip service, who go beyond their rightful tasks in order to impugn the motives and intentions of an author. And what concerns me, also, is that so many books are judged not for what they say, or have to say, but because their central theme troubles the reviewer or librarian, rubs his or her neuroses the wrong way, or makes his life uneasy when he or she simply wants it easy—smooth, slick, and easy.

COCOON WORLDS

I think you and I, public librarian and author, have a good deal in common. I suspect many competent psychoanalysts might tell us that we came to our professions for identical subconscious reasons. Writing books is often the result of an inability to face the world on its own terms, it is a retreat from life, a way to create a cocoon world in which the author can live more happily. In the same way, handling books, living among them in libraries, is simply another means of selecting and creating a world to which one can better adapt, or can cope with more easily. Moreover, you and I, public librarian and author, are dependent on one another. Without us, you are deprived of a favored livelihood and its pleasures; without you, we are deprived of what we need the most, the wonderful people who will listen to our stories.

Yet, for all of this, there is a chasm between us. You say that we put it there, by writing poor books, controversial books, problem books. I say you have put the chasm there, a great many of you, by insisting upon having books your way, neat, quiet, antiseptic (and if they must deal with problems, dear author, bury them behind the historical facade or a style classical and obscure).

It pains me, writing this, to remember how much of my past was lived in both school and public libraries. Until I was 17 I spent months of my life, and found the companions and mentors I loved—Tolstoi, Flaubert, Dickens, Stendahl, Stevenson, Twain, Dumas, and yes, Dreiser, Maugham, Rolland, Hemingway, Huxley, Stephens, Fitzgerald—in the precious shelves and stacks of our library in Kenosha, Wisconsin, and in libraries of Chicago. At college, I was devoted to the libraries of Berkeley, California. In my twenties, I used the libraries of Los Angeles. For one who was poor, money was for lodgings, food, clothes, and for typewriter ribbons, postage, the occasional date.

Only when I began to make a meager living as a magazine writer did my contact with libraries become more limited. I was able to buy my own books, have them in a private library of my own, there to touch them and use them when I wished, to feel the joy of their presence. Thereafter, as I began to write books, my contact with libraries was largely professional, to research for a planned biography in the libraries of Washington, D.C., New York, London, Paris, Rome, Stockholm.

But libraries are not inanimate. They are alive, and what makes them alive, and sets their tone, style, value, are the human beings who direct, run, serve them. A hundred human librarians helped bring me to maturity as a man, and a thousand human librarians collaborated with me to make possible my seven books. This will be horrendous to many of you (like being loved by a leper)— but because of many of you, I was able to gather the factual background on surveys that I used in *The Chapman Report*. It would have been impossible for me to write my last book, a biography entitled *The Twenty-Seventh Wife*, without you. And much of my current novel, *The Prize*, results from your cooperation. There is simply no doubt about it—you are a necessity to me. But now I realize you are something else, also—you are a problem to me.

We are not all of us the same, in any profession, not all formed from the same cookie cutter. I am aware that librarians are not the same in their jobs and duties, in their ideas and tastes, and that all do not have similar feelings about "problem" fiction. I do not lump you all in the same gelatinous mound. I am sure the great majority of you, especially in the universities and schools, but even in the public libraries also, are made of stronger stuff, and deserving of respect from readers and authors alike.

I appreciate how many of you dwell in ultra-conservative communities, and are under fire from vigilante red-necks and organization morons and troublesome patrons with nothing but time on their hands and in their heads. Often, your livelihood is in the balance, and resistance is difficult, and you deserve sympathy—sympathy and the right of self-preservation. You are all engaged in an unceasing defense against the guerrilla attacks of political extremists (both Right and Left), race and religious dogmatists, and the highly moral Grundys and Comstocks, above all the latter.

Still, there are those of you, when accused of condoning the pornographic and the obscene, who stand with Justice William O. Douglas. It was Justice Douglas who remarked: "The idea of using obscenity to bar thoughts of sex is dangerous. A person without sex thoughts is abnormal. Sex thoughts may induce sex practices that make for better marital relations." And there are those of you who are intelligent, progressive, democratic, paying not only lip service but real service to the ideal of freedom of speech. I exempt you from any accusations I make against problem librarians. I wish you were all the librarians on earth. You have my boundless admiration.

The division of those to be admired and those to be admonished is made shining clear by Marjorie Fiske in her valuable volume, *Book Selection and Censorship:* "The key question was whether restrictions are being imposed on librarians, or whether they are imposing restrictions on themselves, that threaten the citizen's right to easy access to as adequate a collection of books and periodicals as his community, his county, or his state can afford." From the Library Journal survey, it is obvious to me that an appalling number of you librarians, especially public librarians, are annoyed, distressed, revolted by controversial fiction. You are the ones who are imposing restrictions on yourselves. You are the problem librarians, you alone, and you are the ones I address.

INTELLECTUAL BIG BROTHERS

Why do I label you problem librarians?

Too often, you stand between the author and his public, to the detriment of both. Many motives inspire you to play obstacle. For one thing, the nature of your calling has made you authoritarian. Unwittingly, you have become intellectual Big Brother or Big Sister. It is not enough for you to react to public taste. You know what is best for the flock. For years, you have immersed yourself in books, your knowledge is extensive, and your prejudices also, and, like a second skin, many of you wear intellectual superiority. You are used to giving your opinions to elderly ladies, lonely gentlemen, harried housewives, eager students, befuddled researchers. You are used to advising and directing. You are in the business of being right, in your tight little planet, and this leads to intolerance. You buy and promote certain books. You reject others, or if forced to buy them, you see that they are hidden or lost.

I am fully aware that 18,000 new books are published in a year, and someone other than the public must have opinions and judgments on what to buy and what to reject, what to recommend and what to turn aside. You must have the right of strong authority, and you have it. I simply say that this corrupts, in tiny ways, because it is misused. You try to impose your standards on pliable personalities. You want an orderly world and orderly books. You are suspicious of literary innovation and harsh realism and ideas that are abrasive or dangerous, and you find the books of the past (already judged) as safer. You are suspicious of whatever is popular.

Above all, you do not want trouble. Maternally, paternally, you wish to shield your card holders from rude reading. You will not face the fact that if we send forth a generation of readers who have been kept hermetically sealed off from troubles and problems by well-meaning librarians, we will have a generation that will be destroyed. For, the world is teeming with troubles and problems; every marriage, every family, every job, every community is agitated by problems. Out there, the stacks are all open. Life has few restrictions. Life is not under the counter. There are race hatred, religious prejudice, sexual aberration, all manners of crime and dishonesty, nuclear madness, ugly nationalism. There are beauty and grace and decency, too, but there are also mighty problems, and make no mistake about it.

There is a Caldwell world out there, and a Kerouac world, and a Metalious world (as she will tell you), and by hiding books about those worlds, you are weakening a generation that should be prepared and knowledgeable of realities. Give that generation your safe, safe books about lazy towns, and corporation fights, and brave young men growing between wars, and doctors concerned with integrity, and adolescents in rebellion, and old family mansions—give them those alone, and you are sending forth a headless generation, one that will be engulfed by life.

This fear of life is what makes certain books offend you, and too many times you stamp "lack of merit" as your rationale. This is your major problem, but you have many others.

Too often, contrary to public demand, you try books in a kangaroo court of your board or own personality. You have too much to read—I agree you are overworked, and underpaid, and that is a national disgrace—and since you cannot read as much as you would like to, you admit that you have to trust outside sources. In the survey, you list your best book selection sources as LIBRARY JOURNAL, Kirkus Service, *Booklist, Saturday Review, New York Times Book Review,* and *Publishers' Weekly.* That is only half of the influence upon you.

You are swayed and influenced, I believe, by maliciously angled reports and word acrobatics in news magazines, in gossip columns, in feature stories. You are unhinged from cool judgment. You are influenced by the private lives of Metalious, Mailer, Henry Miller, by the interviews and angers of O'Hara and others, by sensationalized advertisements slanted to the needs of the competitive market, by wire services' stories on hare-brained local censorship, by columnists who don't read a book a year, by a feeling of dispute in the air.

You don't want brawling, and "problem" fiction is brawling. You want harmony and sensibility. You want antiseptic authors, who have grace and style, who are literary and safe. You shudder with each John O'Hara book, "Must one be so—so vulgar?" It is hard to avoid him, but you try. Yet, I venture to predict that John O'Hara, one of your problem authors, will outlast most of the safe ones, because he has passion, and that is what real living is all about.

Conversely, you are bamboozled by carefully designed "literary" build-ups. If a book has the right imprint, the right advertising tone, the right handful of lobbied reviews, the promise of preciousness—though the book be tedious and involuted, though it be no story at all, though there be little demand for it—you will be fooled into accepting it and recommending it. You want to belong to the Establishment, despite the disservice to your card holders.

Eric Moon wrote in " 'Problem' Fiction": "We deliberately mixed books of literary quality with others that were meretricious potboilers, exploiting sensation with the bestseller list as a goal." What must you librarian readers think of this? Apparently, many of you concur. For, in the same article, the Free Library of Philadelphia states that it rejected *The Chapman Report* and three other books not only for incompetence but for "intentionally sensational writing." I am here to say that you know almost nothing of what impels a writer to write as he does, and you know next to nothing of the creative process.

How are you in Philadelphia able to know what was inside me when I sat, much of a year, writing *The Chapman Report?* What literary X-ray have you to know I was "intentionally sensational"? Or what wizardry does the editor of LIBRARY JOURNAL possess to know that some of the 20 of us were "exploiting sensation" with the bestseller list in mind?

This is the last and saddest of your problems—your utter lack of knowledge of what motivates an author, be he a problem author or a housebroken, library-broken one. What editor or librarian can believe he has the godly perception to know what is in an author's head and heart as he writes? Yet, apparently, many editors and librarians take this wisdom in themselves for granted, and base their judgments on misread motives.

Exploiting sensation? Intentionally designing a book for the bestseller lists? How? As I recently asked an interviewer, "How does one manufacture a bestseller? If one knew, if there were a formula, one might be tempted to avoid years of hardship before. The truth is, I had previously written an honest novel far more overtly sexual than *The Chapman Report,* and it did not sell at all. Sex, per se, cannot sell a novel. Nor can religion. Nor can Lincoln's doctor's dog. There have to be living characters, a good story, and deep sincerity on any literary level. I cannot imagine a prefabricated bestseller. It seems to me you write a tale out of deep inside yourself, as best you can, and hope, and suddenly great masses of people want to read it, and they talk about it, and that is the alchemy of any bestseller."

A librarian who truly believes an independent author of novels, no matter what his talent, will intentionally cheapen and exploit his inner feelings about sex or any subject merely to be thrown royalties, should be defrocked and go over the wall. This librarian does not belong in the world of books, for he does not understand the persons who sweat and burn and suffer over them.

I have a new novel, *The Prize,* and perhaps I will be your problem author again, and you will remain my problem librarians. You will read Kirkus' Service, *Publishers' Weekly,* the ALA *Booklist,* and you may not be sure what to do about this one, and you will worry, because you want peace and quiet and to keep the shelves neat, and some of us won't leave you alone.

But don't worry about us. Because, gentle ladies and good men, the problem is as much yours as our own. If you will accept into your vocabulary one seven letter word—*courage*—you will need worry less about all our four letter words.

I thank you for use of the hall.

36 Law, Liberty and Libraries

(JUNE 15, 1963)

by WILLIAM J. BRENNAN, JR.

This article is drawn from a speech given at a dinner celebrating the 75th anniversary of the Newark (N.J.) Public Library, on May 1, 1963.

It is a fortunate coincidence that we celebrate this birthday of the Newark Public Library on Law Day, 1963. May 1 has become a day on which all of us—not only lawyers and judges and law students, but all citizens —pause to take stock of the importance of the Rule of Law to the functioning of our society and our institutions. It is particularly a time for self-appraisal on the part of my profession—to consider how better as lawyers and judges we may carry out our trust in the service of the Rule of Law. Since ours is a Nation of Laws in which we are trying ever more to secure respect everywhere for the Rule of Law, the day also has aspects of a patriotic event. So it is most appropriate, and a most happy coincidence for me, that the Library—so much an institution which has long been a staunch pillar of freedom—should celebrate its birthday on the very day which the Nation sets aside for recognition of the Rule of Law and its contributions to liberty.

And so I'd like briefly to mention some of the essential contributions a free public library makes to our basic liberties—contributions which perhaps are particularly brought home to those of my profession, both on and off the bench. If May 1 is Law Day as well as the Library's birthday, it has yet a third significance—not one that's pleasing, but one we dare not ignore—it is the day every year that Communists celebrate their advances in the countries which have fallen under their control. I don't think it's farfetched to suggest that nothing better underscores the difference between America's Law Day and the Communists' May Day than the contributions to liberty of the free libraries throughout this country.

I would suggest that the strength and independence of our free public libraries make two contributions which are at the core of the freedom we honor on Law Day, and which are wholly foreign to the Communist May Day. First, it seems to me that the libraries are in a great degree the necessary guardians of academic freedom. As we observe from the increasingly close relationship between the Newark Library and the schools and colleges of the community—public, private and parochial—the resources of the central public library are an absolutely essential part of the educational system. Even for children in schools which have excellent in-school libraries, there is still a vast range of materials which cannot be kept in the school building. These will be available from the public library, or not at all. What school, even with the largest available space and the ablest librarian, can obtain such invaluable materials as Government documents, newspapers and magazines, and foreign-language books? And where in the average school will there be room for fine and rare books, recordings of poetry readings, sheet music and historical or technical films? Again the answer seems obvious—so obvious, perhaps, that one need not state it. But I do pose the question and offer an answer for one reason: however obvious it may seem to you that the public libraries make available to school and college students innumerable materials which can't be kept on the school grounds, the dependence of the schools upon the libraries never ceases to impress me as a quite remarkable phenomenon.

TEACHING THE BILL OF RIGHTS

I am especially concerned about the library's contribution to the school systems in the area of materials about civil rights and individual liberties. Within the past couple of years, a number of groups have taken a new and heartening interest in the status of teaching in the public schools about our basic constitutional freedoms, especially those drawn from the Bill of Rights. Last summer, for example, a Task Force of the National Council for the Social Studies and the Civil Liberties Educational Foundation sponsored a survey to find out how much was being taught about the Bill of Rights in the public schools, and why more was not done at the high school level. The results of the survey were not wholly discouraging, although they reveal that a great deal more needs to be done as soon as funds, personnel and official support will permit.

One question in the survey particularly interested me. It concerned the availability of teaching materials for the teaching of the Bill of Rights. While about half the teachers who responded indicated that they were generally satisfied with the materials now available, many indicated that they could not do a competent job of teaching the Bill of Rights with only the regular civics or history or social studies textbook. A surprising number of the teachers who did express satisfaction with the materials now available also said they relied heavily on film strips, motion pictures, magazines, newspapers and pamphlets to supplement the regular texts. I would imagine that rather few schools, even in the cities and more affluent suburbs would have at hand enough of this sort of material to meet the teacher's needs.

Few people today doubt the vital importance of this field of education to the preparation of responsible citizens. Time and again we have witnessed the sorry effects of a de-emphasis in some of our schools upon individual liberties and the Bill of Rights. Surely there are many reasons why more has not been done along these lines. But one of the major reasons given by the teachers who took part in the survey was the shortage of good teaching materials readily at hand. Here, I would suggest, is one area in which we must look forward to even closer cooperation between the public libraries and the schools than we have had so far—particularly in the less well supported school districts where the schools simply can't afford to provide other than the bare, basic textbooks.

Perhaps I should be a bit more specific about the library's role in servicing teachers of civil liberties and the Bill of Rights. The Task Force to which I referred a moment ago published a set of recommendations last fall, in a booklet entitled *A Program For Improving Bill of Rights Teaching in High Schools*. The editors gave specific attention to the needs for better and more readily available teaching materials. Among other things, they called for development of programmed teaching materials to aid in mastering the factual content of the Bill of Rights, and assistance in the analysis and selection of books, audio-visual materials, pamphlets and periodical literature keyed to curriculum and learning levels. In each of these areas, there would appear to be fruitful avenues for cooperation and interchange between teachers and librarians. I can think of no more valuable function in the education of a democracy than this. It is a task in which the libraries have already played a very important part, and in which I hope their contributions will develop even further in the future.

There is another and quite distinct way in which the strength of our free public libraries points up basic differences between Law Day and May Day. One of the liberties we Americans prize most highly is our freedom to read what we wish and when we wish. It is hard to realize that nothing in the body of the Constitution or the Bill of Rights says anything in terms about a freedom to read, or to listen, or even to think. Yet we know that such liberties are there just as surely as if they were expressly written into the First Amendment. For the freedom to speak would be meaningless without the corollary freedom to listen. And in the same way freedom of the press which we have cherished throughout history would be a hollow right without a corresponding freedom to read without fear of prosecution, censorship, or suspicion. The author and publisher are only as free to write and to print as their readers are to read.

In large part we tend to expect the publishers and booksellers to be the guardians of our liberty to read. I suggest that we have given too little attention to the invaluable role which the public libraries and librarians play in this area. We have seen repeated instances, in the history of other countries as well as our own, in which devoted librarians, archivists and curators have preserved priceless books for posterity when others either did not care about them or would even have caused their destruction. We should give much greater attention to the contribution of our free libraries, from the Library of Congress and the National Archives in Washington on down to the smallest community libraries, in their capacity as what I might call the treasure-houses of the documents of liberty.

There is a more mundane though hardly less important aspect to the library's role as the guardian of freedom to read. Sometimes booksellers, facing the needs of economic survival, become timid in the face of public criticism and refuse to stock certain books regardless of their literary merit. How great then becomes the responsibility of the public library, as the only source then left through which these books may be made available to the community. Then, too, there are books which simply have no market and therefore can't attract a spot on the booksellers' shelves. Yet simply because books may now seem dull or without merit is no reason to take them out of circulation. Indeed, it would be the meanest form of hypocrisy to say that the only books which ought to be available for distribution are those which sell handsomely or invite favorable reviews. To limit the circulation of books and periodicals in that way would impose the most pernicious form of censorship. Yet if the public libraries do not take up where the booksellers feel financially compelled to leave off, we would have exactly that kind of censorship. So it is just as much with respect to the turgid or technical book as with respect to the racy and exotic that the public libraries must ultimately be the guardians of the all-important freedom to read. There is meaning for the professions too in this. For, speaking only of my own, since lawyers must improve their cooperation with several disciplines if they are to be adequate to their role in our society, the public library has a special meaning for them.

We know actually very little about the ways in which the public libraries have carried out these responsibilities. We need to know more, and efforts are now underway, I understand, to find out more. What we do know, however, seems to reflect most creditably upon the courage, independence and integrity of our librarians. For example, at the height of the furor over internal security, with its "book-burning" hysteria directed chiefly at the public libraries, the American Library Association joined forces with the American Book Publishers' Council in drafting and publicizing a courageous statement entitled *The Freedom to Read*. The issuance of that manifesto and other statements fostered the efforts of the National Book Committee and its subcommittee on Freedom to Read—a most distinguished group which includes such publishers as George Shuster and Alfred Knopf, and such leading scholars as Detlev Bronk and Archibald MacLeish. That subcommittee published several years ago a preliminary report under the appropriate title *The Freedom to Read*, edited by Richard McKeon, Robert Merton and Walter Gellhorn. The editors noted that while librarians had been subjected to widespread informal as well as formal pressures to remove from their shelves certain books thought "objectionable" by private groups and individuals, they had withstood the challenge courageously. But the subcommittee had little information on which to rely, and urged the undertaking of surveys which would supply some of the answers.

One such survey has been undertaken covering the State of California, and has resulted in the publication of Marjorie Fiske's important volume, *Book*

Selection and Censorship, an exhaustive survey of the policies of California school and public libraries. Also within the last couple of years the American Library Association has sponsored the publication of a most useful compendium of materials concerning the First Amendment freedoms especially as they relate to writing and publishing—entitled, appropriately, *The First Freedom.* So the American public libraries, both individually and collectively, have responded eloquently to persistent challenges which the currents and pressures of our time have presented to them. It seems to me that we owe a very substantial debt indeed to our libraries and librarians who have so assiduously guarded our intellectual freedoms.

Contrast the canons of our libraries with the policies of the Soviet Union toward the circulation of books and you will see just how clearly the role of the American free public library illuminates the difference between Law Day and May Day. Not only is the Soviet Press designed to serve exclusively as a vehicle of propaganda—what Stalin often described as "a transmission belt between the masses and the Party"—but even the publication of books is permitted only to the extent that it serves the needs of the Party and its rulers. Lenin once wrote, early in the development of Soviet policies toward intellectual freedom:

> Literature must become a part of proletarian activities in general; it must become a wheel and a screw of the single great social democratic mechanism which is driven by the vanguard of the whole worrking class. Literature must become a component part of the organized, planned, unified social democratic Party work.

We had these policies most brutally and dramatically revealed to us at the time of the Soviet Minister of Culture's suppression of Pasternak's great novel *Dr. Zhivago.* The Minister explained his decision in terms which ought to make us stop to realize just how precious, and sometimes how fragile, are our own freedoms to read and to think as we please. The Minister said:

> Our publishing houses publish literature that helps to build a new world, a new society which we call the Communist society. If the work is written on a plane that is not useful for our society and has no use for our society, why should we publish anything of that nature?

It is not hard to understand, then, how easily the freedom to read might be placed in jeopardy were it not for the determination of the great public libraries to keep alive the full spectrum of our literature even when booksellers and others either cannot or care not, or dare not do so.

37 *Censorship Feeds on Complacency*

(OCTOBER 15, 1964)

by JOHN V. LINDSAY

In recent years a wide range of self-appointed groups have exerted various pressures on booksellers, public libraries, and school libraries against the free circulation of certain books. Consider this brief list:

In a high school library in Phoenix, Arizona, such works as *Brave New World, The Magic Mountain, The Short Stories of Ernest Hemingway* have been placed on the restricted list. In Little Rock, Arkansas, a private pressure group protested against the inclusion of *Exodus* and a book called *Great American Negroes* on the library shelves. In California, a small private pressure group attacked such library selections as Richard Wright's *Black Boy* and works by Carl Sandburg, John Steinbeck, Clifford Odets, and William Saroyan. Said the group's spokesman: "A common trait of atheistic totalitarians is an intense preoccupation with sex . . ."

Unhappily, this is a very partial list. Private pressure groups in recent years also have attacked such books as Orwell's *1984*, Hawthorne's *The Scarlet Letter*, Pearl Buck's *The Good Earth*, and Walter Edmonds' *Drums Along the Mohawk*. In these troublesome political days one is too quickly led into assuming a nexus between political movements and censorship. It is there in part, but it is not new in our history. The question is how will we survive it no matter what its motivation.

In the comparatively recent past, tar and feathers, the knout, the club, and the noose were applied by various communities in their efforts to impose narrow orthodoxies on every person. Go back a generation or two and one finds efforts to muzzle the Nonpartisan League organizer in Minnesota, the

Wobbly in Colorado, the Abolitionist in Georgia, the Socialist in Oklahoma, the Catholic in Know-Nothing territory. These efforts were in part political, in part purely moralistic, at least from the viewpoint of the people behind them. From the viewpoint of the unhappy nonconformist they may have been something—indeed anything—else. Whatever the motivation, he was hurt. Most cases of censorship are expressions of the tendency in American life to legislate, or administer without legislation, standards of intellectual morality. Usually reason has prevailed, not without some hard knocks in the process, and principles of free expression have survived. The courts have of course played their role. In most cases the motivation for censorship has been moralistic, not political. Thus, the attack on *Tropic of Cancer* in Honolulu and on *1984* in Minnesota were by independent groups not seeking political goals. In some other cases in recent years the attacks appear to have been linked—at least in ideology—with individuals or collections of individuals who hate this group or that group or this institution or that institution. Some appear to have political goals and seek to operate within or around both major political parties in our country. Most of these "hate" groups are not large in number, but then neither was the Communist party. It doesn't take large numbers to initiate or even achieve, political goals.

These groups of "antis" or "negativists" are not the only force for this distinctly modern form of censorship. As one of the authors and Floor Leaders of the Civil Rights Act of 1964, I think I am entitled loudly to deplore the efforts of a few Negro leaders who attempted to censor books in New York school libraries. I am thinking specifically of the effort to censor Mark Twain's classic, *Huckleberry Finn*, because the characterization of the Negro was found distasteful. We cannot rewrite American history. While I resist the Californian who would deny me Richard Wright's *Black Boy*, I also resist the efforts of civil rights organizations who would deny me *Huckleberry Finn*. The motivation of both the "negativists" and these few Negro leaders was essentially political—one wants to keep out of the American way of life people he doesn't like; the other wants to be let into the American way of life. The difference is of course that the Negro civil rights movement does not pose the country a serious censorship threat. All revolutions, whether peaceful or unpeaceful, tend to breed a few extremists, and the Negro revolution is no exception. Neither is censorship of itself one of the goals of the Negro movement. But it may be one of the goals of some of the "antis" and "negativists," and some of these have the resources and organization to launch censorship campaigns. At the same time, I think the general movement of American history is away from those who would attempt to stifle the free flow of ideas in America.

This does not mean that any thinking person can remain complacent about basic freedoms. They are always threatened. And the point of erosion may shift. An effective national government has been perhaps the key instrument in establishing both civil rights and civil liberties in American life. In our whole history, states and communities have needed this check against the possible tyranny of local majorities. Yet the increasing concentration of power in the central government means there is increased potential from this direction to do evil as well as good. The traditional guardian of personal rights against local majorities itself needs watching. As a Republican with high respect for the philosophy of Lincoln, I see my task in Congress as that of redefining the role of the individual in our half-garrison, part-welfare state. At a time when great complexes of institutional power tend to roll up individuals in their path, the need to reassert individual rights becomes obvious. This is true in both the private and public arenas, where an arbitrary and weighty bureaucracy may blur and submerge individual rights. These massive bureaucratic forces appear under various guises to which we should be alert: "military secrecy," "national security," "international competition," "dominant governmental interest," or just plain expediency.

PERVASIVE THREATS

I believe that the real danger of increasing centralism does not lie in the comparatively modest federal expenditures for the destitute, for education, and for health, but rather in the pervasive threat to individual liberties that stems from undue concentration of military, police, or economic power. A few examples in which I have been involved will illustrate what I mean:

In 1962, in the 87th Congress, the House Committee on Un-American Activities, backed by the Attorney General and the House leadership, tried to push through by unanimous consent a bill that went under the title of "Industrial Security." The bill would have given the government summary power in effect to remove from their jobs, without due process, up to five million Americans employed in private industry and universities on defense contracts or on related research. A small group of us in the House barely beat this bill down by less than a majority vote, under a procedure which requires two-thirds for passage.

In 1963 the House of Representatives passed, by a vote of 340 to 40, again under pressure from the Justice Department, a bill which would toss into the ashcan any semblance of due process for accused employees of the National Security Agency, an organization which handles highly secret military and cold war operations. The measure was backed by the administration and the leadership of both parties in Congress. Another bill with the same backing would have made it a crime merely to order a Federal investigator out of your house or threaten him with an inkwell if it could be said that he was being obstructed in the course of his work.

The Attorney General has continued to press for legislation that will permit the FBI to tap wires without court orders in cases "presenting a threat to the security of the United States"—a phrase which can mean anything at all. Modern electronic listening and eavesdropping devices have made the threat to individual rights posed by unchecked, unlimited use of this power all the more dangerous.

Recently there came to light a widespread practice in the Pentagon of using lie detectors on Pentagon personnel. There was a whole unit which does nothing but train people how to administer lie-detector tests.

Earlier in 1964, the House passed by a vote of 325 to 19 a bill which would require the Postmaster General to notify the sender of mail which is considered "morally offensive" to the recipient of the mail that he, the sender, is forbidden from then on to send any mail of any description, any mail matter at all, to the same recipient unless that recipient should solicit such mail. The matter would then automatically be referred to the Justice Department for civil prosecution. The bill passed despite the fact that the Justice Department said the bill probably is unconstitutional, despite the fact that the Post Office Department said the bill is unworkable, and despite the fact that there is no agreed upon standard of what is or might be "morally offensive." The bill permits the whole weight of the Federal government to be brought against a private citizen by another private citizen. The Postmaster's job is to deliver the mail, not censor it at his own or somebody else's behest.

The Bill of Rights marks off a protected area in which each individual may develop and express himself in his own way. But even that delimited area can be restricted in the absence of a watchful, thoughtful, and vocal public opinion. What is more alarming to me than the threats that are posed to the individual is complacency towards these threats. This complacency has helped feed the problem of censorship. While there is a great deal courts and law-makers can do to protect individual rights, the problem of what books shall appear on library book shelves is largely for the local community to decide. As many constitutional scholars have noted, the First and Fourteenth Amendments to the Constitution prohibit invasions of free speech and press by the Federal and state governments; they do not prohibit invasions of free speech by private pressure groups. In their book, *Censorship,* Morris Ernst and Alan Schwartz point out that "In a society such as ours, where ideas are supposed to prove their value by free and open conflict with other ideas, it is the duty and function of individuals, whether in groups or alone, to project their points of view so long as they act responsibly and with due regard for the rights of others."

No doubt one reason why private censorship groups have proliferated in recent years is that they have not been effectively checked by countervailing efforts by other private groups. It is an unhappy fact that today only a few publishers stand behind their books and defend them in towns and villages where they are attacked. As Ernst and Schwartz point out, the failure of reason and justice in this area is the failure of those interested in the free dissemination of literature to establish a climate of opinion strong enough to counter-balance the activity of the censorious private pressure groups.

The ultimate defense of free speech, then, is a matter for individual citizens. One such citizen called to my attention in this area is Harold W. Tucker of the Queens Borough Public Library, who answered a group which had attacked Henry Miller's *Tropic of Cancer* on the library shelf. Said Tucker:

> Its controversial nature was fully recognized as well as opinions running the full range from condemnation to praise as a literary masterpiece. Precisely be-cause of this wide range of opinion, the book should be available in the public library. Our free society is based on the right of each individual to form his opinion, and I have faith in the ability of our people to think for themselves.

The public library is one of the institutions responsible for the protection of these rights that are basic to our democratic way of life. There are many people in this community who would object strongly to removal of this book, just as you would protest pressures for removal of a book for which you see merit.

Thus, it is important for the future of the reading and thinking public that persons representing all sides of the question make themselves known, heard, and effective. Like the Queens Borough librarian, I favor debate and I believe that debate in itself performs a vital service in setting standards by which most people will voluntarily abide. And I believe that the balance wheel must always be tipped in favor of safeguarding personal rights and liberties, most importantly the right of free speech, so that human beings may live as rational beings, without fear, and with dignity and mutual respect.

CHAPTER

38 *Censorship and Cultural Rebellion*

(JUNE 1, 1965)

by HAROLD E. FEY

At the moment of our greatest responsibility and opportunity for service, we in the United States are confronted with a rebellion against the very elements in our heritage which make the world turn to America in anticipation and hope. It is not only the economic, technical, and scientific attainments which are manifest here, but even more the humanistic and spiritual elements of our culture which impel the people of all continents to cherish more firmly their passionate hope for freedom and sufficiency, for health and learning, for dignity to stand as men among the generality of mankind. Today, it is this humanistic and spiritual significance of America which is under attack from a substantial fraction of our own people. If this nation is not to be altered from within, with incalculable loss to our children and to humanity, we must defeat this rebellion.

The object of this rebellion is to rewrite our history, to substitute a narrow ideology for our intellectual freedom, to shrink the universalism of the democratic faith into the crabbed confines of narrow nationalism. The leaders of this rebellion seize and wave the tattered banners of cultural lag, blow their trumpets of fear and intolerance, and summon the nation to follow them back to yesterday, sweeping all before their hysterical ranks. The ideal is not only a fortress, American in its defense policies and capabilities; it is an America which insulates itself from the international ebb and flow of economic growth, which commits itself to more or less complete political isolation at a time when interdependence is a necessity for survival, which armors itself through censorship against penetration by new ideas, and which blanks out our minds through the incessant propaganda clamor of mass media. In the name of moral reform they propose to abandon minority peoples to the immoralities and injustices practiced for a century by many states. They oppose government participation in the struggles against poverty at home and abroad.

Resistance to learning is not a new thing in Anglo-American history. Leonard Woolf says that "no people has ever despised and distrusted the intellect and intellectuals more than the British." Does he forget that even the ancient Greeks forced Socrates to drink the hemlock "for not worshipping the gods whom the city worships, for introducing religious innovations and for corrupting the young men"? Does he forget our Know-Nothing party of a century ago; our American Protective Association of 75 years ago; our Ku Klux Klan of the 1920's, resurgent again today? Surely he cannot ignore the current proliferation of extremist organizations in this country, now numbering an estimated 3000.

Cultural lag has always existed in our society, as it has in others. But know-nothingism has generally stood on the defensive, has operated under a cloud of public disdain. Fanatics have found plenty of critics who were ready to challenge their half-baked panaceas, to wither their ill-considered utopias, with reason and common sense. But today a movement which was once scattered and sporadic, which won its little triumphs by hit-and-run guerrilla tactics, has acquired muscle, money, some coordination, and a degree of tactical skill. Now it begins to assume the appearance, and more important, the psychology of an organized, large-scale, cultural rebellion capable of destroying the consensus without which our pluralistic society cannot conduct its affairs on a democratic basis.

This new development can accurately be described as philistinism. It has acquired the ability of aggression which was originally attached to the name Philistine. The Philistines were Aryan pirates who forced their way into the settlements of what was once called Canaan and took them over. In the 3000 years since this happened in the eastern Mediterranean, the word Philistine has lost its connotation of aggression, although it continues to mean dull, unimaginative, materialistic, complacent. So Matthew Arnold could rake over the coals the 19th Century Philistines of England as "particularly stiff-necked and perverse in their resistance to light." He rebuked them for their materialism, but not for aggression. It was Byron who understood that it was the aggression of the "barbarian monarchs" which made Rome see "her glories, star by star, expire." The barbarians whom we have the greatest cause to resist are those American philistines who are trying to repeal the 20th Century, which has elected America to defend liberty and equality on a world scale; to repeal the 18th Century, which gave us the Constitution which rooted liberty and equality in our basic law; and to undo the 17th Century, which gave the world the liberal formula which the Constitution expresses.

One of the most trusted reliances of these rebels against rationality is censorship, applied by various degrees and devices, from protest to pressure to outright efforts to pack meetings and capture control of library boards. The object of these endeavors is thought control in the interest of a reactionary creed. Libraries are particularly exposed because the current rebellion against

American cultural and political ideals and institutions is organized on a local, grass roots basis. Its visible national manifestations are only the one-eighth of the iceberg which projects above the water. It is therefore important that we turn once again to the arguments developed by our fathers in the years when the mind of western man was first throwing off the shackles of thought control.

John Milton, whom this generation knows only as a poet, pioneered as a pamphleteer. At a time when political pamphleteering has sunk to the incredible degradation of *None Dare Call It Treason* it is refreshing to be reminded that a pamphlet can have literary distinction, a serious purpose and an interest in truth. Milton recognized that every act of truth-telling is symbolic. He showed his own faith in rationality and in orderly justice in his "Second Defense of the English People."

Milton opposed the idea then prevalent in the Presbyterian Parliament that books should not be published until some official licensed their publication. Such pre-censorship was not only a violation of a civil right, it was in his view also an offense against the nature given man by the Creator. "When God gave him reason, he gave him freedom to choose, for reason is but choosing." He scorned officials who wanted to treat men like children and said if God can "trust (man) with the gift of reason to be his own chooser" men should not enslave their fellows "under a perpetual childhood of prescription."

Milton's strongest argument, in my opinion, was that censorship is wrong chiefly because God is at work in history and censors obstruct his activity. To fulfill his purposes, said Milton, God raises up in every age men of "eminent and ample gifts, and those perhaps neither among the priests nor the pharisees." If we try to "stop their mouths because we fear they come with new and dangerous opinions," he said, it is we who become "the persecutors of the Gospel" in trying to defend it by such methods. "Our testy methods of prohibiting," said Milton, "are unacceptable unto God." They offend against the truth, which is no "fugitive and cloistered virtue" but "is compared in Scripture to a streaming fountain; if her waters flow not in perpetual progression, they sicken into a muddy pool of conformity and tradition." Milton opposed the tyranny of the censors, whose appetites for power knew no bounds, but he also resisted anarchy by insisting that liberty requires inner discipline in accordance with the highest dictates of virtue—a lesson we still need to learn. When full freedom of the press was legally established in England in 1695 and in the United States in 1789, it owed much to men of religion determined to speak and write as conscience demanded they should.

Others who contended for freedom before it was legally established included John Robinson, nonconformist pastor of the Pilgrim fathers, and Roger Williams, founder of Rhode Island. Robinson argued that since God "violates not the liberty of the reasonable soul by superseding the faculties thereof, but approves truth to the understanding and moves the will without violence," men should do the same. Williams, who probably knew Milton, denied secular power to the church and spiritual authority to the state. He insisted that a free conscience was the proper guide to conduct and religious liberty was the bulwark of civil freedom. He declared that the power of the magistrate comes from the association of men in their natural, not their spiritual capacities. So the official is bound to allow complete freedom in religion. "He must defend the civil rights not merely of different varieties of Christians but of "Jews, Turks, anti-Christians, pagans, and even of papists."

The practice of religious and civil liberty in Rhode Island for more than a century before 1789 helped make freedom of speech, press, assembly and petition, and the separation of church and state—the substance of the First Amendment—the cornerstone of our Constitution. And the rationale of freedom thought out and advocated by Milton, Robinson, and Williams constitutes the kind of defense that still could be effective today against the current uprising which would destroy freedom in an effort to preserve it.

NATIONAL ORTHODOXY

Despite the reverence we hold for the great men who blazed the trail for our freedoms, despite the proven validity of the principles on which our liberties are based, censorship by the state or by voluntary group activity is still a danger and at times becomes an actuality. It is always based on the assumption that there is or should be a consensus, a basis of national agreement, on what constitutes national orthodoxy. Through censorship, good as well as evil men have struggled to coerce thought into some pattern of uniformity they considered essential to the life of the nation. National unity is desirable and necessary, but it is achieved and must be achieved on a voluntary basis by the consent of the governed.

Two decades ago, in the midst of war, the Supreme Court ruled against compulsory flag salutes in words which should never be forgotten (West Virginia State Board of Education vs. Barnette, 1943): "As government pressure toward unity becomes greater, so strife becomes more bitter as to whose unity it shall be. Probably no deeper division of our people could proceed from any provocation than from finding it necessary to choose what doctrine and whose program public officials shall compel youth to unite in embracing. Ultimate futility of such attempts to compel coherence is the lesson of every such effort. Those who begin coercive elimination of dissent soon find themselves exterminating dissenters. Compulsory unification of opinion achieves only the unity of the graveyard. If there is any fixed star in our constitutional constellation, it is that no official, high or petty, can prescribe what shall be orthodox in politics, nationalism, religion, or other matters of opinion, or force citizens to confess by word or act their faith therein. If there are (any) circumstances which permit an exception they do not now occur to us."

Our American national orthodoxy, in other words, repudiates orthodoxy. It safeguards democratic procedure and lets ideas stand or fall according to the degree of truth that is in them. This is a formula for a truly open society—a society in which men are free and equal, and in which access to the truth is always open. Ideas freeze when they are encumbered by the sanctions of an official orthodoxy; they become encrusted with special interests and they are made rigid by law and bureaucracy. In this condition, even the greatest conceptions are handicapped in meeting the swift and sweeping changes of the modern world.

Today we have plenty of examples of what happens to nations when they are saddled by orthodoxies. Marxism has frozen the misconceptions of 19th Century English and German industrialism into a rigid ideology. It cannot live within this ideology, as Stalin and Mao Tse-Tung tried and are trying to do, nor break out of entrenched errors, as Khrushchev tried to do. Human nature cannot endure the enforcement of its unnatural materialism, its Godless self-centeredness, its tyrannical cynicism. But the fundamentalistic wing of communist parties terrorizes officials who try to make practical adjustments to reality, making it almost impossible and terribly costly to change. The result is that the communist state moves further and further from reality, away from the people it purports to serve, and in the direction of failure, chaos, and eventual revolution. Americans who fear the exercise of freedom of thought, who seek to restrain that exercise by censorship or other forms of cultural vigilantism, may do so from patriotic motives, but the only result, where their efforts are successful, is to weaken our nation and to discredit democracy as a genuine alternative to Marxism.

Ours is the system which has proved its flexibility by the way it has adapted to the great changes of the past 188 years. Now the rate of change has speeded up enormously and nuclear scientists tell us we stand only at the threshold of the new scientific age. This fact may thrill us or it may terrify us, or our feelings may be a mixture of anticipation and fear. But the one certainty is that these mighty changes are irreversible; that if censorship blocks intelligence in one land it cannot possibly enforce its will in another land. Since this is the case, it is the policy of wisdom to welcome new truth, no matter what its source, to resist every effort to shackle human minds, no matter how alarming their findings. Only we must exert more zeal and courage than ever in making sure that procedure is sound and democratic, that equality of opportunity prevails in education and in access to libraries and other cultural resources, and that religion be encouraged as a guide to conscience and a monitor of our ideals.

POWER AND PROHIBITIONS

The use of the police power of the state to protect children or youth incapable of protecting themselves is repeatedly undertaken, even though the courts generally hold, especially at their higher levels, for freedom from censorship. While the field is one of complexity and difficulty the law is designed to serve freedom and to keep the exercise of governmental power strictly limited. Considering the provocations, the number of prohibitions is surprisingly small. Americans may not publish or distribute seditious or treasonable reading matter, or matter which interferes with the operation of the draft, or which advocates the overthrow of the government by force, or which incites to insurrection. Threats to kill the President are outlawed, and this law may soon be broadened to cover other officials. Matter which is obscene is prohibited. Recently the Supreme Court has undertaken to clarify the confused state of the laws concerning obscenity, with the result that some people complain that it has weakened the ability of the states and cities to control obscenity. Unquestionably the court has curtailed the powers of police to handle such cases themselves and has strengthened the obligation of the courts to rule on them.

According to Dan Lacy, "the courts have made it plain that police and prosecutors may not avoid recourse to the courts by making up lists of publications and ordering or suggesting that they not be sold; that the actual or alleged effect of publications on minors may not be used to ban their sale to adults; that a publication cannot be judged on the basis of excerpts; that a film or publication can lose its constitutional protection only if it is actually obscene, and not by being held 'immoral' or 'sacrilegious'; and that there must be evidence that a bookseller has some knowledge of the content of a publication in order to convict him for its sale as an obscene item. These definitions, as applied by the Supreme Court . . . make it indeed difficult to sustain a conviction for the publication or sale of a work with significant pretensions to literary worth or informational content, or one presenting a serious advocacy of an unorthodox point of view, even though it may have an explicit sexual content or use vulgar language." (*Christian Century*, May 4, 1960.)

Nevertheless, we are not without legal defense against filth. Federal, state, and local governments are well equipped with power to punish with severity the real pornographer. The borderline cases are more difficult and present more problems. While it is generally acknowledged that on moral questions the state can enforce only minimal standards which meet nearly universal acceptance, it can do that much.

A more difficult problem, and one which particularly plagues libraries, is raised by the people who take or try to take censorship into their own hands. The commercialization of sex had driven some good Americans into this form of cultural vigilantism. Armed with lists made by the National Office of Decent Literature (a Catholic organization) they try to pressure police into threatening newsstands or book stores. (NODL officers specifically warn against the practice, but it happens.) Or they organize boycotts against places which ignore their warnings. A telephone campaign directed against a television station kept the film "Martin Luther" from being shown in Chicago on that station, although it later appeared on another station as a result of quick citizen action. Frequently the prohibitions of self-appointed groups get out of hand and for political or doctrinal reasons bar books and films of genuine worth. While citizens undoubtedly have the right to express disapproval in legitimate ways, they would do much more good if they devoted an equal amount of energy to persuade children and other people to know the best of reading, to support and patronize libraries which make reading an enriching experience, to advance the good, the true, and the educational.

John Courtney Murray, the Catholic theologian, who cannot quite bring himself to oppose censorship but comes close to doing it, laid down four rules for voluntary groups. He said each minority group—and all churches are minority groups—has the right to censor for its own members to protect them. (Most Protestants would not concede even this much.) Second, in a pluralist society, no minority group has the right to demand that the government shall impose a general censorship affecting all citizens upon any medium of communication. Third, any minority group has the right to work by persuasion toward the elevation of the standards of public morality. Fourth, no minority group has the right to impose its own religious or moral views on other groups by force, coercion, or violence.

Professor Murray dryly observes that these rules are not made in heaven but on earth by the practical reason of man. He notes the incongruity of the use of coercion in the interests of morality. He is much more concerned that the use of such coercive methods may brand the church as a "power association," fear of which may turn into hatred of the faith. He also points out that a great danger in this field is that reliance on negation and censorship will prevent people from reading and promoting the good and great books.

Religious groups must bear a good deal of responsibility for the rebellion against cultural and political freedom which results so easily in censorship shading into tyranny. The Catholic church poses the most serious threat of censorship, although many of its best leaders oppose such moves. Protestant churches, says Richard Hofstadter in his *Anti-Intellectualism in American Life* (Knopf, 1962), have a large responsibility for the persistent anti-intellectualism which colors our national climate. He says it "first got its strong grip on our ways of thinking because it was fostered by an evangelical religion that also purveyed many humane and democratic sentiments. It made its way into our politics because it became associated with our passion for equality. It has become formidable in our education partly because our educational beliefs are evangelically equalitarian. Hence, as far as possible, our anti-intellectualism must be excised from the benevolent impulses upon which it lives by constant and delicate acts of intellectual surgery which spares these impulses themselves. Only in this way can anti-intellectualism be checked and contained."

We churchmen have also contributed more than our share to the apocalyptic notion of the extremists that everything will suddenly come all right if some great, simple, earthshaking action is taken. Communism is a threat, but it will vanish from the earth if we only "drop the bomb." The Negro civil rights revolution alarms us, but it can be solved by "reversion to states rights." Relief rolls are growing; "put the freeloaders to work on a rockpile." Foreign aid is costly; "withdraw it and let the new nations come up the hard way as we did." (Actually we had foreign aid.) Castro is a threat; "send in the marines." These are all big, simple, attempts for a crash solution to problems which crash answers would only make worse.

A LITTLE LEARNING

Similarly, no crash solution is likely to be found for extremism in America. The permanent revolution of American life must keep its nerve and refuse to be panicked by extremist fantasies which appear in times of great tension or social weariness. Our danger is created not by the wholly ignorant but by the half educated; by the men and women with obsessions and cure-alls, with dreams which are nightmares or Utopias, who think their practical common sense is better than any university education, who hold a conspiratorial view of history, who believe they can restore God to our national life by enacting a prayer amendment.

In such a situation, every logical struggle to maintain the freedom and integrity of our libraries, to preserve academic or press freedom, is just as important as many more highly publicized contests on the floor of Congress. The struggle is for the mind and soul of the American people, who have a commitment to liberty and equality which they will not lightly surrender in this hour of destiny. Winning that struggle to keep the humane, spiritual, and liberal tradition in America, to retain freedom of mind as well as of body, is our mission, our high and wonderful destiny, our service to the world as well as to our children.

39 Who Shall Silence All the Airs and Madrigals?

(JUNE 1, 1965)

by JAKE ZEITLIN

My thoughts on the freedom to read are not all pure black and white. The subject has caused me much anguish and soul-searching. George Meredith's lines from one of his sonnets in *Modern Love* are most apt: "O what a dusty answer gets the soul when hot for certainties in this our life."

My situation might come under the heading of what Edwin Boring, an eminent psychologist, calls "Cognitive Dissonance." This is a condition which occurs when anyone makes an earnest effort to make a choice in an area where good evidence appears on both sides of a question. The healthy person reviews the evidence and makes his choice knowing that it is still an open question. In my experience, the most uncomfortable company is a man who knows what is absolutely right and a woman who knows what is absolutely wrong.

I have been bouncing a number of questions on the freedom to read back and forth in my own mind. Although this has been illuminating to me, my conclusions are not too certain except on one point. And that point is censorship. Censorship, as I define it, is the official and legal power to forbid, suppress, and punish publication, in print, or utterance by any other means, of ideas not approved by an officially designated authority.

The whole question of censorship seems to be obscured by an inflated projection of the image of sex. Now sex is a popular subject, but as the lady from Virginia told the lady from Maine, "Breeding is fun but it isn't everything."

A subtle art of misdirection is being practiced on us. Every time a book like *Lady Chatterley's Lover, Fanny Hill,* or *Tropic of Cancer* becomes the object of the censor it gets front-page headlines. We might be led to believe that only sex is subjected to censorship. By this device we might forget that censorship has as its objective the control of ideas in every realm of human activity. In the past and in the present the censors have sought to suppress free expression in theology, politics, astronomy, economy, biology, and even music. Nowhere has this been more vividly set forth than in Milton's *Areopagitica*:

"If we think to regulate printing, thereby to rectify manners, we must regulate all recreations and pastimes, all that is delightful to man. No music must be heard, no song be set or sung, but what is grave and Doric. There must be licensing dancers, that no (wrong) gesture, motion or deportment be taught . . . it will ask more than the work of 20 licensers to examine all the lutes, the violins, and the guitars in every house. They must not be suffered to prattle as they do, but must be licensed, what they may say. And who shall silence all the airs and madrigals, that whisper softness in the chambers?"

Calvin burned Servetus for his theological ideas, the 17th Century Royalists of London were beheaded for publishing their tracts against the Roundhead parliament, and Charles II had his censors who were equally ruthless against those who dared to question the divine right of kings. Copernicus, Foscarini, Bruno, and Galileo felt the heavy hand of the church upon them. Mendelian inheritance was a proscribed belief in Russia 20 years ago. It is still a little dangerous to walk down the street with a copy of Marx's *Das Kapital* under your arm. Darwinism is far from a safe subject for a biology teacher to discuss in Texas, Georgia, Alabama, and Mississippi, or even the great California educational system.

Censorship as applied to sex is only the periphery of this whole subject. And it is for this reason, if for no other, that I feel we must be staunch in defending the freedom to write, sell, read, and communicate.

There has been much debate about the meaning of the First Amendment to the Constitution, but it is clear that what our First Congress meant to do was to protect Americans from the tyranny of laws which could in any way inhibit, suppress, or punish the free expression of ideas, popular or unpopular, loyal to, or critical of, the government in power. In the 18th Century there was no doubt as to the positive value of freedom. They were too closely acquainted with the implications of tyranny.

The Sedition Act of the Adams administration quickly went down to defeat. As late as 1836, Andrew Jackson's attempt to enact into Federal law a bill suppressing the circulation of Abolitionist tracts was defeated by Congress.

In fact, it is only since 1842 that we have had laws in this country which authorized the Federal authorities to censor publications deemed to be obscene. At first they authorized action only against pictorial material. The power of censorship proliferated during the latter 19th Century, deriving its basic concepts from an English "Common Law" pronouncement.

My role as a bookseller is not the least among those who must defend the right to read. The bookseller is usually the first object of legal action in censorship cases. I feel that we must do battle on the ground where the battle is posed, whether we like it or not. My personal tastes are secondary. When I filed as a plaintiff to clarify my right to sell *Tropic of Cancer*, I did not do so because I think it is a great or brilliant book, nor because I have any great regard for Henry Miller. Our City Attorney is alleged to have reported before a public meeting that I said *Tropic of Cancer* is an obscene book. I did not say that; I said it is a dull book.

I am a member of a generation that finds itself embarrassed at the careless use of four-letter words. There are some books which revolt me. Violence, brutality, insensitivity to pain and the dignity of other human beings, are painful to me.

My wife has an opinion of me which might surprise you. One evening some weeks ago, she came home and found me reading *Who's Afraid of Virginia Woolf?* "What do you think of it?" she asked. "This is what I call a dirty book," I said. She paused a moment before she delivered her crushing blow: "You are a prude." Well, I've lived long enough to be called everything.

Anything which tends to demean and deprave the highest and most ecstatic experience that a human being can have, and I mean the erotic experience, is an affront to me. Yet I cannot convince myself that there is anyone so wise, so universally comprehensive in his judgment, that he can be trusted with the power to tell others: "You shall not express yourself thus, you shall not describe your own experiences; or depict the fantasies which your mind has created; or laugh at what others have set up as respectable; or question old beliefs; or contradict the dogmas of the church, of our society, our economic system, and our political orthodoxy."

I have yet to meet an advocate of censorship who does not feel that it is entirely safe for him to read any book, see any picture, or listen to any speaker. He is convinced that it is for the protection of others that censorship is necessary.

Our courts have discussed and ruled on the question of whether or not a book shall have a redeeming justification in terms of art. What is art and what is not art is the oldest and longest-winded of all debates, and the argument has never been settled. Paul Valery's definition is the best I know: "Art is whatever arouses your sense of despair . . . and gives you succor." To my taste, most pop art is garbage, most abstract impressionism incomprehensible, and most of the new sculpture fit only for a waxworks or a sideshow of freaks. In terms of the question of censorship, my own judgment does not matter.

I am reminded of something that happened in my bookshop on West Sixth Street sometime in 1929. I was exhibiting a group of photographs by Edward Weston. Some of them had been placed in my show window. A little old lady came in and said, "I am going to get the police to arrest you for showing obscene pictures." I said, "Madam, would you mind showing me what you think is obscene?" I thought she would point out one of his anatomical photographs. Instead, she pointed to a picture of two eggs and a cross-section of an artichoke. "Madam," I said, "permit me to compliment you on your active imagination."

I have sometimes tried to argue that good taste shall be the criterion and that good taste is censorship enough. Even that is, I am afraid, not valid for anyone except me. I accept and extoll, or reject and deprecate, that which meets the standards of my conditioning and education. For others with different conditioning and education, good taste is another set of values.

The words of Justice Tobriner, speaking for the Supreme Court of California in the *Tropic of Cancer* decision, have the ring and cadence of Thomas Jefferson's own language in them:

"Indeed, a legal proscription cannot in any event constrict artistic creation. Man's drive for self-expression, which over the centuries has built his monuments, does not stay within set bounds; the creations which yesterday were detested and the obscene become the classics of today. The quicksilver of creativity will not be solidified by legal pronouncement; it will surely and fortunately fail. The new forms of expression, even though formally banned, will, as they always have, remain alive in man's consciousness. The court-made excommunication, if it is too wide or if it interferes with true creativity, will be rejected like incantations of forgotten witch-doctors. Courts must therefore move here with utmost caution; they tread in a field where a lack of restraint can only invite defeat and only impair man's most precious potentiality: his capacity for self-expression."

It may be true that within a limited society faced with the problems of maintaining a unified group and surviving by means of a narrowly restrictive set of standards, the mores and taboos concerning language and symbols are necessary. But in our larger and more abundant society there is no need for this primitive way of behavior.

There is no one area in which one should yield his right to a choice of what ideas he shall be allowed or not be allowed to entertain. My views about censorship are not limited to the area of sex or art or politics or economics or religion or science. If we yield that right in any one area we allow the entire fortress to be breached. In the words of Paul and Schwartz, "Experience has shown that censorship is a self-expanding process." They also say—and I quote from their book, *Federal Censorship: Obscenity in the Mail*—"While no one can very well document the degree of harm, if any, which censorship may have done to our culture by inhibiting expression, the assumption herein is that the very process of censorship can, if legally sanctioned, undermine the concept and institutions of freedom. . . . Policing all reading of all citizens is hardly a worthy goal of government, and the law should eschew such a goal in theory as well as practice."

To echo Luther Evans, a great librarian and a great defender of free ideas, "I will not argue the question of whether this book or that book should be censored. I am against censorship; period."

These views are not the views of all my colleagues in the book trade, and I do not claim to speak for them. Some of them will defend one area of ideas—some another. And there are those who, for the sake of their comfort and their continued economic security, will not take a stand upon any ground against censorship. On the whole, however, the publishers and booksellers of this country stand shoulder to shoulder with the librarians.

It takes great courage for a librarian to stand up against the blue noses, the pecksniffs, and the John Birchers in his community. He puts his job, his livelihood, and often his future, on the line. Were it not for the stand that the organized library profession has taken in this field, I am sure that resistance to censorship would be much less successful.

Compared to the librarians we booksellers are pikers. We are the last of the free enterprisers. We may lose a customer here and there because we choose to take a stand, but it is rarely that we suffer from any serious loss of business. Nobody can fire us, and it is only when we become the object of systematic harassment by the authorities that we face any serious consequences. That rarely happens.

I have been asked, "What do you do about stocking books that you don't like? Isn't it censorship when you refuse to carry, for instance, Ayn Rand's books or *A Choice, Not an Echo?*" I will plead guilty to not taking advantage of some very big bestseller trends in the past, such as Ron Hubbard's *Dianetics*, or *Bridey Murphy*, which sold by the hundreds of copies in many bookstores. My answer is: "I am under no obligation to buy these books. However, if one of my customers orders them, I will supply them." Also, I cannot bring myself to destroy a book however offensive I may find it. I can't even burn a copy of *The Protocols of the Elders of Zion*.

Another question is, "What about the books your children read?" I can tell you that the day I came home and found my 18-year-old son reading Ayn Rand's *The Fountainhead* was a very disturbing one for me. I claim credit, however, for not saying a word to him. And when my young daughter picked out Lawrence Durrell's *Black Book* from our shelf of his writings I refrained, with I admit a considerable struggle, from telling her that in my opinion, it was a piece of Durrell's juvenilia not worth the ink he used to write it. As of now, my son has not embraced Ayn Rand's fascism, nor has my daughter flung herself into a life of moral turpitude.

In conclusion I should like to quote from one of the most lovable men I ever knew. He was a good man who had many doubts about what was right. In spite of these doubts he stood staunchly against bigotry and the littleness of men's minds. He gave the Southwest a solid position in the world of letters by his own writings and by the example he set. I am talking about J. Frank Dobie. He said: "Censorship is never to let people know but always to keep them in ignorance: never to bring light but always darkness. A censor is always a tool—as Churchill called Mussolini, a 'utensil.' Not one censor in history is respected by enlightened men of any nation." And, "I have come to value liberated minds as the supreme good of life on earth. The subject is very complex and proliferates into many areas of living. I would not be satisfied with an autobiography that did not bear witness to my passionate belief in freedom of thought."

This is the testimony of a very wise man given out of the ripeness of his many years of creative living. I offer it to you as a philosophy to which I hope you will join me in a hearty "Amen."

CHAPTER

40 Sex and the Stuffy Librarian

(JUNE 1, 1965)

by EDWARD DE GRAZIA

I had to go to a library to prepare my paper, and I found a book which showed me something that made me a little glad. There are statistics to show that the biggest problem suffered these days by librarians is sex: politics is only the second biggest. And the question of literary merit does not even show. The book, of course, was Marjorie Fiske's *Book Selection and Censorship.*

The Stuffy Librarian is an image apparently not indigenous to me. The stereotype, clinging to my mind's eye since childhood, grew big almost as life again not too long ago when I read the original script for the network television show, *The Defenders*, called "A Book for Burning." That television play, otherwise surprisingly informed in its viewpoints, cast the town librarian as a prude.

You may remember: her name was Miss Tucker. You may also remember that Miss Tucker, who was head librarian of Pine River, was cast down in that show, after delivering this advice concerning the challenged book:

"It's an offensive book dealing with offensive situations in an offensive way. It uses vulgar language. It's insensitive . . . disgusting, and indelicate."

The script created a bit of a stir in the library press, but the main point was, perhaps, obscured. The point has to do with the evolving character of the American librarian, and the most pertinent criticism of that *Defenders* program is that it failed utterly to reflect any bit of that evolution.

But this pathetic picture of Miss Tucker, librarians, is your heritage. It's outdated and absurd, but as stereotype history, is it absolutely wrong? Once upon a time, weren't librarians sort of prudes, and dedicated to circulating mainly the oldest and safest kinds of books? And maybe not bright enough to realize that even those books once were, and still might be, dangerous?

In any event, if Miss Tucker remains your stereotype, people can't be blamed for visiting the library only as a kind of last quiet resort. And maybe they can't be blamed either for telling librarians' what books should or shouldn't be put on their shelves.

Marjorie Fiske showed that books touching on sex get removed from, or purposely never put on library shelves, a great deal more often than books touching on anything else—including communism. Whether this is librarian censorship, subversive of the Library Bill of Rights is a matter I want to deal with. But the fact that books on sex are perhaps the most controversial sort of books being published today doesn't mean that conservative librarians can plot a safe path between the shoals of controversy by steering clear of books on sex, as they did yesterday of books on communism.

The *Newsletter on Intellectual Freedom* for November 1964 reveals very clearly how the Soviets, re-discovering that sex literature is a symptom of our American decadent imperialism, declared it to be "bourgeois." At the same time, as we saw during 1963's Presidential campaign, the leading extreme right-wing groups condemned "pornography" distribution and civil rights fights in the same breath! Maybe the only advice for conservatives is: go into the grocery business. As a librarian you can't be sure today that tomorrow you will not be shot at with both barrels—by the John Birch Society and the Communist Party, USA—for circulating Bill Burroughs' *Naked Lunch*.

If the Library Bill of Rights is to be not only defended but implemented, the librarian may have to expect to make enemies. If he or she does his job; if he or she selects controversial books, whether on sex, politics, or religion, and fights off every attempt to remove them, the librarian *must*, as Eric Moon has said, "not only know that he will displease many of the people much of the time . . . but must be prepared for the consequences."

I hope you will forgive my impulse to put the shoe of censorship on the librarian's own foot, but after I had studied some of your own literature and considered some of the opinions expressed by some of your own most eminent librarians, the gravity of the situation weighed on me. Unless librarians overcome the shortcomings which seem to exist with respect to their own personal and professional convictions and aspirations concerning book selection and rejection policies—that is, unless they first entrench the intellectual freedom principle underlying the Library Bill of Rights securely in their own shops—for every battle won in the courtroom by virtue of legal measures developed and provided through conferences and defense funds, 20 other censorship battles will be privately lost in the librarians' own chambers; and the Library Bill of Rights will be deflated.

I got into this discourse worrying about how Communists and John Birchers might treat librarians carrying William Burroughs' *Naked Lunch*. My suggestion was not all that facetious. Not very long ago, I couldn't find a public library in the Boston area which had a copy of that book around—although it had been very widely and authoritatively reviewed. In fact, as librarian Louis Schreiber was bold enough to point out, in a letter to the Suffolk County District Attorney at about the same time:

"That *Naked Lunch* must be treated as a literary work, and not 'hard-core' pornography, is amply attested by the reviews it received. The *Book Review Digest* for August 1963 cites the following reviews: 1) *Commentary;* 2) *Encounter;* 3) LIBRARY JOURNAL; 4) *New Republic;* 5) *New Statesman;* 6) New York *Herald Tribune's Book Week;* 7) *New York Times Book Review;* 8) *New Yorker;* 9) *Time;* and 10) *Virginia Quarterly Review.*

"Would it not be possible to advance the thesis that there is a *responsibility* on the part of a book dealer to make available to the public all books reviewed in such eminent quarters?"

This book might well be one of the most controversial and disgusting works of our decade. Are librarians, for *those* reasons, "censoring" it—despite its apparent literary and social importance? To paraphrase Mr. Schreiber: is there not a responsibility on the part of a librarian to make available to the public any book reviewed in such eminent quarters?

If they mean to put flesh on their own Bill of Rights, this is the kind of question that librarians must seek honestly to answer. And as a matter of Constitutional law today, it is not at all clear that a librarian does not technically censor and cannot successfully be sued, when he deliberately excludes such a book because of promised or conjectured repercussions. The US Supreme Court's view of the "virulent" character of such self-censorship in the hands of booksellers suggests that the court will take a dim view of librarian censorship if it is presented with a proper case.

The question of what legal measures can be fashioned to backstop the Library Bill of Rights simply loses significance if libraries decline, from timidity or disinterest, from personal lack of faith in the principle of intellectual freedom, to make available avant-garde, controversial works. On the other hand, of course, the formulation of measures to defend all librarians may stiffen the will of many to resist self-censorship and kindle a fresh desire to live your Library Bill of Rights.

Actual experiences with defending the Library Bill of Rights—like that reported by Long Island Librarian Orrin Dow to the Women's National Book Association last October, and those described by librarians Cay Mortenson, Virginia Ross, Ursula Meyer, and Hilda Collins at the last conference in November of the California Library Association—should be heartening to librarians who sense and seek a more dynamic role for the library of tomorrow, having at its core the principle of intellectual freedom.

In my belief, somewhere central to that role lies a professional passion to tutor, not cater to taste; and wake up, not lull the intellect. And to even begin to make of the Library Bill of Rights a living, breathing, growing thing, and of the library—as called for by Article 6—truly "an institution of education for democratic living," librarians must not be afraid of circulating "dangerous" books.

41 *It Is Later Than You Think: An Action Program Against Censorship*

(OCTOBER 1, 1963)

by LEONARD B. ARCHER

"Here's a prediction: within the next three years a California librarian will be forced to resign, or will lose his position, due to a censorship controversy. *It is later than you think.*" Thus warned William R. Eshelman in the January 1963 issue of the *California Librarian.*

California seems to have more than the usual share of people who appear to be unconcerned about basic American rights and freedoms. Even the religious leaders in some cities are demanding that Nikos Kazantzakis' novel, *The Last Temptation of Christ,* be withdrawn from public library shelves because of the book's unorthodox portrayal of Christ.

Eshelman indirectly calls attention to the apathy of librarians everywhere in defending the freedom to read and in failing to take the offensive against censorship bigots. It is not enough, he says, to pass resolutions. It is not enough to make formal statements to legislative committees. It is not enough to appear on behalf of librarians under fire—although all these actions are necessary. Now, says Eshelman, "it is time the Association gave serious thought to the establishment of either an accreditation program for public libraries (the positive approach), or of a committee to investigate and recommend censure (negative, perhaps, but effective)."

Eshelman was referring to the California Library Association but the basic message applies to all state associations and the American Library Association. Attacks on libraries, librarians, schools, and teachers have become so critical as to demand an all-out offensive by concerned librarians and their associations everywhere. Instead of the present weak and apathetic Intellectual Freedom

Committees already in existence in many of the states, each state association should immediately establish an action committee comprising the leading librarians in the state who are not afraid to take a stand, who will be respected, and who will carry weight when they speak.

Our state Intellectual Freedom Committees should be more than academic discussion groups, and there is no reason in the world why they cannot be action committees. For a number of weeks I have been recommending that the Wisconsin Library Association's Intellectual Freedom Committee take a more positive and dynamic stand in defending the freedom to read all over the state. Such positive action is imperative in every state.

It is inexcusable that libraries, librarians, schools, and teachers in the United States get very little help from their Intellectual Freedom Committees to combat these enemies of freedom. Members of the Intellectual Freedom Committee in your state can talk themselves blue-in-the-face, but if an *active* stand is not taken to put the weight of the state association behind every library, librarian, teacher, or school library that is under attack, that committee wastes its time and loses its reason for being: to defend the freedom to read, the freedom of ideas.

Any librarian who has had to fight censorship knows what it is to sweat in a state of nervous tension for days, even weeks, at a time. These people know what it is to get vicious and nasty letters and to be attacked in public. They know what it is to rack their brains for the proper way to defend the basic American right of the freedom to read, the freedom to find out for oneself without being limited by what some narrow-minded individual or group thinks it is safe for others to know. While Rome burns too many of our Intellectual Freedom Committees have *discussions* on the freedom to read!

Some of us, through years of experience in combating misguided people and groups who would establish a coercive concept of American democracy have mastered the art of defending the first amendment to the American Constitution, of defending the freedom to read. However, I am very much concerned about those libraries and those librarians in America who have *not* learned the technique of defending themselves and who are terrified when a pressure group opens up its big guns on the library or school. Every time one of these small town or village libraries or schools gives in to the enemies of freedom it is more difficult for all of us in the library profession. Those of us who have worked out successful methods for combating this evil, and those of us who are charged with the responsibility of the safeguarding of intellectual freedom in our states by our own associations, have an obligation to help these little libraries with more than academic discussions.

Unfortunately, a few of our larger libraries are guilty, also, of giving in to pressure groups from time to time. They, too, need the help of a dynamic and active state-wide committee that is charged with the responsibility of defending the freedom to read. Such a committee should help *any* library, school, librarian or teacher with suggested strategy, suggested news releases, suggested policy statements and a suggested program to be followed in safeguarding the freedom of ideas. My patience is exhausted with namby-pamby librarians and teachers who are afraid of their own shadows, afraid to take a stand on anything. This is no time for pussyfooting. This is the time for librarians to get up on their hind legs, to show that they have something more than shoe-strings for backbones.

Narrow-minded bigots who are attacking libraries and schools have no regard for basic American freedoms and the Bill of Rights. They are playing dirty and they are not going to listen to the gentle reasoning of an ivory-tower Intellectual Freedom Committee. The time is late. Drop some of the things that you are doing and begin an action offensive against these censors NOW.

I suggest that each state be divided into districts, the number depending upon the size of the state, and that the Intellectual Freedom Committee in each state be comprised of a member from each district of the state. The member selected from each district should be a person who can speak and act forcefully when the situation calls for it and who can be tactful when necessary, a person who is respected in his district even when he disagrees with individuals or groups. It will be the responsibility of each district representative to ferret out in the district any censorship activity that is in the planning stage or has already broken out into the open. It will be his obligation regularly to write reports to the chairman of the committee on the situation within his district. He should give aid to the library or school under attack by writing letters to the editor of the local press and to members of the library board or school board in the name of the Intellectual Freedom Committee or the association, and in any way open to him, give support to the librarian under attack. Each of the district representatives will work closely with the local teachers and the local chapter of the National Council of Teachers of English.

It will be the responsibility of the chairman of the Committee to issue a statement, if necessary, in the name of the state library association, and to work closely with the state education association and state chapter of the National Council of Teachers of English, to throw the weight of the state library and teaching associations into the fray. It will be also the responsibility of the chairman of the Committee to see to it that each district representative performs his duties within his district, and to coordinate the clobbering that is necessary.

All members of the Committee will work to get influential citizens and groups to take a stand and to be ready at all times with letters, statements to the press and even statements in meetings where necessary, whenever a library or school comes under attack. By such techniques we can isolate the enemies of freedom. The usual fence-sitters will, early in the fight, get on what they think will be the winning side—and we intend right from the beginning that intellectual freedom is going to be the winning side.

You may get complaints that such activities are time consuming, that librarians have too many other committee responsibilities in their association. I want to say right now that it is time librarians took on fewer responsibilities and did well those that they do assume, instead of getting on every committee under the sun and doing a superficial little something on everything. Those librarians who are so busy that they can't devote enough time to do a good job should be honest enough to say no, not because they're not interested, but because they have enough responsibility with their other duties at the present time. The censorship situation is critical and demands dedication on the part of a few individuals who can work out an action program and a clobbering technique. We need people on our state Intellectual Freedom Committees who believe so strongly in the right of every individual to find out for himself, to read what others think even when he disagrees with them, and to be able to express himself freely, that they are willing to give up some other things in order to restore intellectual stature to our state library association.

Recently I had a conference with the Executive Secretary of our own state chapter of the National Council of Teachers of English. He has assured me that their association would be solidly behind us in our efforts to work out liaison with them and with the Wisconsin Education Association to present a united front against all censorship groups who attack libraries and schools. *Each* state library association should form an alliance now with the state education association and the state chapter of the National Council of Teachers of English in order that the three groups can work together and stand together on all matters of intellectual freedom throughout the state. Every person who is concerned about this critical problem should obtain and read thoroughly an excellent statement prepared by the National Council of Teachers of English, *The Students' Right to Read.*

I should also like to see each state library association adopt a statement of policy similar to that of the California Library Association and the School Library Association of California. The essential factor here is that these associations have given executive power to their Intellectual Freedom and Book Selection Policies Committees to go ahead and do what is necessary in all matters of intellectual freedom.

Anything less than an action committee in the present day is a waste of time. Even now, with supposedly active Intellectual Freedom Committees in our states, some of the smaller libraries are not getting the help they undoubtedly expect from these committees.

Eshelman is right in recommending that the California Library Association give serious thought to the establishment of an accreditation program for public libraries and of a committee to investigate and recommend censure. Although he only recommends one policy or the other, I think state associations should adopt both techniques. In any accreditation policy a library which gives in to a pressure group should be automatically removed from the accredited list and no longer recommended as a place to which any qualified professional librarian would want to go. The extension agency in each state could cooperate with such a policy by refusing to allocate federal funds or state funds to any unaccredited library.

Resolve right now to write, shout, travel, and apply pressure all over your state to make your Intellectual Freedom Committee a do-something committee. It *is* later than you think.

CHAPTER

42 Mr. and Mrs. Grundy
in the Library and in Court

(DECEMBER 15, 1964)

by HENRY MILLER MADDEN

We attended the California Library Association's annual conference of December, 1964, in Los Angeles, and had intended presenting a summary report, if not of the whole conference, of the pre-conference meeting on Intellectual Freedom. Our plans were suddenly changed toward the end of the week, following a virtuoso performance by Henry Miller Madden, librarian of Fresno State College and editor of The California Librarian. *CLA President Everett Moore described Mr. Madden's report to the full conference on the pre-conference meeting as a "superb example of creative reporting." We agree, and we feel that when a job has been done superbly there is little point in trying to do it again. We present here, therefore, some of what Mr. Madden said.—Ed.*

Although the title of this report was chosen long before the preconference was held, it fits the circumstances fairly well. You will recall that Mrs. Grundy is perhaps the most famous nonexistent person in literature. In Thomas Morton's comedy, *Speed the Plough*, written in 1798, Mrs. Ashfield, the wife of one of two rival farmers, constantly alludes to the other farmer's wife in the phrase, "But what will Mrs. Grundy say?" Although Mrs. Grundy never appears on the scene, her name has become proverbial for conventional propriety and morality.

In essence, this conference on Intellectual Freedom reported what Mrs. Grundy is both saying and doing today. Alas, Mrs. Grundy is no longer invisible, nor is she confined to her own sex. Visible Mrs. Grundys and visible Mr. Grundys appear on the scene, in library and in court, and behind them stand an array of invisible counterparts—the writers of anonymous postal cards, the speakers of telephoned invective, the threateners and bullies. And, although this was certainly not brought out by any of the participants in the conference, it was evident by the uncomfortable stirring of the audience that in each of us librarians there is still a jumpy segment in our conscious or subconscious mind which whispers to us—What will Mrs. Grundy say?—when we are confronted with a decision of our own in the cause of intellectual freedom. Not until the day when Mrs. Grundy no longer lurks just off the stage of our own minds can we really say that we are free ourselves and free to defend the freedom of others. Happily, this conference was a demonstration, however, that the librarian's own personal Mrs. Grundy is really becoming decrepit— even though the Mrs. Grundys who creep or storm into the library seem to be more numerous in this age which encourages the illegitimate red, white, and blue—red-baiting, white racism, and blue books.

In essence, then, the preconference dealt directly with two aspects of Grundyism—first, a philosophical and legal survey of the present status of freedom of the press, and, second, a series of case studies in attempted censorship, reported by librarians and trustees who had been in the fight.

The philosophical and legal problems were presented by Robert Kirsch, literary editor of the Los Angeles *Times;* by Paul Ferguson, Professor of English at Los Angeles City College; and Stanley Fleishman, attorney-at-law, and one of the nation's most distinguished specialists in the law of obscenity. I shall deal first with the contributions of these three experts, and reserve for later the case histories which illustrate so graphically the general contentions of the speakers.

Mr. Kirsch provocatively entitled his talk "Custodian, Eunuch, or Lover?" Any bewilderment or puzzling, or any tendency to think that we were to be taken behind the scenes in the Grand Seraglio of the Ottoman Sultans, was quickly removed by Mr. Kirsch's lucid development of the librarian's relation to political and sexual controversy. Quoting Alfred North Whitehead, Mr. Kirsch reminded us that we think in generalities, but we live in detail. We can have a beautifully generalized picture of the library—well supported, a real coffee maker for the coffee hour, and computers to do the trivial work. But the librarian deals with books in detail, and books can generate both light and heat, and from this, in turn, comes the struggle to maintain intellectual freedom. The library—all libraries: public, academic, school—must know how to deal with controversies stemming from any infringement of this freedom.

But what about custodians, eunuchs, and lovers? In the history of the public library, the librarian was first a custodian—a Levite function—he checked out and he checked in, and he was certainly removed not only from the mainstream of American life, but from any stream of it. The absence of controversy, the absence of any sort of provocation, prevented this custodian from demonstrating whether he was a eunuch or a lover. But historical development brought about by a change in the level of literacy, if not in the level of education, attracted people to the hitherto quiet library. People found that books had ideas, that ideas were serpents. The notion prevalent several decades ago was that the custodians of these dangerous objects should be eunuchized to make sure that the custodian attempted no more dangerous role. But now, said Mr. Kirsch, the age of the lover is at hand. We must be lovers because we cannot deny our own convictions and opinions, we cannot simplify the landscape of men and ideas, we must not permit ourselves to become a nation intimidated by books. Among the populace there is widespread either a witless adulation of books or a fear of them. Among the books which emerged in the presidential campaign were many which had an appearance of scholarly apparatus which would fool anyone who had never tripped over a footnote— the type of book which gulled the innocent. At the other extreme is the point of view that the reader is the victim of a conspiracy of intellectuals to twist the minds of the unsuspecting—that the book can change a Jekyll into a Hyde.

Quoting T. P. Smith, Mr. Kirsch reminded that "for souls in growth, great quarrels are great emancipations." In the war to protect free intellectual enquiry, there is no victory—the war keeps on. A cavalier or a lover accepts the fact that the prize is never won. The lover does not woo a neon-lighted library or the computer—he is the spokesman for the life of free intellect.

In comment on Mr. Kirsch's talk, Eric Moon, editor of LIBRARY JOURNAL, pointed out that the librarian should not underestimate the forces which seek to undermine free enquiry. We are not up against stupid "kooks," and we cannot be satisfied with a defensive position. We must draw the battle line for our commitment. We must give a case to doubt, to lack of certainty. Too many librarians are confused about what we are defending. The censor has the advantage of drawing a line around a particular book, while we must fight back from a generalized point of view. He congratulated the California Library Association warmly for its stand on Proposition 14, saying that "it makes a notable contribution toward breaking down our narrow image of ourselves and of our spheres of concern. If we do not understand that discrimination, in any form, against books or people or the free flow of ideas and information, is our business, then we do not understand the basic strength and purpose of libraries."

Kathleen Molz, editor of the *Wilson Library Bulletin,* argued that the process of selection leaves much to be desired and continues to be a mystery to the public. For a reader to be told that "it's against our policy" is hardly a satisfactory explanation, especially as policies seem usually to be unearthed after an attack, not made known before. Too few libraries have a policy that a controversial book should be bought precisely because it is controversial. She was referring not to such a book as *The Carpetbaggers,* but to the current campaign books.

The discussion of Mr. Kirsch's talk was brought to a fitting close by the remark of a librarian in the audience that no amount of exhortation can make a lover out of a eunuch.

There seemed to be no avoidance of provocative titles. Professor Paul Ferguson, who was a party to Jake Zeitlin's suit over *Tropic of Cancer,* entitled his talk "Pornography or Censorship—Which Is Worse?" Avoiding the more moderate term "obscenity," Mr. Ferguson spoke on "pornography," a word derived from the Greek "writing of harlots." Obviously adopting a broad libertarian point of view, he asked if *Hot Dames on a Cold Slab* should be outlawed while *What I Found Out in My Psychoanalysis* is protected. Perhaps the analysis would yield *Hot Dames on a Cold Slab!*

The reasons for censoring usually given are: 1) that the book may change the moral standards of the community; 2) it may offend a sensitive reader—but such sensitive souls are usually not readers; 3) it may stimulate sex thoughts; 4) it may stimulate sex action; and 5) it may injure the young or immature.

But these reasons fall before the present doctrine of clear and present danger, that there must be evidence that such a book can be demonstrated to be measurably harmful. Such a demonstration is almost impossible to make, especially because of the difficulty in defining the term obscenity. As Judge Learned Hand said, "Coming to grips with obscenity is like coming to grips with a greased pig."

New Mexico has never had an obscenity statute, and surely conduct there is not worse than in California. As for the problem of youth, if everything is brought out into the open, into the sunlight, the innocence of ignorance and its attendant dangers will be avoided. Mr. Ferguson mentioned that *Tropic of Cancer* was lying in his house; his teenage daughter picked it up, read a few pages, and put it down. She was bored with it.

Mr. Ferguson pointed out that if all so-called obscene books were to disappear tomorrow, we would still have all the problems of juvenile delinquency and social disorganization. How could we force out all other stimulants to sexual activity? He mentioned a survey of college girls to determine the things which stimulated them sexually. The thing chiefly mentioned was "men," but other answers ranged through "listening to music" to "reading," including such books as the Bible and Motley's *Rise of the Dutch Republic.*

In summation, Mr. Ferguson stated that pornography is to be accepted by society—not just Aristophanes and Rabelais because of their literary value, but books with little or almost no literary value. We cannot say that such books shall be banned because they were written for people who are not sophisticated and have little literary taste.

The speech by Mr. Fleishman came to grips with the basic legal questions in the field of censorship of books dealing with sex. Basing his talk on scores of cases argued before all courts from those of local instance to the Supreme Court of the United States, Mr. Fleishman used as his title, "Obscene Literature and Constitutional Law," the exact title of a book written in 1910 by Theodore Schroeder, an all but forgotten pioneer in the law of obscenity. The basic contentions of Schroeder's book were three in number: 1) the law of obscenity is entirely subjective, and not capable of understanding by men of common intelligence; 2) the government cannot, consistent with the free speech provisions of the Constitution, interfere with sex speech; and 3) there is a link between witchcraft and obscenity, and both have deep religious roots.

Mr. Fleishman outlined the current definition of obscenity, which governs in all courts: 1) The matter must go substantially beyond customary limits of candor in dealing with sex; 2) it must have a predominant appeal to prurient interests; and 3) it must be utterly without redeeming social importance. Each word in the definition must be fully weighed; for example, "utterly" means "utterly"—*utterly* without redeeming social importance. After establishing this definition, Mr. Fleishman moved into a consideration of the relation between religion and obscenity. His contention was that obscenity has become a crime because of religious insistence that it is a sin. He maintained that the United States government, which, because of the First Amendment, may not establish a religion or interfere with religion, could not maintain a morality rooted in religion. Obscenity is not a crime, but a sin in the eyes of religion. Yet the obscenity laws are aimed at saving the reader from his own moral weakness, however private and discreet, rather than from acts which may transgress the law. In short, is legislation, the sole or chief purpose of which is the preservation of religious morality, consistent with the separation of Church and State?

Mr. Fleishman pointed out the basic contradiction in much of the litigation. To some courts the material is so repulsive and revolting—so "indecent" and "nasty" and "nauseating" that it is repellent, while to other courts its offense is that it has an aphrodisiac effect, causing genital commotion or other signs of attraction rather than repulsion. If this is the case, that the same material may be looked upon by some as loathsome and by others as enticing, it is obvious that the word "obscene" evokes passion rather than invites study. In the *Tropic of Cancer* case in Los Angeles, in which Mr. Fleishman represented Mr. Zeitlin, the so-called obscenity provoked the following statement from the eminent Shakespearian scholar of the University of Southern California, Dr. Frank Baxter: "If this book depicts the private life of the average citizen of Los Angeles, I welcome with great joy the hydrogen bomb. I can't believe that it depicted the life of the expatriates in France when this book was written. I can't think that it depicted the artistic life of France.

"Though if it did, it would explain what happened to France at the beginning of World War II, although I think France would have exploded even before that had this been—No, no, this is an odd little corner, unless I am a very simple fellow."

Now *Tropic of Cancer* has been adjudged by the Supreme Court not to be obscene, and such books as *Fanny Hill, Naked Lunch, Hundred Dollar Misunderstanding,* and *Candy* freely circulate. If this is the case, how can prosecutions continue to be brought against so-called obscene books? Many of these books fall into a category outside the normal field of purchase for libraries—the flimsy paperback designed for newsstand sale rather than for review in LIBRARY JOURNAL and for Library of Congress cataloging. They are the so-called "friendless book." Should they be a matter of concern to librarians?

Mr. Fleishman answered his question with a strong affirmation that freedom is indivisible, and that the librarian should come to the support of any bookseller threatened with police harassment or actually brought into court. To Mr. Fleishman, after the Supreme Court decision of June 1964, no book can be adjudged obscene, because no book now on sale exceeds the candor of *Tropic of Cancer*. In short, by sanction of the courts, obscenity is now so defined and interpreted that the First Amendment cannot be subverted by any authoritarian religious interpretation of obscenity. Obscenity may be a sin, but it is not a crime.

The talks by Messrs. Kirsch, Ferguson, and Fleishman completed the philosophical and legal consideration of press freedom. The actual case histories of censorship were presented by Mrs. Cay Mortenson, trustee of the Arcadia Public Library; Virginia Ross, chairman of CLA's Intellectual Freedom Committee; Ursula Meyer, county librarian of Butte County; and Mrs. Hilda Collins, county librarian of Tulare County. Each had been on the firing line, and each had been too busy to do much trumpet blasting.

Mrs. Mortenson had to report a sorry history which shamed the idyllic name of Arcadia. For many months Kazantzakis's novel *The Last Temptation of Christ* had been resting quietly on the shelves of the Arcadia Public Library, occasionally circulating, until two years ago when a middle-aged spinster, a member of the John Birch Society, marched into the library with a list of 41 quotations from the book and demanded that it be withdrawn from the library. From that day, for two years the leading news story of Arcadia had been the controversy over this book. Referred to by the complaining spinster as "that salacious Jesus thing," the book engendered a controversy which affected elections and clogged the normal activities of government. Petitions were circulated, children passed out mimeographed copies of the 41 quotations, the clergy was split, a group called the Americanism Committee of the Watchdogs of Freedom, Inc. threatened the library board, and librarians and trustees became the object of a bitter hate campaign. The members of the City Council, to use their own words, decided to "rise above our principles" and asked that the book be withdrawn from the open shelves. Without wavering, the board and the librarians stood by their commitment to intellectual freedom. Recent elections to the City Council, in which the chief interest was the library controversy, have fortunately put an end to the fight, and the community should rejoice in the dedication to principle which enabled these believers in freedom to withstand invective and threat. Mrs. Mortenson's report, delivered with restrained eloquence but moving feeling, deeply affected the audience.

Virginia Ross reported her appearances before the State Legislature, as chairman of the CLA Intellectual Freedom Committee, in opposition to bills which would have strengthened the state's anti-obscenity laws. Often the only spokesman in opposition to numerous representatives of groups affiliated with Citizens for Decent Literature and other organizations, she was physically threatened and told that "We'll get you." Perhaps less immediately dangerous but not less unsettling, women proponents of censorship refused pointedly and loudly to ride in the same elevator in the State Capitol with Miss Ross.

Ursula Meyer reported her experience in the field of political extremism, rather than in writings concerned with sex. Perhaps the preoccupation with extreme right wing politics of so many persons in Butte County deprives them of a more normal interest in matters of sex. At any rate, it was not *Tropic of Cancer* or *Fanny Hill*, but an obscure right-wing periodical called *Tocsin* which gave rise to Miss Meyer's story. This magazine, published by students at Berkeley, was offered as a gift to the Butte County Free Library. After deliberation, the offer was politely refused on the ground that the library was in an overcrowded old building and that the magazine's point of view was adequately represented by other publications. At about the same time a citizen sent the County Board of Supervisors a letter stating that 32 titles representing a conservative view of American history and social conditions were not in the library. By fortunate chance Miss Meyer was given a copy of the letter, and was able to ascertain that 16 of the titles *were* in the library, some in numerous copies. In advance of the Board meeting, she was able to establish the inaccuracy of the letter and to organize an opposition to it. Although the chambers of the Board were thronged with tennis-shoed ladies from Paradise and other centers of enlightenment in Butte County, Miss Meyer and a few levelheaded supporters were able to convince the Board that all points of view were adequately represented in the library. The trumpet, rather than the tocsin, was sounded in Butte County that night.

The last of the case histories was presented by Hilda Collins, librarian of the Tulare County Free Library. This was the famous, or infamous, case of the *Dictionary of American Slang,* in which the John Birch Society flexed its muscles, Dr. Max Rafferty cheered from the side lines, and other parts of the nation were given the shameful opportunity to laugh at the idiocy of our dear state. As a participant in this incident, I was proud to hear Mrs. Collins' presentation of it. In brief, after Assemblyman Barnes of San Diego had launched his campaign of free advertising for the *Dictionary of American Slang* in Sacramento, the Birchers in Tulare County demanded that the County Board of Education remove it from the high school libraries. To the astonishment of no one in particular, it was found that no high school in Tulare County had a copy of the dictionary. Thus deprived of a target, the Birchers demanded that it be removed from the County Library. The Board of Supervisors scheduled a hearing, and Mrs. Collins presented a statement to be read by the County Clerk, defending the dictionary as a standard work of reference. An instructor in the local junior college spoke eloquently and even belligerently in its defense, directly attacking the local organizer of the John Birch Society who had marshalled his forces in the chamber. The opposition put on a series of evangelistic tirades which would strain the credulity of anyone not present. At the conclusion of the hearing, each Supervisor eloquently stated his opposition to censorship of the type proposed, and reaffirmed the legal right of the county librarian to be the selector of books for the library.

Despite this legal determination, on the following day Mrs. Collins received a telephone call from a physician in Porterville who requested an interview. Mrs. Collins asked him the purpose of the visit, and he told her that he wanted to talk about the *Dictionary.* "I'll bring another doctor with me," he stated. Despite these odds in favor of the medical profession, Mrs. Collins saw the doctor and, in answer to his demand that the *Dictionary* be removed, replied that the matter had been settled and that the *Dictionary* was an accepted reference work. He demanded, "How do you know that it's a reference book? Have you read this dictionary?" After scarcely veiled threats of harm, Mrs. Collins was able to get rid of her visitors.

Although Mrs. Collins did not report it in her talk, I am happy to add that this physician, a self-proclaimed member of the John Birch Society, was later defeated in his race for the Congressional seat in the district comprised of Tulare, Kern, and Kings Counties.

In addition to the formal talks, the program provided seven discussion groups which addressed themselves to such topics as "Political aspects of censorship," "The library and literary trash," "Is intellectual freedom indivisible," and "What to do when the censor comes." Some sample points of view were that a work of literary value has good characterization and style, and depth and understanding, whereas a work of literary trash is a nothing book. In the Contra Costa County Library staff evaluation of *Fanny Hill*, the women staff members said that it was and still is pornography, while the men members considered it an amusing book. A moral issue was raised: if a library does not buy *Candy*, should it offer to borrow it on interlibrary loan? One discussion session dealt with the self-censorship exercised by librarians who buy a book like *Candy*, but keep the cards out of the public catalog until any controversy dies down. In one state, many more libraries have purchased *Memoirs of a Courtesan*, a relatively little-known Japanese work of erotica, than have purchased *Fanny Hill*, which is better known but still controversial. A sample of how to deal with parental objections to a book brought home from the library is to say, "Return the book."

All in all, the preconference was a highly satisfactory meeting—not only a stimulus to thought but a provoker of merriment and laughter. And behind it all was the sound of the trumpet—now muted, now triumphant.

CHAPTER

43 *More Than Lip Service*

(MARCH 1, 1965)

by ERIC MOON

"Some people among our membership believe we are riding this horse too hard." The speaker was Edwin Castagna, reporting to the ALA Council during the Midwinter meeting of the American Library Association in Washington, D.C. in 1965. The horse to which the ALA president referred was intellectual freedom, and Castagna added his personal belief that those who saw the nag as over-ridden were "a very small minority" of the ALA membership.

In the days of the Pony Express, one rider used to wear out many horses in his postal dash across the land. In the gruelling, nonstop, two-day race before the ALA Midwinter meeting, it was the 65 riders who finished exhausted. That old intellectual freedom horse took them all on, welcomed the spur and whip, and finished strong; finished indeed, looking for yet more riders who would take him the full distance of his urgent journey.

The occasion which provoked all this equine metaphor was a special conference sponsored by ALA's Intellectual Freedom Committee. The 65 specially invited participants came from a variety of concerned areas—from church and law, press and publishing, education and libraries. Many organizations were represented; among them the ACLU, the National Education Association, the National Council of Teachers of English, the American Book Publishers Council and—an example of the concern of the citizenry of one state—the New Jersey Right to Read Committee.

The purpose of the conference was "to discuss infringement of intellectual freedom and censorship problems in libraries and to discuss ways and means of implementing the Library Bill of Rights." Specifically, the more immediate purpose, according to the charge from the Intellectual Freedom Committee, was "to work out steps librarians may take when confronted with censorship problems (or perhaps better stated, the immediate purpose was the establishment of a defense mechanism for libraries under attack)."

Prompted by seven principal speakers, each of whom illuminated a different area of the battlefield, four group workshops met in the intervals of these beams of inspiration and information. The groups tried and, we think, succeeded in setting down concrete proposals and programs to move the defence lines forward and, no less important, to strengthen and support the defenders. For once, a theme was something more than an irrelevant, eye-catching piece of bunting hanging over the proceedings: this two-day combination of inspiration and the practical did pay "More Than Lip Service."

The many who had a hand in setting up this special conference deserve commendation, but no one more so than Martha Boaz, chairman of the Intellectual Freedom Committee, who was, in a very real and accurate sense, the driving force. If she can drive the ALA Publishing Department with the same charm, humor, and absolute determination that she used in keeping this conference to the point and to the clock, she may even be able to deliver on her promise to get the papers and proceedings of the conference published by June. Assuming that she can pull off this miracle, we shall quote only briefly here from the main papers, attempting to do no more than pinpoint a few highlights and give a whiff or two of the pungency of the occasion.

NATIONAL COMMUNITY

Dan Lacy, managing director of the American Book Publishers Council, led off the parade of speakers. The only one without a formal paper, he conducted a scholarly ramble through the irrational fields of legal opinions and social attitudes on obscenity. After some familiar history, we reached finally what several speakers were to point out as today's significant landmark—the Supreme Court decision last year in the Jacobellis case, involving the movie "The Lovers." Here, for the first time, "community" standards were defined as "national" rather than local, and emphasis was given to the fact that a work cannot be proscribed unless it is *utterly* without social importance.

The Supreme Court opinion, Lacy pointed out, was signed only by Justices Brennan and Goldberg, but if it holds up as the Court's opinion, it would automatically protect the librarian, since the very act of adding a book to the library's collection might be considered to give that book some social importance. But the comparative freedom from danger of criminal prosecution does not mean that the librarian will be free from pressures. In fact, Lacy said, the growing frustration in some areas over the limitations being placed on the criminal law pertaining to obscenity may very well lead to an increase in the pressure efforts by local groups.

"Can Reading Affect Delinquency?" was the question the second speaker, William C. Kvaraceus, set out to answer. Professor Kvaraceus, director of youth studies at the Lincoln Filene Center for Citizenship and Public Affairs at

Tufts University, declared that "the primitive habit of blaming books . . . for delinquency and crime represents a simple-minded approach to a many-sided and complex phenomenon."

Studies have shown, said Kvaraceus, that "Delinquents more frequently are nonreaders; their basic abilities in reading fall far below their nondelinquent counterparts; and they generally come from homes devoid of reading materials . . . Books are not their best friends; they have become their worst enemies. A case may be drawn showing how nonreading sets a pupil out on the long road to delinquency. Removing books from the reading shelf to save delinquents is a vain and futile gesture, although it may satisfy the missionary zeal of the censor."

Youth was still the focus of attention in the third speech, delivered by Lee A. Burress, Jr., chairman of the English Department at Wisconsin State University, whose subject was "Censorship in the Public Schools." Professor Burress expressed the belief that "the improvement in instruction . . . has made censorship perhaps more of a problem in recent years than it may have been in the past," and he thought that "probably a good school system in our present society might expect to have more trouble than a poor one."

Among the things which contribute to the rise in censorship, Burress cited, for example, ". . . the great increase in the use of genuine books, instead of the artificial, pre-digested, intellectual sawdust which passes for textbooks in so many subjects," and "the militancy of the teachers . . . in greater use of contemporary and controversial books. . . ."

Burress outlined at some length the findings of a recent study by the Wisconsin Council of Teachers of English, which showed that a substantial proportion of the teachers in Wisconsin "feel the continuing presence of censorship pressures." He suggested more studies and more interdisciplinary cooperation, and revealed that a joint committee of the American Association of School Libraries and the National Council of Teachers of English "is in fact currently considering a nationwide study of censorship in the public schools."

"Several educational groups have already considered the possibility of sanctions against school systems that fail to maintain satisfactory working conditions," Burress said. "The definition of satisfactory working conditions ought to be broadened to include intellectual freedom, with especial reference to book selection and book use. If such sanctions are imposed by interdisciplinary groups, they would be more effective than if by one group."

Charles Morgan, Jr. is the director of the Regional Office of the American Civil Liberties Union in Atlanta, Georgia. His assigned subject was "The Freedom to Read and Racial Problems." Dramatic in its delivery, dedicated in its point of view, his paper was only to be surpassed once in the whole program. The book burners, said Morgan, "are not always the little old ladies of the DAR or the young and illiterate of the John Birch Society. . . . Often the book burner is simply an offended human being. Often he should be offended—he may remember loved ones and Auschwitz and Buchenwald."

Or, Morgan continued, "the book burner may be a Negro father in the North, residing in a small town where neither he nor his child noticed there was a difference, who worries over the tensions created by The Movement, the new difficulties and challenges he and his child must face, and the now noticed dialect and references to Negroes in *The Adventures of Huckleberry Finn*. He may see white when he reads an echo of the word 'Sambo' as it was used in Mississippi in the days of slavery. Indeed, the censor may simply be the 'liberal minded' person broadly disposed to tolerance who believes there are valid exceptions to the right of free expression.

"There are other censors who are not searching for a new life but are grasping at remnants of a yesterday which never was. They may be madmen pure and simple. Or, they may be the white southerner frantically clinging to the last straws of his youth."

"The librarian," said Morgan, "is not an innocent bystander aloof from warring men. He should not expect to be. For the library is the major battle-field, its books most important weapons. The First Amendment to the Constitution of the United States forbids governmental censorship. But the road from the Supreme Court of the United States to the public library in a small town in south Alabama is long and tortuous and rarely traveled."

Even after Morgan's stirring paper, the best was yet to come. Everyone we talked to agreed that the next speaker, Dr. Theodore Gill, president of San Francisco Theological Seminary, gave one of the finest papers (and performances) they had seen at *any* conference. The man is an actor, a writer—and a very unusual churchman! His subject, ostensibly, was "Freedom to Read and Religious Problems."

He began by asking the audience "religiously to be fair, to be honest about many if not most of the free-hand censors who advance on your stacks ready to seal them with godly planks pounded with Christian nails. They may be religionists, their labels may be churchly, but the real source of their protest is neither theological nor ecclesiastical. Sometimes it is medical. Many of them are just not very well—not just in their heads, not just in their bodies: in their lives. Sickness is always wrapping itself in religion. Hysteria was long mistaken for sanctity. But you must be able to distinguish between a menopausal flap and a religious cause."

Gill's constantly reiterated theme was that the church and the library shared the same problem. "That is how it is with the sex-obsessed, too. Seeing the world with sick eyes, they see a sick world. Unhealed physicians, they write their bitter, dangerous prescriptions for all. You get the bad word in the libraries, and we get it in the churches. These are not our emissaries to you; they are part of a problem we share with you. Bad religion probably had a good deal to do with the form this particular sickness took, but so too may have some unfortunate reading, and the resultant affliction is gnawing in both our guts. Those who would purge it by limited reading must, if consistent, close churches too."

Gill went on to describe and analyze some of the recent changes in religious thinking, and declared "an enormous reworking is going on in the teaching centers of America's majority religions, a reconceptualizing that will have everything to do with how the churches confront all public issues." He admitted, however, that the church had usually been behind on most social issues, on civil rights, on church-state relations, etc. "Cowstail Christianity again," he called it.

But Gill still hoped, he said, that the church might yet be able to scout out "some forbidden areas" to reconnoiter. "What about sex ethics and attitudes, so wildly open at the moment—and so much involved too in the determination of the freedom to read and the confusion around censorship. Court judgments continue to invoke 'prurience' in their decisions. They are evidently still against it. But what is it? There vagueness sets in, and it may be partly because the good justices honor religious reticence at this point. If so, why not relieve them of that gentility and get on to a clarification that could be important to the freedom to read."

Dr. Gill ended, again with the plea "Don't blame religion for all the problems raised in its name. And don't give up on religion. It is not what it was, and more is yet to be." We could not but believe and feel a renewal of hope.

We moved, next morning, from religion to politics, with Wesley McCune, director of Group Research of Washington, D.C. speaking on "The Freedom to Read and Political Problems." In a democratic society, said McCune, "the problems of freedom to read are intertwined—by definition—with political problems." He concentrated mostly on the extreme right wing, and presented some impressive evidence on its growing support, power, organization, and influence. In fact, the McCune paper was little more than a series of jottings of names of individuals, organizations, and activities which are carrying the extreme right campaign forward. His lists of publishers, book reviewers, books, magazines, and institutions, if put into some organized form for publication, could be immensely useful in the education of librarians for the book selection process.

SHOES OF THE CENSOR

Bringing up the end of this parade of outstanding speakers was Edward de Grazia, a Washington attorney with much experience in defending books against charges of obscenity. Mr. de Grazia delivered his too-long paper, "Enforcing the Library Bill of Rights, or Sex and the Stuffy Librarian," rather flatly, but it contained plenty of meat. He began, as his cutting subtitle suggested he might, by putting "the shoe of censorship first on the other foot, that is, on the librarian's own foot."

"Unless librarians," said de Grazia, "overcome the shortcomings which seem to exist with respect to their own personal and professional convictions and aspirations, concerning book selection and rejection policies—that is, unless they first entrench the intellectual freedom principle underlying the Library Bill of Rights securely in their own shops—for every battle won in the courtroom by virtue of legal measures developed and provided through conferences and defense funds, 20 other censorship battles will be privately lost in the librarians' own chambers; and the Library Bill of Rights will be deflated."

Mr. de Grazia went on to discuss a number of possible measures which would assist in defending librarians, and many of the points he made were taken up during one or other of the group workshops. His final passage dealt with the fluctuations and changes in the law of obscenity in recent years, and their implications for librarians and the Library Bill of Rights. As Lacy had said earlier, de Grazia asserted, "It is my opinion that under present law, no book selected by a librarian for his shelves can Constitutionally be found 'obscene.' Why? Because any such book must have at least some slight redeeming social importance. The very act of library selection testifies to and engrafts such importance upon it."

On the problem of circulating books to children, de Grazia commented that the Supreme Court "has given no sign that it feels children have the same rights as adults to read what they wish, or, and maybe this is the point, that children have the same strength to weather and to choose. . . ." He did feel, however, that librarians could, if they faced the problem squarely, deal with it "in a manner which will not too far discourage children from gaining access to adult sexual literature, science and art, and yet not too much put the librarian in jeopardy of court restraint or suppression."

So much for the speakers and their papers. They provided an exceptional assembly of points of view and represent an arsenal of thought and information for librarians who will read them. Our few quotations here do not, and could not do them justice.

WORKSHOP RECOMMENDATIONS

It was the group workshops which were supposed to produce the "results" of this conference. They made noble efforts, and if only half of the specifics they put forward, succeed in finding their way through ALA's administrative maze, the conference surely will have moved us in some very constructive ways. Some overlapping and conflicts between the recommendations of the four groups remain to be edited and resolved, but a few of the more important items are likely to remain pretty much intact.

The major recommendation, which was immediately pursued by the Intellectual Freedom Committee and presented to the Council during the Midwinter meeting, was that "A full-time legal counsel of ALA, who will devote time wholly to support of the Library Bill of Rights with special emphasis on defense against censorship action, be appointed to be a member of Headquarters Staff and to be responsible to the Executive Director. Counsel to work closely with and be responsive to the needs recognized by the ALA Intellectual Freedom Committee."

The conference backed this up with a further recommendation that "an amount of $2 annually be added to the dues collection from every member of the Association, earmarked exclusively for the implementation of this program."

The conference spelled out a number of suggested duties for the proposed legal counsel. Among them were: 1) To compile a list of volunteer attorneys who may be available for aid and consultation in combatting censorship in local communities; 2) To distribute information on current censorship legal activity to local attorneys and attorneys on boards of trustees; 3) To provide counselling service to local libraries and Intellectual Freedom Committees, national, state, and county, as requested, and to provide for retaining counsel when the situation goes beyond the consulting stage; 4) To keep abreast of legislation on censorship as proposed at federal, state, and city or county levels; 5) To file friend of the court briefs in censorship cases when deemed advisable; and 6) To act as spokesman for ALA in opposing censorship, utilizing all communication media.

One recommendation which came up frequently and in various forms dealt with the possibility of providing job financial security for the individual librarian whose job may be jeopardized by resistance to censorship activity.

The conference also recommended that Intellectual Freedom Committees at all levels be strengthened and made more effective by giving them blanket authority to act in the name of their Associations without being obliged to request executive board approval in each case.

If there was one area in which the conference found itself unable to reach any clear conclusions, it was the sensitive matter of what should be available without restriction for children. One recommendation resulting from this uncertainty was: "Because of the special concern librarians have for intellectual freedom for children, we recommend early convening of a similar conference to work toward a consensus on the extent to which access of children to adult materials should be guided."

Cooperation with other groups in building stronger intellectual freedom defenses was urged time and again, and one specific recommendation was that ALA might urge the National Book Committee to establish a coalition of organizations concerned with the freedom to read—a sort of intellectual freedom NATO.

WESTCHESTER UPDATED

There were a host of other recommendations, but it may be well to wait and see how and in what form they finally emerge, rather than listing them in detail here. One statement, however, should be recorded. It was brought about by the recent developments in legal decisions concerning obscenity and the way in which the law has been enforced in many instances in this area. The statement is, in effect, an updating of part of the famous Westchester "Freedom to Read" statement.

The conference recommended that "a statement, substantially in the following terms, be submitted to the Intellectual Freedom Committee for further consideration and submission to the American Library Association and the American Book Publishers Council for adoption."

The statement itself read: "The recent US Supreme Court rulings giving unconditional constitutional protection to all material dealing with sex in a manner that advocates ideas or that has any literary, artistic, or scientific value or any other form of social importance, is an important step in the right direction. We note, and condemn, however, the abuse of the criminal law by some law enforcement officials and courts to harass those who publish and circulate books so that they are deterred from publishing or distributing works protected by the free speech provisions of the Constitution."

At this close range, this conference appears to be a landmark in the ALA's intellectual freedom journey. Whether it will still appear so from some future point in time depends a great deal on how much action the association forces out of the conference's many positive recommendations.

44 No Stampede in Calgary

(AUGUST, 1966)

by ERIC MOON

Not yet, like ALA, a chronic victim of the preconference plague, the Canadian Library Association did, in 1966, indulge in a warm-up before the main conference bout in Calgary. For two days, June 16–17, some 70 CLA members grappled with formulating a position statement on intellectual freedom which might be acceptable to the association as a whole.

The exercise was necessary and overdue: CLA has groped rather than grappled in this area for several years. At Banff—Canada's little Switzerland, some 75 miles removed from the Stampede City—a new incisiveness emerged. It may be attributed, romantically, to the inspiration of the clean, sharp air and the soaring snow-capped mountains of this beautiful vacationland, but nature's inspiration had considerable human assistance. It came in two forms: leadership, and the withdrawal or muting of a formerly powerful opposition voice.

The principal leaders were incoming CLA president John Archer (librarian of McGill University), who blends persuasive charm and humor with an obvious determination to get things done, and Dean Halliwell (librarian of the University of Victoria), who chaired the difficult discussion meetings at the workshop—and later at the conference proper—with a deceptively flexible steel hand.

The other factor at work at Banff was the unexpected and unaccountable lack of opposition by the strong Catholic contingent which had hitherto slowed down, if not stifled, earlier CLA attempts to formulate a strong intellectual freedom position. On this occasion, Father Edmond Desrochers (Maison

Bellarmin, Montreal) and others were among the most forceful voices arguing for an unequivocal statement.

The Banff workshop began with three general papers, each very different in scope and style, each a useful contribution. Mary Henderson, librarian of the Regina Campus of the University of Saskatchewan, led off with a critique of the ALA position on intellectual freedom.

She described the famous ALA trio—the Labeling Statement, the Freedom to Read Statement, and the Library Bill of Rights—as "very much a product of their times—times when authoritarianism in many and various forms springs like dandelions in the pastures of democracy. They are generalized, broadly idealized, and essentially defensive in tone—a rallying call for a last-ditch fight."

The "central and most positive point" of the ALA statements, said Miss Henderson, "is that the body politic cannot remain healthy without some ferment of ideas. The personal satisfaction of the enquiring mind in free-ranging reading and discussion—as distinct from the value to the body politic—is not even mentioned, which is, when you come to think of it, strange in so otherwise democratic a document."

In a particularly Canadian (un-American?) moment, Miss Henderson declared: "The ALA equates democracy with Americanism and both with ultimate good, at least for Americans—equations which must be increasingly hard to defend in the 60's and the present world situation."

Miss Henderson also put her finger on one clause in the Freedom to Read Statement—"the present laws dealing with obscenity should be vigorously enforced"—which bothered many of those who attended the ALA workshop on intellectual freedom in Washington in 1965. This clause, said Miss Henderson, "seems to take no account of the state-to-state variations in the obscenity laws, and the remarkably ill-equipped officials upon whose judgment the public must depend, at least until a Supreme Court decision has been reached, as to whether or not an item is obscene."

What is the librarian's individual responsibility? Said Miss Henderson: "The ALA position would also seem to imply that whatever is on the statute books is right—but perhaps this too was a McCarthy era reflex born of the fear that any statutory change might be for the worse. Though as public servants we are bound to abide by the law as and while it stands, as private citizens we should not only be watchful to criticize the law intelligently but also be ready to take legitimate action to amend it. Neither the law nor the state is sacrosanct. The principle of individual responsibility which was basic to the Nuremberg trials may one day be turned against Americans and Canadians as well."

The Henderson statement was toughly critical, but fair, and it all led to the fighting conclusion that librarians should act on, "not just talk about their educational role, and participate vigorously in the contemporary battle for the mind."

Claude Aubry, director of the Ottawa Public Library, was billed on the program to talk on "The Canadian position re secularism and church in censorship." He admitted that he was not an authority on politics nor on church matters, and expressed the belief that "most Canadians were always in a rather foggy state of ignorance on these matters."

Instead of his assigned topic, Aubry presented a somewhat philosophical and historical view of censorship, "the fundamental and most common cause of [which] is fear."

He outlined several fear syndromes—religious, political, and social— which he considered invalid justifications for censorship, but found a fourth— "the fear of harming purity and innocence"—as justification for censorship "up to a point." The point seemed to be that "the Church has always tried to save purity and innocence through censorship," and that libraries serving youth should perform a similar role.

The third paper attempted, and brought off, the impossible. James Mac-Eacheron, director of Central Library Services in Fredericton, New Brunswick, presented an amazingly comprehensive and comprehensible summary of the legal and administrative aspects of civil liberties and civil rights in Canada. Even the lawyers present were awed by MacEacheron's audacity and skill. Far too lengthy and complex to be summarized here, the paper's most valuable contribution to this workshop was to place the problem of obscenity in a larger context.

As MacEacheron put it: "What we hear in libraries, too frequently per-haps, are complaints—not really charges or accusations—of obscenity. This situation is likely to remain unchanged until there is either a more liberal or a more restrictive social outlook on the civil liberties and civil rights question as a whole. Hence the importance, it has seemed to me, of treating obscenity as a part of and dependent upon the civil rights and civil liberties situation in general, and upon the right and freedom of speech and the press in particular."

MacEacheron's otherwise dispassionate thesis ended, however, with a grim and appropriate warning. "Information must be directed, planned, and dis-ciplined; it must evolve within a context of liberty . . . and in a milieu as receptive as [this one], we can positively envisage the eventual creation of a ministry of information and public affairs and that of a superior council of social communication." This was not a voice from the past, said MacEacheron, but "the personal remarks of a Speaker of a Provincial Legislature reported on April 28, 1966" in the *Montreal Gazette*.

The speeches were the appetizers, and now the workshop plunged into the main course. Discussion groups met, some of them honing down previous intellectual freedom statements such as that produced by the Ontario Library Association, others working up drafts of their own. The same evening, a "strat-egy committee" (Archer, Halliwell, and others) synthesized what they got from the groups and came back, next morning, with a new target for the assembled workshop to shoot at. The firing was rapid and occasionally random, but old iron-fist Halliwell never let the sights wander too far from the target.

There were two other speakers during the Banff preconference, distin-guished representatives from the legal fraternity. They were interesting, even impressive, but in this reporter's view, not very helpful.

Dean Maxwell Cohen, of McGill University, was of particular interest by virtue of his chairmanship of a special Parliamentary committee which had recently produced a "Report on Hate Propaganda in Canada." A brilliant speaker, he seemed to us, nevertheless, to exude a patronizing air. His view of the workshop as "a process of mutual education" was tenable, but his skeptical view that the conference would probably produce nothing more than healthy exercise for the participants was less welcome.

The other legal representative, Douglas A. Schmeiser, Professor of Criminal Law and Jurisprudence at the University of Saskatchewan, was a little more helpful than Cohen, if only in a negative way. Certainly, he dissipated any complacency that might have been lurking in the audience, with remarks such as: "A substantial majority of people favor censorship. The vast majority of all librarians favor censorship. In Canadian society, librarians are the chief censors."

Well, for all that, Halliwell had drawn a statement out of the participants, and the statement, like the participants, took off for Calgary for the main bout.

There, the intellectual freedom statement weathered a Council meeting, and two open meetings of the membership with only slight amendment. This is the way it finally emerged:

CLA INTELLECTUAL FREEDOM STATEMENT

Intellectual freedom comprehends the right of every person (in the legal meaning of this term), subject to reasonable requirements of public order, to have access to all expressions of knowledge and intellectual creativity, and to express his thoughts publicly.

Intellectual freedom is essential to the health and development of society.

Libraries have a primary role to play in the maintenance and nurture of intellectual freedom.

In declaring its support of these general statements, the CLA-ACB affirms these specific propositions:

1) It is the responsibility of libraries to facilitate the exercise of the right to access by acquiring and making available books and other materials of the widest variety, including those expressing or advocating unconventional or unpopular ideas.

2) It is the responsibility of libraries to facilitate the exercise of the right of expression by making available all facilities and services at their disposal.

3) Libraries should resist all efforts to limit the exercise of these responsibilities, while recognizing the right of criticism by indviduals or groups.

4) Librarians have a professional duty, in addition to their institutional responsibility, to uphold the principles enunciated in this statement.

That wasn't the end of the intellectual freedom story at Calgary. Out of the workshop came the seeds of another "action" resolution which the conference adopted as a kind of rider to the statement of principle.

It was resolved to ask the Government of Canada to recognize the role and the responsibility of libraries as spelled out in the intellectual freedom statement, "by introducing amendments to the Criminal Code specifically exempting libraries from such provisions of the Code as may now or in future restrict or forbid individual citizens from acquiring books or other materials within the scope of the CLA-ACB statement on Intellectual Freedom, such materials to be acquired by libraries for purposes of research."

CHAPTER

45 Clean Down the Drain

(JANUARY 1, 1967)

by EVERETT T. MOORE

The most astonishing result of California's November, 1967 election was the decisive defeat of the "CLEAN" proposition. Writers, librarians, booksellers, publishers, and a host of others who cherish intellectual freedom, were pinching themselves over the surprising failure of Proposition 16, the anti-obscenity measure promoted by an ad hoc organization called CLEAN, Inc. (California League Enlisting Action Now).

Right down to election day, the pre-election polls had indicated easy success for this measure which had the support of the strongest anti-smut forces in the state (led most openly by the Citizens for Decent Literature). It had been opposed by such officials as the District Attorney of Los Angeles County and the City Attorney of San Diego, the District Attorneys Association of California, the board of governors of the State Bar, the Southern California and Northern California-Nevada Councils of Churches, the California Library Association, and the School Librarians' Association of California. Governor Edmund G. Brown had opposed the proposition, but Ronald Reagan, the Gentleman from Hollywood who was then the successful Republican candidate for Governor, had favored it.

The proposition was an initiative measure which had been certified for a statewide vote by the more than 468,000 signatures obtained by CLEAN on petitions circulated earlier in the year. Its chief sponsor was California Assemblyman E. Richard Barnes, for nine years a Methodist pastor in New York, and for 20 years a Navy chaplain. Mr. Barnes had become incensed by the failure of the California Legislature to pass stronger anti-obscenity laws than had been on the books since 1961. He complained that California's former "good and enforceable" obscenity law had been so weakened by amendments as to be all but useless to public prosecutors. His own efforts to "improve" the law in 1963 and 1965 had been rebuffed.

Specifically, Mr. Barnes had sought to have the "utterly without redeeming social importance" phrase eliminated from the present State definition of obscenity. This became one of the objectives of the CLEAN proposition, for its backers said that the law now favored the pornographer, and had so encouraged publishers of obscene matter that California had become the undisputed smut capitol of the United States. Sixty percent of all the pornography distributed in the nation, they said, was produced in California. If this was indeed a two-billion dollar industry, as claimed by the CDL, that meant that California's part in the business was not insignificant.

Some of California's librarians recalled that a year or so ago the librarians of the nation had been taken to task at a convention of the Citizens for Decent Literature at the Waldorf-Astoria in New York by the Rev. Francis X. Lawlor of Chicago, who said he didn't think they knew they had been "betrayed and misrepresented" by the Intellectual Freedom Committee of the American Library Association because it had filed an *amicus curiae* brief before the Supreme Court in defense of *Tropic of Cancer*. They noted with particular interest that Mr. Barnes of California also addressed this national convention of the CDL on the same matter. (They had earlier become acquainted with his concern for controlling obscenity, not only from his legislative activities but because he was the one who touched off the statewide furor a few years ago over *The Dictionary of American Slang*.)

Now the time had come to drive the smut peddlers out of California; and CLEAN was going to have to do it. The lawmakers who had repeatedly refused to listen to the decent people of California would have to be bypassed by a direct appeal to the voters to eliminate "The indiscriminate dissemination of material, the essential character of which is to degrade sex."

Among the staunch supporters of CLEAN was Dr. Max Rafferty, Superintendent of Public Instruction in California, who had sailed to reelection for another four-year term in last June's primary election. (Among his recent honors is his election by *Harper's Magazine,* in November, as Philistine of the Month.) Dr. Rafferty had made his sentiments clear to teachers and librarians by his support of Assemblyman Barnes in the battle over *The Dictionary of American Slang.* "A practicing handbook of sexual perversion," he had called it, and for a brief moment the dictionary became America's raciest reference book. Last April, while he was a candidate for reelection, he had said in a speech to the California Elementary School Administrators Association that "a dirty book is a dirty book." Then he elaborated. "The test for a dirty book is whether it can be read over radio and television or be printed in a newspaper. It's a simple test," he said. He added the helpful information that "outhouse literature is camouflaged today as avant-garde writings," and he declared that we don't need that kind of writing. He declined to name any examples.

Specifically, the CLEAN proposition sought "to proscribe all obscene matter and conduct that is beyond the protection of the free speech and free press guarantees of the First and Fourteenth Amendments of the United States Constitution." "Obscenity" was defined as appeal to "prurient interest," namely, "a shameful or morbid interest in nudity, sex, or excretion which goes substantially beyond customary limits of candor . . ." If the material was designed for a "specially susceptible audience," the appeal of the subject matter was to be judged with reference to such audience; and in the case of minors, appeal was to be weighed against the standard of "an average person of the actual age of the minor." Law enforcement officials pointed out the impossibility of establishing what constitutes an average person of the distributee's age. Reading tastes of adults would presumably have to be adjusted to what minors would be permitted to read.

The definition carefully omitted the qualification that to be declared obscene the material must be "utterly without redeeming social importance."

The initiative proposed to take away from California district and city attorneys any discretion as to whether or not to prosecute obscenity cases. The measure provided that whenever there was reason to believe that any person had knowingly committed any of the acts proscribed therein, and the responsible prosecuting attorney neglected or refused to perform the duties imposed upon him, a civil action might be instituted to require such performance. Refusal to prosecute might lead to dismissal from office. In addition, the lay jury was to be the sole judge in obscenity cases, and the sole judge in fine-fixing.

Many who opposed the proposition pointed out, with varying inflections in their warnings, that if it passed, it would amend existing laws, but if the amended laws were then declared unconstitutional, California would be left without any obscenity law whatsoever.

OPPOSITION PANEL

The opposition was so various that when the California Library Association's Intellectual Freedom Committee presented a panel discussion on Proposition 16 during the Annual CLA Conference, in October, it heard from a half-dozen people who represented many shades of opinion—all opposed to the proposition. (The committee had decided against including proponents of the measure on the panel.) An assistant district attorney of Los Angeles County represented the most "conservative" position, that the measure was not all bad, but that because of the manner in which it was drawn, it appeared unwise to support it. If passed, it would repeal existing obscenity laws. Then, if declared unconstitutional, there would be no way to prosecute the smut peddlers. The most liberal base for opposition was held by a Unitarian minister, who thought the initiative presented a particularly horrifying threat of literary and artistic censorship. Its passage, he believed, would encourage vigilantism and the reckless passing of judgment as to potential dangers in literature and the arts. A newspaperman, a bookstore owner, a representative of the American Jewish Committee, and an Episcopal clergyman presented additional opposing views, each with some significant emphasis on particular defects of the measure.

Perhaps doubts about the constitutionality of the proposition finally contributed the most to its defeat. California voters, seemingly, had for some time been hell-bent for passing measures they passionately believed in, even when they were soberly warned that the propositions would be knocked out by the courts. Two years ago they approved an initiative amendment to the state constitution repealing an anti-discrimination-in-abusing law, and a referendum measure banning pay-TV. Full warnings were sounded about the unconstitutionality of these measures, and both have since been declared unconstitutional by the courts. Perhaps the folly of such costly procedure was realized by more of the voters this time.

The Republican candidate for Lieutenant Governor, Robert H. Finch, an attorney, presented one of the strongest arguments against CLEAN, saying that it was a "radical" law that "plunges into the murky waters of censorship." He called it a sweeping law which would go "far beyond the sincere good motives of its sponsors and supporters."

Finch's running mate, Ronald Reagan, said he was for the proposal, even though some portions of it might be held unconstitutional, because he believed the people should have a chance to express their feelings about the traffic in pornography. To which Mr. Finch replied that the proposition was not a public opinion poll or some kind of a referendum on dirty books—that voting "no" on 16 was not voting "yes" on smut. "The choice before the voters is not between voting 'clean' and voting 'dirty,'" he said. "It is, rather, the act of writing a law on the California statute books. That serious act should not be taken without reading the fine print." This is apparently the message the majority of the voters finally got.

REAGAN THEORY

It was too late in the campaign for candidate Reagan to admit to reading the fine print, but Governor-Elect Reagan said right after the election that he would back anti-pornography legislation along lines proposed by Mr. Finch that would avoid censorship and meet constitutional tests. He acknowledged that defeat of Proposition 16 might have been caused by voters' fear that it would meet the same ruling of unconstitutionality which had nullified 1964's Proposition 14, the anti-anti-discrimination-in-housing amendment.

The question of what finally brought CLEAN to defeat (3,186,583 to 2,475,073) is worthy of treatment by one of tomorrow's doctoral candidates. Every major county in the state turned in a comfortable majority against the proposition with the exception of Orange, stronghold of the right-wing conservatives. Even there, the vote was fairly close (183,209 "yes," 179,770 "no"). Los Angeles County, CLEAN's headquarters, voted against the proposal, 1,110,764 to 995,020. San Francisco voted almost two to one against it, as did Alameda, in which are situated both Oakland and Berkeley.

Some have surmised that the saturation campaign waged by its proponents was overdone. Radio and television spot coverage was exhaustive. The 12-page rotogravure supplement which appeared as a political advertisement for Proposition 16 in several Sunday newspapers in the state two days before the election, was reminiscent of a similar one published by the John Birch Society two years ago. In this one, the Schick Safety Razor Company and Schick Electric, Inc., jointly took a full page of advertising. It was evident that great sums of money were available for the cause.

Whatever the reasons for the defeat, law enforcement officials and civil libertarians joined happily in celebrating their unexpected victory. From now on, there will no doubt be less wholehearted joining of forces as plans for introducing new anti-pornography legislation in Sacramento unfold. The new Lieutenant Governor and the District Attorney of Los Angeles County will certainly have their proposals ready. And it seems not at all unlikely that Assemblyman E. Richard Barnes, himself, will be in there trying harder than ever to save us all from destruction.

CHAPTER

46 Two Cheers for Liberty

(SEPTEMBER 15, 1967)

by EVELYN GELLER

"Librarians, apparently, like sinners, have to reaffirm their belief in virtue from time to time. There was quite definitely an evangelical cast
to this conference." It was not an unfair appraisal that Ervin Gaines (Minneapolis Public Library) made in his wrap-up to the preconference on intellectual
freedom in San Francisco in 1967. Nor was the tone of the meeting inappropriate to its declared purpose—to define "the librarian's responsibility to
adolescents in relation to difficult literature." For it seemed, in many cases, that
it was the librarian's responsibility itself that had to be affirmed in the face of
indifference, fear, or sheer lack of empathy with youth. Spurred by attack—
and sometimes ridicule—from their guest speakers, prodded by even stronger
self-criticism by their colleagues, and warmed by the slogans of responsibility,
many librarians drew from the two days of talk a sense of community to
nourish their return to outposts more provincial than San Francisco, seat of the
"flower people" and psychedelic flights.

What the conference provided besides the stimulus of dialectic remains
moot. Few practical resolutions emerged from it, and the obvious recommendations had already been made before, in other contexts. Few practical
contrasts between the situation of the school and public librarians were made;
few private confessions of cowardice (or conservatism) reached the floor; and
the legitimate fears of librarians were left, as ever, to die in small group
discussion. Above all, the legal limitations on providing reading matter to teens
defined at the conference, concern few of the books that inspire the incursions

of the censors. The more relevant, vast limbo of political and bureaucratic oppression remained, meanwhile, an unexplored terrain, as librarians, through various exercises in pontification, were called on to "only connect" with youth.

A "PRE-FREEDOM" CONFERENCE

It is generally acknowledged that providing youth with reading matter of a controversial or erotic nature is a more complicated and delicate issue than that of censorship *per se*. The proliferation of tawdry reading matter on the newsstands and the liberalization, over the past decade, of what is considered "pornographic" in the bookstore and library, have made the distinction clearer. Even the landmark Roth decision, ruling that adults must not be confined to reading what is suitable for children, implies an area in which restrictions to minors may be imposed—though that area, from a legal point of view, has still to be established.

In recent years, the problem has become more acute as extremists argue the availability of reading matter to teens as an excuse for sterilizing a collection or restricting the teenager's access to the adult collection; as Congress has shown new interest in framing anti-smut legislation intended to protect youth, and in studying "obscenity" more closely; and as various state laws have attempted to define "dirty" books in such specific terms as to jeopardize the holdings of public and school libraries. It was factors like these that, in January 1965, at another ALA censorship conference held in Washington D.C. led to the recommendation of a conference devoted to this special problem.

Since the most liberal selection policy must operate, above all, within legal limitations, we'll skip here to the midpoint of the conference to Stanley Fleishman's discussion of the librarian's legal responsibility to the teenager and his legal rights if he is attacked. Fleishman, a distinguished lawyer who has spent a good part of his life defending erotic literature against charges of obscenity, outlined general obscenity legislation as it applies to teens and described current efforts being made to frame new laws. Almost all states, he noted, have anti-obscenity laws, and the Supreme Court, in the 1957 Roth decision, that obscene works unredeemed by literary or social value are not subject to the protection of the First Amendment. The difficulty has been, of course, in defining the obscene, and while the Court has seemed recently to be retreating from its 1957 decision, its interpretation has been extremely liberal. "Once you have the Marquis de Sade, what's left?"

In deciding whether or not to buy a book, Fleishman emphasized, the librarian need not be constrained by the rulings of a lower court—only by the Supreme Court decision. Not that this is the factor determining a decision, he conceded. "You'll probably say, 'Do we have enough money, or enough space,' or, 'What will the politicians say—will we get any money next year?' But these are not legal issues.

"I don't want to minimize the problems I know exist. . . . Librarians are especially vulnerable to public agencies, politicians who hold their purse-strings, and various pressure groups. And sometimes, librarians share the lack of vision."

Despite his acknowledgements, there ran through Fleishman's talk, like a *cantus firmus*, a serious appeal to professional courage. "The question of legal responsibility contains a broader responsibility," he said,—"The librarian's responsibility to the public. The library is an institution clothed with the public interest. Your first responsibility is to get people into the library to read about their interests, and to have things that will lead them to other ideas. This purpose is present in the existing and the proposed Library Bill of Rights." Fleishman took time out to make a few criticisms of the proposed Library Bill of Rights, including paragraph five, which, he felt, excludes sex and age from the provision that "the rights of an individual to the use of a library should not be denied or abridged because of his race, religion, national origins, or social or political views." "It hasn't been too long," he said, "since we thought women should be protected as we see youth today." The arguments we hear today for protecting youth from exposure were used only recently to separate women from men, he noted, on the Victorian assumption that women had no legitimate interest in sex*.

Yet we know, continued Fleishman, that the teenager *is* interested in all the controversies—sex, drugs, religion, civil rights—around which our fears and doubts focus. If we argue that "bad" literature will "corrupt" him (i.e., result in conduct we want to suppress), we must answer two prior questions: Can we agree on what is "bad"? And can we separate out the cause of an antisocial act?

The literature in this area is not conclusive, Fleishman conceded (this point was made again and again during the conference); but he ventured the opinion that the best way to let adolescents grow healthily is to expose them to the problems that concern them. "There is no law saying a book can be measured by its impact on youth."

Present anti-censorship legislation intended mainly to protect youth, Fleishman pointed out, is not likely to pass Supreme Court review. Whether any such law can remains open to question; but the Supreme Court is in no position to say legislation of this nature is impossible—it can only point to a particular law and find it inadequate. Barring such legislation, he said, the librarian is legally entitled to allow *any* book to circulate to *anyone;* and the teenager should be entitled to his own "bill of rights," guaranteeing access to the library collection and its meeting rooms. He warned that implementation of such a policy would take a great deal of courage, but the risk, he said, might be worth it—if the libraries wanted to hold on to teenagers at all. "They're listening to a different beat."

* *Betty Friedan, in* The Feminine Mystique *(Dell, 1964) has a pertinent comment to make in this connection. Summarizing a study of sex references in the mass media reported in Albert Ellis'* The Folklore of Sex *(Grove, 1961) she observes that "the most striking new sexual phenomenon . . . [between 1950 and 1960] was the increased and evidently 'insatiable' lasciviousness of best-selling novels and periodical fiction, whose audience is primarily women.—EG.*

DEBATE WITHOUT CONFRONTATION

The perspectives aired at the conference did not show great variety in tone—though liberals argued both absolute freedom and a case for some kind of aesthetic controls. Yet a debate did take place, albeit sans confrontation, and to different audiences. On June 23, Edgar Z. Friedenberg (*Coming of Age in America*), professor of sociology at the University of California in Davis, keynoted the intellectual freedom preconference with an attack on the inbred conservatism of librarians, on their willingness to conform to bureaucracy, and on the relevance of print to today's youth. Four days later, addressing the trustees' division of the ALA, Max Rafferty, state superintendent of education in California (whose main distinction may be that he won a conservative of the month award last November from *Harper's* magazine)—junked his prepared speech to inveigh against Friedenberg—or what he had read about Friedenberg in the newspaper—and in the bargain take up the cause of librarianship with a series of astonishing conceits. Indeed, the entire dialogue was that of stereotype *vs.* cliché. That Friedenberg did not know all the literature or all the libraries he criticized, and that Rafferty never anchored himself in the 20th century, may be equally irrelevant. At least the polarities were clear.

Beginning his discourse with fine demagogic flair, Rafferty read four statements Friedenberg had made, asked his audience how many agreed, and concluded: "If I were to stoop to Dr. Friedenberg's terminology, I would say that I just wanted to know how many idiots I was dealing with." Calling Friedenberg "meatheaded," and a "free love apologist and preserver of pornography," Rafferty protected the library profession against his charges. Trimmed down to its essentials, his quotations and rejoinders form the following "dialogue."

1. Friedenberg (as quoted by Rafferty): "The library is just one more place where kids are taught they are second class citizens."

Rafferty: "A library is a place where children are introduced to the wonder and glory of literature, . . . the shimmering tapestry that has been proudly passed from one generation to the next—by our libraries. It hangs upon the walls of the English-speaking world like a great web of dazzling light, coruscating with a million radiant hues. . . . The librarian is the opener of the magic windows, not the humdrum defender of the status quo nor yet the wild-eyed activist of a future punctuated with the blast of riot guns and lit with the lurid glare of Molotov cocktails. How could he teach any child that he is a second-class citizen? The world of literature has no second class citizens, and it is in that enchanted and enchanting universe that the librarian is happily and uniquely at home."

2. Friedenberg: "School libraries are the last place in the world for the act of reading. You can't talk to anyone about what you're reading. Reading is institutionalized, private, isolated, and dull."

Rafferty: "This, of course, is the boiler factory concept of librarianship. It substitutes group discussion for individual communion of reader with author, and jabbering for meditation. It fits in fine, incidentally, with the New Left's 'high decibel' theory of higher education, which substitutes shouting and parading for thinking, and is just what the doctor ordered for the lurching, hairy minority of young people who boast stronger vocal cords than mentalities.

"I suppose that some school libraries are poorly organized, badly administered, and generally dull. So are some university classes. But to blandly damn them all . . . is as arrogantly overinclusive as to condemn all sociology professors because a few of them happen to be blustering nitwits. . . . Professor Friedenberg might profitably address himself to the interesting question of why so many of the young people for whom he acts as a self-appointed Pied Piper are petitioning me to keep their school libraries open longer if these same libraries are institutionalized, isolated, and dull."

3. Friedenberg: "Juvenile books are compendiums of deceit and they are meant to be deceitful. They tell the children how to get along in an evil society."

Rafferty: "For millennia, children got along without books. If they were sufficiently gifted, they grappled successfully with Biblical commentary and adult classics. . . . A happier time for youngsters dawned a century ago, and in that Golden Age a whole new pantheon of youthful gods and goddesses came down from Parnassus and made old Earth a magic place for boys and girls. Wilfred of Ivanhoe . . . Richard Coeur de Leon, . . . the young d'Artagnan, ever ready to draw those flashing blades for truth and glory and the Queen . . . Christopher   Robin . . . Tom   Sawyer . . . Meg,   Joe,   and Beth. . . .

"When in any age have children had such shining exemplars? I'm sure that the shades of Sir Walter Scott and Mark Twain, Dumas and Bunyan, Lewis Carroll and Daniel Defoe would be wryly amused to know that their books are 'compendiums of deceit.' "

4. Friedenberg: "True pornography is essential to American society. Young people should be allowed to read anything they want to read. What can happen to kids when they read a book that can't happen to adults?"

Rafferty: "Every law enforcement officer in the land knows the high probability of finding whole stacks of pornographic books among the personal effects of minors picked up for sex crimes, and the grislier the crime, the higher the probability. Of all the vicious nonsense put forth by the professor . . . this stuff about the intrinsic value of pornography for children is the most nonsensical, and by all odds the most deliberately vicious."

Rafferty also rapped the knuckles of the California Library Association for having denied the harmful effects of reading. To Rafferty, the murders "inspired" by the reading of de Sade; Bluebeard's instructive library in black magic; and the bloody advice of *Mein Kampf* were ample evidence to the contrary. Moreover, "logic would impel librarians to concede that if bad books don't do anybody any harm, then good books certainly don't do anybody any good."

Librarians fear irresponsible censorship, Rafferty said, "which would reduce them to robots moving spasmodically among book stacks and brandishing date stamps." But the only answer, he said, is for librarians to take the initiative and do the censoring themselves. The filth being injected into American publishing must not be made available to children at the taxpayers' expense: "The ninth grade English teacher who assigned *Fanny Hill* or *The Life and Loves of Frank Harris* to his class would probably not only get the sack by his local school district, but also would have his credentials yanked by my office."

What about exposure vs. indoctrination? "I feel about this," said Rafferty, "much as I feel about assigning *Catcher in the Rye*. . . . Certainly it should be assigned—to those students who have read Homer -and Virgil, who have laughed with Dickens and wept with Shakespeare, who have lived with and learned to love the great American writers who have stood the test of time, from Ben Franklin to Mark Twain. Youngsters who are grounded in the culture and wisdom of the past and are ready to judge and evaluate what passes for the literature of the present."

With that he signed off, having given his audience "the hardest thing to come by these days—the other side." What Rafferty didn't know was that the kernel of his talk, which had appeared in his newspaper column in 1966 under the title "Poison—Free with a Card," had been read to the preconference audience and listened to in incredulous silence.

PLASTIC PEOPLE

In Rafferty's remarks, Friedenberg's statements went through a double filter, the newspaper's, and Rafferty's own version of what he had read. So in point 2, for example, he discarded Friedenberg's criticism of the fixed reading period in libraries; in point 3, the statement "Here [in juvenile books] kids learn it is society's intention to punish the unorthodox"; and in point 4 he spliced together three unrelated sentences, omitting Friedenberg's definition of pornography as "literature which arouses sexual excitement in a dehumanizing way." Minor editing; just enough to switch the support of free reading to the advocacy of pornography for children, and ignoring the satire in Friedenberg's statements.

What, then, did the erstwhile California professor (he has moved, by now, to teach at Albany) really say? Basically, he was concerned with extending his points in *Coming of Age in America,* defending the adolescent against his forced dependency and careful socialization (defined by Friedenberg as "the systematic elimination of alternatives") by a host of adult agencies, including libraries, and including literature as a socializing medium. Perhaps his position was not so different from Rafferty's after all. We're all censors, Rafferty was saying with approval in his American Library Trustees Association address—We exercise supervision over manners and morals. You're all censors, Friedenberg said, in effect—you refuse books to teenagers, deny them adult privileges, whether by temperament or accommodation. If for the former reason, you call it "book selection" ("like all bureaucracies, you have your private language to justify your moral lapses"); if for the latter, teenagers learn that the library is just another place where people do what they are told to do, not what they think is right. "The participation of liberals in such restriction makes you what they call 'plastic people.'"

There is a real conflict of interest between the generations, Friedenberg insisted, no matter how much we talk about "misunderstanding" and bridging the gap; and the librarian may be torn between two commitments. The teenager is fighting the plastification of society; the librarian, as adult, participates in the attempt to socialize him by providing a literature that is dishonest (here Friedenberg made his criticism of the juvenile, or junior novel) in denying to any adolescent—except the "bad guy"—the motivations of sex, envy, and greed, and thus encouraging the teen to accept his own infantilization. "What disturbs me," said Friedenberg "is the fact that reading *has* become institutionalized. You have no obligation or right to control or influence except for a critical function. You *can* tell them it's a perfectly awful book." It is not pornography, he added, that threatens the adult society, but precisely the book with uncomfortable personal insights, that depicts the existential plight.

Friedenberg discussed also the McLuhanite idea of distrust by youth of the print medium. They need to learn, he concluded, what people who *are* print-oriented can do with books. "But it has to be the kind of book that *is* most likely to be controversial."

The remaining speakers provided variations and only minor provisos of the Friedenberg theme. Notable among these was Larry Beggs, a young, corduroy-clad Presbyterian minister working with teens in the Haight-Ashbury district of San Francisco—runaway middle-class teens who have copped out on their parents' ambitions, to form a small enclave in the heart of the city. Beggs did a beautiful job of reading from a compilation of California school library book selection policies (those panaceas of anti-censorship efforts) passages that revealed, unconsciously, the patronizing attitude of adults, the conservatism of the policies themselves, and the backwardness of librarians in assessing teenagers' reading tastes. He said sex is often overplayed by adults talking to youth—a projection of their own preoccupations, where adolescents are concerned with other moral issues and with emotional relationships above all. "They don't want to know how the parts fit." Beggs capped his talk with a reading from *Another Country,* revealing the intense morality and sincerity which have eluded so many readers, and ended with this manifesto:

> Let young persons read what their own human curiosity leads them to read. Present to those adults who imagine everyone else to be as disturbed as they are by sexuality—present to these persons, a handful of earthen clay with the gentle suggestion that they are to go work on their own relationship to their body through fashioning and caressing this earthen element. If they have further questions you might furnish them a list of good Jungian analysts in the area, or give them an unexpurgated copy of the book of Genesis which has some rather direct reference to God creating our sexuality, blessing it, and designing it as one of the important and responsible areas of our interpersonal functioning whether we are over or under 18!

Other quotables—Kenneth Rexroth, outspoken and probably the most engaged of the guest speakers: "The drive for censorship has nothing to do

with sex—it stems from the ruthlessness and competitiveness of our society."
The manifestations of violence on film and TV can do "more harm to children
than all the Fanny Hills laid end to end." If you put all books into minors'
hands, he stressed, you need a strong value system, which is not apparent
either in home or school today.

Robert Kirsch (book reviewer, *Los Angeles Times*), who called for an
arena of free communication and expression—a dialogue, though not necessarily agreement, with youth. He upheld the right of the parent, however, to
protect the very young child from violence and pornoviolence.

The most telling viewpoint at the conference, however, came from a
speaker representing the crucial link between the library and the community.
Alex Allain, trustee of the St. Mary Parish Library in Louisiana, and a member
of the Intellectual Freedom Committee, told his audience that trustees would
go to court in behalf of librarians charged with handling "obscene" materials,
but he could not guarantee the same support when controversial material is
handed to teens, or advise a course of action which library boards could be
guaranteed to protect. He also took the line that if we agree literature can have
a beneficial influence we must concede it can harm, and felt that a massive
survey of the effect of literature on teenage behavior was in order. Though he
doubted that any causal relationship could be found, he concluded, "I don't
know what positon we'd take if a correlation were established."

The sharp discrepancy between the materials likely to come up for legal
questioning and those that occasion censorship activity was apparent in the
talks by librarians. Helen Cyr (Oakland Public Schools) pointed out the ironic
contrast between freedom taught in schools and the bureaucratic restrictions
imposed on students' criticisms and school newspapers. She described problems in her own system—parents who protested John Ciardi's *John Jay Petty
and Fiddler Dan* and *You Read To Me, I'll Read To You;* or Milton Meltzer's
Pictorial History of the Negro and Langston Hughes' *Kind Treasure* (the last
two "because they might provoke race hatred"). David Cohen (Plainview
High School, L.I., New York) cited the surveys of school censorship attempts—including Lee Burress' survey of Wisconsin schools, and the National
Council of Teachers of English study of 700 teachers—that found it was the
most creative and dynamic teachers who were the ones to report pressure. He
demanded a posture that would defend intellectual freedom as the colleges
now stress academic freedom.

And on the public library front, both Harriet Covey (Los Angeles County
Library) and Esther Helfand (New York State Library YA consultant) challenged the concept of protection in a society of open communication and sharp
demands on the adolescent. In effect, said Mrs. Covey, the function of young
adult work seems to be censorship, "bridging" a gap that is not as wide as we
imagine it. Boards of education, with tiresome repetitiveness, keep banning the
same titles—*Lord of the Flies*, (Glendale, California), *Raisin in the Sun,
Manchild in the Promised Land* (Washington, D.C.). *Manchild, All Around
the Mulberry Bush, The Group, Another Country*, even *Candy* and *The 100
Dollar Misunderstanding* can be used with the teen. "Why are we clucking
about LSD? Can we protect them at 16, and draft them two years later?"

LOVE AND HUMANITY

"My topic is not intellectual freedom but love and humanity," said Esther Helfand, in beginning the final address of the preconference. It was an emotional speech—and deliberately so, for Miss Helfand's main thesis was that we cannot separate intellect from feeling and will, when it is emotional blocks—sexual insecurity, the clutter of lifetime responses—that color our attitudes toward books and dull our sensitivity to teenagers; and when it is precisely involvement that we want to encourage on the part of youth? How do you reason with an adult who thinks Anne Frank is a fake, she asked, or a principal who refuses to feature a film on premarital pregnancy because the problem is too common in his school? She called for librarians to look at teens as total human beings, and to discuss freely all issues from the Pill to Vietnam to Black Nationalism ("how can librarians afford to be safe in this time of ferment?"). Yet the speech was, in the end, unsettling. For beneath the call to conscience lay a frightening picture of the intransigence of conservatives in positions of authority, and a Cassandra-like mood of prescience without power. That most of the audience should have drawn from the talk only inspiration must attest to hypocrisy or a pathetic ignorance of *Realpolitik*.

THE TRUE DIMENSIONS

If a stranger, unacquainted with the range of selection policies represented by the librarians, had sat in on the small group discussions he would have thought that all these speeches were so much talk. In private, and when it came to specific titles, librarians were often narrow-minded, evasive—passing the buck up or down, or unable to come up with tactical suggestions, or dependent on what they called "personal" judgment.

The most telling session we encountered was run by Eli Oboler, librarian of Idaho State University and a member of ALA's Intellectual Freedom Committee. For a while it seemed, as one person put it, that the discussion was "trending into group therapy," shifting in focus, as the conference seemed to, from intellectual freedom to rapport. But Oboler brought the discussants pretty well into line with a barrage of pointed questions that highlighted the practical dilemmas. Here is a recap of part of this discussion:

Oboler: Let's take LSD and marijuana. There are libraries that won't keep a book on the subject. *Do* you have Timothy Leary?

Public Librarian (hesitantly): I believe so . . . yeah.

Oboler: What about a high school library? Would you be able to defend it for your library?

School Library Supervisor: No. It would be difficult to get the other viewpoints—they're not that good. I wouldn't want the book in the high school library, but I would want it in the public library.

Oboler: Is the school library evading purchase, then? If it rejects the book, for what reason?

School Library Supervisor: A book like that isn't related to the curriculum.
Oboler: Most states have a unit on narcotics.

Silence

School Librarian (after a few moments): It would depend on your teachers there, in the school.

Round Two. Oboler was discussing the problem of gift books, which are often donated by right-wing groups.

Oboler: In Idaho, the John Birch Society asks every librarian to put a copy of *The Blue Book* in its collection. What do you do in cases like that? In a small community, where there is generally only one book on a controversial subject, would you accept books promiscuously?

School Library Supervisor: We use the same criteria as we would for purchase.

Oboler: What if they weren't in your interest? You just said you wouldn't want a book on LSD.

School Library Supervisor: That is my own personal opinion. Another might take it.

Oboler: Would money help in this situation? Could you set aside "mad money" for such contingencies (*i.e.,* to balance the collection when accepting a gift book)?

(*Irresolute discussion.*)

Oboler: What about a book on abortion? A book on perversion?

Trustee (on both high school and public library board): From a political point of view it would be suicide. A board has a responsibility to the community.

Oboler: What about a novel? *Sanctuary* is about sexual perversion. It's by a Nobel Prize winner.

Librarian: I don't buy books.

Trustee: I'd expect the public library to have it; not the school library.

Oboler: Would you buy a history of the U.S. by a communist?

Trustee: I would expect a book about communism by a Communist, not a history of the United States by a Communist.

Oboler: Would you take a history of communism by an American?

Silence

Oboler: Herbert Aptheker, a Communist, has written the best history of the slave rebellion. Would you buy his book?

Silence

School Librarian (after a few moments): Y . . . e . . . e . . . s.

Oboler: If you had to choose, would you take the Communist over the upstanding American?

Silence

Oboler: You see, *these* are the kinds of problems you have.

Echoes of these attitudes were an undertone throughout the conference.

Item: The young adult coordinator in a large Midwestern city discussed with us the library's policy *vis-à-vis* teens: students must have parental consent to gain free acess to the collection; the *adult* book selection librarians designate the titles unsuitable for adolescents. The librarian, who discussed this matter-of-factly and without complaint, made no connection between the procedure and the vehement criticisms of the practice made by the speakers.

Item: A library director whose young adult coordinator was one of the most outspoken at the conference, described his system's procedure: to issue restricted cards only on parental demand. "We find that surprisingly few parents put in the request," said the director. "We pass the responsibility for censoring on to the parent, but he is often reluctant to create still another parent-teen conflict over a library card!" This alternative procedure was not discussed at the conference.

Item: Soon after the conference, we learned that one California county public library, having used a single-card system for everyone, adult and child, was shifting to a restricted access policy requiring parental consent; the change and the reasons for it—a very current change—did not, apparently, seem appropriate for discussion, although the young adult coordinator had helped to organize the conference!

Of the proposals made during the small group sessions, two were of common concern: First, the obvious request for a research study that would put ALA in a stronger position once the congressional inquiry into obscenity got under way; and a request for a strong ALA Intellectual Freedom Office to lend support to librarians. Just what the Office could do for librarians, however, was not spelled out at any point, though it was hoped by the IFC (this apparently was one strong reason for the conference) that the youth divisions could lend added strength to the two-year-old and urgent plea for the establishment of a strong ALA intellectual freedom program. Meanwhile, another important tactical development—the formation of a national freedom to read commission that would involve a number of educational organizations—launched recently by Peter Jennison, assistant director of the National Book Committee, was another subject never discussed.

Nor was the possible irrelevance of an obscenity study to young adult work, in so far as day-to-day censorship problems are concerned, ever considered. It was perhaps symptomatic that two questions—would unrestricted access to the collection mean, eventually, tighter precensorship; and was a closed-shelf policy ever justifiable?—were brought up at the tail end of the conference for possible *future* discussion.

It may not be harsh, at this point, to conclude that whatever good emerges from the conference will not come from the program itself, but from whatever agency decides to bring the most crucial conflicts out into the open. For it seemed, in the end, that while librarians were very brave about sex—lauding their own liberality (or liberation?)—it was "censorship," in turn, that had become the dirty word, symbol of a ubiquitous and unmentionable phenomenon, best left unacknowledged, undiscussed, and unresolved.

CHAPTER

47 *Defending the*
Freedom to Read

(FEBRUARY 1, 1962)

by STUART C. SHERMAN

Human rights have resulted from centuries of struggle and law enforcement. These rights were hard won and may be easily lost.

Ever since the Magna Carta it has been necessary from time to time for man to reaffirm his basic rights to prevent their erosion. This reaffirmation has been expressed through the Bill of Rights, the Emancipation Proclamation, Franklin Roosevelt's Four Freedoms and the United Nations Universal Declaration of Human Rights.

Zechariah Chafee, Jr., one of this country's most distinguished defenders of constitutional freedom, said in 1944 that ". . . liberties of speech, press, and assembly which were universally cherished in my boyhood have been eroded during the past 40 years by law after law, and only scattered protests have been heard."

It was stated with some authority recently that if the Bill of Rights were put to a vote today in Congress there is reason to doubt that it would pass.

The public library is one of the most democratic of American institutions. People don't have to use a library; they choose to do so voluntarily. And because they do, the library has an obligation to preserve their freedom of choice, their freedom to read and to know, and their freedom to think and decide. The public library is, thus, a guardian of certain basic rights.

The word "controversial" is not a valid reason for failing to purchase a book, since there are few subjects which are not controversial to someone. Our shelves would be quite depleted if this factor guided our selection.

Books are not dead things. They contain ideas of great men and of little men. Some ideas and thoughts now accepted were once considered controversial and even revolutionary. Some of the ideas expressed by Charles Darwin, Martin Luther, Thomas Paine, Karl Marx, Galileo and Copernicus have become "books that have changed the world."

Having a book on our shelves implies no automatic approval of its contents, nor should the absence of a book imply our condemnation of it. We have many books on our shelves which contain ideas that conflict with the way we think—even with the American way of life. But our ideas are not the *only* ideas, nor are they necessarily the *best* ideas. Conflict and dissent are often the breeding ground for new ideas. How can we know how to combat our enemies unless we know how they think? For this reason, we don't remove books from our shelves because someone does not like them. It's not our right, nor the right of any individual or group, to tell others what they shall or shall not read.

With the exception of books which represent unquestioned treason, pornography, racial or religious discrimination, or libel, the paramount issue on which libraries must base their decision about a book in question is that it is not our right to decide what people shall or shall not read. Every adult must be permitted the freedom to read according to his choice. Librarians must firmly resist all censorship attempts on the library.

It should be remembered that financial limitations put a restriction on the books which can be bought. This necessitates the exclusion of many books, which may occasionally lead to misunderstanding on the part of the public regarding the intent of the librarian.

On October 31, 1961, Rhode Island Attorney General J. Joseph Nugent declared that in his opinion the *Tropic of Cancer* by Henry Miller was the "foulest, most obscene work" he had ever read. He indicated that he would start a campaign for voluntary withdrawal of the book by newsdealers but, for the time being, he would not seek court action under the State's anti-obscenity statute. His action had been initiated after Westerly police had requested newsdealers to remove the book from their shelves and to limit sales to adults.

On the same day President Barnaby C. Keeney of Brown University stated: "It is not *Tropic of Cancer* that concerns us, but the principle of due process of law. . . ." He announced that the University would not sell the book for the time being, and would try to seek a determination from the Superior Court as to whether the novel was legally obscene.

Public demand for the book began to rise following these announcements. One bookseller received 20 calls in one day; it was reported that a copy of the book has been offered for $20 downtown; the public library reserve list increased to 35; and an out-of-town radio station reported that people were waiting "thirty-five deep" for the book in Providence!

In my regular quarterly report to the Board of Trustees that week, I made the following statement of the library's position concerning the *Tropic of Cancer:*

"The library owns the book; it is not on open shelves; but is available to adults on a reserve basis. It is not available to persons under 18, and it is the library's plan to adhere to this policy.

"It is not the intention of the library to defend or condemn the book, nor to tell mature adults what they may or may not read. It is, however, our intention to defend the freedom to read.

"Our decision to make the book available was based on several criteria. Most knowledgeable critics agree that it is a repulsive book evoking an emetic reaction. The novel pictures a disillusioned American rebelling against society and groping for a meaning to life amid the evil and sordid aspects of Paris in the twenties. If the novel is sordid, it is because the life it reflects is sordid. Many critics also agree that the book has literary merit, that Miller is an influential writer of this century, and that, if considered as a whole, the novel is not believed to be obscene.

"Our decision was also based on the evaluation of the book by competent reviewers on the library staff, and the demand from the community. Furthermore, in August, following the first publication of the book in this country, the United States Justice Department lifted the 27-year-old ban by the US Customs on the importation of the book from France. The decision to place the book in circulation had the approval of the Executive and Library Committee of the Board of Trustees on August 17, 1961.

"The Board of Trustees also upholds the principles of the Library Bill of Rights which states that 'There should be the fullest practicable provision of material presenting all points of view' and that libraries should resist 'abridgement of the free access to ideas and full freedom of expression that are the tradition and heritage of Americans.'

"It is my hope that the library's doors will always be open to those who seek the truth from books containing ideas that may be popular or unpopular."

The Board of Trustees approved the report and "further voted unanimously that *Tropic of Cancer* would be circulated by the library until restrained or enjoined by competent authority or until there is a final judicial determination that the book is obscene."

Evidence of the united front which the library intended to make against the threat is revealed in the following resolution:

"Whereas, We the members of the Staff Association of the Providence Public Library consider the stand being taken by the Librarian and the Board of Trustees on the *Tropic of Cancer* to be in accord with the American Library Association's Bill of Rights;

"Whereas, We feel the freedom to read has been demeaned by the ruling of the Attorney General;

"Resolved, That this Association supports the action taken by the Librarian and the Board of Trustees;

"Be it further resolved, That this Association stands ready to assist the Librarian and the Board of Trustees by whatever means deemed necessary and advisable by the Librarian."

When he learned that the Providence Public Library was circulating a copy of the book, the Attorney General threatened to arrest the Librarian and any borrower, although he admitted he was uncertain how the loan procedure operated. He also stated, through the press, that he was willing to cooperate with the library if it wished to set up a test case.

Among dozens of persons who offered to "borrow" the book in such a test case were a priest, a pregnant mother of four children, a lady over seventy who had, in her own words, "never ridden in a paddy-wagon," and a gentleman who said that he would take the sword his grandfather used in the Dorr Rebellion and run it through anyone who stopped him! The offers were not accepted for reasons that will be explained later.

The library staff was reassured that if anyone were to be arrested it would be the Librarian, and that he would, if necessary, participate directly in the loan process. The Trustees also agreed that they had a strong moral obligation to protect any borrower.

The effect of the ban was to stimulate widespread interest, but the novel did not leave the building for three weeks, probably because some prospective borrowers on the reserve list feared arrest.

On November 3, the Attorney General announced he would not prosecute Brown University and approved the use of the book within the University library building. The writer of a letter to the Editor of the *Providence Journal,* however, noted that "since the 'ban' includes the Providence Public Library, one must assume that Mr. Nugent feels that the 'educative process' is not a function of public libraries" but is "confined solely within university walls."

The library, through its attorneys, then sought a meeting with the Attorney General to review the library's previously announced policy on the circulation of *Tropic of Cancer.*

The conference, attended by the Librarian, President and counsel, did not result in a resolution of the problem. In the Attorney General's own words, the meeting was "affable (but) there was no meeting of minds." After the conference the following statement was released to the press by the library:

"We have explained to Mr. Nugent that the Library's continued circulation of the book to adults on a reserved basis, as approved by the Library's Trustees, is corporate and not individual action. We have stated that we believe any legal action on the Attorney General's part should properly be against the Library itself (that is, the corporation) and not against its staff, its employees or its patrons.

"Whether any such action is brought is, of course, a decision for the Attorney General.

"We have explained to Mr. Nugent that, in the opinion of counsel for the Library, his action in threatening criminal prosecution against the Library's employees and staff, or against any of its patrons for the circulation of this book is a deprivation of fundamental constitutional rights guaranteed by the First and Fourteenth Amendments to the United States Constitution. The clear impact of such threats is to restrict and inhibit the 'freedom to read,' prior to any judicial determination by due process of law as to the nature of the book.

"The Library will adhere to its policy, namely, to circulate the novel to adults on a reserved basis until restrained or enjoined from doing so by competent authority or until there is a final judicial determination that the book is obscene, pursuant to its firm and longstanding commitment to protect the public's 'freedom to read'."

A special meeting of the Board of Trustees was then called to consider the latest developments and possible further action.

Various possibilities of the Library's invoking legal process were considered, but the Board concluded to take no action, and voted to reaffirm its previously announced policy on the book. None of several alternative legal remedies definitely promised a satisfactory resolution. Moreover, the Board wanted to avoid appearing to advocate or defend this particular novel, when the principal objection was to the "banning by threat" as a deprivation of constitutional rights.

At the end of the year there had been no prosecution and the book was still being used by the library.

It is disconcerting to state that too many librarians and trustees, who are eager to uphold the principles in the Library Bill of Rights, are just as eager the next day to avoid involving the library in a controversy. They tend to capitulate and make unfortunate statements under pressure which suggest the way they think the reporter or their community would like them to act. A mockery may thus be made of the library by the librarian himself!

In no area is the work of a librarian so subject to controversy, misunderstanding or misinterpretation as when subjected to the threat of book censorship. Such occasions are nearly always newsworthy, and the eyes and ears of the community are centered on the library for leadership in a controversial area. In no other area of librarianship will the librarian's ablest and most mature judgment be so publicly tested. It is in this area that unfortunate statements are occasionally made under the pressure of a reporter or an irate citizen.

The following statements were among those made by librarians when questioned by a reporter on the availability of Vladimir Nabokov's *Lolita:*

"Absolutely filthy. I'm pretty broadminded, but it made me sick to my stomach . . . it's disgusting to any normal person . . . I would not buy a book (for the library) that I couldn't read myself."

"It's smutty and we consider it trash."

"I don't put a controversial book on the shelves until I read it and I haven't read this one."

"You can add my name to any list of librarians who will not stock the book. I wouldn't want that book in the library."

And a comment from a trustee: "I don't even know anything about the book, but if it's anything like what I've heard, it won't get in the library. I heard that it is trash." When told about the nature of *Lolita* he added: "You can rest assured it won't be put in the library."

This type of careless thinking based on the personal prejudices of librarians or trustees is just as dangerous as the misguided threats of would-be censors, and should have no place in the public library.

Initial judgments about books are usually made by civil authorities who are unfamiliar with contemporary creative writing. They are trained to look for the sordid. But Justice William J. Brennan reminded us that, according to the

US Supreme Court, "Sex and obscenity are not synonymous." Yet, this is the assumption that many would be moralists make when they take unto themselves the "protection" of the morals of others. Those who are familiar with the writing of Dos Passos, Caldwell, Steinbeck, Hemingway, Mailer and Moravia are not likely to be shocked when picking up a book by D. H. Lawrence. They could not fail to see the difference in the literary style and intent of the authors of *Peyton Place* and *Lolita;* nor would they fail to distinguish between outright pornography and an honest attempt to portray a social situation.

The issue frequently involving libraries is the effect of certain books on minors. Should library policies applied to the selection of adult books, be at the same time applied to those for youth? Some "authorities" believe that whatever is improper for youth is also improper for adults. The outworn test which they apply is the loaded question: "Would you give this book to your daughter to read?" The effect of such a policy is to reduce the adult population to reading only what is fit for children.

Library censorship cases are usually of two kinds: complaints that a library *failed* to purchase a certain book, or complaints that a library should *not* have purchased a certain book. Thus, librarians find themselves between two pressures in the community, from the moralists on one hand and from those upholding the freedom of the press. We are wrong if we don't censor and we are wrong if we do. Perhaps a middle of the road approach is the best recourse.

The states have laws to outlaw the sale and distribution of pornographic books. It is not a job for citizens or groups. The chief dangers to our freedom of the press are organizations or individuals who set themselves up to act as judge, jury and police over the community's reading matter. This danger is far greater than that to which a few people might be subjected by reading a risqué novel.

There is wide disagreement among psychiatrists, educators and social scientists, and questionable scientific evidence to substantiate the assumption that there is a correlation between reading and anti-social behavior. There is, however, little or no risk that people are going to commit anti-social acts after reading the type of books that public libraries are likely to purchase.

It is customary in many libraries to consider certain novels dealing with sexual situations, books of anatomy, nude photographs, etc., as candidates for the "restricted shelf." This policy keeps such books out of the hands of minors without restricting adults' freedom to read. It may also serve to minimize complaints.

It is the policy of the Providence Public Library to issue adult cards to a person who is a senior in high school or 18 years old. Persons with adult cards are then eligible to use any book in the library.

Any library at any time is subject to a complaint about a book. It is, therefore, essential to have a set of principles to serve as a guide for the formulation of a mature judgment. Naturally, no policy could apply to all types of censorship threats, but individual complaints may be case-handled within the following framework:

1. See that the Board of Trustees gives its endorsement to the Library Bill

of Rights which was adopted by the Council of the American Library Association on February 3, 1951, and amended at the 1961 Midwinter meeting. Record this approval in the Minutes of the meeting where it may be referred to if necessary.

2. See that the entire staff clearly understands that complaints about books should be referred immediately to the head librarian.

3. Receive the complaint with friendly interest, but give no indication that an error has been made.

4. Be calm and try to avoid argument.

5. Avoid making a statement about a complaint or a release to the press until the facts are reviewed and a statement is prepared in the quiet of one's office. It is better to say nothing than to make a statement you will regret, because the chances are good that you may be quoted in the press.

6. Ask whether the complaint is from an individual or an organization.

7. Request a statement in writing describing the nature of the complaint.

8. Indicate that you will then look into the facts and discuss the matter with your staff and trustees.

9. Inform your trustees immediately.

10. Consult your nearest large library to learn its policy concerning the book.

11. Draft a statement which reflects library policy and, if advisable, submit it to the board for approval.

America is moving rapidly toward what Granville Hicks has called the "dead level of uniformity." Fortunately, the public library is not one of the mass media because its impact is felt by individuals instead of by crowds.

The great strength of democracy is in diversity. Since diversity is the mission of the library, the library is a democratic institution of no mean significance. Few institutions in the community are as capable of resisting leveling influences toward conformity. It must encourage people to leave the superhighways and to explore the less travelled roads which may be rough and uncertain. It must furnish books and ideas to the man who does not conform because he is listening to a different tune. It must defend the freedom of choice and the freedom to read for all Americans.

CHAPTER

48 Ordeal at Long Beach

(JUNE 1, 1965)

by BLANCHE COLLINS

In November of 1962, the Long Beach Public Library, and many other libraries, fought to keep *The Last Temptation of Christ* on its shelves. In Long Beach the episode reached a more intense height than in some other cities when the City Council announced that they would probably ask that the book be taken out of the library. The Council also referred the problem to the City Manager for a report.

Two weeks later, when the subject came up at Council with the City Librarian present to defend the library's position, the Council Chambers were filled. Most of the people present had come to support the library. The City Manager strongly supported the library's position that the book should not be removed.

It is necessary to start with this event, since some of the people who worked on this project against the library are still involved. There have been changes, but the nucleus is the same. Their efforts from that time on have been never-ceasing.

I quote from an article in the Long Beach *Independent Press-Telegram:* "A silver-haired woman member of the John Birch Society is behind the religious battle to ban the *Temptation* from library shelves—Miss Irma K. Bethune of Arcadia frankly admits she started the drive . . . She heatedly denies the group is connected with the ultra-right Birch group but other Birch members are connected with the campaign in other areas."

Of the some 285 cards or letters which the City Council received, demanding that the book be removed, over 80 came from people who did not even live in Long Beach. The mail to the Council supporting the library's position was several times larger. The effort to ban the book failed.

Soon after this episode, a three-page communication was read before the City Council. The following quotations indicate the temper of the communication:

> I also charge that the library is deliberately suppressing literature written in the defense of freedom, and I further charge that the library is deliberately brainwashing its patrons in the evil cause of Communism.

A little further, the writer gets to the crux of the problem, as he sees it:

> I therefore will demand of the Council that it remove immediately those responsible for this attack upon our country.

The Council received and filed this statement. This writer carefully checked shelves and lists, especially at one of the branch libraries and at Main for weeks after this. He also delivered a speech against the library at a recent hearing.

In January of 1964, we began to receive requests to buy *Appendix IX*, a government document of some 19 years ago. It has been recently reproduced in a three-volume edition which sells for $30. It is distributed from a small book shop in Hollywood which is recommended in the May 1962 *Bulletin* of the John Birch Society. It is described by the book shop as, "A meticulously compiled index of the testimony given and the documents furnished to the [House Un-American Activities] Committee." It comprises 2,138 pages, and gives the names of organizations which came to the attention of the Committee, describes each organization, and supplies the membership list of each.

The publicity for the book quotes from *The Martin Dies Story,* by Martin Dies: "After my retirement from the Congress the successor Committee expunged *Appendix IX* from those records and removed it from the Library of Congress and the Document Room." We were able to get a microfilm from the State Library so that we could see what it was. Our decision was that we would not buy it. This too, was taken to the Council by members of this group. My communication to the City Manager says:

> We evaluated carefully and decided that we would not be justified in buying it. Although we do buy items of $30 or more, it is important that material which costs this much has use over a long period.

I go on to say later that ". . . we realize that the demand is a temporary demand."

We were interested in the statement that *Appendix IX* had been "expunged from the record," and wrote to our Congressman to see if his office could find out if this were so. He sent us a report from the Un-American Activities Committee which stated that it was never supposed to be published. The Committee itself had immediately ordered the GPO not to print this Appendix but to return it to official Committee use, and stated, "The Un-American Activities Committee did not destroy the record of the previous committee, as stated in the excerpts of *The Martin Dies Story*." Also:

The reason for withholding the information of *Appendix IX* was that the Dies Special Committee said it was too scurrilous and too many innocent people—the list contained some 20,000 names—would be injured unfairly because information was not accurate in many instances, nor was it documented to the satisfaction of the Committee.

Demands that we buy this document were sent to the City Council. Even after the City Council had received and filed my report to the City Manager and his covering letter in support of the library, people still protested our not having this book.

Another incident which got especial attention from the City Council was a letter filed with it in January 1964, criticizing the communist pamphlet material at one of the branches. The writer mentioned specific items which he wanted removed and others which he wanted purchased. He believed, he said, that ". . . much can be done by our public library to provide more suitable material in the pamphlet file on the study of the policies of Communism." He concluded, "This account illustrates the sort of *censorship* which those of the Socialist-Collectivist persuasion have been practicing upon the citizenery for many years."

Council referred this to the City Manager and, again, we spent many hours preparing a report. We evaluated, pamphlet by pamphlet, the material in the file at the branch mentioned. We were able to prove that the accusation was wrong, that both sides of the specific incidents mentioned in the accusation were covered. The Council again received and filed my report as recommended by the City Manager.

The above is only a partial report of the many incidents in which people of the radical right persuasion condemned and attempted to pressure the Long Beach Public Library. One unique element in the organization of our library is a Book Committee of three members appointed by the City Manager. These people meet once a month to approve the new book list. It is stipulated in the City Charter, and has been for half a century, that the City Librarian has the responsibility of selection but that this Committee must approve.

Delegations of the radical right began coming to the meetings. I allowed them to ask questions, to talk, feeling that it was very hard for me to be ungracious in my own office, and thinking also that it would be well for us to know what they were thinking. Reports came back to me that they were enthused and happy at their reception. In the months that followed they heckled, made speeches, passionately urged the removal of some books from the list, questioned others.

When this had gone on for several months, some of our friends moved in. At one meeting, we had five college professors. An attorney, a doctor, members of the League of Women Voters, members of the Friends of the Library came, so that there were always several present. I let this go on for several months because I thought it well for them to see these people in action, and for them to have a chance to refute the statements and defend the library's policy. This they did magnificently.

Now I am refusing to allow anyone other than the Book Committee to participate, so the meetings seem very dull after the excitement of past months. Under a California State law, all governmental meetings must be open to the public, but the official in charge may refuse to allow participation by the observers.

Now, we arrive at a more recent chapter. In April 1964, the City Council received a letter from the President of the "Education Society of Long Beach" in which the Society presented the charge: "The Education Society of Long Beach, of which the undersigned is president, has evidence and data to prove its contention that de facto censorship of reading material found in the Long Beach Public Library does exist. This censorship is directed toward books and periodicals which present points of view which may be described as pro-American and anti-Communist."

Again, the City Council referred to the City Manager's office. Although the Society's president was contacted immediately for facts, these were not forthcoming at that time. On May 18, the Manager's office sent a letter to the president reminding him of the telephone call in which he had agreed to produce facts. Three months after the original accusation, the president reported to the Manager's office that the Society was ready. A meeting was held in the Executive Chambers of the City Hall with the Executive Assistant to the City Manager presiding, and with the three members of the Library Book Committee and the City Librarian present.

For over two hours, five people presented long, well-prepared papers indicting the library. They and their helpers had worked diligently in the library during these three months collecting "evidence" for the accusations which they had made. They had learned that our records are open. The staff and I had cooperated in every way with them as they built their evidence against us. The Council then decided to call the public hearing these people had been urging.

A newspaper reported the next day: "A *two-year campaign* to gain greater conservative influence in the selection of reading materials for the Long Beach Public Library simmered briefly Tuesday before City Council. It will be the subject of what promises to develop into a long and controversial hearing at 2 P.M. October 20th." The newspaper's prophecy was right. The hearing lasted for five hours. Not only the Council Chambers, which seat about 200 people, were filled, but people were standing around the walls and the hall outside was crowded. There was no way of telling what the percentages were, but people in the audience reported that it was obvious that many were there in support of the library. Three television cameras and many reporters were present.

What is the "Education Society of Long Beach," which we first heard about last last spring? During the hearing a Councilman asked who the officers were. The answer was not forthcoming.

Our accusers have insisted that they are not censoring, that they are not asking us to take books out of the library. This is not so. They have indicted the library vehemently because we purchased *The American Way of Death*, stating that Jessica Mitford is a Communist. They have indicted us because we have Pete Seeger's records and books, and they constantly state that he is a Communist. They have indicted us because we have Langston Hughes' books, stating that he is a Communist. They say that this is not censorship on their part but a misuse of taxpayers' money on our part, since some of the royalties, no doubt, go into Communist coffers. They have indicted us because we have records sponsored by Unesco. One of the several very fine speeches made in defense of the library during the hearing aptly summarized:

> First of all, I believe that this group itself, the Education Society, seeks to impose de facto censorship of books, using one of the oldest and most transparent argumentative devices. The way simply is this, that of creating censorship, first by protesting that something is censored and then by moving in a one-sided group of people to take over and censor in turn. Now this is the way things have happened many times, crying havoc and then repairing the havoc by creating an even deeper formalistic type of control.

It has been interesting to watch the recurrence of one constant theme. Many letters sent to the Council and to me, protesting the Library's having *The Last Temptation of Christ*, either quoted from or included in its entirety a speech by Mr. Leon C. Hill which was given to the Mayflower Society of the District of Columbia in 1956. Its title is "How Are Books Selected for Purchase by Librarians?" To quote: "Librarians, in general, rely mainly upon the reviews and recommendations of the following four guides and these guides to a great extent are framed by a few international 'intellectuals,' profit-seeking promoters, publishers and the like: 1) New York *Times;* 2) New York *Herald Tribune;* 3) *Saturday Review of Literature;* 4) LIBRARY JOURNAL."

Mr. Hill goes on to state: "It so happens that the LIBRARY JOURNAL, intentionally or otherwise, is really a major force in the mass campaign to guide American opinion in the direction of the left-wing precept. Many have wondered, of course, why the reviews in the JOURNAL, almost without exception, recommend left-wing books, and condemn those having a conservative trend. They have also been curious concerning the radical international aspects of the JOURNAL."

The Book Mailer, a distributing center for extreme right books, publishes the *Book Mailer News.* In the January 1964 issue there is an article "Pity the Poor Librarian." LIBRARY JOURNAL is under attack again in this article as the magazine "which more than any other publication, influences your school and public librarians in their selection of books to be purchased for your reading." *Human Events,* September 8, 1961, condemns the same periodicals. It mentions, the *New York Times Book Review,* "which is famous for its bias," the *Saturday Review,* the (then) *New York Herald Tribune Books,* and accuses them of brainwashing. It mentions "the left-wing bias" of LIBRARY JOURNAL.

In one of the papers presented by a member of the Education Society, these four guides are blamed for the fact that the library is "overstocked with works of the liberal persuasion." The paper goes on to say "These two New York papers have a group of reviewers who boost the radical works and criticize, unjustifiably, or give the silent treatment to conservative and 'For America First' works." And, "The LIBRARY JOURNAL, intentionally or otherwise, is really a major force in the mass campaign to guide American opinion in the direction of the left-wing precept. . . . It is alarming and scandalous that this JOURNAL —censoring against almost all conservative or pro-American writings—is accepted as a proper and reliable library guide."

The point I am making is that it is obvious that this did not generate in Long Beach, that there is a pattern in this war on public libraries which goes back several years and extends throughout our country. We have had access to the John Birch Society *Bulletin* and find in it material which ties in with all of this.

In 1965, a member of the Education Society of Long Beach and the City Librarian were interviewed on "News with Mike Wallace." Our accuser emphatically stated that they would win, though it might take a long time. Those of us who have had the privilege of supporting and defending the library policies are equally determined that they will not win. We have enough faith in the public library system and the deep ideals of democracy for which it stands to know that, long after the present radical right groups have disappeared, this library and other libraries throughout the country will still serve, basing their selection policies on the basic principle that the people have a right to choose for themselves.

Much of the burden of the past few years has been on the shoulders of the librarians who assist the public. My job was made easier because I had confidence in them. They have patiently explained our policies, patiently answered questions in regard to books, patiently and with control been the recipients of occasional emotional outbursts. I have constantly reminded them that as librarians it is their responsibility to assist the individual patron in an objective way and that, as we build our book collection, we must think of this radical right element also. They, too, are our patrons. We serve them also.

We have faced up to the Library Bill of Rights in a new way. It becomes a different and much more meaningful thing when you act it out, as we have been forced to do. We have always attempted to act objectively within the rules of this particular library system. This is important. One must have established definite rules and then abide by them. I think that if one does not do this, the fight is lost before it even commences.

These people have learned that their checking of the library need not be done under cover; the staff has cooperated with them in every way possible. During the months in which this group was working on papers to substantiate the accusations which they had already made before the City Council, many hours of staff time were spent assisting them. They presented long lists of books which we checked for them as to whether they were in the library, the number of copies, and the distribution throughout the system. We have learned to quickly identify the person who comes in or who has been sent in to "case the joint." Although the staff has often felt frustrated with the amount of time spent on this so-called "negative area of librarianship" they and I have learned much from these experiences. I have attempted to keep in close contact with the staff.

Major precepts which I have used constantly have been that this must never become a personal conflict; that I, as City Librarian, did not matter, but that the things that the library needed to defend were all important and far bigger than the fate of any one person. I have realized that we must fight the issue on a broad scale and not get caught fighting the little fight on the little branch of the tree. And I have urged my staff to remember that we are fighting and building for the library of tomorrow.

Throughout this period, I had strong support from my boss, the City Manager. With this and a strong staff, what else does a library need to combat this kind of continuous attack? Newspaper support helps. We have always received excellent support from our daily paper. I would hate to face a period such as we have had *without* a strong paper. One day we had five different reporters working on censorship articles.

Lastly, a library needs outstanding community support. We had it. When *The Last Temptation* problem broke, I was dumbfounded. I would have said, "It can't happen in Long Beach." During that first hour, when I evaluated and decided how I should proceed, I considered this community and wondered: did people really understand the freedom to read concept? We had made a very special effort to know the community, to be an integral part of it. This we had done well. We were well-known and the library image was excellent. Had we really done enough talking about basic principles? Did people understand the deep dangers of removing even one book through pressure?

I didn't have to wait very long to find out. The telephone calls started and came pouring in for at least two weeks, as person after person called to express his concern and offer his support. Piles of letters came to me personally. When that crisis was over, a group of supporters formed a Friends of the Library organization so that they would be in a position to uphold the library if other attacks came, and to assist in our new building program.

In the spring of 1965, when we were approaching an even more serious crisis, people who had been attending City Council meetings sprang into action. Unbeknownst to me, groups began working to alert the community. As in the earlier episode, key people sought me out at community gatherings to offer their support. Some made special trips to the library. Many telephoned me. The support was there and it has been unceasing. Whenever we needed people in the Council Chambers, they were there.

Because this is Southern California, where the radical right element is strongest, it has been the privilege of some libraries in this area to carry a large share of the burden. This is the story of what happened in Long Beach. It is well to remember that it might happen some place else.

CHAPTER

49 *A Dime-Store Paul Revere*

(OCTOBER 1, 1967)

by KARL NYREN

On October 3, 1967, Carl Gorton, a trustee elected on May 3 to a five-year term on the board of the Farmingdale Public Library on Long Island, appeared in court in nearby Mineola to answer charges of petty larceny stemming from his confiscation of a copy of *Paris Review* from the library shelves. A week later, he was back to face a charge of assault brought by Mrs. Hortensia R. Stoyan, a children's librarian.

These two cases followed an earlier encounter between Gorton and the courts, in which State Supreme Court Justice William R. Brennan dismissed Gorton's petition to seek direct access to library records "at all hours of the day." Justice Brennan's decision, handed down on August 22, supported the Library Board's regulations that "all trustees may see all files of the library," but only during the regular business hours of the business offices of the library (Mondays through Fridays, from 9:00 A.M. to 5 P.M.), and after first obtaining the records from a library employee. Gorton maintained that these regulations were "arbitrary, capricious, and an abuse of discretion" and "calculated to dilute his effectiveness." Justice Brennan ruled that while a trustee is "entitled to investigate and peruse the records" this "is not to say that the library must remain open 24 hours a day seven days a week to accommodate this worthwhile purpose." He dismissed Gorton's petition on the grounds that it was "utterly devoid of any statement to the effect that he has been denied the right to inspect" the records, that files were refused to him, or that "employees were utilizing the regulation to delay or hinder his investigation."

Regardless of the outcome of Gorton's next encounters with the court, the

cases are only incidents in an ordeal which began last May with the completely
unexpected election of Gorton, an avowed John Birch Society member, to the
Board of Trustees of the library. The intensive campaign of harassment which
Gorton has conducted since his election has almost five more years to go.

The whole situation has an Alice-in-Wonderland quality which would be
funny were it not for the very real peril which it poses to the library. Already
the crude but effective tactics of Gorton's campaign have had results: the
library's budget, which is voted on annually by Farmingdale residents and
which Gorton opposed publicly, was twice rejected, and on its third and final
try, was passed by the narrowest of margins. Had it been defeated, the library
would have had to exist on the same budget as the previous year. With the
built-in escalations in operating costs of any institution, this could only have
meant serious cutbacks in personnel, book purchases, and hours of opening.

Anti-budget campaigning, prior to the third vote, was marked by newspaper ads paid for by Gorton and pamphlets that can best be described as
scurrilous. They attacked the library's budget in a manner senseless to any
intelligent reader, but evidently impressive to a lot of Farmingdale voters.
Bumper stickers, on Gorton's Lincoln Continental and other cars around town,
proclaimed: "Support your local degenerate [library]—vote yes—Farmingdale
Library budget, Aug. 29."

Gorton's strangely effective public appeal has not been his only weapon;
with what seems to be unlimited time at his disposal, he has harassed library
employees, according to the staff, with visits and telephone calls, generally
demanding information in a bullying manner. A statement signed by every
staff member (with the exception of those away on vacation) states that "We
have listened to insults, name-calling, innuendo, and lies, and have overlooked
being intimidated, harassed, and finally having one of our members physically
assaulted."

GARBAGE CAN SEARCH

Mrs. Bernice Fink, a library clerk, says: "We're tired of having him come into
the library, trying to intimidate us and snoop around and stick his tape recorder in front of us. He has rifled the desks of staff members both during the
day and after the library was closed, and has even searched through the
library's garbage cans at night for evidence to use against the staff and
trustees." One result of all this has been the decision of the library staff to join
a union for the protection it might offer. Another has been the sudden
emergence of the library into public prominence, with aroused feelings splitting the community into anti-library and pro-library factions. Library Board
meetings, once unattended by spectators, now draw overflow crowds and
representatives of the news media.

Since Farmingdale is a highly typical American community, with conditions that may well be duplicated in hundreds of other towns and small cities,
its plight is potentially of significance far beyond local concerns. The two
elements that make this plight possible could be duplicated almost anywhere:
a substantial, but not really very large, group of lower middle-class voters

susceptible to anti-intellectual appeals, and one determined agitator who is apparently immune to both embarrassment and reason.

Gorton moved into Farmingdale in 1964; he lives there with his wife and four children. Exactly how he supports his family is a local mystery; he claims to be president of a research company (Carlton Aeronautical Research Laboratory) but no one seems to know where it is, apparently not even his wife. There is suspicion voiced frequently that he is a paid operative of the John Birch Society, but neither this nor his secretiveness seem to lower him in the esteem of his supporters. The humorless approach to library problems of this former Eagle Scout and Scouting leader is characterized as well as anything by his alarm at observing two six-year-old girls in the library giggling as they turned the pages of a book. He reported the incident at a Board of Trustees meeting in August, according to one observer present.

AN "ACT OF GOD"?

His sense of mission is well expressed in a letter published after his election: "Our greatness as a nation depends on those who have not yet been deluged by the 'wave of the future.' I pray that they are yet in the majority and will wake up before it's too late." His actions, he went on to say, are "based on Christian faith, libertarian philosophy, and extensive study of the subversive influences operating throughout our society." Elsewhere, he described his victory as "an act of God that the liberals did not have sufficient insurance to protect against." On another occasion he described himself as having "a moral responsibility to prevent crime."

Gorton himself cites two dates which he considers turning points in his life: 1964, when he read *None Dare Call It Treason,* and March 1967, when he escaped unharmed from the wreckage of a private plane that crashed in upstate New York. After the first experience, he decided to join forces with those opposing communism; after the second, he decided to dedicate his life to God. In a newspaper story which appeared on August 31, Gorton told of some of the amazing events which had happened to him since March, including his discovery of the *Paris Review* in the library. He lashed out at apathy and ignorance, called for control over the library which is dominated by a "minority," and offered to supply copies of the Bible and *None Dare Call It Treason* to anyone who could not find them in the library. His role, as he saw it, was as a "dime-store Paul Revere to Farmingdale."

He first ran for a position on the library board in 1966, but was heavily defeated by the present president, Robert Callahan, a lawyer who had been a board member since 1954. When Gorton ran again this year, opposing another incumbent, Myra Van Nostrand, neither the library board nor anyone else took his candidacy seriously. He had by this time identified himself as a Bircher and a library critic, but beyond making a nuisance of himself, there seemed to be little harm he could do.

In just one year, however, there had been changes in public sentiment. People in Farmingdale, as elsewhere in the country, were concerned as the Vietnam war grew and showed no signs of ending; summer was coming on, with storm signals of riots; and both the Governor and the President were talking about increased taxes. The people who were running things in the country obviously weren't doing very much to protect the way of life of the little home owner who had in a generation or less moved up from rural or city poverty to a mortgage, car, color TV, and unlimited supplies of beer and barbecue in the back yard. The resentment of people who do not participate in the community power structure, even to the extent of voting, who see the library and the schools as institutions for the benefit of others, and to whom a word like "art" suggests depravity, lies well below the surface. Farmingdale, however, has annual elections for school and library boards, and for approval of school and library budgets; a sensational appeal to this resentment, just before election, can bring out a vote that usually stays home. It can also sway the voter who normally marks his ballot with a good-natured vote for the incumbent.

ELECTION FIREWORKS

Gorton saw to it that the sensational appeal was provided. On April 5, three weeks before election time, he plucked a copy of the magazine, *Paris Review*, from the shelf of the South Farmingdale branch of the library. Finding in Dallas E. Wiebe's short story, "Sky Blue on the Dump," a passage describing a boy's fantasy of a modern day Europa enjoying sexual relations with a bull, Gorton showed it to a staff member indignantly and announced that he was confiscating the issue. When the staff member objected, Gorton stated that it would be necessary to use physical force to stop him.

The incident was splashed on the pages of both dailies and weeklies read in Farmingdale, with the announcement that Gorton was to run for a post on the Board of Trustees. In early 1967, few issues could compare with obscenity for their interest to the whole population. Like the war and race problems, it was obviously getting worse and something would have to be done about it.

And the obscenity issue stayed alive after Gorton's election, not at all weakened by a parade of leading clergymen and educators lending public support to the library and avowing that the story in question was a work of art.

"Art," however, wasn't a very reliable touchstone to evoke. The library trustees had considered sponsoring an art program some time earlier; rumor now had it that there were not only nude models walking around the library building, but that a whore house was being operated on the top floor.

At one public meeting where clergymen gave their views on the alleged obscenity in the *Paris Review*, spectators rose to shout "pervert" and "degenerate" at the speaker. These obviously inarticulate protesters were typified by one man who rose and announced ponderously, "you've heard what all these others have to say. Now I want you to hear from someone who isn't either a Catholic, or a Protestant, or a Jew." The audience waited with great interest to hear just what exotic religion he represented. "I am a Baptist," he announced solemnly.

When election day came, Gorton had a few more little things going for him. A strong slate of economy candidates was running for the school board, and urging voters to "vote Row A"; since candidates are placed on the ballot in alphabetical order, Gorton came first in the trustee candidate line-up. Normally, Myra Van Nostrand, the incumbent with three terms behind her, would have come next. But an unexpected third candidate came next: Arthur B. James, a high school teacher. James, although admitting to being a conservative and in basic agreement with Gorton's philosophies, disclaimed, as "a goddamn lie," either Birch Society connections or cooperation with Gorton in splitting the vote which the incumbent would normally get.

The election results showed Gorton getting 1,915 votes, James 1,039, and Van Nostrand 1,703. From a troublesome crank, Gorton was raised to the status of a board member, with a five-year term to serve. In the same election, the library budget was defeated, and this added to his victory.

The *Paris Review* incident stung the rest of the library board into action. On May 10, they voted to censure Gorton publicly for his action in taking the magazine from the library. Gorton had offered to return the issue if the board would keep it out of circulation until they read the offending story and passed judgment on it. But the Board refused, and also refused to read photostatic copies of the page in question which Gorton passed out. Their position was that in the first place the passage couldn't be judged out of context, and that it was up to the professional staff to select and pass on the appropriateness of library materials.

As enlightened as this stand appears to librarians, there is some question whether it was appreciated by library opponents and others whose doubts had been encouraged by Gorton's attack. A rather unfortunate comment was made by trustee Myra Van Nostrand, who was not present for the censure meeting, but who indicated that her vote would have been cast with the other members. "We stick together," she remarked, which was perilously close to an admission that Gorton and others had some reason for seeing the board as an arm of the community's "in" group. Gorton himself referred to the proceedings as a "kangaroo court"—a phrase picked up and repeated by one local editor, who likened the censure vote also to "Nazi Germany in the early days" and "a lynching scene in the old west."

This undercurrent of resentment against established institutions has evidently been an important one. Gorton at one point was asked why he had not joined or even attended the Farmingdale Historical Society meetings. "I felt that I wouldn't be welcome," he responded. His feelings on this subject, and those of his supporters, must certainly have been crystallized even further by the May 18 refusal of the Friends of the Farmingdale Library to accept Gorton's application for membership. The Friends, in so doing, denied Gorton "a soap box for his peculiar views" but they also conceded him a point. And they heard only about three weeks later that a rival group, the Community Association for Responsible Libraries (CARL), had been established, with a former school board president as its leader—and vowing to "spend every cent I have" to defeat the library budget. Acting as "advisor" to the CARL organization was *Carl* Gorton.

One of CARL's activities, prior to the second library budget vote, was the distribution "to adults only" of a pamphlet in which the "objectionable" passage from the *Paris Review* was reprinted.

In letters to the editors of the local papers, the theme of alienation has arisen frequently: "It's not what the educator or the prominent citizen thinks the library system should cost, but what you, as taxpayer, are willing to spend," says one such letter, which also criticizes "so-called cultural growth" as a reason for library expenditures.

Another letter warns against thoughts which "those entrenched in power want you to think." The "in" group, says the same letter, is "evidently afraid of someone they can't control."

A "GOOD CHRISTIAN GENTLEMAN"

Gorton is, of course, cast by these supporters as someone independent of control "by the 'behind the scenes' candidate-selectors," and in one woman's words, "he's a good Christian gentleman and you're trying to crucify him."

A letter signed by Edward H. Werner, who is the Birch Society co-ordinator for the area and who tried three years ago to ban the Nikos Kazantzakis novel *The Last Temptation of Christ* from the library, refers, as do many other letters, to the library board as "a small arrogant clique."

The "public" which is most susceptible to this appeal is represented, in part, by citizens who revealed, in a newspaper poll, that they had never heard of Gorton, his confiscation of the *Paris Review,* nor his unsuccessful court fight over access to the library's files. Many residents admitted that they did not know the location of the library, even though they were standing in the library's parking lot at the time of the newspaper interview. Their feelings of alienation were well typified by one telephone company worker who stated, "People don't really know what is and what isn't in the library." These nonusers of the library are evidently content to let Gorton find out for them; despite all the publicity, library staff members have noticed few new faces coming into the library.

When the library's budget was coming up for its third, and what would have to be its final chance for approval by the voters, Gorton opened up what seemed a promising new front by attacking the "wastefulness" of the library board. He singled out a new reading program being conducted at the South Farmingdale Branch as his main target, and went about assiduously gathering information which would discredit the program. It was in the course of this investigation that the incident occurred which will bring him into court on October 10.

The technique of exploding a dramatic headline just before election backfired this time, as Gorton himself aggrievedly pointed out. He described his predicament in being charged with assault by Mrs. Hortensia R. Stoyan thus: "It is incredible to what length the library 'liberals' will go to discredit me in their third attempt to pass their ill-begotten budget." The assault charge, he maintained, "reveals the same pattern developing, of instituting malicious legal action against me just before the election." Since Mrs. Stoyan is only four feet,

11 inches tall and weighs 87 pounds, she may be the one librarian in New York State Gorton would least like to face in court on a charge of physical assault.

The incident itself began when Gorton went to the library branch on Friday, August 11, 1967, and interrupted a children's program for slow readers by attempting to interview reading consultant John Rothman, who had been hired by the library to work with children, parents, and staff members. Rothman, described by Mrs. Stoyan as "very white in the face," complained to her and said, "I will not talk with Mr. Gorton with the tape recorder on."

Mrs. Stoyan then asked Gorton to turn off the recorder; he refused, and then followed her across the room, "right on my footsteps, right in back of me and almost on top of me, in fact." Mrs. Stoyan said she then turned and attempted to switch the tape recorder off. Gorton, she said, grabbed her wrist and twisted it, shoving her against a nearby table. She attempted to break Gorton's hold on her by using a cane which Gorton carried on his arm. Mrs. Stoyan later went to the East Nassau Medical Center and had a bandage put on her arm.

Gorton, for his part, denied any arm twisting or pushing, claiming he was only trying to protect his tape recorder from confiscation.

Judge Julius R. Lippman, after hearing Mrs. Stoyan's story, signed a warrant for Gorton's arrest on a third-degree assault charge. A detective searched for him all day in vain, with no one, including his wife, admitting to knowledge of his whereabouts. On the following morning, August 16, he surrendered and was arrested, charged, and released on $500 bail. If convicted, Gorton could get a maximum sentence of one year in jail and a $500 fine.

With Gorton's trial coming up in a few days, the library board can probably count on their Bircher trustee losing at least some of the support he may have picked up from responsible citizens. The town's two weeklies, by the time of the third—and successful—budget election, had already swung from consideration of Gorton as a possible truthseeker and underdog to realization that real damage might be done by opposition to the library budget. Support is also rallying in other quarters.

The Friends group, never more than 60 strong, now numbers over 250, and it's in a fighting mood. High school students, at the height of the furor over the *Paris Review* article, demonstrated against Gorton at the library with a "study-in" led by their Student Council president and president-elect.

Religious and educational leaders in the community have continued to back the library strenuously, and groups outside the community have offered support. Among these were a group of eight library directors from neighboring towns, who published a statement; the Jewish War Veterans, who offered valuable advice on Birch Society tactics; and the local county chapter of the American Civil Liberties Union, which issued a statement condemning Gorton's actions.

In the long run—the "very long run"—says library director Orrin Dow, the library will benefit from the struggle. But in the meantime, the library, its staff, and its services, may well suffer from Gorton's attacks.

Support from outside the community is heartening to both librarians and trustees, but they recognize that the battle will be won or lost on home grounds. The voters who are on the fence will not be influenced by out-of-towners, and it will take more than statements of support from civic leaders to sway them.

There are no miracle cures, but the library will intensify its efforts in public relations, to tell the library story and solicit active support. P. R. specialist Betty Rice, of the Nassau Library System, will help develop the library's newsletter, which is distributed to all homeowners in the school district, into a more effective medium. And those lower-income sections of town where Gorton may count on his best support will get more bookmobile service and programs designed to make them aware of what the library has to offer them. In these areas, the library will be stimulated to advance; but in others, there will probably be retreats, minor but real.

Among the less tangible results of having a Bircher on the board, continually searching for ways to discredit the library, will certainly be reluctance on the part of the library staff to take any chances. In book selection, this will almost surely cause second thoughts about purchasing books which will raise the obscenity issue afresh. Interestingly enough, however, books like *The Carpetbaggers* will not suffer; they are considered by Carl Gorton, at least, as all right for the library because there is a "public demand" for them. But *Lady Chatterley's Lover*, he has indicated, "should be restricted to an adult section." Similarly, readers under 18 will probably find their access to adult literature more conscientiously restricted. On June 13, library director Orrin B. Dow told the *Suffolk Sun* that the library had a long standing policy of restricting books such as Henry Miller's *Tropic of Cancer* to persons over 18. "We recognize that there are books that are suitable for youths and others that are suitable for adults," he said, "and if any youth tried to get out of here with an adult book he would be stopped by the librarian at the desk."

Experimentation with new programs or new methods will be much less attractive when an unsuccessful experiement can lead to damaging publicity. And new programs such as increased service to Farmingdale's ghetto areas will be approached more cautiously than ever before, for fear of arousing racial tensions among the predominantly white population.

On Tuesday, September 12, 1967, *LJ* looked in on a meeting of the Farmingdale library trustees. From his entrance ten minutes after the opening of the meeting, until adjournment well after midnight, Gorton attacked the purchase of materials from the Center for Study of Democratic Institutions, the printing and dissemination of library publicity materials, an increase in pay for pages, salary increases for other staff members, and proposed attendance of staff members at professional meetings.

His recommendations included the installation of time clocks in the library, an increase of five hours in the staff workweek (from 35 to 40 hours), and a cut in staff salaries.

Gorton abstained from voting on proposals to open the library on Sundays, and to pay for some minor remodeling out of fine money. About ten people in the audience of 75 were Gorton supporters; one attacked the number of copies of the *Passover Plot* which the library had bought (his figures were inaccurate), and demanded to know why all Birch Society publications donated to the library had not been shelved.

The score for the evening seemed to be heavily in favor of the trustees, who conceded only one point to Gorton: that staff members attending conferences be required to submit written reports within 60 days of attendance. But the pattern for the months to come was clear to see: obstructionism on every possible point, and personal attacks on his critics. The latest of these attacks was made during the meeting, when he called one of the pages, who had criticized him in a letter to a local newspaper, "a liar," yet refused to explain his use of the term.

CHAPTER

50 *Courage and Cowardice*

(FEBRUARY 1, 1963)

by EDWIN CASTAGNA

One day several years ago in the Long Beach Public Library in California where I was City Librarian, a deeply disturbed woman came into my office. She was troubled about a book. It was *The Extraordinary Mr. Morris* by Howard Swiggett. She claimed to be a descendant of Gouverneur Morris, the subject, and she wanted the book removed from the library. She said it told terrible things about her ancestor, and it made him and some of the other Founding Fathers of the Republic look very bad.

I explained the library's book selection policy to her and told her that the book, like all titles in the library, had been selected by the staff after careful consideration, and that it was the work of a qualified author, published by a reputable publisher. This explanation made no impression. My caller said she would report me to her organization, the Daughters of the American Revolution, and to the City Manager, my boss. I agreed this was her right as a citizen, and I urged her to make whatever complaints she thought she should. Feeling I now had a grace period before the blow fell, I got the book from the stacks.

Often I find myself indebted to people who object to books, because I usually read them. I realize I am placing myself in danger of corruption and depravity. But I take the chance. I have a great curiosity about just why people object to certain books. And I always try to look at whatever is controversial.

In this case I was deeply indebted indeed, because *The Extraordinary Mr. Morris* was most remarkable by any standards. As a wealthy man, one of the youngest and most influential members of the Continental Congress, as Minister to France during the Terror, he was a gentleman patriot who lived it up in true 18th century style. But as I read I could see why his descendant seemed so disturbed. She was something out of Grant Wood, thin-lipped, prim, severe, distrustful. Along with his official responsibilities, Gouverneur Morris was a favorite in the boudoir of at least one bewitching French woman. And he tells about his amorous adventures with loving care. In addition to these fascinating details the book tells of Morris's association with George Washington, Jefferson, Monroe, the French Leaders, and other great men of the age. All in all, it seemed a book to make one proud to be an American. It filled me with admiration for this man who was so full of life, and got so much out of it, while representing his country with skill and devotion during a dangerous time.

One of the most extraordinary things about the incident was that the book is based largely upon Gouverneur Morris's own diaries. And the most scandalous incidents, if you consider the Paris exploits scandalous, are given in Morris's own words. With this much information pleasantly acquired, I waited for what might happen next.

What happened was that the unhappy descendant of the Revolutionary hero showed up again madder than ever. And she took a turn for the worse when I told her I had read the book and was grateful to her for having led me to it. I pointed out that it was largely the words of her own ancestor, and that after all he was only doing what was expected of a man of his time and place, and if he were *my* ancestor, I would be very proud indeed, and not want to suppress information about him. If I thought this would in any way mollify the complaining taxpayer, I was dead wrong. She still objected to the book in the library, and left with vague threats of action against a public servant so obviously unqualified and blind to his plain duty. But I never heard from her again.

This experience was not an isolated one. Like most librarians, I expect to be criticized, now and then, because of books bought with public funds under my direction. I have received anonymous notes telling me off for being perverted and subverted. I have been scarified for showing old Charlie Chaplin movies. Breakfast has been spoiled for me by letters to the editor saying I was an unfit person to be in charge of a library. And I have met with more irate, self-designated patriots than I care to remember.

In this incident of *The Extraordinary Mr. Morris*, we can see some of the characteristic approaches and behavior of censors.

1. *A threatening attitude.* They usually try to put the fear of the Lord into you right at the start. And you can see yourself up to your ears in trouble before you can turn a hand.

2. *Belief in personal superiority.* I have never met a censor who thought he was hurt by what he wanted suppressed. But he was convinced others would be gravely injured.

3. *Absolute lack of a sense of humor.* I wonder sometimes how censors can stay alive and be so grim. Laughter to them is a foreign language. A witticism is an indication of treason.

4. *Making the part stand for the whole.* The censor often gets the jump on everybody else by suggesting past questionable associations of an author.

Another favorite device is to point to a supposed subversive phrase or a dirty word here and there that everybody knows anyway. And he tries to make it seem that these often incidental factors are true for the whole book.

5. *The desire to conceal something even if it is true.* Do they see themselves? Some of their own suppressed desires?

6. *Lack of knowledge of literature.* Often censors are incredibly ignorant, without the slightest understanding of the creative mind.

7. *No understanding of history.* Censors don't realize that their game is one of the oldest and most unsuccessful in the world.

8. *No belief in freedom of expression.* Censors usually ride roughshod over the best intellectual traditions of the Western world, the Constitution and the Bill of Rights.

9. *A tendency to bypass and disregard well-established policies and procedures.* Along with their unwillingness to face the facts of history, censors generally don't like to be confronted with obstacles in the way of policies, regulations, and well-established practices.

All librarians with experience are familiar with these tactics and tendencies of the enemies of books.

What happens in libraries is only one chapter in the long history of the attempt of some people to silence some others. In all times and all places of which we have historical knowledge the urge to suppress "dangerous thoughts" has been present. It is an ancient virus that comes back with undiminished virulence after every outbreak has apparently been stamped out. All educated people know that just about every classic, including Homer, Socrates, the Greek dramatists, the Bible, Chaucer, Shakespeare, Mark Twain, Walt Whitman, the Nobel prize winners—O'Neill, Faulkner, Hemingway and Steinbeck—have been expurgated, mutilated, suppressed and censored. And the action has been taken by officials of church and state, by all kinds of groups, and individuals, for just about every reason you could name: corrupting the young, heresy, criticism of officials, erroneous political ideas, scientific discoveries made before their time, and sex, that old favorite and perennial bugaboo.

There have been talented and energetic censors in every age. But my favorite is Shi Huang Ti, who wanted to be known as the first emperor of China. His adviser, Li Ssu, told him how he could bring this about. Li Ssu's advice was as follows:

> Your servant suggests that all books in the bureau of history, save the records of Ch'in, he burned; that all persons in the empire, save those who hold a function under the control of the bureau of the scholars of wide learning, daring to store the Shih, and Shu, and the discussions of the various philosophers, should destroy them with the remission of all penalty.
>
> Those who have not burned them within thirty days after the issuing of the order are to be branded and sent to do forced labor. Books not to be destroyed are those on medicine and pharmacy, divination by the tortoise and milfoil, and agriculture and arboriculture. As for persons who wish to study the laws and ordinances, let them take the officials as their teachers.

The order was issued and a good many books were burned. And, according to some authorities, 460 scholars were also buried alive, "in pits specially dug for the purpose."

The case of Shi Huang Ti is interesting for several reasons. Observe the advice to those who wish to study the laws and ordinances: "let them take the officials as their teachers." Doesn't this sound something like Senator McCarthy during his heyday?

But the most noteworthy thing, it seems to me, about the first emperor, is that he failed, as all censors fail. Robert Frost has written, "Something there is that doesn't like a wall." History shows there is something that likes books. In China not all scholars were willing to throw their precious books into the imperial bonfire. Some hid them in walls and in holes. So the ancient writings were not entirely destroyed and the people of China, after things quieted down, found they were not limited to divining by the tortoise and milfoil, to observing their officials to learn correct behavior, but could learn from history if they would. And these brave scholars and librarians of ancient China, like their courageous successors in every age and place, showed that the censor's role is not an easy one. He is always dealing with a force greater than his own—the force of free minds, unwilling to be silenced.

During our own times librarians, individually and in groups, have been among the most vigorous defenders of the right of access for all people to books they want to read. The names of Robert Downs, Everett Moore, David Clift, Leon Carnovsky, Ruth Brown and others will go down in library history as stout and astute champions of the right to read. We are especially indebted to Eric Moon and John Wakeman, the courageous editors of the LIBRARY JOURNAL and the *Wilson Library Bulletin* who, while they may have ruffled some feathers with their constant concern for library freedom, have been a healthy influence. Along with them, Dan Melcher of the Bowker Company has stubbornly defended freedom of expression. And dozens, perhaps hundreds, of librarians all over the country have placed themselves in jeopardy because they believed there are some things more important than keeping your job. It is encouraging that in almost every case where they have stood up to censors, librarians have won the fight for freedom. They have also gained the respect and admiration of the citizens they serve, by keeping one person or a small group from dictating what a large community shall read.

In defending the freedom of expression, about the worst thing that has happened to any of our librarians is that they have lost their jobs. That's bad enough. But none to my knowledge have yet been buried in "pits dug specially for the purpose."

One of the accomplishments in which American librarians can take pride is the Library Bill of Rights. This statement, an historic document in the history of intellectual freedom, is in the tradition of the Constitution and the Bill of Rights.

The Library Bill of Rights is sometimes displayed, and usually on file, in libraries. But not often enough is it read and pondered. It is strong stuff.

Another landmark in the struggle for intellectual freedom is the "Freedom to Read" statement developed by the American Library Association and the American Book Publishers' Council. This noble document is a useful instrument for anyone faced with a censorship problem because of its clarity, obvious common sense and its patient tone.

Even with such courageous examples before them, and with strong instruments like the Library Bill of Rights and the "Freedom to Read" statement available for use, all too often librarians still fold up under attack. We have too many cases in which librarians have rolled over and played dead the first minute they even heard about possible criticism of a book. Marjorie Fiske in her *Book Selection and Censorship,* possibly the most carefully researched study of public and school librarians, found that a great proportion of censorship is self-censorship by librarians who don't want any trouble. The virus is in all of us and it can come to life at any time. The Fiske study was made in California and deals with California librarians. But the findings are generally applicable to public librarians throughout the country. I have seen librarians squirm and angrily deny and denounce the findings in the Fiske book. Some of the loudest and most outraged were the guiltiest. And just a while ago I had unhappy confirmation of this tendency of librarians themselves to suppress, when I was asked to eliminate a quotation from *Book Selection and Censorship,* in a chapter on a book on public libraries I was invited to write.

Having served as chairman of the advisory committee connected with the Fiske study, I am convinced we still have a lot of work in stiffening the backs of librarians in all the towns across the country, where many of them are apparently shivering in their boots at the very thought of controversy, which they should be among the first to welcome. If the public library is not a place for the dissenting, the heretical, the unorthodox, the critical, for offbeat books with ideas not likely to be found in the mass media, it is not the right kind of place. If the public library does not aggressively seek out and make readily available this kind of material, distasteful as it often is, it is not serving its function. The public librarian who doesn't get in a jam now and then by sticking his neck out, is probably short-changing the taxpayers, who hire him for his intellectual leadership as well as for his technical knowledge. The cautious librarians will be forgotten soon. And their caution will be expensive because it will impoverish rather than enrich the intellectual life of the community.

GATHERING SOUR FRUITS

For some time now the public libraries of the country have been gathering the sour fruits of the literary plantings of Henry Miller. From Maryland to California, there have been raids on bookstores and newsstands by illiterates wearing badges, sent on their pathetic missions by idiots. There have been court cases, decisions made and reversed, suits against libraries and librarians, actions courageous and cowardly by library trustees and librarians. The rash began, of course, when the Grove Press published the *Tropic of Cancer.* This sex-soaked book, you all know by now, because of censors, is based on the middle-aged experiences of an expatriate who, like Gauguin, fled from dull respectability, but unlike Gauguin, ran to Paris instead of from it. He now lives like a serene Oriental sage at Big Sur in California. But he has the library world in an uproar. It is revealing to observe the responses of librarians to the hysterical individuals and groups who have so little faith in our people that they think a book or two will ruin us all.

We are also concerned, whether we live in the Deep South or not, with free access to public libraries by all citizens. It would be ludicrous, if it were not so sad, to see pictures of a library in which all the chairs and tables had been removed so that there should be no contamination of one race by another through their sitting down together. I've always been puzzled that it seems appropriate to those who believe in white superiority for Negro and white to stand and, in some cases, to lie together, but terribly wrong to sit down together. But let us not forget that we have had in many southern cities, brave efforts by Negroes and their friends to achieve the rights spelled out in the Library Bill of Rights. They need our understanding and our help, insofar as we can reach across the great chasm that divides our country and our libraries.

It is a never-ending battle, this battle for free access to books and libraries. It will go on as long as we have freedom of expression for all, those who write their opinions down and those who oppose them. It is a fight we should take upon ourselves with determination even if we cannot do it cheerfully. And we must be honest enough to look within ourselves as well as in others for the negative forces of suppression. If we sometimes get discouraged, let us remember that when we no longer have conflict over ideas, we will no longer have freedom. And if it's too hot in the library we can always get a cool, quiet job some place where people don't get worked up about books and ideas.

Fortunately, censors suggest effective responses by their own behavior. If they threaten, we can stand firm. The bully usually backs up if he can't shout you down. Since censors are convinced of their personal superiority and worried about the danger in reading to everyone but themselves, we have only to ask several questions to show them up. What is the evidence of their personal superiority? And how can they show that anyone will be damaged by reading something that has not debased the censor? Where has it happened?

Having no sense of humor is a serious disadvantage to any antagonist. People who don't realize how ridiculous and over-solemn they are, become easy targets. When *The Rabbit's Wedding* was found to be threatening the sovereign state of Alabama because it showed the mingling of white and black rabbits, the obvious observation that this was splitting hares did a lot to clear the air. To the group in Downey, California, which found the Tarzan books offensive because the ape man and Jane were thought not to have been properly married, one need only reply that since Jane was from Baltimore and the daughter of a clergyman, she could not possibly have been involved in anything that was not on a high moral plane.

CLUMSY SLEIGHT-OF-HAND

The attempt to make the part stand for the whole by pointing out a questionable phrase, a bad word or the author's past is a rather clumsy attempt at sleight-of-hand. The proper response, of course, is to show that it is the whole book that counts and not just one of its parts. And the high courts of the country appear to back up this view.

It is not really in the American tradition to hide things and blink at facts. People who attempt concealment of awkward ideas are usually themselves embarrassed when their ugly work is shown up for what it is. Here the bright light of publicity can be helpful. And usually the press is glad to help out. They know their ox is going to be gored next.

For lack of knowledge of literature there is no cure but good reading. That's our main business, and we should be about it as aggressively as we can so that the active ignoramuses will become an even smaller minority than they are now. The same is true for the lack of understanding of history. Articles and exhibits about censorship, displaying the great books that have been banned will show censorship in its true light.

For those who do not believe in freedom of expression, pity may be the best response. However, pity is passive and we are called upon to act. We must stubbornly fulfill our role as guardians of freedom of expression by never knuckling under to attempted tyranny over the mind of man. The tendency to bypass established policies and procedures is easily countered. When anybody tries to give me a fast shuffle, I tend to become very technical. I ask for complaints in writing. I like to find out just who is protesting. Is it one person or a group? What group? Just who belongs? Since these tactics are well known and ready to be used, we have a great advantage.

All of you can probably think of other effective defenses against censorship or pressure. Recent library literature is full of inspiring examples of protection of the right to read. One of the most constructive things any library can do, of course, is to adopt the Library Bill of Rights as its official policy, or incorporate its substance in the library's statement of objectives and policies.

There will always be more questions than answers in the pressure problem. The public library is subject to popular control. But it is also under direction of professional experts. Here is a built-in guarantee of conflict. How do we bridge this gap between the people who own the place, like the extraordinary Mr. Morris's troubled descendant, and those who run it? Or maybe a better question is, "Can we bridge the gap?"

It would be nice to have a neat wrap-up: a sure-fire solution to be used in all cases. I wish I could offer Castagna's sovereign remedy to relieve pressure on libraries. I'd call it "The Quickest Way with Censors." But I am neither brash nor wise enough to give a pat answer. It is easy, however, to make a prediction. The value of our libraries as democratic institutions will depend upon how bold we are as librarians in shouldering responsibility our fellow citizens place upon us. The degree of courage we display in the face of cowardly tendencies outside and within us will be the measure of our worth as librarians.

51 Censors and Their Tactics

(DECEMBER 15, 1963)

by JACK NELSON

Shortly after the Civil War, a New York publisher advertised "Books prepared for Southern schools by Southern authors, and therefore free from matter offensive to Southern people."

But times have changed, or have they? Regional texts have given way to books competing for a national market, so now the trick is to offend as few people as possible. The result is that many books lack vitality and controversial subjects are treated superficially or not at all.

Textbook publishers do not avoid information about controversial subjects because they believe this is the best way to promote education. They do it because in some cases it is not just the best way, but the only way, they can sell their products.

The publishers face a dilemma. Every time they show the courage to explore controversial subjects in depth, they risk economic setbacks caused by censorship forces. Even relatively minor matters can cost them sales. For example, in Bastrop, La., the school board, learning that the Macmillan Company planned a new line of readers in 1965 which would ignore an old taboo and show white and Negro children playing together, banned the books and urged the rest of the state to do likewise.

NO MATTER HOW YOU SLICE IT, IT'S STILL CENSORSHIP

In our research for *The Censors and the Schools,* Gene Roberts and I found that the pressures for the elimination or censorship of "unpleasant" ideas or facts often come from diametrically opposed forces.

This has been a big factor in the treatment of the Negroes' plight. On the one hand, segregationists clamor to keep out of books pictures of Negroes and whites together, or any mention of an integrated society. On the other hand, the National Association for the Advancement of Colored People has demanded that facts it considers objectionable be excluded from books. As the NAACP has said, the outstanding accomplishments of many Negroes should be dealt with factually and truthfully in school books. But the plight of a majority of Negroes, the discrimination they still face, also should be told, with all the "unpleasant" facts included.

Are we to alter or ban American classics in literature because they contain Negro stereotypes? Or are we to teach them in the context and times in which they were written? After NAACP pressure, the New York City Board of Education dropped Mark Twain's *Huckleberry Finn* as a reading text in elementary and junior high schools, because of a central character in the classic, "Miss Watson's big nigger, named Jim."

In the words of the New York *Times*, "The truth is that *Huckleberry Finn* is one of the deadliest satires that was ever written on some of the nonsense that goes with inequality of the races.

"What happens when Huck's conscience begins to trouble him about running off with another person's slave? Huck decides that if he doesn't undo this crime by letting Miss Watson know where Jim is, he will go to hell. But then he gets to 'thinking over the trip down the river; and I see Jim before me all the time; in the day and in the night time, sometimes moonlight, sometimes storms, and we afloating along talking and singing and laughing . . . and how good he always was.' So Huck tears up the note he was going to send to Miss Watson and then says to himself 'all right, then I'll go to hell.' "

There is too much emphasis today on deleting from a student's experiences, rather than on expanding them. There is justification for pressure to expand the selection of books in school libraries and to include more facts in school books. There is no justification for attempts to ban books and to eliminate facts because they do not conform to some group's ideas about minority group interests, Americanism, or whatnot.

RIGHTWING CENSORS HAVE THE LEAD

While the NAACP and, on occasion, other minority interest groups have campaigned for censorship of books, by far the greatest pressure today emanates from rightwing sources, and is based on political ideology. Unlike the NAACP and other crusading organizations which, for the most part, work independently of each other, the rightwing groups distribute each other's propaganda and carry out concerted campaigns.

In San Antonio, Texas, in 1962, a legislative committee investigating school books for "subversive" contents heard from a score of witnesses armed with propaganda which had originated in Washington, D.C. and at least six different states—from the Watch Washington Club (Columbus, Ohio), the Teacher Publishing Co. (Dallas, Texas), America's Future (New Rochelle,

N.Y.), the Independent American (New Orleans, La.), the Church League of America (Wheaton, Ill.), and Education Information, Inc. (Fullerton, Calif.). Not long before the Texas hearing, materials from these same sources, plus literature from the Daughters of the American Revolution, the Parents for Better Education in California, the Coalition of Patriotic Societies in Florida, and other groups, were used in an attack on books in Meriden, Connecticut.

While some of these groups have different axes to grind, they all find a common cause in the Communist menace as a domestic threat, so that you find a Southern segregationist juxtaposed with a Northern industrialist in a campaign for censorship. A segregationist equates integration with Communism and obligingly includes in the same category the income tax, social security, organized labor and other irritants of the ultraconservatives. An industrialist sees a Red hand in federal taxes and control of industry and business, and he obligingly ascribes the same danger to the Supreme Court decision outlawing segregation. You find a physician worried about socialized medicine, a minister troubled by "obscenities," and ordinary citizens concerned about the patriotism of other citizens. And they all blame it on Communism and together put up a solid front for their demands to censor and ban texts and library books.

One day last year a reporter investigating the activities of censorship groups in Texas called on a news service bureau at the state capital to ask what it had on file on J. Evetts Haley, leader of a militant rightwing organization called Texans for America. The blasé answer was, "Nothing. You can't take Haley seriously. He's not worth keeping a file on." Yet Haley and his Texans for America led successful censorship campaigns against texts and school library books, and helped spark a legislative investigation that turned into a witch-hunt.

Like the news service bureau, most of the Texas press gave Haley relatively little attention. Perhaps they thought a man who publicly advocated "hanging" Chief Justice Earl Warren and smeared Southern Methodist University as "being tainted with left-wingers" should not be taken seriously.

Whatever the reason for the scant attention given to the Haleyites and others who have clamored for censorship, the result has been that well organized forces attacking books in Texas have operated with little organized opposition, free of public scrutiny. And they have forced alterations in many textbooks, the banning of others, and the banning of many school library volumes.

In many other states the same thing has happened to some degree in recent years. During the past five years, school books have come under fire in nearly a third of the state legislatures.

THE PRESS PLAYS IT COOL
OR SOMETIMES PLAYS ALONG

Unfortunately, some newspapers have editorially acquiesced in, and even supported, some of the book censorship campaigns. When Amarillo (Texas) College and four Amarillo high schools withdrew from libraries 10 novels including four Pulitzer Prize winners, the Amarillo *News-Globe* lauded the move in a front-page editorial and proclaimed its own guide for censorship: " . . . sentences too foul to print in the *News-Globe* are too foul for school libraries."

The Los Angeles (Calif.) *Herald and Express* (now the *Herald-Examiner*), in a series of articles opposing the adoption of 13 school books, warned that many phrases and terms were un-American and pro-Communist. It even found a subversive music book in which a song, "Swing the Shining Sickle," which it called "a ditty from behind the Iron Curtain," was found to have replaced, of all things, "God Bless America," in the new edition of the book! The truth was that the song had been composed in 1897 as an American harvest song relating to Thanksgiving.

The Jacksonville (Ala.) *News,* supporting the DAR's current book-banning campaign in Alabama, printed an editorial which, at first glance, I thought must be poking fun at the Daughters. The *News* noted that the DAR "exposes to Alabama parents a sample of socialism, first-grade style, which appears as a story in one of the basic first-grade readers . . . *The New Our New Friends* by Gray, published in 1956 by Scott Foresman." The *News* said the story, called "Ask for It," contains "an objectionable and destructive lesson" about a squirrel named Bobby who was not willing to work.

It seemed that Bobby watched a nut roll out of a birdhouse every time a redbird (the *News* set "redbird" in boldface type) would tap on the door. Bobby tried the redbird's trick and it worked and then, in the words of the story, he thought, "I know how to get my dinner. All I have to do is ask for it." The *News* was shocked. It very soberly asked its readers, "Have you ever heard or read about a more subtle way of undermining the American system of work and profit and replacing it with a collectivist welfare system? Can you recall a socialistic idea more seductively presented to an innocent child?"

A LITTLE CENSORSHIP GOES A LONG WAY

I have cited a few specific examples of censorship campaigns to illustrate the scope of the censorship problems in schools, which the public still fails to recognize. No state escapes the effects of attacks on school books. When censors in Mississippi force a publisher to alter a textbook, that book is sold, as altered, in Missouri and other states.

Last year the Texas State Textbook Committee told a publishing firm it could not market its history book in Texas schools if it did not drop Vera Micheles Dean's name from a supplementary reading list. The publisher agreed to this forced censorship and commented, "Imagine objecting to Vera Dean. But in a case like this, we will have to sacrifice her name in all books. It would be too expensive to make a special edition just for Texas."

Publishers have also deleted references to other authors in order to compete in the big Texas textbook market, and one publishing firm went so far as to say it was "not only willing but anxious to delete any references" to the names of authors whose loyalty might be successfully questioned by the Texans for America.

FIGHTING BACK

In many parts of the country, teachers and school librarians have felt the direct sting of censorship attacks. Gene Roberts and I found that in most cases where teachers and librarians fought back and the press adequately covered the controversy, censorship efforts were thwarted. The same is true, of course, in textbook battles; censors score their most notable successes when they operate with little public exposure.

In Georgia recently a high school teacher was dismissed for making available to his students John Hersey's wartime novel, *A Bell for Adano*. The press gave the matter full coverage, and the teacher fought back. John Hersey was interviewed and was quoted as saying the teacher "has been done a grave injustice by self-appointed censors of the type who are not interested in what a book tries to say as a whole, but are only interested in words taken out of context."

In a page-one column in the Atlanta *Constitution*, publisher Ralph McGill, defending the teacher and the book, wrote in part:

"It is likely the average adult mind, preoccupied with its own guilts and memories of childhood, tends to over-protect to the point of absurdity. High school students never have been and certainly are not in our time unaware of the words, deeds, stupidities, weaknesses, and shabbiness of their communities. They know these as they know those in the community whom they regard as admirable, honest and trustworthy. They know the phonies and they know the whispered gossip. So, lucky is the youngster who has a teacher who tries to interest young minds in reading well written books by established writers— rather than leaving them with no values and direction at all and, therefore, prey to the pornographic and the suggestive."

The issue of Hersey's book and the Georgia teacher was debated editorially and at education meetings. The teacher was reinstated.

A newspaper survey showed that, unfortunately, school librarians in three other Georgia cities removed the book from their shelves to avoid possible criticism during the controversy. And one public librarian said she had not withdrawn the book, but added, "I've put it in a special place and haven't told anyone about it. Isn't that a good way to handle it?" However, librarians, educators and the press did overwhelmingly defend the book, and those who removed it have now returned it to the library shelves.

The point is that in our pursuit of the truth we need to operate with full exposure. Too often a librarian or a teacher quietly discontinues the use of a book—or never begins the use of it—because of pressure. Those who exert these pressures, and who are in fact perverting freedom of the press, would wilt under public scrutiny.

WHAT IS BEHIND RIGHTWING ATTACKS?

Today's pattern of rightwing censorship activities—much of it aimed at library volumes as well as textbooks—evolved after World War II, as much of the country began to drift away from New Deal principles. The critics began to cry collectivism and Communism if they discerned statements which in any way could be twisted or distorted by interpretation into favorable disposition of TVA, socialized medicine, FEPC legislation, the United Nations or other such topics.

The dominant forces that bring this pressure today include the DAR, the John Birch Society, the New Rochelle-based America's Future, and many smaller groups. These organizations, through pressure, have managed to force restrictions on what students may read. And the public still is largely apathetic about such pressure.

The DAR, which regularly mails out a list of almost 170 textbooks it has determined to be "subversive," operates as a respectable patriotic organization whose own values seldom are publicly examined. In 1959, when the DAR first began mailing out its incredible blacklist of books, the American Library Association's *Newsletter on Intellectual Freedom* (Dec. '59) warned of censorship activities and declared, "Of all the programs by organized groups, the DAR textbook investigation, at both the state and national level, was the most specific . . . and the most threatening."

The Daughters' attacks on books need to be evaluated in light of their constant concern about Communist infiltration in religion, mental health programs, public schools and colleges, the Federal Government, metropolitan government, urban renewal, Christmas cards, and all international activities including cultural exchange. It should also be taken into account that the DAR circulates a long list of literature from other ultraconservative groups attacking fluoridation, the U.S. Supreme Court, the Peace Corps, immigration, the UN, the National Council of Churches, the public school system, the National Education Association, and other aspects of American life.

PUTTING THE PRESSURE IN PERSPECTIVE

Pressure groups are an integral part of our society and I am not suggesting that any steps be taken—even if such were possible—to restrict their censorship activities. But these groups and their charges need to be put in perspective for the public.

When, for example, America's Future literature is used in an attack on school books, it is important for the public to know of this organization's fears that the public school system, not just textbooks, is purposely subverting the nation's youth. An official of that organization has written:

"No one who has watched closely what has been going on in our public school system in America these past two decades can escape the feeling that something drastic—and rather terrible—has happened to it. What is more, it is rather difficult to believe that it has happened by accident, that there has not been a planned, slyly executed, and almost successful attempt to deliberately undereducate our children in order to make them into an unquestioning mass who would follow meekly those who wish to turn the American Republic into a socialistic society."

Now any group is entitled to harbor such fears about this country's schools, and even to use such fears as the basis for attacks on books. But the public, in evaluating these attacks, also should be aware of their basis in order to determine whether the group is judging a book on its merits or on the basis of its own fears and prejudices.

I suggest it is important for students themselves—those in elementary and high schools as well as in colleges—to be educated to the threats against unfettered reading. Those who fear that American youths are not capable of judging for themselves what is right and what is wrong condemn the very system they profess to support.

CHAPTER

52 *The Crucial Battle for the Minds of Men*

(JUNE 1, 1965)

by H. WILLIAM AXFORD

Testifying before the Senate Foreign Relations Committee in July, 1965, Carl T. Rowan, director of the United States Information Agency, eloquently described his agency's function as that of projecting the foreign policy interests of the United States in such a manner that "No man chooses tyranny because we have defaulted in telling freedom's story."[1] Mr. Rowan went on to say that he had undertaken a zealous campaign to ensure that every foot of film, every minute of broadcasting, every stick of type that is set, goes to portray this country's strength, its dedication to human freedom, its social progress, its economic vitality, its belief in the rule of law—and most of all the yearning for world peace that guides its every effort.[2]

Occupying a central role in the USIA's activities are its 178 overseas libraries and 70 reading rooms onto whose shelves each year flow more than 200,000 volumes, each of which presumably meets the strict selection standards described by Mr. Rowan. These libraries and reading rooms represent a tremendous propaganda effort in the best sense of that word—an attempt to present American life, American culture, and American goals in such a manner as to create, on the part of others, understanding and sympathy.

While he was quite explicit in describing the type of materials he wanted for the overseas libraries of the USIA, Mr. Rowan, in this testimony, was never forced to answer the crucial question of interest to citizens in general and librarians in particular: By whom and by what processes are the books selected for shipment to the overseas libraries? Those to whom a book burning is an indelible event will remember that it was this very question, "who selects the propaganda?," which was at the center of the storm that engulfed the overseas libraries of the USIA in the early 1950's at the height of the late Senator McCarthy's career.

As this tragic event was building to its climax, William C. Haygood, formerly director of the United States Information Libraries in Spain, pointed out that it was professional librarians who did the book selection for the USIA libraries, people "highly trained in the art of relating books to people and in selecting books in such a manner that the end product may be, in competent hands, a resilient, many-sided teaching instrument of great value."[3] Mr. Haygood goes on to note that the number of librarians involved in the book selection process is only a "handful of overworked, underpaid, completely devoted people," who must select from the enormous volume of current literature 25 to 100 titles a month for the list of recommended publications. In addition to being able to select materials from this cumulative list, the librarians in the field were "allowed a certain amount of latitude in the purchase of locally published translations of books by Americans or about Americans. . . ."[4]

Although the selection process was centralized in Washington, it seems to be true that the USIA overseas libraries at the time of the McCarthy attacks were reasonable facsimiles of the good small or medium sized American public library, containing a broad range of books and other materials carefully chosen according to content and, in most respects, representing the best in American literary and journalistic output. With the basic selection policy being that characterized by an open society, and the selecting being done by professional librarians, the propaganda on the shelves of the overseas libraries did present a positive image of America as a country where freedom was more than a word.

Under Senator McCarthy's assault, however, which began early in 1952, the basic book selection policy for the USIA libraries was to change from one reflecting fundamental American belief in intellectual freedom to one of rigid censorship, reflecting the widespread paranoia affecting American society in the early 1950's. The story of how this came about is a long, complicated, and tragic one, but also an instructive one and its highlights are worth repeating.

Dr. Wilson Compton, director of the International Information Agency, as USIA was called at the time he was director, recalls that it was about mid-1952 that the question of controversial writers began to get some attention with respect to the overseas libraries.[5] Under questioning by Senator Fulbright of Arkansas, Dr. Compton defined controversial writers as those whose loyalty was suspect. Two committees were given the task of studying the problem, the Advisory Commission on Educational Exchange and the Advisory Committee on Books Abroad. These committees presented a recommendation, subsequently rejected by Dr. Compton, that content alone, not authorship, should be the sole criterion for selection. Dr. Compton gave his reasons for this action as follows:

> Now, frankly, I did not buy that one. I said that there were . . . some persons who, however talented they may be and however good writing they are capable of, have flaunted their odd views of their own country in the faces of their fellow men overseas to such an extent that it seems to me it is just inconceivable

that the government of the United States would ever, regardless of quality of writing, put productions of such persons into its libraries overseas or put them on the air through the Voice of America.

Dr. Compton's stand led to the publication of a directive dated February 3, 1953, which contained the following instructions for selecting books for the overseas libraries.

In the selection of materials, writings, art, photographs, films, et cetera, it should be possible as a general rule to draw upon the great body of resources available produced by persons whose *ideological position* (italics mine) is unquestioned, . . .

There were to be exceptions to this general rule and they were as follows:

Materials produced by a person whose ideologies and views are questionable or controversial will not be used unless: a) the material supports importantly, not incidentally, a specific IIA objective, and the converse, i.e., none of the content is detrimental to the objectives of the United States Government; b) the material is substantially better than other material available for the purpose; c) failure to include the material would impair the general credibility of the IIA.

Under continued pressures from Senator McCarthy, this directive was rescinded without knowledge of the Director of IIA and a new one was issued by the State Department to IIA on February 19, 1953 which read, "No material by any Communists, fellow-travelers, et cetera, will be used under any circumstances." This directive caused such an uproar that it too was rescinded and a new one was issued in March, 1953 which permitted the use of "Communist material" solely to "expose Communist propaganda or expose Communist lies," but prohibited "the works of all Communist authors, and any publication which continually publishes Communist propaganda."[6]

It was under this directive and six others subsequently issued in the months immediately following that the program of removing books by offensive authors in the overseas libraries was carried in the summer and fall of 1953.[7] Here, it should be noted that in addition to avowed Communists, the blacklist of authors also covered invokers of the Fifth Amendment, persons convicted of crimes involving the security of the United States and another category never officially admitted but known as "additional data cases." The additional data referred to was any derogatory information which in one way or another reached the USIA Washington office.

This particular list fell into the hands of newsmen in the fall of 1954. Among the names on the list were those of Henry Seidel Canby, Aaron Copeland, Malcolm Cowle, Adolph Denn, Dorothy Canfield Fisher, Martha Foley, Julian Huxley, Saul K. Padover, Dorothy Parker, Frederick L. Schuman, Roger Sessions, Edgar Snow, and George Soule. At one time, the list also included the names of Ernest Hemingway and Henry David Thoreau, whose classic *Walden* was actually withdrawn, on the grounds that it was socialistic, from the expendable libraries which were being given to cultural institutions abroad.[8] The result of this kind of book selection program, aside from the American tragedy it represents, was that the monthly average for volumes shipped overseas in 1953 dropped from 119,913 to 341!

It is safe to say that the image of America being projected overseas was a very, very narrow one, to say the least, and one hardly designed to win the battle for men's minds. In an editorial in the *Saturday Review* at the height of the controversy, Norman Cousins recalled what an enormous weapon a book selection policy geared to intellectual freedom can be. He was participating in a radio debate in India in 1951. His opponent was an avowed Communist who believed that Howard Fast was the greatest living American novelist and that he was banned in his own country. Cousins recalled:

> I rather enjoyed the debate because of the ease with which my opponent could be refuted. The first question was a matter of opinion . . . As for the charge of "banning," its absurdity became apparent in the fact that Fast's writings were between book covers in an American library just around the corner.[9]

The McCarthy episode has passed, but like the lingering remains of a forest fire, its embers are constantly in danger of being fanned into flame by the winds of intolerance and man's fear of what the mind of man produces. Just how close we are to the early 1950's is revealed by the dialog below, reproduced from hearings on the USIA budget for fiscal 1965. The two men involved are Neal Smith, Representative from Iowa, and Andrew May, assistant director for Operations, USIA. The subject under discussion is the USIA program of presentation of copies of subscriptions to newspapers and magazines.

MR. SMITH: *I noticed on page 20 . . . a whole series totalling 857 copies of the* Reader's Digest. *Where would that go, all over the world?*

MR. MAY: *Yes, sir. The bulk of those . . . would go to our information center libraries. The next column indicates those that would go to our bilingual centers. The third column shows those that would be presented to foreign persons by the public relations officer.*

MR. SMITH: *These information libraries are supplied in the hope that citizens of that country will read them?*

MR. MAY: *Yes. That is in recognition of the fact that we have around 23 or 24 million people a year coming into those centers to read.*

MR. SMITH: *How are we going to profit from their reading some of these magazines on the list which specialize in exaggeration, sensationalism, in collecting anti-government information, materials, and articles, and criticizing our government?*

MR. MAY: *I think on the balance the* Reader's Digest *is quite a popular magazine abroad, and people are attracted to come in and read it.*

MR. SMITH: *They like to read things that criticize our government and the way it operates?*

MR. MAY: *I assume they read it for whatever attracts their interest. It has more than that in it.*

MR. SMITH: *Your purpose is to try and influence them to think that democracy is a good thing instead of being all bad?*

MR. MAY: *It is our purpose.*
MR. SMITH: *That is just the opposite, is it not?*
MR. MAY: *I do not follow you to that conclusion, sir.*[10]
The logic is a bit tortuous, but a not unfamiliar phenomenon.

Finally, it should be noted that the overworked staff of professional librarians responsible for book selection for the overseas libraries have been getting some help since 1963. In that year, and every year subsequently, USIA has signed a grant agreement with a nonprofit organization known as Operations and Policy Research, Inc. The amount of the grant has been $54,500 per year. Mr. Andrew May has stated the purpose of the grant as follows:

> The purpose of the contract is to obtain from them book reviews and condensations. We have on our staff book reviewers who review much of the output to arrive at a decision of whether to use a particular book in our program or not. We cannot have on our staff enough specialists to cover every field, so we work through this organization, which has specialists on every subject matter and they will provide us a review on a fee basis.[11]

The fee basis is rather interesting. The scale of charges is $30 per review for a book 200 pages or less; $35 for 201–300 pages; $40 for 301–400 pages; and $50 for anything over 400 pages. During the fiscal year 1963, Operations and Policy Research Inc. supplied USIA with 610 book reviews for a total charge of $52,869.24,[12] or an average of $86.60 per review. In his testimony before the house subcommittee, Mr. May stated that the average cost per review was $35. He arrived at this figure by dividing the number of reviews supplied in fiscal 1963 into $23,890, the actual amount charged to reviews in the final report submitted to USIA for fiscal 1963, and neglected to take into account the additional $29,682 charged basically to administrative costs ($8,800), and salaries ($18,500).[13]

This is an interesting bit of arithmetic, but even more interesting are such questions as these. Why must USIA use a special review service instead of those readily available? Does USIA have a list of criteria for reviewing books? What are these criteria? Finally, who are the experts who are doing the reviewing?

In order to find the answers, a direct inquiry was sent to the USIA. Reproduced below is the "official anonymous and 'cleared' response" to the question: Why does USIA pay $35 for book reviews from Operations & Policy Research Inc.? Why doesn't it use published reviews?

> Actually, USIA does both. For many of the books used by USIA published reviews suffice. For books central to the Agency's purposes and for books used extensively by the Agency, however, more is needed. In order to match books effectively with overseas readers having a variety of cultural and national backgrounds and to carry out the special purpose mission of USIA, it is necessary for the Agency to have, for about 3000 books a year, a fairly detailed description of the book's contents and an evaluation of the book's usefulness in terms of US foreign policy objectives. Most of this reviewing is done by the staff librarians of USIA, forming the basis for use of books in the overseas libraries, the translation programs, the textbook activities, book exhibits, book sales (with

the help of IMG), and in book discussion programs presented by the press, radio and TV services of the Agency.

Some 20 percent of the books so reviewed demand a degree of subject matter competence in certain fields beyond that possessed by our staff librarians. And just as a university librarian would turn to members of the university faculty for advice, so does USIA turn to Operations & Policy Research as its avenue to subject matter expertise. With OPR reviews in hand for about 600 books a year, the Agency can then make its evaluation of any book important to its news-oriented operations, often prior to publication and well in advance of reviews in the scholarly journals normally consulted for this type of information.

The above would appear to be a reasonable justification for the policy of contract book reviews, but not for the high cost of such services. Furthermore, there is some evidence that the effectiveness of the books which pass through the USIA selection process, either external or internal, in creating the desired image of America is not as great as it could be. Writing in the February 1965 issue of the *ALA Bulletin*, John Kenneth Galbraith, U.S. Ambassador to India, told of the following experience:

> When I went to New Delhi . . . we had there a collection of books which we presented as a contribution from the United States, to libraries, to scholars, and to notable people as a guide and help to their thinking. This, I suppose, was one of the most carefully screened collections of books that ever existed. They were all meant to persuade and in a completely safe way. They took an impeccable position on the American character, and morals, and they were stalwart in their view of the cold war. There was not a shadow of suspicion of procommunism. They were also uniformly unreadable.
>
> People who are easily persuaded, who are susceptible to this kind of book . . . are also very easily unpersuaded . . . This is the nature of the susceptible mind, and it will be asked what one has accomplished when one has persuaded these people.[14]

One might seriously question whether a collection such as the one described by Mr. Galbraith would be much of a weapon in the "crucial battle for the minds of men."

REFERENCES

1. US Government Printing Office. Hearings before the subcommittee of the committee on appropriations. US Senate. 88th Congress, Second Session. Part 2, p. 1847.
2. *Ibid.*
3. William C. Haygood, "Enclaves of America Overseas," *Saturday Review*, July 11, 1953, p. 33.
4. *Ibid.*
5. Until otherwise cited, this material is taken from the Hearings before a subcommittee of the committee on foreign relations, US Senate, 83rd Congress, 1st Session on overseas information programs of the United States. Part 2. US Government Printing Office, 1953, p. 388–89.
6. New York *Times*, March 19, 1953, pp. 1, 4.
7. For a country by country survey, and a partial list of authors involved, see New York *Times*, June 22, 1953, the whole of page 8.

8. *The Nation*, 179: 376–79, October 30, 1954.
9. Norman Cousins, "Open the Books," *Saturday Review*, 36: 31, July 11, 1953.
10. US Government Printing Office. Hearings before a subcommittee of the committee on appropriations. House of Representatives. 88th Congress, Second Session, p. 480.
11. *Ibid.*, p. 484.
12. *Ibid.*, p. 485. An unused balance of $1,630.24 was returned to the government at the end of the year.
13. *Ibid.*, p. 485.
14. *ALA Bulletin*, February 1965, p. 113.

CHAPTER

53 *The Hidden Persuaders*
in Book Selection

(SEPTEMBER 15, 1965)

by JEROME CUSHMAN

The emphasis that we place upon the triumvirate of a written book selection policy, the Library Bill of Rights, and the Freedom to Read Statement leads us to a sense of false security. Events in many communities, and they seem to be increasing, find too many libraries forced to abandon the philosophical position propounded by policy statements in the face of actualities that sometimes approach professional ignominy. Statements such as those developed by the library profession are hardly calculated to say Thou Shalt Not to rampaging un-freedom riders. It it true they have acted as a positive road block to censorship when the attempt was halfhearted, or upon occasion when library trustees developed some steel in their backs. A good book selection policy backed by the Library Bill of Rights and the Freedom to Read Statement has at times become an effective weapon in the cause of intellectual freedom. But like the Bill of Rights, the Library Bill of Rights is violated many times a day.

This will not be a discussion of censorship but rather that important and primary function of librarianship called book selection. However, where there is book selection, can the threat of censorship be far behind? There ought to be some studies made which show the direct relationship between censorship attempts and the protection actually provided by brave new words. We may be sure that a public library in its choice of books for purchase can choose to live dangerously or in blissful peace. Past issues of the *Newsletter on Intellectual Freedom* of the American Library Association attest to an amazing variety of offences to individual and group tastes perpetrated by librarians or their book selection committees. And when the righteous wrath of an offended patron is expended upon a staff member, it is little wonder that they do not occasionally become gun-shy as they examine the next group of books for purchase. The Fiske report opened our eyes, but we would be more startled if we knew about the hundreds, or maybe thousands, of unrecorded instances in which the very expectation of controversy affected the book selection process. There is reason to believe that time, present and future, will see an increase in opportunities for librarians to stand before humorless inquisitions from certain segments of the public which, at best question our professional judgment and, at worst, seek community improvement through our enforced and permanent absence.

It might be well, before going into some of the practical aspects of book selection, to reexamine some of the reasons for community jumpiness. There is a confrontation with people and their problems on a scale never before experienced by modern man. Satellite communication has provided us with an immediacy of these problems that shakes us up because we dimly recognize that as we see the problems, we are also involved in seeking the solutions. This bothers us because we do not know much about those people thousands of miles from us, but like the Ancient Mariner, they fix us with their eyes and they threaten our comfort and complacency.

Not only are people from across the world disturbing us by the mere fact that we can now see the hungry faces of their children, but individuals in our own cities and towns are assaulting our ears with loud and concentrated voices. The voices make demands. We doubt our country's ability to grant their requests. The insistence and the proximity of the voices have caught us off balance. We have not arrived at the calm reasoned view, which is apparent to anyone who has even an elementary understanding of our country, that not only is there enough for all, but that we can survive only if the bearers of those voices are enmeshed in the American social, educational, and economic destiny. We do not recognize this and we are disturbed.

Finally, the whirring, buzzing, beeping of electronic equipment serves as an example of that necessary progress which at the same time exacts the cost of depersonalization of the individual. The key to a comfortable life for all mankind lies in the use of tools of science and technology so evident today in North America and Europe, and hopefully, in the rest of the world tomorrow. The key to a valid life for the individual lies in the creative manner in which the inevitabilities of depersonalization are handled.

Book selection in the public library is intimately tied to the above considerations. The library, as never before, must serve as a vast information center for a public confronted by change which is occurring at dazzling speed. Information allays fear and uncertainties. The book is still a sacred vessel because of the imprint that it can make upon the mind of an individual. Its influence is virtually unmeasurable and yet has been at times in history a touchstone for the actions of millions of people. It is not a thing to be put upon a pedestal and worshipped, but rather to be discussed, dissected, argued with, accepted, rejected and always with the view that there will be new books because of new ideas, circumstances, and conditions in the lives of men. A book is a disturber of complacency and status quo. It acerbates uncertainties, causes disagreement, and even rage within a community. Proper book selection needs to take these phenomena into account, and woe to the community where book selection merely reflects the nostalgic symbol of a calm, uncomplicated world. That library is dead, and so is the community.

Book selection, therefore, is a vital endeavor which calls upon the personal resources of education, culture, knowledge, and sometimes courage of its practitioners. There are three main pressures, subtle though they may be, of which every librarian engaged in book selection needs to be aware. They are the pressures of the community, the library board, and the book selection staff itself. All directly or indirectly affect the selection process—and it may be surmised that there are few public libraries in the United States which select books freely in the community and place them for public use without reservation.

The community exerts a powerful force on library book selection, particularly when the book chosen stands a chance of rasping community tensions. What goes on in the minds of a book selection committee in certain areas of the country when *Who Speaks for the South?* by James McBride Dabbs is discussed for possible purchase? Does the fact that the author's former presidency of the Southern Regional Council or the knowledge that this organization is considered a force for integration impinge upon the selection process before the merits of the book are discussed? How can a committee or a librarian order a book for circulation when it is known as a practical certainty that the president of the library board and community leaders will take as a personal insult the book's point concerning the South's failure to come to terms with the 20th Century? Will the librarian whose tenure is usually at the pleasure of the board and who has little or no legal status in the library laws of most states wish to precipitate a discussion that might soon bypass the book in question and concern itself with the librarian's failure to take into account certain community sensibilities? A book selection policy and the Library Bill of Rights and Freedom to Read Statement are frail reeds indeed when a community already on the defensive through the implementation of national policy feels attacked on home grounds. But the issue is not likely to come up, because the book will not be ordered.

What does a book selection staff talk about when it discusses *The Deputy?* If they feel that the play is turgid and stagy, it might be rejected on those terms. If the staff agrees with certain Jewish groups that it calumnizes Pope Pius XII, it might be rejected for that reason. The book selection meeting will hardly discuss whether or not there is a possibility of affecting local religious sensibilities to the book; but in community after community, this larger part of the iceberg becomes a factor in its selection, and it is not endemic to any one communion. It is not necessary to have community protests to alert book selectors to the nay sayers. A community tone easily provides the ready reference.

One of the Notable Books of 1964 was Alexander Werth's *Russia at War, 1941-45*. The annotation says that the book, "pays tribute to the valor of the Russian people in war." Are there communities with sufficient veto power where anything remotely praising Russia is considered not fit for public library consumption? Is it possible for this kind of syndrome to permeate the book selection process of specific libraries? The answer is a suspected yes.

When the mayor of a large Southern city received pressure from a local group to do something about James Baldwin who had visited the city and made some uncomplimentary remarks about it, the answer was to attempt to get the district attorney to arrest a bookseller who was stocking *Another Country*. When the district attorney publicly refused and stated that, in his opinion, the book was not obscene, the office of the city attorney took over. The library got into the act because upon the implied threat of the city attorney and the suggestion of a board member, the book was temporarily withdrawn from the library. The case took almost a year to complete and was thrown out of court because of the prosecution's failure to make a case. Amid the jubilation at winning the case—and the library was of some assistance in this—it was generally forgotten that the public was denied the use of the book for one year—a sort of de facto censorship that incidentally worked.

ON SHAKY GROUND

The political power of a mayor and a city council can stop a public library dead in its tracks. Too many librarians select books with an eye to City Hall because they are aware—and many instances that are reported in our publications and the press attest to their frequency—that their ground, right or wrong, is shaky. Communities are hard to arouse to protect the public library, particularly in terms of principles. It is hard for the public to understand that broken precedents inevitably lead to abuses that may reach to the heart of the ability of the public library to perform its proper tasks. Book selection would perform greater service to the community of the public library if it had the same independence from city hall as does another educational institution, the public school.

Library boards play a hidden role in the book selection process. The selector is aware, through the literature, if not by bitter experience, that it is a most unusual board that stands up to its responsibility in terms of protecting the book selection process of the library without somehow or other compromising it. The board might re-affirm the Library Bill of Rights and the Freedom to Read Statement, announce that it backs up its librarian and his book selection rights, and at the same time pass a resolution which limits the very freedom it so nobly espouses in principle. This makes it easier for a book selection committee to unconsciously avoid clashes with the board's demarcation. Many good books get lost in the book selection shuffle this way. Somehow many boards do not realize that they are in the same position as the Supreme Court—that they must make viable a principle for which the library stands— free and untrammeled reading—and that an untested principle is merely words; furthermore, if the test is not met in practical fashion, then a mockery is made of the principle. Too many boards forget the principle for the immediate gains of noncontroversy, community approbation, and financial support. They do not recognize that they too are teachers and that their actions help the community recognize the difference between sycophancy and courage, ignorance and knowledge, and a library with a free or constricted spirit of inquiry.

And now we discuss the librarians themselves—the ones who because of their professional competence, education, experience, and background are the ones entrusted to the delicate task of building a public library collection that will satisfy the needs of a community in the jangling present. Are we the unsung heroes, the ones who, with clarity of insight and firmness of purpose, choose books for our libraries that measure up to our traditions as educators? A few moments at a book selection meeting will indicate that all of us are prey to some of the identical fears that pervade our community. One hears at a book selection meeting that *City of Night* does not have sufficient validity to be included in a public library collection, despite the fact that, however inept, it is a fictional treatment of male prostitution—a subject not often brought to the attention of the public, that it presents a 20th Century rootlessness that should lead us to a greater understanding of some of the problems of our times, that its staccato jerkiness is not unlike the present, and that perhaps a public library's readers ought to have a chance to participate in the author's limited vision. This also explains the difficulty of book selection as a process, because it is obvious how the writer feels about the example given. This opinion, it would seem, is not shared universally by book selection committees.

We must be careful in assessing rights and wrongs in these matters. A valid case can be made for the rejection of *City of Night* by a library, but we must be sure that the reason for rejection is intellectually honest. Whether or not a teenager will get hold of it, whether a committee will complain to the mayor, or whether or not it is a dirty book is beside the point. The "Selection Not Censorship" article by Lester Asheim of several years ago remains the best statement of the reasons for including a book in a collection.

LITERARY LINUS BLANKET

The open shelf versus closed shelf controversy is another concomitant to book selection. Staff might hesitate to purchase a volume unless it was sure that the book would be relegated to the closed shelf. This playing it safe is more an interest in self-survival than in freedom to read. Chief librarians are resisted when they attempt to do away completely with closed shelves. Many staff members feel that it leaves them too exposed to the elements of community criticism. A closed shelf is a sort of literary Linus blanket, comforting and at the same time justifiable because it gives a modicum of protection. A question might be asked whether a library which has a completely open shelf policy selects books with greater freedom than one with closed shelves? An open shelf policy may indicate fearless selection practices while a closed shelf policy may seem to be timid. On the other hand, the exact opposite could be true: the librarian would be more circumspect because of the open shelf than his counterpart who would be assured some protection if he could tell parents and other groups that he would use the formidable barrier of Library Rules to prevent teenage corruption through books. Can it be the book selection might benefit for the wrong reason?

Where is the librarian in all of this? He usually cannot, and perhaps should not, be active in book selection activities. On the other hand, the librarian cannot abrogate direct responsibility for the results because he is the one professional answerable to the board and the community for the exercise of his judgment. Therefore, he needs to understand the book selection policies as they are affected by the three kinds of pressures upon them and bring them into a meaningful relationship that will enable the library to fulfill its educational task. The policies should be so firmly established that he does not have to spend valuable time putting out censorship brush fires every time a book excites someone in the community.

This means that there must be constant communication between him and the community. Through talks, discussion, public appearances, and writing he may express his ideas concerning the standards he expects from book selection in his library. A community frame of reference is necessary so that freedom to read has the same acceptance in the minds of the public as good library service. Understandably, this frame of reference is not likely to achieve the same approbation as the idea of good library service, but continuous effort should be made to emphasize the point of view that the reader needs to be free to select from as wide a range of materials as possible. The morale effect on the library staff would be invaluable. Its direct result should be more creative selection and in the last analysis, a better total library collection more attuned to the requirements of the present.

The librarian must assist the library board to recognize the importance of unharassed book selection. The board must be helped in the recognition of the primacy of the long view, of the permanent aims of the library as against possible immediate advantages. It must be understood that taking community pressure is a part of their stewardship.

The board represents the library to the community as a part of the peer group whose support makes the library possible. It should not separate the noble words of basic library statements in the area of reading and book selection from that practical implementation which makes the statements valid. The library board should be seen and heard in promoting a professional understanding of the book selection process in their community.

The staff takes its way of life from the chief librarian. He sets the tone of the library, its morale, dedication, professionalism, and, certainly, the terms of growth and direction of the book collection. His encouragement is invaluable to those staff members who would be venturesome in book selection. He can assist the timid ones to new realization of the library as a self-propelled educator. However repugnant staff members feel a certain book to be, the knowledge that the chief librarian would back up a professional decision in favor of its inclusion cannot help but make for a good brand of book selection.

In the face of seemingly active nay sayers to the library's freedom of book selection, it might be well to venture some future projections. At first glance, things seem fairly pessimistic. States are becoming more interested in providing laws against obscenity. Each legislative session sees a rash of bills intended to regulate the sale of obscene materials but which in many cases limits the free access to worthwhile information and literature. The Federal Government got into the act with the passage in April 1965 of H.R. 980 by the House of Representatives. This little gem would make the Postmaster General the arbiter of whether or not the mail sent to us is "obscene, lewd, lascivious, indecent, filthy or vile." Now will he not have some fun decisions to make? It does seem that the library profession is losing ground against those who would restrict acquisition of books, but there is some cause for optimism.

A new intellectual climate has developed in the United States during the last few years. The courts are less and less inclined to define obscenity and more and more interested in protecting due process of law and freedom of speech, which includes freedom to read. Reaction against these decisions can perhaps account for some of the problems libraries are encountering. The decisions have opened literature to wider horizons of experimentation. This inevitably means that trash will take its place alongside the valid, and book selection committees will need to apply literary standards in conjunction with emphasis upon freedom to read. Just because a judge states that a book has a legal right to be published and sold, does not mean that it automatically belongs in the public library.

Another facet of a new intellectual climate is the rising awareness and commitment of the present-day college generation. These young people are aware of the issues of freedom. Contrary to the general belief that, once they are in their communities, they will settle down to solid mediocrity, there are many who believe that these young people—who are giving of themselves in many creative ways—will carry this quiet sense of dedication to the active life of their communities. This speaks well for future public libraries.

Finally our educational system, from kindergarten through the university, seems to have got off the center in which it found itself in the 1950's and is seeking answers that will bring its students up to the demand of present-day society. There is still theorizing, experimentation, and naturally, controversy in our educational pattern, but a corner seems to have been turned, particularly in the increased recognition of the public library as one of the agencies with an educational responsibility. This new partnership presages well for library book selection.

There is no safe sure road for the public library. The buffetings continue. Librarians are still too afraid, and the outspoken ones lose their jobs. But even in this area a new day seems to be dawning. Groups are being formed all over the country to oppose censorship activities in communities. State library associations are heard with greater respect as they oppose short-sighted legislation that restricts freedom of book selection. The American Library Association's Washington Office is performing invaluable service to Congress through its skilled and reasoned advocacy of federal participation in library development. We are looking forward to the day when ALA will help make book selection a safer occupation by assisting librarians who get into trouble through the practice of their profession.

The time has now arrived when the library profession should shed its milk teeth and show fangs when necessary. We no longer need to meekly stretch our necks for the slaughter when a rampaging library board, politicians, or community decide to make over the library in their own image. We should just turn over the library to them, suggest that trained personnel would do well to look elsewhere, and remove that community from accreditation by the American Library Association. We do not have to ask for respect. All we need to do is earn it—through our professional efforts—and wherever we have it, then we can make book selection safe for democracy.

54 Teaching a Commitment to Intellectual Freedom

(OCTOBER 15, 1967)

by DAVID K. BERNINGHAUSEN

In Allen Drury's *Advise and Consent* there is a scene in which the southern Senator is harassing the "intellectual" nominated for the post of Secretary of State. The Senator asks, in a nasty tone of voice: "You are an egghead, aren't you?" And instead of cringing and modestly denying any claims to intellectuality, the nominee replies: "Indeed, I am an egghead. You might say that I am an egghead in full flower, and I hope to shed a little pollen wherever I go."

As professors in library schools, we had better try to shed some pollen. It is our responsibility as intellectuals to persuade our students that they have chosen a profession that commits them to the principle of intellectual freedom. Librarians, while viewed by the general public as people interested in ideas, and therefore as intellectuals, should be humble about the level of intellectuality at which they operate—but they cannot and should not attempt to escape the label or the responsibilities that go with it.

When the college graduate enters library school, he may or he may not have an appreciation of the nature and significance of free scholarship. There is much evidence in our society to indicate that many college graduates do not have this understanding. As a part of the orientation of future librarians to the world of ideas, library educators might deliberately present 20th-Century humanity's *need* for library and information service, for its storehouse of scientific and scholarly knowledge, for every scrap of data that libraries can collect, for free scholars exercising their intelligence on the problems of human society.

Library educators cannot take it for granted that students have an appreciation of the need for, or even the possibility of, *disinterested* scholarship. Of course, the scholar is not *uninterested* in his research. Naturally, he is interested in what he is doing. But he must be disinterested in the sense that he provides all the safeguards possible against bias, against sloppy or inaccurate observations, against imprecise reporting, and against the drawing of conclusions not warranted by the evidence. The scholar is, and must be, disinterested in that he reports as his findings, not what he hopes to find, not what someone else wants him to find, but what the evidence warrants. In short, the scholar requires the freedom to be honest.

Future librarians must be equipped with an understanding of the nature of free scholarship, and also an understanding of the fact that many citizens find it inconceivable that any intellectual could be disinterested. Some of the censors' attacks stem from this failure to appreciate the nature and significance of scholarship.

If we are to teach a commitment to intellectual freedom, what shall be its content? It would be possible, of course, to present here a long list of references to writers such as John Milton, Zechariah Chafee, Thomas Jefferson, John Stuart Mill, etc.

But have our library school students read, for example, *On Liberty?* Our library education standards require a four-year degree for admission, and while it is probably safe to assume that our students are interested in ideas, it is not a justifiable assumption that they have read the classic writers on freedom of speech and thought. Indeed, of the last 150 students to enter the library school at Minnesota, only 14 had read *On Liberty.*

When we assign this small book as required reading in the library school, discussion reveals a rather common reaction to it, as follows: "Well, most of this squares with what I think, myself, however. . . ." And the rest of the comment points to difficulties which Mill failed to clear up. Mill's ideas on freedom of thought have been absorbed into our cultural consciousness, even though our students have not read Mill, and most students seem to feel that they can accept his three chief contentions:

1) Suppression of opinion may blot out truth; no one is infallible and an unconventional opinion may turn out to be true.

2) Even though an opinion is false, truth is served by refuting error; beliefs not founded on reasoned conviction are not held firmly enough to guide human conduct.

3) No opinion is completely true or false; an unconventional opinion may be useful because it contains some particle of truth. Freedom of thought and opinion should not be curbed by collective authority.

Regardless of the degree of acceptance of Mill's ideas, students who have read *On Liberty* have knowledge of his ideas in common, and this is useful for critical and pointed discussion of actual cases. Cases, of course, serve only as illustrations, as guides to the nature of the problem, but they can and should be a part of the program of instruction in library schools which attempt to teach a commitment to intellectual freedom.

From the large number of possible cases I have chosen for illustration here the amendment to the New York State Education Law of 1950. On August 11 of that year, Lewis Wilson, Commissioner of Education, sent to public schools a directive which said:

"Subject to rules and regulations of the Board of Regents, a pupil may be excused from such study of health and hygiene as conflicts with the religion of his parents or guardian. Such conflict must be certified by a proper representative of their religions as defined by Section 2 of the religious corporations law."

The Commissioner's directive stated that he approved the exemption of the children of parents or guardians of the Christian Science faith from instruction in the units of Disease Prevention and Control and three other specified areas.

As a result of this directive, the New York Teachers Guild, the Association of Biology Teachers, and the New York State Civil Liberties Union prepared briefs *amicus curiae* on the issue, presenting these arguments:

a) The law is impractical and discriminatory and it also imposes a censorship on education.

b) The law establishes a precedent for further control by special groups.

c) The law establishes an intolerable iron curtain over ideas which are now part of our common heritage.

The Christian Science leaders argued: "We are not asking for exemption from the teaching of the germ theory of disease nor from any teaching which affects the prevention and control of communicable disease. All we ask is exemption from compulsory study of the symptoms and processes of diseases and the medical treatment of them. We do not wish any alteration in Regents' examinations. As a minority group, we are willing to make any sacrifice for the good of the majority other than the sacrifice of our religious rights."

At first glance it appears to many students that, in this case, John Stuart Mill's emphasis upon freedom of religious choice collides with his ideas on freedom of thought, and library school classes usually have a lively discussion. Questions that are discussed include: How can a school administrator carry out the provisions of this law and avoid embarrassment of any pupil? Does the principal take a religious census of his pupils? If he does, isn't that a violation of the law against discrimination? Does the school send the minority group to the library whenever germs are mentioned? Is this a proper use of the library? Does the librarian have a responsibility to keep away from Christian Scientists books which mention germs?

Also, most library school students have little or no understanding of the fact that legislatures make laws which affect the operations of libraries. The case illuminates this aspect of librarianship, creating a problem for the librarian. Will he be violating the law if he buys books or magazines or films that treat of the germ theory of disease? If this law passed in New York is followed to the letter, is education possible? And a major question raised is: How do we in schools and libraries resolve a conflict between these two cherished principles—a) religious freedom for the individual; and b) freedom of thought in education?

Unless we are willing to accept as valid the contention that *education* and *indoctrination* are synonymous, this conflict is more apparent than actual. A

Christian Scientist pupil who studies the history of the Panama Canal and learns that yellow fever was controlled by killing off the mosquitoes, thus enabling the laborers to build the canal—such a student is still entirely free to believe in and practice his religion. His history teacher cannot coerce him to a belief which he is determined to reject. His freedom of choice as to religion has not been taken away from him.

This case also provides an opportunity for the library school student to learn that the American Library Association has allies in our efforts to preserve the freedom to read in our society. Item number four in the Library Bill of Rights, which urges librarians to cooperate with other individuals and groups, is thus illustrated.

It is also essential that we emphasize in library education that attacks on intellectual freedom in our schools and libraries are contagious, and that they seem to occur in cycles. For several years, for example, the major kind of literature under attack may be political or social, but at another period it may be what is alleged to be obscene.

It is relatively easy to organize the forces *for* censorship, for the appeal can be made in simplistic terms, for example, "Join the Citizens for Decent Literature and Stamp Out Juvenile Delinquency." Frequently, this slogan is supplemented with another, such as, "Obscenity Is Communist-Inspired, Let's Stamp It Out." Such slogans are appealing. They are also deceptively simple, and they seem to suggest that here is a formula which will bring quick salvation. They are appealing because there is in every one of us a desire for the blessed security that comes from absolute assurance that we know how to rid our society of juvenile delinquency.

It is more difficult to organize forces *against* censorship, for to be moved to action on behalf of freedom to read, one must recognize that the relationship between reading and behavior is a complex, rather than a simple matter. One must be sophisticated enough to resist the natural wish to find the one, single cause of evils of this world. One must be able to distinguish between single, or one-to-one causal relationships and multiple causation.

In spite of the inflammatory writings of Frederick Wertham, or the declarations of J. Edgar Hoover, or of Congresswoman Kathryn Granahan, anyone who tries to study the "causes of delinquency" quickly finds that the one point on which almost all authorities agree is that the causes are multiple; that there is no single cause. And moreover, as one student at Minnesota discovered during an investigation of the subject, reading is almost never mentioned as a cause by the serious students of juvenile delinquency. Indeed, it is well-established by many studies that a very large majority of juvenile delinquents are nonreaders or very poor readers.

Here, then, is another idea which should be included in the library school curriculum: The assumption that reading lewd literature causes delinquency is no more than an assumption. There is little or no evidence of a one-to-one causal relationship between reading pornography and juvenile delinquency.

In one year of library school we can hardly expect to cover the subject exhaustively, of course. But we can aim to alert all students to the realization that preserving the freedom to read is and will continue to be a responsibility for librarians. Somehow, our consideration of the subject must take it out of the realm of "academic" study. One way to do this is to refer to actual experiences of former students. For example, here is Miss S., who three months after graduation found her library adult forum program under severe public attack by right wing extremists because she had scheduled three "controversial professors" as speakers. Her head librarian and the public library board supported free speech, and finally one of the speakers won a libel suit against the critics.

Or, here is Mrs. B., a school librarian in a rural community. She gives *Catcher in the Rye* to an English teacher to read, with the result that the teacher complains to the superintendent. In this case the superintendent and the school board were persuaded to study and adopt the Library Bill of Rights and the School Library Bill of Rights as school board policy. Later the English teacher began to read much more widely than ever before.

And, students might well flex their intellects on the case of the student who reads Mill, Chafee, Jefferson, and various articles from library literature on censorship, but still feels committed to protect his patrons by razor-blading certain passages out of Chaucer's *Canterbury Tales*. This case creates a dilemma for the library educator. The young man's convictions must be respected. Even if it were possible to "indoctrinate" him with the lofty ideals expressed in the Library Bill of Rights, as, of course, it is not, would it be appropriate to do so? However, should he be recommended for a library position in a publicly supported institution? He is committed, not to the ideals of the library profession, but to suppress what he doesn't like.

To sharpen this point for our students, library schools should discuss the ethics of librarianship in terms of: *It is unethical for a librarian in a publicly supported library to suppress statements he doesn't like, or to exclude expressions of ideas that are objectionable to any religious or political or other organization to which he belongs. A professional librarian's first commitment must be to intellectual freedom for everyone.* It may also be instructive in this connection to assign some readings on the concept of libraries in the Soviet Union, where all librarians are required to promote only the doctrines approved by the Communist government.

At the 1965 Washington Conference on Freedom of Inquiry, Lee A. Burress stated in his paper that little attention is given to intellectual freedom in the school teacher training programs, and that, in fact, there is more likely to be an emphasis upon the importance of public relations of the school than on the development of professionally competent and independent personalities. Edward R. Murrow's *See It Now* film on California librarians, showing four school librarians timidly appearing in silhouette versus Mrs. Anne Smart who was willing to state her case for censorship in full picture and voice, is a dramatic and sobering lesson for prospective librarians. Here, too, we see school officials seeking to promote smooth public relations at the expense of free inquiry.

If there is any library school which emphasizes public relations above intellectual freedom, its counsel may well take the form of "You risk jeopardiz-

ing freedom of reading by fighting for this not-very-good book." This recommendation deserves full analysis in library schools, for it is probably the most
dangerous to freedom of thought of any that could be found.

It was mentioned above that censorship is contagious. It is also important
to show students that if a climate of opinion favoring censorship, whether it is
censorship of obscenity, scientific literature, or of religious, political, or social
literature, becomes established, our citizen readers will not have available the
necessary information for making wise decisions. As Dan Lacy has pointed out,
the countries which exercise the most thorough controls over publications
about sex are probably Communist China, Russia, Ireland, South Africa, and
Spain. Surely it is not an accident that these countries also practice censorship
in political literature.

Library school students should have the opportunity to learn that censorship is contagious—that it tends to spread from one kind of literature to
others—and that if we accept the Postmaster General, with his thousands of
volunteer helpers, as our literary critics, it is not going to be easy to maintain
our traditional freedom of information.

The library school curriculum should alert students to the distinction
between "approved" and "recommended" lists of books. The Daughters of the
American Revolution, or the National Organization for Decent Literature, or
the Citizens for Decent Literature publish and distribute lists of approved and
unapproved books. Librarians must avoid any issuance of a list of "approved"
titles, for this inevitably suggests that any titles not listed are "unapproved."
Libraries may *recommend* books, but it is a violation of the principle of intellectual freedom for a library or librarian to approve books.

For example, in 1958 the DAR prepared a master list of textbooks, classifying them as "satisfactory" or "unsatisfactory." This organization, like any
other in the United States, has every right to take positions on issues. They can
and do oppose the United Nations and participation in the United Nations by
the United States. They have every right to oppose foreign aid and fluoridation.
Perhaps it will not be a major disaster if they protest against the Tarzan books,
though as Harry Golden writes:

"Some of the DAR ladies took time out from their fight against the United
Nations and fluoridation to demand the elimination of the Tarzan books from
the libraries. The DAR suspects Tarzan and Jane are living together without
benefit of clergy, openly and happily if athletically.

"But as with fluoridation, the ladies are wrong. Jane and Tarzan were
indeed married by Edgar Rice Burroughs in the second Tarzan book and
sometime later Boy floated down from an airplane, which solved the obstacle
of illegitimacy and at the same time gave Boy an advantage in not being
related to Jane and Tarzan and therefore not as neurotic as they. . . ."

But when the DAR presumes to dictate to our school teachers, declaring
that here is a list of 50 satisfactory books and here are 165 unsatisfactory books
now in use in our schools, they go too far. They create a dangerous climate of
censorship. The list of unsatisfactory authors on the DAR list includes Henry
Steele Commager, Allan Nevins, Harold Laski, Morris Ernst, Carl Carmer,

Vera M. Dean, George Counts, Harold Lasswell, and Zechariah Chafee. These writers are highly respected authorities in their fields.

In 1960 the Mississippi legislature—by a vote of 82–44—gave Governor Ross Barnett the power to select all of the state's textbooks. Authors Jack London, Arthur Miller, Carl Sandburg, and Archibald MacLeish seem subversive to some Mississippians and the governor urged: "Clean up our textbooks. Our children must be properly informed of the Southern and true American way of life."

Probably very few of the good people who join volunteer censor groups have read the books of Commager, Chafee, or MacLeish. These are just names—names of authors that someone has put on a list of "unsatisfactory" books. Well-intentioned people who join organizations to control obscenity are seldom aware of the contagious character of censorship, and library schools have an obligation to reveal to their students that wherever a society has a weakness or a blind spot, it tends to feel that censorship is necessary. Once it adopts the practice in one field, it seems necessary in other fields, as illustrated by historian James Silver in his book *Mississippi, the Closed Society*. Censorship is contagious.

And speaking of blind spots, since library education must accept the responsibility for teaching documentation, some documentalists have a curious notion that they do not need to know anything about the problems of censorship in libraries—that this is a problem for public and school libraries only. This is not so. Witness the banning of the *Bulletin of Atomic Scientists* in various libraries. For a more dramatic illustration, consider the story of Dr. Edward U. Condon, driven out of his job as director of the U.S. Bureau of Standards because people less well-informed than he thought his interest in Russian scientific literature grounds for suspicion.

Dr. Condon's contributions to scholarship were very considerable. His record was scrutinized in three full-scale loyalty investigations, and in each he received full clearance. Library educators must be sure that they teach an understanding by documentalists that the director of the U.S. Bureau of Standards, our scientists, and our librarians are failing to do their jobs if they are *not* interested in securing and distributing Russian scientific literature.

Documentalists, and all other librarians, must learn that censorship is contagious, and that the Library Bill of Rights applies to all media collected or distributed by libraries. Although written for a public library, the policy of the Palisades Free Library, New York, is pertinent:

"[The responsibility of the Library] . . . is to serve all the community, not to promote—and above all, not to censor—any particular political, moral, philosophical, or religious convictions or opinions. It is not the purpose of the Library to stimulate or to cater to trivial, antisocial, prurient, or immoral interests. But no one, least of all a free public library, has the right to judge what another may or may not read or hear.

"If a member of the Library wishes to find out for himself whether a certain publication is worthless, tasteless, vicious, or inaccurate, it is the function of the Library to give him an opportunity to do so. Furthermore, history shows that many books which have been most controversial or objectionable to some persons or groups have in due course been recognized to be among those books which most, rather than least, belong in public libraries. If an idea is truly dangerous or evil, the best protection against it is a public which has been exposed to it and has rejected it; the worst protection is a public which has been shielded from exposure to it by official or self-appointed guardians.

"Therefore, in the event that anyone in or out of the community should object to the Library's acquisition or retention of a certain publication on moral, political, religious, or philosophical grounds, the objection should be recognized as an indication that the publication in question may well be of more than routine interest and may be likely to be requested by members of the community who wish to judge its merits and demerits for themselves."

This policy statement illuminates what was (before its 1967 revision) an unfortunate aspect of the otherwise very valuable policy statement of the ALA, the Library Bill of Rights. When this policy was reaffirmed in 1948, the phrase "of sound factual authority" was debated by the Committee on Intellectual Freedom, and it was decided that it should be left in the statement. Unfortunately, there are many documents which may not be "of sound factual authority" which should be and must be in libraries. One example is Houston Chamberlain's *Foundations of the Nineteenth Century,* a work which expounds an anti-Semitic philosophy of history, and which was used by Hitler as a basis for his persecution of the Jews. But dare we suppress this book, or *Mein Kampf,* or the writings of white supremacy exponents, or other documents on the grounds that they are not "of sound factual authority?"

By way of illustration, in Belleville, Illinois, the public librarian, a Roman Catholic, refused to place in the library the periodical *Church and State,* an unsolicited gift subscription. He believed that this publication, the official organ of Protestants and other Americans United for Separation of Church and State was disqualified because it was not "of sound factual authority." As Ervin Gaines pointed out, his argument for exclusion was based upon the Library Bill of Rights (as it then read).

This case provides a fine opportunity for library science students to gain a sense of participation in the ongoing process of librarianship. The ALA statement against prejudicial labeling, or the Freedom to Read statement were once debatable and debated. For the beginning library student, however, they may very well be merely "of historical interest." Not so, however, with that phrase, "of sound factual authority," which has now been removed from the Library Bill of Rights.

Outbreaks of censorship are likely to occur when nonreaders discover the world of books and ideas. As has been pointed out elsewhere, it is a predictable result of the expansion of library services through federal aid to libraries, that there will be even more attempts at censorship. As a school system is staffed with better prepared teachers, teachers who stimulate the intellectual processes of their students by introducing books such as *1984,* or *Catcher in the Rye,* instead of sticking to the "safe" and noncontroversial textbooks, there will be more attempts at censorship.

Library school students, our future librarians, need this kind of perspective. They also need to learn that the censors who frequently try to impose their own prejudices and their own limitations upon everyone else are frequently very few in number, representing a tiny fraction of our society, which, even though it has not read Mill's *On Liberty*, basically believes in the value of freedom of thought. Also, they need to learn that publicity can be an effecive weapon against the censor.

Finally, in any consideration of "Teaching a Commitment to Intellectual Freedom," some attention should be given to the nature of truth and scholarship. This is, of course, a large subject, and actually should be the result of any liberal education. Here, it can only be sketched in broad outlines.

If we view truth as a quality of a proposition—as a quality that a proposition possesses to some degree, not in any absolute sense—we will not be so ready to demand the suppression of certain propositions. Consider: truths are stated in sentences, made up of words, formed to communicate ideas from speaker or writer to listeners or readers. There is a natural tendency on the part of all of us to underestimate or to forget the difficulties of communication as a process—difficulties which begin with the speaker's perception of the world outside his own head, or perhaps we should say, with the speaker's faulty perception—often *mis*perceptions of external reality. We all recognize that our perceptions are only partially consistent with that reality, and that other perceivers may see things differently.

But in the communications process, the observer "sees" what he sees, depending upon his past experience and his present purposes, and he then tries to state propositions which communicate his ideas to others. His propositions are stated in words, picture, gestures, facial expressions, etc. Semantic difficulties inevitably arise. The propositions may be "true"; that is, they may possess the quality of correspondence with reality to a greater or lesser degree. They are never *precise*. And the recipient of the attempted communication has his own past experiences and present purposes and moods and mind-sets. Inevitably, he perceives the propositions as "true" wholly, or in part, according to his own "frame of reference."

If library educators are to teach a commitment to intellectual freedom, then they need to study and teach the communications process in detail, and to encourage students to reject the notion that there are "impartial facts." This is not to say that facts as such do not exist, but when they are described in sentences, or in films, or by whatever media, the propositions enunciated inevitably carry with them the incitement to believe or reject, as noted by Alfred North Whitehead. Or, as William James noted, the little word *and* follows along after every proposition. *Truth* is a quality that a proposition possesses, to some degree, under certain specified or understood conditions.

For example, suppose we have a bucket of water heated to a temperature of 80 degrees. Mr. A and Mr. B put a hand into the water, and Mr. A says it is cold. Mr. B says it is hot. And an argument ensues, perhaps ending in a physical fight.

But let us suppose that we have three buckets of water, one at 60 degrees, one at 80 degrees, and one at 100 degrees. If I hold one hand in the 60 degree bucket and one hand in the 100 degree bucket for a minute, and then put both hands into the middle bucket, how do I describe the temperature? My perceptions of temperature are contradictory. My left hand sensations lead me to say it is hot water in the middle bucket, but my right hand sensations tell me it is cold. Of course, there is a way I can express my perceptions. I can say: "To my left hand, the water in this middle bucket feels warm. But to my right hand it feels cold." These propositions are much more precise, more accurate, than to say: "This water is cold," or "This water is hot."

And when reader A dips into *Catcher in the Rye* he may say, after reading one page, "This book is obscene. Ban it!" Reader B, however, may say, "This is an honest book. It is a valuable book." In each case, the reader is reacting to the stimuli provided by the book in terms of his past experiences, his purposes, his moods, his degree of sophistication as a reader, his own frame of reference.

The librarian needs to understand these reactions. If he does, he is better prepared to resist reader A's efforts to persuade him to "protect" his library patrons by banning the book.

As educators of future librarians, we need to note the findings by Remmers and Radler, that, in 1958, teenagers believed, by a majority of 60 percent to 27 percent, that "Police and other groups have sometimes banned or censored certain books and movies in their cities, and *that they should have the power to do this.*" It would be foolish for us to hope that, when today's youth reach our library school classes, all of them have relinquished this attitude. We therefore have a responsibility, as intellectuals, to provide our students with the perspective necessary for understanding the meaning and significance of intellectual freedom and scholarship, declaring positively that: "We believe that what people read is deeply important; that ideas can be dangerous; but that the suppression of ideas is fatal to a democratic society. Freedom itself is a dangerous way of life, but it is ours."

CHAPTER

55 *A Unique Course*
on Intellectual Freedom
and Censorship

by KENNETH KISTER

For a hundred years or thereabouts, American librarianship has officially professed that censorship is an intolerable evil, and that intellectual freedom should be supported vigorously and defended without reservation against those who would limit or deny it. This belief—consistent with American political theory as expressed by Locke out of Jefferson (with the Bill of Rights as midwife)—rests on the notion that libraries are important agents of intellectual communication and, as such, must be free, within the bounds of the law, to circulate any and all ideas, opinions, and facts, no matter how disturbing, offensive, unpopular, or heretical they might be. Toward this end, the profession has issued or endorsed numerous statements, such as the Library Bill of Rights and the Students' Right to Read, which embody various intellectual freedom principles.

That most librarians have not always lived up to the high principles and felicitous phrases found in these documents is not especially surprising or culpable: compromise and expediency are unavoidable, even necessary components of the democratic process, where minority rights and majority power are often in conflict.[1] But what is surprising and culpable—indeed, shocking— is the *ready willingness* with which many librarians violate professed principles of intellectual freedom. This is not a new or an original observation, and the evidence that librarians frequently yield, without visible protest, to extralegal pressure exerted by organized vigilante groups or influential individuals, and cheerfully practice the most invidious and effective form of censorship, self-censorship, needs no detailed recounting here. The authoritative Fiske Report,[2] although now a decade old and limited to California school and public libraries, stands as the empirical cornerstone of this criticism, while more recent studies conducted in other parts of the country offer supportive data.[3] Put bluntly, the library profession has recognized its obligation to resist censorship and foster intellectual freedom by word but not deed: the performance to date has been less than admirable, marked more by shoddy casuistry and sanctimonious ignorance than by honesty and sincere dedication to principle.

Reasons for this alarming disparity between announced principles and actual practice have not been neatly documented, although some credible assumptions can be made. First, librarianship is a gentle profession dominated by gentle people. From its early origins, when libraries were simply storehouses for books and manuscripts, and librarians were erudite bibliographers intent upon keeping the cloister quiet and the books tidy, to the positivistic modern age when American libraries assumed the genteel role of helping to educate and entertain the lower and middle classes, and librarians took on a predominantly feminine form, library work has had a distinctively benign, complacent, nonaggressive quality about it. Quite naturally, library practitioners reflect and value these traits. But adherence to intellectual freedom tenets requires a toughness, an assertiveness, a combativeness which most gentle people find either distasteful or impossible. Sometimes (the important times), intellectual freedom must be fought for, but librarians are not fighters by nature.

Second, librarianship is an inherently conservative profession dominated by instinctively conservative people. Historically, preservation of man's accumulated knowledge and wisdom was the rationale for libraries, and today preservation remains an essential library function. Those attracted to the field are usually preservers by instinct, a desirable aptitude from a professional standpoint. This conservative "preserver instinct" among librarians, however, goes well beyond the professional activity of preserving books and other materials: American librarians—recruited principally from that middle class stratum which places highest priority on political order and stability and social conformity—tend to react with hostility or suspicion toward ideas and opinions which question or threaten established value systems. Robert D. Leigh, something of a minor guru when I was in library school, spoke for the profession when twenty years ago he inveighed against "irresponsible freedom":

> . . . in our culture, occasional instances of publications much worse than silly can certainly be absorbed, if the general trend of publication is sound and true. But a major trend in published output that promotes the breakdown of cherished standards of truth about life and its values, represents an irresponsibility which destroys any claim for immunity from social and even governmental action.[4]

The problem with this thinking is, of course, that maintaining "cherished standards of truth" by suppressing "irresponsibility" contradicts a fundamental premise of intellectual freedom, which holds that any "truth" is meaningful only if it can withstand open and repeated challenge, regardless of the fact that prevailing authority considers the challenge silly or unsound or irresponsible or worse.[5] Dedication to intellectual freedom presumes a genuine tolerance for social and political diversity and change—a tolerance which most librarians lack.

Third, many librarians view the library as a passive rather than an active agent of communication. Librarians have been diligent husbanders of recorded knowledge and reasonably keen (albeit unimaginative) organizers of information, and it is true also that they have been vocal, sometimes persuasive propagandists for book reading as a happy, constructive activity. But librarians have been much less zealous or successful in their efforts to communicate vital knowledge and information to people: irrelevant and corny displays, timid and unattractive book lists, painfully dull book talks, and reference service where questions are treated as either demeaning chores or unwarranted intrusions hardly constitute an enterprising approach to knowledge/information transmission and dissemination—an approach, nonetheless, commonplace in American libraries.[6] Indeed, for the great majority of people, the concept of the library as an essential information source is as foreign as the thought of naked dancing girls entertaining at a PTA meeting. Unfortunately for everyone concerned, the absence of a strong professional sense of the library as an active communications medium has militated against development of a strong intellectual freedom commitment, since such a commitment derives from and is nourished by the desire to communicate effectively and, if necessary, forcefully.[7] Put another way: passive communicators develop passive commitments to free expression, and librarians are passive communicators at best.

A fourth and final assumption concerning the profession's dismal record on upholding reputed principles of intellectual freedom is that, by and large, librarians do not understand the idea of intellectual freedom or the complex, sophisticated and confluent principles involved. Mere endorsement of imposing documents like the Library Bill of Rights and the Freedom to Read statement is a thin claim indeed to comprehending intellectual freedom: such documents are doubtless useful in that they provide convenient, rather simplistic codifications of germane principles; but such documents do not provide automatic understanding and appreciation of the principles themselves. Neither do they furnish necessary insight into the difficult, sometimes agonizingly sensitive issues which arise when these theoretical principles are applied. All too often, in fact, endorsement of the Library Bill of Rights and similar documents is an intellectually empty action, a platitudinous gesture: the words sound nice and appear to be harmless, and, of course, it is comforting to be on the side of "freedom," along with Socrates, John Milton, Jefferson, John Stuart Mill, D. H. Lawrence, Vashti McCollum, Herbert Marcuse, et al. But intellectual freedom is not an amusing game designed to make librarians (or anyone else) feel happy or proud, although some library literature on the subject might lead one to believe otherwise. Intellectual freedom is, however, a remarkably powerful and radical idea which is at once profoundly simple and enormously complicated. Adherence to intellectual freedom requires both a positive commitment to the power of the idea and a genuine understanding of the functioning of the idea. Furthermore, this understanding requires interdisciplinary knowledge of the definitions and *raisons d'etre* of the principles involved; the practical and theoretical extent of these principles; the arguments, attitudes, and methodologies which contravene them; and the numerous critical areas where they are infringed, either openly or subtly. The record indicates that librarians seldom possess this range and depth of understanding.

All of the general assumptions made here about why librarians readily and willingly violate or ignore officially endorsed principles of intellectual freedom —the gentle, conservative nature of the profession and its practitioners, the passive approach to communication, and ignorance or superficial understanding of the principles themselves—interrelate and interact with one another, forming a rather tight, self-preservative pattern. Unquestionably, for example, the middle-class conservatism which pervades the profession contributes directly and indirectly to maintaining a passive attitude toward the library's communications function and vice versa. But as a library educator I am most concerned with the assumption that librarians lack understanding of intellectual freedom, not only because this is the most crucial assumption—it is possible, of course, for nonaggressive, conservative librarians to develop a viable commitment to intellectual freedom, but it is not possible to develop this commitment if the principles involved are not clearly understood—but also because this is where the educator possibly can be most effective.

That professional library education has failed heretofore to prepare librarians for understanding intellectual freedom and the body of theory underlying its principles requires little elaboration here. Suffice it to say that library educators have tended to equate teaching intellectual freedom with waving around the Library Bill of Rights and other treasured documents, expecting students to develop an unshakable dedication to noble principles as a result of this process.[8] This well-meaning but shallow, glad-handing approach to teaching intellectual freedom does not work, and, clearly, it never has. Especially today, when students are actively participating in civil rights causes and seriously questioning the academic community's hierarchical, anti-democratic power structure, this kind of teaching is as intellectually insulting and debilitating as forced memorization of the Anglo-American cataloging rules or required burbling over Helen Haines and the i-love-books line. Perhaps the kindest observation which can be made about the traditional approach to teaching intellectual freedom is that it has been irrelevant.

Dissatisfaction with conventional library teaching of intellectual freedom—coupled with the recognition that understanding intellectual freedom requires conscientious study and thought, and the conviction that the library school is properly the place for librarians to begin this study/thought process —resulted in the Simmons course entitled "Intellectual Freedom and Censorship," which was added to the School's curriculum last year, and is believed to be the first library course entirely devoted to the subject. The course, proposed in 1966 and developed in 1967, was first offered on an experimental basis in the spring (January–May) 1968 semester, and is currently a four-credit elective open to students with degree candidacy or postgraduate standing.[9]

Since its announcement in the library press in 1967, "Intellectual Freedom and Censorship" has created considerable interest and enthusiasm among some librarians and library educators around the country. The following is intended to share the course outline more fully with my colleagues and intellectual freedom cognoscenti in the field, and, moreover, to stimulate interest in reassessing library education's responsibility and approach to this vital, pervasive area of professional concern. Those who have followed the trend of my remarks thus far will understand that the syllabus is not presented here as a final or comprehensive answer to how or what to teach: panaceas are unfortunately in short supply all over these days, and teaching intellectual freedom is certainly no exception.

AIMS OF THE COURSE

The ostensible aims of the course are to consider the broad historical development, current status, and future implications of intellectual freedom concepts; to analyze the often perplexing, almost always wide-ranging ramifications of these concepts in action; and to explore the various internal and external restrictions imposed upon acknowledged intellectual freedom principles, especially at the present time. An underlying, unspoken, related aim of the course—the most important but least easily evaluated or directly implemented aim—is to encourage each student to evolve an individually satisfying, workable, and coherent personal/professional philosophy concerning intellectual freedom, so that as a librarian he will be prepared to make consistent judgments about freedom and censorship questions on the basis of understanding and confidence, not fear and ignorance. The individual student's evolving philosophy might not always coincide with my own; indeed, it would be remarkable if it did, since understanding and philosophical discernment cannot be "taught," in the academic sense of that word.

The aim of the course, then, is not to evangelize for glorious intellectual freedom and rail against the gross iniquities of censorship—the concepts, principles, definitions, history, methods, and attitudes involved are much too subtle and complex for a simple either/or, good/bad, right/wrong approach— nor is the aim to produce librarians who occasionally, smugly, purchase the latest controversial novel in order to strike a grand blow for intellectual freedom and the right to read, while unwittingly perpetuating the library (the *whole* library) as a sterile middle-class retreat. Rather, the aim is to enlarge the student's perspective, develop his critical awareness, and increase his appreciation of the difficult, often ambiguous points at issue. Admittedly, these aims are not modest ones, but they are worth pursuing. As is always the case, achievement will depend largely on the individual student's motivation, capabilities, background, and so on. I do have some faith, however, that those who seriously examine the history and sociology of freedom and censorship will come to value intellectual freedom more fully, and, perhaps, adhere to its tenets more readily.

ORGANIZATION AND CONTENT OF THE COURSE

The general organization of the course is loosely structured, although there is a deliberately progressive order of study, beginning with the historical develop-

ment of concepts of intellectual freedom and attitudes toward censorship, and
moving to 1) legal and political concepts, theories, and attitudes, with particular emphasis on the American judicial system and its interpretations of First
Amendment provisions; 2) extralegal and illegal political and social controls, as
evidenced by both organized pressure groups and the "tyranny of the majority";
and 3) internal psychological controls and the phenomenon of self-censorship.
This organizational pattern has several virtues, not least of which is that it
progresses naturally from the most open, definable form of censorship activity
(legal) to the most clandestine, elusive form (internal). Finally, sexual expression and questions of obscenity—the area of human expression which has most
concerned the censor in modern times—are studied in depth toward the end of
the course, in order that the overlapping and meshing of legal, extralegal, and
internal attitudes and controls can be more precisely understood and related to
other problem areas.

"Intellectual Freedom and Censorship" ordinarily meets fifteen times (for
two-and-one-half hour periods) during a semester, and, therefore, I have
divided the content into a like number of sections here.[10]

1) *Historical Background from Plato to the Reformation*

Definitions of intellectual freedom and censorship; types of censorship; the
Platonic concept of man as a "public" entity accountable to public authority for
his beliefs, expressions, and actions; Plato's guide to censorship, the *Republic;*
an uneasy backward glance at Socrates, the free speech martyr; censorship
activity in Greece and Rome; the rise of Christianity and the Church's increasing intolerance; Renaissance attitudes; the coming of the Protestant Reformation and the concept of man's private religious conscience. Lecture.

2) *Roots of Modern Concepts*

The trends: the rise of secularism, the advent of strong political states,
printing and the idea of universal literacy, the scientific method and the spirit
of objective inquiry, the emergence of an economically powerful middle class,
the political theories of the Enlightenment; the men: Galileo against ecclesiastical authority, John Locke and "natural" political rights, Rousseau and his
"contract," Hobbes and the quest for authority, Mill and the social utility of
liberty. Students read Brecht's *Galileo,* Milton's *Areopagitica,* and Mill's *On
Liberty.* (See Appendix I for required reading list.) Lecture and discussion.
(See Appendixes II and III for sample discussion questions.)

3) *Majority Power and Minority Rights*

Introduction to the U.S. judicial system and its dual role as guardian of
both social order and individual freedom; the Supreme Court and its history,
powers, and limits; the Bill of Rights, with emphasis on the First and Fourteenth Amendments; legal theories advanced to resolve conflicts between the
Bill of Rights guarantees and social order prerequisites. Student reports on
McCloskey's *American Supreme Court* and Emerson's *Toward a General
Theory of the First Amendment.* (See Appendix VII for list of student reports.) Discussion.

Contravention of the judiciary's function by extralegal or illegal actions by
official, quasi-official, or private organizations; methods, characteristics, and
behavioral patterns of the extralegal censor; uses and abuses of police power as

an illustration. Student report on Chevigny's *Police Power* or Cray's *Big Blue Line*. Discussion. (See Appendix IV.)

4) *Religious Liberty*

The centrality of religious freedom in the American constitutional system; the Supreme Court's position and some landmark cases: *Watson v. Jones, Reynolds, Cochran, Everson, McCollum, Schempp*, the various Jehovah's Witnesses cases; the rationale and vitality of Jefferson's "wall of separation"; the validity of the "slippery slope" argument; problems in defining "religion"; recent legislative and judicial developments. Students read Konvitz's *Expanding Liberties*, Chapter I. Student reports on McCollum's *One Woman's Fight* and Howe's *The Garden and the Wilderness*. Lecture and discussion. (See Appendix V.)

5) *Freedom of Speech*

Legal definitions and theories concerning "speech"; the Supreme Court's recent attempts to delineate between "pure" and "symbolic" speech; the force of the Clear and Present Danger doctrine since the Schenck case in 1919 and Justice Holmes's famous "shouting fire" in a crowded theater analogy; the significance of recent civil rights cases in determining legal attitudes toward speech as opposed to action. Students read Konvitz's *Expanding Liberties*, Chapter VII. Lecture and discussion. (See Appendix VI.)

The Court's record on defending political dissent, from the Sedition Act of 1798 and the sedition acts of World War I to the Internal Security Act of 1950 and the draft card burning cases of 1965 and 1968; national security prerequisites and the Clear and Present Danger doctrine; the Court's sensitivity to the mood of the American political majority. Student reports on Murray's *Red Scare*, Bosworth's *America's Concentration Camps*, and Allen's *Concentration Camps U.S.A.* Lecture and discussion.

6) *Freedom of the Press*

Theories of the press: authoritarian, libertarian, social responsibility, and Soviet Communist; development of the social responsibility theory in this country, from the Zenger case to the present; the extent of press freedom in America; the problem areas: government restrictions and manipulation, new legal concepts of libel and the evolving right to privacy, conflict between press freedom and the right to a fair trial in reporting crime news, the Federal Communications Commission's "Fairness Doctrine" and licensing power, monopolistic (or oligopolistic) tendencies in media ownership, and news and entertainment programs depicting social violence. Students read McClellan's *Censorship in the United States*, pp. 94–150. Student reports on Siebert's *Four Theories of the Press* and Alexander's *Brief Narrative of the Case and Trial of John Peter Zenger*. Discussion.

7) *Loyalty and Freedom of Association*

Definitions of loyalty; the psychological roots of the "loyalty compulsion"; patriots, traitors, and "traitriots"; loyalties in conflict. Student report on Grodzins' *The Loyal and the Disloyal*. Discussion.

Developing legal concepts concerning the right to associate and to form loyalties, without fear of governmental or social reprisal based on the presumption of guilt by association; landmark cases: *N.A.A.C.P. v. Alabama* and

N.A.A.C.P. v. *Button;* emergence of the "breathing space" doctrine and the "preferred liberties" concept; Communist Party membership and the Court's shifting record, as revealed in the Dennis, Yates, and Robel cases. Students read Konvitz's *Expanding Liberties,* Chapters II and IV. Lecture and discussion.

8) *Academic Freedom*

The newest constitutionally protected freedom; the analogy with religious liberty and the operative "wall of separation" concept; the procedural nature of academic freedom; the rise and fall of loyalty oaths; student activism and the extents of academic freedom. Students read Konvitz's *Expanding Liberties,* Chapter III and McClellan's *Censorship in the United States,* pp. 189–213. Student reports on Kirk's *Academic Freedom* and Hofstader's *Academic Freedom in the Age of the College.* Discussion.

9) *Political Freedom and Censorship Abroad*

A world survey, with emphasis on Western Europe and the Soviet sphere; comparison of European, Soviet, and American attitudes toward the individual's role and place in society and the implications for intellectual freedom in each of these civilizations; Gletkin, Rubashov, maintenance of the political system, and commitment to self. Students read Koestler's *Darkness at Noon.* Student reports on Bunn and Andrews' *Politics and Civil Liberties in Europe* and Sakharov's *Progress, Coexistence and Intellectual Freedom.* Lecture and discussion.

10) *Conformity v. Freedom in the Modern World*

Political, social, and psychological definitions of freedom; the prerequisites of freedom; the inner stresses of freedom; the psychological urge to conform; agents for building and maintaining conformity: majority disapproval, sacred and inflexible political dogma, social and religious codes of behavior, authoritarian bureaucracy, the "repressive toleration" of democratic liberalism, educational and political conditioning, human emulation of the machine's efficiency and interchangeability. Students read Kafka's *Trial* and Meerloo's *Rape of the Mind.* Student reports on Fromm's *Escape from Freedom* and Marcuse's *One-Dimensional Man.* Lecture and discussion.

11) *Moral Censorship, Obscenity, and the Law*

Evolution of legal definitions and concepts of obscenity: common law attitudes, the *Hicklin Rule,* nineteenth century American legislation, the debt to Schroeder, Learned Hand's challenge to the Victorian standard in *United States* v. *Kennerley,* the *Ulysses*/Woolsey breakthrough in 1933, the Warren Court's *Roth* and *Alberts* cases, refining Roth, the Ginzburg aberration, sanctioning the "variable obscenity" theory. Students read Ernst and Schwartz's *Censorship: the Search for the Obscene,* Konvitz's *Expanding Liberties,* Chapter V, and McClellan's *Censorship in the United States,* pp. 54–94. Student reports on Schroeder's *'Obscene' Literature and Constitutional Law* and Rembar's *End of Obscenity.* Discussion.

The effects of obscenity on human behavior; the social scientist's frustrating quest for "scientific" evidence to prove or disprove a causal relationship between "obscene" material and criminal sex acts; the government's Commission on Obscenity and Pornography. Students read the Kronhausens' *Pornog-*

raphy and the Law. Student reports on Gebhard's *Sex Offenders* and Lorang's *Burning Ice.* Lecture and discussion.

12) *The Nature of Pornography and Hard-core Censors*

History and characteristics of pornography; possible social value and importance of pornography; class consciousness and pornographic styles; the censor's arguments and methods; the nineteenth century vice-society movement: its history and psychology; the current organizations. Students read Boyer's *Purity in Print* and McClellan's *Censorship in the United States,* pp. 9–53. Students examine pornography collection. (See Appendix VIII.) Student reports on Marcus's *Other Victorians* and Ullerstam's *Erotic Minorities.* Lecture and discussion.

13) *Moral Censorship and the Visual Media*

Film censorship in this country: First Amendment protection denied until 1952; landmark legal cases, with emphasis on *Burstyn* v. *Wilson;* prior censorship and self-regulation predominate; the pernicious effects of self-regulatory codes on the film art; the new classification system; blue movies and "sexploitation" films; the special power of the picture as compared with print. Students read Randall's *Censorship of the Movies.* Student report on Walker's *Sex in the Movies.* Lecture and discussion.

14) *Violence! the New "Obscenity"*

Definitions of violence; physical and psychological ramifications; America's violent history: causal effects and double standards; the "contagion" of violence; television and motion pictures as purveyors of violence: the First Amendment and Clear and Present Danger clash once again. Student report on Wertham's *Sign for Cain.* Lecture and discussion.

15) *Summing Up: the Librarian in a Censorious World*

The librarian's professional functions and obligations; reasons for the poor record to date; analysis of the assumptions; the conservative arguments; alternatives. Students read Fiske's *Book Selection and Censorship* and McClellan's *Censorship in the United States,* pp. 173–188. Student report on Shera's "Intellectual Freedom—Intellectual? Free?" in *Wilson Library Bulletin.* Discussion.

METHODS OF TEACHING

As the detailed course outline above indicates, "Intellectual Freedom and Censorship" is principally a reading and discussion course. Lectures, which are ordinarily brief and to the point, supplement outside reading material, as do the concise oral student reports on pertinent individual titles.[11]

Class discussion is focused by means of specially designed discussion questions. (See Appendixes II–VI for examples.) These questions are circulated well in advance of the class meeting to which they pertain, and are related to scheduled reading assignments and student reports. Discussion in the classroom is conducted with as much informality and latitude as possible: the objective is a thoughtful, uninhibited airing of ideas relevant to the subject matter of the course. I would add that the instructor attempts to be nondoctrinaire most of the time, although he does not always succeed.

In addition, two or three guest speakers are invited to meet with the class each semester. Speakers thus far have included Paul S. Boyer, Professor of History at the University of Massachusetts at Amherst and author of *Purity in Print;* Wayne Hansen, Editor of *Avatar*, an interesting and substantial hippie sheet which prints four-letter words and, predictably, ran into a confluence of censorship problems; Lawrence Clark Powell, author and distinguished librarian, who spoke about his youthful flirtation with the American Communist Party and the McCarthy Era repercussions; and Leo Renaud, former Vice President of the National Organization of Citizens for Decent Literature, who talked about smut.

A research paper which reflects high standards of scholarship is required. These papers usually run from fifteen to thirty pages or more in typewritten form, although no specified length is required. The student is free to choose the subject of his paper; a list of suggested topics is issued, however, for the purposes of guidance and stimulation. Suggested topics include: "The Velikovsky Affair," "Why the Fifth Amendment?," "Book Censorship in Ireland," "The Right to Travel," "Senator Joseph McCarthy, Communism, and the Constitution," "The Ladies Chatterley, Fanny Hill, and Pamela," "Homosexuals and Civil Rights," "What To Do About Hate Literature?," "Censoring History in the Schools," "Girodias and the Olympia Press," "The Philosophy and Psychology of Civil Disobedience," "Anthony Comstock and A. Mitchell Palmer: Heroes in Their Time," "John Locke's Influence on American Libertarianism," "Freedom of Information and the U.S. Government," "The Post Office and the Obscenity Business," "Japanese Relocation: Injustice or Necessity?," "CLEAN in California," "The Psychology of Dirty Words," "The Nature and Power of Propaganda," "Literary Censorship in the USSR," "Ginzburg, Mishkin, and Fanny Hill: Three Funny Cases for the Nine Men," and "The Lord Chamberlain v. the British Theatre."

An examination is scheduled and administered at the end of the course, but it is an optional requirement. Students are evaluated on the basis of their general performance in class and the quality of the research paper; the examination, for those who choose to take it, simply adds another grading criterion. The three-hour examination emphasizes required reading assignments.

CONCLUSIONS

"Intellectual Freedom and Censorship," as the foregoing attests, is not a "library" course *per se.* Indeed, until the final class meeting, libraries are rarely mentioned. I have stated elsewhere that "Intellectual freedom, if it's worth anything at all, should be taught from an intellectual point of view."[12] I would add to that statement this thought: librarianship is an interdisciplinary field, if it is nothing else, and those who are unable or unwilling to make the necessary relationships between general intellectual theory and professional library work ought not, perhaps, to become librarians in the first place.

It is much too early to make precise assessments about the possible successes and failures of the course or its ultimate impact. Students who have completed the course thus far—for the most part, interested and intelligent individuals with a desire and capacity for handling complex, abstract ideas— have been genuinely enthusiastic about the results:

> I looked at some of my old opinions in a new light and found that I had changed my mind on some of them, such as censorship of the "obscene." It helped me to develop a more rational basis for forming attitudes and opinions. I liked the presentation of facts, philosophies of great thinkers of the past and present, diverse points of view, and encouragement of discussions in class with an interesting interchange of ideas.

This quotation, taken from a written student evaluation of the course, is typical in many respects of general student response.[13] Critiques from other students include these representative comments:

> Although the course did not cause me to revise my thinking on the subject of censorship, I now have some concrete information to back my arguments.

> While I began the course as an opponent of censorship, and ended up feeling the same way (if not more so), learning the how and why of the other person's point of view has been valuable.

> I have been rethinking my whole set of values since taking this course. My term paper was, to me, in terms of my own personal self and my own ideas as related to my field—high school librarianship—and my personal and social life, the hardest and most valuable piece of work I've done at library school.

> Personally, the course has helped me to gain a new perspective—especially on civil rights issues. The importance and impact of Supreme Court decisions means more to me now; especially the fact that a dissenting opinion may eventually become the basis of a new decision as the times change. I have also become more conscious of the fact that it isn't enough to have ideals and principles; there comes a time when you must act or lose them.

> I feel as if I've received from the course what I was seeking—an ability to handle professionally questions of intellectual freedom and censorship. In my first year of library work, I was involved in a censorship episode regarding James Michener's *Hawaii;* I did defend the book, but to no avail. I often wished afterwards that I could have handled the situation more professionally. Now, if I had it to do over, I think I could handle the situation more maturely.

These comments, and others like them, are encouraging and gratifying. But the proof of the pudding, as the old saw goes, is in the eating. Whether the individuals who have taken the course "Intellectual Freedom and Censorship" actually are more articulate, confident, cognizant adherents of intellectual freedom concepts and the principles contained in the Library Bill of Rights and similar documents, cannot be known for some time, if ever.

Finally, to repeat: the course "Intellectual Freedom and Censorship" is not presented here as a cure-all for the library profession's chronic case of censorshipitis. The censorship syndrome is integrally related to the personality problems of the profession, and a single course, no matter how fine, will not make everything all well again. If Paul Boyer is right, however, when he states in his introduction to *Purity in Print* that "Much scattered evidence—from the bench, the legislatures, the intellectual community, and the grassroots level—suggests to me that we may be on the threshold of a period of greatly intensified censorship activity," then it is time for librarians and library educators to begin the search for some basic healing remedies. I believe that the course "Intellectual Freedom and Censorship" points in the right direction.

APPENDIX I

Required Reading List

Boyer, Paul S. *Purity in Print; the Vice-Society Movement and Censorship in America*. New York: Scribners, 1968.

Brecht, Bertolt. *Galileo*. English version by Charles Laughton; edited with an introduction by Eric Bentley. New York: Grove Pr., 1966.

Ernst, Morris L. and Schwartz, Alan. *Censorship: the Search for the Obscene*. Introduction by Philip Scharper. New York: Macmillan, 1964.

Fiske, Marjorie. *Book Selection and Censorship: a Study of School and Public Libraries in California*. Berkeley and Los Angeles: Univ. of California Pr., 1959.

Kafka, Franz. *The Trial*. New York: Modern Library, 1964. (Originally published in 1937.)

Koestler, Arthur. *Darkness at Noon*. Translated by Daphne Hardy. New York: Bantam Books, 1966. (Originally published in 1941.)

Konvitz, Milton R. *Expanding Liberties*. New York: Viking Pr., 1966.

Kronhausen, Eberhard and Phyllis. *Pornography and the Law*. Rev. ed. New York: Ballantine, 1964.

McClellan, Grant S. (ed.) *Censorship in the United States*. (The Reference Shelf, Vol. XXXIX, No. 3.) New York: H. W. Wilson, 1967.

Meerloo, Joost. *The Rape of the Mind; the Psychology of Thought Control, Menticide, and Brainwashing*. New York: Grosset & Dunlap, 1956.

Mill, John Stuart. *On Liberty*. Edited by Alburey Castell. New York: Appleton-Century-Crofts, 1947. (Originally published in 1859.)

Milton, John. *Areopagitica*. Edited by John W. Hales. New York and London: Oxford Univ. Pr., 1961.

Randall, Richard S. *Censorship of the Movies; the Social and Political Control of a Mass Media*. Madison: Univ. of Wisconsin Pr., 1968.

APPENDIX II

Sample Discussion Question

"THEY SHOWED ME THE INSTRUMENTS":
THE SILENCE OF GALILEO

Unlike Socrates, history's first great martyr for intellectual freedom, Galileo did not die for his convictions. Instead, he recanted. And as Brecht would tell the story, Galileo lived to regret his action:

In my day astronomy emerged into the market place. At that particular time, had one man put up a fight, it could have had wide repercussions. I have come to believe that I was never in real danger; for some years I was as strong as the authorities, and I surrendered my knowledge to the powers that be, to use it, no, not *use* it, *abuse* it, as it suits their ends. I have betrayed my profession. Any man who does what I have done must not be tolerated in the ranks of the science.

As you perhaps know, in 1968 the Roman Catholic Church authorized Franz Cardinal Konig of Vienna to convene a commission which would reverse the Church's judgment against Galileo and his ideas—a judgment which has stood for three centuries. Cardinal Konig put the Church's current attitude this way:

> The Church has no reason whatsoever to shun a revision of the disputed Galileo verdict. To the contrary, the case provides the Church with an opportunity to explain its claim to infallibility in its realm and to define its limits.

Does this contemplated action by the Church—three hundred years too late—really matter? Does it matter, really matter, that the prevailing authority —seventeenth century ecclesiastical law—censored Galileo? Did not "science" triumph despite the conservative attitudes and repressive actions of the Church?

Do you agree that Galileo's actions make him unfit for the profession of science? What were his obligations to "science"?

Do you buy Brecht's contention that Galileo recanted because he feared physical pain? Is it correct to call Galileo a coward?

Brecht's Galileo says that "for some years I was as strong as the authorities": would he have had the same obligations to science and the principle of free inquiry if he had lacked this stature? Would the risks have been greater? Would Church authorities have acted differently, perhaps?

At one point in the play, Brecht's Galileo comments that "The plight of the multitude is old as the rocks, and is believed to be basic as the rocks. But now they have learned to doubt. They snatched the telescopes out of our hands and had them trained on their tormentors: prince, official, public moralist." Has the freedom to doubt increased since Galileo's time? Has this freedom reduced or weakened "the authorities"? In our age of civil liberties and constitutional guarantees for the individual, could a Galileo be silenced? By whom? How?

APPENDIX III

Sample Discussion Question

THE CLASSIC ARGUMENTS:
MILTON AND MILL

Libertarians are fond of quoting and citing John Stuart Mill's *On Liberty* and John Milton's *Areopagitica*. While there is no doubt that these two essays are among the most powerful defenses of freedom of expression in the English language, both should be examined closely for limitations and flaws in argumentation.

What are Milton's principal arguments against censorship? Does he argue for total lack of restraints? If not, what exceptions does he note? What are the chief criticisms that you would make concerning his arguments?

Consider the same questions for Mill, and then apply both men's argumentation to the following contemporary censorship case:

> Radio station WBAI in New York City broadcast a poem entitled "Anti-Semitism." The poem written by a fifteen-year-old Negro student and read over the air by a Negro teacher, was "dedicated" to Albert Shanker, President of the United Federation of Teachers. The poem begins: "Hey Jew boy with that yarmulka on your head/You pale-faced Jew boy/I wish you were dead." Later, the station broadcast a discussion program in which one participant suggested that Hitler had not exterminated enough Jews: "He didn't make enough lampshades out of them."

> Outrage greeted these broadcasts, with strong protests condemning the radio station coming quickly from the New York Jewish community and municipal officials. One prominent Jewish leader wondered: "Is WBAI the ghost of Joseph Goebbel's Nazi radio network with a Federal license?" Jack Gould, the *New York Times* media analyst, wrote that ". . . ventilation of prejudice toward either Jews or Negroes need not take the form of epithets and advocacy of genocide over the airwaves. To broadcast to the mass the gutter verbiage of hatred is a sell-out to opportunistic sensationalism, the protest of WBAI to the contratry notwithstanding."

> Speaking for WBAI's board of directors, its chairman, Dr. Harold Taylor, former President of Sarah Lawrence College, refused to eliminate anti-Semitic expressions and opinions from future broadcasts. Dr. Taylor suggested that proscribing such views would "fall into the trap of those who would refine the rawness of truth in order to make it socially convenient. To be informed of the existence and extent of dangerous social forces is the first step toward coping with them."

APPENDIX IV

Sample Discussion Question

POLICE POWER: EXTRALEGAL CHALLENGE
TO THE CONSTITUTIONAL SYSTEM

The judiciary does not have a spotless record, of course, as a defender of intellectual freedom. In the area of political expression, for example, the Supreme Court failed miserably in its encounter with the Sedition Act of 1798; the Court upheld the conviction of the Haymarket anarchists (four were hanged, but three were later freed by Governor John Peter Atgeld); it aided in the constraint of political dissent during and after World War I; it sanctioned the internment of Japanese-Americans during World War II; it sustained the conviction of the Communist Ten for violation of the Smith Act in 1951. Yet, objectively speaking, it can be said that the judiciary has a reasonably good record on civil liberties questions, except perhaps in times of national emergency. In recent years especially, the High Court has acted to protect, secure, and expand individual liberties, using the thin wedge of case law to restrain repressive forces.

A much greater threat to intellectual freedom is government agencies and private organizations which seek to impose their views on the individual through extralegal or illegal means.

Possibly the most dangerous and uncontrollable extralegal pressure is exerted by law enforcement agencies, such as the FBI, the U.S. Bureau of Narcotics, and state and local police forces. When these powerful, official agencies overstep the fine line between law enforcement and extralegal activity, the delicate constitutional system breaks down, because "due process of law" is denied. Extralegal or illegal police power takes many forms, including willful disregard of judicial rulings; use of illegal information gathering techniques, such as wiretapping and electronic eavesdropping; intimidation through police raids and police presence; police harassment; and even police riots.

Evidence that extralegal use of police power destroys the constitutional process is overwhelming and incontestable. Paul Chevigny, in his book *Police Power*, notes that one study showed that thirty-seven percent of the policemen interviewed believed that "disrespect for police" was sufficient justification for "roughing up a guy." Chevigny also points out:

> In dozens of cases a verbal act of defiance is followed by summary punishment and arrest, and the charges against the offender, of course, are drawn so as to account for the events in the street as well as for any injuries to the defendant. Sometimes those who protest the actions of the police are drawn into the orbit of defiance and are arrested as well. The arrest not only punishes their defiance but eliminates them as effective witnesses.

There seems to be little doubt, as Edgar Friedenberg put it in his article "Hooked on Law Enforcement" in *The Nation* (October 16, 1967), that "people do not become law-enforcement officers anywhere in order to serve as guardians of liberty."

Why do police and other enforcement agents sometimes misuse their power? Is it possible to restrain extralegal use of police power? What is the power of the courts in this area? How thin is the line between enforcement and interpretation of the law? Which is more important to you: social and political order or freedom of expression? When Chicago demonstrators at the 1968 Democratic National Convention shouted such phrases as "Fuck these Nazis!," "Kill the pigs," "Fuck you, pig," and "Fuck, fuck, fuck!" at the police, how should (or could) the situation have been handled? What is involved when the police publicly use obscenities and "fighting words"? For example, at Chicago one policeman was quoted as telling a "hippie-type" girl, "You better get your fucking dirty cunt out of here." (See *trans-action*, January, 1969, p. 39.) Recently, the sheriff of Fairfax County, Virginia, ordered a haircut for a male prisoner serving a one-day sentence: "It is my policy to have uniformity in the jail and I do cut hair," the sheriff said. Is this an extralegal or illegal use of police power? Are there any constitutional principles involved in this instance?

APPENDIX V

Sample Discussion Question

HOW STRONG IS JEFFERSON'S "WALL OF SEPARATION"?

As you know, the First Amendment clearly states that "Congress shall make no law respecting an establishment of religion, or prohibiting the free exercise thereof." Thomas Jefferson interpreted this First Amendment provision as "building a wall of separation between Church and State," an interpretation which has been incorporated into U.S. constitutional law, and one which is zealously assented to by many laymen. In his postlude to McCollum's *One Woman's Fight,* Paul Blanshard, for example, speaks for a large segment of public opinion when he says:

> It is evident from Vashti McCollum's story that the fruits of her great victory in the Supreme Court cannot be preserved except by organized effort. Organized sectarianism, Protestant and Catholic, continues to chip away at the wall of separation between church and state. An organized defense of the Constitution is a necessity.

But Robert Frost, as you might recall, asked "Before I built a wall I'd ask to know / What I was walling in or walling out." Taking the cue from Frost, then, we should ask: Why the separation principle? Why the wall? Whom does it benefit? Society? In what way? Ecclesiastics? How? Mark DeWolfe Howe, the late Professor of Law at Harvard, has some interesting thoughts about this last question in his collection of lectures entitled *The Garden and the Wilderness: Religion and Government in American Constitutional History.*

Before considering how strong Jefferson's famous wall is today, it seems appropriate to ask: What is religion? What constitutes religious conviction? According to Konvitz, the various Jehovah's Witnesses cases decided by the Supreme Court since 1938 exemplify "the centrality of religious freedom in the complex of constitutional liberties and in American society." What, then, comes under the purview of religious freedom? Is, for example, Timothy Leary's League for Spiritual Discovery (LSD) a religion? Is Scientology a religion? Is Pacifism a religious conviction? Robert G. Ingersoll, the fine old radical, questioned the existence of God and said that "Religion can never reform mankind because religion is slavery." But he did urge his fellow men "to find the subtle threads that join the distant with the now, to increase knowledge, to take burdens from the weak, to develop the brain, to defend the right, to make a palace for the soul." "This is real religion," Ingersoll said. "This is real worship." What is religion?

After conceding the difficulties encountered in defining "religion," and if we conclude that the separation principle has any value as a constitutional doctrine, we should inquire into the status of Jefferson's wall today. How strong is it? Churchmen today are active in social protest movements; receive lucrative tax exemptions from the state; maintain educational institutions which receive public tax money for building construction, textbooks, and, in some instances, teachers' salaries. Konvitz wonders if "slippery slope" is a fallacious argument or legitimate reasoning in connection with the separation principle. We should consider the question carefully, beginning with the "child-benefit" theory (first introduced in 1930 in the Cochran case) and then proceeding to more contemporary issues and cases.

APPENDIX VI

Sample Discussion Question

SPEECH V. ACTION

The American constitutional system protects free speech, the First Amendment reading: "Congress shall make no law . . . abridging the freedom of speech." The provision is simple, uncomplicated, and absolute. Yet it has caused more judicial debate, more constitutional agony and pain, and more interpretative second thoughts than any of the other Bill of Rights guarantees.

The principle issues concerning the deceptively straightforward free speech provision are rooted in disagreements about definitions. What is speech? Are there different kinds of speech? If so, are they all protected by the First Amendment? Is there "pure" speech as opposed to "symbolic" speech? When does expression become action? Is, for example, draft card burning or a lunch-counter sit-in or flag desecration or commandeering a campus building by students a form of protected speech, expressing dissatisfaction or dissent, or is it an action liable to criminal prosecution? Judges, scholars, students, and the man in the street differ over these questions. Recently, Federal Judge Marvin E. Frankel, when ruling on Columbia University's right to discipline student protesters, commented that "debate on public issues should be uninhibited, robust and wide-open," but he added (and this was his decisive point):

> I must make clear, however, the gross error of believing that every kind of conduct (however nonverbal and physically destructive or obstructive) must be treated simply as protected "speech" because those engaged in it intend to express some view or position.

> It is surely nonsense of the most literal kind that a court of law should subordinate the rule of law in favor of more "fundamental principles" of revolutionary action designed to forcibly oust governments, courts and all.

Supreme Court Justice Abe Fortas looks at this question from a slightly different point of view:

The college youth who is protesting against the college administration or the war in Vietnam or the draft has, of course, the full scope of First Amendment rights. He is entitled to the full protection of the state and the courts in the exercise of speech and symbolic speech, however hostile. But he is not entitled to immunity if he directly and willfully incites violence or insists upon deliberately disrupting the work or movement of others.

He may be motivated by the highest moral principles. He may be passionately inspired. He may, indeed, be right in the eyes of history or morality or philosophy. These are not controlling. It is the state's duty to arrest and punish those who violate the laws designed to protect private safety and public order.

Justice Fortas concludes his thinking (taken here from his article "The Limits of Civil Disobedience" which appeared in the *New York Times Magazine*, May 12, 1968) with this comment: "Dissent and dissenters have no monopoly on freedom. They must tolerate opposition. They must accept dissent from their dissent."

Yet another perspective is found in Ralph W. Conant's article "Rioting, Insurrection and Civil Disobedience," in *The American Scholar*, Summer, 1968. Conant, who is Associate Director of the Lemberg Center for the Study of Violence at Brandeis University, points out:

> . . . we have often rationalized *post factum* the use of violence by aggrieved segments of the population *when the cause was regarded as a just one in terms of our deeply held egalitarian values*. The anti-draft riots during the Civil War are one example. . . . Two or three generations from now, the ghetto riots (and even the spasmodic insurrection that is bound to follow) will be seen as having contributed to the perfection of our system of egalitarian values. Thus, I conclude that violence in the cause of hewing to our most cherished goals of freedom, justice and equal opportunity for all our citizens is and will remain as indispensable a corrective ingredient in our system as peaceful acts of civil disobedience.

Consider the positions noted above, in light of the Clear and Present Danger doctrine discussed by Konvitz. Consider also the High Court's arguments in the various sit-in cases, beginning with *Garner* v. *Louisiana*. In your opinion, should the Court legitimatize Conant's position, as expressed above?

APPENDIX VII

Individual Student Reports: Reading List

Alexander, James. *A Brief Narrative of the Case and Trial of John Peter Zenger, Printer of The New York Weekly Journal.* Edited by Stanley N. Katz. Cambridge: Harvard Univ. Pr., 1963.

Allen, Charles R., Jr. *Concentration Camps U.S.A.* Privately printed, 1966.

Bosworth, Allan R. *America's Concentration Camps.* New York: Norton, 1967.

Bunn, Ronald F. and Andrews, William (eds.). *Politics and Civil Liberties in Europe; Four Case Studies.* Princeton: Van Nostrand, 1967.

Chevigny, Paul. *Police Power*. New York: Pantheon, 1968.

Cray, Ed. *The Big Blue Line: Police Power vs. Human Rights*. New York: Coward-McCann, 1967.

Emerson, Thomas I. *Toward a General Theory of the First Amendment*. New York: Vintage Books, 1966.

Fromm, Erich. *Escape From Freedom*. New York: Holt, 1941.

Gebhard, Paul H., *et al. Sex Offenders: an Analysis of Types*. New York: Harper, 1965. (Chapters 1–3; 18; 31.)

Grodzins, Morton. *The Loyal and the Disloyal; Social Boundaries of Patriotism and Treason*. Cleveland: World, 1966.

Hofstadter, Richard. *Academic Freedom in the Age of the College*. New York: Columbia Univ. Pr., 1955.

Howe, Mark DeWolfe. *The Garden and the Wilderness: Religion and Government in American Constitutional History*. Chicago: Univ. of Chicago Pr., 1965.

Kirk, Russell. *Academic Freedom; an Essay in Definition*. New York: Regnery, 1955.

Lorang, Sister Mary Corde. *Burning Ice: the Moral and Emotional Effects of Reading*. New York: Scribners, 1968.

McCloskey, Robert G. *The American Supreme Court*. Chicago: Univ. of Chicago, 1960.

McCollum, Vashti Cromwell. *One Woman's Fight*. Rev. ed., with preface by George Axtelle; postlude by Paul Blanshard. Boston: Beacon Pr., 1961.

Marcus, Steven. *The Other Victorians; a Study of Sexuality and Pornography in Mid-Nineteenth-Century England*. New York: Basic Books, 1964.

Marcuse, Herbert. *One-Dimensional Man; Studies in the Ideology of Advanced Industrial Society*. Boston: Beacon Pr., 1964.

Murray, Robert K. *Red Scare; a Study of National Hysteria, 1919–1920*. Minneapolis: Univ. of Minnesota, 1955.

Rembar, Charles. *The End of Obscenity; the Trials of Lady Chatterley, Tropic of Cancer and Fanny Hill*. New York: Random, 1968.

Sakharov, Andrei D. *Progress, Coexistence and Intellectual Freedom*. Translated by the New York Times; introduction, afterword, and notes by Harrison Salisbury. New York: Norton, 1968.

Schroeder, Theodore. *'Obscene' Literature and Constitutional Law*. New York: Privately printed, 1910.

Shera, Jesse. "Intellectual Freedom—Intellectual? Free?," *Wilson Library Bulletin*, XLII (November, 1967), 323+.

Siebert, Fred S., Peterson, Theodore, and Schramm, Wilbur. *Four Theories of the Press*. Urbana: Univ. of Illinois Pr., 1956.

Ullerstam, Lars. *The Erotic Minorities*. New York: Grove, 1966.

Walker, Alexander. *Sex in the Movies; the Celluloid Sacrifice*. Baltimore: Penguin Books, 1968.

Wertham, Frederick. *A Sign for Cain; an Exploration of Human Violence*. New York: Macmillan, 1966.

APPENDIX VIII

Pornography Collection

In their article "Pornography—Raging Menace or Paper Tiger" in *Trans-action* (July/August, 1967), John Gagnon and William Simon make the point that "In middle class circles, many young men and the majority of females may grow up without ever having seen hard-core pornography," and the Kronhausens state (in *Pornography and the Law*) that "It is crucial to an understanding of the problem at hand that the difference between pornography and erotic realism be made clear from three aspects, namely, intent, content, and effect, and it has been our experience that *this can only be done by an examination of both kinds of writing.*"

With these two thoughts in mind, a small collection of pornography has been developed at the Library School at Simmons. The collection includes items which represent various levels and degrees of the pornographic art, both written and pictorial. Students examine the collection individually, in order to form a more perfect judgment about what is and what is not pornographic.

In addition, examples of pornography are found in Marcus's *The Other Victorians;* Ullerstam's *The Erotic Minorities;* and the Kronhausens' *Pornography and the Law.*

REFERENCES

1. William D. North, legal counsel to the American Library Association, has wisely advised: "In order to win our fight for intellectual freedom, we must obtain the support of lawmakers, educators, library trustees and the public. To obtain such support, we must buy time—time to install adequate selection procedures and policies; time to open communications with civic, religious, educational and political bodies; time to win the confidence of the public. To buy the time necessary to do all this, an occasional defeat may be encountered, a strategic withdrawal may be inevitable; but this need not be the end. Intellectual freedom is indeed a feeble concept if it cannot survive compromise." "Intellectual Freedom" (column) *ALA Bulletin*, LXII (September, 1968), 950.
2. Marjorie Fiske, *Book Selection and Censorship: a Study of School and Public Libraries in California* (Berkeley and Los Angeles: Univ. of California Pr., 1959).
3. For example, the study *Dissent and Sex*, conducted by the New Jersey Library Association's Committee on Restrictive Library Practices and issued in mimeograph form in 1966, lends support to Fiske's conclusions. Although not as intensive as Fiske's study, the New Jersey survey analyzed controversial book and periodical holdings in various sized public libraries in the state. The results were predictable. As the introduction to *Dissent and Sex* notes, "All librarians are against censorship in principle. Few are in practice."
4. Robert D. Leigh, "Intellectual Freedom," *ALA Bulletin*, XLII (September 1, 1948), 365.
5. I hasten to add that there are several or more types of human expression which are legally proscribed, such as slander and libel, misrepresentation and fraud,

revelation of trade secrets and classified information, plagiarism, and "obscenity." There is, however, no legal restriction on offensive or irresponsible expression, unless it falls into one of these categories.

6. As Samuel Rothstein has pointed out, this does not obtain in most special libraries. Yet, the librarian's image as an obstacle to getting information in public and academic libraries appears to be secure, at least for the near future.

7. Contrast, for instance, the attitude of the professional journalist with the librarian's.

8. The questionnaire survey "What are the Accredited Library Schools Teaching in the Area of Intellectual Freedom and Censorship?" conducted several years ago by Dorothy Bendix documents this point. With the exception of the Fiske Report and Robert Downs's fine anthology *The First Freedom*, the materials used in most library schools are thin on content and parochial in outlook. "Teaching the Concept of Intellectual Freedom: the State of the Art," *ALA Bulletin*, LXIII (March, 1969), 356.

9. I owe more than a footnote of gratitude to Kenneth R. Shaffer, Director of the School of Library Science at Simmons, for permitting me to experiment with the course, and for his encouragement during the developmental stages.

10. The course syllabus presented here is not static; it will doubtless change, perhaps radically, in the future. The outline here simply represents the course as taught in 1969.

11. Oral reports are limited to approximately fifteen minutes, unless the title involved is exceptionally difficult. Throughout the discussion (and the semester), each student reporter serves as a knowledgeable resource person on the subject of his book.

12. In the text of LeRoy Charles Merritt's review of the Fiske Report when it was reprinted in 1968. "Fiske Revisited," *Library Journal*, XCIII (July, 1968), 2625.

13. Although student evaluations of the course, almost without exception, have been positive overall, there have been minor criticisms of various aspects of the course. For example, students have questioned the value of certain titles on the reading lists; in addition, the student report technique has received a number of adverse comments.

Contributors

Raymond B. Agler, formerly an Adult Assistant at the Gardenville Branch of the Enoch Pratt Free Library, Baltimore, Maryland and then a Branch Librarian at the Hyde Park Branch of the Boston Public Library, Boston, Massachusetts, is presently an Inter-Library Loan Officer at the Boston Public Library, Boston, Massachusetts.

John F. Anderson, formerly Director of the Knoxville Public Library, Knoxville, Tennessee, is presently City Librarian of the San Francisco Public Library, San Francisco, California.

Leonard B. Archer is the Director of the Oshkosh Public Library, Oshkosh, Wisconsin. He is active in intellectual freedom activities in Wisconsin, and served as the Chairman of the Wisconsin Library Association Intellectual Freedom Committee from 1963–1965.

H. William Axford, formerly Director of Library Service at the University of Denver, Colorado, is presently the Director of Library Services at Florida Atlantic University, Boca Raton, Florida.

Sanford Berman, formerly Periodicals Librarian at the University of California at Los Angeles, is presently the Assistant Librarian at the University of Zambia, Lusaka, Zambia.

David K. Berninghausen, a former chairman of the ALA Committee on Intellectual Freedom, is the Director of the University of Minnesota Library School, Minneapolis, Minnesota.

John N. Berry III has served as Assistant Director, Simmons College Library; Lecturer at Simmons College School of Library Science; and Editor of the *Bay State Librarian* prior to joining the R. R. Bowker Co. in 1964. A former Assistant Editor of *Library Journal* and Managing Editor of Bowker New Book Projects, Mr. Berry is now Editor-in-Chief of *Library Journal*.

Donald V. Black, formerly Physics Librarian at the University of California at Los Angeles, and editor of the *ALA Newsletter on Intellectual Freedom* from 1961–62, is presently with the System Development Corporation, Santa Monica, California.

William J. Brennan, Jr. is a Justice of the Supreme Court of the United States.

Dorothy Broderick, formerly an Associate Professor of Library Science at St. John's University, Jamaica, New York, a Children's Consultant for the New York State Library in Albany, New York, and then an Associate Professor at the School of Library Science, Case-Western Reserve University, Cleveland, Ohio, is visiting lecturer (1969–1970) at the University of Wisconsin-Madison.

Edwin Castagna President of ALA from 1964–1965, is currently Chairman of ALA's Intellectual Freedom Committee and the Director of the Enoch Pratt Free Library, Baltimore, Maryland.

Blanche Collins has recently retired from her position as City Librarian of the Long Beach Public Library, Long Beach, California. She held the position from 1960 to 1969.

Jerome Cushman, formerly the Librarian of the New Orleans Public Library, New Orleans, Louisiana, is presently a lecturer in children's literature at the School of Library Science, University of California at Los Angeles.

Edward de Grazia, censorship lawyer, is well-known for his defenses of *Tropic of Cancer* and *Naked Lunch*. He is also the author of *Censorship Landmarks* (R. R. Bowker Co.).

Robert B. Downs is the Dean of the Library Administration at the University of Illinois Library, Urbana, Illinois. He is also the author of *The First Freedom*,

Molders of the Modern Mind, Books That Changed the World, Famous Books, and *How to Do Library Research.* Mr. Downs is a former Chairman of the ALA Intellectual Freedom Committee. An annual award for outstanding contributions in intellectual freedom has recently been established in his name.

Henry P. Durkin is the Publicity Director for Walker & Co., New York, New York.

William L. Emerson, formerly head of the Science Department at the Long Beach Public Library, Long Beach, California, is presently District Librarian of the Palos Verdes District Library, Palos Verdes, California.

Dr. Harold E. Fey, formerly the editor of *The Christian Century,* joined the faculty of Christian Theological Seminary, Indianapolis, Indiana, in 1964 and is presently Professor Emeritus of Christian Ethics at Christian Theological Seminary.

Ervin J. Gaines is the Director of the Minneapolis Public Library, Minneapolis, Minnesota. He is a former intellectual freedom columnist for the *ALA Bulletin* and former Chairman of the ALA Intellectual Freedom Committee. Mr. Gaines is currently revising *Banned Books* (R. R. Bowker).

Evelyn Geller is the Editor of *School Library Journal.*

Barbara Hagist is the Coordinator of Community Services at the Tulsa City-County Library System, Tulsa, Oklahoma.

Theodore C. Hines, formerly an Assistant Professor at the Graduate School of Library Service, Rutgers University, New Brunswick, New Jersey, is presently an Assistant Professor at the School of Library Service, Columbia University, New York, New York.

George M. Holloway is Head of the Regional Film Center, The Free Library of Philadelphia, Philadelphia, Pennsylvania.

Inge Judd is a librarian in the Language and Literature Division of the Queens Borough Public Library, Jamaica, New York.

William A. Katz is a Professor at the School of Library Science, State University of New York at Albany, New York. He is the editor of *Journal on Education for Librarianship, RQ,* the official publication of the ALA Reference Series Division, "Magazines," a regular column in *Library Journal,* and the author of *Magazines for Libraries* (R. R. Bowker).

James J. Kilpatrick, formerly the editor of the *Richmond News Leader,* Richmond, Virginia, is presently a correspondent with the *Washington Star* syndicate.

Kenneth Kister is an Assistant Professor at the School of Library Science, Simmons College, Boston, Massachusetts and author of *Social Issues and Library Problems* (R. R. Bowker Co.).

Ronald A. Landor is the Head of Adult Reference Services at the Orange County Public Library, Orange, California.

John V. Lindsay, formerly a Republican Congressman from New York, is now the Mayor of New York City.

Henry Miller Madden, a former editor of *The California Librarian* who played a prominent role in the defense of intellectual freedom in the California trial *Ballantine* v. *Hogue* (1964), is now the Librarian of the Fresno State College Library, Fresno, California.

Daniel Melcher joined the R. R. Bowker Company in 1947 and served as publisher of *Library Journal* and a director of the company. He was the President of Bowker from 1963 to 1968, when he became Chairman of Bowker as a part of the Xerox Educational Division until his retirement in 1969.

Margaret E. Monroe, formerly Associate Professor at the Graduate School of Library Service, Rutgers University, New Brunswick, New Jersey, is presently Director of The Library School of the University of Wisconsin-Madison.

Eric Moon was the Editor of *Library Journal* from October 1959 to January 1969, when he became the director of editorial development of R. R. Bowker Co. Mr. Moon is now executive officer of Scarecrow Press, a division of Grolier Educational Corp.

Everett T. Moore is the Assistant Librarian at the University of California at Los Angeles. He is the former editor of the *ALA Newsletter on Intellectual Freedom* and a former columnist on intellectual freedom for the *ALA Bulletin.* Mr. Moore is also the editor of a forthcoming issue of *Library Trends* which will deal with intellectual freedom.

Jack Nelson, co-author with Gene Roberts, Jr. of the book, *Censors and the Schools,* was formerly a reporter for the *Atlanta Constitution,* Atlanta, Georgia and is now a reporter for the *Los Angeles Times,* Atlanta Bureau, Atlanta, Georgia.

Karl Nyren is Associate Editor of *Library Journal*.

Eli M. Oboler is the Librarian of the State University Library, Idaho State University, Pocatello, Idaho. Currently serving on the ALA Intellectual Freedom Committee, Mr. Oboler has been an active force in this organization since he joined in 1965.

Anne Pellowski, formerly the storytelling specialist for the New York Public Library, is presently the Director-Librarian for the Information Center on Children's Cultures at UNESCO, New York, New York. She is also the author of *The World of Children's Literature* (R. R. Bowker Co.).

John C. Pine, who formerly worked in the Literature Division of the Rochester Public Library, Rochester, New York, is presently Head of Adult Services at the Smithtown Library, Smithtown, New York.

Stuart C. Sherman, a former Librarian of the Providence Public Library, Providence, Rhode Island, is now the Librarian of the John Hay Library at Brown University, Providence, Rhode Island.

Ray Smith, previously Director of the Mason City Public Library, Mason City, Iowa and then Director of the Dakota-Scott Regional Library, West St. Paul, Minnesota, is now a member of the faculty at the School of Library Science, Immaculate Heart College, Los Angeles, California.

Gordon Stevenson, previously Director of the Art and Music Department at the Kansas City Public Library, Kansas City, Missouri and then Co-ordinator of Reader Services at the same institution, is currently a Fellow at the Indiana University Graduate Library School, Bloomington, Indiana.

Zada Taylor was the Librarian at the West Valley Regional Branch of the Los Angeles Public Library, Los Angeles, California, leaving in 1967 for extensive travel and research.

Carol Wall, formerly Assistant Librarian at the Auburn Community College Library, Auburn, New York, is presently Reference Librarian at the Shippensburg State College Library, Shippensburg, Pennsylvania.

Irving Wallace is a well-known author of many best-sellers, including *The Chapman Report, The Prize* and *The Seven Minutes* which is about a censorship case.

Jake Zeitlin is a noted bookseller in Los Angeles, California.